WILLIAM SHAKESPEARE
Poetry selected by TED HUGHES

WILLIAM SHAKESPEARE

Poetry selected by TED HUGHES

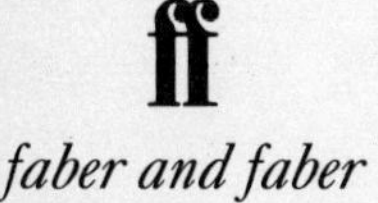

faber and faber

for Roy Davids

First published in 1971
as *A Choice of Shakespeare's Verse*
by Faber and Faber Limited
3 Queen Square London WC1N 3AU
This edition first published in 2000

Photoset by Parker Typesetting Service, Leicester
Printed in Italy

All rights reserved
Introduction © Ted Hughes, 1991; The Estate of Ted Hughes, 2000
This selection © Faber and Faber Ltd, 1971, 1991

This book is sold subject to the condition that it shall not, by way of trade or otherwise, be lent, resold, hired out or otherwise circulated without the publisher's prior consent in any form of binding or cover other than that in which it is published and without a similar condition including this condition being imposed on the subsequent purchaser

A CIP record for this book
is available from the British Library

ISBN 0–571–20368–X

10 9 8 7 6 5 4 3 2 1

Contents

The text of this Selection follows that of the Oxford Standard Authors edition of the Complete Works of Shakespeare: acknowledgements are due to the Oxford University Press for their permission.

Introduction

It has never been easy to settle Shakespeare into the succession of poets in English. According to most anthologies, he wrote only sonnets and songs for his plays. The reasons for this reluctance of anthologists to break into the sacred precincts of his drama and start looting portable chunks from the holy structures would make a curious chapter in the history of England's attitudes to its national hero.

Yet when the great speeches of his plays are taken out of context they are no more difficult to understand and appropriate than poems by other great poets. In many cases they are very much easier. Is it more difficult to pick up, and make part of one's mental furnishings, the following:

To-morrow, and to-morrow, and to-morrow,
Creeps in this petty pace from day to day,
To the last syllable of recorded time;
And all our yesterdays have lighted fools
The way to dusty death. Out, out, brief candle!
Life's but a walking shadow, a poor player
That struts and frets his hour upon the stage
And then is heard no more; it is a tale
Told by an idiot, full of sound and fury,
Signifying nothing.

(*Macbeth*, v.v. Macbeth)

than it is to come to terms with Yeats's 'Death':

Nor dread nor hope attend
A dying animal;
A man awaits his end
Dreading and hoping all;
Many times he died,
Many times rose again.

A great man in his pride
Confronting murderous men
Casts derision upon
Supersession of breath;
He knows death to the bone –
Man has created death.

or with Eliot's:

Phlebas the Phoenician, a fortnight dead,
Forgot the cry of gulls, and the deep sea swell
And the profit and loss.
                                        A current under sea
Picked his bones in whispers. As he rose and fell
He passed the stages of his age and youth
Entering the whirlpool.
                                        Gentile or Jew
O you who turn the wheel and look to windward,
Consider Phlebas, who was once handsome and tall as you.

('The Waste Land', IV)

In fact, if one specifies that 'To-morrow, and to-morrow, and to-morrow' is spoken by Macbeth as he faces the leafy army that will put an end to his spellbound, murderous career (having just heard that his wife, who prompted the course of action that converted him from the King's loyal champion to a regicidal tyrant, has died), it actually limits the use of the passage for a reader. Its relevance is then confined to Macbeth's unique predicament in a sacrosanct, old-fashioned play, rather than applied generally to the reader's own immediate plight, as an ephemeral creature, facing the abyss, on a spinning ball of self-delusion.

Obviously, by reading the passage out of context, one is missing the great imaginative experience of the drama – but one is missing that anyway. The speech on its own is something else, read in less than a minute, learned in less than five, still wonderful, and a pure bonus.

Accordingly, I have collected here a wide range of speeches (from all the plays except two or three) that seem to me self-sufficient outside their dramatic context and capable of striking up a life of their own in the general experience of the reader. In among, I have distributed many of the sonnets and songs.

Ted Hughes, August 1991

WILLIAM SHAKESPEARE

1

Now the hungry lion roars,
  And the wolf behowls the moon;
Whilst the heavy ploughman snores,
  All with weary task fordone,
Now the wasted brands do glow,
  Whilst the screech-owl, screeching loud,
Puts the wretch that lies in woe
  In remembrance of a shroud.
Now it is the time of night
  That the graves, all gaping wide,
Every one lets forth his sprite,
  In the church-way paths to glide:
And we fairies, that do run
  By the triple Hecate's team,
From the presence of the sun,
  Following darkness like a dream,
Now are frolic; not a mouse
Shall disturb this hallow'd house;
I am sent with broom before,
To sweep the dust behind the door.

2

Music to hear, why hear'st thou music sadly?
Sweets with sweets war not, joy delights in joy:
Why lov'st thou that which thou receiv'st not gladly,
Or else receiv'st with pleasure thine annoy?
If the true concord of well-tuned sounds,
By unions married, do offend thine ear,
They do not sweetly chide thee, who confounds
In singleness the parts that thou shouldst bear.
Mark how one string, sweet husband to another,
Strikes each in each by mutual ordering;
Resembling sire and child and happy mother,
Who, all in one, one pleasing note do sing:

Whose speechless song, being many, seeming one,
Sings this to thee: 'Thou single wilt prove none.'

3

Well, say there is no kingdom then for Richard;
What other pleasures can the world afford?
I'll make my heaven in a lady's lap,
And deck my body in gay ornaments,
And witch sweet ladies with my words and looks.
O miserable thought! and more unlikely
Than to accomplish twenty golden crowns.
Why, love forswore me in my mother's womb:
And, for I should not deal in her soft laws,
She did corrupt frail nature with some bribe,
To shrink mine arm up like a wither'd shrub;
To make an envious mountain on my back,
Where sits deformity to mock my body;
To shape my legs of an unequal size;
To disproportion me in every part,
Like to a chaos, or an unlick'd bear-whelp
That carries no impression like the dam.
And am I then a man to be belov'd?
O monstrous fault! to harbour such a thought.
Then, since this earth affords no joy to me
But to command, to check, to o'erbear such
As are of better person than myself,
I'll make my heaven to dream upon the crown;
And, whiles I live, to account this world but hell,
Until my mis-shap'd trunk that bears this head
Be round impaled with a glorious crown.
And yet I know not how to get the crown,
For many lives stand between me and home:
And I, like one lost in a thorny wood,
That rents the thorns and is rent with the thorns,
Seeking a way and straying from the way;

4

Not knowing how to find the open air,
But toiling desperately to find it out,
Torment myself to catch the English crown:
And from that torment I will free myself,
Or hew my way out with a bloody axe.
Why, I can smile, and murder while I smile,
And cry, 'Content,' to that which grieves my heart,
And wet my cheeks with artificial tears,
And frame my face to all occasions.
I'll drown more sailors than the mermaid shall;
I'll slay more gazers than the basilisk;
I'll play the orator as well as Nestor,
Deceive more slily than Ulysses could,
And, like a Sinon, take another Troy.
I can add colours to the chameleon,
Change shapes with Proteus for advantages,
And set the murd'rous Machiavel to school.
Can I do this, and cannot get a crown?
Tut! were it further off, I'll pluck it down.

4

Sin of self-love possesseth all mine eye
And all my soul and all my every part;
And for this sin there is no remedy,
It is so grounded inward in my heart.
Methinks no face so gracious is as mine,
No shape so true, no truth of such account;
And for myself mine own worth do define,
As I all other in all worths surmount.
But when my glass shows me myself indeed,
Beated and chopp'd with tann'd antiquity,
Mine own self-love quite contrary I read;
Self so self-loving were iniquity.
'Tis thee, myself, – that for myself I praise,
Painting my age with beauty of thy days.

5

But, soft! what light through yonder window breaks?
It is the east, and Juliet is the sun!
Arise, fair sun, and kill the envious moon,
Who is already sick and pale with grief,
That thou her maid art far more fair than she:
Be not her maid, since she is envious;
Her vestal livery is but sick and green,
And none but fools do wear it; cast it off.
It is my lady; O! it is my love:
O! that she knew she were.
She speaks, yet she says nothing: what of that?
Her eye discourses; I will answer it.
I am too bold, 'tis not to me she speaks:
Two of the fairest stars in all the heaven,
Having some business, do entreat her eyes
To twinkle in their spheres till they return.
What if her eyes were there, they in her head?
The brightness of her cheek would shame those stars
As daylight doth a lamp; her eyes in heaven
Would through the airy region stream so bright
That birds would sing and think it were not night.
See! how she leans her cheek upon her hand:
O! that I were a glove upon that hand,
That I might touch that cheek.

6

Shall I compare thee to a summer's day?
Thou art more lovely and more temperate:
Rough winds do shake the darling buds of May,
And summer's lease hath all too short a date:
Sometime too hot the eye of heaven shines,
And often is his gold complexion dimm'd:
And every fair from fair sometime declines,
By chance, or nature's changing course untrimm'd;

But thy eternal summer shall not fade,
Nor lose possession of that fair thou ow'st,
Nor shall death brag thou wander'st in his shade,
When in eternal lines to time thou grow'st;
So long as men can breathe, or eyes can see,
So long lives this, and this gives life to thee.

7

I do affect the very ground, which is base, where her shoe, which is baser, guided by her foot, which is basest, doth tread. I shall be forsworn, – which is a great argument of falsehood, – if I love. And how can that be true love which is falsely attempted? Love is a familiar; Love is a devil: there is no evil angel but Love. Yet was Samson so tempted, and he had an excellent strength; yet was Solomon so seduced, and he had a very good wit. Cupid's butt-shaft is too hard for Hercules' club, and therefore too much odds for a Spaniard's rapier. The first and second clause will not serve my turn; the passado he respects not, the duello he regards not: his disgrace is to be called boy, but his glory is, to subdue men. Adieu, valour! rust, rapier! be still, drum! for your manager is in love; yea, he loveth. Assist me some extemporal god of rime, for I am sure I shall turn sonneter. Devise, wit; write, pen; for I am for whole volumes in folio.

8

Let me not to the marriage of true minds
Admit impediments. Love is not love
Which alters when it alteration finds,
Or bends with the remover to remove:
O, no! it is an ever-fixed mark,
That looks on tempests and is never shaken;
It is the star to every wandering bark,
Whose worth's unknown, although his height be taken.
Love's not Time's fool, though rosy lips and cheeks

Within his bending sickle's compass come;
Love alters not with his brief hours and weeks,
But bears it out even to the edge of doom.
  If this be error, and upon me prov'd,
  I never writ, nor no man ever lov'd.

9

Thy life did manifest thou lov'dst me not,
And thou wilt have me die assur'd of it.
Thou hid'st a thousand daggers in thy thoughts,
Which thou hast whetted on thy stony heart,
To stab at half an hour of my life.
What! canst thou not forbear me half an hour?
Then get thee gone and dig my grave thyself,
And bid the merry bells ring to thine ear
That thou art crowned, not that I am dead.
Let all the tears that should bedew my hearse
Be drops of balm to sanctify thy head:
Only compound me with forgotten dust;
Give that which gave thee life unto the worms.
Pluck down my officers, break my decrees;
For now a time is come to mock at form.
Harry the Fifth is crown'd! Up, vanity!
Down, royal state! all you sage counsellors, hence!
And to the English court assemble now,
From every region, apes of idleness!
Now, neighbour confines, purge you of your scum:
Have you a ruffian that will swear, drink, dance,
Revel the night, rob, murder, and commit
The oldest sins the newest kind of ways?
Be happy, he will trouble you no more;
England shall double gild his treble guilt.
England shall give him office, honour, might;
For the fifth Harry from curb'd licence plucks
The muzzle of restraint, and the wild dog

Shall flesh his tooth in every innocent.
O my poor kingdom! sick with civil blows,
When that my care could not withhold thy riots,
What wilt thou do when riot is thy care?
O! thou wilt be a wilderness again,
Peopled with wolves, thy old inhabitants.

10

When I do count the clock that tells the time,
And see the brave day sunk in hideous night;
When I behold the violet past prime,
And sable curls, all silver'd o'er with white;
When lofty trees I see barren of leaves,
Which erst from heat did canopy the herd,
And summer's green all girded up in sheaves,
Borne on the bier with white and bristly beard,
Then of thy beauty do I question make,
That thou among the wastes of time must go,
Since sweets and beauties do themselves forsake
And die as fast as they see others grow;
  And nothing 'gainst Time's scythe can make defence
  Save breed, to brave him when he takes thee hence.

11

— Swearest thou, ungracious boy? henceforth ne'er look on me. Thou are violently carried away from grace: there is a devil haunts thee in the likeness of a fat old man; a tun of man is thy companion. Why dost thou converse with that trunk of humours, that bolting-hutch of beastliness, that swoln parcel of dropsies, that huge bombard of sack, that stuffed cloakbag of guts, that roasted Manningtree ox with the pudding in his belly, that reverend vice, that grey iniquity, that father ruffian, that vanity in years? Wherein is he good but to taste sack and drink it? wherein neat and cleanly but to carve a capon and eat it? wherein cunning but in craft? wherein crafty but in villany? wherein villanous but in all things? wherein worthy but in nothing?

— I would your Grace would take me with you: whom means your Grace?

— That villanous abominable misleader of youth, Falstaff, that old white-bearded Satan.

— My lord, the man I know.

— I know thou dost.

— But to say I know more harm in him than in myself were to say more than I know. That he is old, the more the pity, his white hairs do witness it; but that he is, saving your reverence, a whoremaster, that I utterly deny. If sack and sugar be a fault, God help the wicked! If to be old and merry be a sin, then many an old host that I know is damned: if to be fat be to be hated, then Pharaoh's lean kine are to be loved. No, my good lord; banish Peto, banish Bardolph, banish Poins; but for sweet Jack Falstaff, kind Jack Falstaff, true Jack Falstaff, valiant Jack Falstaff, and therefore more valiant, being, as he is, old Jack Falstaff, banish not him thy Harry's company: banish not him thy Harry's company: banish plump Jack, and banish all the world.

— I do, I will.

12

When I have seen by Time's fell hand defac'd
The rich-proud cost of outworn buried age;
When sometime lofty towers I see down-raz'd,
And brass eternal slave to mortal rage;
When I have seen the hungry ocean gain
Advantage on the kingdom of the shore,
And the firm soil win of the watery main,
Increasing store with loss, and loss with store;
When I have seen such interchange of state,
Or state itself confounded to decay;
Ruin hath taught me thus to ruminate –

That Time will come and take my love away.
  This thought is as a death, which cannot choose
  But weep to have that which it fears to lose.

13

'Guilty thou art of murder and of theft,
Guilty of perjury and subornation,
Guilty of treason, forgery, and shift,
Guilty of incest, that abomination;
An accessary by thine inclination
  To all sins past, and all that are to come,
  From the creation to the general doom.

'Mis-shapen Time, copesmate of ugly Night,
Swift subtle post, carrier of grisly care,
Eater of youth, false slave to false delight,
Base watch of woes, sin's pack-horse, virtue's snare;
Thou nursest all, and murderest all that are;
  O! hear me, then, injurious, shifting Time,
  Be guilty of my death, since of my crime.

'Why hath thy servant, Opportunity,
Betray'd the hours thou gav'st me to repose?
Cancell'd my fortunes, and enchained me
To endless date of never-ending woes?
Time's office is to fine the hate of foes;
  To eat up errors by opinion bred,
  Not spend the dowry of a lawful bed.

'Time's glory is to calm contending kings,
To unmask falsehood and bring truth to light,
To stamp the seal of time in aged things,
To wake the morn and sentinel the night,
To wrong the wronger till he render right,
  To ruinate proud buildings with thy hours,
  And smear with dust their glittering golden towers;

'To fill with worm-holes stately monuments,
To feed oblivion with decay of things,
To blot old books and alter their contents,
To pluck the quills from ancient ravens' wings,
To dry the old oak's sap and cherish springs,
  To spoil antiquities of hammer'd steel,
  And turn the giddy round of Fortune's wheel;

'To show the beldam daughters of her daughter,
To make the child a man, the man a child,
To slay the tiger that doth live by slaughter,
To tame the unicorn and lion wild,
To mock the subtle, in themselves beguil'd,
  To cheer the ploughman with increaseful crops,
  And waste huge stones with little water-drops.

'Why work'st thou mischief in thy pilgrimage,
Unless thou couldst return to make amends?
One poor retiring minute in an age
Would purchase thee a thousand thousand friends,
Lending him wit that to bad debtors lends:
  O! this dread night, wouldst thou one hour come back,
  I could prevent this storm and shun thy wrack.

'Thou ceaseless lackey to eternity,
With some mischance cross Tarquin in his flight:
Devise extremes beyond extremity,
To make him curse this cursed crimeful night:
Let ghastly shadows his lewd eyes affright,
  And the dire thought of his committed evil
  Shape every bush a hideous shapeless devil.

'Disturb his hours of rest with restless trances,
Afflict him in his bed with bedrid groans;
Let there bechance him pitiful mischances
To make him moan, but pity not his moans;
Stone him with harden'd hearts, harder than stones;
  And let mild women to him lose their mildness.
  Wilder to him than tigers in their wildness.

'Let him have time to tear his curled hair,
Let him have time against himself to rave,
Let him have time of Time's help to despair,
Let him have time to live a loathed slave,
Let him have time a beggar's orts to crave,
  And time to see one that by alms doth live
  Disdain to him disdained scraps to give.

'Let him have time to see his friends his foes,
And merry fools to mock at him resort;
Let him have time to mark how slow time goes
In time of sorrow, and how swift and short
His time of folly and his time of sport;
  And ever let his unrecalling crime
  Have time to wail the abusing of his time.

'O Time! thou tutor both to good and bad,
Teach me to curse him that thou taught'st this ill;
At his own shadow let the thief run mad,
Himself himself seek every hour to kill:
Such wretched hands such wretched blood should spill;
  For who so base would such an office have
  As slanderous deathsman to so base a slave?

'The baser is he, coming from a king,
To shame his hope with deeds degenerate:
The mightier man, the mightier is the thing
That makes him honour'd, or begets him hate;
For greatest scandal waits on greatest state.
  The moon being clouded presently is miss'd,
  But little stars may hide them when they list.

'The crow may bathe his coal-black wings in mire,
And unperceiv'd fly with the filth away;
But if the like the snow-white swan desire,
The stain upon his silver down will stay.
Poor grooms are sightless night, kings glorious day.
  Gnats are unnoted wheresoe'er they fly,
  But eagles gaz'd upon with every eye.

'Out, idle words! servants to shallow fools,
Unprofitable sounds, weak arbitrators!
Busy yourselves in skill-contending schools;
Debate where leisure serves with dull debaters;
To trembling clients be you mediators:
  For me, I force not argument a straw,
  Since that my case is past the help of law.

14

Like as the waves make towards the pebbled shore,
So do our minutes hasten to their end;
Each changing place with that which goes before,
In sequent toil all forwards do contend.
Nativity, once in the main of light,
Crawls to maturity, wherewith being crown'd,
Crooked eclipses 'gainst his glory fight,
And Time that gave doth now his gift confound.
Time doth transfix the flourish set on youth
And delves the parallels in beauty's brow,
Feeds on the rarities of nature's truth,
And nothing stands but for his scythe to mow:
  And yet to times in hope my verse shall stand,
  Praising thy worth, despite his cruel hand.

15

I am amaz'd, methinks, and lose my way
Among the thorns and dangers of this world.
How easy dost thou take all England up!
From forth this morsel of dead royalty,
The life, the right and truth of all this realm
Is fled to heaven; and England now is left
To tug and scamble and to part by the teeth
The unow'd interest of proud swelling state.
Now for the bare-pick'd bone of majesty
Doth dogged war bristle his angry crest,

And snarleth in the gentle eyes of peace:
Now powers from home and discontents at home
Meet in one line; and vast confusion waits, –
As doth a raven on a sick-fallen beast, –
The imminent decay of wrested pomp.
Now happy he whose cloak and ceinture can
Hold out this tempest.

16

Not marble, nor the gilded monuments
Of princes, shall outlive this powerful rime;
But you shall shine more bright in these contents
Than unswept stone, besmear'd with sluttish time.
When wasteful war shall statues overturn,
And broils root out the work of masonry,
Nor Mars his sword nor war's quick fire shall burn
The living record of your memory.
'Gainst death and all-oblivious enmity
Shall you pace forth; your praise shall still find room
Even in the eyes of all posterity
That wear this world out to the ending doom.
So, till the judgment that yourself arise,
You live in this, and dwell in lovers' eyes.

17

But I remember, when the fight was done,
When I was dry with rage and extreme toil,
Breathless and faint, leaning upon my sword,
Came there a certain lord, neat, and trimly dress'd,
Fresh as a bridegroom; and his chin, new reap'd,
Show'd like a stubble-land at harvest-home:
He was perfumed like a milliner,
And 'twixt his finger and his thumb he held
A pouncet-box, which ever and anon
He gave his nose and took't away again;

Who therewith angry, when it next came there,
Took it in snuff: and still he smil'd and talk'd;
And as the soldiers bore dead bodies by,
He call'd them untaught knaves, unmannerly,
To bring a slovenly unhandsome corpse
Betwixt the wind and his nobility.
With many holiday and lady terms
He question'd me; among the rest, demanded
My prisoners in your majesty's behalf.
I then all smarting with my wounds being cold,
To be so pester'd with a popinjay,
Out of my grief and my impatience
Answer'd neglectingly, I know not what,
He should, or he should not; for he made me mad
To see him shine so brisk and smell so sweet
And talk so like a waiting-gentlewoman
Of guns, and drums, and wounds, – God save the mark! –
And telling me the sovereign'st thing on earth
Was parmaceti for an inward bruise;
And that it was great pity, so it was,
This villanous saltpetre should be digg'd
Out of the bowels of the harmless earth,
Which many a good tall fellow had destroy'd
So cowardly; and but for these vile guns,
He would himself have been a soldier.

18

Petruchio is coming, in a new hat and an old jerkin; a pair of old breeches thrice turned; a pair of boots that have been candle-cases, one buckled, another laced; an old rusty sword ta'en out of the town-armoury, with a broken hilt, and chapeless; with two broken points: his horse hipped with an old mothy saddle and stirrups of no kindred; besides, possessed with the glanders and like to mose in the chine; troubled with the lampass, infected with the fashions, full of windgalls, sped with spavins, rayed with the yellows, past cure of the fives, stark spoiled with the staggers, begnawn with the bots, swayed in the back, and shoulder-shotten; near-legged before, and with a half-checked bit, and a head-stall of sheep's leather, which, being restrained to keep him from stumbling, hath been often burst and now repaired with knots; one girth six times pieced, and a woman's crupper of velure, which hath two letters for her name fairly set down in studs, and here and there pieced with pack-thread.

19

Now hear our English king;
For thus his royalty doth speak in me.
He is prepar'd; and reason too he should:
This apish and unmannerly approach,
This harness'd masque and unadvised revel,
This unhair'd sauciness and boyish troops,
The king doth smile at; and is well prepar'd
To whip this dwarfish war, these pigmy arms,
From out the circle of his territories.
That hand which had the strength, even at your door,
To cudgel you and make you take the hatch;
To dive, like buckets, in concealed wells;
To crouch in litter of your stable planks;
To lie like pawns lock'd up in chests and trunks;
To hug with swine; to seek sweet safety out
In vaults and prisons; and to thrill and shake,
Even at the crying of your nation's crow,
Thinking this voice an armed Englishman:
Shall that victorious hand be feebled here
That in your chambers gave you chastisement?
No! Know, the gallant monarch is in arms,
And like an eagle o'er his aiery towers,
To souse annoyance that comes near his nest.

And you degenerate, you ingrate revolts,
You bloody Neroes, ripping up the womb
Of your dear mother England, blush for shame:
For your own ladies and pale-visag'd maids
Like Amazons come tripping after drums,
Their thimbles into armed gauntlets change,
Their needles to lances, and their gentle hearts
To fierce and bloody inclination.

20

That very time I saw, but thou couldst not,
Flying between the cold moon and the earth,
Cupid all arm'd: a certain aim he took
At a fair vestal throned by the west,
And loos'd his love-shaft smartly from his bow,
As it should pierce a hundred thousand hearts;
But I might see young Cupid's fiery shaft
Quench'd in the chaste beams of the wat'ry moon,
And the imperial votaress passed on,
In maiden meditation, fancy-free.
Yet mark'd I where the bolt of Cupid fell:
It fell upon a little western flower,
Before milk-white, now purple with love's wound,
And maidens call it, Love-in-idleness.
Fetch me that flower; the herb I show'd thee once:
The juice of it on sleeping eyelids laid
Will make or man or woman madly dote
Upon the next live creature that it sees.
Fetch me this herb.

21

— Bless our poor virginity from underminers and blowers up! Is there no military policy, how virgins might blow up men?

— Virginity being blown down, man will quicklier be

blown up: marry, in blowing him down again, with the breach yourselves made, you lose your city. It is not politic in the commonwealth of nature to preserve virginity. Loss of virginity is rational increase, and there was never virgin got till virginity was first lost. That you were made of is metal to make virgins. Virginity, by being once lost, may be ten times found: by being ever kept, it is ever lost. 'Tis too cold a companion: away with't!

— I will stand for't a little, though therefore I die a virgin.

— There's little can be said in't; 'tis against the rule of nature. To speak on the part of virginity is to accuse your mothers, which is most infallible disobedience. He that hangs himself is a virgin: virginity murders itself, and should be buried in highways, out of all sanctified limit, as a desperate offendress against nature. Virginity breeds mites, much like a cheese, consumes itself to the very paring, and so dies with feeding his own stomach. Besides, virginity is peevish, proud, idle, made of self-love, which is the most inhibited sin in the canon. Keep it not; you cannot choose but lose by't! Out with't! within the year it will make itself two, which is a goodly increase, and the principal itself not much the worse. Away with't!

— How might one do, sir, to lose it to her own liking?

— Let me see: marry, ill, to like him that ne'er it likes. 'Tis a commodity that will lose the gloss with lying; the longer kept, the less worth: off with't, while 'tis vendible; answer the time of request. Virginity, like an old courtier, wears her cap out of fashion; richly suited, but unsuitable: just like the brooch and the toothpick, which wear not now. Your date is better in your pie and your porridge than in your cheek: and your virginity, your old virginity, is like one of our French withered pears; it looks ill, it eats drily; marry, 'tis a withered pear; it was formerly better; marry, yet 'tis a withered pear. Will you anything with it?

22

My tongue-tied Muse in manners holds her still,
Whilst comments of your praise, richly compil'd,
Deserve their character with golden quill,
And precious phrase by all the Muses fil'd.
I think good thoughts, while others write good words,
And, like unletter'd clerk, still cry 'Amen'
To every hymn that able spirit affords,
In polish'd form of well-refined pen.
Hearing you prais'd, I say, ''Tis so, 'tis true,'
And to the most of praise add something more;
But that is in my thought, whose love of you,
Though words come hindmost, holds his rank before.
  Then others for the breath of words respect,
  Me for my dumb thoughts, speaking in effect.

23

I cannot tell what you and other men
Think of this life; but, for my single self,
I had as lief not be as live to be
In awe of such a thing as I myself.
I was born free as Caesar; so were you:
We both have fed as well, and we can both
Endure the winter's cold as well as he:
For once, upon a raw and gusty day,
The troubled Tiber chafing with her shores,
Caesar said to me, 'Dar'st thou, Cassius, now
Leap in with me into this angry flood,
And swim to yonder point?' Upon the word,
Accoutred as I was, I plunged in
And bade him follow; so, indeed he did.
The torrent roar'd, and we did buffet it
With lusty sinews, throwing it aside
And stemming it with hearts of controversy;
But ere we could arrive the point propos'd,

Caesar cried, 'Help me, Cassius, or I sink!'
I, as Æneas, our great ancestor,
Did from the flames of Troy upon his shoulder
The old Anchises bear, so from the waves of Tiber
Did I the tired Caesar. And this man
Is now become a god, and Cassius is
A wretched creature and must bend his body
If Caesar carelessly but nod on him.
He had a fever when he was in Spain,
And when the fit was on him, I did mark
How he did shake; 'tis true, this god did shake;
His coward lips did from their colour fly,
And that same eye whose bend doth awe the world
Did lose his lustre; I did hear him groan;
Ay, and that tongue of his that bade the Romans
Mark him and write his speeches in their books,
Alas! it cried, 'Give me some drink, Titinius,'
As a sick girl. Ye gods, it doth amaze me,
A man of such a feeble temper should
So get the start of the majestic world,
And bear the palm alone.

24

But be contented: when that fell arrest
Without all bail shall carry me away,
My life hath in this line some interest,
Which for memorial still with thee shall stay.
When thou reviewest this, thou dost review
The very part was consecrate to thee:
The earth can have but earth, which is his due;
My spirit is thine, the better part of me:
So then thou hast but lost the dregs of life,
The prey of worms, my body being dead;
The coward conquest of a wretch's knife,
Too base of thee to be remembered.

The worth of that is that which it contains,
And that is this, and this with thee remains

25

A fool, a fool! I met a fool i' the forest,
A motley fool; a miserable world!
As I do live by food, I met a fool;
Who laid him down and bask'd him in the sun,
And rail'd on Lady Fortune in good terms,
In good set terms, and yet a motley fool.
'Good morrow, fool,' quoth I. 'No, sir,' quoth he,
'Call me not fool till heaven hath sent me fortune.'
And then he drew a dial from his poke,
And, looking on it with lack-lustre eye,
Says very wisely, 'It is ten o'clock;
Thus may we see,' quoth he, 'how the world wags:
'Tis but an hour ago since it was nine,
And after one hour more 'twill be eleven;
And so from hour to hour we ripe and ripe,
And then from hour to hour we rot and rot,
And thereby hangs a tale.' When I did hear
The motley fool thus moral on the time,
My lungs began to crow like chanticleer,
That fools should be so deep-contemplative,
And I did laugh sans intermission
An hour by his dial. O noble fool!
A worthy fool! Motley's the only wear.

26

No more be griev'd at that which thou hast done:
Roses have thorns, and silver fountains mud;
Clouds and eclipses stain both moon and sun,
And loathsome canker lives in sweetest bud.
All men make faults, and even I in this,
Authorizing thy trespass with compare,

Myself corrupting, salving thy amiss,
Excusing thy sins more than thy sins are;
For to thy sensual fault I bring in sense, –
Thy adverse party is thy advocate, –
And 'gainst myself a lawful plea commence:
Such civil war is in my love and hate,
  That I an accessary needs must be
  To that sweet thief which sourly robs from me.

27

I have been studying how I may compare
This prison where I live unto the world:
And for because the world is populous,
And here is not a creature but myself,
I cannot do it; yet I'll hammer it out.
My brain I'll prove the female to my soul;
My soul the father: and these two beget
A generation of still-breeding thoughts,
And these same thoughts people this little world
In humours like the people of this world.
For no thought is contented. The better sort,
As thoughts of things divine, are intermix'd
With scruples, and do set the word itself
Against the word:
As thus, 'Come, little ones,' and then again,
'It is as hard to come as for a camel
To thread the postern of a needle's eye.'
Thoughts tending to ambition, they do plot
Unlikely wonders; how these vain weak nails
May tear a passage through the flinty ribs
Of this hard world, my ragged prison walls;
And, for they cannot, die in their own pride.
Thoughts tending to content flatter themselves
That they are not the first of fortune's slaves,
Nor shall not be the last; like silly beggars

Who sitting in the stocks refuge their shame,
That many have and others must sit there:
And in this thought they find a kind of ease,
Bearing their own misfortune on the back
Of such as have before endur'd the like.
Thus play I in one person many people,
And none contented: sometimes am I king;
Then treason makes me wish myself a beggar,
And so I am: then crushing penury
Persuades me I was better when a king;
Then am I king'd again; and by and by
Think that I am unking'd by Bolingbroke,
And straight am nothing: but whate'er I be,
Nor I nor any man that but man is
With nothing shall be pleas'd, till he be eas'd
With being nothing.

28

They that have power to hurt and will do none,
That do not do the thing they most do show,
Who, moving others, are themselves as stone,
Unmoved, cold, and to temptation slow;
They rightly do inherit heaven's graces,
And husband nature's riches from expense;
They are the lords and owners of their faces,
Others but stewards of their excellence.
The summer's flower is to the summer sweet,
Though to itself it only live and die,
But if that flower with base infection meet,
The basest weed outbraves his dignity:
For sweetest things turn sourest by their deeds;
Lilies that fester smell far worse than weeds.

29

Good faith, this same young sober-blooded boy doth not love me; nor a man cannot make him laugh; but that's no marvel, he drinks no wine. There's never none of these demure boys come to any proof; for thin drink doth so over-cool their blood, and making many fish-meals, that they fall into a kind of male green-sickness; and then, when they marry, they get wenches. They are generally fools and cowards, which some of us should be too but for inflammation. A good sherris-sack hath a two-fold operation in it. It ascends me into the brain; dries me there all the foolish and dull and crudy vapours which environ it; makes it apprehensive, quick, forgetive, full of nimble fiery and delectable shapes; which, deliver'd o'er to the voice, the tongue, which is the birth, becomes excellent wit. The second property of your excellent sherris is, the warming of the blood; which, before cold and settled, left the liver white and pale, which is the badge of pusillanimity and cowardice: but the sherris warms it and makes it course from the inwards to the parts extreme. It illumineth the face, which, as a beacon, gives warning to all the rest of this little kingdom, man, to arm; and then the vital commoners and inland petty spirits muster me all to their captain, the heart, who, great and puffed up with this retinue, doth any deed of courage; and this valour comes of sherris. So that skill in the weapon is nothing without sack, for that sets it a-work; and learning, a mere hoard of gold kept by a devil till sack commences it and sets it in act and use. Hereof comes it that Prince Harry is valiant; for the cold blood he did naturally inherit of his father, he hath, like lean, sterile, and bare land, manured, husbanded, and tilled, with excellent endeavour of drinking good and good store of fertile sherris, that he is become very hot and valiant. If I had a thousand sons, the first human principle I would teach them should be, to forswear thin potations and to addict themselves to sack.

30

If music be the food of love, play on;
Give me excess of it, that, surfeiting,
The appetite may sicken, and so die.
That strain again! it had a dying fall:
O! it came o'er my ear like the sweet sound
That breathes upon a bank of violets,
Stealing and giving odour. Enough! no more:
'Tis not so sweet now as it was before.
O spirit of love! how quick and fresh art thou,
That, notwithstanding thy capacity
Receiveth as the sea, nought enters there,
Of what validity and pitch soe'er,
But falls into abatement and low price,
Even in a minute: so full of shapes is fancy,
That it alone is high fantastical.

31

Let those who are in favour with their stars
Of public honour and proud titles boast,
Whilst I, whom fortune of such triumph bars,
Unlook'd for joy in that I honour most.
Great princes' favourites their fair leaves spread
But as the marigold at the sun's eye,
And in themselves their pride lies buried,
For at a frown they in their glory die.
The painful warrior famoused for fight,
After a thousand victories once foil'd,
Is from the book of honour razed quite,
And all the rest forgot for which he toil'd:
  Then happy I, that love and am belov'd,
  Where I may not remove nor be remov'd.

32

Come away, come away, death,
And in sad cypress let me be laid;
Fly away, fly away, breath;
I am slain by a fair cruel maid.
My shroud of white, stuck all with yew,
O! prepare it.
My part of death, no one so true
Did share it.

Not a flower, not a flower sweet,
On my black coffin let there be strown;
Not a friend, not a friend greet
My poor corse, where my bones shall be thrown.
A thousand thousand sighs to save,
Lay me, O! where
Sad true lover never find my grave,
To weep there.

33

For do but note a wild and wanton herd,
Or race of youthful and unhandled colts,
Fetching mad bounds, bellowing and neighing loud,
Which is the hot condition of their blood;
If they but hear perchance a trumpet sound,
Or any air of music touch their ears,
You shall perceive them make a mutual stand,
Their savage eyes turn'd to a modest gaze
By the sweet power of music: therefore the poet
Did feign that Orpheus drew trees, stones, and floods;
Since nought so stockish, hard, and full of rage,
But music for the time doth change his nature.
The man that hath no music in himself,
Nor is not mov'd with concord of sweet sounds,
Is fit for treasons, strategems, and spoils;

The motions of his spirit are dull as night,
And his affections dark as Erebus:
Let no such man be trusted. Mark the music.

34

Are not these woods
More free from peril than the envious court?
Here feel we but the penalty of Adam,
The seasons' difference; as, the icy fang
And churlish chiding of the winter's wind,
Which, when it bites and blows upon my body,
Even till I shrink with cold, I smile and say
'This is no flattery: these are counsellors
That feelingly persuade me what I am.'
Sweet are the uses of adversity,
Which like the toad, ugly and venomous,
Wears yet a precious jewel in his head;
And this our life exempt from public haunt,
Finds tongues in trees, books in the running brooks,
Sermons in stones, and good in every thing.
I would not change it.

35

Was it the proud full sail of his great verse,
Bound for the prize of all too precious you,
That did my ripe thoughts in my brain inhearse,
Making their tomb the womb wherein they grew?
Was it his spirit, by spirits taught to write
Above a mortal pitch, that struck me dead?
No, neither he, nor his compeers by night
Giving him aid, my verse astonished.
He, nor that affable familiar ghost,
Which nightly gulls him with intelligence,
As victors of my silence cannot boast;
I was not sick of any fear from thence:

But when your countenance fill'd up his line,
Then lack'd I matter; that enfeebled mine.

36

Now is the winter of our discontent
Made glorious summer by this sun of York;
And all the clouds that lour'd upon our house
In the deep bosom of the ocean buried.
Now are our brows bound with victorious wreaths;
Our bruised arms hung up for monuments;
Our stern alarums changed to merry meetings;
Our dreadful marches to delightful measures.
Grim-visag'd war hath smooth'd his wrinkled front;
And now, – instead of mounting barbed steeds,
To fright the souls of fearful adversaries, –
He capers nimbly in a lady's chamber
To the lascivious pleasing of a lute.
But I, that am not shap'd for sportive tricks,
Nor made to court an amorous looking-glass;
I, that am rudely stamp'd, and want love's majesty
To strut before a wanton ambling nymph;
I, that am curtail'd of this fair proportion,
Cheated of feature by dissembling nature,
Deform'd, unfinish'd, sent before my time
Into this breathing world, scarce half made up,
And that so lamely and unfashionable
That dogs bark at me, as I halt by them;
Why, I, in this weak piping time of peace,
Have no delight to pass away the time,
Unless to see my shadow in the sun
And descant on mine own deformity:
And therefore, since I cannot prove a lover,
To entertain these fair well-spoken days,
I am determined to prove a villian,
And hate the idle pleasures of these days.

37

Then hate me when thou wilt; if ever, now;
Now, while the world is bent my deeds to cross,
Join with the spite of fortune, make me bow,
And do not drop in for an after-loss:
Ah! do not, when my heart hath 'scap'd this sorrow,
Come in the rearward of a conquer'd woe;
Give not a windy night a rainy morrow,
To linger out a purpos'd overthrow.
If thou wilt leave me, do not leave me last,
When other petty griefs have done their spite,
But in the onset come: so shall I taste
At first the very worst of fortune's might;
  And other strains of woe, which now seem woe,
  Compar'd with loss of thee will not seem so.

38

When a man's servant shall play the cur with him, look you, it goes hard; one that I brought up of a puppy; one that I saved from drowning, when three or four of his blind brothers and sisters went to it. I have taught him, even as one would say precisely, 'Thus would I teach a dog.' I was sent to deliver him as a present to Mistress Silvia from my master; and I came no sooner into the dining-chamber but he steps me to her trencher and steals her capon's leg. O! 'tis a foul thing when a cur cannot keep himself in all companies. I would have, as one should say, one that takes upon him to be a dog indeed, to be, as it were, a dog at all things. If I had not had more wit than he, to take a fault upon me that he did, I think verily he had been hanged for't: sure as I live, he had suffered for't: you shall judge. He thrusts me himself into the company of three or four gentleman-like dogs under the duke's table: he had not been there – bless the mark – a pissing-while, but all the chamber smelt him. 'Out with the dog!' says one; 'What cur is that?' says another; 'Whip him out,' says the third; 'Hang him up,' says the duke. I, having been acquainted with the smell before, knew it was Crab, and goes me to the fellow that whips the dogs: 'Friend,' quoth I, 'you mean to whip the dog?' 'Ay, marry, do I,' quoth he. 'You do him the more wrong,' quoth I; ' 'twas I did the thing you wot of.' He makes me no more ado, but whips me out of the chamber. How many masters would do this for his servant? Nay, I'll be sworn, I have sat in the stocks for puddings he hath stolen, otherwise he had been executed; I have stood on the pillory for geese he hath killed, otherwise he had suffered for't; thou thinkest not of this now. Nay, I remember the trick you served me when I took my leave of Madam Silvia: did not I bid thee still mark me and do as I do? When didst thou see me heave up my leg and make water against a gentlewoman's farthingale? Didst thou ever see me do such a trick?

39

Blow, blow, thou winter wind,
Thou art not so unkind
As man's ingratitude;
Thy tooth is not so keen,
Because thou art not seen,
Although thy breath be rude.
Heigh-ho! sing, heigh-ho! unto the green holly:
Most friendship is feigning, most loving mere folly.
Then heigh-ho! the holly!
This life is most jolly.

Freeze, freeze, thou bitter sky,
That dost not bite so nigh
As benefits forgot:
Though thou the waters warp,
Thy sting is not so sharp
As friend remember'd not.
Heigh-ho! sing, heigh-ho! unto the green holly:

Most friendship is feigning, most loving mere folly.
Then heigh-ho! the holly!
This life is most jolly.

40

When to the sessions of sweet silent thought
I summon up remembrance of things past,
I sigh the lack of many a thing I sought,
And with old woes new wail my dear times' waste:
Then can I drown an eye, unus'd to flow,
For precious friends hid in death's dateless night,
And weep afresh love's long since cancell'd woe,
And moan the expense of many a vanish'd sight:
Then can I grieve at grievances foregone,
And heavily from woe to woe tell o'er
The sad account of fore-bemoaned moan,
Which I new pay as if not paid before.
But if the while I think on thee, dear friend,
All losses are restor'd and sorrows end.

41

Lovers and madmen have such seething brains,
Such shaping fantasies, that apprehend
More than cool reason ever comprehends.
The lunatic, the lover, and the poet,
Are of imagination all compact:
One sees more devils than vast hell can hold,
That is, the madman; the lover, all as frantic,
Sees Helen's beauty in a brow of Egypt:
The poet's eye, in a fine frenzy rolling,
Doth glance from heaven to earth, from earth to heaven;
And, as imagination bodies forth
The forms of things unknown, the poet's pen
Turns them to shapes, and gives to airy nothing
A local habitation and a name.

Such tricks hath strong imagination,
That, if it would but apprehend some joy,
It comprehends some bringer of that joy;
Or in the night, imagining some fear,
How easy is a bush suppos'd a bear!

42

Say that thou didst forsake me for some fault,
And I will comment upon that offence:
Speak of my lameness, and I straight will halt,
Against thy reasons making no defence.
Thou canst not, love, disgrace me half so ill,
To set a form upon desired change,
As I'll myself disgrace, knowing thy will,
I will acquaintance strangle, and look strange;
Be absent from thy walks; and in my tongue
Thy sweet beloved name no more shall dwell,
Lest I, too much profane, should do it wrong,
And haply of our old acquaintance tell.
For thee, against myself I'll vow debate,
For I must ne'er love him whom thou dost hate.

43

Whenas thine eye hath chose the dame,
And stall'd the deer that thou should'st strike,
Let reason rule things worthy blame,
As well as fancy, partial wight:
Take counsel of some wiser head,
Neither too young nor yet unwed.

And when thou com'st thy tale to tell,
Smooth not thy tongue with filed talk,
Lest she some subtle practice smell;
A cripple soon can find a halt:
But plainly say thou lov'st her well,
And set the person forth to sell.

What though her frowning brows be bent,
Her cloudy looks will clear ere night;
And then too late she will repent
That thus dissembled her delight;
  And twice desire, ere it be day,
  That which with scorn she put away.

What though she strive to try her strength,
And ban and brawl, and say thee nay,
Her feeble force will yield at length,
When craft hath taught her thus to say,
  'Had women been so strong as men,
  In faith, you had not had it then.'

And to her will frame all thy ways;
Spare not to spend, and chiefly there
Where thy desert may merit praise,
By ringing in thy lady's ear:
  The strongest castle, tower, and town,
  The golden bullet beats it down.

Serve always with assured trust,
And in thy suit be humble true;
Unless thy lady prove unjust,
Seek never thou to choose anew.
  When time shall serve, be thou not slack
  To proffer, though she put thee back.

The wiles and guiles that women work,
Dissembled with an outward show,
The tricks and toys that in them lurk,
The cock that treads them shall not know.
  Have you not heard it said full oft,
  A woman's nay doth stand for nought?

Think, women love to match with men
And not to live so like a saint:
Here is no heaven; they holy then

Begin when age doth them attaint.
Were kisses all the joys in bed,
One woman would another wed.

But, soft! enough! too much, I fear;
For if my mistress hear my song,
She will not stick to ring my ear,
To teach my tongue to be so long:
Yet will she blush, here be it said,
To hear her secrets so bewray'd.

44

My mistress' eyes are nothing like the sun;
Coral is far more red than her lips' red:
If snow be white, why then her breasts are dun;
If hairs be wires, black wires grow on her head.
I have seen roses damask'd, red and white,
But no such roses see I in her cheeks;
And in some perfumes is there more delight
Than in the breath that from my mistress reeks.
I love to hear her speak, yet well I know
That music hath a far more pleasing sound:
I grant I never saw a goddess go, –
My mistress, when she walks, treads on the ground:
And yet, by heaven, I think my love as rare
As any she belied with false compare.

45

It was a lover and his lass,
With a hey, and a ho, and a hey nonino,
That o'er the green corn-field did pass,
In the spring time, the only pretty ring time,
When birds do sing, hey ding a ding, ding;
Sweet lovers love the spring.

Between the acres of the rye,
  With a hey, and a ho, and a hey nonino,
These pretty country folks would lie,
  In the spring time, &c.

This carol they began that hour,
  With a hey, and a ho, and a hey nonino,
How that a life was but a flower
  In the spring time, &c.

And therefore take the present time,
  With a hey, and a ho, and a hey nonino;
For love is crowned with the prime
  In the spring time, &c.

46

My love is strengthen'd, though more weak in seeming;
I love not less, though less the show appear:
That love is merchandiz'd whose rich esteeming
The owner's tongue doth publish everywhere.
Our love was new, and then but in the spring,
When I was wont to greet it with my lays;
As Philomel in summer's front doth sing,
And stops her pipe in growth of riper days:
Not that the summer is less pleasant now
Than when her mournful hymns did hush the night,
But that wild music burthens every bough,
And sweets grown common lose their dear delight.
  Therefore, like her, I sometime hold my tongue,
  Because I would not dull you with my song.

47

Forsooth, in love! I, that have been love's whip;
A very beadle to a humorous sigh;
A critic, nay, a night-watch constable,
A domineering pedant o'er the boy,

Than whom no mortal so magnificent!
This wimpled, whining, purblind, wayward boy,
This senior-junior, giant-dwarf, Dan Cupid;
Regent of love-rimes, lord of folded arms,
The anointed sovereign of sighs and groans,
Liege of all loiterers and malcontents,
Dread prince of plackets, king of codpieces,
Sole imperator and great general
Of trotting 'paritors: O my little heart!
And I to be a corporal of his field,
And wear his colours like a tumbler's hoop!
What I! I love! I sue! I seek a wife!
A woman that is like a German clock,
Still a-repairing, ever out of frame,
And never going aright, being a watch,
But being watch'd that it may still go right!
Nay, to be perjur'd, which is worst of all;
And, among three, to love the worst of all;
A wightly wanton with a velvet brow,
With two pitch balls stuck in her face for eyes;
Ay, and, by heaven, one that will do the deed
Though Argus were her eunuch and her guard:
And I to sigh for her! to watch for her!
To pray for her! Go to; it is a plague
That Cupid will impose for my neglect
Of his almighty dreadful little might.
Well I will love, write, sigh, pray, sue, and groan:
Some men must love my lady, and some Joan.

48

The forward violet thus did I chide:
Sweet thief, whence didst thou steal thy sweet that smells,
If not from my love's breath? The purple pride
Which on thy soft cheek for complexion dwells
In my love's veins thou hast too grossly dy'd.

The lily I condemned for thy hand,
And buds of marjoran had stol'n thy hair;
The roses fearfully on thorns did stand,
One blushing shame, another white despair;
A third, nor red nor white, had stol'n of both,
And to his robbery had annex'd thy breath;
But, for his theft, in pride of all his growth
A vengeful canker eat him up to death.
  More flowers I noted, yet I none could see
  But sweet or colour it had stol'n from thee.

49

O mistress mine! where are you roaming?
O! stay and hear; your true love's coming,
  That can sing both high and low.
Trip no further, pretty sweeting;
Journeys end in lovers meeting,
  Every wise man's son doth know.

What is love? 'tis not hereafter;
Present mirth hath present laughter;
  What's to come is still unsure:
In delay there lies no plenty;
Then come kiss me, sweet and twenty,
  Youth's a stuff will not endure.

50

The expense of spirit in a waste of shame
Is lust in action; and till action, lust
Is perjur'd, murderous, bloody, full of blame,
Savage, extreme, rude, cruel, not to trust;
Enjoy'd no sooner but despised straight;
Past reason hunted; and no sooner had,
Past reason hated, as a swallow'd bait,
On purpose laid to make the taker mad:

Mad in pursuit, and in possession so;
Had, having, and in quest to have, extreme;
A bliss in proof, – and prov'd, a very woe;
Before, a joy propos'd; behind, a dream.
All this the world well knows; yet none knows well
To shun the heaven that leads men to this hell.

51

— Methought that I had broken from the Tower,
And was embark'd to cross to Burgundy;
And in my company my brother Gloucester,
Who from my cabin tempted me to walk
Upon the hatches: hence we look'd toward England,
And cited up a thousand heavy times,
During the wars of York and Lancaster,
That had befall'n us. As we pac'd along
Upon the giddy footing of the hatches,
Methought that Gloucester stumbled; and, in falling,
Struck me, that thought to stay him, overboard,
Into the tumbling billows of the main.
Lord, Lord! methought what pain it was to drown:
What dreadful noise of water in mine ears!
What sights of ugly death within mine eyes!
Methought I saw a thousand fearful wracks;
A thousand men that fishes gnaw'd upon;
Wedges of gold, great anchors, heaps of pearl,
Inestimable stones, unvalu'd jewels,
All scatter'd in the bottom of the sea.
Some lay in dead men's skulls; and in those holes
Where eyes did once inhabit, there were crept,
As 'twere in scorn of eyes, reflecting gems,
That woo'd the slimy bottom of the deep,
And mock'd the dead bones that lay scatter'd by.
— Had you such leisure in the time of death
To gaze upon those secrets of the deep?

— Methought I had; and often did I strive
To yield the ghost; but still the envious flood
Stopt in my soul, and would not let it forth
To find the empty, vast, and wandering air;
But smother'd it within my panting bulk,
Which almost burst to belch it in the sea.
— Awak'd you not with this sore agony?
— No, no, my dream was lengthen'd after life;
O! then began the tempest to my soul.
I pass'd, methought, the melancholy flood,
With that grim ferryman which poets write of,
Unto the kingdom of perpetual night.
The first that there did greet my stranger soul,
Was my great father-in-law, renowned Warwick;
Who cried aloud, 'What scourge for perjury
Can this dark monarchy afford false Clarence?'
And so he vanish'd: then came wandering by
A shadow like an angel, with bright hair
Dabbled in blood; and he shriek'd out aloud,
'Clarence is come, – false, fleeting, perjur'd Clarence,
That stabb'd me in the field by Tewksbury; –
Seize on him! Furies, take him unto torment.'
With that, methought, a legion of foul fiends
Environ'd me, and howled in mine ears
Such hideous cries, that, with the very noise
I trembling wak'd, and, for a season after
Could not believe but that I was in hell,
Such terrible impression made my dream.

52

What's in the brain, that ink may character,
Which hath not figur'd to thee my true spirit?
What's new to speak, what new to register,
That may express my love, or thy dear merit?
Nothing, sweet boy; but yet, like prayers divine,

I must each day say o'er the very same;
Counting no old thing old, thou mine, I thine,
Even as when first I hallow'd thy fair name.
So that eternal love in love's fresh case
Weighs not the dust and injury of age,
Nor gives to necessary wrinkles place,
But makes antiquity for aye his page;
  Finding the first conceit of love there bred,
  Where time and outward form would show it dead.

53

Nay, sure, he's not in hell: he's in Arthur's bosom, if ever man went to Arthur's bosom. A' made a finer end and went away an it had been any christom child; a' parted even just between twelve and one, even at the turning o' the tide: for after I saw him fumble with the sheets and play with flowers and smile upon his fingers' ends, I knew there was but one way; for his nose was as sharp as a pen, and a' babbled of green fields. 'How now, Sir John!' quoth I: 'what man! be of good cheer.' So a' cried out, 'God, God, God!' three or four times: now I, to comfort him, bid him a' should not think of God, I hoped there was no need to trouble himself with any such thoughts yet. So a' bade me lay more clothes on his feet: I put my hand into the bed and felt them, and they were as cold as any stone; then I felt to his knees, and so upward, and upward, and all was as cold as any stone.

54

Let not my love be call'd idolatry,
Nor my beloved as an idol show,
Since all alike my songs and praises be
To one, of one, still such, and ever so.
Kind is my love to-day, to-morrow kind,
Still constant in a wondrous excellence;
Therefore my verse, to constancy confin'd,

One thing expressing, leaves out difference.
'Fair, kind, and true,' is all my argument,
'Fair, kind, and true,' varying to other words;
And in this change is my invention spent,
Three themes in one, which wondrous scope affords.
'Fair, kind, and true,' have often liv'd alone,
    Which three till now never kept seat in one.

55

SPRING

When daisies pied and violets blue
    And lady-smocks all silver-white
And cuckoo-buds of yellow hue
    Do paint the meadows with delight,
The cuckoo then, on every tree,
Mocks married men; for thus sings he,
                    Cuckoo;
Cuckoo, cuckoo: O, word of fear,
Unpleasing to a married ear!

When shepherds pipe on oaten straws,
    And merry larks are ploughmen's clocks,
When turtles tread, and rooks, and daws,
    And maidens bleach their summer smocks,
The cuckoo then, on every tree,
Mocks married men; for thus sings he,
                    Cuckoo;
Cuckoo, cuckoo: O, word of fear,
Unpleasing to a married ear!

WINTER

When icicles hang by the wall,
    And Dick the shepherd blows his nail,
And Tom bears logs into the hall,
    And milk comes frozen home in pail,

When blood is nipp'd, and ways be foul,
Then nightly sings the staring owl,
Tu-who;
Tu-whit, tu-who – a merry note,
While greasy Joan doth keel the pot.

When all aloud the wind doth blow,
And coughing drowns the parson's saw,
And birds sit brooding in the snow,
And Marion's nose looks red and raw,
When roasted crabs hiss in the bowl,
Then nightly sings the staring owl,
Tu-who;
Tu-whit, tu-who – a merry note,
While greasy Joan doth keel the pot.

— The words of Mercury are harsh after the songs of Apollo. You, that way: we, this way.

56

Poor soul, the centre of my sinful earth,
Fool'd by these rebel powers that thee array,
Why dost thou pine within and suffer dearth,
Painting thy outward walls so costly gay?
Why so large cost, having so short a lease,
Dost thou upon thy fading mansion spend?
Shall worms, inheritors of this excess,
Eat up thy charge? Is this thy body's end?
Then, soul, live thou upon thy servant's loss,
And let that pine to aggravate thy store;
Buy terms divine in selling hours of dross;
Within be fed, without be rich no more:
So shalt thou feed on Death, that feeds on men,
And Death once dead, there's no more dying then.

57

Now entertain conjecture of a time
When creeping murmur and the poring dark
Fills the wide vessel of the universe.
From camp to camp, through the foul womb of night,
The hum of either army stilly sounds,
That the fix'd sentinels almost receive
The secret whispers of each other's watch:
Fire answers fire, and through their paly flames
Each battle sees the other's umber'd face:
Steed threatens steed, in high and boastful neighs
Piercing the night's dull ear; and from the tents
The armourers, accomplishing the knights,
With busy hammers closing rivets up,
Give dreadful note of preparation.
The country cocks do crow, the clocks do toll,
And the third hour of drowsy morning name,
Proud of their numbers, and secure in soul,
The confident and over-lusty French
Do the low-rated English play at dice;
And chide the cripple tardy-gaited night
Who, like a foul and ugly witch, doth limp
So tediously away. The poor condemned English,
Like sacrifices, by their watchful fires
Sit patiently, and inly ruminate
The morning's danger, and their gesture sad
Investing lank-lean cheeks and war-worn coats
Presenteth them unto the gazing moon
So many horrid ghosts. O! now, who will behold
The royal captain of this ruin'd band
Walking from watch to watch, from tent to tent,
Let him cry 'Praise and glory on his head!'
For forth he goes and visits all his host,
Bids them good morrow with a modest smile,
And calls them brothers, friends, and countrymen.

Upon his royal face there is no note
How dread an army hath enrounded him;
Nor doth he dedicate one jot of colour
Unto the weary and all-watched night:
But freshly looks and overbears attaint
With cheerful semblance and sweet majesty;
That every wretch, pining and pale before,
Beholding him, plucks comfort from his looks.
A largess universal, like the sun
His liberal eye doth give to every one,
Thawing cold fear. Then mean and gentle all,
Behold, as may unworthiness define,
A little touch of Harry in the night.
And so our scene must to the battle fly;
Where, – O for pity, – we shall much disgrace,
With four or five most vile and ragged foils,
Right ill dispos'd in brawl ridiculous,
The name of Agincourt.

58

Devouring Time, blunt thou the lion's paws,
And make the earth devour her own sweet brood;
Pluck the keen teeth from the fierce tiger's jaws,
And burn the long-liv'd phoenix in her blood;
Make glad and sorry seasons as thou fleets,
And do whate'er thou wilt, swift-footed Time,
To the wide world and all her fading sweets;
But I forbid thee one most heinous crime:
O! carve not with thy hours my love's fair brow,
Nor draw no lines there with thine antique pen;
Him in thy course untainted do allow
For beauty's pattern to succeeding men.
  Yet, do thy worst, old Time: despite thy wrong,
  My love shall in my verse ever live young.

59

All the world's a stage,
And all the men and women merely players:
They have their exits and their entrances;
And one man in his time plays many parts,
His acts being seven ages. At first the infant,
Mewling and puking in the nurse's arms.
And then the whining school-boy, with his satchel,
And shining morning face, creeping like snail
Unwillingly to school. And then the lover,
Sighing like furnace, with a woeful ballad
Made to his mistress' eyebrow. Then a soldier,
Full of strange oaths, and bearded like the pard,
Jealous in honour, sudden and quick in quarrel,
Seeking the bubble reputation
Even in the cannon's mouth. And then the justice,
In fair round belly with good capon lin'd,
With eyes severe, and beard of formal cut,
Full of wise saws and modern instances;
And so he plays his part. The sixth age shifts
Into the lean and slipper'd pantaloon,
With spectacles on nose and pouch on side,
His youthful hose well sav'd, a world too wide
For his shrunk shank; and his big manly voice,
Turning again toward childish treble, pipes
And whistles in his sound. Last scene of all,
That ends this strange eventful history,
Is second childishness and mere oblivion,
Sans teeth, sans eyes, sans taste, sans everything.

60

Tir'd with all these, for restful death I cry
As to behold desert a beggar born,
And needy nothing trimm'd in jollity,
And purest faith unhappily forsworn,

And gilded honour shamefully misplac'd,
And maiden virtue rudely strumpeted,
And right perfection wrongfully disgraced,
And strength by limping sway disabled,
And art made tongue-tied by authority,
And folly – doctor-like – controlling skill,
And simple truth miscall'd simplicity,
And captive good attending captain ill:
  Tir'd with all these, from these would I be gone,
  Save that, to die, I leave my love alone.

61

Upon the king! let us our lives, our souls,
Our debts, our careful wives,
Our children, and our sins lay on the king!
We must bear all. O hard condition!
Twin-born with greatness, subject to the breath
Of every fool, whose sense no more can feel
But his own wringing. What infinite heart's ease
Must kings neglect that private men enjoy!
And what have kings that privates have not too,
Save ceremony, save general ceremony?
And what art thou, thou idle ceremony?
What kind of god art thou, that suffer'st more
Of mortal griefs than do thy worshippers?
What are thy rents? what are thy comings-in?
O ceremony! show me but thy worth:
What is thy soul of adoration?
Art thou aught else but place, degree, and form,
Creating awe and fear in other men?
Wherein thou art less happy, being fear'd,
Than they in fearing.
What drink'st thou oft, instead of homage sweet,
But poison'd flattery? O! be sick, great greatness,
And bid thy ceremony give thee cure.

Think'st thou the fiery fever will go out
With titles blown from adulation?
Will it give place to flexure and low-bending?
Canst thou, when thou command'st the beggar's knee,
Command the health of it? No, thou proud dream,
That play'st so subtly with a king's repose;
I am a king that find thee; and I know
'Tis not the balm, the sceptre and the ball,
The sword, the mace, the crown imperial,
The intertissued robe of gold and pearl,
The farced title running 'fore the king,
The throne he sits on, nor the tide of pomp
That beats upon the high shore of this world,
No, not all these, thrice-gorgeous ceremony,
Not all these, laid in bed majestical,
Can sleep so soundly as the wretched slave,
Who with a body fill'd and vacant mind
Gets him to rest, cramm'd with distressful bread;
Never sees horrid night, the child of hell,
But, like a lackey, from the rise to set
Sweats in the eye of Phœbus, and all night
Sleeps in Elysium; next day after dawn,
Doth rise and help Hyperion to his horse,
And follows so the ever-running year
With profitable labour to his grave:
And, but for ceremony, such a wretch,
Winding up days with toil and nights with sleep,
Had the fore-hand and vantage of a king.
The slave, a member of the country's peace,
Enjoys it; but in gross brain little wots
What watch the king keeps to maintain the peace,
Whose hours the peasant best advantages.

62

Some glory in their birth, some in their skill,
Some in their wealth, some in their body's force;

Some in their garments, though new-fangled ill;
Some in their hawks and hounds, some in their horse;
And every humour hath his adjunct pleasure,
Wherein it finds a joy above the rest:
But these particulars are not my measure;
All these I better in one general best.
Thy love is better than high birth to me,
Richer than wealth, prouder than garments' cost,
Of more delight than hawks or horses be;
And having thee, of all men's pride I boast:
  Wretched in this alone, that thou mayst take
  All this away, and me most wretched make.

63

— I did dislike the cut of a certain courtier's beard: he sent me word, if I said his beard was not cut well, he was in the mind it was: this is called 'the retort courteous'. If I sent him word again, it was not well cut, he would send me word, he cut it to please himself: this is called the 'quip modest'. If again, it was not well cut, he disabled my judgment: this is called the 'reply churlish'. If again, it was not well cut, he would answer, I spake not true: this is called the 'reproof valiant': if again, it was not well cut, he would say, I lie: this is called the 'countercheck quarrelsome': and so to the 'lie circumstantial', and the 'lie direct'.

— And how oft did you say his beard was not well cut?

— I durst go no further than the 'lie circumstantial', nor he durst not give me the 'lie direct'; and so we measured swords and parted.

— Can you nominate in order now the degrees of the lie?

— O sir, we quarrel in print; by the book, as you have books for good manners: I will name you the degrees. The first, the 'retort courteous'; the second, the 'quip modest'; the third, the 'reply churlish'; the fourth, the 'reproof valiant'; the fifth, the 'countercheck quarrelsome'; the sixth, the 'lie with circumstance'; the seventh, the 'lie direct'. All these you may avoid but the lie direct; and you may avoid that too, with an 'if'. I knew when seven justices could not take up a quarrel; but when the parties were met themselves, one of them thought but of an 'if', as 'If you said so, then I said so'; and they shook hands and swore brothers. Your 'if' is the only peace-maker; much virtue in 'if'.

64

Once more unto the breach, dear friends, once more;
Or close the wall up with our English dead!
In peace there's nothing so becomes a man
As modest stillness and humility:
But when the blast of war blows in our ears,
Then imitate the action of the tiger;
Stiffen the sinews, summon up the blood,
Disguise fair nature with hard-favour'd rage;
Then lend the eye a terrible aspect;
Let it pry through the portage of the head
Like the brass cannon; let the brow o'erwhelm it
As fearfully as doth a galled rock
O'erhang and jutty his confounded base,
Swill'd with the wild and wasteful ocean.
Now set the teeth and stretch the nostril wide,
Hold hard the breath, and bend up every spirit
To his full height! On, on, you noblest English!
Whose blood is fet from fathers of war-proof;
Fathers that, like so many Alexanders,
Have in these parts from morn till even fought,
And sheath'd their swords for lack of argument.
Dishonour not your mothers; now attest
That those whom you call'd fathers did beget you.
Be copy now to men of grosser blood,
And teach them how to war. And you, good yeomen,
Whose limbs were made in England, show us here

The mettle of your pasture; let us swear
That you are worth your breeding; which I doubt not;
For there is none of you so mean and base
That hath not noble lustre in your eyes.
I see you stand like greyhounds in the slips,
Straining upon the start. The game's afoot:
Follow your spirit; and, upon this charge
Cry 'God for Harry! England and Saint George!'

65

Since brass, nor stone, nor earth, nor boundless sea,
But sad mortality o'ersways their power,
How with this rage shall beauty hold a plea,
Whose action is no stronger than a flower?
O! how shall summer's honey breath hold out
Against the wrackful siege of battering days,
When rocks impregnable are not so stout,
Nor gates of steel so strong, but Time decays?
O fearful meditation! where, alack,
Shall Time's best jewel from Time's chest lie hid?
Or what strong hand can hold his swift foot back?
Or who his spoil of beauty can forbid?
  O! none, unless this miracle have might,
  That in black ink my love may still shine bright.

66

O! pardon me, thou bleeding piece of earth,
That I am meek and gentle with these butchers;
Thou art the ruins of the noblest man
That ever lived in the tide of times.
Woe to the hand that shed this costly blood!
Over thy wounds now do I prophesy,
Which like dumb mouths do ope their ruby lips,
To beg the voice and utterance of my tongue,
A curse shall light upon the limbs of men;

Domestic fury and fierce civil strife
Shall cumber all the parts of Italy;
Blood and destruction shall be so in use,
And dreadful objects so familiar,
That mothers shall but smile when they behold
Their infants quarter'd with the hands of war;
All pity chok'd with custom of fell deeds:
And Caesar's spirit, ranging for revenge,
With Ate by his side come hot from hell,
Shall in these confines with a monarch's voice
Cry 'Havoc!' and let slip the dogs of war;
That this foul deed shall smell above the earth
With carrion men, groaning for burial.

67

Were't aught to me I bore the canopy,
With my extern the outward honouring,
Or laid great bases for eternity,
Which prove more short than waste or ruining?
Have I not seen dwellers on form and favour
Lose all and more by paying too much rent,
For compound sweet foregoing simple savour
Pitiful thrivers, in their gazing spent?
No; let me be obsequious in thy heart,
And take thou my oblation, poor but free,
Which is not mix'd with seconds, knows no art,
But mutual render, only me for thee.
  Hence, thou suborn'd informer! a true soul
  When most impeach'd stands least in thy control.

68

If we are mark'd to die, we are enow
To do our country loss; and if to live,
The fewer men, the greater share of honour.
God's will! I pray thee, wish not one man more.

By Jove, I am not covetous for gold,
Nor care I who doth feed upon my cost;
It yearns me not if men my garments wear;
Such outward things dwell not in my desires:
But if it be a sin to covet honour,
I am the most offending soul alive.
No, faith, my coz, wish not a man from England:
God's peace! I would not lose so great an honour
As one man more, methinks, would shake from me,
For the best hope I have. O! do not wish one more:
Rather proclaim it, Westmoreland, through my host,
That he which hath no stomach to this fight,
Let him depart: his passport shall be made,
And crowns for convoy put into his purse:
We would not die in that man's company
That fears his fellowship to die with us.
This day is call'd the feast of Crispian:
He that outlives this day, and comes safe home,
Will stand a tip-toe when this day is nam'd,
And rouse him at the name of Crispian.
He that shall live this day, and see old age,
Will yearly on the vigil feast his neighbours,
And say, 'To-morrow is Saint Crispian':
Then will he strip his sleeve and show his scars,
And say, 'These wounds I had on Crispin's day.'
Old men forget: yet all shall be forgot,
But he'll remember with advantages
What feats he did that day. Then shall our names,
Familiar in his mouth as household words,
Harry the king, Bedford and Exeter,
Warwick and Talbot, Salisbury and Gloucester,
Be in their flowing cups freshly remember'd.
This story shall the good man teach his son;
And Crispin Crispian shall ne'er go by,
From this day to the ending of the world,
But we in it shall be remembered;

We few, we happy few, we band of brothers;
For he to-day that sheds his blood with me
Shall be my brother; be he ne'er so vile
This day shall gentle his condition:
And gentlemen in England now a-bed
Shall think themselves accurs'd they were not here,
And hold their manhoods cheap whiles any speaks
That fought with us upon Saint Crispin's day.

69

What potions have I drunk of Siren tears,
Distill'd from limbecks foul as hell within,
Applying fears to hopes, and hopes to fears,
Still losing when I saw myself to win!
What wretched errors hath my heart committed,
Whilst it hath thought itself so blessed never!
How have mine eyes out of their spheres been fitted,
In the distraction of this madding fever!
O benefit of ill! now I find true
That better is by evil still made better
And ruin'd love, when it is built anew,
Grows fairer than at first, more strong, far greater.
  So I return rebuk'd to my content,
  And gain by ill thrice more than I have spent.

70

What need I be so forward with him that calls not on me? Well, 'tis no matter; honour pricks me on. Yea, but how if honour prick me off when I come on? how then? Can honour set to a leg? No. Or an arm? No. Or take away the grief of a wound? No. Honour hath no skill in surgery then? No. What is honour? a word. What is that word, honour? Air. A trim reckoning! Who hath it? he that died o' Wednesday. Doth he feel it? No. Doth he hear it? No. It is insensible then? Yea, to the dead. But will it not live with the living? No. Why?

Detraction will not suffer it. Therefore I'll none of it: honour is a mere scutcheon; and so ends my catechism.

71

If my dear love were but the child of state,
It might for Fortune's bastard be unfather'd,
As subject to Time's love or to Time's hate,
Weeds among weeds, or flowers with flowers gather'd.
No, it was builded far from accident;
It suffers not in smiling pomp, nor falls
Under the blow of thralled discontent,
Whereto the inviting time our fashion calls:
It fears not policy, that heretic,
Which works on leases of short number'd hours,
But all alone stands hugely politic,
That it nor grows with heat, nor drowns with showers.
  To this I witness call the fools of time,
  Which die for goodness, who have liv'd for crime.

72

Tell me where is fancy bred,
Or in the heart or in the head?
How begot, how nourished?
    Reply, reply.
It is engender'd in the eyes,
With gazing fed; and fancy dies
In the cradle where it lies.
    Let us all ring fancy's knell:
    I'll begin it, – Ding, dong, bell.
Ding, dong, bell.

73

That time of year thou mayst in me behold
When yellow leaves, or none, or few, do hang
Upon those boughs which shake against the cold,

Bare ruin'd choirs, where late the sweet birds sang.
In me thou see'st the twilight of such day
As after sunset fadeth in the west;
Which by and by black night doth take away,
Death's second self, that seals up all in rest.
In me thou see'st the glowing of such fire,
That on the ashes of his youth doth lie,
As the death-bed whereon it must expire
Consum'd with that which it was nourish'd by.
  This thou perceiv'st, which makes thy love more strong,
  To love that well which thou must leave ere long.

74

— Even or odd of all days in the year,
Come Lammas-eve at night shall she be fourteen.
Susan and she – God rest all Christian souls! –
Were of an age. Well, Susan is with God;
She was too good for me. But, as I said,
On Lammas-eve at night shall she be fourteen;
That shall she, marry; I remember it well.
'Tis since the earthquake now eleven years;
And she was wean'd, I never shall forget it,
Of all the days of the year, upon that day;
For I had then laid wormwood to my dug,
Sitting in the sun under the dove-house wall;
My lord and you were then at Mantua.
Nay, I do bear a brain: – but, as I said,
When it did taste the wormwood on the nipple
Of my dug and felt it bitter, pretty fool!
To see it tetchy and fall out with the dug.
'Shake,' quoth the dove-house: 'twas no need, I trow
To bid me trudge:
And since that time it is eleven years;
For then she could stand high lone; nay, by the rood,
She could have run and waddled all about;

For even the day before she broke her brow:
And then my husband – God be with his soul!
A' was a merry man – took up the child:
'Yea,' quoth he, 'dost thou fall upon thy face?
Thou wilt fall backward when thou hast more wit;
Wilt thou not, Jule?' and, by my halidom,
The pretty wretch left crying, and said 'Ay.'
To see now how a jest shall come about!
I warrant, an I should live a thousand years,
I never should forget it: 'Wilt thou not, Jule?' quoth he;
And, pretty fool, it stinted and said 'Ay.'
— Enough of this; I pray thee, hold thy peace.
— Yes, madam. Yet I cannot chose but laugh,
To think it should leave crying, and say 'Ay.'
And yet, I warrant, it had upon its brow
A bump as big as a young cockerel's stone;
A parlous knock; and it cried bitterly:
'Yea,' quoth my husband, 'fall'st upon thy face?
Thou wilt fall backwards when thou com'st to age;
Wilt thou not, Jule?' it stinted and said 'Ay.'

75

'Tis better to be vile than vile esteem'd,
When not to be receives reproach of being;
And the just pleasure lost, which is so deem'd
Not by our feeling, but by others' seeing:
For why should others' false adulterate eyes
Give salutation to my sportive blood?
Or on my frailties why are frailer spies,
Which in their wills count bad what I think good?
No, I am that I am, and they that level
At my abuses reckon up their own:
I may be straight though they themselves be bevel;
By their rank thoughts my deeds must not be shown;
Unless this general evil they maintain,
All men are bad and in their badness reign.

76

The quality of mercy is not strain'd,
It droppeth as the gentle rain from heaven
Upon the place beneath: it is twice bless'd;
It blesseth him that gives and him that takes:
'Tis mightiest in the mightiest; it becomes
The throned monarch better than his crown;
His sceptre shows the force of temporal power,
The attribute to awe and majesty,
Wherein doth sit the dread and fear of kings;
But mercy is above this sceptred sway,
It is enthroned in the hearts of kings,
It is an attribute to God himself,
And earthly power doth then show likest God's
When mercy seasons justice.

77

Thine eyes I love, and they, as pitying me,
Knowing thy heart torments me with disdain,
Have put on black and loving mourners be,
Looking with pretty ruth upon my pain.
And truly not the morning sun of heaven
Better becomes the grey cheeks of the east,
Nor that full star that ushers in the even,
Doth half that glory to the sober west,
As those two mourning eyes become thy face:
O! let it then as well beseem thy heart
To mourn for me, since mourning doth thee grace,
And suit thy pity like in every part.
  Then will I swear beauty herself is black,
  And all they foul that thy complexion lack.

78

Of comfort no man speak:
Let's talk of graves, of worms, and epitaphs;
Make dust our paper, and with rainy eyes
Write sorrow on the bosom of the earth;
Let's choose executors and talk of wills:
And yet not so – for what can we bequeath
Save our deposed bodies to the ground?
Our lands, our lives, and all are Bolingbroke's,
And nothing can we call our own but death,
And that small model of the barren earth
Which serves as paste and cover to our bones.
For God's sake, let us sit upon the ground
And tell sad stories of the death of kings:
How some have been depos'd, some slain in war,
Some haunted by the ghosts they have depos'd,
Some poison'd by their wives, some sleeping kill'd;
All murder'd: for within the hollow crown
That rounds the mortal temples of a king
Keeps Death his court, and there the antick sits,
Scoffing his state and grinning at his pomp;
Allowing him a breath, a little scene,
To monarchize, be fear'd, and kill with looks,
Infusing him with self and vain conceit
As if this flesh which walls about our life
Were brass impregnable; and humour'd thus
Comes at the last, and with a little pin
Bores through his castle wall, and farewell king!
Cover your heads, and mock not flesh and blood
With solemn reverence: throw away respect,
Tradition, form, and ceremonious duty,
For you have but mistook me all this while:
I live with bread like you, feel want,
Taste grief, need friends: subjected thus,
How can you say to me I am a king?

79

In faith, I do not love thee with mine eyes,
For they in thee a thousand errors note;
But 'tis my heart that loves what they despise,
Who, in despite of view, is pleas'd to dote.
Nor are mine ears with thy tongue's tune delighted;
Nor tender feeling, to base touches prone.
Nor taste nor smell desire to be invited
To any sensual feast with thee alone:
But my five wits nor my five senses can
Dissuade one foolish heart from serving thee,
Who leaves unsway'd the likeness of a man,
Thy proud heart's slave and vassal wretch to be:
  Only my plague thus far I count my gain,
  That she that makes me sin awards me pain.

80

I do see the bottom of Justice Shallow. Lord, Lord! how subject we old men are to this vice of lying. This same starved justice hath done nothing but prate to me of the wildness of his youth and the feats he hath done about Turnbull Street; and every third word a lie, duer paid to the hearer than the Turk's tribute. I do remember him at Clement's Inn like a man made after supper of a cheese-paring: when a' was naked he was for all the world like a forked radish, with a head fantastically carved upon it with a knife: a' was so forlorn that his dimensions to any thick sight were invincible: a' was the very genius of famine; yet lecherous as a monkey, and the whores called him mandrake: a' came ever in the rearward of the fashion and sung those tunes to the over-scutched huswives that he heard the carmen whistle, and sware they were his fancies or his good-nights. And now is this Vice's dagger become a squire, and talks as familiarly of John a Gaunt as if he had been sworn brother to him; and I'll be sworn a' never saw him but once in the Tilt-yard, and then he burst his head for crowding among the marshal's men. I saw it and told John a Gaunt he beat his own name; for you might have thrust him and all his apparel into an eel-skin; the case of a treble hautboy was a mansion for him, a court; and now has he land and beefs.

81

Grant them remov'd, and grant that this your noise
Hath chid down all the majesty of England;
Imagine that you see the wretched strangers,
Their babies at their backs, with their poor luggage,
Plodding to th' ports and coasts for transportation,
And that you sit as kings in your desires,
Authority quite silenc'd by your brawl,
And you in ruff of your opinions clothed,
What had you got? I'll tell you. You had taught
How insolence and strong hand should prevail,
How order should be quell'd – and by this pattern
Not one of you should live an aged man;
For other ruffians, as their fancies wrought,
With selfsame hand, self reasons and self right
Would shark on you, and men like ravenous fishes
Would feed on one another . . . you'll put down strangers,
Kill them, cut their throats, possess their houses,
And lead the majesty of law in liom
To slip him like a hound. Say now the king
(As he is clement, if th'offender mourn)
Should so much come too short of your great trespass
As but to banish you – whither would you go?
What country, by the nature of your error,
Should give you harbour? Go you to France or Flanders,
To any German prince, to Spain or Portugal,
Nay, anywhere that not adheres to England,
Why, you must needs be strangers. Would you be pleas'd
To find a nation of such barbarous temper

That, breaking out in hideous violence,
Would not afford you an abode on earth,
Whet their detested knives against your throats,
Spurn you like dogs, and like as if that God
Ow'd not nor made not you, nor that the elements
Were not all appropriate to your comforts,
But charter'd unto them – what would you think
To be thus us'd? This is the strangers' case,
And this your mountainish inhumanity.

82

No longer mourn for me when I am dead
Than you shall hear the surly sullen bell
Give warning to the world that I am fled
From this vile world, with vilest worms to dwell:
Nay, if you read this line, remember not
The hand that writ it; for I love you so,
That I in your sweet thoughts would be forgot,
If thinking on me then should make you woe.
O! if, – I say, you look upon this verse,
When I perhaps compounded am with clay,
Do not so much as my poor name rehearse,
But let your love even with my life decay;
  Lest the wise world should look into your moan,
  And mock you with me after I am gone.

83

No, not an oath: if not the face of men,
The sufferance of our souls, the time's abuse,
If these be motives weak, break off betimes,
And every man hence to his idle bed;
So let high-sighted tyranny range on,
Till each man drop by lottery. But if these,
As I am sure they do, bear fire enough
To kindle cowards and to steel with valour

The melting spirits of women, then, countrymen,
What need we any spur but our own cause
To prick us to redress? what other bond
Than secret Romans, that have spoke the word
And will not palter? and what other oath
Than honesty to honesty engag'd,
That this shall be, or we will fall for it?
Swear priests and cowards and men cautelous,
Old feeble carrions and such suffering souls
That welcome wrongs; unto bad causes swear
Such creatures as men doubt; but do not stain
The even virtue of our enterprise,
Nor th' insuppressive mettle of our spirits,
To think that or our cause or our performance
Did need an oath; when every drop of blood
That every Roman bears, and nobly bears,
Is guilty of a several bastardy,
If he do break the smallest particle
Of any promise that hath pass'd from him.

84

Not mine own fears, nor the prophetic soul
Of the wide world dreaming on things to come,
Can yet the lease of my true love control,
Suppose'd as forfeit to a confin's doom.
The mortal moon hath her eclipse endur'd,
And the sad augurs mock their own presage;
Incertainties now crown themselves assur'd,
And peace proclaims olives of endless age.
Now with the drops of this most balmy time
My love looks fresh, and Death to me subscribes,
Since, spite of him, I'll live in this poor rime,
While he insults o'er dull and speechless tribes:
And thou in this shalt find thy monument,
When tyrants' crests and tombs of brass are spent.

85

Friends, Romans, countrymen, lend me your ears;
I come to bury Caesar, not to praise him.
The evil that men do lives after them,
The good is oft interred with their bones;
So let it be with Caesar. The noble Brutus
Hath told you Caesar was ambitious;
If it were so, it was a grievous fault,
And grievously hath Caesar answered it.
Here, under leave of Brutus and the rest, –
For Brutus is an honourable man;
So are they all, all honourable men, –
Come I to speak in Caesar's funeral.
He was my friend, faithful and just to me:
But Brutus says he was ambitious;
And Brutus is an honourable man.
He hath brought many captives home to Rome,
Whose ransoms did the general coffers fill:
Did this in Caesar seem ambitious?
When that the poor have cried, Caesar hath wept;
Ambition should be made of sterner stuff:
Yet Brutus says he was ambitious;
And Brutus is an honourable man.
You all did see that on the Lupercal
I thrice presented him a kingly crown,
Which he did thrice refuse: was this ambition?
Yet Brutus says he was ambitious;
And, sure, he is an honourable man.
I speak not to disprove what Brutus spoke,
But here I am to speak what I do know.
You all did love him once, not without cause:
What cause withholds you then to mourn for him?
O judgment! thou art fled to brutish beasts,
And men have lost their reason. Bear with me;
My heart is in the coffin there with Caesar,
And I must pause till it come back to me.

86

Two loves I have of comfort and despair,
Which like two spirits do suggest me still:
The better angel is a man right fair,
The worser spirit a woman, colour'd ill.
To win me soon to hell, my female evil
Tempteth my better angel from my side,
And would corrupt my saint to be a devil,
Wooing his purity with her foul pride.
And whether that my angel be turn'd fiend
Suspect I may, but not directly tell;
But being both from me, both to each friend,
I guess one angel in another's hell:
  Yet this shall I ne'er know, but live in doubt,
  Till my bad angel fire my good one out.

87

Nay, you shall hear, Master Brook, what I have suffered to bring this woman to evil for your good. Being thus crammed in the basket, a couple of Ford's knaves, his hinds, were called forth by their mistress to carry me in the name of foul clothes to Datchetlane: they took me on their shoulders; met the jealous knave their master in the door, who asked them once or twice what they had in their basket. I quaked for fear lest the lunatic knave would have searched it; but Fate, ordaining he should be a cuckold, held his hand. Well; on went he for a search, and away went I for foul clothes. But mark the sequel, Master Brook: I suffered the pangs of three several deaths: first, an intolerable fright, to be detected with a jealous rotten bell-wether; next, to be compassed, like a good bilbo, in the circumference of a peck, hilt to point, heel to head; and then, to be stopped in, like a strong distillation, with stinking clothes that fretted in their own grease: think of that, a man of my kidney, think of that, that am as subject to heat as butter; a man of continual dissolution and thaw: it was a miracle to 'scape suffocation. And in the height of this bath, when I was more than half stewed in grease, like a Dutch dish, to be thrown into the Thames, and cooled, glowing hot, in that surge, like a horse-shoe; think of that, hissing hot, think of that, Master Brook!

88

When that I was and a little tiny boy,
With hey, ho, the wind and the rain;
A foolish thing was but a toy,
For the rain it raineth every day.

But when I came to man's estate,
With hey, ho, the wind and the rain;
'Gainst knaves and thieves men shut their gate,
For the rain it raineth every day.

But when I came, alas! to wive,
With hey, ho, the wind and the rain;
By swaggering could I never thrive,
For the rain it raineth every day.

But when I came unto my beds,
With hey, ho, the wind and the rain;
With toss-pots still had drunken heads,
For the rain it raineth every day.

A great while ago the world begun,
With hey, ho, the wind and the rain;
But that's all one, our play is done,
And we'll strive to please you every day.

89

Thou blind fool, Love, what dost thou to mine eyes,
That they behold, and see not what they see?
They know what beauty is, see where it lies,
Yet what the best is take the worst to be.

If eyes, corrupt by over-partial looks,
Be anchor'd in the bay where all men ride,
Why of eyes' falsehood hast thou forged hooks,
Whereto the judgment of my heart is tied?
Why should my heart think that a several plot
Which my heart knows the wide world's common place?
Or mine eyes, seeing this, say this is not,
To put fair truth upon so foul a face?
In things right true my heart and eyes have err'd,
And to this false plague are they now transferr'd.

90

This royal throne of kings, this scepter'd isle,
This earth of majesty, this seat of Mars,
This other Eden, demi-paradise,
This fortress built by Nature for herself
Against infection and the hand of war,
This happy breed of men, this little world,
This precious stone set in the silver sea,
Which serves it in the office of a wall,
Or as a moat defensive to a house,
Against the envy of less happier lands,
This blessed plot, this earth, this realm, this England,
This nurse, this teeming womb of royal kings,
Fear'd by their breed and famous by their birth,
Renowned for their deeds as far from home, –
For Christian service and true chivalry, –
As is the sepulchre in stubborn Jewry
Of the world's ransom, blessed Mary's Son:
This land of such dear souls, this dear, dear land,
Dear for her reputation through the world,
Is now leas'd out, – I die pronouncing it, –
Like to a tenement, or pelting farm:
England, bound in with the triumphant sea,
Whose rocky shore beats back the envious siege

Of watery Neptune, is now bound in with shame,
With inky blots, and rotten parchment bonds:
That England, that was wont to conquer others,
Hath made a shameful conquest of itself.

91

When my love swears that she is made of truth,
I do believe her, though I know she lies,
That she might think me some untutor'd youth,
Unlearned in the world's false subtleties.
Thus vainly thinking that she thinks me young,
Although she knows my days are past the best,
Simply I credit her false-speaking tongue:
On both sides thus is simple truth suppress't.
But wherefore says she not she is unjust?
And wherefore say not I that I am old?
O! love's best habit is in seeming trust,
And age in love loves not to have years told:
  Therefore I lie with her, and she with me,
  And in our faults by lies we flatter'd be.

92

If I begin the battery once again,
I will not leave the half-achieved Harfleur
Till in her ashes she lie buried.
The gates of mercy shall be all shut up,
And the flesh'd soldier, rough and hard of heart,
In liberty of bloody hand shall range
With conscience wide as hell, mowing like grass
Your fresh-fair virgins and your flowering infants.
What is it then to me, if impious war,
Array'd in flames like to the prince of fiends,
Do, with his smirch'd complexion, all fell feats
Enlink'd to waste and desolation?
What is't to me, when you yourselves are cause,

If your pure maidens fall into the hand
Of hot and forcing violation?
What rein can hold licentious wickedness
When down the hill he holds his fierce career?
We may as bootless spend our vain command
Upon the enraged soldiers in their spoil
As send precepts to the leviathan
To come ashore. Therefore, you men of Harfleur,
Take pity of your town and of your people,
Whiles yet my soldiers are in my command;
Whiles yet the cool and temperate wind of grace
O'erblows the filthy and contagious clouds
Of heady murder, spoil, and villany.
If not, why, in a moment, look to see
The blind and bloody soldier with foul hand
Defile the locks of your shrill-shrieking daughters;
Your fathers taken by the silver beards,
And their most reverend heads dash'd to the walls;
Your naked infants spitted upon pikes,
Whiles the mad mothers with their howls confus'd
Do break the clouds, as did the wives of Jewry
At Herod's bloody-hunting slaughtermen.
What say you? will you yield, and this avoid?

93

O me! what eyes hath Love put in my head,
Which have no correspondence with true sight;
Or, if they have, where is my judgment fled,
That censures falsely what they see aright?
If that be fair whereon my false eyes dote,
What means the world to say it is not so?
If it be not, then love doth well denote
Love's eye is not so true as all men's: no.
How can it? O! how can Love's eye be true,
That is so vex'd with watching and with tears?

No marvel then, though I mistake my view;
The sun itself sees not till heaven clears.
  O cunning Love! with tears thou keep'st me blind,
  Lest eyes well-seeing thy foul faults should find.

94

Yon island carrions desperate of their bones,
Ill-favour'dly become the morning field;
Their ragged curtains poorly are let loose,
And our air shakes them passing scornfully:
Big Mars seems bankrupt in their beggar'd host,
And faintly through a rusty beaver peeps:
The horsemen sit like fixed candlesticks,
With torch-staves in their hand; and their poor jades
Lob down their heads, dropping the hides and hips,
The gum down-roping from their pale-dead eyes,
And in their pale dull mouths the gimmal bit
Lies foul with chew'd grass, still and motionless;
And their executors, the knavish crows,
Fly o'er them, all impatient for their hour.

95

I think Crab my dog be the sourest-natured dog that lives: my mother weeping, my father wailing, my sister crying, our maid howling, our cat wringing her hands, and all our house in a great perplexity, yet did not this cruel-hearted cur shed one tear. He is a stone, a very pebble stone, and has no more pity in him than a dog; a Jew would have wept to have seen our parting: why, my grandam, having no eyes, look you, wept herself blind at my parting. Nay, I'll show you the manner of it. This shoe is my father; no, this left shoe is my father: no, no, this left shoe is my mother; nay, that cannot be so neither: – yes, it is so; it is so; it hath the worser sole. This shoe, with the hole in, is my mother, and this my father. A vengeance on't! there 'tis: now, sir, this staff is my sister;

for, look you, she is as white as a lily and as small as a wand: this hat is Nan, our maid: I am the dog; no, the dog is himself, and I am the dog, – O! the dog is me, and I am myself: ay, so, so. Now come I to my father; 'Father, your blessing'; now should not the shoe speak a word for weeping: now should I kiss my father; well, he weeps on. Now come I to my mother; – O, that she could speak now like a wood woman! Well, I kiss her; why, there 'tis; here's my mother's breath up and down. Now come I to my sister; mark the moan she makes: Now the dog all this while sheds not a tear nor speaks a word; but see how I lay the dust with my tears.

96

My love is as a fever, longing still
For that which longer nurseth the disease;
Feeding on that which doth preserve the ill,
The uncertain sickly appetite to please.
My reason, the physician to my love,
Angry that his prescriptions are not kept,
Hath left me, and I desperate now approve
Desire is death, which physic did except.
Past cure I am, now Reason is past care,
And frantic-mad with evermore unrest;
My thoughts and my discourse as madmen's are,
At random from the truth vainly express'd;
  For I have sworn thee fair, and thought thee bright,
  Who art as black as hell, as dark as night.

97

Other slow arts entirely keep the brain,
And therefore, finding barren practisers,
Scarce show a harvest of their heavy toil;
But love, first learned in a lady's eyes,
Lives not alone immured in the brain,
But, with the motion of all elements,

Courses as swift as thought in every power,
And gives to every power a double power,
Above their functions and their offices.
It adds a precious seeing to the eye;
A lover's eyes will gaze an eagle blind;
A lover's ear will hear the lowest sound,
When the suspicious head of theft is stopp'd:
Love's feeling is more soft and sensible
Than are the tender horns of cockled snails:
Love's tongue proves dainty Bacchus gross in taste.
For valour, is not Love a Hercules,
Still climbing trees in the Hesperides?
Subtle as Sphinx; as sweet and musical
As bright Apollo's lute, strung with his hair;
And when Love speaks, the voice of all the gods
Makes heaven drowsy with the harmony.

98

In loving thee thou know'st I am forsworn,
But thou art twice forsworn, to me love swearing;
In act thy bed-vow broke, and new faith torn,
In vowing new hate after new love bearing.
But why of two oaths' breach do I accuse thee,
When I break twenty? I am perjur'd most;
For all my vows are oaths but to misuse thee,
And all my honest faith in thee is lost:
For I have sworn deep oaths of thy deep kindness,
Oaths of thy love, thy truth, thy constancy;
And, to enlighten thee, gave eyes to blindness,
Or made them swear against the thing they see;
For I have sworn thee fair; more perjur'd I,
To swear against the truth so foul a lie!

99

She is the fairies' midwife, and she comes
In shape no bigger than an agate-stone
On the fore-finger of an alderman,
Drawn with a team of little atomies
Athwart men's noses as they lie asleep:
Her waggon-spokes made of long spinners' legs;
The cover, of the wings of grasshoppers;
The traces, of the smallest spider's web;
The collars, of the moonshine's watery beams;
Her whip, of cricket's bone; the lash, of film;
Her waggoner, a small grey-coated gnat,
Not half so big as a round little worm
Prick'd from the lazy finger of a maid;
Her chariot is an empty hazel-nut,
Made by the joiner squirrel or old grub,
Time out o' mind the fairies' coach-makers.
And in this state she gallops night by night
Through lovers' brains, and then they dream of love;
O'er courtiers' knees, that dream on curtsies straight;
O'er lawyers' fingers, who straight dream on fees;
O'er ladies' lips, who straight on kisses dream;
Which oft the angry Mab with blisters plagues,
Because their breaths with sweetmeats tainted are.
Sometimes she gallops o'er a courtier's nose,
And then dreams he of smelling out a suit;
And sometimes comes she with a tithe-pig's tail,
Tickling a parson's nose as a' lies asleep,
Then dreams he of another benefice;
Sometime she driveth o'er a soldier's neck,
And then dreams he of cutting foreign throats,
Of breaches, ambuscadoes, Spanish blades,
Of healths five fathom deep; and then anon
Drums in his ear, at which he starts and wakes;
And, being thus frighted, swears a prayer or two,

And sleeps again. This is that very Mab
That plats the manes of horses in the night;
And bakes the elf-locks in foul sluttish hairs,
Which once untangled much misfortune bodes;
This is the hag, when maids lie on their backs,
That presses them and learns them first to bear,
Making them women of good carriage:
This is she –

100

Farewell! thou art too dear for my possessing,
And like enough thou know'st thy estimate:
The charter of thy worth gives thee releasing;
My bonds in thee are all determinate.
For how do I hold thee but by thy granting?
And for that riches where is my deserving?
The cause of this fair gift in me is wanting,
And so my patent back again is swerving.
Thyself thou gav'st, thy own worth then not knowing,
Or me, to whom thou gav'st it, else mistaking;
So thy great gift, upon misprision growing,
Comes home again, on better judgment making.
  Thus have I had thee, as a dream doth flatter,
  In sleep a king, but, waking, no such matter.

101

I would I had that corporal soundness now,
As when thy father and myself in friendship
First tried our soldiership! He did look far
Into the service of the time and was
Discipled of the bravest: he lasted long;
But on us both did haggish age steal on,
And wore us out of act. It much repairs me
To talk of your good father. In his youth
He had the wit which I can well observe

To-day in our young lords; but they may jest
Till their own scorn return to them unnoted
Ere they can hide their levity in honour.
So like a courtier, contempt nor bitterness
Were in his pride or sharpness; if they were,
His equal had awak'd them; and his honour,
Clock to itself, knew the true minute when
Exception bid him speak, and at this time
His tongue obey'd his hand: who were below him
He us'd as creatures of another place,
And bow'd his eminent top to their low ranks,
Making them proud of his humility,
In their poor praise he humbled. Such a man
Might be a copy to these younger times,
Which, follow'd well, would demonstrate them now
But goers backward . . .
Would I were with him! He would always say, –
Methinks I hear him now: his plausive words
He scatter'd not in ears, but grafted them,
To grow there and to bear. 'Let me not live,' –
Thus his good melancholy oft began,
On the catastrophe and heel of pastime,
When it was out, – 'Let me not live,' quoth he,
'After my flame lacks oil, to be the snuff
Of younger spirits, whose apprehensive senses
All but new things disdain; whose judgements are
Mere fathers of their garments; whose constancies
Expire before their fashions.' This he wish'd:
I, after him, do after him wish too,
Since I nor wax nor honey can bring home,
I quickly were dissolved from my hive,
To give some labourers room.

102

And suddenly; where injury of chance
Puts back leave-taking, justles roughly by
All time of pause, rudely beguiles our lips
Of all rejoindure, forcibly prevents
Our lock'd embrasures, strangles our dear vows
Even in the birth of our own labouring breath.
We two, that with so many thousand sighs
Did buy each other, must poorly sell ourselves
With the rude brevity and discharge of one.
Injurious time now with a robber's haste
Crams his rich thievery up, he knows not how:
As many farewells as be stars in heaven,
With distinct breath and consign'd kisses to them,
He fumbles up into a loose adieu,
And scants us with a single famish'd kiss,
Distasted with the salt of broken tears.

103

Love is too young to know what conscience is;
Yet who knows not conscience is born of love?
Then, gentle cheater, urge not my amiss,
Lest guilty of my faults thy sweet self prove:
For, thou betraying me, I do betray
My nobler part to my gross body's treason;
My soul doth tell my body that he may
Triumph in love; flesh stays no further reason,
Bur rising at thy name doth point out thee
As his triumphant prize. Proud of this pride,
He is contented thy poor drudge to be,
To stand in thy affairs, fall by thy side.
  No want of conscience hold it that I call
  Her 'love' for whose dear love I rise and fall.

104

Fie, fie upon her!
There's language in her eye, her cheek, her lip,
Nay, her foot speaks; her wanton spirits look out
At every joint and motive of her body.
O! these encounterers, so glib of tongue,
That give a coasting welcome ere it comes,
And wide unclasp the tables of their thoughts
To every tickling reader, set them down
For sluttish spoils of opportunity
And daughters of the game.

105

Be absolute for death; either death or life
Shall thereby be the sweeter. Reason thus with life:
If I do lose thee, I do lose a thing
That none but fools would keep: a breath thou art,
Servile to all the skyey influences,
That dost this habitation, where thou keep'st,
Hourly afflict. Merely, thou art death's fool;
For him thou labour'st by thy flight to shun,
And yet run'st toward him still. Thou art not noble;
For all th' accommodations that thou bear'st
Are nurs'd by baseness. Thou art by no means valiant;
For thou dost fear the soft and tender fork
Of a poor worm. Thy best of rest is sleep,
And that thou oft provok'st; yet grossly fear'st
Thy death, which is no more. Thou art not thyself;
For thou exist'st on many a thousand grains
That issue out of dust. Happy thou art not;
For what thou hast not, still thou striv'st to get,
And what thou hast, forget'st. Thou art not certain;
For thy complexion shifts to strange effects,
After the moon. If thou art rich, thou'rt poor;
For, like an ass whose back with ingots bows,

Thou bear'st thy heavy riches but a journey,
And death unloads thee. Friend has thou none;
For thine own bowels, which do call thee sire,
The mere effusion of thy proper loins,
Do curse the gout, serpigo, and the rheum,
For ending thee no sooner. Thou hast nor youth nor age;
But, as it were, an after-dinner's sleep,
Dreaming on both; for all thy blessed youth
Becomes as aged, and doth beg the alms
Of palsied eld; and when thou art old and rich,
Thou hast neither heat, affection, limb, nor beauty,
To make thy riches pleasant. What's yet in this
That bears the name of life? Yet in this life
Lie hid moe thousand deaths: yet death we fear,
That makes these odds all even.

106

— Come, how wouldst thou praise me?

— I am about it; but indeed my invention
Comes from my pate as birdlime does from frize;
It plucks out brains and all: but my muse labours,
And thus she is deliver'd.
If she be fair and wise, fairness and wit,
The one's for use, the other useth it.

— Well prais'd! How if she be black and witty?

— If she be black, and thereto have a wit,
She'll find a white that shall her blackness fit.

— How if fair and foolish?

— She never yet was foolish that was fair,
For even her folly help'd her to an heir.

— These are old fond paradoxes to make fools laugh i' the alehouse. What miserable praise hast thou for her that's foul and foolish?

— There's none so foul and foolish thereunto
But does foul pranks which fair and wise ones do.

— O heavy ignorance! thou praisest the worst best. But what praise couldst thou bestow on a deserving woman indeed, one that in the authority of her merit, did justly put on the vouch of very malice itself?

— She that was ever fair and never proud,
Had tongue at will and yet was never loud,
Never lack'd gold and yet went never gay,
Fled from her wish and yet said 'Now I may,'
She that being anger'd, her revenge being nigh,
Bade her wrong stay and her displeasure fly,
She that in wisdom never was so frail
To change the cod's head for the salmon's tail,
She that could think and ne'er disclose her mind,
See suitors following and not look behind,
She was a wight, if ever such wight were, –

— To do what?

— To suckle fools and chronicle small beer.

107

I have of late, – but wherefore I know not, – lost all my mirth, forgone all custom of exercises; and indeed it goes so heavily with my disposition that this goodly frame, the earth, seems to me a sterile promontory; this most excellent canopy, the air, look you, this brave o'erhanging firmament, this majestical roof fretted with golden fire, why, it appears no other thing to me but a foul and pestilent congregation of vapours. What a piece of work is a man! How noble in reason! how infinite in faculty! in form, in moving, how express and admirable! in action how like an angel! in apprehension how like a god! the beauty of the world! the paragon of animals! And yet, to me, what is this quintessence of dust? man delights not me; no, nor woman neither, though, by your smiling, you seem to say so.

108

O! that I thought it could be in a woman –
As if it can I will presume in you –
To feed for aye her lamp and flames of love;
To keep her constancy in plight and youth,
Outliving beauty's outward, with a mind
That doth renew swifter than blood decays:
Or that persuasion could but thus convince me,
That my integrity and truth to you
Might be affronted with the match and weight
Of such a winnow'd purity in love;
How were I then uplifted! but, alas!
I am as true as truth's simplicity,
And simpler than the infancy of truth.

109

— He eats nothing but doves, love; and that breeds hot blood, and hot blood begets hot thoughts, and hot thoughts beget hot deeds, and hot deeds is love.

— Is this the generation of love? hot blood? hot thoughts, and hot deeds? Why, they are vipers: is love a generation of vipers?

110

If I be false, or swerve a hair from truth,
When time is old and hath forgot itself,
When waterdrops have worn the stones of Troy,
And blind oblivion swallow'd cities up,
And mighty states characterless are grated
To dusty nothing, yet let memory,
From false to false, among false maids in love

Upbraid my falsehood! when they have said 'as false
As air, as water, wind, or sandy earth,
As fox to lamb, as wolf to heifer's calf,
Pard to the hind, or stepdame to her son';
Yea, let them say, to stick the heart of falsehood,
'As false as Cressid.'

111

I follow him to serve my turn upon him;
We cannot all be masters, nor all masters
Cannot be truly follow'd. You shall mark
Many a duteous and knee-crooking knave,
That, doting on his own obsequious bondage,
Wears out his time, much like his master's ass,
For nought but provender, and when he's old, cashier'd;
Whip me such honest knaves. Others there are
Who, trimm'd in forms and visages of duty,
Keep yet their hearts attending on themselves,
And, throwing but shows of service on their lords,
Do well thrive by them, and when they have lin'd their coats
Do themselves homage: these fellows have some soul;
And such a one do I profess myself. For, sir,
It is as sure as you are Roderigo,
Were I the Moor, I would not be Iago:
In following him, I follow but myself;
Heaven is my judge, not I for love and duty,
But seeming so, for my peculiar end:
For when my outward action doth demonstrate
The native act and figure of my heart
In compliment extern, 'tis not long after
But I will wear my heart upon my sleeve
For daws to peck at: I am not what I am.

112

Aye, but to die, and go we know not where;
To lie in cold obstruction and to rot;
This sensible warm motion to become
A kneaded clod; and the delighted spirit
To bathe in fiery floods, or to reside
In thrilling region of thick-ribbed ice;
To be imprison'd in the viewless winds,
And blown with restless violence round about
The pendant world; or to be worse than worst
Of those that lawless and incertain thoughts
Imagine howling: 'tis too horrible!
The weariest and most loathed worldly life
That age, ache, penury and imprisonment
Can lay on nature is a paradise
To what we fear of death.

113

Take, O take those lips away,
  That so sweetly were forsworn;
And those eyes, the break of day,
  Lights that do mislead the morn:
But my kisses bring again,
                bring again,
Seals of love, but seal'd in vain,
                seal'd in vain.

114

But I do think it is their husbands' faults
If wives do fall. Say that they slack their duties;
And pour our treasures into foreign laps,
Or else break out in peevish jealousies,
Throwing restraint upon us; or, say they strike us,
Or scant our former having in despite;

Why, we have galls, and though we have some grace,
Yet have we some revenge. Let husbands know
Their wives have sense like them; they see and smell,
And have their palates both for sweet and sour,
As husbands have. What is it that they do
When they change us for others? Is it sport?
I think it is; and doth affection breed it?
I think it doth; is't frailty that thus errs?
It is so too; and have not we affections,
Desires for sport, and frailty, as men have?
Then, let them use us well; else let them know,
The ills we do, their ills instruct us so.

115

There, my blessing with thee!
And these few precepts in thy memory
Look thou character. Give thy thoughts no tongue,
Nor any unproportion'd thought his act.
Be thou familiar, but by no means vulgar;
The friends thou hast, and their adoption tried,
Grapple them to thy soul with hoops of steel;
But do not dull thy palm with entertainment
Of each new-hatch'd, unfledg'd comrade. Beware
Of entrance to a quarrel, but, being in,
Bear't that th' opposed may beware of thee.
Give every man thine ear, but few thy voice;
Take each man's censure, but reserve thy judgment.
Costly thy habit as thy purse can buy,
But not express'd in fancy; rich, not gaudy;
For the apparel oft proclaims the man,
And they in France of the best rank and station
Are most select and generous, chief in that.
Neither a borrower, nor a lender be;
For loan oft loses both itself and friend,
And borrowing dulls the edge of husbandry.

This above all: to thine own self be true,
And it must follow, as the night the day,
Thou canst not then be false to any man.
Farewell; my blessing season this in thee!

116

Had it pleas'd heaven
To try me with affliction, had he rain'd
All kinds of sores, and shames, on my bare head,
Steep'd me in poverty to the very lips,
Given to captivity me and my utmost hopes,
I should have found in some part of my soul
A drop of patience; but, alas! to make me
The fixed figure for the time of scorn
To point his slow and moving finger at;
Yet could I bear that too; well, very well.
But there, where I have garner'd up my heart,
Where either I must live or bear no life,
The fountain from the which my current runs
Or else dries up; to be discarded thence!
Or keep it as a cistern for foul toads
To knot and gender in!

117

O! beware, my lord, of jealousy;
It is the green-ey'd monster which doth mock
The meat it feeds on; that cuckold lives in bliss
Who, certain of his fate, loves not his wronger;
But, O! what damned minutes tell he o'er
Who dotes, yet doubts; suspects, yet soundly loves!
Poor and content is rich, and rich enough,
Bur riches fineless is as poor as winter.
To him that ever fears he shall be poor.
Good heaven, the souls of all my tribe defend
From jealousy!

118

O! that this too too solid flesh would melt,
Thaw and resolve itself into a dew;
Or that the Everlasting had not fix'd
His canon 'gainst self-slaughter! O God! O God!
How weary, stale, flat, and unprofitable
Seem to me all the uses of this world.
Fie on't! O fie! 'tis an unweeded garden,
That grows to seed; things rank and gross in nature
Possess it merely. That it should come to this!
But two months dead: nay, not so much, not two:
So excellent a king; that was, to this,
Hyperion to a satyr; so loving to my mother
That he might not beteem the winds of heaven
Visit her face too roughly. Heaven and earth!
Must I remember? why, she would hang on him,
As if increase of appetite had grown
By what it fed on; and yet, within a month,
Let me not think on't: Frailty, thy name is woman!
A little month; or ere those shoes were old
With which she follow'd my poor father's body,
Like Niobe, all tears; why she, even she, –
O God! a beast, that wants discourse of reason,
Would have mourn'd longer, – married with mine uncle,
My father's brother, but no more like my father
Than I to Hercules: within a month,
Ere yet the salt of most unrighteous tears
Had left the flushing in her galled eyes,
She married. O! most wicked speed, to post
With such dexterity to incestuous sheets.
It is not nor it cannot come to good;
But break, my heart, for I must hold my tongue!

119

Who is Silvia? what is she,
  That all our swains commend her?
Holy, fair, and wise is she:
  The heaven such grace did lend her,
That she might admired be.

Is she kind as she is fair?
  For beauty lives with kindness:
Love doth to her eyes repair,
  To help him of his blindness;
And, being help'd, inhabits there.

Then to Silvia let us sing,
  That Silvia is excelling;
She excels each mortal thing
  Upon the dull earth dwelling;
To her let us garlands bring.

120

We have strict statutes and most biting laws, –
The needful bits and curbs to headstrong steeds, –
Which for this fourteen years we have let sleep;
Even like an o'ergrown lion in a cave,
That goes not out to prey. Now, as fond fathers,
Having bound up the threat'ning twigs of birch,
Only to stick it in their children's sight
For terror, not to use, in time the rod
Becomes more mock'd than fear'd; so our decrees,
Dead to infliction, to themselves are dead,
And liberty plucks justice by the nose;
The baby beats the nurse, and quite athwart
Goes all decorum.

121

Good name in man and woman, dear my lord,
Is the immediate jewel of their souls:
Who steals my purse steals trash; 'tis something, nothing;
'Twas mine, 'tis his, and has been slave to thousands;
But he that filches from me my good name
Robs me of that which not enriches him,
And makes me poor indeed.

122

Virtue, a fig! 'tis in ourselves that we are thus, or thus. Our bodies are our gardens, to the which our wills are gardeners; so that if we will plant nettles or sow lettuce, set hyssop and weed up thyme, supply it with one gender of herbs or distract it with many, either to have it sterile with idleness or manured with industry, why, the power and corrigible authority of this lies in our wills. If the balance of our lives had not one scale of reason to poise another of sensuality, the blood and baseness of our natures would conduct us to most preposterous conclusions; but we have reason to cool our raging motions, our carnal stings, our unbitted lusts, whereof I take this that you call love to be a sect or scion.

123

O thou foul thief! where hast thou stow'd my daughter?
Damned as thou art, thou hast enchanted her;
For I'll refer me to all things of sense,
If she in chains of magic were not bound,
Whether a maid so tender, fair, and happy,
So opposite to marriage that she shunn'd
The wealthy curled darlings of our nation,
Would ever have, to incur a general mock,
Run from her guardage to the sooty bosom
Of such a thing as thou; to fear, not to delight.

Judge me the world, if 'tis not gross in sense
That thou hast practis'd on her with foul charms,
Abus'd her delicate youth with drugs or minerals
That weaken motion: I'll have't disputed on;
'Tis probable, and palpable to thinking.
I therefore apprehend and do attach thee
For an abuser of the world, a practiser
Of arts inhibited and out of warrant.
Lay hold upon him: if he do resist,
Subdue him at his peril.

124

O! what a rogue and peasant slave am I:
Is it not monstrous that this player here,
But in a fiction, in a dream of passion,
Could force his soul so to his own conceit
That from her working all his visage wann'd,
Tears in his eyes, distraction in's aspect,
A broken voice, and his whole function suiting
With forms to his conceit? and all for nothing!
For Hecuba!
What's Hecuba to him or he to Hecuba
That he should weep for her? What would he do
Had he the motive and the cue for passion
That I have? He would drown the stage with tears,
And cleave the general ear with horrid speech,
Make mad the guilty and appal the free,
Confound the ignorant, and amaze indeed
The very faculties of eyes and ears.
Yet I,
A dull and muddy-mettled rascal, peak,
Like John-a-dreams, unpregnant of my cause,
And can say nothing; no, not for a king,
Upon whose property and most dear life
A damn'd defeat was made. Am I a coward?

Who calls me villain? breaks my pate across?
Plucks off my beard and blows it in my face?
Tweaks me by the nose? gives me the lie i' the throat,
As deep as to the lungs? Who does me this?
Ha!
Swounds, I should take it, for it cannot be
But I am pigeon-liver'd, and lack gall
To make oppression bitter, or ere this
I should have fatted all the region kites
With this slave's offal. Bloody, bawdy villain!
Remorseless, treacherous, lecherous, kindless villain!
O! vengeance!
Why, what an ass am I! This is most brave
That I, the son of a dear father murder'd,
Prompted to my revenge by heaven and hell,
Must, like a whore, unpack my heart with words,
And fall a-cursing, like a very drab,
A scullion!
Fie upon't! foh! About, my brain!

125

If I do prove her haggard
Though that her jesses were my dear heart-strings,
I'd whistle her off and let her down the wind,
To prey at fortune. Haply, for I am black,
And have not those soft parts of conversation
That chamberers have, or, for I am declin'd
Into the vale of years – yet that's not much –
She's gone, I am abus'd; and my relief
Must be to loathe her. O curse of marriage!
That we can call these delicate creatures ours,
And not their appetites. I had rather be a toad,
And live upon the vapour of a dungeon,
Than keep a corner in the thing I love
For others' uses. Yet, 'tis the plague of great ones;

Prerogativ'd are they less than the base;
'Tis destiny unshunnable, like death:
Even then this forked plague is fated to us
When we do quicken.

126

Degree being vizarded,
The unworthiest shows as fairly in the mask.
The heavens themselves, the planets, and this centre
Observe degree, priority, and place,
Insisture, course, proportion, season, form,
Office, and custom, in all line of order:
And therefore is the glorious planet Sol
In noble eminence enthron'd and spher'd
Amidst the other; whose med'cinable eye
Corrects the ill aspects of planets evil,
And posts, like the commandment of a king,
Sans check, to good and bad: but when the planets
In evil mixture to disorder wander,
What plagues, and what portents, what mutiny,
What raging of the sea, shaking of earth,
Commotion in the winds, freights, changes, horrors,
Divert and crack, rend and deracinate
The unity and married calm of states
Quite from their fixture! O! when degree is shak'd,
Which is the ladder to all high designs,
The enterprise is sick. How could communities,
Degrees in schools, and brotherhoods in cities,
Peaceful commerce from dividable shores,
The primogenitive and due of birth,
Prerogative of age, crowns, sceptres, laurels,
But by degree, stand in authentic place?
Take but degree away, untune that string,
And, hark! what discord follows; each thing meets
In mere oppugnancy: the bounded waters

Should lift their bosoms higher than the shores,
And make a sop of all this solid globe:
Strength should be lord of imbecility,
And the rude son should strike his father dead:
Force should be right; or rather, right and wrong –
Between whose endless jar justice resides –
Should lose their names, and so should justice too.
Then every thing includes itself in power,
Power into will, will into appetite;
And appetite, a universal wolf,
So doubly seconded with will and power,
Must make perforce a universal prey,
And last eat up himself.

127

I am giddy, expectation whirls me round.
The imaginary relish is so sweet
That it enchants my sense. What will it be
When that the watery palate tastes indeed
Love's thrice-repured nectar? death, I fear me,
Swounding destruction, or some joy too fine,
Too subtle-potent, tun'd too sharp in sweetness
For the capacity of my ruder powers:
I fear it much; and I do fear besides
That I shall lose distinction in my joys;
As doth a battle, when they charge on heaps
The enemy flying.

128

— Lay thy finger thus, and let thy soul be instructed. Mark me with what violence she first loved the Moor but for bragging and telling her fantastical lies; and will she love him still for prating? let not thy discreet heart think it. Her eye must be fed; and what delight shall she have to look on the devil? When the blood is made dull with the act of sport, there should be, again to inflame it, and to give satiety a fresh appetite, loveliness in favour, sympathy in years, manners, and beauties; all which the Moor is defective in. Now, for want of these required conveniences, her delicate tenderness will find itself abused, begin to heave the gorge, disrelish and abhor the Moor; very nature will instruct her in it, and compel her to some second choice. Now, sir, this granted, as it is a most pregnant and unforced position, who stands so eminently in the degree of this fortune as Cassio does? a knave very voluble, no further conscionable than in putting on the mere form of civil and humane seeming, for the better compassing of his salt and most hidden loose affection? why, none; why, none: a slipper and subtle knave, a finder-out of occasions, that has an eye can stamp and counterfeit advantages, though true advantage never present itself; a devilish knave! Besides, the knave is handsome, young, and hath all those requisites in him that folly and green minds look after; a pestilent complete knave! and the woman hath found him already.

— I cannot believe that in her; she is full of most blessed condition.

—Blessed fig's end! the wine she drinks is made of grapes; if she had been blessed she would never have loved the Moor; blessed pudding! Didst thou not see her paddle with the palm of his hand? didst not mark that?

— Yes, that I did; but that was but courtesy.

—Lechery, by this hand! an index and obscure prologue to the history of lust and foul thoughts. They met so near with their lips, that their breaths embraced together. Villanous thoughts, Roderigo! when these mutualities so marshal the way, hard at hand comes the master and main exercise, the incorporate conclusion. Pish!

129

— O! courage, courage, princes; great Achilles
Is arming, weeping, cursing, vowing vengeance:

Patroclus' wounds have rous'd his drowsy blood,
Together with his mangled Myrmidons,
That noseless, handless, hack'd and chipp'd, come to him,
Crying on Hector. Ajax hath lost a friend,
And foams at mouth, and he is arm'd and at it,
Roaring for Troilus, who hath done to-day
Mad and fantastic execution,
Engaging and redeeming of himself
With such a careless force and forceless care
As if that luck, in very spite of cunning,
Bade him win all.
— Go, bear Patroclus' body to Achilles;
And bid the snail-pac'd Ajax arm for shame.
There is a thousand Hectors in the field:
Now here he fights on Galathe his horse,
And there lacks work; anon he's there afoot,
And there they fly or die, like scaled sculls
Before the belching whale; then is he yonder,
And there the strawy Greeks, ripe for his edge,
Fall down before him, like the mower's swath:
Here, there, and everywhere, he leaves and takes,
Dexterity so obeying appetite
That what he will he does; and does so much
That proof is called impossibility.
— Renew, renew! the fierce Polydamas
Hath beat down Menon; bastard Margarelon
Hath Doreus prisoner,
And stands colossus-wise, waving his beam,
Upon the pashed corses of the kings
Epistrophus and Cedius; Polixenes is slain;
Amphimachus, and Thoas, deadly hurt;
Patroclus ta'en, or slain; and Palamedes
Sore hurt and bruis'd; the dreadful Sagittary
Appals our numbers: haste we, Diomed,
To reinforcement, or we perish all.

130

Get thee to a nunnery: why wouldst thou be a breeder of sinners? I am myself indifferent honest; but yet I could accuse me of such things that it were better my mother had not borne me. I am very proud, revengeful, ambitious; with more offences at my beck than I have thoughts to put them in, imagination to give them shape, or time to act them in. What should such fellows as I do crawling between heaven and earth? We are arrant knaves, all; believe none of us. Go thy ways to a nunnery.

If thou dost marry, I'll give thee this plague for thy dowry: be thou as chaste as ice, as pure as snow, thou shalt not escape calumny. Get thee to a nunnery, go; farewell. Or, if thou wilt needs marry, marry a fool; for wise men know well enough what monsters you make of them. To a nunnery, go; and quickly too. Farewell.

I have heard of your paintings too, well enough; God hath given you one face, and you make yourselves another: you jig, you amble, and you lisp, and nickname God's creatures, and make your wantonness your ignorance. Go to, I'll no more on't; it hath made me mad. I say, we will have no more marriages; those that are married already, all but one, shall live; the rest shall keep as they are. To a nunnery, go.

131

The ample proposition that hope makes
In all designs begun on earth below
Fails in the promis'd largeness: checks and disasters
Grow in the veins of actions highest rear'd;
As knots, by the conflux of meeting sap,
Infect the sound pine and divert his grain
Tortive and errant from his course of growth.
Nor, princes, is it matter new to us
That we come short of our suppose so far
That after seven years' siege yet Troy walls stand;

Sith every action that hath gone before
Whereof we have record, trial did draw
Bias and thwart, not answering the aim,
And that unbodied figure of the thought
That gave't surmised shape. Why then, you princes,
Do you with cheeks abash'd behold our works,
And call them shames? which are indeed nought else
But the protractive trials of great Jove,
To find persistive constancy in men:
The fineness of which metal is not found
In Fortune's love; for then, the bold and coward,
The wise and fool, the artist and unread,
The hard and soft, seem all affin'd and kin:
But, in the wind and tempest of her frown,
Distinction, with a broad and powerful fan,
Puffing at all, winnows the light away;
And what hath mass or matter, by itself
Lies rich in virtue and unmingled.

132

How all occasions do inform against me,
And spur my dull revenge! What is a man,
If his chief good and market of his time
Be but to sleep and feed? a beast, no more.
Sure he that made us with such large discourse,
Looking before and after, gave us not
That capability and god-like reason
To fust in us unus'd. Now, whe'r it be
Bestial oblivion, or some craven scruple
Of thinking too precisely on the event,
A thought, which, quarter'd, hath but one part wisdom,
And ever three parts coward, I do not know
Why yet I live to say 'This thing's to do';
Sith I have cause and will and strength and means
To do't. Examples gross as earth exhort me:

Witness this army of such mass and charge
Led by a delicate and tender prince,
Whose spirit with divine ambition puff'd
Makes mouths at the invisible event,
Exposing what is mortal and unsure
To all that fortune, death and danger dare,
Even for an egg-shell. Rightly to be great
Is not to stir without great argument,
But greatly to find quarrel in a straw
When honour's at the stake. How stand I then,
That have a father kill'd, a mother stain'd,
Excitements of my reason and my blood,
And let all sleep, while, to my shame, I see
The imminent death of twenty thousand men,
That, for a fantasy and trick of fame,
Go to their graves like beds, fight for a plot
Whereon the numbers cannot try the cause,
Which is not tomb enough and continent
To hide the slain? O! from this time forth,
My thoughts be bloody, or be nothing worth!

133

Time hath, my lord, a wallet at his back,
Wherein he puts alms for oblivion,
A great siz'd monster of ingratitudes:
Those scraps are good deeds past; which are devour'd
As fast as they are made, forgot as soon
As done: perseverance, dear my lord,
Keeps honour bright: to have done, is to hang
Quite out of fashion, like a rusty mail
In monumental mockery. Take the instant way;
For honour travels in a strait so narrow
Where one but goes abreast: keep, then, the path;
For emulation hath a thousand sons
That one by one pursue: if you give way,

Or hedge aside from the direct forthright,
Like to an enter'd tide they all rush by
And leave you hindmost;
Or, like a gallant horse fall'n in first rank,
Lie there for pavement to the abject rear,
O'errun and trampled on: then what they do in present,
Though less than yours in past, must o'ertop yours;
For time is like a fashionable host,
That slightly shakes his parting guest by the hand,
And with his arms outstretch'd, as he would fly,
Grasps in the comer: welcome ever smiles,
And farewell goes out sighing. O! let not virtue seek
Remuneration for the thing it was;
For beauty, wit,
High birth, vigour of bone, desert in service,
Love, friendship, charity, are subjects all
To envious and calumniating time.
One touch of nature makes the whole world kin,
That all with one consent praise new-born gawds,
Though they are made and moulded of things past,
And give to dust that is a little gilt
More laud than gilt o'er-dusted.
The present eye praises the present object

134

This heavy-headed revel east and west
Makes us traduc'd and tax'd of other nations;
They clepe us drunkards, and with swinish phrase
Soil our addition; and indeed it takes
From our achievements, though perform'd at height,
The pith and marrow of our attribute.
So, oft if chances in particular men,
That for some vicious mole of nature in them,
As, in their birth, – wherein they are not guilty,
Since nature cannot choose his origin, –

By the o'ergrowth of some complexion,
Oft breaking down the pales and forts of reason,
Or by some habit that too much o'er-leavens
The form of plausive manners; that these men,
Carrying, I say, the stamp of one defect,
Being nature's livery, or fortune's star,
Their virtues else, be they as pure as grace,
As infinite as man may undergo,
Shall in the general censure take corruption
From that particular fault: the dram of eale
Doth all the noble substance of a doubt,
To his own scandal.

135

O Pandarus! I tell thee, Pandarus, –
When I do tell thee, there my hopes lie drown'd,
Reply not in how many fathoms deep
They lie indrench'd. I tell thee I am mad
In Cressid's love: thou answer'st, she is fair;
Pour'st in the open ulcer of my heart
Her eyes, her hair, her cheek, her gait, her voice;
Handlest in thy discourse, O! that her hand,
In whose comparison all whites are ink,
Writing their own reproach; to whose soft seizure
The cygnet's down is harsh, and spirit of sense
Hard as the palm of ploughman; this thou tell'st me,
As true thou tell'st me, when I say I love her;
But, saying thus, instead of oil and balm,
Thou lay'st in every gash that love hath given me
The knife that made it.

136

In the reproof of chance
Lies the true proof of men: the sea being smooth,
How many shallow bauble boats dare sail

Upon her patient breast, making their way
With those of nobler bulk!
But let the ruffian Boreas once enrage
The gentle Thetis, and anon behold
The strong-ribb'd bark through liquid mountains cut
Bounding between the two moist elements,
Like Perseus' horse: where's then the saucy boat
Whose weak untimber'd sides but even now
Co-rivall'd greatness? either to harbour fled,
Or made a toast for Neptune. Even so
Doth valour's show and valour's worth divide
In storms of fortune; for in her ray and brightness
The herd hath more annoyance by the breese
Than by the tiger; but when the splitting wind
Makes flexible the knees of knotted oaks,
And flies fled under shade, why then the thing of courage,
As rous'd with rage, with rage doth sympathize,
And with an accent tun'd in self-same key,
Retorts to chiding fortune.

137

To be, or not to be: that is the question:
Whether 'tis nobler in the mind to suffer
The slings and arrows of outrageous fortune,
Or to take arms against a sea of troubles,
And by opposing end them? To die: to sleep;
No more; and, by a sleep to say we end
The heart-ache and the thousand natural shocks
That flesh is heir to, 'tis a consummation
Devoutly to be wish'd. To die, to sleep;
To sleep: perchance to dream: ay, there's the rub;
For in that sleep of death what dreams may come
When we have shuffled off this mortal coil,
Must give us pause. There's the respect
That makes calamity of so long life;

For who would bear the whips and scorns of time,
The oppressor's wrong, the proud man's contumely,
The pangs of dispriz'd love, the law's delay,
The insolence of office, and the spurns
The patient merit of the unworthy takes,
When he himself might his quietus make
With a bare bodkin? who would fardels bear,
To grunt and sweat under a weary life,
But that the dread of something after death,
The undiscover'd country from whose bourn
No traveller returns, puzzles the will,
And makes us rather bear those ills we have
Than fly to others that we know not of?
Thus conscience does make cowards of us all;
And thus the native hue of resolution
Is sicklied o'er with the pale cast of thought,
And enterprises of great pith and moment
With this regard their currents turn awry,
And lose the name of action.

138

Could great men thunder
As Jove himself does, Jove would ne'er be quiet,
For every pelting, petty officer
Would use his heaven for thunder; nothing but thunder.
Merciful heaven!
Thou rather with thy sharp and sulphurous bolt
Split'st the unwedgeable and gnarled oak
Than the soft myrtle; but man, proud man,
Drest in a little brief authority,
Most ignorant of what he's most assur'd,
His glassy essence, like an angry ape,
Plays such fantastic tricks before high heaven
As make the angels weep; who, with our spleens,
Would all themselves laugh mortal.

139

It is the cause, it is the cause, my soul;
Let me not name it to you, you chaste stars!
It is the cause. Yet I'll not shed her blood,
Nor scar that whiter skin of hers than snow,
And smooth as monumental alabaster.
Yet she must die, else she'll betray more men.
Put out the light, and then put out the light:
If I quench thee, thou flaming minister,
I can again thy former light restore,
Should I repent me; but once put out thy light,
Thou cunning'st pattern of excelling nature,
I know not where is that Promethean heat
That can thy light relume. When I have pluck'd the rose,
I cannot give it vital growth again,
It needs must wither: I'll smell it on the tree.
[*Kisses her.*]
O balmy breath, that dost almost persuade
Justice to break her sword! One more, one more.
Be thus when thou art dead, and I will kill thee,
And love thee after. One more, and this the last:
So sweet was ne'er so fatal.

140

The rugged Pyrrhus, he, whose sable arm,
Black as his purpose, did the night resemble
When he lay couched in the ominous horse,
Hath now this dread and black complexion smear'd
With heraldry more dismal; head to foot
Now is he total gules; horridly trick'd
With blood of fathers, mothers, daughters, sons,
Bak'd and impasted with the parching streets,
That lend a tyrannous and damned light
To their vile murders: roasted in wrath and fire,
And thus o'er-sized with coagulate gore,

With eyes like carbuncles, the hellish Pyrrhus
Old grandsire Priam seeks.
. . . Anon, he finds him
Striking too short at Greeks; his antique sword,
Rebellious to his arm, lies where it falls,
Repugnant to command. Unequal match'd,
Pyrrhus at Priam drives; in rage strikes wide;
But with the whiff and wind of his fell sword
The unnerved father falls. Then senseless Ilium,
Seeming to feel this blow, with flaming top
Stoops to his base, and with a hideous crash
Takes prisoner Pyrrhus' ear: for lo! his sword,
Which was declining on the milky head
Of reverend Priam, seem'd i' the air to stick:
So, as a painted tyrant, Pyrrhus stood,
And like a neutral to his will and matter,
Did nothing.
But, as we often see, against some storm,
A silence in the heavens, the rack stand still,
The bold winds speechless and the orb below
As hush as death, anon the dreadful thunder
Doth rend the region; so, after Pyrrhus' pause,
Aroused vengeance set him new a-work;
And never did the Cyclops' hammers fall
On Mars's armour, forg'd for proof eterne,
With less remorse than Pyrrhus' bleeding sword
Now falls on Priam.
Out, out, thou strumpet, Fortune! All you gods,
In general synod, take away her power;
Break all the spokes and fellies from her wheel,
And bowl the round nave down the hill of heaven,
As low as to the fiends!
But who, O! who had seen the mobled queen
Run barefoot up and down, threat'ning the flames
With bisson rheum; a clout upon that head
Where late the diadem stood; and, for a robe,

About her lank and all o'er-teemed loins,
A blanket, in the alarm of fear caught up;
Who this had seen, with tongue in venom steep'd,
'Gainst Fortune's state would treason have pronounc'd:
But if the gods themselves did see her then,
When she saw Pyrrhus make malicious sport
In mincing with his sword her husband's limbs,
The instant burst of clamour that she made –
Unless things mortal move them not at all –
Would have made milch the burning eyes of heaven,
And passion in the gods.

141

There is a willow grows aslant a brook
That shows his hoar leaves in the glassy stream;
There with fantastic garlands did she come,
Of crow-flowers, nettles, daisies, and long purples,
That liberal shepherds give a grosser name,
But our cold maids do dead men's fingers call them:
There, on the pendent boughs her coronet weeds
Clambering to hang, an envious sliver broke,
When down her weedy trophies and herself
Fell in the weeping brook. Her clothes spread wide,
And, mermaid-like, awhile they bore her up;
Which time she chanted snatches of old tunes,
As one incapable of her own distress,
Or like a creature native and indu'd
Unto that element; but long it could not be
Till that her garments, heavy with their drink,
Pull'd the poor wretch from her melodious lay
To muddy death.

142

Her father lov'd me; oft invited me;
Still question'd me the story of my life

From year to year, the battles, sieges, fortunes
That I have pass'd.
I ran it through, even from my boyish days
To the very moment that he bade me tell it;
Wherein I spake of most disastrous chances,
Of moving accidents by flood and field,
Of hair-breadth 'scapes i' the imminent deadly breach,
Of being taken by the insolent foe
And sold to slavery, of my redemption thence
And portance in my travel's history;
Wherein of antres vast and desarts idle,
Rough quarries, rocks and hills whose heads touch heaven,
It was my hint to speak, such was the process;
And of the Cannibals that each other eat,
The Anthropophagi, and men whose heads
Do grow beneath their shoulders. This to hear
Would Desdemona seriously incline;
But still the house-affairs would draw her thence;
Which ever as she could with haste dispatch,
She'd come again, and with a greedy ear
Devour up my discourse. Which I observing,
Took once a pliant hour, and found good means
To draw from her a prayer of earnest heart
That I would all my pilgrimage dilate,
Whereof by parcels she had something heard,
But not intentively: I did consent;
And often did beguile her of her tears,
When I did speak of some distressful stroke
That my youth suffer'd. My story being done,
She gave me for my pains a world of sighs:
She swore, in faith, 'twas strange, 'twas passing strange;
'Twas pitiful, 'twas wondrous pitiful:
She wish'd she had not heard it, yet she wish'd
That heaven had made her such a man; she thank'd me,
And bade me, if I had a friend that lov'd her,
I should but teach him how to tell my story,

And that would woo her. Upon this hint I spake:
She lov'd me for the dangers I had pass'd,
And I lov'd her that she did pity them.
This only is the witchcraft I have us'd.

143

O! my offence is rank, it smells to heaven;
It hath the primal eldest curse upon't;
A brother's murder! Pray can I not,
Though inclination be as sharp as will:
My stronger guilt defeats my strong intent;
And, like a man to double business bound,
I stand in pause where I shall first begin,
And both neglect. What if this cursed hand
Were thicker than itself with brother's blood,
Is there not rain enough in the sweet heavens
To wash it white as snow? Whereto serves mercy
But to confront the visage of offence?
And what's in prayer but this two-fold force,
To be forestalled, ere we come to fall,
Or pardon'd, being down? Then, I'll look up;
My fault is past. But, O! what form of prayer
Can serve my turn? 'Forgive me my foul murder'?
That cannot be; since I am still possess'd
Of those effects for which I did the murder,
My crown, mine own ambition, and my queen.
May one be pardon'd and retain the offence?
In the corrupted currents of the world
Offence's gilded hand may shove by justice,
And oft 'tis seen the wicked prize itself
Buys out the law; but 'tis not so above;
There is no shuffling, there the action lies
In his true nature, and we ourselves compell'd
Even to the teeth and forehead of our faults
To give in evidence. What then? what rests?

Try what repentance can: what can it not?
Yet what can it, when one can not repent?
O wretched state! O bosom black as death!
O limed soul, that struggling to be free
Art more engaged! Help, angels! make assay;
Bow, stubborn knees; and heart with strings of steel
Be soft as sinews of the new-born babe.
All may be well.

144

Alas! poor Yorick. I knew him, Horatio; a fellow of infinite jest, of most excellent fancy; he hath borne me on his back a thousand times; and now, how abhorred in my imagination it is! my gorge rises at it. Here hung those lips that I have kissed I know not how oft. Where be your gibes now? your gambols? your songs? your flashes of merriment, that were wont to set the table on a roar? Not one now, to mock your own grinning? quite chapfallen? Now get you to my lady's chamber, and tell her, let her paint an inch thick, to this favour she must come; make her laugh at that.

145

Soft you; a word or two before you go.
I have done the state some service, and they know't;
No more of that. I pray you, in your letters,
When you shall these unlucky deeds relate,
Speak of me as I am; nothing extenuate,
Nor set down aught in malice: then, must you speak
Of one that lov'd not wisely but too well;
Of one not easily jealous, but, being wrought,
Perplex'd in the extreme; of one whose hand,
Like the base Indian, threw a pearl away
Richer than all his tribe; of one whose subdu'd eyes
Albeit unused to the melting mood,
Drop tears as fast as the Arabian trees

Their med'cinable gum. Set you down this;
And say besides, that in Aleppo once,
Where a malignant and a turban'd Turk
Beat a Venetian and traduc'd the state,
I took by the throat the circumcised dog,
And smote him thus. [*Stabs himself.*]

146

Thrice the brinded cat hath mew'd.
Thrice and once the hedge-pig whin'd.
Harper cries: 'Tis time, 'tis time.
Round about the cauldron go;
In the poison'd entrails throw.
Toad, that under cold stone
Days and nights hast thirty-one
Swelter'd venom sleeping got,
Boil thou first i' the charmed pot.
  Double, double toil and trouble;
  Fire burn and cauldron bubble.

Fillet of a fenny snake,
In the cauldron boil and bake;
Eye of newt, and toe of frog,
Wool of bat, and tongue of dog,
Adder's fork, and blind-worm's sting,
Lizard's leg, and howlet's wing,
For a charm of powerful trouble,
Like a hell-broth boil and bubble.
  Double, double toil and trouble;
  Fire burn and cauldron bubble.

Scale of dragon, tooth of wolf,
Witches' mummy, maw and gulf
Of the ravin'd salt-sea shark,
Root of hemlock digg'd i' the dark,
Liver of blaspheming Jew,

Gall of goat, and slips of yew
Sliver'd in the moon's eclipse,
Nose of Turk, and Tartar's lips,
Finger of birth-strangled babe
Ditch-deliver'd by a drab,
Make the gruel thick and slab:
Add thereto a tiger's chaudron,
For the ingredients of our cauldron.
  Double, double toil and trouble;
  Fire burn and cauldron bubble.
  Cool it with a baboon's blood,
  Then the charm is firm and good.

147

These late eclipses in the sun and moon portend no good to us: though the wisdom of nature can reason it thus and thus, yet nature finds itself scourged by the sequent effects. Love cools, friendship falls off, brothers divide: in cities, mutinies; in countries, discord; in palaces, treason; and the bond cracked between son and father. This villain of mine comes under the prediction; there's son against father: the king falls from bias of nature; there's father against child. We have seen the best of our time: machinations, hollowness, treachery, and all ruinous disorders, follow us disquietly to our graves.

148

The night has been unruly: where we lay,
Our chimneys were blown down; and, as they say,
Lamentings heard i' the air; strange screams of death,
And prophesying with accents terrible
Of dire combustion and confus'd events
New hatch'd to the woeful time. The obscure bird
Clamour'd the livelong night: some say the earth
Was feverous and did shake.

149

O blessed breeding sun! draw from the earth
Rotten humidity; below thy sister's orb
Infect the air! Twinn'd brothers of one womb,
Whose procreation, residence and birth,
Scarce is dividant, touch them with several fortunes;
The greater scorns the lesser: not nature,
To whom all sores lay siege, can bear great fortune,
But by contempt of nature.
Raise me this beggar, and deny't that lord;
The senator shall bear contempt hereditary,
The beggar native honour.
It is the pasture lards the rother's sides,
The want that makes him lean. Who dares, who dares,
In purity of manhood stand upright,
And say, 'This man's a flatterer?' if one be,
So are they all; for every grize of fortune
Is smooth'd by that below: the learned pate
Ducks to the golden fool: all is oblique;
There's nothing level in our cursed natures
But direct villany. Therefore, be abhorr'd
All feasts, societies, and throngs of men!
His semblable, yea, himself, Timon disdains:
Destruction fang mankind! Earth, yield me roots!
[*Digging.*]
Who seeks for better of thee, sauce his palate
With thy most operant poison! What is here?
Gold! yellow, glittering, precious gold! No, gods,
I am no idle votarist. Roots, you clear heavens!
Thus much of this will make black white, foul fair,
Wrong right, base noble, old young, coward valiant.
Ha! you gods, why this? What this, you gods? Why, this
Will lug your priests and servants from your sides,
Pluck stout men's pillows from below their head:
This yellow slave

Will knit and break religions; bless the accurs'd;
Make the hoar leprosy ador'd; place thieves,
And give them title, knee, and approbation,
With senators on the bench; this is it
That makes the wappen'd widow wed again;
She, whom the spital-house and ulcerous sores
Would cast the gorge at, this embalms and spices
To the April day again. Come, damned earth,
Thou common whore of mankind, that putt'st odds
Among the rout of nations, I will make thee
Do thy right nature.

150

When I do stare, see how the subject quakes.
I pardon that man's life. What was thy cause?
Adultery?
Thou shalt not die: die for adultery! No:
The wren goes to't, and the small gilded fly
Does lecher in my sight.
Let copulation thrive; for Gloucester's bastard son
Was kinder to his father than my daughters
Got 'tween the lawful sheets.
To't luxury, pell-mell! for I lack soldiers.
Behold yond simpering dame,
Whose face between her forks presageth snow;
That minces virtue, and does shake the head
To hear of pleasure's name;
The fitchew nor the soiled horse goes to't
With a more riotous appetite.
Down from the waist they are Centaurs,
Though women all above:
But to the girdle do the gods inherit,
Beneath is all the fiends':
There's hell, there's darkness, there is the sulphurous pit,
Burning, scalding, stench, consumption; fie, fie, fie! pah, pah!

Give me an ounce of civet, good apothecary, to sweeten my imagination.

151

Glamis thou art, and Cawdor; and shalt be
What thou art promis'd. Yet do I fear thy nature;
It is too full o' the milk of human kindness
To catch the nearest way; thou wouldst be great,
Art not without ambition, but without
The illness should attend it; what thou wouldst highly,
That thou wouldst holily; wouldst not play false,
And yet wouldst wrongly win; thou'dst have, great Glamis,
That which cries, 'Thus thou must do, if thou have it';
And that which rather thou dost fear to do
Than wishest should be undone. Hie thee hither,
That I may pour my spirits in thine ear,
And chastise with the valour of my tongue
All that impedes thee from the golden round,
Which fate and metaphysical aid doth seem
To have thee crown'd withal.

152

If thou wert the lion, the fox would beguile thee; if thou wert the lamb, the fox would eat thee; if thou wert the fox, the lion would suspect thee, when peradventure thou wert accused by the ass; if thou wert the ass, thy dulness would torment thee, and still thou livedst but as a breakfast to the wolf; if thou wert the wolf, thy greediness would afflict thee, and oft thou shouldst hazard thy life for thy dinner; wert thou the unicorn, pride and wrath would confound thee and make thine own self the conquest of thy fury; wert thou a bear, thou wouldst be killed by the horse; wert thou a horse, thou wouldst be seized by the leopard; wert thou a leopard, thou wert german to the lion, and the spots of thy kindred were jurors on thy life; all thy safety were remotion, and thy defence absence. What beast couldst thou be, that were not subject to a beast? and what a beast art thou already, that seest not thy loss in transformation!

153

Thou, Nature, art my goddess; to thy law
My services are bound. Wherefore should I
Stand in the plague of custom, and permit
The curiosity of nations to deprive me,
For that I am some twelve or fourteen moonshines
Lag of a brother? Why bastard? wherefore base?
When my dimensions are as well compact,
My mind as generous, and my shape as true,
As honest madam's issue? Why brand they us
With base? with baseness? bastardy? base, base?
Who in the lusty stealth of nature take
More composition and fierce quality
Than doth, within a dull, stale, tired bed,
Go to the creating a whole tribe of fops,
Got 'tween asleep and wake? Well then,
Legitimate Edgar, I must have your land:
Our father's love is to the bastard Edmund
As to the legitimate. Fine word, 'legitimate!'
Well, my legitimate, if this letter speed,
And my invention thrive, Edmund the base
Shall top the legitimate: – I grow, I prosper;
Now, gods, stand up for bastards!

154

— This castle hath a pleasant seat; the air
Nimbly and sweetly recommends itself
Unto our gentle senses.
— This guest of summer,
The temple-haunting martlet, does approve
By his lov'd mansionry that the heaven's breath

Smells wooingly here: no jutty, frieze,
Buttress, nor coign of vantage, but this bird
Hath made his pendent bed and procreant cradle:
Where they most breed and haunt, I have observ'd
The air is delicate

155

— Where's the king?
— Contending with the fretful elements;
Bids the wind blow the earth into the sea,
Or swell the curled waters 'bove the main,
That things might change or cease; tears his white hair,
Which the impetuous blasts, with eyeless rage,
Catch in their fury, and make nothing of;
Strives in his little world of man to out-scorn
The to-and-fro-conflicting wind and rain.
This night, wherein the cub-drawn bear would couch,
The lion and the belly-pinched wolf
Keep their fur dry, unbonneted he runs,
And bids what will take all.

156

Was the hope drunk,
Wherein you dress'd yourself? hath it slept since,
And wakes it now, to look so green and pale
At what it did so freely? From this time
Such I account thy love. Art thou afeard
To be the same in thine own act and valour
As thou art in desire? Wouldst thou have that
Which thou esteem'st the ornament of life,
And live a coward in thine own esteem,
Letting 'I dare not' wait upon 'I would,'
Like the poor cat i' the adage?
. . . What beast was't, then,
That made you break this enterprise to me?

When you durst do it then you were a man;
And, to be more than what you were, you would
Be so much more the man. Nor time nor place
Did then adhere, and yet you would make both;
They have made themselves, and that their fitness now
Does unmake you. I have given suck, and know
How tender 'tis to love the babe that milks me:
I would, while it was smiling in my face,
Have pluck'd my nipple from his boneless gums,
And dash'd the brains out, had I so sworn as you
Have done to this.

157

Let the great gods,
That keep this dreadful pother o'er our heads,
Find out their enemies now. Tremble, thou wretch,
That hast within thee undivulged crimes,
Unwhipp'd of justice; hide thee, thou bloody hand;
Thou perjur'd, and thou simular of virtue
That art incestuous; caitiff, to pieces shake,
That under covert and convenient seeming
Hast practis'd on man's life; close pent-up guilts,
Rive your concealing continents, and cry
These dreadful summoners grace. I am a man
More sinn'd against than sinning.

158

Speak the speech, I pray you, as I pronounced it to you, trippingly on the tongue; but if you mouth it, as many of your players do, I had as lief the town-crier spoke my lines. Nor do not saw the air too much with your hand, thus; but use all gently: for in the very torrent, tempest, and – as I may say – whirlwind of passion, you must acquire and beget a temperance, that may give it smoothness. O! it offends me to the soul to hear a robustious periwig-pated fellow tear a passion to tatters, to very rags, to split the ears of the groudlings, who for the most part are capable of nothing but inexplicable dumb-shows and noise: I would have such a fellow whipped for o'er-doing Termagant; it out-Herods Herod: pray you, avoid it . . .

Be not too tame neither, but let your own discretion be your tutor: suit the action to the word, the word to the action; with this special observance, that you o'erstep not the modesty of nature; for anything so overdone is from the purpose of playing, whose end, both at the first and now, was and is, to hold, as 'twere, the mirror up to nature; to show virtue her own feature, scorn her own image, and the very age and body of the time his form and pressure. Now, this overdone, or come tardy off, though it make the unskilful laugh, cannot but make the judicious grieve; the censure of which one must in your allowance o'erweigh a whole theatre of others. O! there be players that I have seen play, and heard others praise, and that highly, not to speak it profanely, that, neither having the accent of Christians nor the gait of Christian, pagan, nor man, have so strutted and bellowed that I have thought some of nature's journeymen had made men and not made them well, they imitated humanity so abominably.

159

Hold up, you sluts,
Your aprons mountant: you are not oathable,
Although, I know, you'll swear, terribly swear
Into strong shudders and to heavenly agues
The immortal gods that hear you, spare your oaths,
I'll trust to your conditions: be whores still;
And he whose pious breath seeks to convert you,
Be strong in whore, allure him, burn him up;
Let your close fire predominate his smoke,
And be no turncoats: yet may your pains, six months,

Be quite contrary: and thatch your poor thin roofs
With burdens of the dead; some that were hang'd,
No matter; wear them, betray with them: whore still;
Paint till a horse may mire upon your face:
A pox of wrinkles!
Consumptions sow
In hollow bones of man; strike their sharp shins,
And mar men's spurring. Crack the lawyer's voice,
That he may never more false title plead,
Nor sound his quillets shrilly: hoar the flamen,
That scolds against the quality of flesh,
And not believes himself: down with the nose,
Down with it flat; take the bridge quite away
Of him that, his particular to foresee,
Smells from the general weal: make curl'd-pate ruffians bald,
And let the unscarr'd braggarts of the war
Derive some pain from you: plague all,
That your activity may defeat and quell
The source of all erection. There's more gold;
Do you damn others, and let this damn you,
And ditches grave you all!

160

If it were done when 'tis done, then 'twere well
It were done quickly; if the assassination
Could trammel up the consequence, and catch
With his surcease success; that but this blow
Might be the be-all and the end-all here,
But here, upon this bank and shoal of time,
We'd jump the life to come. But in these cases
We still have judgement here; that we but teach
Bloody instructions, which, being taught, return
To plague the inventor; this even-handed justice
Commends the ingredients of our poison'd chalice
To Your own lips. He's here in double trust:

First, as I am his kinsman and his subject,
Strong both against the deed; then, as his host,
Who should against his murderer shut the door,
Not bear the knife myself. Besides, this Duncan
Hath borne his faculties so meek, hath been
So clear in his great office, that his virtues
Will plead like angels trumpet-tongu'd against
The deep damnation of his taking-off;
And pity, like a naked new-born babe,
Striding the blast, or heaven's cherubin, hors'd
Upon the sightless couriers of the air,
Shall blow the horrid deed in every eye,
That tears shall drown the wind. I have no spur
To prick the sides of my intent, but only
Vaulting ambition, which o'er-leaps itself
And falls on the other.

161

Blow, winds, and crack your cheeks! rage! blow!
You cataracts and hurricanoes, spout
Till you have drench'd our steeples, drown'd the cocks!
You sulphurous and thought-executing fires,
Vaunt-couriers to oak-cleaving thunderbolts,
Singe my white head! And thou, all-shaking thunder,
Strike flat the thick rotundity o' the world!
Crack nature's moulds, all germens spill at once
That make ingrateful man!

162

— That which hath made them drunk hath made me bold,
What hath quench'd them hath given me fire. Hark! Peace!
It was the owl that shriek'd, the fatal bellman,
Which gives the stern'st good-night. He is about it:
The doors are open, and the surfeited grooms

Do mock their charge with snores: I have drugg'd their
  possets,
That death and nature do contend about them,
Whether they live or die.
  — Who's there? what, ho!
  — Alack! I am afraid they have awak'd,
And 'tis not done; the attempt and not the deed
Confounds us. Hark! I laid their daggers ready;
He could not miss them. Had he not resembled
My father as he slept I had done't. My husband!
  — I have done the deed. Didst thou not hear a noise?
  — I heard the owl scream and the crickets cry.
Did not you speak?
  — When?
  — Now.
  — As I descended?
  — Ay.
  — Hark!
Who lies i' the second chamber?
  — Donalbain.
  — [*Looking on his hands.*] This is a sorry sight.
  — A foolish thought to say a sorry sight.
  —There's one did laugh in's sleep, and one cried
  'Murder!'
That they did wake each other: I stood and heard them;
But they did say their prayers, and address'd them
Again to sleep.
  — There are two lodg'd together.
  — One cried 'God bless us!' and 'Amen' the other:
As they had seen me with these hangman's hands.
Listening their fear, I could not say 'Amen',
When they did say 'God bless us!'
  — Consider it not so deeply.
  — But wherefore could not I pronounce 'Amen'?
I had most need of blessing, and 'Amen'
Stuck in my throat.

— These deeds must not be thought
After these ways; so, it will make us mad.
— Methought I heard a voice cry 'Sleep no more!
Macbeth does murder sleep,' the innocent sleep,
Sleep that knits up the ravell'd sleave of care,
The death of each day's life, sore labour's bath,
Balm of hurt minds, great nature's second course,
Chief nourisher in life's feast, –
— What do you mean?
— Still it cried, 'Sleep no more!' to all the house:
'Glamis hath murder'd sleep, and therefore Cawdor
Shall sleep no more, Macbeth shall sleep no more!'

163

Hoy-day! what a sweep of vanity comes this way:
They dance! they are mad women.
Like madness is the glory of this life,
As this pomp shows to a little oil and root.
We make ourselves fools to disport ourselves;
And spend our flatteries to drink those men
Upon whose age we void it up again,
With poisonous spite and envy.
Who lives that's not depraved or depraves?
Who dies that bears not one spurn to their graves
Of their friend's gift?
I should fear those that dance before me now
Would one day stamp upon me: it has been done;
Men shut their doors against a setting sun.

164

Wisdom and goodness to the vile seem vile;
Filths savour but themselves. What have you done?
Tigers, not daughters, what have you perform'd?
A father, and a gracious aged man,
Whose reverence the head-lugg'd bear would lick,

Most barbarous, most degenerate! have you madded.
Could my good brother suffer you to do it?
A man, a prince, by him so benefited!
If that the heavens do not their visible spirits
Send quickly down to tame these vile offences,
It will come,
Humanity must perforce prey on itself,
Like monsters of the deep.

165

— Who gives anything to poor Tom? whom the foul fiend hath led through fire and through flame, through ford and whirlpool, o'er bog and quagmire; that hath laid knives under his pillow, and halters in his pew; set ratsbane by his porridge; made him proud of heart, to ride on a bay trotting-horse over four-inched bridges, to course his own shadow for a traitor. Bless thy five wits! Tom's a-cold. O! do de, do de, do de. Bless thee from whirlwinds, starblasting, and taking! Do poor Tom some charity, whom the foul fiend vexes. There could I have him now, and there, and there again, and there . . .

Take heed o' the foul fiend. Obey thy parents; keep thy word justly; swear not; commit not with man's sworn spouse; set not thy sweet heart on proud array. Tom's a-cold.

— What hast thou been?

— A serving man, proud in heart and mind; that curled my hair, wore gloves in my cap, served the lust of my mistress's heart, and did the act of darkness with her; swore as many oaths as I spake words, and broke them in the sweet face of heaven; one that slept in the contriving of lust, and waked to do it. Wine loved I deeply, dice dearly, and in woman out-paramoured the Turk: false of heart, light of ear, bloody of hand; hog in sloth, fox in stealth, wolf in greediness, dog in madness, lion in prey. Let not the creaking of shoes nor the rustling of silks betray thy poor heart to woman: keep thy foot out of brothels, thy hand out of plackets, thy pen from lenders' books, and defy the foul fiend. Still through the hawthorn blows the cold wind; says suum, mun ha no nonny. Dolphin my boy, my boy; sessa! let him trot by . . .

— What are you there? Your names?

— Poor Tom; that eats the swimming frog; the toad, the tadpole, the wall-newt, and the water; that in the fury of his heart, when the foul fiend rages, eats cow-dung for sallets; swallows the old rat and the ditch-dog; drinks the green mantle of the standing pool; who is whipped from tithing to tithing, and stock-punished, and imprisoned; who hath had three suits to his back, six shirts to his body, horse to ride, and weapon to wear;

> But mice and rats and such small deer
> Have been Tom's food for seven long year.

Beware my follower. Peace, Smulkin! peace, thou fiend.

166

We have scotch'd the snake, not kill'd it:
She'll close and be herself, whilst our poor malice
Remains in danger of her former tooth.
But let the frame of things disjoint, both the worlds suffer,
Ere we will eat our meal in fear, and sleep
In the affliction of these terrible dreams
That shake us nightly. Better be with the dead,
Whom we, to gain our peace, have sent to peace,
Than on the torture of the mind to lie
In restless ecstasy. Duncan is in his grave;
After life's fitful fever he sleeps well;
Treason has done his worst: not steel, nor poison,
Malice domestic, foreign levy, nothing
Can touch him further.

167

Let me look back upon thee. O thou wall,
That girdlest in those wolves, dive in the earth,
And fence not Athens! Matrons, turn incontinent!
Obedience fail in children! slaves and fools,
Pluck the grave wrinkled senate from the bench,
And minister in their steads! To general filths
Convert, o' the instant, green virginity!
Do't in your parents' eyes! Bankrupts, hold fast;
Rather than render back, out with your knives,
And cut your trusters' throats! Bound servants, steal! –
Large-handed robbers your grave masters are, –
And pill by law. Maid, to thy master's bed;
Thy mistress is o' the brothel! Son of sixteen,
Pluck the lin'd crutch from thy old limping sire,
With it beat out his brains! Piety, and fear,
Religion to the gods, peace, justice, truth,
Domestic awe, night-rest and neighbourhood,
Instruction, manners, mysteries and trades,
Degrees, observances, customs and laws,
Decline to your confounding contraries,
And let confusion live! Plagues incident to men,
Your potent and infectious fevers heap
On Athens, ripe for stroke! Thou cold sciatica,
Cripple our senators, that their limbs may halt
As lamely as their manners! Lust and liberty
Creep in the minds and marrows of our youth,
That 'gainst the stream of virtue they may strive,
And drown themselves in riot! Itches, blains,
Sow all the Athenian bosoms, and their crop
Be general leprosy! Breath infect breath,
That their society, as their friendship, may
Be merely poison! Nothing I'll bear from thee
But nakedness, thou detestable town!
Take thou that too, with multiplying bans!

Timon will to the woods; where he shall find
The unkindest beast more kinder than mankind.

168

This is the excellent foppery of the world, that, when we are sick in fortune, – often the surfeit of our own behaviour, – we make guilty of our disasters the sun, the moon, and the stars; as if we were villains by necessity, fools by heavenly compulsion, knaves, thieves, and treachers by spherical predominance, drunkards, liars, and adulterers by an enforced obedience of planetary influence; and all that we are evil in, by a divine thrusting on: an admirable evasion of whoremaster man, to lay his goatish disposition to the charge of a star! My father compounded with my mother under the dragon's tail, and my nativity was under *ursa major*; so that it follows I am rough and lecherous. 'Sfoot! I should have been that I am had the maidenliest star in the firmament twinkled on my bastardizing.

169

— A man may see how this world goes with no eyes. Look with thine ears: see how yond justice rails upon yon simple thief. Hark, in thine ear: change places; and, handy-dandy, which is the justice, which is the thief? Thou hast seen a farmer's dog bark at a beggar?

— Ay, sir.

— And the creature run from the cur? There thou mightst behold the great image of authority; a dog's obey'd in office.
Thou rascal beadle, hold thy bloody hand!
Why dost thou lash that whore? Strip thine own back;
Thou hotly lust'st to use her in that kind
For which thou whipp'st her. The usurer hangs the cozener.
Through tatter'd clothes small vices do appear;
Robes and furr'd gowns hide all. Plate sin with gold,
And the strong lance of justice hurtless breaks;

Arm it in rags, a pigmy's straw doth pierce it.
None does offend, none, I say none; I'll able 'em:
Take that of me, my friend, who have the power
To seal the accuser's lips. Get thee glass eyes;
And, like a scurvy politician, seem
To see the things thou dost not.

170

Poor naked wretches, whereso'er you are,
That bide the pelting of this pitiless storm,
How shall your houseless heads and unfed sides,
Your loop'd and window'd raggedness, defend you
From seasons such as these? O! I have ta'en
Too little care of this. Take physic, pomp;
Expose thyself to feel what wretches feel,
That thou mayst shake the superflux to them,
And show the heavens more just.

171

Put up thy gold: go on – here's gold, – go on;
Be as a planetary plague, when Jove
Will o'er some high-vic'd city hang his poison
In the sick air: let not thy sword skip one.
Pity not honour'd age for his white beard;
He is a usurer. Strike me the counterfeit matron;
It is her habit only that is honest,
Herself's a bawd. Let not the virgin's cheek
Make soft thy trenchant sword; for those milk-paps,
That through the window-bars bore at men's eyes,
Are not within the leaf of pity writ,
But set them down horrible traitors. Spare not the babe,
Whose dimpled smiles from fools exhaust their mercy;
Think it a bastard, whom the oracle
Hath doubtfully pronounc'd thy throat shall cut,
And mince it sans remorse. Swear against objects;

Put armour on thine ears and on thine eyes,
Whose proof nor yells of mothers, maids, nor babes,
Nor sight of priests in holy vestments bleeding,
Shall pierce a jot. There's gold to pay thy soldiers:
Make large confusion; and, thy fury spent,
Confounded be thyself!

172

Had I but died an hour before this chance
I had liv'd a blessed time; for, from this instant,
There's nothing serious in mortality,
All is but toys; renown and grace is dead,
The wine of life is drawn, and the mere lees
Is left this vault to brag of.

173

O! reason not the need; our basest beggars
Are in the poorest thing superfluous:
Allow not nature more than nature needs,
Man's life is cheap as beast's. Thou art a lady;
If only to go warm were gorgeous,
Why, nature needs not what thou gorgeous wear'st
Which scarcely keeps thee warm. But, for true need, –
You heavens, give me that patience, patience I need!
You see me here, you gods, a poor old man,
As full of grief as age; wretched in both!
If it be you that stir these daughters' hearts
Against their father, fool me not so much
To bear it tamely; touch me with noble anger,
And let not women's weapons, water-drops,
Stain my man's cheeks! No, you unnatural hags,
I will have such revenges on you both
That all the world shall – I will do such things, –
What they are yet I know not, – but they shall be
The terrors of the earth. You think I'll weep;

No, I'll not weep:
I have full cause of weeping, but this heart
Shall break into a hundred thousand flaws
Or ere I'll weep. O fool! I shall go mad.

174

The raven himself is hoarse
That croaks the fatal entrance of Duncan
Under my battlements. Come, you spirits
That tend on mortal thoughts! unsex me here,
And fill me from the crown to the toe top full
Of direst cruelty; make thick my blood,
Stop up the access and passage to remorse,
That no compunctious visitings of nature
Shake my fell purpose, nor keep peace between
The effect and it! Come to my woman's breasts,
And take my milk for gall, you murdering ministers,
Wherever in your sightless substances
You wait on nature's mischief! Come, thick night,
And pall thee in the dunnest smoke of hell,
That my keen knife see not the wound it makes,
Nor heaven peep through the blanket of the dark,
To cry, 'Hold, hold!'

175

— What three things does drink especially provoke?

— Marry, sir, nose-painting, sleep, and urine. Lechery, sir, it provokes, and unprovokes; it provokes the desire, but it takes away the performance. Therefore much drink may be said to be an equivocator with lechery; it makes him, and it mars him; it sets him on, and it takes him off; it persuades him, and disheartens him; makes him stand to, and not stand to; in conclusion, equivocates him in a sleep, and giving him the lie, leaves him.

176

Hear, Nature, hear! dear goddess, hear!
Suspend thy purpose, if thou didst intend
To make this creature fruitful!
Into her womb convey sterility!
Dry up in her the organs of increase,
And from her derogate body never spring
A babe to honour her! If she must teem,
Create her child of spleen, that it may live
And be a thwart disnatur'd torment to her!
Let it stamp wrinkles in her brow of youth,
With cadent tears fret channels in her cheeks,
Turn all her mother's pains and benefits
To laughter and contempt, that she may feel
How sharper than a serpent's tooth it is
To have a thankless child!

177

Common mother, thou,
Whose womb unmeasurable, and infinite breast,
Teems, and feeds all; whose self-same mettle,
Whereof thy proud child, arrogant man, is puff'd,
Engenders the black toad and adder blue,
The gilded newt and eyeless venom'd worm,
With all the abhorred births below crisp heaven
Whereon Hyperion's quickening fire doth shine;
Yield him, who all thy human sons doth hate,
From forth thy plenteous bosom, one poor root!
Ensear thy fertile and conceptious womb,
Let it no more bring out ingrateful man!
Go great with tigers, dragons, wolves, and bears;
Teem with new monsters, whom thy upward face
Hath to the marbled mansion all above
Never presented! O! a root; dear thanks:
Dry up thy marrows, vines and plough-torn leas;

Whereof ingrateful man, with liquorish draughts
And morsels unctuous, greases his pure mind,
That from it all consideration slips!

178

Why, thou wert better in thy grave than to answer with thy uncovered body this extremity of the skies. Is man no more than this? Consider him well. Thou owest the worm no silk, the beast no hide, the sheep no wool, the cat no perfume. Ha! here's three on's are sophisticated; thou art the thing itself; unaccommodated man is no more but such a poor, bare, forked animal as thou art. Off, off, you lendings! Come, unbutton here.

179

Thou hast cast away thyself, being like thyself;
A madman so long, now a fool. What! think'st
That the bleak air, thy boisterous chamberlain,
Will put thy shirt on warm? will these moss'd trees,
That have outliv'd the eagle, page thy heels
And skip when thou point'st out? will the cold brook,
Candied with ice, caudle thy morning taste
To cure the o'er night's surfeit? Call the creatures
Whose naked natures live in all the spite
Of wreakful heaven, whose bare unhoused trunks
To the conflicting elements expos'd,
Answer mere nature; bid them flatter thee.

180

How fearful
And dizzy 'tis to cast one's eye so low!
The crows and choughs that wing the midway air
Show scarce so gross as beetles; half way down
Hangs one that gathers samphire, dreadful trade!

Methinks he seems no bigger than his head.
The fishermen that walk upon the beach
Appear like mice, and yond tall anchoring bark
Diminish'd to her cock, her cock a buoy
Almost too small for sight. The murmuring surge,
That on the unnumber'd idle pebbles chafes,
Cannot be heard so high. I'll look no more,
Lest my brain turn, and the deficient sight
Topple down headlong.

181

Is this a dagger which I see before me,
The handle toward my hand? Come, let me clutch thee:
I have thee not, and yet I see thee still.
Art thou not, fatal vision, sensible
To feeling as to sight? or art thou but
A dagger of the mind, a false creation,
Proceeding from the heat-oppressed brain?
I see thee yet, in form as palpable
As this which now I draw.
Thou marshall'st me the way that I was going;
And such an instrument I was to use.
Mine eyes are made the fools o' the other senses,
Or else worth all the rest: I see thee still;
And on thy blade and dudgeon gouts of blood,
Which was not so before. There's no such thing:
It is the bloody business which informs
Thus to mine eyes. Now o'er the one half-world
Nature seems dead, and wicked dreams abuse
The curtain'd sleep; witchcraft celebrates
Pale Hecate's offerings; and wither'd murder,
Alarum'd by his sentinel, the wolf,
Whose howl's his watch, thus with his stealthy pace,
With Tarquin's ravishing strides, towards his design
Moves like a ghost. Thou sure and firm-set earth,

Hear not my steps, which way they walk, for fear
The very stones prate of my whereabout,
And take the present horror from the time,
Which now suits with it.

182

No, no, no, no! Come, let's away to prison;
We two alone will sing like birds i' the cage:
When thou dost ask me blessing, I'll kneel down,
And ask of thee forgiveness: so we'll live,
And pray, and sing, and tell old tales, and laugh
At gilded butterflies, and hear poor rogues
Talk of court news; and we'll talk with them too,
Who loses and who wins; who's in, who's out;
And take upon's the mystery of things,
As if we were God's spies: and we'll wear out,
In a wall'd prison, packs and sets of great ones
That ebb and flow by the moon.

183

— The queen, my lord, is dead.
— She should have died hereafter;
There would have been a time for such a word.
To-morrow, and to-morrow, and to-morrow,
Creeps in this petty pace from day to day,
To the last syllable of recorded time;
And all our yesterdays have lighted fools
The way to dusty death. Out, out, brief candle!
Life's but a walking shadow, a poor player
That struts and frets his hour upon the stage,
And then is heard no more; it is a tale
Told by an idiot, full of sound and fury,
Signifying nothing.

184

I have liv'd long enough: my way of life
Is fall'n into the sear, the yellow leaf;
And that which should accompany old age,
As honour, love, obedience, troops of friends,
I must not look to have; but, in their stead,
Curses, not loud but deep, mouth-honour, breath,
Which the poor heart would fain deny, and dare not.

185

Thou God of this great vast, rebuke these surges,
Which wash both heaven and hell; and thou, that hast
Upon the winds command, bind them in brass,
Having call'd them from the deep. O! still
Thy deafening, dreadful thunders; gently quench
Thy nimble, sulphurous flashes. O! how Lychorida,
How does my queen? Thou stormest venomously;
Wilt thou spit all thyself? The seaman's whistle
Is as a whisper in the ears of death,
Unheard. Lychorida! Lucina, O!
Divinest patroness, and midwife gentle
To those that cry by night, convey thy deity
Aboard our dancing boat; make swift the pangs
Of my queen's travails!

186

Be not afeard: the isle is full of noises,
Sounds and sweet airs, that give delight, and hurt not.
Sometimes a thousand twangling instruments
Will hum about mine ears; and sometimes voices,
That, if I then had wak'd after long sleep,
Will make me sleep again: and then, in dreaming,
The clouds methought would open and show riches
Ready to drop upon me; that, when I wak'd
I cried to dream again.

187

The barge she sat in, like a burnish'd throne,
Burn'd on the water; the poop was beaten gold,
Purple the sails, and so perfumed, that
The winds were love-sick with them; the oars were silver,
Which to the tune of flutes kept stroke, and made
The water which they beat to follow faster,
As amorous of their strokes. For her own person,
It beggar'd all description; she did lie
In her pavilion, – cloth-of-gold of tissue, –
O'er-picturing that Venus where we see
The fancy outwork nature; on each side her
Stood pretty-dimpled boys, like smiling Cupids,
With divers-colour'd fans, whose wind did seem
To glow the delicate cheeks which they did cool,
And what they undid did.
Her gentlewomen, like the Nereides,
So many mermaids, tended her i' the eyes,
And made their bends adornings; at the helm
A seeming mermaid steers; the silken tackle
Swell with the touches of those flower-soft hands,
That yarely frame the office. From the barge
A strange invisible perfume hits the sense
Of the adjacent wharfs. The city cast
Her people out upon her, and Antony,
Enthron'd i' the market-place, did sit alone,
Whistling to the air; which, but for vacancy,
Had gone to gaze on Cleopatra too
And made a gap in nature.
Upon her landing, Antony sent to her,
Invited her to supper; she replied
It should be better he became her guest,
Which she entreated. Our courteous Antony,
Whom ne'er the word of 'No' woman heard speak,
Being barber'd ten times o'er, goes to the feast,

And, for his ordinary, pays his heart
For what his eyes eat only. I saw her once
Hop forty paces through the public street;
And having lost her breath, she spoke, and panted
That she did make defect perfection,
And, breathless, power breathe forth.
Age cannot wither her, nor custom stale
Her infinite variety; other women cloy
The appetites they feed, but she makes hungry
Where most she satisfies; for vilest things
Become themselves in her, that the holy priests
Bless her when she is riggish.

188

What! are men mad? Hath nature given them eyes
To see this vaulted arch, and the rich crop
Of sea and land, which can distinguish 'twixt
The fiery orbs above and the twinn'd stones
Upon the number'd beach? and can we not
Partition make with spectacles so precious
'Twixt fair and foul?
It cannot be i' the eye; for apes and monkeys
'Twixt two such shes would chatter this way and
Contemn with mows the other; nor i' the judgment,
For idiots in this case of favour would
Be wisely definite; nor i' the appetite;
Sluttery to such neat excellence oppos'd
Should make desire vomit emptiness,
Not so allur'd to feed. The cloyed will, –
That satiate yet unsatisfied desire, that tub
Both fill'd and running, – ravening first the lamb,
Longs after for the garbage.

189

What you do
Still betters what is done. When you speak, sweet,
I'd have you do it ever: when you sing,
I'd have you buy and sell so; so give alms;
Pray so; for the ordering your affairs,
To sing them too: when you do dance, I wish you
A wave o' the sea, that you might ever do
Nothing but that; move still, still so,
And own no other function: each your doing,
So singular in each particular,
Crowns what you are doing in the present deed,
That all your acts are queens.

190

This double worship,
Where one part does disdain with cause, the other
Insult without all reason; where gentry, title, wisdom,
Cannot conclude, but by the yea and no
Of general ignorance, – it must omit
Real necessities, and give way the while
To unstable slightness: purpose so barr'd, it follows
Nothing is done to purpose. Therefore, beseech you, –
You that will be less fearful than discreet,
That love the fundamental part of state
More than you doubt the change on't, that prefer
A noble life before a long, and wish
To jump a body with a dangerous physic
That's sure of death without it, at once pluck out
The multitudinous tongue; let them not lick
The sweet which is their poison. Your dishonour
Mangles true judgment, and bereaves the state
Of that integrity which should become it,
Not having the power to do the good it would,
For the ill which doth control 't.

191

Dost thou forget
From what a torment I did free thee?
Thou dost; and think'st it much to tread the ooze
Of the salt deep,
To run upon the sharp wind of the north,
To do me business in the veins o' th' earth
When it is bak'd with frost.
Hast thou forgot
The foul witch Sycorax, who with age and envy
Was grown into a hoop? hast thou forgot her?
I must,
Once in a month, recount what thou hast been,
Which thou forget'st. This damn'd witch, Sycorax,
For mischiefs manifold and sorceries terrible
To enter human hearing, from Argier,
Thou know'st, was banish'd: for one thing she did
They would not take her life. Is not this true?
This blue-ey'd hag was hither brought with child
And here was left by the sailors. Thou, my slave,
As thou report'st thyself, wast then her servant:
And, for thou wast a spirit too delicate
To act her earthy and abhorr'd commands,
Refusing her grand hests, she did confine thee,
By help of her more potent ministers,
And in her most unmitigable rage,
Into a cloven pine; within which rift
Imprison'd thou didst painfully remain
A dozen years; within which space she died
And left thee there, where thou didst vent thy groans
As fast as mill-wheels strike. Then was this island, –
Save for the son that she did litter here,
A freckled whelp hag-born, – not honour'd with
A human shape.
He that Caliban,

Whom now I keep in service. Thou best know'st
What torment I did find thee in; thy groans
Did make wolves howl and penetrate the breasts
Of ever-angry bears: it was a torment
To lay upon the damn'd, which Sycorax
Could not again undo; it was mine art,
When I arriv'd and heard thee, that made gape
The pine, and let thee out.
If thou more murmur'st, I will rend an oak
And peg thee in his knotty entrails till
Thou hast howl'd away twelve winters.

192

Where think'st thou he is now? Stands he, or sits he?
Or does he walk? or is he on his horse?
O happy horse, to bear the weight of Antony!
Do bravely, horse, for wot'st thou whom thou mov'st?
The demi-Atlas of this earth, the arm
And burgonet of men. He's speaking now,
Or murmuring 'Where's my serpent of old Nile?'
For so he calls me. Now I feed myself
With most delicious poison. Think on me,
That am with Phœbus' amorous pinches black,
And wrinkled deep in time? Broad-fronted Caesar,
When thou wast here above the ground I was
A morsel for a monarch, and great Pompey
Would stand and make his eyes grow in my brow;
There would he anchor his aspect and die
With looking on his life.

193

You common cry of curs! whose breath I hate
As reek o' the rotten fens, whose loves I prize
As the dead carcases of unburied men
That do corrupt my air, I banish you;

And here remain with your uncertainty!
Let every feeble rumour shake your hearts!
Your enemies, with nodding of their plumes,
Fan you into despair! Have the power still
To banish your defenders; till at length
Your ignorance, – which finds not, till it feels, –
Making but reservation of yourselves, –
Still your own foes, – deliver you as most
Abated captives to some nation
That won you without blows! Despising,
For you, the city, thus I turn my back:
There is a world elsewhere.

194

. . . he no more remembers his mother now than an eight-year-old horse. The tartness of his face sours ripe grapes: when he walks, he moves like an engine, and the ground shrinks before his treading: he is able to pierce a corslet with his eye; talks like a knell, and his hum is a battery. He sits in his state, as a thing made for Alexander. What he bids be done is finished with his bidding. He wants nothing of a god but eternity and a heaven to throne in.

195

Had I this cheek
To bathe my lips upon; this hand, whose touch,
Whose every touch, would force the feeler's soul
To the oath of loyalty; this object, which
Takes prisoner the wild motion of mine eye,
Firing it only here; should I – damn'd then –
Slaver with lips as common as the stairs
That mount the Capitol; join gripes with hands
Made hard with hourly falsehood, – falsehood, as
With labour; – then by-peeping in an eye,
Base and illustrous as the smoky light

That's fed with stinking tallow; it were fit
That all the plagues of hell should at one time
Encounter such revolt.

196

He that will give good words to thee will flatter
Beneath abhorring. What would you have, you curs,
That like nor peace nor war? the one affrights you,
The other makes you proud. He that trusts to you,
Where he should find you lions, finds you hares;
Where foxes, geese: you are no surer, no,
Than is the coal of fire upon the ice,
Or hailstone in the sun. Your virtue is,
To make him worthy whose offence subdues him,
And curse that justice did it. Who deserves greatness
Deserves your hate; and your affections are
A sick man's appetite, who desires most that
Which would increase his evil. He that depends
Upon your favours swims with fins of lead
And hews down oaks with rushes. Hang ye! Trust ye?
With every minute you do change a mind,
And call him noble that was now your hate,
Him vile that was your garland.

197

O, it is monstrous! monstrous!
Methought the billows spoke and told me of it;
The winds did sing it to me; and the thunder,
That deep and dreadful organ-pipe, pronounc'd
The name of Prosper: it did bass my trespass.
Therefore my son i' th' ooze is bedded; and
I'll seek him deeper than e'er plummet sounded.
And with him there lie mudded.

198

All places yield to him ere he sits down;
And the nobility of Rome are his:
The senators and patricians love him too:
The tribunes are no soldiers; and their people
Will be as rash in the repeal as hasty
To expel him thence. I think he'll be to Rome
As is the osprey to the fish, who takes it
By sovereignty of nature. First he was
A noble servant to them, but he could not
Carry his honours even; whether 'twas pride,
Which out of daily fortune ever taints
The happy man; whether defect of judgment,
To fail in the disposing of those chances
Which he was lord of; or whether nature,
Not to be other than one thing, not moving
From the casque to the cushion, but commanding peace
Even with the same austerity and garb
As he controll'd the war; but one of these,
As he hath spices of them all, not all,
For I dare so far free him, made him fear'd,
So hated, and so banish'd: but he has a merit
To choke it in the utterance. So our virtues
Lie in the interpretation of the time;
And power, unto itself most commendable,
Hath not a tomb so evident as a chair
To extol what it hath done.

199

Is whispering nothing?
Is leaning cheek to cheek? is meeting noses?
Kissing with inside lip? stopping the career
Of laughter with a sigh? – a note infallible
Of breaking honesty, – horsing foot on foot?
Skulking in corners? wishing clocks more swift?

Hours, minutes? noon, midnight? and all eyes
Blind with the pin and web but theirs, theirs only,
That would unseen be wicked? is this nothing?
Why, then the world and all that's in't is nothing;
The covering sky is nothing; Bohemia nothing;
My wife is nothing; nor nothing have these nothings,
If this be nothing.

200

I would I had some flowers o' the spring that might
Become your time of day; and yours, and yours,
That wear upon your virgin branches yet
Your maidenheads growing: O Proserpina!
For the flowers now that frighted thou let's fall
From Dis's waggon! daffodils,
That come before the swallow dares, and take
The winds of March with beauty; violets dim,
But sweeter than the lids of Juno's eyes
Or Cytherea's breath; pale prime-roses,
That die unmarried, ere they can behold
Bright Phœbus in his strength, a malady
Most incident to maids; bold oxlips and
The crown imperial; lilies of all kinds,
The flower-de-luce being one. O! these I lack
To make you garlands of, and my sweet friend,
To strew him o'er and o'er!

201

Antony,
Leave thy lascivious wassails. When thou once
Wast beaten from Modena, where thou slew'st
Hirtius and Pansa, consuls, at thy heel
Did famine follow, whom thou fought'st against,
Though daintily brought up, with patience more
Than savages could suffer; thou didst drink

The stale of horses and the gilded puddle
Which beasts would cough at; thy palate then did deign
The roughest berry on the rudest hedge;
Yea, like the stag, when snow the pasture sheets,
The barks of trees thou browsed'st; on the Alps
It is reported thou didst eat strange flesh,
Which some did die to look on; and all this –
It wounds thy honour that I speak it now –
Was borne so like a soldier, that thy cheek
So much as lank'd not.

202

Inch-thick, knee-deep, o'er head and ears a fork'd one!
Go play, boy, play; thy mother plays, and I
Play too, but so disgrac'd a part, whose issue
Will hiss me to my grave: contempt and clamour
Will be my knell. Go play, boy, play. There have been,
Or I am much deceiv'd, cuckolds ere now;
And many a man there is even at this present,
Now, while I speak this, holds his wife by the arm,
That little thinks she has been sluic'd in's absence,
And his pond fish'd by his next neighbour, by
Sir Smile, his neighbour: nay, there's comfort in't,
Whiles other men have gates, and those gates open'd,
As mine, against their will. Should all despair
That have revolted wives the tenth of mankind
Would hang themselves. Physic for't there is none;
It is a bawdy planet, that will strike
Where 'tis predominant; and 'tis powerful, think it,
From east, west, north, and south: be it concluded,
No barricado for a belly: know't;
It will let in and out the enemy
With bag and baggage. Many a thousand on's
Have the disease and feel't not.

203

When daffodils begin to peer,
  With heigh! the doxy, over the dale,
Why, then comes in the sweet o' the year;
  For the red blood reigns in the winter's pale.

The white sheet bleaching on the hedge,
  With heigh! the sweet birds, O, how they sing!
Doth set my pugging tooth on edge;
  For a quart of ale is a dish for a king.

The lark, that tirra-lirra chants,
  With, heigh! with, heigh! the thrush and the jay,
Are summer songs for me and my aunts,
  While we lie tumbling in the hay.

204

The crickets sing, and man's o'er-labour'd sense
Repairs itself by rest. Our Tarquin thus
Did softly press the rushes ere he waken'd
The chastity he wounded. Cytherea,
How bravely thou becom'st thy bed! fresh lily,
And whiter than the sheets! That I might touch!
But kiss: one kiss! Rubies unparagon'd,
How dearly they do't! 'Tis her breathing that
Perfumes the chamber thus; the flame of the taper
Bows toward her, and would under-peep her lids,
To see the enclosed lights, now canopied
Under these windows, white and azure lac'd
With blue of heaven's own tinct. But my design,
To note the chamber: I will write all down:
Such and such pictures; there the window; such
Th' adornment of her bed; the arras, figures,
Why, such and such; and the contents o' the story.
Ah! but some natural notes about her body,
Above ten thousand meaner moveables

Would testify, to enrich mine inventory.
O sleep! thou ape of death, lie dull upon her;
And be her senses but as a monument
Thus in a chapel lying. Come off, come off; –
{*Taking off her bracelet.*]
As slipper as the Gordian knot was hard!
'Tis mine; and this will witness outwardly,
As strongly as the conscience does within,
To the madding of her lord. On her left breast
A mole cinque-spotted, like the crimson drops
I' the bottom of a cowslip: here's a voucher;
Stronger than ever law could make: this secret
Will force him think I have pick'd the lock and ta'en
The treasure of her honour. No more. To what end?
Why should I write this down, that's riveted,
Screw'd to my memory? She hath been reading late
The tale of Tereus; here the leaf's turn'd down
Where Philomel gave up. I have enough:
To the trunk again, and shut the spring of it.
Swift, swift, you dragons of the night, that dawning
May bare the raven's eye! I lodge in fear;
Though this a heavenly angel, hell is here.
[*Clock strikes.*]
One, two, three: time, time!

205

I saw him beat the surges under him,
And ride upon their backs: he trod the water,
Whose enmity he flung aside, and breasted
The surge most swoln that met him: his bold head
'Bove the contentious waves he kept, and oar'd
Himself with his good arms in lusty stroke
To the shore, that o'er his wave-worn basis bow'd,
As stooping to relieve him. I not doubt
He came alive to land.

Is there no way for men to be, but women
Must be half-workers? We are all bastards; all,
And that most venerable man which I
Did call my father was I know not where
When I was stamp'd; some coiner with his tools
Made me a counterfeit; yet my mother seem'd
The Dian of that time; so doth my wife
The nonpareil of this. O! vengeance, vengeance;
Me of my lawful pleasure she restrain'd
And pray'd me oft forbearance; did it with
A pudency so rosy the sweet view on't
Might well have warm'd old Saturn; that I thought her
As chaste as unsunn'd snow. O! all the devils!
This yellow Iachimo, in an hour, – was't not?
Or less – at first? – perchance he spoke not, but
Like a full-acorn'd boar, a German one,
Cried 'O!' and mounted; found no opposition
But what he look'd for should oppose and she
Should from encounter guard. Could I find out
The woman's part in me! For there's no motion
That tends to vice in man but I affirm
It is the woman's part; be it lying, note it,
The woman's; flattering, hers; deceiving, hers;
Lust and rank thoughts, hers, hers; revenges, hers;
Ambitions, covetings, change of prides, disdain,
Nice longing, slanders, mutability,
All faults that man may name, nay, that hell knows,
Why, hers, in part, or all; but rather, all;
For even to vice
They are not constant, but are changing still
One vice but of a minute old for one
Not half so old as that. I'll write against them,
Detest them, curse them. Yet 'tis greater skill
In a true hate to pray they have their will:
The very devils cannot plague them better.

144

207

If by your art, my dearest father, you have
Put the wild waters in this roar, allay them.
The sky, it seems, would pour down stinking pitch,
But that the sea, mounting to th' welkin's cheek,
Dashes the fire out. O! I have suffer'd
With those that I saw suffer: a brave vessel,
Who had, no doubt, some noble creatures in her,
Dash'd all to pieces. O! the cry did knock
Against my very heart. Poor souls, they perish'd.
Had I been any god of power, I would
Have sunk the sea within the earth, or e'er
It should the good ship so have swallow'd and
The fraughting souls within her.

208

These three,
Three thousand confident, in act as many, –
For three performers are the file when all
The rest do nothing, – with this word, 'Stand, stand!'
Accommodated by the place, more charming
With their own nobleness, – which could have turn'd
A distaff to a lance, – gilded pale looks,
Part shame, part spirit renew'd; that some, turn'd coward
But by example, – O! a sin of war,
Damn'd in the first beginners, – 'gan to look
The way that they did, and to grin like lions
Upon the pikes o' the hunters. Then began
A stop i' the chaser, a retire, anon,
A rout, confusion thick; forthwith they fly
Chickens, the way which they stoop'd eagles; slaves,
The strides they victors made. And now our cowards –
Like fragments in hard voyages – became
The life o' the need; having found the back door open
Of the unguarded hearts, Heavens! how they wound;

Some slain before; some dying; some their friends
O'er-borne i' the former wave; ten, chas'd by one,
Are now each one the slaughter-man of twenty;
Those that would die or ere resist are grown
The mortal bugs o' the field.

209

There was a time when all the body's members
Rebell'd against the belly; thus accus'd it:
That only like a gulf it did remain
I' the midst o' the body, idle and unactive,
Still cupboarding the viand, never bearing
Like labour with the rest, where the other instruments
Did see and hear, devise, instruct, walk, feel,
And, mutually participate, did minister
Unto the appetite and affection common
Of the whole body. The belly answer'd . . .
With a kind of smile,
Which ne'er came from the lungs, but even thus –
For, look you, I may make the belly smile
As well as speak – it tauntingly replied
To the discontented members, the mutinous parts
That envied his receipt; even so most fitly
As you malign our senators for that
They are not such as you . . .
Note me this, good friend;
Your most grave belly was deliberate,
Not rash like his accusers, and thus answer'd:
'True is it, my incorporate friends,' quoth he,
'That I receive the general food at first,
Which you do live upon; and fit it is;
Because I am the store-house and the shop
Of the whole body: but, if you do remember,
I send it through the rivers of your blood,
Even to the court, the heart, to the seat o' the brain;

And, through the cranks and offices of man,
The strongest nerves and small inferior veins
From me receive that natural competency
Whereby they live. And though that all at once,
You, my good friends,' – this says the belly, mark me. –
'Though all at once cannot
See what I do deliver out to each,
Yet I can make my audit up, that all
From me do back receive the flour of all,
And leave me but the bran.'

210

Fear no more the heat o' the sun,
  Nor the furious winter's rages;
Thou thy worldly task hast done,
  Home art gone, and ta'en thy wages;
Golden lads and girls all must
  As chimney-sweepers, come to dust.

Fear no more the frown o' the great,
  Thou art past the tyrant's stroke:
Care no more to clothe and eat;
  To thee the reed is as the oak;
The sceptre, learning, physic, must
  All follow this, and come to dust.

Fear no more the lightning-flash,
  Nor the all-dreaded thunder-stone;
Fear not slander, censure rash;
  Thou hast finsh'd joy and moan:
All lovers young, all lovers must
  Consign to thee, and come to dust.

No exorcizer harm thee!
  Nor no witchcraft charm thee!
Ghost unlaid forbear thee!
  Nothing ill come near thee!

Quiet consummation have;
And renowned be thy grave!

211

Safely in harbour
Is the king's ship; in the deep nook, where once
Thou call'dst me up at midnight to fetch dew
From the still-vex'd Bermoothes; there she's hid:
The mariners all under hatches stow'd;
Who, with a charm join'd to their suffer'd labour,
I have left asleep: and for the rest o' the fleet
Which I dispers'd, they all have met again,
And are upon the Mediterranean flote,
Bound sadly home for Naples,
Supposing that they saw the king's ship wrack'd,
And his great person perish.

212

I dream'd there was an Emperor Antony:
O! such another sleep, that I might see
But such another man.
His face was as the heavens, and therein stuck
A sun and moon, which kept their course, and lighted
The little O, the earth.
His legs bestrid the ocean; his rear'd arm
Crested the world; his voice was propertied
As all the tuned spheres, and that to friends;
But when he meant to quail and shake the orb,
He was as rattling thunder. For his bounty,
There was no winter in't, an autumn 'twas
That grew the more by reaping; his delights
Were dolphin-like, they show'd his back above
The element they liv'd in; in his livery
Walk'd crowns and crownets, realms and islands were
As plates dropp'd from his pocket.

213

— Where should this music be? i' th' air, or th' earth?
It sounds no more; – and sure, it waits upon
Some god o' th' island. Sitting on a bank,
Weeping again the king my father's wrack,
This music crept by me upon the waters,
Allaying both their fury, and my passion,
With its sweet air: thence I have follow'd it. –
Or it hath drawn me rather, – but 'tis gone.
No, it begins again.
— Full fathom five thy father lies;
Of his bones are coral made:
Those are pearls that were his eyes:
Nothing of him that doth fade,
But doth suffer a sea-change
Into something rich and strange.
Sea-nymphs hourly ring his knell:
[*Burden*:] ding-dong.
Hark! now I hear them, – ding-dong, bell.

214

With fairest flowers
While summer lasts and I live here, Fidele,
I'll sweeten thy sad grave; thou shalt not lack
The flower that's like thy face, pale primrose, nor
The azur'd hare-bell, like thy veins, no, nor
The leaf of eglantine, whom not to slander,
Out-sweeten'd not thy breath: the ruddock would,
With charitable bill, – O bill! sore-shaming
Those rich-left heirs, that let their fathers lie
Without a monument, – bring thee all this;
Yea, and furr'd moss besides, when flowers are none,
To winter-ground thy corse.

215

Ye elves of hills, brooks, standing lakes, and groves;
And ye, that on the sands with printless foot
Do chase the ebbing Neptune and do fly him
When he comes back; you demi-puppets, that
By moonshine do the green sour ringlets make
Whereof the ewe not bites; and you, whose pastime
Is to make midnight mushrooms; that rejoice
To hear the solemn curfew; by whose aid, –
Weak masters though ye be – I have bedimm'd
The noontide sun, call'd forth the mutinous winds,
And 'twixt the green sea and the azur'd vault
Set roaring war: to the dread-rattling thunder
Have I given fire and rifted Jove's stout oak
With his own bolt; the strong-bas'd promontory
Have I made shake; and by the spurs pluck'd up
The pine and cedar; graves at my command
Have wak'd their sleepers, op'd, and let them forth
By my so potent art. But this rough magic
I here abjure; and, when I have requir'd
Some heavenly music, – which even now I do, –
To work mine end upon their senses that
This airy charm is for, I'll break my staff,
Bury it certain fathoms in the earth,
And, deeper than did ever plummet sound,
I'll drown my book.

216

A terrible child-bed hast thou had, my dear;
No light, no fire: the unfriendly elements
Forgot thee utterly; nor have I time
To give thee hallow'd to thy grave, but straight
Must cast thee, scarcely coffin'd, in the ooze;
Where, for a monument upon thy bones,
And aye-remaining lamps, the belching whale

And humming water must o'erwhelm thy corpse,
Lying with simple shells!

217

Our revels now are ended. These our actors,
As I foretold you, were all spirits and
Are melted into air, into thin air:
And, like the baseless fabric of this vision,
The cloud-capp'd towers, the gorgeous palaces,
The solemn temples, the great globe itself,
Yea, all which it inherit, shall dissolve
And, like this insubstantial pageant faded,
Leave not a rack behind. We are such stuff
As dreams are made on, and our little life
Is rounded with a sleep.

218

The Phœnix and the Turtle

Let the bird of loudest lay,
On the sole Arabian tree,
Herald sad and trumpet be,
To whose sound chaste wings obey.

But thou shrieking harbinger,
Foul precurrer of the fiend,
Augur of the fever's end,
To this troop come thou not near.

From this session interdict
Every fowl of tyrant wing,
Save the eagle, feather'd king:
Keep the obsequy so strict.

Let the priest in surplice white
That defunctive music can,

Be the death-divining swan,
Lest the requiem lack his right.

And thou treble-dated crow,
That thy sable gender mak'st
With the breath thou giv'st and tak'st,
'Mongst our mourners shalt thou go.

Here the anthem doth commence:
Love and constancy is dead;
Phœnix and the turtle fled
In a mutual flame from hence.

So they lov'd, as love in twain
Had the essence but in one;
Two distincts, division none:
Number there in love was slain.

Hearts remote, yet not asunder;
Distance, and no space was seen
'Twixt the turtle and his queen:
But in them it were a wonder.

So between them love did shine,
That the turtle saw his right
Flaming in the phœnix' sight;
Either was the other's mine.

Property was thus appall'd,
That the self was not the same;
Single nature's double name
Neither two nor one was call'd.

Reason, in itself confounded,
Saw division grow together;
To themselves yet either neither,
Simple were so well compounded,

That it cried, 'How true a twain
Seemeth this concordant one!

Love hath reason, reason none,
If what parts can so remain.'

Whereupon it made this threne
To the phœnix and the dove,
Co-supremes and stars of love,
As chorus to their tragic scene.

THRENOS

Beauty, truth, and rarity
Grace in all simplicity,
Here enclos'd in cinders lie.

Death is now the phœnix' nest;
And the turtle's loyal breast
To eternity doth rest,

Leaving no posterity:
'Twas not their infirmity,
It was married chastity.

Truth may seem, but cannot be;
Beauty brag, but 'tis not she;
Truth and beauty buried be.

To this urn let those repair
That are either true or fair;
For these dead birds sigh a prayer.

Sources

1 *A Midsummer Night's Dream*, v.ii. Puck
2 Sonnet VIII
3 *Henry VI*, Pt 3, III.ii. Richard, Duke of Gloucester
4 Sonnet LXII
5 *Romeo and Juliet*, II.ii. Romeo
6 Sonnet XVIII
7 *Love's Labour's Lost*, I.ii. Armado
8 Sonnet CXVI
9 *Henry IV*, Pt 2, IV.v. King Henry
10 Sonnet XII
11 *Henry IV*, Pt 1. II.iv. Prince Hal, Falstaff
12 Sonnet LXIV
13 *Rape of Lucrece*, lines 918–1022
14 Sonnet LX
15 *King John*, IV.iii. The Bastard
16 Sonnet LV
17 *Henry IV*, Pt 1, I.iii. Hotspur
18 *The Taming of the Shrew*, III.ii. Biondello
19 *King John*, V.ii. The Bastard
20 *Midsummer Night's Dream*, II.i. Oberon
21 *All's Well That Ends Well*, I.i. Helena, Parolles
22 Sonnet LXXXV
23 *Julius Caesar*, I.ii. Cassius
24 Sonnet LXXIV
25 *As You Like It*, II.vi. Jaques
26 Sonnet XXXV
27 *Richard II*, V.V. King Richard
28 Sonnet XCIV
29 *Henry IV*, Pt 2, IV.iii Falstaff
30 *Twelfth Night*, I.i. Orsino
31 Sonnet XXV
32 *Twelfth Night*, II,iv. Clown
33 *Merchant of Venice*, V.i. Lorenzo
34 *As You Like It*, II.i Duke Senior
35 Sonnet LXXXVI
36 *Richard III*, I.i. Richard, Duke of Gloucester
37 Sonnet XC
38 *Two Gentlemen of Verona*, IV.iv. Launce
39 *As You Like It*, II.vii. Amiens
40 Sonnet XXX

41 *Midsummer Night's Dream*, V.i. Theseus
42 Sonnet LXXXIX
43 Poem IV, from *Sonnets to Sundry Notes of Music*
44 Sonnets CXXX
45 *As You Like It*, V.iii. Second Page's Song
46 Sonnet CII
47 *Love's Labour's Lost*, III.i. Berowne
48 Sonnet XCIX
49 *Twelfth Night*, II.iii. Clown's Song
50 Sonnet CXXIX
51 *Richard II*, I.iv. Clarence, Brakenbury
52 Sonnet CVIII
53 *Henry V*, II.iii. Hostess
54 Sonnet CV
55 *Love's Labour's Lost*, V.ii. Song, Armado
56 Sonnet CXLVI
57 *Henry V*, IV. Chorus
58 Sonnet XIX
59 *As You Like It*, II.vii. Jaques
60 Sonnet LXVI
61 *Henry V*, IV.i. King Henry
62 Sonnet XCI
63 *As You Like It*, V.iv. Touchstone, Jaques
64 *Henry V*, III.i. King Henry
65 Sonnet LXV
66 *Julius Caesar*, III.i. Antony
67 Sonnet CXXV
68 *Henry V*, IV.iii. King Henry
69 Sonnet CXIX
70 *Henry IV*, Pt 1, V.i. Falstaff
71 Sonnet CXXIV
72 *Merchant of Venice*, III.ii. Song
73 Sonnet LXXIII
74 *Romeo and Juliet*, I.iii. Nurse, Lady Capulet
75 Sonnet CXXI
76 *Merchant of Venice*, IV.i. Portia
77 Sonnet CXXXII
78 *Richard II*, III.ii. King Richard
79 Sonnet CXLI
80 *Henry IV*, Pt 2, III.ii. Falstaff
81 *Sir Thomas More*, IV More
82 Sonnet LXXI
83 *Julius Caesar*, II.i. Brutus
84 Sonnet CVII

85 *Julius Caesar*, III.ii. Antony
86 Sonnet CXLIV
87 *Merry Wives of Windsor*, III.v. Falstaff
88 *Twelfth Night*, V.i. Song
89 Sonnet CXXXVII
90 *Richard II*, II.i. Gaunt
91 Sonnet CXXXVIII
92 *Henry V*, III.iii. King Henry
93 Sonnet CXLVIII
94 *Henry V*, IV.ii. Grandpré
95 *Two Gentlemen of Verona*, II.iii. Launce
96 Sonnet CXLVII
97 *Love's Labour's Lost*, IV.iii. Berowne
98 Sonnet CLII
99 *Romeo and Juliet*, I.iv. Mercutio
100 Sonnet LXXXVII
101 *All's Well That Ends Well*, I.ii. King
102 *Troilus and Cressida*, IV.iii. Troilus
103 Sonnet CLI
104 *Troilus and Cressida*, IV.v. Ulysses
105 *Measure for Measure*, III.i. Duke
106 *Othello*, II.i. Iago, Desdemona, Emilia
107 *Hamlet*, II.ii. Hamlet
108 *Troilus and Cressida*, III.ii. Troilus
109 *Troilus and Cressida*, III.i. Paris, Pandarus
110 *Troilus and Cressida*, III.ii Cressida
111 *Othello*, I.i. Iago
112 *Measure for Measure*, III.i. Claudio
113 *Measure for Measure*, IV.i. Song
114 *Othello*, IV.iii. Emilia
115 *Hamlet*, I.iii. Polonius
116 *Othello*, IV.ii. Othello
117 *Othello*, III.iii. Iago
118 *Hamlet*, I.ii. Hamlet
119 *Two Gentlemen of Verona*, IV.ii. Song
120 *Measure for Measure*, I.iii. Duke
121 *Othello*, III.iii. Iago
122 *Othello*, I.i. Iago
123 *Othello*, I.ii. Brabantio
124 *Hamlet*, II.ii. Hamlet
125 *Othello*, III.iii. Othello
126 *Troilus and Cressida*, I.iii. Ulysses
127 *Troilus and Cressida*, III.ii. Troilus
128 *Othello*, II.i. Iago, Roderigo

129 *Troilus and Cressida*, V.v. Agamemnon, Nestor, Ulysses
130 *Hamlet*, III.i. Hamlet
131 *Troilus and Cressida*, I.iii. Agamemnon
132 *Hamlet*, IV.iv. Hamlet
133 *Troilus and Cressida*, III.iii. Ulysses
134 *Hamlet*, I.iv. Hamlet
135 *Troilus and Cressida*, I.i. Troilus
136 *Troilus and Cressida*, I.iii. Nestor
137 *Hamlet*, III.i. Hamlet
138 *Measure for Measure*, II.ii. Isabella
139 *Othello*, V.ii. Othello
140 *Hamlet*, II.ii. Hamlet
141 *Hamlet*, IV.vii. Queen
142 *Othello*, I.iii. Othello
143 *Hamlet*, III.iii. King
144 *Hamlet*, V.i. Hamlet
145 *Othello*, V.ii. Othello
146 *Macbeth*, IV.i. Witches
147 *King Lear*, I.ii. Gloucester
148 *Macbeth*, II.iii. Lennox
149 *Timon of Athens*, IV.iii. Timon
150 *King Lear*, IV.vi. King Lear
151 *Macbeth*, I.v. Lady Macbeth
152 *Timon*, IV.iii. Apemantus
153 *King Lear*, I.ii. Edmund
154 *Macbeth*, I.vi. Duncan, Banquo
155 *King Lear*, III.i. Kent, Gentleman
156 *Macbeth*, I.vii. Lady Macbeth
157 *King Lear*, III.ii. King Lear
158 *Hamlet*, III.iii. Hamlet
159 *Timon of Athens*, IV.iii. Timon
160 *Macbeth*, I.vii. Macbeth
161 *King Lear*, III.ii. King Lear
162 *Macbeth*, II.ii. Macbeth, Lady Macbeth
163 *Timon of Athens*, I.ii. Apemantus
164 *King Lear*, IV.ii. Albany
165 *King Lear*, III.iv. Edgar
166 *Macbeth*, III.ii. Macbeth
167 *Timon of Athens*, IV.i. Timon
168 *King Lear*, I.ii. Edmund
169 *King Lear*, IV.vi. King Lear, Gloucester
170 *King Lear*, III.iv. King Lear
171 *Timon of Athens*, IV.iii. Timon
172 *Macbeth*, II.iii. Macbeth

173 *King Lear*, II.iv. King Lear
174 *Macbeth*, I.v. Lady Macbeth
175 *Macbeth*, II.iii. Macduff, Porter
176 *King Lear*, I.iv. King Lear
177 *Timon of Athens*, IV.iii. Timon
178 *King Lear*, III.iv. King Lear
179 *Timon of Athens*, IV.iii. Apemantus
180 *King Lear*, IV.vi. Edgar
181 *Macbeth*, II.i. Macbeth
182 *King Lear*, V.iii. King Lear
183 *Macbeth*, V.v. Macbeth
184 *Macbeth*, V.iii. Macbeth
185 *Pericles*, III.i. Pericles
186 *The Tempest*, III.ii. Caliban
187 *Antony and Cleopatra*, II.ii. Enobarbus
188 *Cymbeline*, I.vi. Iachimo
189 *Winter's Tale*, IV.iii. Florizel
190 *Coriolanus*, III.i. Coriolanus
191 *The Tempest*, I.ii. Prospero
192 *Antony and Cleopatra*, I.v. Cleopatra
193 *Coriolanus*, III.iii. Coriolanus
194 *Coriolanus*, V.iv. Menenius
195 *Cymbeline*, I.vi. Iachimo
196 *Coriolanus*, I.i. Coriolanus
197 *The Tempest*, III.iii. Alonso
198 *Coriolanus*, IV.vii. Aufidius
199 *Winter's Tale*, I.ii. Leontes
200 *Winter's Tale*, IV.iii. Perdita
201 *Antony and Cleopatra*, I.iv. Caesar
202 *Winter's Tale*, I.ii. Leontes
203 *Winter's Tale*, IV.ii. Song
204 *Cymbeline*, II.ii. Iachimo
205 *The Tempest*, II.i. Francisco
206 *Cymbeline*, III.i. Posthumous
207 *The Tempest*, I.ii. Miranda
208 *Cymbeline*, V.iii. Posthumous
209 *Coriolanus*, I.i. Menenius
210 *Cymbeline*, IV.ii. Song
211 *The Tempest*, I.ii. Ariel
212 *Antony and Cleopatra*, V.ii. Cleopatra
213 *The Tempest*, I.ii. Ferdinand, Ariel
214 *Cymbeline*, IV.ii. Arviragus
215 *The Tempest*, V.i. Prospero
216 *Pericles*, III.i. Pericles

217 *The Tempest*, IV.i. Prospero
218 *The Phoenix and the Turtle*, from *Sonnets to Sundry Notes of Music*

Index of First Lines

EZRA POUND Poems selected by THOM GUNN

EZRA POUND

Poems selected by THOM GUNN

faber and faber

First published in 2000
by Faber and Faber Limited
3 Queen Square London WC1N 3AU

Photoset by Parker Typesetting Service, Leicester
Printed in Italy

All rights reserved

Introduction and this selection © Thom Gunn, 2000
The poems of Ezra Pound are taken from the following publications:
Selected Poems, ed. T. S. Eliot, © Ezra Pound, 1928;
Collected Shorter Poems (US edition, *Personae*), © Ezra Pound, 1926, 1935, 1952, 1968, 1971; *Homage to Sextus Propertius*, © Ezra Pound, 1934, 1964; *A Draft of XXX Cantos*, © Ezra Pound, 1933; *The Fifth Decad of Cantos*, © Ezra Pound, 1937; *The Pisan Cantos*, © Ezra Pound, 1948; *Drafts and Fragments of Cantos CX–CXVII*, © Ezra Pound, 1970; *The Cantos of Ezra Pound*, © The Ezra Pound Literary Property Trust, 1986

Thom Gunn is hereby identified as editor of this work in accordance with Section 77 of the Copyright, Designs and Patents Act 1988

This book is sold subject to the condition that it shall not, by way of trade or otherwise, be lent, resold, hired out or otherwise circulated without the publisher's prior consent in any form of binding or cover other than that in which it is published and without a similar condition including this condition being imposed on the subsequent purchaser

A CIP record for this book
is available from the British Library

ISBN 0–571–20430–9

10 9 8 7 6 5 4 3 2 1

Contents

Introduction

At the end of the twentieth century's first decade, Ezra Pound moved to London, a young American in his mid-twenties. He did so, he said, because he hoped to meet there the greatest living poet, W. B. Yeats. He succeeded in this fairly soon, and became a friend. He met, too, Thomas Hardy and Henry James, two living classics. England would also have been a source of poetic energy because of Robert Browning, twenty years dead but an influence deeper and more lasting on Pound than any of the others. Pound's was seldom a poetry of personal utterance until the Pisan Cantos of the 1940s, when the crisis of the prison-cage forced him into a new kind of writing. Meanwhile, Browning's dramatic poetry had taught Pound how to speak through the mouths of others: a troubadour-warrior, a Chinese river-merchant's wife, Sextus Propertius, or an Italian Renaissance prince. His first commercially published book was called *Personae* – persona being the name of the mask a Roman actor wore, thence coming to refer to the part played. It has since become a fashionable critical term – too fashionable, as if a poem is necessarily spoken through another voice than that of the author, but in Pound's case it usually was. He was willing to try any kind of voice, and at the same time he conducted an extensive apprenticeship translating, imitating, adapting, and inventing new kinds of versification. Even more than most young poets, he sought out what was available, and extended it in testing it.

In the course of his search, he almost inadvertently founded Imagism, a school consisting of his friend H.D., her husband, and himself, of which the most famous exemplary poem is his own 'In a Station of the Metro' (1913), consisting of two images that through juxtaposition constitute a visual comparison. The idea behind Imagism, at its simplest, and it always remained pretty simple, was this: the poet sees an image and has a reaction to it; the poet presents the image as vividly as possible on paper; then, without being told how to react, the reader reacts to the image in the same way as the poet. It was a tiny movement with a tiny life-span which produced tiny poems; but it was to be the most influential poetic movement of the century, in subject matter confining itself to the sensory at the expense of the conceptual, in style emphasizing clarity and compression, and in form carrying with it the implicit necessity of free verse, which was still young and experimental at that time, and by no means the drab norm it is nowadays.

The influence of Imagism was discernible on Pound's translations from the ancient Chinese, a group of poems published in 1915 as *Cathay*. At the time of writing, Pound knew no Chinese, but he had been entrusted with the notebooks of Ernest Fenollosa by his widow, who – clearly a woman of discrimination – could see a resemblance between their contents and the kind of thing that Pound was doing. Fenollosa had been an honoured American scholar of Japanese antiquities who had eventually decided to study ancient Chinese poetry (then little known in the West) and had taken tutorials from Japanese professors of Chinese, being conducted word by word through the originals to produce his own literal translation into English which Pound now proceeded to versify with sensitivity and intelligence. He reproduced in his versions a characteristic note of restrained wistfulness which echoes through the work of subsequent Western poets, from William Carlos Williams to Gary Snyder. Selected physical details did the job of emotion or thought. In 'Taking Leave of a Friend', the feeling is sufficiently implied by the imagery, so that overt expression of regret would be superfluous. This project produced its own kind of free verse, each line being heavily end-stopped and tending to consist of a distinct item parallel to those of other lines, as Donald Davie has pointed out. Other kinds of free verse were to be invented for other kinds of poem, improvised but definably different forms.

In *Homage to Sextus Propertius* (1917), the line is more garrulous, as is suitable to a poetry of wit, gossip, and opinion. The book is an arrangement of poems spliced together from the Latin of Propertius, translation as interpretation. In them Propertius becomes a dramatic character, as scornful of the Emperor Augustus' imperialism as Pound is of the British imperialism of his own time. It is a far from literal translation (the reader will readily notice the anachronistic frigidaires and Roman policemen in Tibet); and the voice of Propertius is at times lively, pompous, eloquent, pedantic, subtle, and broadly comic. The shifts in tone are occasionally puzzling. We may contrast the compressed power of poem VI with the opening lines of IX and wonder about the relationship, or lack of it: if the second of these is a parody, is it Propertius himself parodying somebody, or is it Pound's parody of Latin translation in English?

Toward the end of that marvellous first decade of publication, Pound started his most ambitious work, the *Cantos*, which was to occupy his poetic energies for the rest of his life. He called it an epic, but defined epic only as 'a poem containing history'. You might retort that a bag of groceries *contains*, but that the only relationship between its contents is in the needs of the person who purchased them. The *Cantos* contains – besides history – myth, anecdote, excerpts from many kinds of document, and even poems of various sorts that can stand on their own (for example 'Tudor indeed is gone'), a long-meditated translation from Cavalcanti, versions of Chinese landscape poems, and so on. What to make of all this assortment? The commentators who have found most continuity in the work as a whole have identified the poet with the Odysseus of the first Canto, adventuring and (in Pound's words) sailing after knowledge. Odysseus goes down to the underworld to give speech to the dead: the first line of the first Canto is 'And then went down to the ship', and the Canto itself is a translation of the eleventh book of the *Odyssey* – though from the Renaissance Latin of Andreas Divus, rather than from the original of Homer. How does a poet perceive what he explores while he explores it? Pound would answer 'not as land looks on a map/but as sea bord seen by men sailing' (Canto LIX). So here we are with Pound, translating the archaic into an archaic measure (that of 'The Seafarer'), and suddenly flipping through the pages in his volume, published in 1538, to a translation of a Homeric Hymn to Aphrodite – something as unexpected as the discovery round some unmapped point of a sheltered bay or a dangerous shoal on the coast. Unexpected but appropriate, in that he is sailing not only after knowledge but after beauty also, for Aphrodite is the goddess of beauty.

The Old English line becomes rhythmically looser, in the second Canto developing step by step into a new and flexible free verse line. The arrangement of subject matter was experimental, too: as in the early poem about the Paris Metro, the procedure is often to place one detail by another apparently unrelated, and expect the reader to make the connection. The connection is always easier to make on a rereading, in that we have meanwhile been able to work out a thematic core to each Canto, sometimes obvious and sometimes not. The second Canto centres on a metamorphosis out of Ovid – the boy-god hitching his way across the seas is Dionysus, requiring our worship, might we say lord of the imagination in his combination of wine and poetry? The thirteenth Canto collects precepts by Kung Fu (Confucius) defining 'order', to form something structurally a bit similar to a Platonic dialogue. Each Canto is composed, in its different way, of fragments carefully put together, and it might have struck a contemporary that Pound's juxtaposition of them was similar to the collagist or paste-up techniques common in the visual arts of the time.

We are not, even now, accustomed to works of verse assembled in this way; but it is important, as with any poetry to which we are new, to read with an unreasonable trust, giving ourselves to it in the act of reading aloud, thus discovering the main activity while attempting to share in it; some of the imagery will fall into place as a matter of course, while other details may be postponed as so far resistant to explanation. We understand what we can, pursuing the gist as we recreate the sound.

The rewards are already great. We read in the second Canto:

> Fish-scales over groin muscles,
> lynx-purr amid sea . . .

Here, in sentence fragments, we have the transformation of the sailors into fish occurring simultaneously with the appearance of the god's big cats in the vineyard that the ship is becoming. The absence of finite verbs suggests not only the incompleteness of the images but a process going beyond human control. A wondering dreaminess of tone coincides with precision of image and language.

A good deal of the *Cantos* is concerned with economics. In 1918, Pound came across the work of Major C. H. Douglas, deviser of a scheme of monetary reform called Social Credit. Briefly, his theory arose from the belief that the value of money should be based on real goods and real work, and not on paper money or credit. Pound came to think that usury (in Latin *usura*) was the main cause of the ills of the world. The usurer, whether bank or individual money-lender, charges interest, and such interest, which is not worked for, leads to false and arbitrary values, not only in economics, but in language and art, and in fact all other aspects of our lives.

His dislike of capitalism caused Pound to be attracted to Fascism and to Mussolini himself, who was populist and anti-capitalist. And, since part of the fabric of Fascism was racism, it strengthened his dislike of Jews, associated with money-lending since the Middle Ages.

The group of Cantos directly or indirectly concerned with

usury, XLV, XLVII, and LI, dates from the 1930s, when Pound lived in Rapallo. Canto XLV, as has often been remarked, with its archaisms and its parallel clauses, its rage and its denunciations, is reminiscent of the rhetoric of the Old Testament prophet, Pound's newest persona, raving about the city's sins in the open streets.

Canto XLVII is among Pound's most remarkable works. It can be read as a self-sufficient poem, and a few careful readings aloud will make the outlines clear and leave few obscurities. If it contains fragments of Greek, we are told at once how to pronounce them, and we soon realize that they are incantatory, being exclamations of religious adoration for Adonis. Taking its starting point from the same incidents of the *Odyssey* as Canto I, this Canto concerns ancient wisdom, from Hesiod's advice about the dates of ploughing to descriptions of the votive candles placed in small jars that floated out to sea in a July festival of the Madonna, a ceremony still performed annually in Rapallo as late as 1933. We return again and again to the connections between death and fertility. 'The light has entered the cave. Io! Io!' Religious and orgasmic ecstasy are one. The god enters the cave, the plough enters the earth, the man enters the woman, Odysseus enters the porch of the underworld, we all enter the ground in our death, and in doing so make it fertile.

This Canto is grouped among the anti-usury Cantos, clearly to contrast with them. This is *real* value. Wheat at the altar, olives on the trees, semen in the womb – these are the contrast to paper money, of which the growth is *contra naturam*, against nature. Canto LI is a good deal more dense, the purpose of its juxtapositions needing to be puzzled over at greater length. The bulk of it is taken up by a contrast between a reprise of the prophetic denunciation from Canto XLV and a block of phrases from an 1828 guide to the making of artificial trout flies, exemplifying the careful craftsman who captures the rich products of the world by his creation of lures through organic materials. The difference between styles is extreme, but it is left up to us to get the gist of the contrast in the material. Other items included in this Canto are brief and sometimes obscure in allusion. The poem ends with two Chinese characters which signify 'right name' – the proper wording that is as necessary to honest discussion as it is to good poetry. Accurate language is part of the world's health, and to call something by its right name is part of true knowledge.

Pound was still in Rapallo during World War II, and made a series of eccentric propaganda broadcasts over Radio Rome to America. Since he was still a citizen of the United States, he was thus open to a charge of treason. In 1945 he was arrested by the US Army and held in an army prison camp at Pisa, where he was placed in solitary confinement in a large outdoor cage. He was later allowed the privacy of a small tent within this cage. It was in such circumstances that he awaited his removal to the United States and that he composed what are now known as the Pisan Cantos, which were not to be published for several years. After his return, he was judged mentally unfit to stand trial, and was kept in St Elizabeth's Hospital for the insane, in Washington, for almost the next thirteen years.

The Pisan Cantos were completely unforeseen, as were the conditions of their writing. By contrast to the carefully planned organization of the earlier Cantos, these formed an almost continuous unit of reflection, proceeding as a stream of consciousness (that is, by association), and for the first time consistently personal in point of view. Pound was writing in every expectation of a death sentence, and amid the ruin of his political hopes, deluded though they may have been.

> As a lone ant from a broken anthill,
> from the wreckage of Europe
> ego scriptor.

His material is partly from the daily life of the prison camp:

details about the guards and fellow prisoners, gossip about who is on sick call, notations about the birth of a wasp, the appearance of lizards or ants by or in his cage.

> When the mind swings by a grass-blade
>   an ant's forefoot shall save you

by the beauty and adequacy of its mere being, a fact in the world, not in the mind. He also writes partly of the past – memories above all of his days in England before World War I, of Yeats, Maurice Hewlett, Wilfred Scawen Blunt and his wife Lady Anne. Included here is a snatch of song about the violence of sixteenth-century England, however much the Tudors had managed to reconcile the opposed roses of York and Lancaster from the Wars of the Roses. In his tent he hallucinates the eyes of a goddess, reproaching him for his faults, to whom he seeks to justify himself. It is worth noting that both these excerpts depend for much of their strength on the iambic line he had by no means abandoned when he sought out other forms of versification earlier in his career.

Pound believed that literature was news that stays news, and surely by now he has proved himself among those who continue newsworthy. He was probably the single most influential poet of the century, the generous encourager of poets from Frost to Zukofsky, the friend of Williams and Bunting, the editor of *The Waste Land*. His poetry is often difficult, but the payment for study and annotation is normally made to us in full. His politics were abhorrent, but if we forgive Hazlitt for his admiration of Napoleon then we should be prepared to do likewise to Pound for his delusions about Mussolini. And at least he apologized for his anti-Semitism at the last minute, which is more than his genteeler contemporaries did. In any case, he is demonstrably a poet of the highest order. A short selection from his poems, 'The Return', 'The Spring', *Cathay*, Propertius VI, the description of the metamorphosis on Acoetes' ship, the whole of Canto XLVII, innumerable passages from the Pisan

Cantos – these just for a start are enough to keep him among the headlines for a few centuries.

With further reading of Pound, the reader will be helped, as I have been, by the writings of Michael Alexander, Donald Davie, George Dekker, Christine Froula, Hugh Kenner, Noel Stock, and the several Guides and Companions to the *Cantos*. William Cookson has been kind with his advice.

Thom Gunn

1

Mesmerism

'And a cat's in the water-butt.' – ROBERT BROWNING

Aye you're a man that! ye old mesmerizer
Tyin' your meanin' in seventy swadelin's,
One must of needs be a hang'd early riser
To catch you at worm turning. Holy Odd's bodykins!

'Cat's i' the water butt!' Thought's in your verse-barrel,
Tell us this thing rather, then we'll believe you,
You, Master Bob Browning, spite your apparel
Jump to your sense and give praise as we'd lief do.

You wheeze as a head-cold long-tonsilled Calliope,
But God! what a sight you ha' got o' our in'ards,
Mad as a hatter but surely no Myope,
Broad as all ocean and leanin' man-kin'ards.

Heart that was big as the bowels of Vesuvius,
Words that were wing'd as her sparks in eruption,
Eagled and thundered as Jupiter Pluvius,
Sound in your wind past all signs o' corruption.

Here's to you, Old Hippety-Hop o' the accents,
True to the Truth's sake and crafty dissector,
You grabbed at the gold sure; had no need to pack cents
Into your versicles.
Clear sight's elector!

To Whistler, American

On the loan exhibit of his paintings at the Tate Gallery.

You also, our first great,
Had tried all ways;
Tested and pried and worked in many fashions,
And this much gives me heart to play the game.

Here is a part that's slight, and part gone wrong,
And much of little moment, and some few
Perfect as Dürer!

'In the Studio' and these two portraits, if I had my choice!
And then these sketches in the mood of Greece?

You had your searches, your uncertainties,
And this is good to know – for us, I mean,
Who bear the brunt of our America
And try to wrench her impulse into art.

You were not always sure, not always set
To hiding night or tuning 'symphonies';
Had not one style from birth, but tried and pried
And stretched and tampered with the media.

You and Abe Lincoln from that mass of dolts
Show us there's chance at least of winning through.

Sestina: Altaforte

LOQUITUR: En *Bertrans de Born.*

Dante Alighieri put this man in hell for that he was a stirrer up of strife.

Eccovi!

Judge ye!

Have I dug him up again?

The scene is at his castle, Altaforte. 'Papiols' is his jongleur.
'The Leopard,' the device *of Richard Cœur de Lion.*

I

Damn it all! all this our South stinks peace.
You whoreson dog, Papiols, come! Let's to music!
I have no life save when the swords clash.
But ah! when I see the standards gold, vair, purple, opposing
And the broad fields beneath them turn crimson,
Then howl I my heart nigh mad with rejoicing.

II

In hot summer have I great rejoicing
When the tempests kill the earth's foul peace,
And the lightnings from black heav'n flash crimson,
And the fierce thunders roar me their music
And the winds shriek through the clouds mad, opposing,
And through all the riven skies God's swords clash.

III

Hell grant soon we hear again the swords clash!
And the shrill neighs of destriers in battle rejoicing,
Spiked breast to spiked breast opposing!
Better one hour's stour than a year's peace
With fat boards, bawds, wine and frail music!
Bah! there's no wine like the blood's crimson!

IV

And I love to see the sun rise blood-crimson.
And I watch his spears through the dark clash
And it fills all my heart with rejoicing
And pries wide my mouth with fast music
When I see him so scorn and defy peace,
His lone might 'gainst all darkness opposing.

V

The man who fears war and squats opposing
My words for stour, hath no blood of crimson
But is fit only to rot in womanish peace
Far from where worth's won and the swords clash
For the death of such sluts I go rejoicing;
Yea, I fill all the air with my music.

VI

Papiols, Papiols, to the music!
There's no sound like to swords swords opposing,
No cry like the battle's rejoicing
When our elbows and swords drip the crimson
And our charges 'gainst 'The Leopard's' rush clash.
May God damn for ever all who cry 'Peace!'

VII

And let the music of the swords make them crimson!
Hell grant soon we hear again the swords clash!
Hell blot black for alway the thought 'Peace'!

Ballad of the Goodly Fere

Simon Zelotes speaketh it somewhile after the Crucifixion.
Fere = Mate, Companion.

Ha' we lost the goodliest fere o' all
For the priests and the gallows tree?
Aye lover he was of brawny men,
O' ships and the open sea.

When they came wi' a host to take Our Man
His smile was good to see,
'First let these go!' quo' our Goodly Fere,
'Or I'll see ye damned,' says he.

Aye he sent us out through the crossed high spears
And the scorn of his laugh rang free,
'Why took ye not me when I walked about
Alone in the town?' says he.

Oh we drunk his 'Hale' in the good red wine
When we last made company,
No capon priest was the Goodly Fere
But a man o' men was he.

I ha' seen him drive a hundred men
Wi' a bundle o' cords swung free,
That they took the high and holy house
For their pawn and treasury.

They'll no' get him a' in a book I think
Though they write it cunningly;
No mouse of the scrolls was the Goodly Fere
But aye loved the open sea.

If they think they ha' snared our Goodly Fere
They are fools to the last degree.
'I'll go to the feast,' quo' our Goodly Fere,
'Though I go to the gallows tree.'

'Ye ha' seen me heal the lame and blind,
And wake the dead,' says he,
'Ye shall see one thing to master all:
'Tis how a brave man dies on the tree.'

A son of God was the Goodly Fere
That bade us his brothers be.
I ha' seen him cow a thousand men.
I have seen him upon the tree.

He cried no cry when they drave the nails
And the blood gushed hot and free,
The hounds of the crimson sky gave tongue
But never a cry cried he.

I ha' seen him cow a thousand men
On the hills o' Galilee,
They whined as he walked out calm between,
Wi' his eyes like the grey o' the sea,

Like the sea that brooks no voyaging
With the winds unleashed and free,
Like the sea that he cowed at Genseret
Wi' twey words spoke' suddently.

A master of men was the Goodly Fere,
A mate of the wind and sea,
If they think they ha' slain our Goodly Fere
They are fools eternally.

I ha' seen him eat o' the honey-comb
Sin' they nailed him to the tree.

Rome

From the French of Joachim du Bellay

'Troica Roma resurges.' – PROPERTIUS

O thou new comer who seek'st Rome in Rome
And find'st in Rome no thing thou canst call Roman;
Arches worn old and palaces made common,
Rome's name alone within these walls keeps home.

Behold how pride and ruin can befall
One who hath set the whole world 'neath her laws,
All-conquering, now conquerèd, because
She is Time's prey and Time consumeth all.

Rome that art Rome's one sole last monument,
Rome that alone hast conquered Rome the town,
Tiber alone, transient and seaward bent,
Remains of Rome. O world, thou unconstant mime!
That which stands firm in thee Time batters down,
And that which fleeteth doth outrun swift time.

Portrait d'une Femme

Your mind and you are our Sargasso Sea,
London has swept about you this score years
And bright ships left you this or that in fee:
Ideas, old gossip, oddments of all things,
Strange spars of knowledge and dimmed wares of price.
Great minds have sought you – lacking someone else.
You have been second always. Tragical?
No. You preferred it to the usual thing:
One dull man, dulling and uxorious,
One average mind – with one thought less, each year.
Oh, you are patient, I have seen you sit
Hours, where something might have floated up.
And now you pay one. Yes, you richly pay.
You are a person of some interest, one comes to you
And takes strange gain away:
Trophies fished up; some curious suggestion;
Fact that leads nowhere; and a tale or two,
Pregnant with mandrakes, or with something else
That might prove useful and yet never proves,
That never fits a corner or shows use,
Or finds its hour upon the loom of days:
The tarnished, gaudy, wonderful old work;
Idols and ambergris and rare inlays,
These are your riches, your great store; and yet
For all this sea-hoard of deciduous things,
Strange woods half sodden, and new brighter stuff:
In the slow float of differing light and deep,
No! there is nothing! In the whole and all,
Nothing that's quite your own.
                    Yet this is you.

The Seafarer

From the Anglo-Saxon

May I for my own self song's truth reckon,
Journey's jargon, how I in harsh days
Hardship endured oft.
Bitter breast-cares have I abided,
Known on my keel many a care's hold,
And dire sea-surge, and there I oft spent
Narrow nightwatch nigh the ship's head
While she tossed close to cliffs. Coldly afflicted,
My feet were by frost benumbed.
Chill its chains are; chafing sighs
Hew my heart round and hunger begot
Mere-weary mood. Lest man know not
That he on dry land loveliest liveth,
List how I, care-wretched, on ice-cold sea,
Weathered the winter, wretched outcast
Deprived of my kinsmen;
Hung with hard ice-flakes, where hail-scur flew,
There I heard naught save the harsh sea
And ice-cold wave, at whiles the swan cries,
Did for my games the gannet's clamour,
Sea-fowls' loudness was for me laughter,
The mews' singing all my mead-drink.
Storms, on the stone-cliffs beaten, fell on the stern
In icy feathers; full oft the eagle screamed
With spray on his pinion.
                                        Not any protector
May make merry man faring needy.
This he little believes, who aye in winsome life
Abides 'mid burghers some heavy business,
Wealthy and wine-flushed, how I weary oft
Must bide above brine.
Neareth nightshade, snoweth from north,

Frost froze the land, hail fell on earth then,
Corn of the coldest. Nathless there knocketh now
The heart's thought that I on high streams
The salt-wavy tumult traverse alone.
Moaneth alway my mind's lust
That I fare forth, that I afar hence
Seek out a foreign fastness.
For this there's no mood-lofty man over earth's midst,
Not though he be given his good, but will have in his youth greed;
Nor his deed to the daring, nor his king to the faithful
But shall have his sorrow for sea-fare
Whatever his lord will.
He hath not heart for harping, nor in ring-having
Nor winsomeness to wife, nor world's delight
Nor any whit else save the wave's slash,
Yet longing comes upon him to fare forth on the water.
Bosque taketh blossom, cometh beauty of berries,
Fields to fairness, land fares brisker,
All this admonisheth man eager of mood,
The heart turns to travel so that he then thinks
On flood-ways to be far departing.
Cuckoo calleth with gloomy crying,
He singeth summerward, bodeth sorrow,
The bitter heart's blood. Burgher knows not –
He the prosperous man – what some perform
Where wandering them widest draweth.
So that but now my heart burst from my breastlock,
My mood 'mid the mere-flood,
Over the whale's acre, would wander wide.
On earth's shelter cometh oft to me,
Eager and ready, the crying lone-flyer,
Whets for the whale-path the heart irresistibly,
O'er tracks of ocean; seeing that anyhow
My lord deems to me this dead life
On loan and on land, I believe not

That any earth-weal eternal standeth
Save there be somewhat calamitous
That, ere a man's tide go, turn it to twain.
Disease or oldness or sword-hate
Beats out the breath from doom-gripped body.
And for this, every earl whatever, for those speaking after –
Laud of the living, boasteth some last word,
That he will work ere he pass onward,
Frame on the fair earth 'gainst foes his malice,
Daring ado, . . .
So that all men shall honour him after
And his laud beyond them remain 'mid the English,
Aye, for ever, a lasting life's-blast,
Delight 'mid the doughty.
                                        Days little durable,
And all arrogance of earthen riches,
There come now no kings nor Cæsars
Nor gold-giving lords like those gone.
Howe'er in mirth most magnified,
Whoe'er lived in life most lordliest,
Drear all this excellence, delights undurable!
Waneth the watch, but the world holdeth.
Tomb hideth trouble. The blade is layed low.
Earthly glory ageth and seareth.
No man at all going the earth's gait,
But age fares against him, his face paleth,
Grey-haired he groaneth, knows gone companions,
Lordly men, are to earth o'ergiven,
Nor may he then the flesh-cover, whose life ceaseth,
Nor eat the sweet nor feel the sorry,
Nor stir hand nor think in mid heart,
And though he strew the grave with gold,
His born brothers, their buried bodies
Be an unlikely treasure hoard.

The Return

See, they return; ah, see the tentative
        Movements, and the slow feet,
        The trouble in the pace and the uncertain
        Wavering!

See, they return, one, and by one,
With fear, as half-awakened;
As if the snow should hesitate
And murmur in the wind,
                        and half turn back;
These were the 'Wing'd-with-Awe,'
                        Inviolable.

Gods of the wingèd shoe!
With them the silver hounds,
                        sniffing the trace of air!

Haie! Haie!
        These were the swift to harry;
These the keen-scented;
These were the souls of blood.

Slow on the leash,
                        pallid the leash-men!

[epigraph to *Lustra*]

And the days are not full enough
And the nights are not full enough
And life slips by like a field mouse
            Not shaking the grass.

The Garret

Come, let us pity those who are better off than we are.
Come, my friend, and remember
        that the rich have butlers and no friends,
And we have friends and no butlers.
Come, let us pity the married and the unmarried.

Dawn enters with little feet
        like a gilded Pavlova,
And I am near my desire.
Nor has life in it aught better
Than this hour of clear coolness,
        the hour of waking together.

The Garden

En robe de parade. – SAMAIN

Like a skein of loose silk blown against a wall
She walks by the railing of a path in Kensington Gardens,
And she is dying piece-meal
        of a sort of emotional anæmia.

And round about there is a rabble
Of the filthy, sturdy, unkillable infants of the very poor.
They shall inherit the earth.

In her is the end of breeding.
Her boredom is exquisite and excessive.
She would like some one to speak to her,
And is almost afraid that I
        will commit that indiscretion.

The Spring

'Ηρι μεν αί τε κυδώνιαι – IBYCUS

Cydonian Spring with her attendant train,
Maelids and water-girls,
Stepping beneath a boisterous wind from Thrace,
Throughout this sylvan place
Spreads the bright tips,
And every vine-stock is
Clad in new brilliancies.
                                        And wild desire
Falls like black lightning.
O bewildered heart,
Though every branch have back what last year lost,
She, who moved here amid the cyclamen,
Moves only now a clinging tenuous ghost.

April

Nympharum membra disjecta

Three spirits came to me
And drew me apart
To where the olive boughs
Lay stripped upon the ground:
Pale carnage beneath bright mist.

Les Millwin

The little Millwins attend the Russian Ballet.
The mauve and greenish souls of the little Millwins
Were seen lying along the upper seats
Like so many unused boas.

The turbulent and undisciplined host of art students –
The rigorous deputation from 'Slade' –
Was before them.

With arms exalted, with fore-arms
Crossed in great futuristic X's, the art students
Exulted, they beheld the splendours of *Cleopatra*.

And the little Millwins beheld these things;
With their large and anæmic eyes they looked out upon this
  configuration.

Let us therefore mention the fact,
For it seems to us worthy of record.

The Study in Aesthetics

The very small children in patched clothing,
Being smitten with an unusual wisdom,
Stopped in their play as she passed them
And cried up from their cobbles:

Guarda! Ahi, guarda! ch' è be'a![1]

But three years after this
I heard the young Dante, whose last name I do not know –
For there are, in Sirmione, twenty-eight young Dantes and
thirty-four Catulli;
And there had been a great catch of sardines,
And his elders
Were packing them in the great wooden boxes
For the market in Brescia, and he
Leapt about, snatching at the bright fish
And getting in both of their ways;
And in vain they commanded him to *sta fermo!*
And when they would not let him arrange
The fish in the boxes
He stroked those which were already arranged,
Murmuring for his own satisfaction
This identical phrase:

Ch' è be'a.

And at this I was mildly abashed.

1. Bella

Liu Ch'e

The rustling of the silk is discontinued,
Dust drifts over the court-yard,
There is no sound of foot-fall, and the leaves
Scurry into heaps and lie still,
And she the rejoicer of the heart is beneath them:

A wet leaf that clings to the threshold.

In a Station of the Metro

The apparition   of these faces   in the crowd   :
Petals   on a wet, black   bough   .

[First version: *Poetry*, 1913]

Alba

As cool as the pale wet leaves
                                        of lily-of-the-valley
She lay beside me in the dawn.

Coitus

The gilded phaloi of the crocuses
                    are thrusting at the spring air.
Here is there naught of dead gods
But a procession of festival,
A procession, O Giulio Romano,
Fit for your spirit to dwell in.
Dione, your nights are upon us.

The dew is upon the leaf.
The night about us is restless.

Society

The family position was waning,
And on this account the little Aurelia,
Who had laughed on eighteen summers,
Now bears the palsied contact of Phidippus.

The Gypsy

'Est-ce que vous avez vu des autres – des camarades – avec des singes ou des ours?'

A STRAY GIPSY, AD 1912

That was the top of the walk, when he said:
'Have you seen any others, any of our lot,
With apes or bears?'
          – A brown upstanding fellow
Not like the half-castes,
          up on the wet road near Clermont.
The wind came, and the rain,
And mist clotted about the trees in the valley,
And I'd the long ways behind me,
          gray Arles and Biaucaire,
And he said, 'Have you seen any of our lot?'
I'd seen a lot of his lot . . .
          ever since Rhodez,
Coming down from the fair
          of St John,
With caravans, but never an ape or a bear.

Alba

(from 'Langue d'Oc')

When the nightingale to his mate
Sings day-long and night late
My love and I keep state
In bower,
In flower,
'Till the watchman on the tower
Cry:
        'Up! Thou rascal, Rise,
        I see the white
            Light
            And the night
                Flies.'

2 *from* Cathay

For the most part from the Chinese of Rihaku [Li Po], from the notes of the late Ernest Fenollosa, and the decipherings of the professors Mori and Ariga

Song of the Bowmen of Shu

Here we are, picking the first fern-shoots
And saying: When shall we get back to our country?
Here we are because we have the Ken-nin for our foemen,
We have no comfort because of these Mongols.
We grub the soft fern-shoots,
When anyone says 'Return,' the others are full of sorrow.
Sorrowful minds, sorrow is strong, we are hungry and
thirsty.
Our defence is not yet made sure, no one can let his friend
return.
We grub the old fern-stalks.
We say: Will we be let to go back in October?
There is no ease in royal affairs, we have no comfort.
Our sorrow is bitter, but we would not return to our country.
What flower has come into blossom?
Whose chariot? The General's.
Horses, his horses even, are tired. They were strong.
We have no rest, three battles a month.
By heaven, his horses are tired.
The generals are on them, the soldiers are by them.
The horses are well trained, the generals have ivory arrows
and quivers ornamented with fish-skin.
The enemy is swift, we must be careful.
When we set out, the willows were drooping with spring,
We come back in the snow,
We go slowly, we are hungry and thirsty,
Our mind is full of sorrow, who will know of our grief?

By Bunno, reputedly 1100 BC

The Beautiful Toilet

Blue, blue is the grass about the river
And the willows have overfilled the close garden.
And within, the mistress, in the midmost of her youth,
White, white of face, hesitates, passing the door.
Slender, she puts forth a slender hand;

And she was a courtezan in the old days,
And she has married a sot,
Who now goes drunkenly out
And leaves her too much alone.

By Mei Sheng, 140 BC

The River Song

This boat is of shato-wood, and its gunwales are cut
magnolia,
Musicians with jewelled flutes and with pipes of gold
Fill full the sides in rows, and our wine
Is rich for a thousand cups.
We carry singing girls, drift with the drifting water,
Yet Sennin needs
A yellow stork for a charger, and all our seamen
Would follow the white gulls or ride them.
Kutsu's prose song
Hangs with the sun and moon.

King So's terraced palace
is now but barren hill,
But I draw pen on this barge
Causing the five peaks to tremble,
And I have joy in these words
like the joy of blue islands.
(If glory could last forever
Then the waters of Han would flow northward.)
*

And I have moped in the Emperor's garden, awaiting an
order-to-write!
I looked at the dragon-pond, with its willow-coloured water
Just reflecting the sky's tinge,
And heard the five-score nightingales aimlessly singing.

The eastern wind brings the green colour into the island
grasses at Yei-shu,
The purple house and the crimson are full of Spring softness.
South of the pond the willow-tips are half-blue and bluer,
Their cords tangle in mist, against the brocade-like palace.
Vine-strings a hundred feet long hang down from carved
railings,

And high over the willows, the fine birds sing to each other, and listen,
Crying – 'Kwan, Kuan,' for the early wind, and the feel of it.
The wind bundles itself into a bluish cloud and wanders off.
Over a thousand gates, over a thousand doors are the sounds of spring singing,
And the Emperor is at Ko.
Five clouds hang aloft, bright on the purple sky,
The imperial guards come forth from the golden house with their armour a-gleaming.
The Emperor in his jewelled car goes out to inspect his flowers,
He goes out to Hori, to look at the wing-flapping storks,
He returns by way of Sei rock, to hear the new nightingales,
For the gardens at Jo-run are full of new nightingales,
Their sound is mixed in this flute,
Their voice is in the twelve pipes here.

By Rihaku, 8th century AD

The River-Merchant's Wife: A Letter

While my hair was still cut straight across my forehead
I played about the front gate, pulling flowers.
You came by on bamboo stilts, playing horse,
You walked about my seat, playing with blue plums.
And we went on living in the village of Chokan:
Two small people, without dislike or suspicion.

At fourteen I married My Lord you.
I never laughed, being bashful.
Lowering my head, I looked at the wall.
Called to, a thousand times, I never looked back.

At fifteen I stopped scowling,
I desired my dust to be mingled with yours
Forever and forever and forever.
Why should I climb the look out?

At sixteen you departed,
You went into far Ku-to-yen, by the river of swirling eddies,
And you have been gone five months.
The monkeys make sorrowful noise overhead.
You dragged your feet when you went out.
By the gate now, the moss is grown, the different mosses,
Too deep to clear them away!
The leaves fall early this autumn, in wind.
The paired butterflies are already yellow with August
Over the grass in the West garden;
They hurt me. I grow older.
If you are coming down through the narrows of the river
   Kiang,
Please let me know beforehand,
And I will come out to meet you
                As far as Cho-fu-Sa.

By Rihaku

Poem by the Bridge at Ten-Shin

March has come to the bridge head,
Peach boughs and apricot boughs hang over a thousand
  gates,
At morning there are flowers to cut the heart,
And evening drives them on the eastward-flowing waters.
Petals are on the gone waters and on the going,
        And on the back-swirling eddies,
But to-day's men are not the men of the old days,
Though they hang in the same way over the bridge-rail.

The sea's colour moves at the dawn
And the princes still stand in rows, about the throne,
And the moon falls over the portals of Sei-go-yo,
And clings to the walls and the gate-top.
With head gear glittering against the cloud and sun,
The lords go forth from the court, and into far borders.
They ride upon dragon-like horses,
Upon horses with head-trappings of yellow metal,
And the streets make way for their passage.
        Haughty their passing,
Haughty their steps as they go in to great banquets,
To high halls and curious food,
To the perfumed air and girls dancing,
To clear flutes and clear singing;
To the dance of the seventy couples;
To the mad chase through the gardens.
Night and day are given over to pleasure
And they think it will last a thousand autumns,
        Unwearying autumns.
For them the yellow dogs howl portents in vain,
And what are they compared to the lady Riokushu,
        That was cause of hate!
Who among them is a man like Han-rei

Who departed alone with his mistress,
With her hair unbound, and he his own skiffsman!

By Rihaku

The Jewel Stairs' Grievance

The jewelled steps are already quite white with dew,
It is so late that the dew soaks my gauze stockings,
And I let down the crystal curtain
And watch the moon through the clear autumn.

By Rihaku

NOTE – Jewel stairs, therefore a palace. Grievance, therefore there is something to complain of. Gauze stockings, therefore a court lady, not a servant who complains. Clear autumn, therefore he has no excuse on account of weather. Also she has come early, for the dew has not merely whitened the stairs, but has soaked her stockings. The poem is especially prized because she utters no direct reproach.

Lament of the Frontier Guard

By the North Gate, the wind blows full of sand,
Lonely from the beginning of time until now!
Trees fall, the grass goes yellow with autumn.
I climb the towers and towers
        to watch out the barbarous land:
Desolate castle, the sky, the wide desert.
There is no wall left to this village.
Bones white with a thousand frosts,
High heaps, covered with trees and grass;
Who brought this to pass?
Who has brought the flaming imperial anger?
Who has brought the army with drums and with kettle-
  drums?
Barbarous kings.
A gracious spring, turned to blood-ravenous autumn,
A turmoil of wars-men, spread over the middle kingdom,
Three hundred and sixty thousand,
And sorrow, sorrow like rain.
Sorrow to go, and sorrow, sorrow returning.
Desolate, desolate fields,
And no children of warfare upon them,
        No longer the men for offence and defence.
Ah, how shall you know the dreary sorrow at the North Gate,
With Riboku's name forgotten,
And we guardsmen fed to the tigers.

By Rihaku

Exile's Letter

To So-Kin of Rakuyo, ancient friend, Chancellor of Gen.
Now I remember that you built me a special tavern
By the south side of the bridge at Ten-Shin.
With yellow gold and white jewels, we paid for songs and
  laughter
And we were drunk for month on month, forgetting the
  kings and princes.
Intelligent men came drifting in from the sea and from the
  west border,
And with them, and with you especially
There was nothing at cross purpose,
And they made nothing of sea-crossing or of mountain-
  crossing,
If only they could be of that fellowship,
And we all spoke out our hearts and minds, and without
  regret.
And then I was sent off to South Wei,
        smothered in laurel groves,
And you to the north of Raku-hoku,
Till we had nothing but thoughts and memories in common.
And then, when separation had come to its worst,
We met, and travelled into Sen-Go,
Through all the thirty-six folds of the turning and twisting
  waters,
Into a valley of the thousand bright flowers,
That was the first valley;
And into ten thousand valleys full of voices and pine-winds.
And with silver harness and reins of gold,
Out came the East of Kan foreman and his company.
And there came also the 'True man' of Shi-yo to meet me,
Playing on a jewelled mouth-organ.
In the storied houses of San-Ko they gave us more Sennin
  music,

Many instruments, like the sound of young phœnix broods.
The foreman of Kan Chu, drunk, danced
because his long sleeves wouldn't keep still
With that music playing,
And I, wrapped in brocade, went to sleep with my head on his lap,
And my spirit so high it was all over the heavens,
And before the end of the day we were scattered like stars, or rain.
I had to be off to So, far away over the waters,
You back to your river-bridge.

And your father, who was brave as a leopard,
Was governor in Hei Shu, and put down the barbarian rabble.
And one May he had you send for me,
despite the long distance.
And what with broken wheels and so on, I won't say it wasn't hard going,
Over roads twisted like sheep's guts.
And I was still going, late in the year,
in the cutting wind from the North,
And thinking how little you cared for the cost,
and you caring enough to pay it.
And what a reception:
Red jade cups, food well set on a blue jewelled table,
And I was drunk, and had no thought of returning.
And you would walk out with me to the western corner of the castle,
To the dynastic temple, with water about it clear as blue jade,
With boats floating, and the sound of mouth-organs and drums,
With ripples like dragon-scales, going grass green on the water,
Pleasure lasting, with courtezans, going and coming without hindrance,

With the willow flakes falling like snow,
And the vermilioned girls getting drunk about sunset,
And the water, a hundred feet deep, reflecting green
  eyebrows
– Eyebrows painted green are a fine sight in young
  moonlight,
Gracefully painted –
And the girls singing back at each other,
Dancing in transparent brocade,
And the wind lifting the song, and interrupting it,
Tossing it up under the clouds.
        And all this comes to an end.
        And is not again to be met with.
I went up to the court for examination,
Tried Layu's luck, offered the Choyo song,
And got no promotion,
        and went back to the East Mountains
        White-headed.
And once again, later, we met at the South bridge-head.
And then the crowd broke up, you went north to San palace,
And if you ask how I regret that parting:
It is like the flowers falling at Spring's end
        Confused, whirled in a tangle.
What is the use of talking, and there is no end of talking,
There is no end of things in the heart.
I call in the boy,
Have him sit on his knees here
        To seal this,
And send it a thousand miles, thinking.

By Rihaku

Taking Leave of a Friend

Blue mountains to the north of the walls,
White river winding about them;
Here we must make separation
And go out through a thousand miles of dead grass.

Mind like a floating wide cloud,
Sunset like the parting of old acquaintances
Who bow over their clasped hands at a distance.
Our horses neigh to each other
        as we are departing.

Rihaku

Sennin Poem by Kakuhaku

The red and green kingfishers
          flash between the orchids and clover,
One bird casts its gleam on another.

Green vines hang through the high forest,
They weave a whole roof to the mountain,
The lone man sits with shut speech,
He purrs and pats the clear strings.
He throws his heart up through the sky,
He bites through the flower pistil
          and brings up a fine fountain.

The red-pine-tree god looks at him and wonders.
He rides through the purple smoke to visit the sennin,
He takes 'Floating Hill' by the sleeve,
He claps his hand on the back of the great water sennin.

But you, you dam'd crowd of gnats,
Can you even tell the age of a turtle?

A Ballad of the Mulberry Road

The sun rises in south east corner of things
To look on the tall house of the Shin
For they have a daughter named Rafu,
        (pretty girl)
She made the name for herself: 'Gauze Veil,'
For she feeds mulberries to silkworms.
She gets them by the south wall of the town.
With green strings she makes the warp of her basket,
She makes the shoulder-straps of her basket
        from the boughs of Katsura,
And she piles her hair up on the left side of her head-piece.

Her earrings are made of pearl,
Her underskirt is of green pattern-silk,
Her overskirt is the same silk dyed in purple,
And when men going by look on Rafu
        They set down their burdens,
They stand and twirl their moustaches.

(Fenollosa Mss, very early)

Old Idea of Choan by Rosoriu

I

The narrow streets cut into the wide highway at Choan,
Dark oxen, white horses,
        drag on the seven coaches with outriders.
The coaches are perfumed wood,
The jewelled chair is held up at the crossway,
Before the royal lodge:
A glitter of golden saddles, awaiting the princess;
They eddy before the gate of the barons.
The canopy embroidered with dragons
        drinks in and casts back the sun.
Evening comes.
        The trappings are bordered with mist.
The hundred cords of mist are spread through
        and double the trees,
Night birds, and night women,
Spread out their sounds through the gardens.

II

Birds with flowery wing, hovering butterflies
        crowd over the thousand gates,
Trees that glitter like jade,
        terraces tinged with silver,
The seed of a myriad hues,
A net-work of arbours and passages and covered ways,
Double towers, winged roofs,
        border the net-work of ways:
A place of felicitous meeting.
Riu's house stands out on the sky,
        with glitter of colour
As Butei of Kan had made the high golden lotus
        to gather his dews,

Before it another house which I do not know:
How shall we know all the friends
          whom we meet on strange roadways?

To-Em-Mei's 'The Unmoving Cloud'

'Wet springtime,' says To-Em-Mei,
'Wet spring in the garden.'

I

The clouds have gathered, and gathered,
and the rain falls and falls,
The eight ply of the heavens
are all folded into one darkness,
And the wide, flat road stretches out.
I stop in my room toward the East, quiet, quiet,
I pat my new cask of wine.
My friends are estranged, or far distant,
I bow my head and stand still.

II

Rain, rain, and the clouds have gathered,
The eight ply of the heavens are darkness,
The flat land is turned into river.
'Wine, wine, here is wine!'
I drink by my eastern window.
I think of talking and man,
And no boat, no carriage, approaches.

III

The trees in my east-looking garden
are bursting out with new twigs,
They try to stir new affection,
And men say the sun and moon keep on moving
because they can't find a soft seat.
The birds flutter to rest in my tree,
and I think I have heard them saying,

‘It is not that there are no other men
But we like this fellow the best,
But however we long to speak
He can not know of our sorrow.’

T’ao Yuan Ming, AD 365–427

3 *from* Homage to Sextus Propertius

Orfeo

'Quia pauper amavi.'

I

Shades of Callimachus, Coan ghosts of Philetas
It is in your grove I would walk,
I who come first from the clear font
Bringing the Grecian orgies into Italy,
                    and the dance into Italy.
Who hath taught you so subtle a measure,
                    in what hall have you heard it;
What foot beat out your time-bar,
                    what water has mellowed your whistles?

Out-weariers of Apollo will, as we know, continue their
  Martian generalities,
  We have kept our erasers in order.
A new-fangled chariot follows the flower-hung horses;
A young Muse with loves clustered about her
                    ascends with me into the æther, . . .
And there is no high-road to the Muses.

Annalists will continue to record Roman reputations,
Celebrities from the Trans-Caucasus will belaud Roman
  celebrities
And expound the distentions of Empire,
But for something to read in normal circumstances?
For a few pages brought down from the forked hill unsullied?
I ask a wreath which will not crush my head.
                    And there is no hurry about it;
I shall have, doubtless, a boom after my funeral,
Seeing that long standing increases all things
                    regardless of quality.
And who would have known the towers
                    pulled down by a deal-wood horse;
Or of Achilles withstaying waters by Simois
Or of Hector spattering wheel-rims,

Or of Polydmantus, by Scamander, or Helenus and
Deiphoibos?
Their door-yards would scarcely know them, or Paris.
Small talk O Ilion, and O Troad
twice taken by Oetian gods,
If Homer had not stated your case!

And I also among the later nephews of this city
shall have my dog's day,
With no stone upon my contemptible sepulchre;
My vote coming from the temple of Phoebus in Lycia, at
Patara,
And in the mean time my songs will travel,
And the devirginated young ladies will enjoy them
when they have got over the strangeness,
For Orpheus tamed the wild beasts –
and held up the Threician river;
And Cithaeron shook up the rocks by Thebes
and danced them into a bulwark at his pleasure,
And you, O Polyphemus? Did harsh Galatea almost
Turn to your dripping horses, because of a tune, under Aetna?
We must look into the matter.
Bacchus and Apollo in favour of it,
There will be a crowd of young women doing homage to my
palaver,
Though my house is not propped up by Taenarian columns
from Laconia (associated with Neptune and Cerberus),
Though it is not stretched upon gilded beams:
My orchards do not lie level and wide
as the forests of Phaeacia,
the luxurious and Ionian,
Nor are my caverns stuffed stiff with a Marcian vintage,
My cellar does not date from Numa Pompilius,
Nor bristle with wine jars,
Nor is it equipped with a frigidaire patent;

Yet the companions of the Muses
        will keep their collective nose in my books,
And weary with historical data, they will turn to my
    dance tune.

Happy who are mentioned in my pamphlets,
    the songs shall be a fine tomb-stone over their beauty.
        But against this?
Neither expensive pyramids scraping the stars in their route,
Nor houses modelled upon that of Jove in East Elis,
Nor the monumental effigies of Mausolus,
                are a complete elucidation of death.

Flame burns, rain sinks into the cracks
And they all go to rack ruin beneath the thud of the years.
Stands genius a deathless adornment,
        a name not to be worn out with the years.

III

Midnight, and a letter comes to me from our mistress:
    Telling me to come to Tibur:
                                    At once!!
'Bright tips reach up from twin towers,
Anienan spring water falls into flat-spread pools.'

What *is* to be done about it?
    Shall I entrust myself to entangled shadows,
Where bold hands may do violence to my person?

Yet if I postpone my obedience
                    because of this respectable terror,
I shall be prey to lamentations worse than a nocturnal
  assailant.
And I shall be in the wrong,
                        and it will last a twelve month,
For her hands have no kindness me-ward,

Nor is there anyone to whom lovers are not sacred at
  midnight
    And in the Via Sciro.
If any man would be a lover
                    he may walk on the Scythian coast,
No barbarism would go to the extent of doing him harm,
The moon will carry his candle,
                the stars will point out the stumbles,
Cupid will carry lighted torches before him
                    and keep mad dogs off his ankles.
Thus all roads are perfectly safe
                                and at any hour;
Who so indecorous as to shed the pure gore of a suitor?!
    Cypris is his cicerone.
What if undertakers follow my track,
                        such a death is worth dying.

She would bring frankincense and wreaths to my tomb,
    She would sit like an ornament on my pyre.

Gods' aid, let not my bones lie in a public location
With crowds too assiduous in their crossing of it;
For thus are tombs of lovers most desecrated.

May a woody and sequestered place cover me with its foliage
Or may I inter beneath the hummock
                    of some as yet uncatalogued sand;
At any rate I shall not have my epitaph in a high road.

IV

Difference of Opinion With Lygdamus

Tell me the truths which you hear of our constant young
 lady,
  Lygdamus,
And may the bought yoke of a mistress lie with
  equitable weight on your shoulders;
For I am swelled up with inane pleasurabilities
  and deceived by your reference
To things which you think I would like to believe.

No messenger should come wholly empty,
  and a slave should fear plausibilities;
Much conversation is as good as having a home.
 Out with it, tell it to me, all of it, from the beginning,
I guzzle with outstretched ears.
Thus? She wept into uncombed hair,
  And you saw it.
Vast waters flowed from her eyes?
  You, you Lygdamus
Saw her stretched on her bed, –
  it was no glimpse in a mirror;
No gawds on her snowy hands, no orfevrerie,
Sad garment draped on her slender arms.
Her escritoires lay shut by the bed-feet.
Sadness hung over the house, and the desolated female
 attendants
Were desolated because she had told them her dreams.

She was veiled in the midst of that place,
Damp woolly handkerchiefs were stuffed into her undryable
 eyes,
And a querulous noise responded to our solicitous
 reprobations.

For which things you will get a reward from me,
Lygdamus?
To say many things is equal to having a home.
And the other woman 'has not enticed me
by her pretty manners,
She has caught me with herbaceous poison,
she twiddles the spiked wheel of a rhombus,
She stews puffed frogs, snake's bones, the moulted feathers of screech owls,

She binds me with ravvles of shrouds.
Black spiders spin in her bed!
Let her lovers snore at her in the morning!
May the gout cramp up her feet!
Does he like me to sleep here alone,
Lygdamus?
Will he say nasty things at my funeral?'

And you expect me to believe this
after twelve months of discomfort?

VI

When, when, and whenever death closes our eyelids,
Moving naked over Acheron
Upon the one raft, victor and conquered together,
Marius and Jugurtha together,
                    one tangle of shadows.

Caesar plots against India,
Tigris and Euphrates shall, from now on, flow at his bidding,
Tibet shall be full of Roman policemen,
The Parthians shall get used to our statuary
                    and acquire a Roman religion;
One raft on the veiled flood of Acheron,
        Marius and Jugurtha together.

Nor at my funeral either will there be any long trail,
                    bearing ancestral lares and images;
No trumpets filled with my emptiness,
Nor shall it be on an Atalic bed;
        The perfumed cloths shall be absent.
A small plebeian procession.
        Enough, enough and in plenty
There will be three books at my obsequies
Which I take, my not unworthy gift, to Persephone.

You will follow the bare scarified breast
Nor will you be weary of calling my name, nor too weary
        To place the last kiss on my lips
When the Syrian onyx is broken.

            'He who is now vacant dust
            Was once the slave of one passion:'
Give that much inscription
            'Death why tardily come?'

You, sometimes, will lament a lost friend,
For it is a custom:
This care for past men,

Since Adonis was gored in Idalia, and the Cytharean
Ran crying with out-spread hair,
In vain, you call back the shade,
In vain, Cynthia. Vain call to unanswering shadow,
Small talk comes from small bones.

IX

1

The twisted rhombs ceased their clamour of
accompaniment;
The scorched laurel lay in the fire-dust;
The moon still declined to descend out of heaven,

But the black ominous owl hoot was audible.

And one raft bears our fates
on the veiled lake toward Avernus
Sails spread on Cerulean waters, I would shed tears
for two;
I shall live, if she continue in life,
If she dies, I shall go with her.
Great Zeus, save the woman,
or she will sit before your feet in a veil,
and tell out the long list of her troubles.

2

Persephone and Dis, Dis, have mercy upon her,
There are enough women in hell,
quite enough beautiful women,
Iope, and Tyro, and Pasiphae, and the formal girls of Achaia,
And out of Troad, and from the Campania,
Death has his tooth in the lot,
Avernus lusts for the lot of them,
Beauty is not eternal, no man has perennial fortune,
Slow foot, or swift foot, death delays but for a season.

3

My light, light of my eyes,
you are escaped from great peril,
Go back to Great Dian's dances bearing suitable gifts,
Pay up your vow of night watches
to Dian goddess of virgins,
And unto me also pay debt:
The ten nights of your company you have
promised me.

X

Light, light of my eyes, at an exceeding late hour I was
wandering,
And intoxicated,
and no servant was leading me,
And a minute crowd of small boys came from opposite,
I do not know what boys,
And I am afraid of numerical estimate,
And some of them shook little torches,
and others held onto arrows,
And the rest laid their chains upon me,
and they were naked, the lot of them,
And one of the lot was given to lust.

'That incensed female has consigned him to our pleasure.'
So spoke. And the noose was over my neck.
And another said 'Get him plumb in the middle!
Shove along there, shove along!'
And another broke in upon this:
'He thinks that we are not gods.'
'And she has been waiting for the scoundrel,
and in a new Sidonian night cap,
And with more than Arabian odours,
God knows where he has been.
She could scarcely keep her eyes open
enter that much for his bail.
Get along now!'

We were coming near to the house,
and they gave another yank to my cloak,
And it was morning, and I wanted to see if she was alone, and resting,
And Cynthia was alone in her bed.
I was stupefied.
I had never seen her looking so beautiful,
No, not when she was tunick'd in purple.

Such aspect was presented to me, me recently emerged from my visions,
You will observe that pure form has its value.

'You are a very early inspector of mistresses.
Do you think I have adopted your habits?'
There were upon the bed no signs of a voluptuous encounter,
No signs of a second incumbent.

She continued:
'No incubus has crushed his body against me,
Though spirits are celebrated for adultery.
And I am going to the temple of Vesta ...'
and so on.

Since that day I have had no pleasant nights.

XII

Who, who will be the next man to entrust his girl to a friend?
Love interferes with fidelities;
The gods have brought shame on their relatives;
Each man wants the pomegranate for himself;
Amiable and harmonious people are pushed incontinent
  into duels,
A Trojan and adulterous person came to Menelaus under the
  rites of hospitium,
And there was a case in Colchis, Jason and that woman in
  Colchis;
And besides, Lynceus,
                    you were drunk.

Could you endure such promiscuity?
                    She was not renowned for fidelity;
But to jab a knife in my vitals, to have passed on a swig of
  poison,
Preferable, my dear boy, my dear Lynceus,
Comrade, comrade of my life, of my purse, of my person;
But in one bed, in one bed alone, my dear Lynceus,
        I deprecate your attendance;
I would ask a like boon of Jove.

And you write of Achelöus, who contended with Hercules,
You write of Adrastus' horses and the funeral rites of
  Achenor,
And you will not leave off imitating Aeschylus.
        Though you make a hash of Antimachus,
You think you are going to do Homer.
        And still a girl scorns the gods,
Of all these young women
      not one has enquired the cause of the world,
Nor the modus of lunar eclipses
        Nor whether there be any patch left of us

After we cross the infernal ripples,
nor if the thunder fall from predestination;
Nor anything else of importance.

Upon the Actian marshes Virgil is Phoebus' chief of police,
He can tabulate Caesar's great ships.
He thrills to Ilian arms,
He shakes the Trojan weapons of Aeneas,
And casts stores on Lavinian beaches.
Make way, ye Roman authors,
clear the street, O ye Greeks,
For a much larger Iliad is in the course of construction
(and to Imperial order)
Clear the streets, O ye Greeks!

And you also follow him 'neath Phrygian pine shade:
Thyrsis and Daphnis upon whittled reeds,
And how ten sins can corrupt young maidens;
Kids for a bribe and pressed udders,
Happy selling poor loves for cheap apples.

Tityrus might have sung the same vixen;
Corydon tempted Alexis,
Head farmers do likewise, and lying weary amid their oats
They get praise from tolerant Hamadryads.
Go on, to Ascraeus' prescription, the ancient,
respected, Wordsworthian:
'A flat field for rushes, grapes grow on the slope.'

And behold me, small fortune left in my house.
Me, who had no general for a grandfather!
I shall triumph among young ladies of indeterminate
character,
My talent acclaimed in their banquets,
I shall be honoured with yesterday's wreaths.
And the god strikes to the marrow.

Like a trained and performing tortoise,
I would make verse in your fashion, if she should command it,
With her husband asking a remission of sentence,
And even this infamy would not attract numerous readers
Were there an erudite or violent passion,
For the nobleness of the populace brooks nothing below its own altitude.
One must have resonance, resonance and sonority ... like a goose.

Varro sang Jason's expedition,
Varro, of his great passion Leucadia,
There is song in the parchment; Catullus the highly indecorous,
Of Lesbia, known above Helen;
And in the dyed pages of Calvus,
Calvus mourning Quintilia,
And but now Gallus had sung of Lycoris.
Fair, fairest Lycoris –
The waters of Styx poured over the wound:
And now Propertius of Cynthia, taking his stand among these.

4 from *The Cantos*

Canto I

And then went down to the ship,
Set keel to breakers, forth on the godly sea, and
We set up mast and sail on that swart ship,
Bore sheep aboard her, and our bodies also
Heavy with weeping, so winds from sternward
Bore us out onward with bellying canvas,
Circe's this craft, the trim-coifed goddess.
Then sat we amidships, wind jamming the tiller,
Thus with stretched sail, we went over sea till day's end.
Sun to his slumber, shadows o'er all the ocean,
Came we then to the bounds of deepest water,
To the Kimmerian lands, and peopled cities
Covered with close-webbed mist, unpiercèd ever
With glitter of sun-rays
Nor with stars stretched, nor looking back from heaven
Swartest night stretched over wretched men there.
The ocean flowing backward, came we then to the place
Aforesaid by Circe.
Here did they rites, Perimedes and Eurylochus,
And drawing sword from my hip
I dug the ell-square pitkin;
Poured we libations unto each the dead,
First mead and then sweet wine, water mixed with white
  flour.
Then prayed I many a prayer to the sickly death's-heads;
As set in Ithaca, sterile bulls of the best
For sacrifice, heaping the pyre with goods,
A sheep to Tiresias only, black and a bell-sheep.
Dark blood flowed in the fosse,
Souls out of Erebus, cadaverous dead, of brides,
Of youths and of the old who had borne much;
Souls stained with recent tears, girls tender,
Men many, mauled with bronze lance heads,

Battle spoil, bearing yet dreory arms,
These many crowded about me; with shouting,
Pallor upon me, cried to my men for more beasts;
Slaughtered the herds, sheep slain of bronze;
Poured ointment, cried to the gods,
To Pluto the strong, and praised Proserpine;
Unsheathed the narrow sword,
I sat to keep off the impetuous impotent dead,
Till I should hear Tiresias.
But first Elpenor came, our friend Elpenor,
Unburied, cast on the wide earth,
Limbs that we left in the house of Circe,
Unwept, unwrapped in sepulchre, since toils urged other.
Pitiful spirit. And I cried in hurried speech:
'Elpenor, how art thou come to this dark coast?
Cam'st thou afoot, outstripping seamen?'
          And he in heavy speech:
'Ill fate and abundant wine. I slept in Circe's ingle.
Going down the long ladder unguarded,
I fell against the buttress,
Shattered the nape-nerve, the soul sought Avernus.
But thou, O King, I bid remember me, unwept, unburied,
Heap up mine arms, be tomb by sea-bord, and inscribed:
A man of no fortune, and with a name to come.
And set my oar up, that I swung mid fellows.'

And Anticlea came, whom I beat off, and then Tiresias
   Theban,
Holding his golden wand, knew me, and spoke first:
'A second time? why? man of ill star,
Facing the sunless dead and this joyless region?
Stand from the fosse, leave me my bloody bever
For soothsay.'
          And I stepped back,
And he strong with the blood, said then: 'Odysseus
Shalt return through spiteful Neptune, over dark seas,

Lose all companions.' Then Anticlea came.
Lie quiet Divus. I mean, that is Andreas Divus,
In officina Wecheli, 1538, out of Homer.
And he sailed, by Sirens and thence outward and away
And unto Circe.
            Venerandam,
In the Cretan's phrase, with the golden crown, Aphrodite,
Cypri munimenta sortita est, mirthful, oricalchi, with golden
Girdles and breast bands, thou with dark eyelids
Bearing the golden bough of Argicida. So that:

Canto II

Hang it all, Robert Browning,
        there can be but the one 'Sordello'.
But Sordello, and my Sordello?
Lo Sordels si fo di Mantovana.
So-shu churned in the sea.
Seal sports in the spray-whited circles of cliff-wash,
Sleek head, daughter of Lir,
        eyes of Picasso
Under black fur-hood, lithe daughter of Ocean;
And the wave runs in the beach-groove:
'Eleanor, ἑλέναυς and ἑλέπτολις!'
        And poor old Homer blind, blind, as a bat,
Ear, ear for the sea-surge, murmur of old men's voices:
'Let her go back to the ships,
Back among Grecian faces, lest evil come on our own,
Evil and further evil, and a curse cursed on our children,
Moves, yes she moves like a goddess
And has the face of a god
        and the voice of Schoeney's daughters,
And doom goes with her in walking,
Let her go back to the ships,
        back among Grecian voices.'
That by the beach-run, Tyro,
        Twisted arms of the sea-god,
Lithe sinews of water, gripping her, cross-hold,
And the blue-gray glass of the wave tents them,
Glare azure of water, cold-welter, close cover.
Quiet sun-tawny sand-stretch,
The gulls broad out their wings,
        nipping between the splay feathers;
Snipe come for their bath,
        bend out their wing-joints,
Spread wet wings to the sun-film,

And by Scios,
          to left of the Naxos passage,
Naviform rock overgrown,
          algæ cling to its edge,
There is a wine-red glow in the shallows,
          a tin flash in the sun-dazzle.

The ship landed in Scios,
          men wanting spring-water,
And by the rock-pool a young boy loggy with vine-must,
          'To Naxos? Yes, we'll take you to Naxos,
Cum' along lad.' 'Not that way!'
'Aye, that way is Naxos.'
          And I said: 'It's a straight ship.'
And an ex-convict out of Italy
          knocked me into the fore-stays,
(He was wanted for manslaughter in Tuscany)
          And the whole twenty against me,
Mad for a little slave money.
          And they took her out of Scios
And off her course . . .
          And the boy came to, again, with the racket,
And looked out over the bows,
          and to eastward, and to the Naxos passage.
God sleight then, god-sleight:
          Ship stock fast in sea-swirl,
Ivy upon the oars, King Pentheus,
          grapes with no seed but sea-foam,
Ivy in scupper-hole.
Aye, I, Acœtes, stood there,
          and the god stood by me,
Water cutting under the keel,
Sea-break from stern forrards,
          wake running off from the bow,
And where was gunwale, there now was vine-trunk,
And tenthril where cordage had been,

grape-leaves on the rowlocks,
Heavy vine on the oarshafts,
And, out of nothing, a breathing,
hot breath on my ankles,
Beasts like shadows in glass,
a furred tail upon nothingness.
Lynx-purr, and heathery smell of beasts,
where tar smell had been,
Sniff and pad-foot of beasts,
eye-glitter out of black air.
The sky overshot, dry, with no tempest,
Sniff and pad-foot of beasts,
fur brushing my knee-skin,
Rustle of airy sheaths,
dry forms in the *æther*.
And the ship like a keel in ship-yard,
slung like an ox in smith's sling,
Ribs stuck fast in the ways,
grape-cluster over pin-rack,
void air taking pelt.
Lifeless air become sinewed,
feline leisure of panthers,
Leopards sniffing the grape shoots by scupper-hole,
Crouched panthers by fore-hatch,
And the sea blue-deep about us,
green-ruddy in shadows,
And Lyæus: 'From now, Acœtes, my altars,
Fearing no bondage,
Fearing no cat of the wood,
Safe with my lynxes,
feeding grapes to my leopards,
Olibanum is my incense,
the vines grow in my homage.'

The back-swell now smooth in the rudder-chains,
Black snout of a porpoise

where Lycabs had been,
Fish-scales on the oarsmen.
And I worship.
I have seen what I have seen.
When they brought the boy I said:
'He has a god in him,
though I do not know which god.'
And they kicked me into the fore-stays.
I have seen what I have seen:
Medon's face like the face of a dory,
Arms shrunk into fins. And you, Pentheus,
Had as well listen to Tiresias, and to Cadmus,
or your luck will go out of you.
Fish-scales over groin muscles,
lynx-purr amid sea . . .
And of a later year,
pale in the wine-red algæ,
If you will lean over the rock,
the coral face under wave-tinge,
Rose-paleness under water-shift,
Ileuthyeria, fair Dafne of sea-bords,
The swimmer's arms turned to branches,
Who will say in what year,
fleeing what band of tritons,
The smooth brows, seen, and half seen,
now ivory stillness.

So-shu churned in the sea, So-shu also,
using the long moon for a churn-stick . . .
Lithe turning of water,
sinews of Poseidon,
Black azure and hyaline,
glass wave over Tyro,
Close cover, unstillness,
bright welter of wave-cords,
Then quiet water,

quiet in the buff sands,
Sea-fowl stretching wing-joints,
splashing in rock-hollows and sand-hollows
In the wave-runs by the half-dune;
Glass-glint of wave in the tide-rips against sunlight,
pallor of Hesperus,
Grey peak of the wave,
wave, colour of grape's pulp,

Olive grey in the near,
far, smoke grey of the rock-slide,
Salmon-pink wings of the fish-hawk
cast grey shadows in water,
The tower like a one-eyed great goose
cranes up out of the olive-grove,

And we have heard the fauns chiding Proteus
in the smell of hay under the olive-trees.
And the frogs singing against the fauns
in the half-light.
And . . .

Canto XIII

Kung walked
        by the dynastic temple
and into the cedar grove,
        and then out by the lower river,
And with him Khieu Tchi
        and Tian the low speaking
And 'we are unknown,' said Kung,
'You will take up charioteering?
        Then you will become known,
Or perhaps I should take up charioteering, or archery?
Or the practice of public speaking?'
And Tseu-lou said, 'I would put the defences in order,'
And Khieu said, 'If I were lord of a province
I would put it in better order than this is.'
And Tchi said, 'I should prefer a small mountain temple,
With order in the observances,
        with a suitable performance of the ritual,'
And Tian said, with his hand on the strings of his lute
The low sounds continuing
        after his hand left the strings,
And the sound went up like smoke, under the leaves,
And he looked after the sound:
        'The old swimming hole,
And the boys flopping off the planks,
Or sitting in the underbrush playing mandolins.'
        And Kung smiled upon all of them equally.
And Thseng-sie desired to know:
        'Which had answered correctly?'
And Kung said, 'They have all answered correctly,
That is to say, each in his nature.'
And Kung raised his cane against Yuan Jang,
        Yuan Jang being his elder,
For Yuan Jang sat by the roadside pretending to

be receiving wisdom.
And Kung said
'You old fool, come out of it,
Get up and do something useful.'
And Kung said
'Respect a child's faculties
From the moment it inhales the clear air,
But a man of fifty who knows nothing
Is worthy of no respect.'
And 'When the prince has gathered about him
All the savants and artists, his riches will be fully employed.'
And Kung said, and wrote on the bo leaves:
'If a man have not order within him
He can not spread order about him;
And if a man have not order within him
His family will not act with due order;
And if the prince have not order within him
He can not put order in his dominions.'
And Kung gave the words 'order'
and 'brotherly deference'
And said nothing of the 'life after death'.
And he said
'Anyone can run to excesses,
It is easy to shoot past the mark,
It is hard to stand firm in the middle.'

And they said: 'If a man commit murder
Should his father protect him, and hide him?'
And Kung said:
'He should hide him.'

And Kung gave his daughter to Kong-Tchang
Although Kong-Tchang was in prison.
And he gave his niece to Nan-Young
although Nan-Young was out of office.
And Kung said 'Wang ruled with moderation,
In his day the State was well kept,

And even I can remember
A day when the historians left blanks in their writings,
I mean for things they didn't know,
But that time seems to be passing.'
And Kung said, 'Without character you will
be unable to play on that instrument
Or to execute the music fit for the Odes.
The blossoms of the apricot
blow from the east to the west,
And I have tried to keep them from falling.'

Canto XLV

With *Usura*

With usura hath no man a house of good stone
each block cut smooth and well fitting
that design might cover their face,
with usura
hath no man a painted paradise on his church wall
harpes et luz
or where virgin receiveth message
and halo projects from incision,
with usura
seeth no man Gonzaga his heirs and his concubines
no picture is made to endure nor to live with
but it is made to sell and sell quickly
with usura, sin against nature,
is thy bread ever more of stale rags
is thy bread dry as paper,
with no mountain wheat, no strong flour
with usura the line grows thick
with usura is no clear demarcation
and no man can find site for his dwelling.
Stonecutter is kept from his stone
weaver is kept from his loom
WITH USURA
wool comes not to market
sheep bringeth no gain with usura
Usura is a murrain, usura
blunteth the needle in the maid's hand
and stoppeth the spinner's cunning. Pietro Lombardo
came not by usura
Duccio came not by usura
nor Pier della Francesca; Zuan Bellin' not by usura
nor was 'La Calunnia' painted.

Came not by usura Angelico; came not Ambrogio Praedis,
Came no church of cut stone signed: *Adamo me fecit.*
Not by usura St Trophime
Not by usura Saint Hilaire,
Usura rusteth the chisel
It rusteth the craft and the craftsman
It gnaweth the thread in the loom
None learneth to weave gold in her pattern;
Azure hath a canker by usura; cramoisi is unbroidered
Emerald findeth no Memling
Usura slayeth the child in the womb
It stayeth the young man's courting
It hath brought palsey to bed, lyeth
between the young bride and her bridegroom
CONTRA NATURAM
They have brought whores for Eleusis
Corpses are set to banquet
at behest of usura.

N.B. Usury: A charge for the use of purchasing power, levied without regard to production; often without regard to the possibilities of production. (Hence the failure of the Medici bank.)

Canto XLVII

Who even dead, yet hath his mind entire!
This sound came in the dark
First must thou go the road
to hell
And to the bower of Ceres' daughter Proserpine,
Through overhanging dark, to see Tiresias,
Eyeless that was, a shade, that is in hell
So full of knowing that the beefy men know less than he,
Ere thou come to thy road's end.
Knowledge the shade of a shade,
Yet must thou sail after knowledge
Knowing less than drugged beasts. *phtheggometha thasson*
φθελλώμεθα θᾶσσον
The small lamps drift in the bay
And the sea's claw gathers them.
Neptunus drinks after neap-tide.
Tamuz! Tamuz!!
The red flame going seaward.
By this gate art thou measured.
From the long boats they have set lights in the water,
The sea's claw gathers them outward.
Scilla's dogs snarl at the cliff's base,
The white teeth gnaw in under the crag,
But in the pale night the small lamps float seaward
τυ Διώνα
TU DIONA

και Μοῖρα τ' Ἄδονιν
KAI MOIRA T' ADONIN

The sea is streaked red with Adonis,
The lights flicker red in small jars.
Wheat shoots rise new by the altar,
        flower from the swift seed.
Two span, two span to a woman,
Beyond that she believes not. Nothing is of any importance.
To that is she bent, her intention,
To that art thou called ever turning intention,
Whether by night the owl-call, whether by sap in shoot,
Never idle, by no means by no wiles intermittent
Moth is called over mountain
The bull runs blind on the sword, *naturans*
To the cave art thou called, Odysseus,
By Molü hast thou respite for a little,
By Molü art thou freed from the one bed
        that thou may'st return to another
The stars are not in her counting,
        To her they are but wandering holes.
Begin thy plowing
When the Pleiades go down to their rest,
Begin thy plowing
40 days are they under seabord,
Thus do in fields by seabord
And in valleys winding down toward the sea.
When the cranes fly high
        think of plowing.
By this gate art thou measured
Thy day is between a door and a door
Two oxen are yoked for plowing
Or six in the hill field
White bulk under olives, a score for drawing down stone,
Here the mules are gabled with slate on the hill road.
Thus was it in time.
And the small stars now fall from the olive branch,
Forked shadow falls dark on the terrace

More black than the floating martin
        that has no care for your presence,
His wing-print is black on the roof tiles
And the print is gone with his cry.
So light is thy weight on Tellus
Thy notch no deeper indented
Thy weight less than the shadow
Yet hast thou gnawed through the mountain,
        Scilla's white teeth less sharp.
Hast thou found a nest softer than cunnus
Or hast thou found better rest
Hast'ou a deeper planting, doth thy death year
Bring swifter shoot?
Hast thou entered more deeply the mountain?

The light has entered the cave. Io! Io!
The light has gone down into the cave,
Splendour on splendour!
By prong have I entered these hills:
That the grass grow from my body,
That I hear the roots speaking together,
The air is new on my leaf,
The forked boughs shake with the wind.
Is Zephyrus more light on the bough, Apeliota
more light on the almond branch?
By this door have I entered the hill.
Falleth,
Adonis falleth.
Fruit cometh after. The small lights drift out with the tide,
sea's claw has gathered them outward,
Four banners to every flower
The sea's claw draws the lamps outward.
Think thus of thy plowing
When the seven stars go down to their rest
Forty days for their rest, by seabord
And in valleys that wind down toward the sea

καὶ Μοῖρα τ' Ἄδονιν
KAI MOIRA T' ADONIN
When the almond bough puts forth its flame,
When the new shoots are brought to the altar,
τυ Διωνα, καὶ Μοῖρα
TU DIONA, KAI MOIRA
καὶ Μοῖρα τ' Ἄδονιν
KAI MOIRA T' ADONIN
that hath the gift of healing,
that hath the power over wild beasts.

Canto LI

Shines
in the mind of heaven   God
who made it
more than the sun
in our eye.
Fifth element; mud; said Napoleon
With usury has no man a good house
made of stone, no paradise on his church wall
With usury the stone cutter is kept from his stone
the weaver is kept from his loom by usura
Wool does not come into market
the peasant does not eat his own grain
The girl's needle goes blunt in her hand
The looms are hushed one after another
ten thousand after ten thousand
Duccio was not by usura
Nor was 'La Calunnia' painted.
Neither Ambrogio Praedis nor Angelico
had their skill by usura
Nor St Trophime its cloisters;
Nor St Hilaire its proportion.
Usury rusts the man and his chisel
It destroys the craftsman; destroying craft
Azure is caught with cancer. Emerald comes to no Memling
Usury kills the child in the womb
And breaks short the young man's courting
Usury brings age into youth; it lies between the bride
and the bridegroom
Usury is against Nature's increase.
Whores for Eleusis;
Under usury no stone is cut smooth
Peasant has no gain from his sheep herd
        Blue dun; number 2 in most rivers

for dark days; when it is cold
A starling's wing will give you the colour
or duck widgeon; if you take feather from under the wing
Let the body be of blue fox fur, or a water rat's
or grey squirrel's. Take this with a portion of mohair
and a cock's hackle for legs.
12th of March to 2nd of April
Hen pheasant's feather does for a fly,
green tail, the wings flat on the body
Dark fur from a hare's ear for a body
a green shaded partridge feather
        grizzled yellow cock's hackle
green wax; harl from a peacock's tail
bright lower body; about the size of pin
the head should be. can be fished from seven a.m.
till eleven; at which time the brown marsh fly comes on.
As long as the brown continues, no fish will take Granham

That hath the light of the doer; as it were
a form cleaving to it.
Deo similis quodam modo
hic intellectus adeptus
Grass; nowhere out of place. Thus speaking in Konigsberg
Zwischen die Volkern erzielt wird
a modus vivendi.
circling in eddying air; in a hurry;
the 12: close eyed in the oily wind
these were the regents; and a sour song from the folds
        of his belly
sang Geryone: I am the help of the aged;
I pay men to talk peace;
Mistress of many tongues; merchant of chalcedony
I am Geryon twin with usura,
You who have lived in a stage set.

A thousand were dead in his folds;
in the eel-fishers basket
Time was of the League of Cambrai:

from Canto LXXX

[Only shadows enter my tent
                                        as men pass between me and the sunset,]
beyond the eastern barbed wire
        a sow with nine boneen
matronly as any duchess at Claridge's

and for that Christmas at Maurie Hewlett's
Going out from Southampton
they passed the car by the dozen
        who would not have shown weight on a scale
                                        riding, riding
                                                for Noel the green holly
        Noel, Noel, the green holly
        A dark night for the holly

That would have been Salisbury plain, and I have not
    thought of
        the Lady Anne for this twelve years
                Nor of Le Portel
How tiny the panelled room where they stabbed him
                In her lap, almost, La Stuarda
        Si tuit li dolh ehl planh el marrimen
                for the leopards and broom plants

Tudor indeed is gone and every rose,
Blood-red, blanch-white that in the sunset glows
Cries: 'Blood, Blood, Blood!' against the gothic stone
Of England, as the Howard or Boleyn knows.

Nor seeks the carmine petal to infer;
Nor is the white bud Time's inquisitor
Probing to know if its new-gnarled root
Twists from York's head or belly of Lancaster;

Or if a rational soul should stir, perchance,
Within the stem or summer shoot to advance
Contrition's utmost throw, seeking in thee
But oblivion, not thy forgiveness, FRANCE.

as the young lizard extends his leopard spots
    along the grass-blade seeking the green midge half an
        ant-size
and the Serpentine will look just the same
and the gulls be as neat on the pond
and the sunken garden unchanged
and God knows what else is left of our London
        my London, your London
and if her green elegance
    remains on this side of my rain ditch
    puss lizard will lunch on some other T-bone

sunset grand couturier.

from Canto LXXXI

Ed ascoltando al leggier mormorio
        there came new subtlety of eyes into my tent,
whether of spirit or hypostasis,
        but what the blindfold hides
or at carneval
                                nor any pair showed anger
        Saw but the eyes and stance between the eyes,
colour, diastasis,
        careless or unaware it had not the
    whole tent's room
nor was place for the full Ειδώς
interpass, penetrate
        casting but shade beyond the other lights
                sky's clear
                night's sea
                green of the mountain pool
                shone from the unmasked eyes in half-mask's
                    space.
What thou lovest well remains,
                                        the rest is dross
What thou lov'st well shall not be reft from thee
What thou lov'st well is thy true heritage
Whose world, or mine or theirs
                                    or is it of none?
First came the seen, then thus the palpable
        Elysium, though it were in the halls of hell,
What thou lovest well is thy true heritage
What thou lov'st well shall not be reft from thee

The ant's a centaur in his dragon world.
Pull down thy vanity, it is not man
Made courage, or made order, or made grace,
        Pull down thy vanity, I say pull down.

Learn of the green world what can be thy place
In scaled invention or true artistry,
Pull down thy vanity,
                              Paquin pull down!
The green casque has outdone your elegance.

'Master thyself, then others shall thee beare'
      Pull down thy vanity
Thou art a beaten dog beneath the hail,
A swollen magpie in a fitful sun,
Half black half white
Nor knowst'ou wing from tail
Pull down thy vanity
                  How mean thy hates
Fostered in falsity,
                  Pull down thy vanity,
Rathe to destroy, niggard in charity,
Pull down thy vanity,
                  I say pull down.

But to have done instead of not doing
                  this is not vanity
To have, with decency, knocked
That a Blunt should open
            To have gathered from the air a live tradition
or from a fine old eye the unconquered flame
This is not vanity.
      Here error is all in the not done,
all in the diffidence that faltered.

from Canto LXXXIII

and Brother Wasp is building a very neat house
of four rooms, one shaped like a squat indian bottle
La vespa, *la* vespa, mud, swallow system
so that dreaming of Bracelonde and of Perugia
and the great fountain in the Piazza
or of old Bulagaio's cat that with a well timed leap
could turn the lever-shaped door handle
It comes over me that Mr Walls must be a ten-strike
with the signorinas
and in the warmth after chill sunrise
an infant, green as new grass,
has stuck its head or tip
out of Madame La Vespa's bottle

mint springs up again
in spite of Jones' rodents
as had the clover by the gorilla cage
with a four-leaf

When the mind swings by a grass-blade
an ant's forefoot shall save you
the clover leaf smells and tastes as its flower

The infant has descended,
from mud on the tent roof to Tellus,
like to like colour he goes amid grass-blades
greeting them that dwell under XTHONOS   ΧΘΟΝΟΣ
ΟΙ ΧΘΟΝΙΟΙ;   to carry our news
εἰς χθονιους   to them that dwell under the earth
begotten of air, that shall sing in the bower
of Kore,   Περσεφόνεια
and have speech with Tiresias, Thebae
Cristo Re, Dio Sole

in about $\frac{1}{2}$ a day she has made her adobe
(la vespa) the tiny mud-flask

and that day I wrote no further

From Canto CXV

The scientists are in terror
        and the European mind stops
Wyndham Lewis chose blindness
        rather than have his mind stop.
Night under wind mid garofani,
        the petals are almost still
Mozart, Linnaeus, Sulmona,
When one's friends hate each other
        how can there be peace in the world?
Their asperities diverted me in my green time.
A blown husk that is finished
        but the light sings eternal
a pale flare over marshes
        where the salt hay whispers to tide's change
Time, space,
        neither life nor death is the answer.
And of man seeking good,
        doing evil.
In meiner Heimat
            where the dead walked
                    and the living were made of cardboard.

W. H. AUDEN Poems selected by JOHN FULLER

W. H. AUDEN

Poems selected by JOHN FULLER

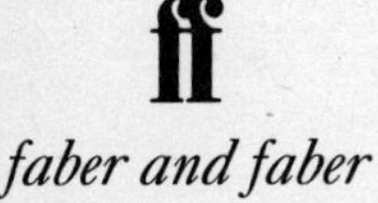

faber and faber

First published in 2000
by Faber and Faber Limited
3 Queen Square London WC1N 3AU

Photoset by Parker Typesetting Service, Leicester
Printed in Italy

All rights reserved

This selection and introduction © John Fuller, 2000
Poems copyright © 1977, 1991, the Estate of W. H. Auden

John Fuller is hereby identified as editor of
this work in accordance with Section 77
of the Copyright, Designs and Patents Act 1988

This book is sold subject to the condition that it shall not, by way of trade or otherwise, be lent, resold, hired out or otherwise circulated without the publisher's prior consent in any form of binding or cover other than that in which it is published and without a similar condition including this condition being imposed on the subsequent purchaser

A CIP record for this book
is available from the British Library
ISBN 0-571-20348-5

10 9 8 7 6 5 4 3 2 1

Contents

Textual Note

Early texts of poems from the 1930s have been preferred, but with the titles given to them in Auden's most recent collected editions. All poems and extracts may be found in either *The English Auden* or *Collected Poems*, with the exception of 'Getting Dressed' (my title for the extract from 'In the year of my youth . . .', published in *The Review of English Studies*, ns. vol. xxix, no. 115, August 1978).

Introduction

Auden's range was astonishing. He wrote poems of all kinds, from couplet squibs to book-length 'abstract drama', from advertising songs to oratorios, from film commentary to formal elegy, from comic verse letter to dream allegory, from limericks to libretti, from *vers d'occasion* to political satire. He remoulded the ode, the sonnet-sequence, the dramatic chorus and the prose poem for his age, and more or less invented the mode we tend to call the 'paysage moralisé'. To offer a faithful representation of his work in fewer than a hundred pages is clearly impossible. It would be like representing the art of a three-star Michelin chef (who had mastered the *haute cuisine* of several continents, remembered the regional cooking of his childhood, and could produce a memorable dish from a commonplace larder) by a single three-course lunch.

Readers who are new to Auden might be well advised to plunge into some of the longer works: the immersion is invigorating. Thus, my selection might quite reasonably have simply contained (for example) the ground-breaking charade *Paid on Both Sides*, the engagingly opinionated and autobiographical 'Letter to Lord Byron', the panoramic and moving sonnet-sequence 'In Time of War', the pained and fantastical *ars poetica* 'Caliban to the Audience' from 'The Sea and the Mirror', the Crucifixion sequence 'Horae Canonicae' . . . But I would already have long run out of space, without having offered a single love-lyric or biographical poem, both forms in which Auden was supreme.

Of all possible approaches, I have chosen one which I believe would have pleased him: the 96 pages of text are a little more than two pages for each of the years of his mature writing life, from 1927 to 1973, therefore I have undertaken to include something for every one of those years. Spare pages have gone towards a weighting in the period 1933 to 1939, when his work still seems the most prolific and relevant.

The result, even so, is necessarily a thin spread, but the reader will get a good idea of most of Auden's gifts and obsessions. The lifelong love affair with lead-mining, with its psycho-geological ramifications, can be traced in 'The Watershed', 'England to me is my own tongue' from 'New Year Letter', the songs from *The Age of Anxiety*, and 'In Praise of Limestone'. Response to public events in 1938 ('Here war is simple like a monument') contrasts with response to public events in 1968 ('August 1968'). There are strikingly different approaches, early and late, to such subjects as human knowledge of death ('The Cultural Presupposition' and 'Address to the Beasts'), coming to terms with lost love ('Taller To-day' and 'Since') or the political urgency of choice ('Spain 1937' and 'Aubade'). And of course there are many more complex comparisons across the years to be made between the different forms of poetic analysis and celebration in his work.

Difference there is. Auden was our first major poet to have a scientific education. For him, both Self and Not-Self were infinitely open to whatever clinical approaches the mental laboratory could contrive. Poetic imitation was like a controlled experiment, in which emotions, ideas and beliefs could be tested to breaking-point, and functional variety became itself a test of the poet's social utility.

Auden was a chameleon-like and self-conscious artist, not a Kandinsky but a Picasso, not a Schoenberg but a Stravinsky. You might say that modernism has provided the automobile of literature with a fifth gear, but that post-modernism also likes to get out all the old road maps. In this sense, Auden is also our first post-modernist poet. In the 1930s, in a restless quest for settled belief, he was driven by the investigative and forensic possibilities of all the varied genres, voices and forms of the English poetic tradition. From the 1940s onwards he believed that he had arrived, and so was eventually content to be driven largely by his material.

But he had always been, nonetheless, a poet for whom ideas were crucial; and he never failed to worship the language without whose enchantment ideas in poetry will fail to impress. In his maturity, his poetic ideals were democratic, and for a time he made distinctly greater advances against the commonplace public rejection of modern poetry as difficult, unpleasant and élitist than Yeats or Eliot had managed to do. His aim was 'the thoughts of a wise man in the language of the common people', an impossible ideal that nonetheless made the Auden of the Thirties a household name for apt metaphor, concision and suggestiveness.

What is it we feel we require from an Auden poem? Something political, perhaps, something understated, but dramatic. And accurately coloured with deceptively simple moral observations and quietly charged implications. Something perhaps like 'Gare du Midi' (see p. 30). The station of the title is a Brussels station, the one at which a bureaucrat from Nazi Germany might arrive. 'He walks out briskly to infect a city': before World War One you feared chemical warfare; before World War Two you feared appeasement. The line boldly talks about the one in terms of the other. Mustard gas? Or a diplomat, not with attachés but with a sinister little attaché *case*? The poem itself is like a case. It is a dramatised diplomatic exemplum of a political débâcle.

And yet Auden is not always so simple. The complexities of his thinking and the range of his reading sometimes present syntactic and conceptual hurdles to the reader. If you start reading a late essay-poem like 'The Aliens' (see p. 89) you will soon find yourself thinking that you should perhaps have taken a deeper mental breath before beginning, so as to get through the first six-line sentence at a steady pace. And yet this sentence, though it takes up a variety of related notions in its sweep (our rational relationship with plants and their response to our scientific knowledge, the absolute theological disaster of the Fall, and so on), is no more difficult than it has to be, and is finally not really so difficult after all. Its tone is humorous and tolerant ('the grace of chlorophyll') and restores the sinning Adam for a knowing moment to the innocent garden he once lost.

These are just two sides of a many-sided poet who never failed to remember that poetry must give pleasure. Auden was not often or for long granted personal happiness, but he rarely exploited poetry for the purpose of complaint. In his early poems he recorded a process of alienation, retreat and renewal; in his middle period he encountered the fallible public world that we all create and must inhabit; in his later poems he sought on every occasion for a reason to give thanks. In their different ways these periods are alike in their devotion to the poetic vocation as a sacred trust, and in the conscious choice of perfection of the work over the perfection of the life.

And yet there was for Auden always a danger in poetry becoming too introspective or high-minded. He believed, in a perfectly practical way, that its function was moral and parabolic, and that it could work instructively on any of the many levels at which the human mind functions ('Even a limerick | ought to be something a man of | honour, awaiting death from cancer or a firing squad, | could read without contempt'). In 1936, speaking to the Workers' Educational Association, he put it another way: 'Really to appreciate archdeacons, you must know some barmaids, and vice versa. The same applies to poetry.'

John Fuller

W. H. AUDEN

The Watershed

Who stands, the crux left of the watershed,
On the wet road between the chafing grass
Below him sees dismantled washing-floors,
Snatches of tramline running to the wood,
An industry already comatose,
Yet sparsely living. A ramshackle engine
At Cashwell raises water; for ten years
It lay in flooded workings until this,
Its latter office, grudgingly performed,
And further here and there, though many dead
Lie under the poor soil, some acts are chosen
Taken from recent winters; two there were
Cleaned out a damaged shaft by hand, clutching
The winch the gale would tear them from; one died
During a storm, the fells impassable,
Not at his village, but in wooden shape
Through long abandoned levels nosed his way
And in his final valley went to ground.

Go home, now, stranger, proud of your young stock,
Stranger, turn back again, frustrate and vexed:
This land, cut off, will not communicate,
Be no accessory content to one
Aimless for faces rather there than here.
Beams from your car may cross a bedroom wall,
They wake no sleeper; you may hear the wind
Arriving driven from the ignorant sea
To hurt itself on pane, on bark of elm
Where sap unbaffled rises, being Spring;
But seldom this. Near you, taller than grass,
Ears poise before decision, scenting danger.

The Secret Agent

Control of the passes was, he saw, the key
To this new district, but who would get it?
He, the trained spy, had walked into the trap
For a bogus guide, seduced with the old tricks.

At Greenhearth was a fine site for a dam
And easy power, had they pushed the rail
Some stations nearer. They ignored his wires.
The bridges were unbuilt and trouble coming.

The street music seemed gracious now to one
For weeks up in the desert. Woken by water
Running away in the dark, he often had
Reproached the night for a companion
Dreamed of already. They would shoot, of course,
Parting easily who were never joined.

Taller To-day

Taller to-day, we remember similar evenings,
Walking together in the windless orchard
Where the brook runs over the gravel, far from the glacier.

Again in the room with the sofa hiding the grate,
Look down to the river when the rain is over,
See him turn to the window, hearing our last
Of Captain Ferguson.

It is seen how excellent hands have turned to commonness.
One staring too long, went blind in a tower,
One sold all his manors to fight, broke through, and faltered.

Nights come bringing the snow, and the dead howl
Under the headlands in their windy dwelling
Because the Adversary put too easy questions
On lonely roads.

But happy now, though no nearer each other,
We see the farms lighted all along the valley;
Down at the mill-shed the hammering stops
And men go home.

Noises at dawn will bring
Freedom for some, but not this peace
No bird can contradict: passing, but is sufficient now
For something fulfilled this hour, loved or endured.

Shut Your Eyes and Open Your Mouth

Sentries against inner and outer,
At stated interval is feature;
And how shall enemy on these
Make sudden raid or lasting peace?
For bribery were vain to try
Against the incorruptible eye
Too amply paid with tears, the chin
Has hairs to hide its weakness in,
And proud bridge and indignant nostril
Nothing to do but to look noble.
But in between these lies the mouth;
Watch that, that you may parley with:
There strategy comes easiest,
Though it seem stern, was seen compressed
Over a lathe, refusing answer,
It will release the ill-fed prisoner,
It will do murder or betray
For either party equally,
Yielding at last to a close kiss
It will admit tongue's soft advance,
So longed for, given in abandon,
Given long since, had it but known.

This Lunar Beauty

This lunar beauty
Has no history
Is complete and early;
If beauty later
Bear any feature
It had a lover
And is another.

This like a dream
Keeps other time
And daytime is
The loss of this;
For time is inches
And the heart's changes
Where ghost has haunted
Lost and wanted.

But this was never
A ghost's endeavour
Nor finished this,
Was ghost at ease;
And till it pass
Love shall not near
The sweetness here
Nor sorrow take
His endless look.

Argument, Part iii

Came one after a ruined harvest, with a schoolroom globe, a wizard, sorry. From the nipping North Righteousness running. But where that warm boy of the summer château? Found on wet roads early this morning, patches of oil, the face of an avenger, downwards. Speech of worn tools in a box, thoughts from the trap.

Sound of guns in the city, the voice of the demonstrator, 'Gentlemen, to-morrow we shall tie the carotid.' What memory of self-regard from the locked room, shaken by lorries, from the depressed areas?

Suspicion of one of our number, away for week-ends. Catching sight of Him on the lawn with the gardener, from the upper rooms of a house. His insane dislike of birds. His fondness for verbal puzzles. Friendly joking converting itself into a counterplot, the spore of fear. Then in the hot weeks, the pavement blistering and the press muzzled, the sudden disaster, surprising as a comic turn. Shutting the door on the machines, we stood in the silence, thinking of nothing. (Murder of a rook by weasels.) Some taking refuge in thankful disillusion, others in frank disbelief, the youngest getting drunk. Hysterical attempts of two women to reach Him. The slow seeping in of their sly condolences, of the mass hatred of the villas. A child's sense of failure after burning a slug in a candle.

Daylight, striking at the eye from far-off roofs, why did you blind us, think: we who on the snow-line were in love with death, despised vegetation, we forgot His will; who came to us in an extraordinary dream, calming the plunging dangerous horses, greeting our arrival on a reedy shore. His sharing from His own provisions after the blizzard's march. The thrashing He gave the dishonest contractor who promised marvels in an old boy's tie. The old peasant couple's belief in His magical powers. His ability to smell a wet knife at a distance of half a mile. His refusal to wear anything but silk next to His skin. His reverent stories of the underpaid drunken usher who taught Him all. His tale of the Three Sorb Trees. His words after we had failed Him at the Roman bridge.

Love, that notable forked one, riding away from the farm, the ill word said, fought at the frozen dam, transforms itself to influenza and guilty rashes. Seduction of a postmistress on the lead roof of a church-tower, and an immature boy wrapping himself in a towel, ashamed at the public baths. From these stony acres, a witless generation, plant-like in beauty.

On the steps of His stone the boys play prisoner's base, turning their backs on the inscription, unconscious of sorrow as the sea of drowning. Passage to music of an unchaste hero from a too-strict country. March, long black piano, silhouetted head; cultured daughter of a greying ironmaster, march through fields. The hammer settles on the white-hot ingot. The telescope focuses accurately upon a recent star. On skyline of detritus, a truck, nose up. Loiterer at carved gates, immune stranger, follow. It is nothing, your loss. The priest's mouth opens in the green graveyard, but the wind is against it.

Epilogue

‘O where are you going?’ said reader to rider,
‘That valley is fatal where furnaces burn,
Yonder’s the midden whose odours will madden,
That gap is the grave where the tall return.’

‘O do you imagine’, said fearer to farer,
‘That dusk will delay on your path to the pass,
Your diligent looking discover the lacking
Your footsteps feel from granite to grass?’

‘O what was that bird’, said horror to hearer,
‘Did you see that shape in the twisted trees?
Behind you swiftly the figure comes softly,
The spot on your skin is a shocking disease?’

‘Out of this house’ – said rider to reader
‘Yours never will’ – said farer to fearer
‘They’re looking for you’ – said hearer to horror
As he left them there, as he left them there.

Getting Dressed

Now picking from chair, I passed over head
The loose-fitting shirt of light flannel,
Pickle-red from soaking in a secret die
Distilled from coal-tar, the exact shade
Calculated in a notebook, known before seen
By men to whom thermometers are more than women.
Wound round neck the wort-blue tie,
Knotting at the windpipe in a neat bow.
Then I pulled on the hairy breeches
Smelling of peat from skua-breeding Harris,
Caught round the waist with a calf-leather belt
That joined at the navel with a nickel clip,
And in the region which is touched for the reflex of the knee
Fastened with tabs. Took from drawer
The closely-woven mudproof stockings,
Carried from corner the climber's boots,
Polished with grease and pride of craftsman,
Hand-made in rainy Esthwaite to last a lifetime,
Studded on the soles in concentric horseshoes
With three-pronged nails, and now beginning
At the middle of the instep from ankle to knee
Carefully the spiral khaki puttees
I wound and fastened; fetched the jacket
Matching the breeches, and the motorist's cap;
Shook out a handkerchief of Irish linen
And started downstairs to find my friend.

O What is That Sound

O what is that sound which so thrills the ear
  Down in the valley drumming, drumming?
Only the scarlet soldiers, dear,
      The soldiers coming.

O what is that light I see flashing so clear
  Over the distance brightly, brightly?
Only the sun on their weapons, dear,
      As they step lightly.

O what are they doing with all that gear;
  What are they doing this morning, this morning?
Only the usual manœuvres, dear,
      Or perhaps a warning.

O why have they left the road down there;
  Why are they suddenly wheeling, wheeling?
Perhaps a change in the orders, dear;
      Why are you kneeling?

O haven't they stopped for the doctor's care;
  Haven't they reined their horses, their horses?
Why, they are none of them wounded, dear,
      None of these forces.

O is it the parson they want with white hair;
  Is it the parson, is it, is it?
No, they are passing his gateway, dear,
      Without a visit.

O it must be the farmer who lives so near;
  It must be the farmer so cunning, so cunning?
They have passed the farm already, dear,
      And now they are running.

O where are you going? stay with me here!
  Were the vows you swore me deceiving, deceiving?
No, I promised to love you, dear,
    But I must be leaving.

O it's broken the lock and splintered the door,
  O it's the gate where they're turning, turning;
Their feet are heavy on the floor
    And their eyes are burning.

A Summer Night
(To Geoffrey Hoyland)

Out on the lawn I lie in bed,
Vega conspicuous overhead
  In the windless nights of June;
Forests of green have done complete
The day's activity; my feet
  Point to the rising moon.

Lucky, this point in time and space
Is chosen as my working place;
  Where the sexy airs of summer,
The bathing hours and the bare arms,
The leisured drives through a land of farms,
  Are good to the newcomer.

Equal with colleagues in a ring
I sit on each calm evening,
  Enchanted as the flowers
The opening light draws out of hiding
From leaves with all its dove-like pleading
  Its logic and its powers.

That later we, though parted then
May still recall these evenings when
  Fear gave his watch no look;
The lion griefs loped from the shade
And on our knees their muzzles laid,
  And Death put down his book.

Moreover, eyes in which I learn
That I am glad to look, return
  My glances every day;
And when the birds and rising sun
Waken me, I shall speak with one
  Who has not gone away.

Now North and South and East and West
Those I love lie down to rest;
  The moon looks on them all:
The healers and the brilliant talkers,
The eccentrics and the silent walkers,
  The dumpy and the tall.

She climbs the European sky;
Churches and power stations lie
  Alike among earth's fixtures:
Into the galleries she peers,
And blankly as an orphan stares
  Upon the marvellous pictures.

To gravity attentive, she
Can notice nothing here; though we
  Whom hunger cannot move,
From gardens where we feel secure
Look up, and with a sigh endure
  The tyrannies of love:

And, gentle, do not care to know,
Where Poland draws her Eastern bow,
  What violence is done;
Nor ask what doubtful act allows
Our freedom in this English house,
  Our picnics in the sun.

The creepered wall stands up to hide
The gathering multitudes outside
  Whose glances hunger worsens;
Concealing from their wretchedness
Our metaphysical distress,
  Our kindness to ten persons.

And now no path on which we move
But shows already traces of
  Intentions not our own,

Thoroughly able to achieve
What our excitement could conceive,
   But our hands left alone.

For what by nature and by training
We loved, has little strength remaining:
   Though we would gladly give
The Oxford colleges, Big Ben,
And all the birds in Wicken Fen,
   It has no wish to live.

Soon through the dykes of our content
The crumpling flood will force a rent,
   And, taller than a tree,
Hold sudden death before our eyes
Whose river-dreams long hid the size
   And vigours of the sea.

But when the waters make retreat
And through the black mud first the wheat
   In shy green stalks appears;
When stranded monsters gasping lie,
And sounds of riveting terrify
   Their whorled unsubtle ears:

May this for which we dread to lose
Our privacy, need no excuse
   But to that strength belong;
As through a child's rash happy cries
The drowned voices of his parents rise
   In unlamenting song.

After discharges of alarm,
All unpredicted may it calm
   The pulse of nervous nations;
Forgive the murderer in his glass,
Tough in its patience to surpass
   The tigress her swift motions.

'May with its light behaving'

May with its light behaving
Stirs vessel, eye, and limb;
The singular and sad
Are willing to recover,
And to the swan-delighting river
The careless picnics come,
The living white and red.

The dead remote and hooded
In their enclosures rest; but we
From the vague woods have broken,
Forests where children meet
And the white angel-vampires flit;
We stand with shaded eye,
The dangerous apple taken.

The real world lies before us;
Animal motions of the young,
The common wish for death,
The pleasured and the haunted;
The dying master sinks tormented
In the admirers' ring,
The unjust walk the earth.

And love that makes impatient
The tortoise and the roe, and lays
The blonde beside the dark,
Urges upon our blood,
Before the evil and the good
How insufficient is
The endearment and the look.

The Cultural Presupposition

Happy the hare at morning, for she cannot read
The Hunter's waking thoughts. Lucky the leaf
Unable to predict the fall. Lucky indeed
The rampant suffering suffocating jelly
Burgeoning in pools, lapping the grits of the desert:
The elementary sensual cures,
The hibernations and the growth of hair assuage:
Or best of all the mineral stars disintegrating quietly into light
But what shall man do, who can whistle tunes by heart,
Know to the bar when death shall cut him short, like the cry of the shearwater?
We will show you what he has done.
How comely are his places of refuge and the tabernacles of his peace,
The new books upon the morning table, the lawns and the afternoon terraces!
Here are the playing-fields where he may forget his ignorance
To operate within a gentleman's agreement: twenty-two sins have here a certain licence.
Here are the thickets where accosted lovers combatant
May warm each other with their wicked hands,
Here are the avenues for incantation and workshops for the cunning engravers.
The galleries are full of music, the pianist is storming the keys, the great cellist is crucified over his instrument,
That none may hear the ejaculations of the sentinels
Nor the sigh of the most numerous and the most poor; the thud of their falling bodies
Who with their lives have banished hence the serpent and the faceless insect.

On This Island

Look, stranger, at this island now
The leaping light for your delight discovers,
Stand stable here
And silent be,
That through the channels of the ear
May wander like a river
The swaying sound of the sea.

Here at the small field's ending pause
Where the chalk wall falls to the foam, and its tall ledges
Oppose the pluck
And knock of the tide,
And the shingle scrambles after the suck-
ing surf, and the gull lodges
A moment on its sheer side.

Far off like floating seeds the ships
Diverge on urgent voluntary errands;
And the full view
Indeed may enter
And move in memory as now these clouds do,
That pass the harbour mirror
And all the summer through the water saunter.

'Fish in the unruffled lakes'

Fish in the unruffled lakes
The swarming colours wear,
Swans in the winter air
A white perfection have,
And the great lion walks
Through his innocent grove;
Lion, fish, and swan
Act, and are gone
Upon Time's toppling wave.

We till shadowed days are done,
We must weep and sing
Duty's conscious wrong,
The devil in the clock,
The Goodness carefully worn
For atonement or for luck;
We must lose our loves,
On each beast and bird that moves
Turn an envious look.

Sighs for folly said and done
Twist our narrow days;
But I must bless, I must praise
That you, my swan, who have
All gifts that to the swan
Impulsive Nature gave,
The majesty and pride,
Last night should add
Your voluntary love.

Funeral Blues

Stop all the clocks, cut off the telephone,
Prevent the dog from barking with a juicy bone,
Silence the pianos and with muffled drum
Bring out the coffin, let the mourners come.

Let aeroplanes circle moaning overhead
Scribbling on the sky the message He Is Dead,
Put crêpe bows round the white necks of the public doves,
Let the traffic policemen wear black cotton gloves.

He was my North, my South, my East and West,
My working week and my Sunday rest,
My noon, my midnight, my talk, my song;
I thought that love would last for ever: I was wrong.

The stars are not wanted now; put out every one,
Pack up the moon and dismantle the sun,
Pour away the ocean and sweep up the wood;
For nothing now can ever come to any good.

Detective Story

For who is ever quite without his landscape,
The straggling village street, the house in trees,
All near the church, or else the gloomy town house,
The one with the Corinthian pillars, or
The tiny workmanlike flat: in any case
A home, the centre where the three or four things
That happen to a man do happen? Yes,
Who cannot draw the map of his life, shade in
The little station where he meets his loves
And says good-bye continually, and mark the spot
Where the body of his happiness was first discovered?

An unknown tramp? A rich man? An enigma always
And with a buried past – but when the truth,
The truth about our happiness comes out
How much it owed to blackmail and philandering.

The rest's traditional. All goes to plan:
The feud between the local common sense
And that exasperating brilliant intuition
That's always on the spot by chance before us;
All goes to plan, both lying and confession,
Down to the thrilling final chase, the kill.

Yet on the last page just a lingering doubt
That verdict, was it just? The judge's nerves,
That clue, that protestation from the gallows,
And our own smile . . . why yes . . .
But time is always killed. Someone must pay for
Our loss of happiness, our happiness itself.

Spain 1937

Yesterday all the past. The language of size
Spreading to China along the trade-routes; the diffusion
        Of the counting-frame and the cromlech;
Yesterday the shadow-reckoning in the sunny climates.

Yesterday the assessment of insurance by cards,
The divination of water; yesterday the invention
        Of cart-wheels and clocks, the taming of
Horses; yesterday the bustling world of the navigators.

Yesterday the abolition of fairies and giants;
The fortress like a motionless eagle eyeing the valley,
        The chapel built in the forest;
Yesterday the carving of angels and of frightening gargoyles;

The trial of heretics among the columns of stone;
Yesterday the theological feuds in the taverns
        And the miraculous cure at the fountain;
Yesterday the Sabbath of Witches. But to-day the struggle.

Yesterday the installation of dynamos and turbines;
The construction of railways in the colonial desert;
        Yesterday the classic lecture
On the origin of Mankind. But to-day the struggle.

Yesterday the belief in the absolute value of Greek;
The fall of the curtain upon the death of a hero;
        Yesterday the prayer to the sunset
And the adoration of madmen. But to-day the struggle.

As the poet whispers, startled among the pines
Or, where the loose waterfall sings, compact, or upright
        On the crag by the leaning tower:
'O my vision. O send me the luck of the sailor.'

And the investigator peers through his instruments
At the inhuman provinces, the virile bacillus
Or enormous Jupiter finished:
'But the lives of my friends. I inquire, I inquire.'

And the poor in their fireless lodgings dropping the sheets
Of the evening paper: 'Our day is our loss. O show us
History the operator, the
Organiser, Time the refreshing river.'

And the nations combine each cry, invoking the life
That shapes the individual belly and orders
The private nocturnal terror:
'Did you not found once the city state of the sponge,

'Raise the vast military empires of the shark
And the tiger, establish the robin's plucky canton?
Intervene. O descend as a dove or
A furious papa or a mild engineer: but descend.'

And the life, if it answers at all, replies from the heart
And the eyes and the lungs, from the shops and squares of the city:
'O no, I am not the Mover,
Not to-day, not to you. To you I'm the

'Yes-man, the bar-companion, the easily-duped:
I am whatever you do; I am your vow to be
Good, your humorous story;
I am your business voice; I am your marriage.

'What's your proposal? To build the Just City? I will.
I agree. Or is it the suicide pact, the romantic
Death? Very well, I accept, for
I am your choice, your decision: yes, I am Spain.'

Many have heard it on remote peninsulas,
On sleepy plains, in the aberrant fishermen's islands,
In the corrupt heart of the city;
Have heard and migrated like gulls or the seeds of a flower.

They clung like burrs to the long expresses that lurch
Through the unjust lands, through the night, through the
alpine tunnel;
They floated over the oceans;
They walked the passes: they came to present their lives.

On that arid square, that fragment nipped off from hot
Africa, soldered so crudely to inventive Europe,
On that tableland scored by rivers,
Our fever's menacing shapes are precise and alive.

To-morrow, perhaps, the future: the research on fatigue
And the movements of packers; the gradual exploring of all
the
Octaves of radiation;
To-morrow the enlarging of consciousness by diet and
breathing.

To-morrow the rediscovery of romantic love;
The photographing of ravens; all the fun under
Liberty's masterful shadow;
To-morrow the hour of the pageant-master and the
musician.

To-morrow for the young the poets exploding like bombs,
The walks by the lake, the winter of perfect communion;
To-morrow the bicycle races
Through the suburbs on summer evenings: but to-day the
struggle.

To-day the inevitable increase in the chances of death;
The conscious acceptance of guilt in the fact of murder;
To-day the expending of powers
On the flat ephemeral pamphlet and the boring meeting.

To-day the makeshift consolations; the shared cigarette;
The cards in the candle-lit barn and the scraping concert,
The masculine jokes; to-day the
Fumbled and unsatisfactory embrace before hurting.

The stars are dead; the animals will not look:
We are left alone with our day, and the time is short and
History to the defeated
May say Alas but cannot help or pardon.

The Sphinx

Did it once issue from the carver's hand
Healthy? Even the earliest conquerors saw
The face of a sick ape, a bandaged paw,
A Presence in the hot invaded land.

The lion of a tortured stubborn star,
It does not like the young, nor love, nor learning:
Time hurt it like a person; it lies, turning
A vast behind on shrill America,

And witnesses. The huge hurt face accuses,
And pardons nothing, least of all success.
The answers that it utters have no uses

To those who face akimbo its distress:
'Do people like me?' No. The slave amuses
The lion: 'Am I to suffer always?' Yes.

‘Here war is simple like a monument’

Here war is simple like a monument:
A telephone is speaking to a man;
Flags on a map assert that troops were sent;
A boy brings milk in bowls. There is a plan

For living men in terror of their lives,
Who thirst at nine who were to thirst at noon,
And can be lost and are, and miss their wives,
And, unlike an idea, can die too soon.

But ideas can be true although men die,
And we can watch a thousand faces
Made active by one lie:

And maps can really point to places
Where life is evil now:
Nanking; Dachau.

Musée des Beaux Arts

About suffering they were never wrong,
The Old Masters: how well they understood
Its human position; how it takes place
While someone else is eating or opening a window or just
walking dully along;
How, when the aged are reverently, passionately waiting
For the miraculous birth, there always must be
Children who did not specially want it to happen, skating
On a pond at the edge of the wood:
They never forgot
That even the dreadful martyrdom must run its course
Anyhow in a corner, some untidy spot
Where the dogs go on with their doggy life and the torturer's
horse
Scratches its innocent behind on a tree.

In Brughel's *Icarus*, for instance: how everything turns away
Quite leisurely from the disaster; the ploughman may
Have heard the splash, the forsaken cry,
But for him it was not an important failure; the sun shone
As it had to on the white legs disappearing into the green
Water; and the expensive delicate ship that must have seen
Something amazing, a boy falling out of the sky,
Had somewhere to get to and sailed calmly on.

Gare du Midi

A nondescript express in from the South,
Crowds round the ticket barrier, a face
To welcome which the mayor has not contrived
Bugles or braid: something about the mouth
Distracts the stray look with alarm and pity.
Snow is falling. Clutching a little case,
He walks out briskly to infect a city
Whose terrible future may have just arrived.

Refugee Blues

Say this city has ten million souls,
Some are living in mansions, some are living in holes:
Yet there's no place for us, my dear, yet there's no place for us.

Once we had a country and we thought it fair,
Look in the atlas and you'll find it there:
We cannot go there now, my dear, we cannot go there now.

In the village churchyard there grows an old yew,
Every spring it blossoms anew:
Old passports can't do that, my dear, old passports can't do that.

The consul banged the table and said:
'If you've got no passport you're officially dead':
But we are still alive, my dear, but we are still alive.

Went to a committee; they offered me a chair;
Asked me politely to return next year:
But where shall we go to-day, my dear, but where shall we go to-day?

Came to a public meeting; the speaker got up and said:
'If we let them in, they will steal our daily bread';
He was talking of you and me, my dear, he was talking of you and me.

Thought I heard the thunder rumbling in the sky;
It was Hitler over Europe, saying: 'They must die';
We were in his mind, my dear, we were in his mind.

Saw a poodle in a jacket fastened with a pin,
Saw a door opened and a cat let in:
But they weren't German Jews, my dear, but they weren't German Jews.

Went down to the harbour and stood upon the quay,
Saw the fish swimming as if they were free:
Only ten feet away, my dear, only ten feet away.

Walked through a wood, saw the birds in the trees;
They had no politicians and sang at their ease:
They weren't the human race, my dear, they weren't the human race.

Dreamed I saw a building with a thousand floors,
A thousand windows and a thousand doors;
Not one of them was ours, my dear, not one of them was ours.

Stood on a great plain in the falling snow;
Ten thousand soldiers marched to and fro:
Looking for you and me, my dear, looking for you and me.

In Memory of W. B. Yeats

(d. Jan. 1939)

1

He disappeared in the dead of winter:
The brooks were frozen, the air-ports almost deserted,
And snow disfigured the public statues;
The mercury sank in the mouth of the dying day.
O all the instruments agree
The day of his death was a dark cold day.

Far from his illness
The wolves ran on through the evergreen forests,
The peasant river was untempted by the fashionable quays;
By mourning tongues
The death of the poet was kept from his poems.

But for him it was his last afternoon as himself,
An afternoon of nurses and rumours;
The provinces of his body revolted,
The squares of his mind were empty,
Silence invaded the suburbs,
The current of his feeling failed: he became his admirers.

Now he is scattered among a hundred cities
And wholly given over to unfamiliar affections;
To find his happiness in another kind of wood
And be punished under a foreign code of conscience.
The words of a dead man
Are modified in the guts of the living.

But in the importance and noise of to-morrow
When the brokers are roaring like beasts on the floor of the Bourse,
And the poor have the sufferings to which they are fairly accustomed,

And each in the cell of himself is almost convinced of his freedom;
A few thousand will think of this day
As one thinks of a day when one did something slightly unusual.

O all the instruments agree
The day of his death was a dark cold day.

2

You were silly like us: your gift survived it all;
The parish of rich women, physical decay,
Yourself; mad Ireland hurt you into poetry.
Now Ireland has her madness and her weather still,
For poetry makes nothing happen: it survives
In the valley of its saying where executives
Would never want to tamper; it flows south
From ranches of isolation and the busy griefs,
Raw towns that we believe and die in; it survives,
A way of happening, a mouth.

3

Earth, receive an honoured guest;
William Yeats is laid to rest:
Let the Irish vessel lie
Emptied of its poetry.

Time that is intolerant
Of the brave and innocent,
And indifferent in a week
To a beautiful physique,

Worships language and forgives
Everyone by whom it lives;
Pardons cowardice, conceit,
Lays its honours at their feet.

Time that with this strange excuse
Pardoned Kipling and his views,
And will pardon Paul Claudel,
Pardons him for writing well.

In the nightmare of the dark
All the dogs of Europe bark,
And the living nations wait,
Each sequestered in its hate;

Intellectual disgrace
Stares from every human face,
And the seas of pity lie
Locked and frozen in each eye.

Follow, poet, follow right
To the bottom of the night,
With your unconstraining voice
Still persuade us to rejoice;

With the farming of a verse
Make a vineyard of the curse,
Sing of human unsuccess
In a rapture of distress;

In the deserts of the heart
Let the healing fountain start,
In the prison of his days
Teach the free man how to praise.

Epitaph on a Tyrant

Perfection, of a kind, was what he was after,
And the poetry he invented was easy to understand;
He knew human folly like the back of his hand,
And was greatly interested in armies and fleets;
When he laughed, respectable senators burst with laughter,
And when he cried the little children died in the streets.

'Carry her over the water'

Carry her over the water,
  And set her down under the tree,
Where the culvers white all day and all night,
  And the winds from every quarter,
Sing agreeably, agreeably, agreeably of love.

Put a gold ring on her finger,
  And press her close to your heart,
While the fish in the lake their snapshots take,
  And the frog, that sanguine singer,
Sings agreeably, agreeably, agreeably of love.

The streets shall all flock to your marriage,
  The houses turn round to look,
The tables and chairs say suitable prayers,
  And the horses drawing your carriage
Sing agreeably, agreeably, agreeably of love.

'England to me is my own tongue'

England to me is my own tongue,
And what I did when I was young.
If now, two aliens in New York,
We meet, Elizabeth , and talk
Of friends who suffer in the torn
Old Europe where we both were born,
What this refutes or that confirms,
I can but think our talk in terms
Of images that I have seen,
And England tells me what we mean.
Thus, squalid beery BURTON stands
For shoddy thinking of all brands;
The wreck of RHONDDA for the mess
We make when for a short success
We split our symmetry apart,
Deny the Reason or the Heart;
YE OLDË TUDOR TEA-SHOPPE for
The folly of dogmatic law,
While graceless BOURNEMOUTH is the sloth
Of men or bureaucrats or both.

No matter where, or whom I meet,
Shop-gazing in a Paris street,
Bumping through Iceland in a bus,
At teas where clubwomen discuss
The latest Federation Plan,
In Pullman washrooms, man to man,
Hearing how circumstance has vexed
A broker who is oversexed,
In houses where they do not drink,
Whenever I begin to think
About the human creature we
Must nurse to sense and decency,

An English area comes to mind,
I see the nature of my kind
As a locality I love,
Those limestone moors that stretch from BROUGH
To HEXHAM and the ROMAN WALL,
There is my symbol of us all.
There, where the EDEN leisures through
Its sandstone valley, is my view
Of green and civil life that dwells
Below a cliff of savage fells
From which original address
Man faulted into consciousness.
Along the line of lapse the fire
Of life's impersonal desire
Burst through his sedentary rock
And, as at DUFTON and at KNOCK,
Thrust up between his mind and heart
Enormous cones of myth and art.
Always my boy of wish returns
To those peat-stained deserted burns
That feed the WEAR and TYNE and TEES,
And, turning states to strata, sees
How basalt long oppressed broke out
In wild revolt at CAULDRON SNOUT,
And from the relics of old mines
Derives his algebraic signs
For all in man that mourns and seeks,
For all of his renounced techniques,
Their tramways overgrown with grass,
For lost belief, for all Alas,
The derelict lead-smelting mill,
Flued to its chimney up the hill,
That smokes no answer any more
But points, a landmark on BOLTS LAW,
The finger of all questions. There
In ROOKHOPE I was first aware

Of Self and Not-self, Death and Dread:
Adits were entrances which led
Down to the Outlawed, to the Others,
The Terrible, the Merciful, the Mothers;
Alone in the hot day I knelt
Upon the edge of shafts and felt
The deep *Urmutterfurcht* that drives
Us into knowledge all our lives,
The far interior of our fate
To civilise and to create,
Das Weibliche that bids us come
To find what we're escaping from.
There I dropped pebbles, listened, heard
The reservoir of darkness stirred;
*'O deine Mutter kehrt dir nicht
Wieder. Du selbst bin ich, dein' Pflicht
Und Liebe. Brach sie nun mein Bild.'*
And I was conscious of my guilt.

If I Could Tell You

Time will say nothing but I told you so,
Time only knows the price we have to pay;
If I could tell you I would let you know.

If we should weep when clowns put on their show,
If we should stumble when musicians play,
Time will say nothing but I told you so.

There are no fortunes to be told, although,
Because I love you more than I can say,
If I could tell you I would let you know.

The winds must come from somewhere when they blow,
There must be reasons why the leaves decay;
Time will say nothing but I told you so.

Perhaps the roses really want to grow,
The vision seriously intends to stay;
If I could tell you I would let you know.

Suppose the lions all get up and go,
And all the brooks and soldiers run away;
Will Time say nothing but I told you so?
If I could tell you I would let you know.

Atlantis

Being set on the idea
   Of getting to Atlantis,
You have discovered of course
   Only the Ship of Fools is
Making the voyage this year,
As gales of abnormal force
   Are predicted, and that you
   Must therefore be ready to
Behave absurdly enough
   To pass for one of The Boys,
At least appearing to love
   Hard liquor, horseplay and noise.

Should storms, as may well happen,
   Drive you to anchor a week
In some old harbour-city
   Of Ionia, then speak
With her witty scholars, men
Who have proved there cannot be
   Such a place as Atlantis:
   Learn their logic, but notice
How their subtlety betrays
   A simple enormous grief;
Thus they shall teach you the ways
   To doubt that you may believe.

If, later, you run aground
   Among the headlands of Thrace
Where with torches all night long
   A naked barbaric race
Leaps frenziedly to the sound
Of conch and dissonant gong;
   On that stony savage shore
   Strip off your clothes and dance, for

Unless you are capable
    Of forgetting completely
About Atlantis, you will
    Never finish your journey.

Again, should you come to gay
    Carthage or Corinth, take part
In their endless gaiety;
    And if in some bar a tart,
As she strokes your hair, should say
'This is Atlantis, dearie,'
    Listen with attentiveness
    To her life-story: unless
You become acquainted now
    With each refuge that tries to
Counterfeit Atlantis, how
    Will you recognize the true?

Assuming you beach at last
    Near Atlantis, and begin
The terrible trek inland
    Through squalid woods and frozen
Tundras where all are soon lost;
If, forsaken then, you stand,
    Dismissal everywhere,
    Stone and snow, silence and air,
Remember the noble dead
    And honour the fate you are,
Travelling and tormented,
    Dialectic and bizarre.

Stagger onward rejoicing;
    And even then if, perhaps
Having actually got
    To the last col, you collapse
With all Atlantis gleaming
Below you yet you cannot

Descend, you should still be proud
Even to have been allowed
Just to peep at Atlantis
In a poetic vision:
Give thanks and lie down in peace,
Having seen your salvation.

All the little household gods
Have started crying, but say
Good-bye now, and put to sea.
Farewell, dear friend, farewell: may
Hermes, master of the roads
And the four dwarf Kabiri,
Protect and serve you always;
And may the Ancient of Days
Provide for all you must do
His invisible guidance,
Lifting up, friend, upon you
The light of His countenance.

The Lesson

The first time that I dreamed, we were in flight,
And fagged with running; there was civil war,
A valley full of thieves and wounded bears.

Farms blazed behind us; turning to the right,
We came at once to a tall house, its door
Wide open, waiting for its long-lost heirs.

An elderly clerk sat on the bedroom stairs
Writing; but we had tiptoed past him when
He raised his head and stuttered – 'Go away'.

We wept and begged to stay:
He wiped his pince-nez, hesitated, then
Said no, he had no power to give us leave;
Our lives were not in order; we must leave.

*

The second dream began in a May wood;
We had been laughing; your blue eyes were kind,
Your excellent nakedness without disdain.

Our lips met, wishing universal good;
But, on their impact, sudden flame and wind
Fetched you away and turned me loose again

To make a focus for a wide wild plain,
Dead level and dead silent and bone dry,
Where nothing could have suffered, sinned, or grown.
On a high chair alone
I sat, a little master, asking why
The cold and solid object in my hands
Should be a human hand, one of your hands.

*

And the last dream was this: we were to go
To a great banquet and a Victory Ball
After some tournament or dangerous test.

Our cushions were of crimson velvet, so
We must have won; though there were crowns for all,
Ours were of gold, of paper all the rest.

Fair, wise or funny was each famous guest,
Love smiled at Courage over priceless glass,
And rockets died in hundreds to express
Our learned carelessness.
A band struck up; all over the green grass
A sea of paper crowns rose up to dance:
Ours were too heavy; we did not dance.

*

I woke. You were not there. But as I dressed
Anxiety turned to shame, feeling all three
Intended one rebuke. For had not each
In its own way tried to teach
My will to love you that it cannot be,
As I think, of such consequence to want
What anyone is given, if they want?

Miranda's Song

My Dear One is mine as mirrors are lonely,
As the poor and sad are real to the good king,
And the high green hill sits always by the sea.

Up jumped the Black Man behind the elder tree,
Turned a somersault and ran away waving;
My Dear One is mine as mirrors are lonely.

The Witch gave a squawk; her venomous body
Melted into light as water leaves a spring,
And the high green hill sits always by the sea.

At his crossroads, too, the Ancient prayed for me;
Down his wasted cheeks tears of joy were running:
My Dear One is mine as mirrors are lonely.

He kissed me awake, and no one was sorry;
The sun shone on sails, eyes, pebbles, anything,
And the high green hill sits always by the sea.

So, to remember our changing garden, we
Are linked as children in a circle dancing:
My Dear One is mine as mirrors are lonely,
And the high green hill sits always by the sea.

'As yet the young hero's'

As yet the young hero's
Brow is unkissed by battle,
But he knows how necessary
Is his defiance of fate
And, serene already, he sails
Down the gorge between the august
Faces carved in the cliffs
Towards the lordship of the world.

And the gentle majority are not
Afraid either, but, owl-like
And sedate in their glass globes
The wedded couples wave
At the bandits racing by
With affection, and the learned relax
On pinguid plains among
A swarm of flying flowers.

But otherwise is it with the play
Of the child whom chance decrees
To say what all men suffer:
For he wishes against his will
To be lost, and his fear leads him
To dales of driving rain
Where peasants with penthouse eyebrows
Sullenly guard the sluices.

And his steps follow the stream
Past rusting apparatus
To its gloomy beginning, the original
Chasm where brambles block
The entrance to the underworld;
There the silence blesses his sorrow,
And holy to his dread is that dark
Which will neither promise nor explain.

Prospector's Ballad

When Laura lay on her ledger side
And nicely threw her north cheek up,
How pleasing the plight of her promising grove
And how rich the random I reached with a rise.

The Fall of Rome

(for Cyril Connolly)

The piers are pummelled by the waves;
In a lonely field the rain
Lashes an abandoned train;
Outlaws fill the mountain caves.

Fantastic grow the evening gowns;
Agents of the Fisc pursue
Absconding tax-defaulters through
The sewers of provincial towns.

Private rites of magic send
The temple prostitutes to sleep;
All the literati keep
An imaginary friend.

Cerebrotonic Cato may
Extol the Ancient Disciplines,
But the muscle-bound Marines
Mutiny for food and pay.

Caesar's double-bed is warm
As an unimportant clerk
Writes *I DO NOT LIKE MY WORK*
On a pink official form.

Unendowed with wealth or pity,
Little birds with scarlet legs,
Sitting on their speckled eggs,
Eye each flu-infected city.

Altogether elsewhere, vast
Herds of reindeer move across
Miles and miles of golden moss,
Silently and very fast.

In Praise of Limestone

If it form the one landscape that we, the inconstant ones,
   Are consistently homesick for, this is chiefly
Because it dissolves in water. Mark these rounded slopes
   With their surface fragrance of thyme and, beneath,
A secret system of caves and conduits; hear the springs
   That spurt out everywhere with a chuckle,
Each filling a private pool for its fish and carving
   Its own little ravine whose cliffs entertain
The butterfly and the lizard; examine this region
   Of short distances and definite places:
What could be more like Mother or a fitter background
   For her son, the flirtatious male who lounges
Against a rock in the sunlight, never doubting
   That for all his faults he is loved; whose works are but
Extensions of his power to charm? From weathered outcrop
   To hill-top temple, from appearing waters to
Conspicuous fountains, from a wild to a formal vineyard,
   Are ingenious but short steps that a child's wish
To receive more attention than his brothers, whether
   By pleasing or teasing, can easily take.

Watch, then, the band of rivals as they climb up and down
   Their steep stone gennels in twos and threes, at times
Arm in arm, but never, thank God, in step; or engaged
   On the shady side of a square at midday in
Voluble discourse, knowing each other too well to think
   There are any important secrets, unable
To conceive a god whose temper-tantrums are moral
   And not to be pacified by a clever line
Or a good lay: for, accustomed to a stone that responds,
   They have never had to veil their faces in awe
Of a crater whose blazing fury could not be fixed;
   Adjusted to the local needs of valleys

Where everything can be touched or reached by walking,
   Their eyes have never looked into infinite space
Through the lattice-work of a nomad's comb; born lucky,
   Their legs have never encountered the fungi
And insects of the jungle, the monstrous forms and lives
   With which we have nothing, we like to hope, in common.
So, when one of them goes to the bad, the way his mind
works
   Remains comprehensible: to become a pimp
Or deal in fake jewellery or ruin a fine tenor voice
   For effects that bring down the house, could happen to all
But the best and the worst of us . . .
That is why, I suppose,
   The best and worst never stayed here long but sought
Immoderate soils where the beauty was not so external,
   The light less public and the meaning of life
Something more than a mad camp. 'Come!' cried the granite
wastes,
   'How evasive is your humor, how accidental
Your kindest kiss, how permanent is death.' (Saints-to-be
   Slipped away sighing.) 'Come!' purred the clays and
gravels,
'On our plains there is room for armies to drill; rivers
   Wait to be tamed and slaves to construct you a tomb
In the grand manner: soft as the earth is mankind and both
   Need to be altered.' (Intendant Caesars rose and
Left, slamming the door.) But the really reckless were
fetched
   By an older colder voice, the oceanic whisper:
'I am the solitude that asks and promises nothing;
   That is how I shall set you free. There is no love;
There are only the various envies, all of them sad.'

   They were right, my dear, all those voices were right
And still are; this land is not the sweet home that it looks,
   Nor its peace the historical calm of a site

Where something was settled once and for all: A backward
And dilapidated province, connected
To the big busy world by a tunnel, with a certain
Seedy appeal, is that all it is now? Not quite:
It has a worldly duty which in spite of itself
It does not neglect, but calls into question
All the Great Powers assume; it disturbs our rights. The poet,
Admired for his earnest habit of calling
The sun the sun, his mind Puzzle, is made uneasy
By these marble statues which so obviously doubt
His antimythological myth; and these gamins,
Pursuing the scientist down the tiled colonnade
With such lively offers, rebuke his concern for Nature's
Remotest aspects: I, too, am reproached, for what
And how much you know. Not to lose time, not to get caught,
Not to be left behind, not, please! to resemble
The beasts who repeat themselves, or a thing like water
Or stone whose conduct can be predicted, these
Are our Common Prayer, whose greatest comfort is music
Which can be made anywhere, is invisible,
And does not smell. In so far as we have to look forward
To death as a fact, no doubt we are right: But if
Sins can be forgiven, if bodies rise from the dead,
These modifications of matter into
Innocent athletes and gesticulating fountains,
Made solely for pleasure, make a further point:
The blessed will not care what angle they are regarded from,
Having nothing to hide. Dear, I know nothing of
Either, but when I try to imagine a faultless love
Or the life to come, what I hear is the murmur
Of underground streams, what I see is a limestone landscape.

Cattivo Tempo

Sirocco brings the minor devils:
A slamming of doors
At four in the morning
Announces they are back,
Grown insolent and fat
On cheesy literature
And corny dramas,
Nibbar, demon
Of ga-ga and bêtise,
Tubervillus, demon
Of gossip and spite.

Nibbar to the writing-room
Plausibly to whisper
The nearly fine,
The almost true;
Beware of him, poet,
Lest, reading over
Your shoulder, he find
What makes him glad,
The manner arch,
The meaning blurred,
The poem bad.

Tubervillus to the dining-room
Intently to listen,
Waiting his cue;
Beware of him, friends,
Lest the talk at his prompting
Take the wrong turning,
The unbated tongue
In mischief blurt
The half-home-truth,
The fun turn ugly,
The jokes hurt.

Do not underrate them; merely
To tear up the poem,
To shut the mouth
Will defeat neither:
To have got you alone
Self-confined to your bedroom
Manufacturing there
From lewdness or self-care
Some whining unmanaged
Imp of your own,
That too is their triumph.

The proper riposte is to bore them;
To scurry the dull pen
Through dull correspondence,
To wag the sharp tongue
In pigeon Italian,
Asking the socialist
Barber to guess
Or the monarchist fisherman to tell
When the wind will change,
Outwitting hell
With human obviousness.

Their Lonely Betters

As I listened from a beach-chair in the shade
To all the noises that my garden made,
It seemed to me only proper that words
Should be withheld from vegetables and birds.

A robin with no Christian name ran through
The Robin-Anthem which was all it knew,
And rustling flowers for some third party waited
To say which pairs, if any, should get mated.

Not one of them was capable of lying,
There was not one which knew that it was dying
Or could have with a rhythm or a rhyme
Assumed responsibility for time.

Let them leave language to their lonely betters
Who count some days and long for certain letters;
We, too, make noises when we laugh or weep:
Words are for those with promises to keep.

Fleet Visit

The sailors come ashore
Out of their hollow ships,
Mild-looking middle-class boys
Who read the comic strips;
One baseball game is more
To them than fifty Troys.

They look a bit lost, set down
In this unamerican place
Where natives pass with laws
And futures of their own;
They are not here because
But only just-in-case.

The whore and ne'er-do-well
Who pester them with junk
In their grubby ways at least
Are serving the Social Beast;
They neither make nor sell –
No wonder they get drunk.

But their ships on the vehement blue
Of this harbor actually gain
From having nothing to do;
Without a human will
To tell them whom to kill
Their structures are humane

And, far from looking lost,
Look as if they were meant
To be pure abstract design
By some master of pattern and line,
Certainly worth every cent
Of the billions they must have cost.

Lauds

Among the leaves the small birds sing;
The crow of the cock commands awaking:
In solitude, for company.

Bright shines the sun on creatures mortal;
Men of their neighbors become sensible:
In solitude, for company.

The crow of the cock commands awaking;
Already the mass-bell goes dong-ding:
In solitude, for company.

Men of their neighbors become sensible;
God bless the Realm, God bless the People:
In solitude, for company.

Already the mass-bell goes dong-ding;
The dripping mill-wheel is again turning:
In solitude, for company.

God bless the Realm, God bless the People;
God bless this green world temporal:
In solitude, for company.

The dripping mill-wheel is again turning;
Among the leaves the small birds sing:
In solitude, for company.

Streams

(for Elizabeth Drew)

Dear water, clear water, playful in all your streams,
as you dash or loiter through life who does not love
 to sit beside you, to hear you and see you,
 pure being, perfect in music and movement?

Air is boastful at times, earth slovenly, fire rude,
but you in your bearing are always immaculate,
 the most well-spoken of all the older
 servants in the household of Mrs Nature.

Nobody suspects you of mocking him, for you still
use the same vocables you were using the day
 before that unexpected row which
 downed every hod on half-finished Babel,

and still talk to yourself: nowhere are you disliked;
arching your torso, you dive from a basalt sill,
 canter across white chalk, slog forward
 through red marls, the aboriginal pilgrim,

at home in all sections, but for whom we should be
idolaters of a single rock, kept apart
 by our landscapes, excluding as alien
 the tales and diets of all other strata.

How could we love the absent one if you did not keep
coming from a distance, or quite directly assist,
 as when past Iseult's tower you floated
 the willow pash-notes of wanted Tristram?

And Homo Ludens, surely, is your child, who make
fun of our feuds by opposing identical banks
 and transferring the loam from Huppim
 to Muppim and back each time you crankle.

Growth cannot add to your song: as unchristened brooks
already you whisper to ants what, as Brahma's son,
descending his titanic staircase
into Assam, to Himalayan bears you thunder.

And not even man can spoil you: his company
coarsens roses and dogs but, should he herd you through a sluice
to toil at a turbine, or keep you
leaping in gardens for his amusement,

innocent still is your outcry, water, and there
even, to his soiled heart raging at what it is,
tells of a sort of world, quite other,
altogether different from this one

with its envies and passports, a polis like that
to which, in the name of scholars everywhere,
Gaston Paris pledged his allegiance
as Bismarck's siege-guns came within earshot.

Lately, in that dale of all Yorkshire's the loveliest,
where, off its fell-side helter-skelter, Kisdon Beck
jumps into Swale with a boyish shouting,
sprawled out on grass, I dozed for a second,

and found myself following a croquet tournament
in a calm enclosure, with thrushes popular:
of all the players in that cool valley
the best with the mallet was my darling.

While, on the wolds that begirdled it, wild old men
hunted with spades and hammers, monomaniac each,
for a megalith or a fossil,
and bird-watchers crept through mossy beech-woods.

Suddenly, over the lawn we started to run
for, lo, through the trees, in a cream and golden coach

drawn by two baby locomotives,
the god of mortal doting approached us,

flanked by his bodyguard, those hairy armigers in green
who laugh at thunderstorms and weep at a blue sky:
He thanked us for our cheers of homage,
and promised X and Y a passion undying.

With a wave of his torch he commanded a dance;
so round in a ring we flew, my dear on my right,
when I awoke. But fortunate seemed that
day because of my dream and enlightened,

and dearer, water, than ever your voice, as if
glad – though goodness knows why – to run with the human race,
wishing, I thought, the least of men their
figures of splendor, their holy places.

A Permanent Way

Self-drivers may curse their luck,
Stuck on new-fangled trails,
But the good old train will jog
To the dogma of its rails,

And steam so straight ahead
That I cannot be led astray
By tempting scenes which occur
Along any permanent way.

Intriguing dales escape
Into hills of the shape I like,
Though, were I actually put
Where a foot-path leaves the pike

For some steep romantic spot,
I should ask what chance there is
Of at least a ten-dollar cheque
Or a family peck of a kiss:

But, forcibly held to my tracks,
I can safely relax and dream
Of a love and a livelihood
To fit that wood or stream;

And what could be greater fun,
Once one has chosen and paid,
Than the inexpensive delight
Of a choice one might have made?

The Old Man's Road

Across the Great Schism, through our whole landscape,
Ignoring God's Vicar and God's Ape,

Under their noses, unsuspected,
The Old Man's Road runs as it did

When a light subsoil, a simple ore
Were still in vogue: true to His wherefore,

By stiles, gates, hedge-gaps it goes
Over ploughland, woodland, cow meadows,

Past shrines to a cosmological myth
No heretic today would be caught dead with,

Near hill-top rings that were so safe then,
Now stormed easily by small children

(Shepherds use bits in the high mountains,
Hamlets take stretches for Lovers' Lanes),

Then through cities threads its odd way,
Now without gutters, a Thieves' Alley,

Now with green lamp-posts and white curb,
The smart Crescent of a high-toned suburb,

Giving wide berth to an old Cathedral,
Running smack through a new Town Hall,

Unlookable for, by logic, by guess:
Yet some strike it, and are struck fearless.

No life can know it, but no life
That sticks to this course can be made captive,

And who wander with it are not stopped at
Borders by guards of some Theocrat,

Crossing the pass so almost where
His searchlight squints but no closer

(And no further where it might by chance):
So in summer sometimes, without hindrance,

Apotropaically scowling, a tinker
Shuffles past, in the waning year

Potters a coleopterist, poking
Through yellow leaves, and a youth in spring

Trots by after a new excitement,
His true self, hot on the scent.

The Old Man leaves his Road to those
Who love it no less since it lost purpose,

Who never ask what History is up to,
So cannot act as if they knew:

Assuming a freedom its Powers deny,
Denying its Powers, they pass freely.

There Will Be No Peace

Though mild clear weather
Smile again on the shire of your esteem
And its colors come back, the storm has changed you:
You will not forget, ever,
The darkness blotting out hope, the gale
Prophesying your downfall.

You must live with your knowledge.
Way back, beyond, outside of you are others,
In moonless absences you never heard of,
Who have certainly heard of you,
Beings of unknown number and gender:
And they do not like you.

What have you done to them?
Nothing? Nothing is not an answer:
You will come to believe – how can you help it? –
That you did, you did do something;
You will find yourself wishing you could make them laugh,
You will long for their friendship.

There will be no peace.
Fight back, then, with such courage as you have
And every unchivalrous dodge you know of,
Clear in your conscience on this:
Their cause, if they had one, is nothing to them now;
They hate for hate's sake.

Limbo Culture

The tribes of Limbo, travellers report,
On first encounter seem much like ourselves;
They keep their houses practically clean,
Their watches round about a standard time,
They serve you almost appetising meals:
But no one says he saw a Limbo child.

The language spoken by the tribes of Limbo
Has many words far subtler than our own
To indicate how much, how little, something
Is pretty closely or not quite the case,
But none you could translate by *Yes* or *No*,
Nor do its pronouns distinguish between Persons.

In tales related by the tribes of Limbo,
Dragon and Knight set to with fang and sword
But miss their rival always by a hair's-breadth,
Old Crone and Stripling pass a crucial point,
She seconds early and He seconds late,
A magic purse mistakes the legal tender:

'And so,' runs their concluding formula,
'Prince and Princess are nearly married still.'
Why this concern, so marked in Limbo culture,
This love for inexactness? Could it be
A Limbo tribesman only loves himself?
For that, we know, cannot be done exactly.

Walks

I choose the road from here to there
When I've a scandalous tale to bear,
Tools to return or books to lend
To someone at the other end.

Returning afterwards, although
I meet my footsteps toe to toe,
The road looks altogether new
Now that is done I meant to do.

But I avoid it when I take
A walker's walk for walking's sake:
The repetition it involves
Raises a doubt it never solves.

What good or evil angel bid
Me stop exactly when I did?
What would have happened had I gone
A kilometre further on?

No, when a fidget in the soul
Or cumulus clouds invite a stroll,
The route I pick goes roundabout
To finish where it started out.

It gets me home, this curving track,
Without my having to turn back,
Nor does it leave it up to me
To say how long my walk shall be,

Yet satisfies a moral need
By turning behavior into deed,
For I have boxed the compass when
I enter my front door again.

The heart, afraid to leave her shell,
Demands a hundred yards as well
Between my personal abode
And either sort of public road,

Making, when it is added too,
The straight a T, the round a Q,
Allowing me in rain or shine
To call both walks entirely mine,

A lane no traveller would use,
Where prints that do not fit my shoes
Have looked for me and, like enough,
Were made by someone whom I love.

Dame Kind

Steatopygous, sow-dugged
and owl-headed,
To Whom – Whom else? – the first innocent blood
was formally shed
By a chinned mammal that hard times
had turned carnivore,
From Whom his first promiscuous orgy
begged a downpour
To speed the body-building cereals
of a warmer age:
Now who put *us*, we should like to know,
in *Her* manage?

Strait-laced She never was
and has not grown more so
Since the skeptical academies got wind
of the *Chi-Rho*
St Cuckoo's wooden church for Her
where on Green Sundays
Bald hermits celebrate a wordless
cult in Her praise:
So pocket your fifty sonnets, Bud;
tell Her a myth
Of unpunishable gods and all the girls
they interfered with.

Haven't we spotted Her Picked Winners
whom She cossets, ramparts
And does the handsome by? Didn't the darlings
have cold hearts?
. . . ONE BOMB WOULD BE ENOUGH . . . Now look
who's thinking gruesome!
Brother, you're worse than a lonesome Peeper
or a He-Virgin

Who nightly abhors the Primal Scene
in medical Latin:
She mayn't be all She might be but
She *is* our Mum.

You can't tell *us* your hypochondriac
Blue-Stocking from Provence
Who makes the clock-work arcadies go round
is worth twopence;
You won't find a steady in *that* museum
unless you prefer
Tea with a shapeless angel to bedtime
with a lovely monster:
Before you catch it for your mim look
and gnostic chirrup,
Ask the Kind Lady who fitted you out
to fix you up.

Supposing even (through misdirections
or your own mischief)
You do land in that anomalous duchy,
Her remotest fief,
Where four eyes encounter in two
one mirror perilous
As the clear rock-basin that stultified
frigid Narcissus,
Where tongues stammer on a First Name,
bereft of guile,
And common snub-nosed creatures are abashed
at a face in profile,

Even there, as your blushes invoke its Guardian
(whose true invocable
Name is singular for each true heart
and false to tell)
To sacre your courtship ritual so
it deserve a music

More solemn than the he-hawing
of a salesman's limerick,
Do a bow to the Coarse Old Party that wrought you
an alderliefest
Of the same verbose and sentient kidney,
grateful not least

For all the dirty work She did.
How many hundreds
Of lawful, unlawful, both equally
loveless beds,
Of lying endearments, crooked questions,
crookeder answers,
Of bawling matches, sarcastic silences,
megrims, tears,
How much half-witted horse-play and sheer
bloody misrule
It took to bring you two together
both on schedule?

You

Really, must you,
Over-familiar
Dense companion,
Be there always?
The bond between us
Is chimerical surely:
Yet I cannot break it.

Must I, born for
Sacred play,
Turn base mechanic
So you may worship
Your secular bread,
With no thought
Of the value of time?

Thus far I have known your
Character only
From its pleasanter side,
But you know I know
A day will come
When you grow savage
And hurt me badly.

Totally stupid?
Would that you were:
But, no, you plague me
With tastes I was fool enough
Once to believe in.
Bah!, blockhead:
I know where you learned them.

Can I trust you even
On creaturely fact?
I suspect strongly

You hold some dogma
Of positive truth,
And feed me fictions:
I shall never prove it.

Oh, I know how you came by
A sinner's cranium,
How between two glaciers
The master-chronometer
Of an innocent primate
Altered its tempi:
That explains nothing.

Who tinkered and why?
Why am I certain,
Whatever your faults are,
The fault is mine,
Why is loneliness not
A chemical discomfort,
Nor Being a smell?

A Change of Air

Corns, heartburn, sinus headaches, such minor ailments
Tell of estrangement between your name and you,
Advise a change of air: heed them, but let
The modesty of their discomfort warn you
Against the flashy errands of your dreams.

To grow a sailor's beard, don monkish garb,
Or trade in an agglutinative tongue
With a stone-age culture, would be molly-coddling:
To go Elsewhere is to withdraw from movement;
A side-step, a short one, will convey you thither.

Although its chaffinches, maybe, have learned
The dialect of another river-basin,
A fault transformed the local building stone,
It has a priest, a post-mistress, an usher,
Its children know they are not to beg from strangers.

Within its average elsewhereishness
Your name is as a mirror answers, yourself
How you behave in shops, the tips you give:
It sides with neither, being outside both,
But welcomes both with healing disregard.

Nor, when you both return here (for you will)
Where luck and instinct originally brought you,
Will it salute your reconciliation
With farewell rites, or populate your absence
With reverent and irreverent anecdote.

No study of your public re-appearance
Will show, as judgement on a cure demands,
A sudden change in love, ideas, or diet:
Your sojourn Elsewhere will remain a wordless
Hiatus in your voluble biography.

Fanatic scholarship at most may prove
That you resigned from some Committee, unearth
A letter from the Grand-Duke to his cousin,
Remarking, among more important gossip,
That you seem less amusing than you were.

The Birth of Architecture

(for John Bayley)

From gallery-grave and the hunt of a wren-king
 to Low Mass and trailer-camp
is hardly a tick by the carbon-clock, but I
 don't count that way nor do you:
already it is millions of heart-beats ago
 back to the Bicycle Age,
before which is no *After* for me to measure,
 just a still prehistoric *Once*
where anything could happen. To you, to me,
 Stonehenge and Chartres Cathedral,
the Acropolis, Blenheim, the Albert Memorial
 are works by the same Old Man
under different names: we know what He did,
 what, even, He thought He thought,
but we don't see why. (To get that, one would have
 to be selfish in His way,
without concrete or grapefruit.) It's our turn now
 to puzzle the unborn. No world
wears as well as it should but, mortal or not,
 a world has still to be built
because of what we can see from our windows,
 that Immortal Commonwealth
which is there regardless: it's in perfect taste
 and it's never boring but
it won't quite do. Among its populations
 are masons and carpenters
who build the most exquisite shelters and safes,
 but no architects, any more
than there are heretics or bounders: to take
 umbrage at death, to construct
a second nature of tomb and temple, lives
 must know the meaning of *If*.

POSTSCRIPT

Some thirty inches from my nose
The frontier of my Person goes,
And all the untilled air between
Is private *pagus* or demesne.
Stranger, unless with bedroom eyes
I beckon you to fraternise,
Beware of rudely crossing it:
I have no gun, but I can spit.

Recitative by Death

Ladies and gentlemen, you have made most remarkable
   Progress, and progress, I agree, is a boon;
You have built more automobiles than are parkable,
   Crashed the sound-barrier, and may very soon
   Be setting up juke-boxes on the Moon:
But I beg to remind you that, despite all that,
I, Death, still am and will always be Cosmocrat.

Still I sport with the young and daring; at my whim,
   The climber steps upon the rotten boulder,
The undertow catches boys as they swim,
   The speeder steers onto the slippery shoulder:
   With others I wait until they are older
Before assigning, according to my humor,
To one a coronary, to one a tumor.

Liberal my views upon religion and race;
   Tax-posture, credit-rating, social ambition
Cut no ice with me. We shall meet face to face,
   Despite the drugs and lies of your physician,
   The costly euphemisms of the mortician:
Westchester matron and Bowery bum,
Both shall dance with me when I rattle my drum.

Et in Arcadia Ego

Who, now, seeing Her so
Happily married,
Housewife, helpmate to Man,

Can imagine the screeching
Virago, the Amazon,
Earth-Mother was?

Her jungle-growths
Are abated, Her exorbitant
Monsters abashed,

Her soil mumbled,
Where crops, aligned precisely,
Will soon be orient:

Levant or couchant,
Well-daunted thoroughbreds
Graze on mead and pasture,

A church-clock sub-divides the day,
Up the lane at sundown
Geese podge home.

As for Him:
What has happened to the Brute
Epics and nightmares tell of?

No bishops pursue
Their archdeacons with axes,
In the crumbling lair

Of a robber baron
Sightseers picnic
Who carry no daggers.

I well might think myself
A humanist
Could I manage not to see

How the autobahn
Thwarts the landscape
In godless Roman arrogance,

The farmer's children
Tip-toe past the shed
Where the gelding-knife is kept.

Since

On a mid-December day,
frying sausages
for myself, I abruptly
felt under fingers
thirty years younger the rim
of a steering-wheel,
on my cheek the parching wind
of an August noon,
as passenger beside me
You as then you were.

Slap across a veg-growing
alluvial plain
we raced in clouds of white dust,
and geese fled screaming
as we missed them by inches,
making a bee-line
for mountains gradually
enlarging eastward,
joyfully certain nightfall
would occasion joy.

It did. In a flagged kitchen
we were served broiled trout
and a rank cheese: for a while
we talked by the fire,
then, carrying candles, climbed
steep stairs. Love was made
then and there: so halcyoned,
soon we fell asleep
to the sound of a river
swabbling through a gorge.

Since then, other enchantments
have blazed and faded,
enemies changed their address,
and War made ugly
an uncountable number
of unknown neighbors,
precious as us to themselves:
but round your image
there is no fog, and the Earth
can still astonish.

Of what, then, should I complain,
pottering about
a neat suburban kitchen?
Solitude? Rubbish!
It's social enough with real
faces and landscapes
for whose friendly countenance
I at least can learn
to live with obesity
and a little fame.

River Profile

Our body is a moulded river – NOVALIS

Out of a bellicose fore-time, thundering
head-on collisions of cloud and rock in an
up-thrust, crevasse-and-avalanche, troll country,
deadly to breathers,

it whelms into our picture below the melt-line,
where tarns lie frore under frowning cirques, goat-bell,
wind-breaker, fishing-rod, miner's-lamp country,
already at ease with

the mien and gestures that become its kindness,
in streams, still anonymous, still jumpable,
flows as it should through any declining country
in probing spirals.

Soon of a size to be named and the cause of
dirty in-fighting among rival agencies,
down a steep stair, penstock-and-turbine country,
it plunges ram-stam,

to foam through a wriggling gorge incised in softer
strata, hemmed between crags that nauntle heaven,
robber-baron, tow-rope, portage-way country,
nightmare of merchants.

Disemboguing from foothills, now in hushed meanders,
now in riffling braids, it vaunts across a senile
plain, well-entered, chateau-and-cider-press country,
its regal progress

gallanted for a while by quibbling poplars,
then by chimneys: led off to cool and launder
retort, steam-hammer, gasometer country,
it changes color.

Polluted, bridged by girders, banked by concrete,
now it bisects a polyglot metropolis,
ticker-tape, taxi, brothel, foot-lights country,
à-la-mode always.

Broadening or burrowing to the moon's phases,
turbid with pulverised wastemantle, on through
flatter, duller, hotter, cotton-gin country
it scours, approaching

the tidal mark where it puts off majesty,
disintegrates, and through swamps of a delta,
punting-pole, fowling-piece, oyster-tongs country,
wearies to its final

act of surrender, effacement, atonement
in a huge amorphous aggregate no cuddled
attractive child ever dreams of, non-country,
image of death as

a spherical drew-drop of life. Unlovely
monsters, our tales believe, can be translated
too, even as water, the selfless mother
of all especials.

A Mosaic for Marianne Moore

(on the occasion of her eightieth birthday, November 15th, 1967)

The concluded gardens of personal liking
are enchanted habitats
where real toads may catch imaginary flies
and the climate will accommodate the tiger
and the polar-bear.

So in the middle of yours (where it is human
to sit) we see you sitting
in a wide-brimmed hat beneath a monkey-puzzle,
at your feet the beasts you animated for us
by thinking of them.

Your lion with ferocious chrysanthemum head,
your jerboa, erect on
his Chippendale claw, your pelican behaving
like charred paper, your musk-ox who smells of water,
your fond nautilus,

cope with what surprises them and greet the stranger
in a mid-western accent,
even that bum, the unelephantine creature
who is certainly here to worship and often
selected to mourn.

Egocentric, eccentric, he will name a cat
Peter, a new car *Edsel*,
emphasise his own birthday and a few others
he thinks deserve it, as to-day we stress your name,
Miss Marianne Moore

who, fastidious but fair, are unaffronted
by those whose disposition
it is to affront, who beg the cobra's pardon,
are always on time and never would yourself write
error with four *r*'s.

For poems, dolphin-graceful as carts from Sweden,
our thank-you should be a right
good salvo of barks: it's much too muffled to say
'how well and with what unfreckled integrity
it has all been done.'

August 1968

The Ogre does what ogres can,
Deeds quite impossible for Man,
But one prize is beyond his reach,
The Ogre cannot master Speech.
About a subjugated plain,
Among its desperate and slain,
The Ogre stalks with hands on hips,
While drivel gushes from his lips.

Pseudo-Questions

Who could possibly approve of Metternich
and his Thought Police? Yet in a liberal
milieu would Adalbert Stifter have written
his noble idylls?

Vice-versa, what God-fearing Magistrate
would dream of shaking hands with a financial
crook and Anti-Semite? Yet Richard Wagner
wrought masterpieces.

Wild horses could not drag me to debates on
Art and Society: critics with credos,
Christian or Marxist, should keep their trap shut,
lest they spout nonsense.

The Aliens

(for William Gray)

Wide though the interrupt be that divides us, runers and
counters,
from the Old World of the Plants, all lapped in a tolerant
silence,
where, by the grace of chlorophyll, few of them ever have
taken
life and not one put a sceptical question, we nod them as
neighbours
who, to conclude from their friendly response to a gardener's
handling,
like to be given the chance to get more than a self-education.
As for the hot-blooded Beasts, we didn't need Darwin to tell
us
horses and rabbits and mice are our cognates, the double-
voiced song-birds
cousins, however removed: unique as we seem, we, too, are
shovelled out into the cold, poodle-naked, as male or as
female,
grab at and gobble up proteins, drop dung, perform the
ungainly
brute-with-two-backs until, dared and doddered by age, we
surrender,
lapse into stagnant stuff, while they by retaining a constant
visible shape through a lifetime, accord with our human idea
of
having a Self. They also, we cannot but fancy, are peering
at a horizon as we do, aware of, however obscurely,
more than they must be concerned with, and vaguely elated
at being
someone who's up and about: yes, even their humblest have,
surely,
nosed a few steps on the hazardous foreright to courage,

utterance, joy and collateral love. That is why, in our folk-
tales,
toads and squirrels can talk, in our epics the great be
compared to
lions or foxes or eagles.
But between us and the Insects,
namely nine-tenths of the living, there grins a prohibitive
fracture
empathy cannot transgress: (What Saint made a friend of a
roach or
preached to an ant-hill?) Unrosed by a shame, unendorsed
by a sorrow,
blank to a fear of failure, they daunt alike the believer's
faith in a fatherly providence and the atheist's dogma of
purely
random events. To begin as a crawling insatiable eater,
then to be buried and mortify, then to emerge from the cere-
cloth
winged and mateable, brilliantly coloured, a sipper of juices,
yet a compulsive hunter and hoarder, must do havoc to any
unitive sense. To insert them, excuse those unamiable towns
where
sex is reserved for the Few and the many animate tool-kits
perish from overwear, one is tempted to cook up a Gnostic
myth of an earlier Fall, preceding by aeons the Reptiles:
Adam, a crab-like creature who'd just wriggled out of a
steamy
ocean where he had failed at making a living and now lay
moribund, choked, on a shore without song. Unto whom the
Seducer,
not our romantic Satan but a clever cartesian Archon,
coaxingly thus: *Not doing very well, are you, poor deathling,*
no, and unlikely to do any better, thanks to the schemes of
We-Know-Whom. (He's a Precious but logic was never His
forte.)
Freedom may manage in Heaven with Incorporeals, but for

ghosted extended matter the consequence is to be doomed to
err where an error is mortal. But trust me and live, for I do
know
clearly what needs to be done. If I programme your ganglia for
you,
you shall inherit the earth.
Such a myth, we all know, is no
answer.
What they mean to themselves or to God is a meaningless
question:
they to us are quite simply what we must never become.

Short Ode to the Cuckoo

No one now imagines you answer idle questions
– *How long shall I live? How long remain single?*
Will butter be cheaper? – nor does your shout make
husbands uneasy.

Compared with arias by the great performers
such as the merle, your two-note act is kid-stuff:
our most hardened crooks are sincerely shocked by
your nesting habits.

Science, Aesthetics, Ethics, may huff and puff but they
cannot extinguish your magic: you marvel
the commuter as you wondered the savage.
Hence, in my diary,

where I normally enter nothing but social
engagements and, lately, the death of friends, I
scribble year after year when I first hear you,
of a holy moment.

Aubade

(In Memoriam Eugen Rosenstock-Huessy)

Beckoned anew to a World
where wishes alter nothing,
expelled from the padded cell
of Sleep and re-admitted
to involved Humanity,
again, as wrote Augustine,
I know that I am and will,
I am willing and knowing,
I will to be and to know,
facing in four directions,
outwards and inwards in Space,
observing and reflecting,
backwards and forwards through Time,
recalling and forecasting.

Out there, to the Heart, there are
no dehumanised Objects,
each one has its Proper Name,
there is no Neuter Gender:
Flowers fame their splendid shades,
Trees are proud of their posture,
Stones are delighted to lie
just where they are. Few bodies
comprehend, though, an order,
few can obey or rebel,
so, when they must be managed,
Love is no help: We must opt
to eye them as mere Others,
must count, weigh, measure, compel.

Within a Place, not of Names
but of Personal Pronouns,
where I hold council with Me

and recognise as present
Thou and Thou comprising We,
unmindful of the meinie,
all those We think of as They.
No voice is raised in quarrel,
but quietly We converse,
by turns relate tall stories,
at times just sit in silence,
and on fit occasion I
sing verses *sotto-voce*,
made on behalf of Us all.

But Time, the domain of Deeds,
calls for a complex Grammar
with many Moods and Tenses,
and prime the Imperative.
We are free to choose our paths
but choose We must, no matter
where they lead, and the tales We
tell of the Past must be true.
Human Time is a City
where each inhabitant has
a political duty
nobody else can perform,
made cogent by Her Motto:
Listen, Mortals, Lest Ye Die.

Address to the Beasts

For us who, from the moment
we first are worlded,
lapse into disarray,

who seldom know exactly
what we are up to,
and, as a rule, don't want to,

what a joy to know,
even when we can't see or hear you,
that you are around,

though very few of you
find us worth looking at,
unless we come too close.

To you all scents are sacred
except our smell and those
we manufacture.

How promptly and ably
you execute Nature's policies,
and are never

lured into misconduct
except by some unlucky
chance imprinting.

Endowed from birth with good manners,
you wag no snobbish elbows,
don't leer,

don't look down your nostrils,
nor poke them into another
creature's business.

Your own habitations
are cosy and private, not
pretentious temples.

Of course, you have to take lives
to keep your own, but never
kill for applause.

Compared with even your greediest,
how Non-U
our hunting gentry seem.

Exempt from taxation,
you have never felt the need
to become literate,

but your oral cultures
have inspired our poets to pen
dulcet verses,

and, though unconscious of God
your Sung Eucharists are
more hallowed than ours.

Instinct is commonly said
to rule you: I would call it
Common Sense.

If you cannot engender
a genius like Mozart,
neither can you

plague the earth
with brilliant sillies like Hegel
or clever nasties like Hobbes.

Shall we ever become adulted,
as you all soon do?
It seems unlikely.

Indeed, one balmy day,
we might well become
not fossils, but vapour.

Distinct now,
in the end we shall join you
(how soon all corpses look alike),

but you exhibit no signs
of knowing that you are sentenced.
Now, could that be why

we upstarts are often
jealous of your innocence,
but never envious?

No, Plato, No

I can't imagine anything
   that I would less like to be
than a disincarnate Spirit,
   unable to chew or sip
or make contact with surfaces
   or breathe the scents of summer
or comprehend speech and music
   or gaze at what lies beyond.
No, God has placed me exactly
   where I'd have chosen to be:
the sub-lunar world is such fun,
   where Man is male or female
and gives Proper Names to all things.

   I can, however, conceive
that the organs Nature gave Me,
   my ductless glands, for instance,
slaving twenty-four hours a day
   with no show of resentment
to gratify Me, their Master,
   and keep Me in decent shape,
(not that I give them their orders,
   I wouldn't know what to yell),
dream of another existence
   than that they have known so far:
yes, it well could be that my Flesh
   is praying for 'Him' to die,
so setting Her free to become
   irresponsible Matter.

SYLVIA PLATH Poems selected by TED HUGHES

SYLVIA PLATH

Poems selected by TED HUGHES

faber and faber

First published in 1985
by Faber and Faber Limited
3 Queen Square London WC1N 3AU
This edition first published in 2000

Photoset by Parker Typesetting Service, Leicester
Printed in Italy

All rights reserved

© The Estate of Sylvia Plath, 1960, 1965, 1971, 1981, 1985

This book is sold subject to the condition that it shall not, by way of trade or otherwise, be lent, resold, hired out or otherwise circulated without the publisher's prior consent in any form of binding or cover other than that in which it is published and without a similar condition including this condition being imposed on the subsequent purchaser

A CIP record for this book
is available from the British Library
ISBN 0–571–20358-2

10 9 8 7 6 5 4 3 2 1

Contents

Publisher's Note

The poems in this selection are arranged in chronological order of composition rather than of publication. For all of the poems apart from 'Miss Drake Proceeds to Supper' (1956) and 'Resolve' (1956), which have been published in *Sylvia Plath: Collected Poems*, dates of composition and the collections in which they originally appeared are given below.

The Colossus (London, 1960; New York, 1962): 'Spinster' (1956), 'Maudlin' (1956), 'Night Shift' (1957), 'Full Fathom Five' (1958), 'Suicide off Egg Rock' (1959), 'The Hermit at Outermost House' (1959), 'Medallion' (1959), 'The Manor Garden' (1959), 'The Stones' (1959), 'The Burnt-Out Spa' (1959)

Ariel (London and New York, 1965): 'You're' (1960), 'Morning Song' (1961), 'Tulips' (1961), 'The Moon and the Yew Tree' (1961), 'Little Fugue' (1962), 'Elm' (1962), 'Poppies in July' (1962), 'A Birthday Present' (1962), 'The Bee Meeting' (1962), 'Daddy' (1962), 'Cut' (1962), 'Ariel' (1962), 'Poppies in October' (1962), 'Nick and the Candlestick' (1962), 'Letter in November' (1962), 'Death & Co.' (1962), 'Sheep in Fog' (1963), 'The Munich Mannequins' (1963), 'Words' (1963), 'Edge' (1963)

Crossing the Water (London and New York, 1971): 'Face Lift' (1961), 'Insomniac' (1961), 'Wuthering Heights' (1961), 'Finisterre' (1961), 'Mirror' (1961), 'The Babysitters' (1961), 'An Appearance' (1962), 'Crossing the Water' (1962), 'Among the Narcissi' (1962)

Winter Trees (London, 1971; New York, 1972): 'Lesbos' (1962), 'By Candlelight' (1962), 'Mary's Song' (1962), 'Winter Trees' (1962)

SYLVIA PLATH

Miss Drake Proceeds to Supper

No novice
In those elaborate rituals
Which allay the malice
Of knotted table and crooked chair,
The new woman in the ward
Wears purple, steps carefully
Among her secret combinations of eggshells
And breakable humming birds,
Footing sallow as a mouse
Between the cabbage-roses
Which are slowly opening their furred petals
To devour and drag her down
Into the carpet's design.

With bird-quick eye cocked askew
She can see in the nick of time
How perilous needles grain the floorboards
And outwit their brambled plan;
Now through her ambushed air,
Adazzle with bright shards
Of broken glass,
She edges with wary breath,
Fending off jag and tooth,
Until, turning sideways,
She lifts one webbed foot after the other
Into the still, sultry weather
Of the patients' dining room.

Spinster

Now this particular girl
During a ceremonious April walk
With her latest suitor
Found herself, of a sudden, intolerably struck
By the birds' irregular babel
And the leaves' litter.

By this tumult afflicted, she
Observed her lover's gestures unbalance the air,
His gait stray uneven
Through a rank wilderness of fern and flower.
She judged petals in disarray,
The whole season, sloven.

How she longed for winter then! –
Scrupulously austere in its order
Of white and black
Ice and rock, each sentiment within border,
And heart's frosty discipline
Exact as a snowflake.

But here – a burgeoning
Unruly enough to pitch her five queenly wits
Into vulgar motley –
A treason not to be borne. Let idiots
Reel giddy in bedlam spring:
She withdrew neatly.

And round her house she set
Such a barricade of barb and check
Against mutinous weather
As no mere insurgent man could hope to break
With curse, fist, threat
Or love, either.

Maudlin

Mud-mattressed under the sign of the hag
In a clench of blood, the sleep-talking virgin
Gibbets with her curse the moon's man,
Faggot-bearing Jack in his crackless egg:

Hatched with a claret hogshead to swig
He kings it, navel-knit to no groan,
But at the price of a pin-stitched skin
Fish-tailed girls purchase each white leg.

Resolve

Day of mist: day of tarnish

with hands
unserviceable, I wait
for the milk van

the one-eared cat
laps its gray paw

and the coal fire burns

outside, the little hedge leaves are
become quite yellow
a milk-film blurs
the empty bottles on the windowsill

no glory descends

two water drops poise
on the arched green
stem of my neighbor's rose bush

o bent bow of thorns

the cat unsheathes its claws
the world turns

today
today I will not
disenchant my twelve black-gowned examiners
or bunch my fist
in the wind's sneer.

Night Shift

It was not a heart, beating,
That muted boom, that clangor
Far off, not blood in the ears
Drumming up any fever

To impose on the evening.
The noise came from outside:
A metal detonating
Native, evidently, to

These stilled suburbs: nobody
Startled at it, though the sound
Shook the ground with its pounding.
It took root at my coming

Till the thudding source, exposed,
Confounded inept guesswork:
Framed in windows of Main Street's
Silver factory, immense

Hammers hoisted, wheels turning,
Stalled, let fall their vertical
Tonnage of metal and wood;
Stunned the marrow. Men in white

Undershirts circled, tending
Without stop those greased machines,
Tending, without stop, the blunt
Indefatigable fact.

Full Fathom Five

Old man, you surface seldom.
Then you come in with the tide's coming
When seas wash cold, foam-

Capped: white hair, white beard, far-flung,
A dragnet, rising, falling, as waves
Crest and trough. Miles long

Extend the radial sheaves
Of your spread hair, in which wrinkling skeins
Knotted, caught, survives

The old myth of origins
Unimaginable. You float near
As keeled ice-mountains

Of the north, to be steered clear
Of, not fathomed. All obscurity
Starts with a danger:

Your dangers are many. I
Cannot look much but your form suffers
Some strange injury

And seems to die: so vapors
Ravel to clearness on the dawn sea.
The muddy rumors

Of your burial move me
To half-believe: your reappearance
Proves rumors shallow,

For the archaic trenched lines
Of your grained face shed time in runnels:
Ages beat like rains

On the unbeaten channels
Of the ocean. Such sage humor and
Durance are whirlpools

To make away with the ground-
Work of the earth and the sky's ridgepole.
Waist down, you may wind

One labyrinthine tangle
To root deep among knuckles, shinbones,
Skulls. Inscrutable,

Below shoulders not once
Seen by any man who kept his head,
You defy questions;

You defy other godhood.
I walk dry on your kingdom's border
Exiled to no good.

Your shelled bed I remember.
Father, this thick air is murderous.
I would breathe water.

Suicide off Egg Rock

Behind him the hotdogs split and drizzled
On the public grills, and the ochreous salt flats,
Gas tanks, factory stacks – that landscape
Of imperfections his bowels were part of –
Rippled and pulsed in the glassy updraught.
Sun struck the water like a damnation.
No pit of shadow to crawl into,
And his blood beating the old tattoo
I am, I am, I am. Children
Were squealing where combers broke and the spindrift
Raveled wind-ripped from the crest of the wave.
A mongrel working his legs to a gallop
Hustled a gull flock to flap off the sandspit.

He smoldered, as if stone-deaf, blindfold,
His body beached with the sea's garbage,
A machine to breathe and beat forever.
Flies filing in through a dead skate's eyehole
Buzzed and assailed the vaulted brainchamber.
The words in his book wormed off the pages.
Everything glittered like blank paper.

Everything shrank in the sun's corrosive
Ray but Egg Rock on the blue wastage.
He heard when he walked into the water.

The forgetful surf creaming on those ledges.

The Hermit at Outermost House

Sky and sea, horizon-hinged
Tablets of blank blue, couldn't,
Clapped shut, flatten this man out.

The great gods, Stone-Head, Claw-Foot,
Winded by much rock-bumping
And claw-threat, realized that.

For what, then, had they endured
Dourly the long hots and colds,
Those old despots, if he sat

Laugh-shaken on his doorsill,
Backbone unbendable as
Timbers of his upright hut?

Hard gods were there, nothing else.
Still he thumbed out something else.
Thumbed no stony, horny pot,

But a certain meaning green.
He withstood them, that hermit.
Rock-face, crab-claw verged on green.

Gulls mulled in the greenest light.

Medallion

By the gate with star and moon
Worked into the peeled orange wood
The bronze snake lay in the sun

Inert as a shoelace; dead
But pliable still, his jaw
Unhinged and his grin crooked,

Tongue a rose-colored arrow.
Over my hand I hung him.
His little vermilion eye

Ignited with a glassed flame
As I turned him in the light;
When I split a rock one time

The garnet bits burned like that.
Dust dulled his back to ochre
The way sun ruins a trout.

Yet his belly kept its fire
Going under the chainmail,
The old jewels smoldering there

In each opaque belly-scale:
Sunset looked at through milk glass.
And I saw white maggots coil

Thin as pins in the dark bruise
Where his innards bulged as if
He were digesting a mouse.

Knifelike, he was chaste enough,
Pure death's-metal. The yardman's
Flung brick perfected his laugh.

The Manor Garden

The fountains are dry and the roses over.
Incense of death. Your day approaches.
The pears fatten like little buddhas.
A blue mist is dragging the lake.

You move through the era of fishes,
The smug centuries of the pig –
Head, toe and finger
Come clear of the shadow. History

Nourishes these broken flutings,
These crowns of acanthus,
And the crow settles her garments.
You inherit white heather, a bee's wing,

Two suicides, the family wolves,
Hours of blankness. Some hard stars
Already yellow the heavens.
The spider on its own string

Crosses the lake. The worms
Quit their usual habitations.
The small birds converge, converge
With their gifts to a difficult borning.

The Stones

This is the city where men are mended.
I lie on a great anvil.
The flat blue sky-circle

Flew off like the hat of a doll
When I fell out of the light. I entered
The stomach of indifference, the wordless cupboard.

The mother of pestles diminished me.
I became a still pebble.
The stones of the belly were peaceable,

The head-stone quiet, jostled by nothing.
Only the mouth-hole piped out,
Importunate cricket

In a quarry of silences.
The people of the city heard it.
They hunted the stones, taciturn and separate,

The mouth-hole crying their locations.
Drunk as a foetus
I suck at the paps of darkness.

The food tubes embrace me. Sponges kiss my lichens away.
The jewelmaster drives his chisel to pry
Open one stone eye.

This is the after-hell: I see the light.
A wind unstoppers the chamber
Of the ear, old worrier.

Water mollifies the flint lip,
And daylight lays its sameness on the wall.
The grafters are cheerful,

Heating the pincers, hoisting the delicate hammers.
A current agitates the wires
Volt upon volt. Catgut stitches my fissures.

A workman walks by carrying a pink torso.
The storerooms are full of hearts.
This is the city of spare parts.

My swaddled legs and arms smell sweet as rubber.
Here they can doctor heads, or any limb.
On Fridays the little children come

To trade their hooks for hands.
Dead men leave eyes for others.
Love is the uniform of my bald nurse.

Love is the bone and sinew of my curse.
The vase, reconstructed, houses
The elusive rose.

Ten fingers shape a bowl for shadows.
My mendings itch. There is nothing to do.
I shall be good as new.

The Burnt-Out Spa

An old beast ended in this place:

A monster of wood and rusty teeth.
Fire smelted his eyes to lumps
Of pale blue vitreous stuff, opaque
As resin drops oozed from pine bark.

The rafters and struts of his body wear
Their char of karakul still. I can't tell
How long his carcass has foundered under
The rubbish of summers, the black-leaved falls.

Now little weeds insinuate
Soft suede tongues between his bones.
His armorplate, his toppled stones
Are an esplanade for crickets.

I pick and pry like a doctor or
Archaeologist among
Iron entrails, enamel bowls,
The coils and pipes that made him run.

The small dell eats what ate it once.
And yet the ichor of the spring
Proceeds clear as it ever did
From the broken throat, the marshy lip.

It flows off below the green and white
Balustrade of a sag-backed bridge.
Leaning over, I encounter one
Blue and improbable person

Framed in a basketwork of cat-tails.
O she is gracious and austere,
Seated beneath the toneless water!
It is not I, it is not I.

No animal spoils on her green doorstep.
And we shall never enter there
Where the durable ones keep house.
The stream that hustles us

Neither nourishes nor heals.

You're

Clownlike, happiest on your hands,
Feet to the stars, and moon-skulled,
Gilled like a fish. A common-sense
Thumbs-down on the dodo's mode.
Wrapped up in yourself like a spool,
Trawling your dark as owls do.
Mute as a turnip from the Fourth
Of July to All Fools' Day,
O high-riser, my little loaf.

Vague as fog and looked for like mail.
Farther off than Australia.
Bent-backed Atlas, our traveled prawn.
Snug as a bud and at home
Like a sprat in a pickle jug.
A creel of eels, all ripples.
Jumpy as a Mexican bean.
Right, like a well-done sum.
A clean slate, with your own face on.

Face Lift

You bring me good news from the clinic,
Whipping off your silk scarf, exhibiting the tight white
Mummy-cloths, smiling: I'm all right.
When I was nine, a lime-green anesthetist
Fed me banana gas through a frog-mask. The nauseous vault
Boomed with bad dreams and the Jovian voices of surgeons.
Then mother swam up, holding a tin basin.
O I was sick.

They've changed all that. Traveling
Nude as Cleopatra in my well-boiled hospital shift,
Fizzy with sedatives and unusually humorous,
I roll to an anteroom where a kind man
Fists my fingers for me. He makes me feel something precious
Is leaking from the finger-vents. At the count of two
Darkness wipes me out like chalk on a blackboard . . .
I don't know a thing.

For five days I lie in secret,
Tapped like a cask, the years draining into my pillow.
Even my best friend thinks I'm in the country.
Skin doesn't have roots, it peels away easy as paper.
When I grin, the stitches tauten. I grow backward. I'm twenty,
Broody and in long skirts on my first husband's sofa, my fingers
Buried in the lambswool of the dead poodle;
I hadn't a cat yet.

Now she's done for, the dewlapped lady
I watched settle, line by line, in my mirror –
Old sock-face, sagged on a darning egg.
They've trapped her in some laboratory jar.

Let her die there, or wither incessantly for the next fifty years,
Nodding and rocking and fingering her thin hair.
Mother to myself, I wake swaddled in gauze,
Pink and smooth as a baby.

Morning Song

Love set you going like a fat gold watch.
The midwife slapped your footsoles, and your bald cry
Took its place among the elements.

Our voices echo, magnifying your arrival. New statue.
In a drafty museum, your nakedness
Shadows our safety. We stand round blankly as walls.

I'm no more your mother
Than the cloud that distills a mirror to reflect its own slow
Effacement at the wind's hand.

All night your moth-breath
Flickers among the flat pink roses. I wake to listen:
A far sea moves in my ear.

One cry, and I stumble from bed, cow-heavy and floral
In my Victorian nightgown.
Your mouth opens clean as a cat's. The window square

Whitens and swallows its dull stars. And now you try
Your handful of notes;
The clear vowels rise like balloons.

Tulips

The tulips are too excitable, it is winter here.
Look how white everything is, how quiet, how snowed-in.
I am learning peacefulness, lying by myself quietly
As the light lies on these white walls, this bed, these hands.
I am nobody; I have nothing to do with explosions.
I have given my name and my day-clothes up to the nurses
And my history to the anesthetist and my body to surgeons.

They have propped my head between the pillow and the
  sheet-cuff
Like an eye between two white lids that will not shut.
Stupid pupil, it has to take everything in.
The nurses pass and pass, they are no trouble,
They pass the way gulls pass inland in their white caps,
Doing things with their hands, one just the same as another,
So it is impossible to tell how many there are.

My body is a pebble to them, they tend it as water
Tends to the pebbles it must run over, smoothing them
  gently.
They bring me numbness in their bright needles, they bring
  me sleep.
Now I have lost myself I am sick of baggage –
My patent leather overnight case like a black pillbox,
My husband and child smiling out of the family photo;
Their smiles catch onto my skin, little smiling hooks.

I have let things slip, a thirty-year-old cargo boat
Stubbornly hanging on to my name and address.
They have swabbed me clear of my loving associations.
Scared and bare on the green plastic-pillowed trolley
I watched my teaset, my bureaus of linen, my books
Sink out of sight, and the water went over my head.
I am a nun now, I have never been so pure.

I didn't want any flowers, I only wanted
To lie with my hands turned up and be utterly empty.
How free it is, you have no idea how free –
The peacefulness is so big it dazes you,
And it asks nothing, a name tag, a few trinkets.
It is what the dead close on, finally; I imagine them
Shutting their mouths on it, like a Communion tablet.

The tulips are too red in the first place, they hurt me.
Even through the gift paper I could hear them breathe
Lightly, through their white swaddlings, like an awful baby.
Their redness talks to my wound, it corresponds.
They are subtle: they seem to float, though they weigh me
  down,
Upsetting me with their sudden tongues and their color,
A dozen red lead sinkers round my neck.

Nobody watched me before, now I am watched.
The tulips turn to me, and the window behind me
Where once a day the light slowly widens and slowly thins,
And I see myself, flat, ridiculous, a cut-paper shadow
Between the eye of the sun and the eyes of the tulips,
And I have no face, I have wanted to efface myself.
The vivid tulips eat my oxygen.

Before they came the air was calm enough,
Coming and going, breath by breath, without any fuss.
Then the tulips filled it up like a loud noise.
Now the air snags and eddies round them the way a river
Snags and eddies round a sunken rust-red engine.
They concentrate my attention, that was happy
Playing and resting without committing itself.

The walls, also, seem to be warming themselves.
The tulips should be behind bars like dangerous animals;
They are opening like the mouth of some great African cat,
And I am aware of my heart: it opens and closes

Its bowl of red blooms out of sheer love of me.
The water I taste is warm and salt, like the sea,
And comes from a country far away as health.

Insomniac

The night sky is only a sort of carbon paper,
Blueblack, with the much-poked periods of stars
Letting in the light, peephole after peephole –
A bonewhite light, like death, behind all things.
Under the eyes of the stars and the moon's rictus
He suffers his desert pillow, sleeplessness
Stretching its fine, irritating sand in all directions.

Over and over the old, granular movie
Exposes embarrassments – the mizzling days
Of childhood and adolescence, sticky with dreams,
Parental faces on tall stalks, alternately stern and tearful,
A garden of buggy roses that made him cry.
His forehead is bumpy as a sack of rocks.
Memories jostle each other for face-room like obsolete film
  stars.

He is immune to pills: red, purple, blue –
How they lit the tedium of the protracted evening!
Those sugary planets whose influence won for him
A life baptized in no-life for a while,
And the sweet, drugged waking of a forgetful baby.
Now the pills are worn-out and silly, like classical gods.
Their poppy-sleepy colors do him no good.

His head is a little interior of gray mirrors.
Each gesture flees immediately down an alley
Of diminishing perspectives, and its significance
Drains like water out the hole at the far end.
He lives without privacy in a lidless room,
The bald slots of his eyes stiffened wide-open
On the incessant heat-lightning flicker of situations.

Nightlong, in the granite yard, invisible cats
Have been howling like women, or damaged instruments.

Already he can feel daylight, his white disease,
Creeping up with her hatful of trivial repetitions.
The city is a map of cheerful twitters now,
And everywhere people, eyes mica-silver and blank,
Are riding to work in rows, as if recently brainwashed.

Wuthering Heights

The horizons ring me like faggots,
Tilted and disparate, and always unstable.
Touched by a match, they might warm me,
And their fine lines singe
The air to orange
Before the distances they pin evaporate,
Weighting the pale sky with a solider color.
But they only dissolve and dissolve
Like a series of promises, as I step forward.

There is no life higher than the grasstops
Or the hearts of sheep, and the wind
Pours by like destiny, bending
Everything in one direction.
I can feel it trying
To funnel my heat away.
If I pay the roots of the heather
Too close attention, they will invite me
To whiten my bones among them.

The sheep know where they are,
Browsing in their dirty wool-clouds,
Gray as the weather.
The black slots of their pupils take me in.
It is like being mailed into space,
A thin, silly message.
They stand about in grandmotherly disguise,
All wig curls and yellow teeth
And hard, marbly baas.

I come to wheel ruts, and water
Limpid as the solitudes
That flee through my fingers.
Hollow doorsteps go from grass to grass;

Lintel and sill have unhinged themselves.
Of people the air only
Remembers a few odd syllables.
It rehearses them moaningly:
Black stone, black stone.

The sky leans on me, me, the one upright
Among all horizontals.
The grass is beating its head distractedly.
It is too delicate
For a life in such company;
Darkness terrifies it.
Now, in valleys narrow
And black as purses, the house lights
Gleam like small change.

Finisterre

This was the land's end: the last fingers, knuckled and
  rheumatic,
Cramped on nothing. Black
Admonitory cliffs, and the sea exploding
With no bottom, or anything on the other side of it,
Whitened by the faces of the drowned.
Now it is only gloomy, a dump of rocks –
Leftover soldiers from old, messy wars.
The sea cannons into their ear, but they don't budge.
Other rocks hide their grudges under the water.

The cliffs are edged with trefoils, stars and bells
Such as fingers might embroider, close to death,
Almost too small for the mists to bother with.
The mists are part of the ancient paraphernalia –
Souls, rolled in the doom-noise of the sea.
They bruise the rocks out of existence, then resurrect them.
They go up without hope, like sighs.
I walk among them, and they stuff my mouth with cotton.
When they free me, I am beaded with tears.

Our Lady of the Shipwrecked is striding toward the horizon,
Her marble skirts blown back in two pink wings.
A marble sailor kneels at her foot distractedly, and at his foot
A peasant woman in black
Is praying to the monument of the sailor praying.
Our Lady of the Shipwrecked is three times life size,
Her lips sweet with divinity.
She does not hear what the sailor or the peasant is saying –
She is in love with the beautiful formlessness of the sea.

Gull-colored laces flap in the sea drafts
Beside the postcard stalls.
The peasants anchor them with conches. One is told:

'These are the pretty trinkets the sea hides,
Little shells made up into necklaces and toy ladies.
They do not come from the Bay of the Dead down there,
But from another place, tropical and blue,
We have never been to.
These are our crêpes. Eat them before they blow cold.'

The Moon and the Yew Tree

This is the light of the mind, cold and planetary.
The trees of the mind are black. The light is blue.
The grasses unload their griefs on my feet as if I were God,
Prickling my ankles and murmuring of their humility.
Fumy, spiritous mists inhabit this place
Separated from my house by a row of headstones.
I simply cannot see where there is to get to.

The moon is no door. It is a face in its own right,
White as a knuckle and terribly upset.
It drags the sea after it like a dark crime; it is quiet
With the O-gape of complete despair. I live here.
Twice on Sunday, the bells startle the sky –
Eight great tongues affirming the Resurrection.
At the end, they soberly bong out their names.

The yew tree points up. It has a Gothic shape.
The eyes lift after it and find the moon.
The moon is my mother. She is not sweet like Mary.
Her blue garments unloose small bats and owls.
How I would like to believe in tenderness –
The face of the effigy, gentled by candles,
Bending, on me in particular, its mild eyes.

I have fallen a long way. Clouds are flowering
Blue and mystical over the face of the stars.
Inside the church, the saints will be all blue,
Floating on their delicate feet over the cold pews,
Their hands and faces stiff with holiness.
The moon sees nothing of this. She is bald and wild.
And the message of the yew tree is blackness – blackness and
silence.

Mirror

I am silver and exact. I have no preconceptions.
Whatever I see I swallow immediately
Just as it is, unmisted by love or dislike.
I am not cruel, only truthful –
The eye of a little god, four-cornered.
Most of the time I meditate on the opposite wall.
It is pink, with speckles. I have looked at it so long
I think it is a part of my heart. But it flickers.
Faces and darkness separate us over and over.

Now I am a lake. A woman bends over me,
Searching my reaches for what she really is.
Then she turns to those liars, the candles or the moon.
I see her back, and reflect it faithfully.
She rewards me with tears and an agitation of hands.
I am important to her. She comes and goes.
Each morning it is her face that replaces the darkness.
In me she has drowned a young girl, and in me an old
  woman
Rises toward her day after day, like a terrible fish.

The Babysitters

It is ten years, now, since we rowed to Children's Island.
The sun flamed straight down that noon on the water off
  Marblehead.
That summer we wore black glasses to hide our eyes.
We were always crying, in our spare rooms, little put-upon
  sisters,
In the two huge, white, handsome houses in Swampscott.
When the sweetheart from England appeared, with her
  cream skin and Yardley cosmetics,
I had to sleep in the same room with the baby on a too-short
  cot,
And the seven-year-old wouldn't go out unless his jersey
  stripes
Matched the stripes of his socks.

O it was richness! – eleven rooms and a yacht
With a polished mahogany stair to let into the water
And a cabin boy who could decorate cakes in six-colored
  frosting.
But I didn't know how to cook, and babies depressed me.
Nights, I wrote in my diary spitefully, my fingers red
With triangular scorch marks from ironing tiny ruchings and
  puffed sleeves.
When the sporty wife and her doctor husband went on one
  of their cruises
They left me a borrowed maid named Ellen, 'for protection',
And a small Dalmatian.

In your house, the main house, you were better off.
You had a rose garden and a guest cottage and a model
  apothecary shop
And a cook and a maid, and knew about the key to the
  bourbon.
I remember you playing 'Ja Da' in a pink piqué dress

On the gameroom piano, when the 'big people' were out,
And the maid smoked and shot pool under a green-shaded
lamp.
The cook had one wall eye and couldn't sleep, she was so
nervous.
On trial, from Ireland, she burned batch after batch of
cookies
Till she was fired.

O what has come over us, my sister!
On that day-off the two of us cried so hard to get
We lifted a sugared ham and a pineapple from the grownups'
icebox
And rented an old green boat. I rowed. You read
Aloud, crosslegged on the stern seat, from the *Generation of
Vipers*.
So we bobbed out to the island. It was deserted –
A gallery of creaking porches and still interiors,
Stopped and awful as a photograph of somebody laughing,
But ten years dead.

The bold gulls dove as if they owned it all.
We picked up sticks of driftwood and beat them off,
Then stepped down the steep beach shelf and into the water.
We kicked and talked. The thick salt kept us up.
I see us floating there yet, inseparable – two cork dolls.
What keyhole have we slipped through, what door has shut?
The shadows of the grasses inched round like hands of a
clock,
And from our opposite continents we wave and call.
Everything has happened.

Little Fugue

The yew's black fingers wag;
Cold clouds go over.
So the deaf and dumb
Signal the blind, and are ignored.

I like black statements.
The featurelessness of that cloud, now!
White as an eye all over!
The eye of the blind pianist

At my table on the ship.
He felt for his food.
His fingers had the noses of weasels.
I couldn't stop looking.

He could hear Beethoven:
Black yew, white cloud,
The horrific complications.
Finger-traps – a tumult of keys.

Empty and silly as plates,
So the blind smile.
I envy the big noises,
The yew hedge of the Grosse Fuge.

Deafness is something else.
Such a dark funnel, my father!
I see your voice
Black and leafy, as in my childhood,

A yew hedge of orders,
Gothic and barbarous, pure German.
Dead men cry from it.
I am guilty of nothing.

The yew my Christ, then.
Is it not as tortured?
And you, during the Great War
In the California delicatessen

Lopping the sausages!
They color my sleep,
Red, mottled, like cut necks.
There was a silence!

Great silence of another order.
I was seven, I knew nothing.
The world occurred.
You had one leg, and a Prussian mind.

Now similar clouds
Are spreading their vacuous sheets.
Do you say nothing?
I am lame in the memory.

I remember a blue eye,
A briefcase of tangerines.
This was a man, then!
Death opened, like a black tree, blackly.

I survive the while,
Arranging my morning.
These are my fingers, this my baby.
The clouds are a marriage dress, of that pallor.

An Appearance

The smile of iceboxes annihilates me.
Such blue currents in the veins of my loved one!
I hear her great heart purr.

From her lips ampersands and percent signs
Exit like kisses.
It is Monday in her mind: morals

Launder and present themselves.
What am I to make of these contradictions?
I wear white cuffs, I bow.

Is this love then, this red material
Issuing from the steel needle that flies so blindingly?
It will make little dresses and coats,

It will cover a dynasty.
How her body opens and shuts –
A Swiss watch, jeweled in the hinges!

O heart, such disorganization!
The stars are flashing like terrible numerals.
ABC, her eyelids say.

Crossing the Water

Black lake, black boat, two black, cut-paper people.
Where do the black trees go that drink here?
Their shadows must cover Canada.

A little light is filtering from the water flowers.
Their leaves do not wish us to hurry:
They are round and flat and full of dark advice.

Cold worlds shake from the oar.
The spirit of blackness is in us, it is in the fishes.
A snag is lifting a valedictory, pale hand;

Stars open among the lilies.
Are you not blinded by such expressionless sirens?
This is the silence of astounded souls.

Among the Narcissi

Spry, wry, and gray as these March sticks,
Percy bows, in his blue peajacket, among the narcissi.
He is recuperating from something on the lung.

The narcissi, too, are bowing to some big thing:
It rattles their stars on the green hill where Percy
Nurses the hardship of his stitches, and walks and walks.

There is a dignity to this; there is a formality –
The flowers vivid as bandages, and the man mending.
They bow and stand: they suffer such attacks!

And the octogenarian loves the little flocks.
He is quite blue; the terrible wind tries his breathing.
The narcissi look up like children, quickly and whitely.

Elm

for Ruth Fainlight

I know the bottom, she says. I know it with my great tap root:

It is what you fear.
I do not fear it: I have been there.

Is it the sea you hear in me,
Its dissatisfactions?
Or the voice of nothing, that was your madness?

Love is a shadow.
How you lie and cry after it
Listen: these are its hooves: it has gone off, like a horse.

All night I shall gallop thus, impetuously,
Till your head is a stone, your pillow a little turf,
Echoing, echoing.

Or shall I bring you the sound of poisons?
This is rain now, this big hush.
And this is the fruit of it: tin-white, like arsenic.

I have suffered the atrocity of sunsets.
Scorched to the root
My red filaments burn and stand, a hand of wires.

Now I break up in pieces that fly about like clubs.
A wind of such violence
Will tolerate no bystanding: I must shriek.

The moon, also, is merciless: she would drag me
Cruelly, being barren.
Her radiance scathes me. Or perhaps I have caught her.

I let her go. I let her go
Diminished and flat, as after radical surgery.
How your bad dreams possess and endow me.

I am inhabited by a cry.
Nightly it flaps out
Looking, with its hooks, for something to love.

I am terrified by this dark thing
That sleeps in me;
All day I feel its soft, feathery turnings, its malignity.

Clouds pass and disperse.
Are those the faces of love, those pale irretrievables?
Is it for such I agitate my heart?

I am incapable of more knowledge.
What is this, this face
So murderous in its strangle of branches? –

Its snaky acids kiss.
It petrifies the will. These are the isolate, slow faults
That kill, that kill, that kill.

Poppies in July

Little poppies, little hell flames,
Do you do no harm?

You flicker. I cannot touch you.
I put my hands among the flames. Nothing burns.

And it exhausts me to watch you
Flickering like that, wrinkly and clear red, like the skin of a mouth.

A mouth just bloodied.
Little bloody skirts!

There are fumes that I cannot touch.
Where are your opiates, your nauseous capsules?

If I could bleed, or sleep! –
If my mouth could marry a hurt like that!

Or your liquors seep to me, in this glass capsule,
Dulling and stilling.

But colorless. Colorless.

A Birthday Present

What is this, behind this veil, is it ugly, is it beautiful?
It is shimmering, has it breasts, has it edges?

I am sure it is unique, I am sure it is just what I want.
When I am quiet at my cooking I feel it looking, I feel it
thinking

'Is this the one I am to appear for,
Is this the elect one, the one with black eye-pits and a scar?

Measuring the flour, cutting off the surplus,
Adhering to rules, to rules, to rules.

Is this the one for the annunciation?
My god, what a laugh!'

But it shimmers, it does not stop, and I think it wants me.
I would not mind if it was bones, or a pearl button.

I do not want much of a present, anyway, this year.
After all I am alive only by accident.

I would have killed myself gladly that time any possible way.
Now there are these veils, shimmering like curtains,

The diaphanous satins of a January window
White as babies' bedding and glittering with dead breath. O
ivory!

It must be a tusk there, a ghost-column.
Can you not see I do not mind what it is.

Can you not give it to me?
Do not be ashamed – I do not mind if it is small.

Do not be mean, I am ready for enormity.
Let us sit down to it, one on either side, admiring the gleam,

The glaze, the mirrory variety of it.
Let us eat our last supper at it, like a hospital plate.

I know why you will not give it to me,
You are terrified

The world will go up in a shriek, and your head with it,
Bossed, brazen, an antique shield,

A marvel to your great-grandchildren.
Do not be afraid, it is not so.

I will only take it and go aside quietly.
You will not even hear me opening it, no paper crackle,

No falling ribbons, no scream at the end.
I do not think you credit me with this discretion.

If you only knew how the veils were killing my days.
To you they are only transparencies, clear air.

But my god, the clouds are like cotton.
Armies of them. They are carbon monoxide.

Sweetly, sweetly I breathe in,
Filling my veins with invisibles, with the million

Probable motes that tick the years off my life.
You are silver-suited for the occasion. O adding machine –

Is it impossible for you to let something go and have it go whole?
Must you stamp each piece in purple,

Must you kill what you can?
There is this one thing I want today, and only you can give it to me.

It stands at my window, big as the sky.
It breathes from my sheets, the cold dead center

Where spilt lives congeal and stiffen to history.
Let it not come by the mail, finger by finger.

Let it not come by word of mouth, I should be sixty
By the time the whole of it was delivered, and too numb to
  use it.

Only let down the veil, the veil, the veil.
If it were death

I would admire the deep gravity of it, its timeless eyes.
I would know you were serious.

There would be a nobility then, there would be a birthday.
And the knife not carve, but enter

Pure and clean as the cry of a baby,
And the universe slide from my side.

The Bee Meeting

Who are these people at the bridge to meet me? They are the villagers –
The rector, the midwife, the sexton, the agent for bees.
In my sleeveless summery dress I have no protection,
And they are all gloved and covered, why did nobody tell me?
They are smiling and taking out veils tacked to ancient hats.

I am nude as a chicken neck, does nobody love me?
Yes, here is the secretary of bees with her white shop smock,
Buttoning the cuffs at my wrists and the slit from my neck to my knees.
Now I am milkweed silk, the bees will not notice.
They will not smell my fear, my fear, my fear.

Which is the rector now, is it that man in black?
Which is the midwife, is that her blue coat?
Everybody is nodding a square black head, they are knights in visors,
Breastplates of cheesecloth knotted under the armpits.
Their smiles and their voices are changing. I am led through a beanfield.

Strips of tinfoil winking like people,
Feather dusters fanning their hands in a sea of bean flowers,
Creamy bean flowers with black eyes and leaves like bored hearts.
Is it blood clots the tendrils are dragging up that string?
No, no, it is scarlet flowers that will one day be edible.

Now they are giving me a fashionable white straw Italian hat
And a black veil that molds to my face, they are making me one of them.
They are leading me to the shorn grove, the circle of hives.
Is it the hawthorn that smells so sick?
The barren body of hawthorn, etherizing its children.

Is it some operation that is taking place?
It is the surgeon my neighbors are waiting for,
This apparition in a green helmet,
Shining gloves and white suit.
Is it the butcher, the grocer, the postman, someone I know?

I cannot run, I am rooted, and the gorse hurts me
With its yellow purses, its spiky armory.
I could not run without having to run forever.
The white hive is snug as a virgin,
Sealing off her brood cells, her honey, and quietly humming.

Smoke rolls and scarves in the grove.
The mind of the hive thinks this is the end of everything.
Here they come, the outriders, on their hysterical elastics.
If I stand very still, they will think I am cow-parsley,
A gullible head untouched by their animosity,

Not even nodding, a personage in a hedgerow.
The villagers open the chambers, they are hunting the queen.
Is she hiding, is she eating honey? She is very clever.
She is old, old, old, she must live another year, and she knows it.
While in their fingerjoint cells the new virgins

Dream of a duel they will win inevitably,
A curtain of wax dividing them from the bride flight,
The upflight of the murderess into a heaven that loves her.
The villagers are moving the virgins, there will be no killing.
The old queen does not show herself, is she so ungrateful?

I am exhausted, I am exhausted –
Pillar of white in a blackout of knives.
I am the magician's girl who does not flinch.
The villagers are untying their disguises, they are shaking hands.
Whose is that long white box in the grove, what have they accomplished, why am I cold.

Daddy

You do not do, you do not do
Any more, black shoe
In which I have lived like a foot
For thirty years, poor and white,
Barely daring to breathe or Achoo.

Daddy, I have had to kill you.
You died before I had time –
Marble-heavy, a bag full of God,
Ghastly statue with one gray toe
Big as a Frisco seal

And a head in the freakish Atlantic
Where it pours bean green over blue
In the waters off beautiful Nauset.
I used to pray to recover you.
Ach, du.

In the German tongue, in the Polish town
Scraped flat by the roller
Of wars, wars, wars.
But the name of the town is common.
My Polack friend

Says there are a dozen or two.
So I never could tell where you
Put your foot, your root,
I never could talk to you.
The tongue stuck in my jaw.

It stuck in a barb wire snare.
Ich, ich, ich, ich,
I could hardly speak.
I thought every German was you.
And the language obscene

An engine, an engine
Chuffing me off like a Jew.
A Jew to Dachau, Auschwitz, Belsen.
I began to talk like a Jew.
I think I may well be a Jew.

The snows of the Tyrol, the clear beer of Vienna
Are not very pure or true.
With my gipsy ancestress and my weird luck
And my Taroc pack and my Taroc pack
I may be a bit of a Jew.

I have always been scared of *you*,
With your Luftwaffe, your gobbledygoo.
And your neat mustache
And your Aryan eye, bright blue.
Panzer-man, panzer-man, O You –

Not God but a swastika
So black no sky could squeak through.
Every woman adores a Fascist,
The boot in the face, the brute
Brute heart of a brute like you.

You stand at the blackboard, daddy,
In the picture I have of you,
A cleft in your chin instead of your foot
But no less a devil for that, no not
Any less the black man who

Bit my pretty red heart in two.
I was ten when they buried you.
At twenty I tried to die
And get back, back, back to you.
I thought even the bones would do.

But they pulled me out of the sack,
And they stuck me together with glue.
And then I knew what to do.

I made a model of you,
A man in black with a Meinkampf look

And a love of the rack and the screw.
And I said I do, I do.
So daddy, I'm finally through.
The black telephone's off at the root,
The voices just can't worm through.

If I've killed one man, I've killed two –
The vampire who said he was you
And drank my blood for a year,
Seven years, if you want to know.
Daddy, you can lie back now.

There's a stake in your fat black heart
And the villagers never liked you.
They are dancing and stamping on you.
They always *knew* it was you.
Daddy, daddy, you bastard, I'm through.

Lesbos

Viciousness in the kitchen!
The potatoes hiss.
It is all Hollywood, windowless,
The fluorescent light wincing on and off like a terrible
  migraine,
Coy paper strips for doors –
Stage curtains, a widow's frizz.
And I, love, am a pathological liar,
And my child – look at her, face down on the floor,
Little unstrung puppet, kicking to disappear –
Why she is schizophrenic,
Her face red and white, a panic,
You have stuck her kittens outside your window
In a sort of cement well
Where they crap and puke and cry and she can't hear.
You say you can't stand her,
The bastard's a girl.
You who have blown your tubes like a bad radio
Clear of voices and history, the staticky
Noise of the new.
You say I should drown the kittens. Their smell!
You say I should drown my girl.
She'll cut her throat at ten if she's mad at two.
The baby smiles, fat snail,
From the polished lozenges of orange linoleum.
You could eat him. He's a boy.
You say your husband is just no good to you.
His Jew-Mama guards his sweet sex like a pearl.
You have one baby, I have two.
I should sit on a rock off Cornwall and comb my hair.
I should wear tiger pants, I should have an affair.
We should meet in another life, we should meet in air,
Me and you.

Meanwhile there's a stink of fat and baby crap.
I'm doped and thick from my last sleeping pill.
The smog of cooking, the smog of hell.
Floats our heads, two venomous opposites,
Our bones, our hair.
I call you Orphan, orphan. You are ill.
The sun gives you ulcers, the wind gives you T.B.
Once you were beautiful.
In New York, in Hollywood, the men said: 'Through?
Gee baby, you are rare.'
You acted, acted, acted for the thrill.
The impotent husband slumps out for a coffee.
I try to keep him in,
An old pole for the lightning,
The acid baths, the skyfuls off of you.
He lumps it down the plastic cobbled hill,
Flogged trolley. The sparks are blue.
The blue sparks spill,
Splitting like quartz into a million bits.
O jewel! O valuable!
That night the moon
Dragged its blood bag, sick
Animal
Up over the harbor lights.
And then grew normal,
Hard and apart and white.
The scale-sheen on the sand scared me to death.
We kept picking up handfuls, loving it,
Working it like dough, a mulatto body,
The silk grits.
A dog picked up your doggy husband. He went on.

Now I am silent, hate
Up to my neck,
Thick, thick.
I do not speak.

I am packing the hard potatoes like good clothes,
I am packing the babies,
I am packing the sick cats.
O vase of acid,
It is love you are full of. You know who you hate.
He is hugging his ball and chain down by the gate
That opens to the sea
Where it drives in, white and black,
Then spews it back.
Every day you fill him with soul-stuff, like a pitcher.
You are so exhausted.
Your voice my ear-ring,
Flapping and sucking, blood-loving bat.
That is that. That is that.
You peer from the door,
Sad hag, 'Every woman's a whore.
I can't communicate.'

I see your cute décor
Close on you like the fist of a baby
Or an anemone, that sea
Sweetheart, that kleptomaniac.
I am still raw.
I say I may be back.
You know what lies are for.

Even in your Zen heaven we shan't meet.

Cut

for Susan O'Neill Roe

What a thrill –
My thumb instead of an onion.
The top quite gone
Except for a sort of a hinge

Of skin,
A flap like a hat,
Dead white.
Then that red plush.

Little pilgrim,
The Indian's axed your scalp.
Your turkey wattle
Carpet rolls

Straight from the heart.
I step on it,
Clutching my bottle
Of pink fizz.

A celebration, this is.
Out of a gap
A million soldiers run,
Redcoats, every one.

Whose side are they on?
O my
Homunculus, I am ill.
I have taken a pill to kill

The thin
Papery feeling.
Saboteur,
Kamikaze man –

The stain on your
Gauze Ku Klux Klan
Babushka
Darkens and tarnishes and when

The balled
Pulp of your heart
Confronts its small
Mill of silence

How you jump –
Trepanned veteran,
Dirty girl,
Thumb stump.

By Candlelight

This is winter, this is night, small love –
A sort of black horsehair,
A rough, dumb country stuff
Steeled with the sheen
Of what green stars can make it to our gate.
I hold you on my arm.
It is very late.
The dull bells tongue the hour.
The mirror floats us at one candle power.

This is the fluid in which we meet each other,
This haloey radiance that seems to breathe
And lets our shadows wither
Only to blow
Them huge again, violent giants on the wall.
One match scratch makes you real.
At first the candle will not bloom at all –
It snuffs its bud
To almost nothing, to a dull blue dud.

I hold my breath until you creak to life,
Balled hedgehog,
Small and cross. The yellow knife
Grows tall. You clutch your bars.
My singing makes you roar.
I rock you like a boat
Across the Indian carpet, the cold floor,
While the brass man
Kneels, back bent, as best he can

Hefting his white pillar with the light
That keeps the sky at bay,
The sack of black! It is everywhere, tight, tight!
He is yours, the little brassy Atlas –

Poor heirloom, all you have,
At his heels a pile of five brass cannonballs,
No child, no wife.
Five balls! Five bright brass balls!
To juggle with, my love, when the sky falls.

Ariel

Stasis in darkness.
Then the substanceless blue
Pour of tor and distances.

God's lioness,
How one we grow,
Pivot of heels and knees! – The furrow

Splits and passes, sister to
The brown arc
Of the neck I cannot catch,

Nigger-eye
Berries cast dark
Hooks –

Black sweet blood mouthfuls,
Shadows.
Something else

Hauls me through air –
Thighs, hair;
Flakes from my heels.

White
Godiva, I unpeel –
Dead hands, dead stringencies.

And now I
Foam to wheat, a glitter of seas.
The child's cry

Melts in the wall.
And I
Am the arrow,

The dew that flies
Suicidal, at one with the drive
Into the red

Eye, the cauldron of morning.

Poppies in October

Even the sun-clouds this morning cannot manage such
  skirts.
Nor the woman in the ambulance
Whose red heart blooms through her coat so astoundingly –

A gift, a love gift
Utterly unasked for
By a sky

Palely and flamily
Igniting its carbon monoxides, by eyes
Dulled to a halt under bowlers.

O my God, what am I
That these late mouths should cry open
In a forest of frost, in a dawn of cornflowers.

Nick and the Candlestick

I am a miner. The light burns blue.
Waxy stalactites
Drip and thicken, tears

The earthen womb
Exudes from its dead boredom.
Black bat airs

Wrap me, raggy shawls,
Cold homicides.
They weld to me like plums.

Old cave of calcium
Icicles, old echoer.
Even the newts are white,

Those holy Joes.
And the fish, the fish –
Christ! they are panes of ice,

A vice of knives,
A piranha
Religion, drinking

Its first communion out of my live toes.
The candle
Gulps and recovers its small altitude,

Its yellows hearten.
O love, how did you get here?
O embryo

Remembering, even in sleep,
Your crossed position.
The blood blooms clean

In you, ruby.
The pain
You wake to is not yours.

Love, love,
I have hung our cave with roses,
With soft rugs –

The last of Victoriana.
Let the stars
Plummet to their dark address,

Let the mercuric
Atoms that cripple drip
Into the terrible well,

You are the one
Solid the spaces lean on, envious.
You are the baby in the barn.

Letter in November

Love, the world
Suddenly turns, turns color. The streetlight
Splits through the rat's-tail
Pods of the laburnum at nine in the morning.
It is the Arctic,

This little black
Circle, with its tawn silk grasses – babies' hair.
There is a green in the air,
Soft, delectable.
It cushions me lovingly.

I am flushed and warm.
I think I may be enormous,
I am so stupidly happy,
My wellingtons
Squelching and squelching through the beautiful red.

This is my property.
Two times a day
I pace it, sniffing
The barbarous holly with its viridian
Scallops, pure iron,

And the wall of old corpses.
I love them.
I love them like history.
The apples are golden,
Imagine it –

My seventy trees
Holding their gold-ruddy balls
In a thick gray death-soup,
Their million
Gold leaves metal and breathless.

O love, O celibate.
Nobody but me
Walks the waist-high wet.
The irreplaceable
Golds bleed and deepen, the mouths of Thermopylae.

Death & Co.

Two, of course there are two.
It seems perfectly natural now –
The one who never looks up, whose eyes are lidded
And balled, like Blake's,
Who exhibits

The birthmarks that are his trademark –
The scald scar of water,
The nude
Verdigris of the condor.
I am red meat. His beak

Claps sidewise: I am not his yet.
He tells me how badly I photograph.
He tells me how sweet
The babies look in their hospital
Icebox, a simple

Frill at the neck,
Then the flutings of their Ionian
Death-gowns,
Then two little feet.
He does not smile or smoke.

The other does that,
His hair long and plausive.
Bastard
Masturbating a glitter,
He wants to be loved.

I do not stir.
The frost makes a flower,
The dew makes a star,
The dead bell,
The dead bell.

Somebody's done for.

Mary's Song

The Sunday lamb cracks in its fat.
The fat
Sacrifices its opacity . . .

A window, holy gold.
The fire makes it precious,
The same fire

Melting the tallow heretics,
Ousting the Jews.
Their thick palls float

Over the cicatrix of Poland, burnt-out
Germany.
They do not die.

Gray birds obsess my heart,
Mouth-ash, ash of eye.
They settle. On the high

Precipice
That emptied one man into space
The ovens glowed like heavens, incandescent.

It is a heart,
This holocaust I walk in,
O golden child the world will kill and eat.

Winter Trees

The wet dawn inks are doing their blue dissolve.
On their blotter of fog the trees
Seem a botanical drawing –
Memories growing, ring on ring,
A series of weddings.

Knowing neither abortions nor bitchery,
Truer than women,
They seed so effortlessly!
Tasting the winds, that are footless,
Waist-deep in history –

Full of wings, otherworldliness.
In this, they are Ledas.
O mother of leaves and sweetness
Who are these pietàs?
The shadows of ringdoves chanting, but easing nothing.

Sheep in Fog

The hills step off into whiteness.
People or stars
Regard me sadly, I disappoint them.

The train leaves a line of breath.
O slow
Horse the color of rust,

Hooves, dolorous bells –
All morning the
Morning has been blackening,

A flower left out.
My bones hold a stillness, the far
Fields melt my heart.

They threaten
To let me through to a heaven
Starless and fatherless, a dark water.

The Munich Mannequins

Perfection is terrible, it cannot have children.
Cold as snow breath, it tamps the womb

Where the yew trees blow like hydras,
The tree of life and the tree of life

Unloosing their moons, month after month, to no purpose.
The blood flood is the flood of love,

The absolute sacrifice.
It means: no more idols but me,

Me and you.
So, in their sulfur loveliness, in their smiles

These mannequins lean tonight
In Munich, morgue between Paris and Rome,

Naked and bald in their furs,
Orange lollies on silver sticks,

Intolerable, without mind.
The snow drops its pieces of darkness,

Nobody's about. In the hotels
Hands will be opening doors and setting

Down shoes for a polish of carbon
Into which broad toes will go tomorrow.

O the domesticity of these windows,
The baby lace, the green-leaved confectionery,

The thick Germans slumbering in their bottomless Stolz.
And the black phones on hooks

Glittering
Glittering and digesting

Voicelessness. The snow has no voice.

Words

Axes
After whose stroke the wood rings,
And the echoes!
Echoes traveling
Off from the center like horses.

The sap
Wells like tears, like the
Water striving
To re-establish its mirror
Over the rock

That drops and turns,
A white skull,
Eaten by weedy greens.
Years later I
Encounter them on the road –

Words dry and riderless,
The indefatigable hoof-taps.
While
From the bottom of the pool, fixed stars
Govern a life.

Edge

The woman is perfected.
Her dead

Body wears the smile of accomplishment,
The illusion of a Greek necessity

Flows in the scrolls of her toga,
Her bare

Feet seem to be saying:
We have come so far, it is over.

Each dead child coiled, a white serpent,
One at each little

Pitcher of milk, now empty.
She has folded

Them back into her body as petals
Of a rose close when the garden

Stiffens and odors bleed
From the sweet, deep throats of the night flower.

The moon has nothing to be sad about,
Staring from her hood of bone.

She is used to this sort of thing.
Her blacks crackle and drag.

TED HUGHES Poems selected by SIMON ARMITAGE

TED HUGHES

Poems selected by

SIMON ARMITAGE

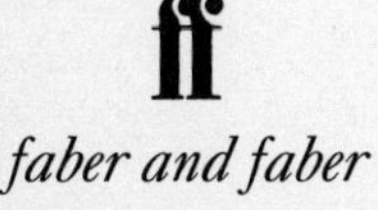
faber and faber

First published in 2000
by Faber and Faber Limited
3 Queen Square London WC1N 3AU

Photoset by Parker Typesetting Service, Leicester
Printed in Italy

All rights reserved

Introduction and selection © Simon Armitage, 2000
Poems © The Estate of Ted Hughes, 1995, 1997

Simon Armitage is hereby identified as editor of
this work in accordance with Section 77
of the Copyright, Designs and Patents Act 1988

This book is sold subject to the condition that it shall not, by way of trade or otherwise, be lent, resold, hired out or otherwise circulated without the publisher's prior consent in any form of binding or cover other than that in which it is published and without a similar condition including this condition being imposed on the subsequent purchaser

A CIP record for this book
is available from the British Library
ISBN 0-571-20363-9

10 9 8 7 6 5 4 3 2 1

Contents

Introduction

Putting together and publishing a selection of Ted Hughes's poetry today is a very different task than it would have been twenty years ago. When Hughes died in 1998, he was as valued and admired as at any time in his career, and his two final collections, *Tales from Ovid* and *Birthday Letters*, had met with resounding acclaim. In that respect alone, the task of assembling this book comes with all sorts of extra frisson and significance.

During the seventies and eighties, however, to speak up on behalf of Hughes, whether as a reader or writer, was to take a position. To support Hughes's poetry was to support the man himself, a man whose ideologies could have been described as unfashionable, and whose poetic style was seen by some as stubborn and entrenched. Hughes himself had become increasingly private and his poetry seemed to be in hiding with him. The criticisms over his role in the death of his first wife, Sylvia Plath, had reached fever pitch, especially in the United States, and even those with little or no knowledge of his poetry were quick to offer an opinion of it. For many, he represented the antithesis of contemporary ideology and modern political thought. His acceptance of the Laureateship in 1984 and his well-documented interest in hunting, shooting and fishing were easily caricatured. In that era, to be seen promoting the work of the man could have been construed as an act of defiance almost, rather than the act of celebration it is today. How quickly and how strangely situations turn about.

Possibly the tide will turn again, but Hughes's poetry has reached a new high-water mark in recent years. *Birthday Letters* is now one of the biggest-selling poetry titles of all time, with sales climbing towards the half-a-million mark. Its readership might well include a substantial number of ghouls, voyeurs and gossips with a less than literary interest in

Hughes's candid descriptions of his relationship with Plath – the white heat of their time together and her subsequent suicide – and the book also contains details of a second relationship which ended in still greater tragedy. But it is the quality of the writing that brought *Birthday Letters* such recognition, a quality of extraordinariness that for many of Hughes's supporters has been present throughout. It is worth noting that aside from the steady, sometimes obligatory admiration of his contemporaries, interest in Hughes's work has been renewed and revitalized by a younger generation of writers, many of whom have talked about the importance and influence of his poetry. The swag-bag of prizes and plaudits that Hughes carried off for those last two publications – pretty much a clean sweep of the board in the case of *Birthday Letters* – owed much to a new wave of poets, keen to make public an affiliation they had felt for years. It was a case of poets having their say, poetry putting its own house in order. Once that had happened, the ingrained polarity of the media seemed to reverse overnight, and suddenly it was acceptable for ordinary people to be seen in public places reading a book of poetry – and one written by Ted Hughes at that.

But if editing this volume is a thrill, there is also a sense of trepidation and responsibility associated with the project. Throughout his life, Hughes practised (quite rightly) a strict control over his work, being extremely careful as to its context, its presentation, and its timing. Poems were kept on a tight leash, invitations to read were very often declined, launch-dates were calculated by means of star-charts and zodiacal coincidences. For a writer of Hughes's stature, there are surprisingly few critical books on the market; those which do exist are engrossing and distinctive, for the main part, but have not come from the usual sources or been written by the usual suspects. (The number of available discourses on Plath makes an interesting comparison.) With Hughes no longer around to shepherd his poetry, that situation will surely change, and no doubt his death-knell will sound to some like a starting-pistol, triggering several unauthorized biographies. Some may be with us sooner than we like; biographers, like obituary writers, have a tendency to jump the gun, and don't always wait for the death before getting stuck into the life. We can only hope that any such books do proper justice to their subject.

Perhaps there has been a sense, within the world of writing and further afield, that Ted Hughes was not a man to be messed with, and therefore that his poetry wasn't something to be messed with either. It is an image at odds with the supportive, generous and enigmatic person that many found him to be, but an image that persisted nevertheless, possibly as an extension of his subject matter and poetic style. As far as I am aware, there are no previous selections of his work in which Hughes didn't have either complete control or at least a meaningful, supervisory presence, a presence which I still feel, and one that I need to respect. Hughes's *New Selected Poems* was published just three years before his death. Some writers, in their later life, have attempted a kind of self-revisionism that borders on the insane, making final, definitive selections of their work that have mystified and antagonized scholars and readers. Hughes, however, was as sharp as ever and possibly at his shrewdest during his later years, as the timing of *Birthday Letters* demonstrates, and there is every reason to trust in the final judgement he made concerning the poems he believed to be most successful. It is not the purpose of this volume to revise that judgement, but simply to further refine it into a more concentrated form, and to add a small amount of catalytic material into the equation. Ideally, I would have liked to have included pieces from some of Hughes's theatre works, and at least one short story, probably 'The Deadfall'. But for the moment there is a greater pressure to concentrate on the poems, and hopefully readers will be persuaded to investigate other dimensions of his work, just as Hughes himself investigated the boundaries of his talent through explorations into drama and prose.

Even when out of favour with the opinion-makers, Hughes still attracted the kind of attention that most poets would kill for, and every move he made was guaranteed a certain amount of notice, from serious reviews of his books, to journalists standing on the graveyard wall adjoining his house to take photographs through the windows. In fact, right from the appearance of his first book, *The Hawk in the Rain*, he was famous. Hughes was onto something that set him apart from his contemporaries. His concerns with animal instincts, ancient lore and the manifestations of nature were at variance with the sociological preoccupation of fellow poets, and his language – a sort of agricultural dialect of the Bible – was a far cry from the up-to-the-minute vocabularies of his peers. His interest in European poetry was undoubtedly helpful in the shaping and development of his voice, especially in *Crow*, where Hughes was at his most robust, uncompromising and apocalyptic.

Interestingly, though, and despite the complex philosophical subjects of his work, it was in the classrooms of Britain where Hughes's poetry found much of its loyal audience. My own experience as an uninspired and uninspiring secondary school student is one shared by many of the same age group, in the way that Hughes's poems were the first captivating moments in English literature, and were read and described by teachers who could not hide their enthusiasm for the work or their eagerness to share it. Poems like 'Wind', 'The Bull Moses', 'The Horses' and of course 'Hawk Roosting' are not only fastened in the imagination of a whole generation, but for some, like myself, were a kind of Rosetta Stone – the means by which the surrounding world could suddenly be translated, understood, and experienced. It is a particular virtue of Hughes's poetry, and one that he shares with only the very best poets, that clarity and complexity can exist simultaneously, like clear, still water, into which a person can see to a ponderous depth. No one could ever accuse Hughes of simplicity or superficiality, and yet his poems have an immediacy that students, even of a young age, find alluring and true. They draw the reader in, like black holes, whose event-horizons are instant, but whose intensities are infinite and utterly absorbing. His Noah-like cataloguing of the animal kingdom is of course a further lure to younger readers. Hughes was a determined educationalist; his book *Poetry in the Making*, taken from programmes written for the Schools' Broadcasting Department, is a valuable text for poets of any age, would-be or established, and his books for children represent a sizeable proportion of his output. As a follower of his work, I find it impossible not to see this as strategic, rather than accidental or sentimental, and part of Hughes's ambition to enter the world of intuition, innocence, and possibility.

I have come a long way in this introduction without, except for the scattering of adjectives, describing the work. Possibly the poems speak for themselves by now and need no further explanation, possibly an overview of Hughes's writing through his dozens of books is beyond the scope of this commentary, or possibly the detailing of poetic intent and achievement can only lead to a narrowing of interpretation rather than the ever-expanding experience that poetry should provide. In any case, such is the range of Hughes's poetry that a partial synopsis would not serve it well. His profound interest in history and prehistory, his arguments as to the monarchistic structure of the human imagination, his take on nature, his almost obsessional fixation with the First World War, his observations as to the sexual-courtship practised by poets through their work, are just a few of the interwoven and tangled threads. They need teasing out carefully, with due process.

But one theme which is worth enlarging on is the issue of Hughes's fascination with the supernatural and the paranormal. From an early age, Hughes demonstrated an uncommon interest in all things other-worldly, an interest furthered by his choice of studies at university and his background reading. Anyone who spent any time with him will have experienced this at first hand; his conversations were full of the weird and wonderful, from poltergeists to pixies, from witchcraft to ouija boards, from astrology to apparitions, from dousing to divination, and so on. It would be easy to pass this off as so much hocus-pocus, serving no literary purpose other than providing reams of subject-matter and bumping up the poet's credentials as a latter-day witch-doctor. But Hughes wasn't someone who pursued interests casually or without reason, and his dabblings in the occult were, to him, nothing less than an essential part of his task. Hughes aligned himself with the ancient role of the poet. He looked even further than the metaphysical potential of poetry to a kind of writing that had the power to heal and transform, to change perceptions and to alter states. He saw beyond the power to communicate, aiming instead for a kind of 'contact', or sensual comprehension, where poem and reader took possession of each other through the medium of poetry, or through the poet as medium. And he saw language as one of the least understood powers in the universe, ranking alongside electrical, gravitational, atomic and magnetic energy as a force to be manipulated and controlled. His view of the poet as shaman was one he took seriously, and many of his poems are unembarrassed shamanic flights of fancy into the spirit-world, excursions to the 'other side', where he might properly inhabit the nature of his subject, be it animal, vegetable or mineral, be it jaguar, snowdrop or rocky crag. He had a clear vision of his duties, and one of those duties was to convince his audience. Hughes was well aware of the potency and authority of his speaking voice, not to mention his personality, and put these attributes to good use. It was all part of the job. People had to believe in him. The word magic these days might conjure up images of a man pulling rabbits from a top hat or producing cards from under his cuffs. But Hughes's magic was his writing. He made little black marks against clean white pages, marks that somehow detailed the absolute matter and manner of a bird or an eel or a foal or a wolf or a bear. At later dates and in distant locations, when we looked at those marks, when we read the poems, those creatures came to life. Out of nothing. Has any other magician ever pulled off a greater trick?

Hughes, for me, was the man from over the top of the hill, from the next Yorkshire valley, and his poems made me want to read. Later, it was homesickness that drew me back to his work, and by that time his poems were making me want to write. I think we shared a nostalgia for the same part of the world, even if that patch of the planet held a different significance for us.

The first time I saw him was on a school English trip to Hebden Bridge, where he read his poems in a moth-eaten cinema, sitting on a creaking wooden chair in front of a threadbare velvet curtain. Over the next twenty years I met him about a dozen times, in some very obscure circumstances and peculiar company. We had certain common interests, but our meetings were always lopsided, by definition, because one of my interests was him. On the last occasion, I sat and listened as he made his last recorded reading, the poems from *Tales from Ovid* that were taped at his home and broadcast on BBC Radio 4. Hughes lowered his head to the microphone, and like the storyteller he truly was, told the whole story, beginning to end, with barely a fluff. Those cassettes are now available to all, but for all their slick packaging and promotion, they have for me the quality of a rare bootleg. Anyone listening carefully will be able to hear not just Hughes's voice at its ghostly, intimate best, but also the sounds of the Devon landscape going on around him. At one point there's a tractor. A little later, church bells. And eventually, right on cue, a crow comes winging its way through the stereo, in one ear and out through the other. It's a compelling testament to the work of a poet whose great exploit was to bring the inner workings of the human brain out into the wide world, and at the same time draw the outside world into the mind.

Simon Armitage

TED HUGHES

The Thought-Fox

I imagine this midnight moment's forest:
Something else is alive
Beside the clock's loneliness
And this blank page where my fingers move.

Through the window I see no star:
Something more near
Though deeper within darkness
Is entering the loneliness:

Cold, delicately as the dark snow
A fox's nose touches twig, leaf;
Two eyes serve a movement, that now
And again now, and now, and now

Sets neat prints into the snow
Between trees, and warily a lame
Shadow lags by stump and in hollow
Of a body that is bold to come

Across clearings, an eye,
A widening deepening greenness,
Brilliantly, concentratedly,
Coming about its own business

Till, with a sudden sharp hot stink of fox
It enters the dark hole of the head.
The window is starless still; the clock ticks,
The page is printed.

The Jaguar

The apes yawn and adore their fleas in the sun.
The parrots shriek as if they were on fire, or strut
Like cheap tarts to attract the stroller with the nut.
Fatigued with indolence, tiger and lion

Lie still as the sun. The boa-constrictor's coil
Is a fossil. Cage after cage seems empty, or
Stinks of sleepers from the breathing straw.
It might be painted on a nursery wall.

But who runs like the rest past these arrives
At a cage where the crowd stands, stares, mesmerized,
As a child at a dream, at a jaguar hurrying enraged
Through prison darkness after the drills of his eyes

On a short fierce fuse. Not in boredom –
The eye satisfied to be blind in fire,
By the bang of blood in the brain deaf the ear –
He spins from the bars, but there's no cage to him

More than to the visionary his cell:
His stride is wildernesses of freedom:
The world rolls under the long thrust of his heel.
Over the cage floor the horizons come.

Famous Poet

Stare at the monster: remark
How difficult it is to define just what
Amounts to monstrosity in that
Very ordinary appearance. Neither thin nor fat,
Hair between light and dark,

And the general air
Of an apprentice – say, an apprentice house-
Painter amid an assembly of famous
Architects: the demeanour is of mouse,
Yet is he monster.

First scrutinize those eyes
For the spark, the effulgence: nothing. Nothing there
But the haggard stony exhaustion of a near-
Finished variety artist. He slumps in his chair
Like a badly hurt man, half life-size.

Is it his dreg-boozed inner demon
Still tankarding from tissue and follicle
The vital fire, the spirit electrical
That puts the gloss on a normal hearty male?
Or is it women?

The truth – bring it on
With black drapery, drums and funeral tread
Like a great man's coffin – no, no, he is not dead
But in this truth surely half-buried:
Once, the humiliation

Of youth and obscurity,
The autoclave of heady ambition trapped,
The fermenting of the yeasty heart stopped –
Burst with such pyrotechnics the dull world gaped
And 'Repeat that!' still they cry.

But all his efforts to concoct
The old heroic bang from their money and praise
From the parent's pointing finger and the child's amaze,
Even from the burning of his wreathed bays,
Have left him wrecked: wrecked,

And monstrous, so,
As a Stegosaurus, a lumbering obsolete
Arsenal of gigantic horn and plate
From a time when half the world still burned, set
To blink behind bars at the zoo.

The Horses

I climbed through woods in the hour-before-dawn dark.
Evil air, a frost-making stillness,

Not a leaf, not a bird, –
A world cast in frost. I came out above the wood

Where my breath left tortuous statues in the iron light.
But the valleys were draining the darkness

Till the moorline – blackening dregs of the brightening
grey –
Halved the sky ahead. And I saw the horses:

Huge in the dense grey – ten together –
Megalith-still. They breathed, making no move,

With draped manes and tilted hind-hooves,
Making no sound.

I passed: not one snorted or jerked its head.
Grey silent fragments

Of a grey silent world.

I listened in emptiness on the moor-ridge.
The curlew's tear turned its edge on the silence.

Slowly detail leafed from the darkness. Then the sun
Orange, red, red erupted.

Silently, and splitting to its core tore and flung cloud,
Shook the gulf open, showed blue,

And the big planets hanging –
I turned

Stumbling in the fever of a dream, down towards
The dark woods, from the kindling tops,

And came to the horses.
                                        There, still they stood,
But now steaming and glistening under the flow of light,

Their draped stone manes, their tilted hind-hooves
Stirring under a thaw while all around them

The frost showed its fires. But still they made no sound.
Not one snorted or stamped,

Their hung heads patient as the horizons
High over valleys, in the red levelling rays –

In din of the crowded streets, going among the years, the faces,
May I still meet my memory in so lonely a place

Between the streams and the red clouds, hearing curlews,
Hearing the horizons endure.

Wind

This house has been far out at sea all night,
The woods crashing through darkness, the booming hills,
Winds stampeding the fields under the window
Floundering black astride and blinding wet

Till day rose; then under an orange sky
The hills had new places, and wind wielded
Blade-light, luminous black and emerald,
Flexing like the lens of a mad eye.

At noon I scaled along the house-side as far as
The coal-house door. Once I looked up –
Through the brunt wind that dented the balls of my eyes
The tent of the hills drummed and strained its guyrope,

The fields quivering, the skyline a grimace,
At any second to bang and vanish with a flap:
The wind flung a magpie away and a black-
Back gull bent like an iron bar slowly. The house

Rang like some fine green goblet in the note
That any second would shatter it. Now deep
In chairs, in front of the great fire, we grip
Our hearts and cannot entertain book, thought,

Or each other. We watch the fire blazing,
And feel the roots of the house move, but sit on,
Seeing the window tremble to come in,
Hearing the stones cry out under the horizons.

October Dawn

October is marigold, and yet
A glass half full of wine left out

To the dark heaven all night, by dawn
Has dreamed a premonition

Of ice across its eye as if
The ice-age had begun its heave.

The lawn overtrodden and strewn
From the night before, and the whistling green

Shrubbery are doomed. Ice
Has got its spearhead into place.

First a skin, delicately here
Restraining a ripple from the air;

Soon plate and rivet on pond and brook;
Then tons of chain and massive lock

To hold rivers. Then, sound by sight
Will Mammoth and Sabre-tooth celebrate

Reunion while a fist of cold
Squeezes the fire at the core of the world,

Squeezes the fire at the core of the heart,
And now it is about to start.

Bayonet Charge

Suddenly he awoke and was running – raw
In raw-seamed hot khaki, his sweat heavy,
Stumbling across a field of clods towards a green hedge
That dazzled with rifle fire, hearing
Bullets smacking the belly out of the air –
He lugged a rifle numb as a smashed arm;
The patriotic tear that had brimmed in his eye
Sweating like molten iron from the centre of his chest –

In bewilderment then he almost stopped –
In what cold clockwork of the stars and the nations
Was he the hand pointing that second? He was running
Like a man who has jumped up in the dark and runs
Listening between his footfalls for the reason
Of his still running, and his foot hung like
Statuary in mid-stride. Then the shot-slashed furrows

Threw up a yellow hare that rolled like a flame
And crawled in a threshing circle, its mouth wide
Open silent, its eyes standing out.
He plunged past with his bayonet towards the green hedge,
King, honour, human dignity, etcetera
Dropped like luxuries in a yelling alarm
To get out of that blue crackling air
His terror's touchy dynamite.

Mayday on Holderness

This evening, motherly summer moves in the pond.
I look down into the decomposition of leaves –
The furnace door whirling with larvae.

From Hull's sunset smudge
Humber is melting eastward, my south skyline:
A loaded single vein, it drains
The effort of the inert North – Sheffield's ores.
Bog pools, dregs of toadstools, tributary
Graves, dunghills, kitchens, hospitals.
The unkillable North Sea swallows it all.
Insects, drunken, drop out of the air.

Birth-soils,
The sea-salts, scoured me, cortex and intestine,
To receive these remains.
As the incinerator, as the sun,
As the spider, I had a whole world in my hands.
Flowerlike, I loved nothing.
Dead and unborn are in God comfortable.
What a length of gut is growing and breathing –
This mute eater, biting through the mind's
Nursery floor, with eel and hyena and vulture,
With creepy-crawly and the root,
With the sea-worm, entering its birthright.

The stars make pietas. The owl announces its sanity.

The crow sleeps glutted and the stoat begins.
There are eye-guarded eggs in these hedgerows,
Hot haynests under the roots in burrows.
Couples at their pursuits are laughing in the lanes.

The North Sea lies soundless. Beneath it
Smoulder the wars: to heart-beats, bomb, bayonet.

'Mother, Mother!' cries the pierced helmet.
Cordite oozings of Gallipoli,

Curded to beastings, broached my palate,
The expressionless gaze of the leopard,
The coils of the sleeping anaconda,
The nightlong frenzy of shrews.

February

The wolf with its belly stitched full of big pebbles;
Nibelung wolves barbed like black pineforest
Against a red sky, over blue snow; or that long grin
Above the tucked coverlet – none suffice.

A photograph: the hairless, knuckled feet
Of the last wolf killed in Britain spoiled him for wolves:
The worst since has been so much mere Alsatian.
Now it is the dream cries 'Wolf!' where these feet

Print the moonlit doorstep, or run and run
Through the hush of parkland, bodiless, headless;
With small seeming of inconvenience
By day, too, pursue, siege all thought;

Bring him to an abrupt poring stop
Over engravings of gibbet-hung wolves,
As at a cage where the scraggy Spanish wolf
Danced, smiling, brown eyes doggily begging

A ball to be thrown. These feet, deprived,
Disdaining all that are caged, or storied, or pictured,
Through and throughout the true world search
For their vanished head, for the world

Vanished with the head, the teeth, the quick eyes –
Now, lest they choose his head,
Under severe moons he sits making
Wolf-masks, mouths clamped well onto the world.

Dick Straightup

Past eighty, but never in eighty years –
Eighty winters on the windy ridge
Of England – has he buttoned his shirt or his jacket.
He sits in the bar-room seat he has been
Polishing with his backside sixty-odd years
Where nobody else sits. White is his head,
But his cheek high, hale as when he emptied
Every Saturday the twelve-pint tankard at a tilt,
Swallowed the whole serving of thirty eggs,
And banged the big bass drum for Heptonstall –
With a hundred other great works, still talked of.
Age has stiffened him, but not dazed or bent,
The blue eye has come clear of time:
At a single pint, now, his memory sips slowly,
His belly strong as a tree bole.

He survives among hills, nourished by stone and height.
The dust of Achilles and Cuchulain
Itches in the palms of scholars; thin clerks exercise
In their bed-sitters at midnight, and the meat salesman can
Loft fully four hundred pounds. But this one,
With no more application than sitting,
And drinking, and singing, fell in the sleet, late,
Dammed the pouring gutter; and slept there; and,
   throughout
A night searched by shouts and lamps, froze,
Grew to the road with welts of ice. He was chipped out at
   dawn
Warm as a pie and snoring.

The gossip of men younger by forty years –
Loud in his company since he no longer says much –
Empties, refills and empties their glasses.
Or their strenuous silence places the dominoes

(That are old as the house) into patterns
Gone with the game; the darts that glint to the dartboard
Pin no remarkable instant. The young men sitting
Taste their beer as by imitation,
Borrow their words as by impertinence
Because he sits there so full of legend and life
Quiet as a man alone.

He lives with sixty and seventy years ago,
And of everything he knows three quarters is in the grave,
Or tumbled down, or vanished. To be understood
His words must tug up the bottom-most stones of this
  village,
This clutter of blackstone gulleys, peeping curtains,
And a graveyard bigger and deeper than the village
That sways in the tide of wind and rain some fifty
Miles off the Irish sea.
                                        The lamp above the pub-door
Wept yellow when he went out and the street
Of spinning darkness roared like a machine
As the wind applied itself. His upright walk,
His strong back, I commemorate now,
And his white blown head going out between a sky and an
  earth
That were bundled into placeless blackness, the one
Company of his mind.

Obit

Now, you are strong as the earth you have entered.

This is a birthplace picture. Green into blue
The hills run deep and limpid. The weasel's
Berry-eyed red lock-head, gripping the dream
That holds good, goes lost in the heaved calm

Of the earth you have entered.

Hawk Roosting

I sit in the top of the wood, my eyes closed.
Inaction, no falsifying dream
Between my hooked head and hooked feet:
Or in sleep rehearse perfect kills and eat.

The convenience of the high trees!
The air's buoyancy and the sun's ray
Are of advantage to me;
And the earth's face upward for my inspection.

My feet are locked upon the rough bark.
It took the whole of Creation
To produce my foot, my each feather:
Now I hold Creation in my foot

Or fly up, and revolve it all slowly –
I kill where I please because it is all mine.
There is no sophistry in my body:
My manners are tearing off heads –

The allotment of death.
For the one path of my flight is direct
Through the bones of the living.
No arguments assert my right:

The sun is behind me.
Nothing has changed since I began.
My eye has permitted no change.
I am going to keep things like this.

The Bull Moses

A hoist up and I could lean over
The upper edge of the high half-door,
My left foot ledged on the hinge, and look in at the byre's
Blaze of darkness: a sudden shut-eyed look
Backward into the head.
                              Blackness is depth
Beyond star. But the warm weight of his breathing,
The ammoniac reek of his litter, the hotly-tongued
Mash of his cud, steamed against me.
Then, slowly, as onto the mind's eye –
The brow like masonry, the deep-keeled neck:
Something come up there onto the brink of the gulf,
Hadn't heard of the world, too deep in itself to be called to,
Stood in sleep. He would swing his muzzle at a fly
But the square of sky where I hung, shouting, waving,
Was nothing to him; nothing of our light
Found any reflection in him.
                              Each dusk the farmer led him
Down to the pond to drink and smell the air,
And he took no pace but the farmer
Led him to take it, as if he knew nothing
Of the ages and continents of his fathers,
Shut, while he wombed, to a dark shed
And steps between his door and the duckpond;
The weight of the sun and the moon and the world
  hammered
To a ring of brass through his nostrils. He would raise
His streaming muzzle and look out over the meadows,
But the grasses whispered nothing awake, the fetch
Of the distance drew nothing to momentum
In the locked black of his powers. He came strolling gently
  back,
Paused neither toward the pig-pens on his right,

Nor toward the cow-byres on his left: something
Deliberate in his leisure, some beheld future
Founding in his quiet.
                                        I kept the door wide,
Closed it after him and pushed the bolt.

View of a Pig

The pig lay on a barrow dead.
It weighed, they said, as much as three men.
Its eyes closed, pink white eyelashes.
Its trotters stuck straight out.

Such weight and thick pink bulk
Set in death seemed not just dead.
It was less than lifeless, further off.
It was like a sack of wheat.

I thumped it without feeling remorse.
One feels guilty insulting the dead,
Walking on graves. But this pig
Did not seem able to accuse.

It was too dead. Just so much
A poundage of lard and pork.
Its last dignity had entirely gone.
It was not a figure of fun.

Too dead now to pity.
To remember its life, din, stronghold
Of earthly pleasure as it had been,
Seemed a false effort, and off the point.

Too deadly factual. Its weight
Oppressed me – how could it be moved?
And the trouble of cutting it up!
The gash in its throat was shocking, but not pathetic.

Once I ran at a fair in the noise
To catch a greased piglet
That was faster and nimbler than a cat,
Its squeal was the rending of metal.

Pigs must have hot blood, they feel like ovens.
Their bite is worse than a horse's –
They chop a half-moon clean out.
They eat cinders, dead cats.

Distinctions and admirations such
As this one was long finished with.
I stared at it a long time. They were going to scald it,
Scald it and scour it like a doorstep.

November

The month of the drowned dog. After long rain the land
Was sodden as the bed of an ancient lake,
Treed with iron and birdless. In the sunk lane
The ditch – a seep silent all summer –

Made brown foam with a big voice: that, and my boots
On the lane's scrubbed stones, in the gulleyed leaves,
Against the hill's hanging silence;
Mist silvering the droplets on the bare thorns

Slower than the change of daylight.
In a let of the ditch a tramp was bundled asleep;
Face tucked down into beard, drawn in
Under his hair like a hedgehog's. I took him for dead,

But his stillness separated from the death
Of the rotting grass and the ground. A wind chilled,
And a fresh comfort tightened through him,
Each hand stuffed deeper into the other sleeve.

His ankles, bound with sacking and hairy band,
Rubbed each other, resettling. The wind hardened;
A puff shook a glittering from the thorns,
And again the rains' dragging grey columns

Smudged the farms. In a moment
The fields were jumping and smoking; the thorns
Quivered, riddled with the glassy verticals.
I stayed on under the welding cold

Watching the tramp's face glisten and the drops on his coat
Flash and darken. I thought what strong trust
Slept in him – as the trickling furrows slept,
And the thorn-roots in their grip on darkness;

And the buried stones, taking the weight of winter;
The hill where the hare crouched with clenched teeth.
Rain plastered the land till it was shining
Like hammered lead, and I ran, and in the rushing wood

Shuttered by a black oak leaned.
The keeper's gibbet had owls and hawks
By the neck, weasels, a gang of cats, crows:
Some, stiff, weightless, twirled like dry bark bits

In the drilling rain. Some still had their shape,
Had their pride with it; hung, chins on chests,
Patient to outwait these worst days that beat
Their crowns bare and dripped from their feet.

Snowdrop

Now is the globe shrunk tight
Round the mouse's dulled wintering heart.
Weasel and crow, as if moulded in brass,
Move through an outer darkness
Not in their right minds,
With the other deaths. She, too, pursues her ends,
Brutal as the stars of this month,
Her pale head heavy as metal.

Pike

Pike, three inches long, perfect
Pike in all parts, green tigering the gold.
Killers from the egg: the malevolent aged grin.
They dance on the surface among the flies.

Or move, stunned by their own grandeur
Over a bed of emerald, silhouette
Of submarine delicacy and horror.
A hundred feet long in their world.

In ponds, under the heat-struck lily pads –
Gloom of their stillness:
Logged on last year's black leaves, watching upwards.
Or hung in an amber cavern of weeds

The jaws' hooked clamp and fangs
Not to be changed at this date;
A life subdued to its instrument;
The gills kneading quietly, and the pectorals.

Three we kept behind glass,
Jungled in weed: three inches, four,
And four and a half: fed fry to them –
Suddenly there were two. Finally one.

With a sag belly and the grin it was born with.
And indeed they spare nobody.
Two, six pounds each, over two feet long,
High and dry and dead in the willow-herb –

One jammed past its gills down the other's gullet:
The outside eye stared: as a vice locks –
The same iron in this eye
Though its film shrank in death.

A pond I fished, fifty yards across,
Whose lilies and muscular tench
Had outlasted every visible stone
Of the monastery that planted them –

Stilled legendary depth:
It was as deep as England. It held
Pike too immense to stir, so immense and old
That past nightfall I dared not cast

But silently cast and fished
With the hair frozen on my head
For what might move, for what eye might move.
The still splashes on the dark pond,

Owls hushing the floating woods
Frail on my ear against the dream
Darkness beneath night's darkness had freed,
That rose slowly towards me, watching.

Thistles

Against the rubber tongues of cows and the hoeing hands of men
Thistles spike the summer air
Or crackle open under a blue-black pressure.

Every one a revengeful burst
Of resurrection, a grasped fistful
Of splintered weapons and Icelandic frost thrust up

From the underground stain of a decayed Viking.
They are like pale hair and the gutturals of dialects.
Every one manages a plume of blood.

Then they grow grey, like men.
Mown down, it is a feud. Their sons appear,
Stiff with weapons, fighting back over the same ground.

Her Husband

Comes home dull with coal-dust deliberately
To grime the sink and foul towels and let her
Learn with scrubbing brush and scrubbing board
The stubborn character of money.

And let her learn through what kind of dust
He has earned his thirst and the right to quench it
And what sweat he has exchanged for his money
And the blood-weight of money. He'll humble her

With new light on her obligations.
The fried, woody chips, kept warm two hours in the oven,
Are only part of her answer.
Hearing the rest, he slams them to the fire back

And is away round the house-end singing
'Come back to Sorrento' in a voice
Of resounding corrugated iron.
Her back has bunched into a hump as an insult.

For they will have their rights.
Their jurors are to be assembled
From the little crumbs of soot. Their brief
Goes straight up to heaven and nothing more is heard of it.

Public Bar TV

On a flaked ridge of the desert

Outriders have found foul water. They say nothing;
With the cactus and the petrified tree
Crouch numbed by a wind howling all
Visible horizons equally empty.

The wind brings dust and nothing
Of the wives, the children, the grandmothers
With the ancestral bones, who months ago
Left the last river,

Coming at the pace of oxen.

Second Glance at a Jaguar

Skinful of bowls he bowls them,
The hip going in and out of joint, dropping the spine
With the urgency of his hurry
Like a cat going along under thrown stones, under cover,
Glancing sideways, running
Under his spine. A terrible, stump-legged waddle
Like a thick Aztec disemboweller,
Club-swinging, trying to grind some square
Socket between his hind legs round,
Carrying his head like a brazier of spilling embers,
And the black bit of his mouth, he takes it
Between his back teeth, he has to wear his skin out,
He swipes a lap at the water-trough as he turns,
Swivelling the ball of his heel on the polished spot,
Showing his belly like a butterfly.
At every stride he has to turn a corner
In himself and correct it. His head
Is like the worn down stump of another whole jaguar,
His body is just the engine shoving it forward,
Lifting the air up and shoving on under,
The weight of his fangs hanging the mouth open,
Bottom jaw combing the ground. A gorged look,
Gangster, club-tail lumped along behind gracelessly,
He's wearing himself to heavy ovals,
Muttering some mantra, some drum-song of murder
To keep his rage brightening, making his skin
Intolerable, spurred by the rosettes, the Cain-brands,
Wearing the spots off from the inside,
Rounding some revenge. Going like a prayer-wheel,
The head dragging forward, the body keeping up,
The hind legs lagging. He coils, he flourishes
The blackjack tail as if looking for a target,
Hurrying through the underworld, soundless.

Fern

Here is the fern's frond, unfurling a gesture,
Like a conductor whose music will now be pause
And the one note of silence
To which the whole earth dances gravely.

The mouse's ear unfurls its trust,
The spider takes up her bequest,
And the retina
Reins the creation with a bridle of water.

And, among them, the fern
Dances gravely, like the plume
Of a warrior returning, under the low hills,

Into his own kingdom.

Theology

No, the serpent did not
Seduce Eve to the apple.
All that's simply
Corruption of the facts.

Adam ate the apple.
Eve ate Adam.
The serpent ate Eve.
This is the dark intestine.

The serpent, meanwhile,
Sleeps his meal off in Paradise –
Smiling to hear
God's querulous calling.

Heptonstall

Black village of gravestones.
Skull of an idiot
Whose dreams die back
Where they were born.

Skull of a sheep
Whose meat melts
Under its own rafters.
Only the flies leave it.

Skull of a bird,
The great geographies
Drained to sutures
Of cracked windowsills.

Life tries.

Death tries.

The stone tries.

Only the rain never tires.

Full Moon and Little Frieda

A cool small evening shrunk to a dog bark and the clank of a bucket –
And you listening.
A spider's web, tense for the dew's touch.
A pail lifted, still and brimming – mirror
To tempt a first star to a tremor.

Cows are going home in the lane there, looping the hedges with their warm wreaths of breath –
A dark river of blood, many boulders,
Balancing unspilled milk.

'Moon!' you cry suddenly, 'Moon! Moon!'

The moon has stepped back like an artist gazing amazed at a work

That points at him amazed

Wodwo

What am I? Nosing here, turning leaves over
Following a faint stain on the air to the river's edge
I enter water. What am I to split
The glassy grain of water looking upward I see the bed
Of the river above me upside down very clear
What am I doing here in mid-air? Why do I find
this frog so interesting as I inspect its most secret
interior and make it my own? Do these weeds
know me and name me to each other have they
seen me before, do I fit in their world? I seem
separate from the ground and not rooted but dropped
out of nothing casually I've no threads
fastening me to anything I can go anywhere
I seem to have been given the freedom
of this place what am I then? And picking
bits of bark off this rotten stump gives me
no pleasure and it's no use so why do I do it
me and doing that have coincided very queerly
But what shall I be called am I the first
have I an owner what shape am I what
shape am I am I huge if I go
to the end on this way past these trees and past these trees
till I get tired that's touching one wall of me
for the moment if I sit still how everything
stops to watch me I suppose I am the exact centre
but there's all this what is it roots
roots roots roots and here's the water
again very queer but I'll go on looking

Two Legends

I

Black was the without eye
Black the within tongue
Black was the heart
Black the liver, black the lungs
Unable to suck in light
Black the blood in its loud tunnel
Black the bowels packed in furnace
Black too the muscles
Striving to pull out into the light
Black the nerves, black the brain
With its tombed visions
Black also the soul, the huge stammer
Of the cry that, swelling, could not
Pronounce its sun.

II

Black is the wet otter's head, lifted.
Black is the rock, plunging in foam.
Black is the gall lying on the bed of the blood.

Black is the earth-globe, one inch under,
An egg of blackness
Where sun and moon alternate their weathers

To hatch a crow, a black rainbow
Bent in emptiness
over emptiness
But flying

Examination at the Womb-Door

Who owns these scrawny little feet? *Death.*
Who owns this bristly scorched-looking face? *Death.*
Who owns these still-working lungs? *Death.*
Who owns this utility coat of muscles? *Death.*
Who owns these unspeakable guts? *Death.*
Who owns these questionable brains? *Death.*
All this messy blood? *Death.*
These minimum-efficiency eyes? *Death.*
This wicked little tongue? *Death.*
This occasional wakefulness? *Death.*

Given, stolen, or held pending trial?
Held.

Who owns the whole rainy, stony earth? *Death.*
Who owns all of space? *Death.*

Who is stronger than hope? *Death.*
Who is stronger than the will? *Death.*
Stronger than love? *Death.*
Stronger than life? *Death.*

But who is stronger than death?
Me, evidently.

Pass, Crow.

Crow's First Lesson

God tried to teach Crow how to talk.
'Love,' said God. 'Say, Love.'
Crow gaped, and the white shark crashed into the sea
And went rolling downwards, discovering its own depth.

'No, no,' said God. 'Say Love. Now try it. LOVE.'
Crow gaped, and a bluefly, a tsetse, a mosquito
Zoomed out and down
To their sundry flesh-pots.

'A final try,' said God. 'Now, LOVE.'
Crow convulsed, gaped, retched and
Man's bodiless prodigious head
Bulbed out onto the earth, with swivelling eyes,
Jabbering protest –

And Crow retched again, before God could stop him.
And woman's vulva dropped over man's neck and tightened.
The two struggled together on the grass.
God struggled to part them, cursed, wept –

Crow flew guiltily off.

That Moment

When the pistol muzzle oozing blue vapour
Was lifted away
Like a cigarette lifted from an ashtray

And the only face left in the world
Lay broken
Between hands that relaxed, being too late

And the trees closed forever
And the streets closed forever

And the body lay on the gravel
Of the abandoned world
Among abandoned utilities
Exposed to infinity forever

Crow had to start searching for something to eat.

Crow and the Birds

When the eagle soared clear through a dawn distilling of emerald.
When the curlew trawled in seadusk through a chime of wineglasses
When the swallow swooped through a woman's song in a cavern
And the swift flicked through the breath of a violet

When the owl sailed clear of tomorrow's conscience
And the sparrow preened himself of yesterday's promise
And the heron laboured clear of the Bessemer upglare
And the bluetit zipped clear of lace panties
And the woodpecker drummed clear of the rotovator and the rose-farm
And the peewit tumbled clear of the laundromat

While the bullfinch plumped in the apple bud
And the goldfinch bulbed in the sun
And the wryneck crooked in the moon
And the dipper peered from the dewball
Crow spraddled head-down in the beach-garbage, guzzling a dropped ice-cream.

In Laughter

Cars collide and erupt luggage and babies
In laughter
The steamer upends and goes under saluting like a stuntman
In laughter
The nosediving aircraft concludes with a boom
In laughter
People's arms and legs fly off and fly on again
In laughter
The haggard mask on the bed rediscovers its pang
In laughter, in laughter
The meteorite crashes
With extraordinarily ill-luck on the pram

The ears and eyes are bundled up
Are folded up in the hair,
Wrapped in the carpet, the wallpaper, tied with the lampflex
Only the teeth work on
And the heart, dancing on in its open cave
Helpless on the strings of laughter

While the tears are nickel-plated and come through doors
with a bang

And the wails stun with fear
And the bones
Jump from the torment flesh has to stay for

Stagger some distance and fall in full view

Still laughter scampers around on centipede boots
Still it runs all over on caterpillar tread
And rolls back onto the mattress, legs in the air

But it's only human

And finally it's had enough – enough!
And slowly sits up, exhausted,
And slowly starts to fasten buttons,
With long pauses,

Like somebody the police have come for.

Crow's Last Stand

Burning
          burning
                    burning
                              there was finally something
The sun could not burn, that it had rendered
Everything down to – a final obstacle
Against which it raged and charred

And rages and chars

Fragment of an Ancient Tablet

Above – the well-known lips, delicately downed.
Below – beard between thighs.

Above – her brow, the notable casket of gems.
Below – the belly with its blood-knot.

Above – many a painful frown.
Below – the ticking bomb of the future.

Above – her perfect teeth, with the hint of a fang at the
corner.
Below – the millstones of two worlds.

Above – a word and a sigh.
Below – gouts of blood and babies.

Above – the face, shaped like a perfect heart.
Below – the heart's torn face.

Lovesong

He loved her and she loved him
His kisses sucked out her whole past and future or tried to
He had no other appetite
She bit him she gnawed him she sucked
She wanted him complete inside her
Safe and sure forever and ever
Their little cries fluttered into the curtains

Her eyes wanted nothing to get away
Her looks nailed down his hands his wrists his elbows
He gripped her hard so that life
Should not drag her from that moment
He wanted all future to cease
He wanted to topple with his arms round her
Off that moment's brink and into nothing
Or everlasting or whatever there was
Her embrace was an immense press
To print him into her bones
His smiles were the garrets of a fairy palace
Where the real world would never come
Her smiles were spider bites
So he would lie still till she felt hungry
His words were occupying armies
Her laughs were an assassin's attempts
His looks were bullets daggers of revenge
Her glances were ghosts in the corner with horrible secrets
His whispers were whips and jackboots
Her kisses were lawyers steadily writing
His caresses were the last hooks of a castaway
Her love-tricks were the grinding of locks
And their deep cries crawled over the floors
Like an animal dragging a great trap

His promises were the surgeon's gag
Her promises took the top off his skull
She would get a brooch made of it
His vows pulled out all her sinews
He showed her how to make a love-knot
Her vows put his eyes in formalin
At the back of her secret drawer
Their screams stuck in the wall
Their heads fell apart into sleep like the two halves
Of a lopped melon, but love is hard to stop

In their entwined sleep they exchanged arms and legs
In their dreams their brains took each other hostage

In the morning they wore each other's face

The Lovepet

Was it an animal was it a bird?
She stroked it. He spoke to it softly.
She made her voice its happy forest.
He brought it out with sugarlump smiles.
Soon it was licking their kisses.

She gave it the strings of her voice which it swallowed
He gave it the blood of his face it grew eager
She gave it the liquorice of her mouth it began to thrive
He opened the aniseed of his future
And it bit and gulped, grew vicious, snatched
The focus of his eyes
She gave it the steadiness of her hand
He gave it the strength of his spine it ate everything

It began to cry what could they give it
They gave it their calendars it bolted their diaries
They gave it their sleep it gobbled their dreams
Even while they slept
It ate their bodyskin and the muscle beneath
They gave it vows its teeth clashed its starvation
Through every word they uttered

It found snakes under the floor it ate them
It found a spider horror
In their palms and ate it

They gave it double smiles and blank silence
It chewed holes in their carpets
They gave it logic
It ate the colour of their hair
They gave it every argument that would come
They gave it shouting and yelling they meant it
It ate the faces of their children
They gave it their photograph albums they gave it their
  records

It ate the colour of the sun
They gave it a thousand letters they gave it money
It ate their future complete it waited for them
Staring and starving
They gave it screams it had gone too far
It ate into their brains
It ate the roof
It ate lonely stone it ate wind crying famine
It went furiously off

They wept they called it back it could have everything
It stripped out their nerves chewed chewed flavourless
It bit at their numb bodies they did not resist
It bit into their blank brains they hardly knew

It moved bellowing
Through a ruin of starlight and crockery

It drew slowly off they could not move

It went far away they could not speak

Littleblood

O littleblood, hiding from the mountains in the mountains
Wounded by stars and leaking shadow
Eating the medical earth.

O littleblood, little boneless little skinless
Ploughing with a linnet's carcase
Reaping the wind and threshing the stones.

O littleblood, drumming in a cow's skull
Dancing with a gnat's feet
With an elephant's nose with a crocodile's tail.

Grown so wise grown so terrible
Sucking death's mouldy tits.

Sit on my finger, sing in my ear, O littleblood.

The Scream

There was the sun on the wall – my childhood's
Nursery picture. And there my gravestone
Shared my dreams, and ate and drank with me happily.

All day the hawk perfected its craftsmanship
And even through the night the miracle persisted.

Mountains lazed in their smoky camp.
Worms in the ground were doing a good job.

Flesh of bronze, stirred with a bronze thirst,
Like a newborn baby at the breast,
Slept in the sun's mercy.

And the inane weights of iron
That come suddenly crashing into people, out of nowhere,
Only made me feel brave and creaturely.

When I saw little rabbits with their heads crushed on roads
I knew I rode the wheel of the galaxy.

Calves' heads all dew-bristled with blood on counters
Grinned like masks where sun and moon danced.

And my mate with his face sewn up
Where they'd opened it to take something out
Lifted a hand –

He smiled, in half-coma,
A stone temple smile.

Then I, too, opened my mouth to praise –
But a silence wedged my gullet.

Like an obsidian dagger, dry, jag-edged,
A silent lump of volcanic glass,

The scream
Vomited itself.

Bride and Groom Lie Hidden for Three Days

She gives him his eyes, she found them
Among some rubble, among some beetles

He gives her her skin
He just seemed to pull it down out of the air and lay it over her
She weeps with fearfulness and astonishment

She has found his hands for him, and fitted them freshly at the wrists
They are amazed at themselves, they go feeling all over her

He has assembled her spine, he cleaned each piece carefully
And sets them in perfect order
A superhuman puzzle but he is inspired
She leans back twisting this way and that, using it and laughing, incredulous

Now she has brought his feet, she is connecting them
So that his whole body lights up

And he has fashioned her new hips
With all fittings complete and with newly wound coils, all shiningly oiled
He is polishing every part, he himself can hardly believe it
They keep taking each other to the sun, they find they can easily
To test each new thing at each new step

And now she smooths over him the plates of his skull
So that the joints are invisible
And now he connects her throat, her breasts and the pit of her stomach
With a single wire

She gives him his teeth, tying their roots to the centrepin of his body

He sets the little circlets on her fingertips

She stitches his body here and there with steely purple silk

He oils the delicate cogs of her mouth

She inlays with deep-cut scrolls the nape of his neck

He sinks into place the inside of her thighs

So, gasping with joy, with cries of wonderment
Like two gods of mud
Sprawling in the dirt, but with infinite care

They bring each other to perfection.

A March Calf

Right from the start he is dressed in his best – his blacks and
his whites
Little Fauntleroy – quiffed and glossy,
A Sunday suit, a wedding natty get-up,
Standing in dunged straw

Under cobwebby beams, near the mud wall,
Half of him legs,
Shining-eyed, requiring nothing more
But that mother's milk come back often.

Everything else is in order, just as it is.
Let the summer skies hold off, for the moment.
This is just as he wants it.
A little at a time, of each new thing, is best.

Too much and too sudden is too frightening –
When I block the light, a bulk from space,
To let him in to his mother for a suck,
He bolts a yard or two, then freezes,

Staring from every hair in all directions,
Ready for the worst, shut up in his hopeful religion,
A little syllogism
With a wet blue-reddish muzzle, for God's thumb.

You see all his hopes bustling
As he reaches between the worn rails towards
The topheavy oven of his mother.
He trembles to grow, stretching his curl-tip tongue –

What did cattle ever find here
To make this dear little fellow
So eager to prepare himself?
He is already in the race, and quivering to win –

His new purpled eyeball swivel-jerks
In the elbowing push of his plans.
Hungry people are getting hungrier,
Butchers developing expertise and markets,

But he just wobbles his tail – and glistens
Within his dapper profile
Unaware of how his whole lineage
Has been tied up.

He shivers for feel of the world licking his side.
He is like an ember – one glow
Of lighting himself up
With the fuel of himself, breathing and brightening.

Soon he'll plunge out, to scatter his seething joy,
To be present at the grass,
To be free on the surface of such a wideness,
To find himself himself. To stand. To moo.

The River in March

Now the river is rich, but her voice is low.
It is her Mighty Majesty the sea
Travelling among the villages incognito.

Now the river is poor. No song, just a thin mad whisper.
The winter floods have ruined her.
She squats between draggled banks, fingering her rags and
 rubbish.

And now the river is rich. A deep choir.
It is the lofty clouds, that work in heaven,
Going on their holiday to the sea.

The river is poor again. All her bones are showing.
Through a dry wig of bleached flotsam she peers up ashamed
From her slum of sticks.

Now the river is rich, collecting shawls and minerals.
Rain brought fatness, but she takes ninety-nine percent
Leaving the fields just one percent to survive on.

And now she is poor. Now she is East wind sick.
She huddles in holes and corners. The brassy sun gives her a
 headache.
She has lost all her fish. And she shivers.

But now once more she is rich. She is viewing her lands.
A hoard of king-cups spills from her folds, it blazes, it cannot
 be hidden.
A salmon, a sow of solid silver,

Bulges to glimpse it.

Apple Dumps

After the fiesta, the beauty-contests, the drunken wrestling
Of the blossom
Come some small ugly swellings, the dwarfish truths
Of the prizes.

After blushing and confetti, the breeze-blown bridesmaids, the shadowed snapshots
Of the trees in bloom
Come the gruelling knuckles, and the cracked housemaid's hands,
The workworn morning plainness of apples.

Unearthly was the hope, the wet star melting the gland,
Staggering the offer –
But pawky the real returns, not easy to see,
Dull and leaf-green, hidden, still-bitter, and hard.

The orchard flared wings, a new heaven, a dawn-lipped apocalypse
Kissing the sleeper –
The apples emerge, in the sun's black shade, among stricken trees,
A straggle of survivors, nearly all ailing.

Barley

Barley grain is like seeds of gold bullion.
When you turn a heap with a shovel it pours
With the heavy magic of wealth.
Every grain is a sleeping princess –
Her kingdom is still to come.
She sleeps with sealed lips.
Each grain is like a mouth sealed
Or an eye sealed.
In each mouth the whole bible of barley.
In each eye, the whole sun of barley.
From each single grain, given time,
You could feed the earth.

You treat them rough, dump them into the drill,
Churn them up with a winter supply
Of fertiliser, and steer out onto the tilth
Trailing your wake of grains.

When the field's finished, fresh-damp,
Its stillness is no longer stillness.
The coverlet has been drawn tight again
But now over breathing and dreams.
And water is already bustling to sponge the newcomers.
And the soil, the ancient nurse,
Is assembling everything they will need.
And the angel of earth
Is flying through the field, kissing each one awake.
But it is a hard nursery.
Night and day all through winter huddling naked
They have to listen to pitiless lessons
Of the freezing constellations
And the rain. If it were not for the sun
Who visits them daily, briefly,
To pray with them, they would lose hope

And give up. With him
They recite the Lord's prayer
And sing a psalm. And sometimes at night
When the moon haunts their field and stares down
Into their beds
They sing a psalm softly together
To keep up their courage.

Once their first leaf shivers they sing less
And start working. They cannot miss a day.
They have to get the whole thing right.
Employed by the earth, employed by the sky,
Employed by barley, to be barley.
And now they begin to show their family beauty.
They come charging over the field, under the wind, like
 warriors –
'Terrible as an army with banners',
Barbaric, tireless, Amazon battalions.

And that's how they win their kingdom.
Then they put on gold, for their coronation.
Each one barbed, feathered, a lithe weapon,
Puts on the crown of her kingdom.
Then the whole fieldful of queens
Swirls in a dance
With their invisible partner, the wind,
Like a single dancer.

That is how barley inherits the kingdom of barley.

Football at Slack

Between plunging valleys, on a bareback of hill
Men in bunting colours
Bounced, and their blown ball bounced.

The blown ball jumped, and the merry-coloured men
Spouted like water to head it.
The ball blew away downwind –

The rubbery men bounced after it.
The ball jumped up and out and hung on the wind
Over a gulf of treetops.
Then they all shouted together, and the ball blew back.

Winds from fiery holes in heaven
Piled the hills darkening around them
To awe them. The glare light
Mixed its mad oils and threw glooms.
Then the rain lowered a steel press.

Hair plastered, they all just trod water
To puddle glitter. And their shouts bobbed up
Coming fine and thin, washed and happy

While the humped world sank foundering
And the valleys blued unthinkable
Under depth of Atlantic depression –

But the wingers leapt, they bicycled in air
And the goalie flew horizontal

And once again a golden holocaust
Lifted the cloud's edge, to watch them.

Sunstruck

The freedom of Saturday afternoons
Starched to cricket dazzle, nagged at a theorem –
Shaggy valley parapets
Pending like thunder, narrowing the spin-bowler's angle.

The click, disconnected, might have escaped –
A six! And the ball slammed flat!
And the bat in flinders! The heart soaring!
And everybody jumping up and running –

Fleeing after the ball, stampeding
Through the sudden hole in Saturday – but
Already clapped into hands and the trap-shout
The ball jerked back to the stumper on its elastic.

Everything collapsed that bit deeper
Towards Monday.

Misery of the brassy sycamores!
Misery of the swans and the hard ripple!

Then again Yes Yes a wild YES –
The bat flashed round the neck in a tight coil,
The stretched shout snatching for the North Sea –
But it fell far short, even of Midgley.

And the legs running for dear life, twinkling white
In the cage of wickets
Were cornered again by the ball, pinned to the crease,
Blocked by the green and white pavilion.

Cross-eyed, mid-stump, sun-descending headache!
Brain sewn into the ball's hide
Hammering at four corners of abstraction
And caught and flung back, and caught, and again caught

To be bounced on baked earth, to be clubbed
Toward the wage-mirage sparkle of mills
Toward Lord Savile's heather
Toward the veto of the poisonous Calder

Till the eyes, glad of anything, dropped
From the bails
Into the bottom of a teacup,
To sandwich crusts for the canal cygnets.

The bowler had flogged himself to a dishclout.
And the burned batsmen returned, with changed faces,
'Like men returned from a far journey',
Under the long glare walls of evening

To the cool sheet and the black slot of home.

When Men Got to the Summit

Light words forsook them.
They filled with heavy silence.

Houses came to support them,
But the hard, foursquare scriptures fractured
And the cracks filled with soft rheumatism.

Streets bent to the task
Of holding it all up
Bracing themselves, taking the strain
Till their vertebrae slipped.

The hills went on gently
Shaking their sieve.

Nevertheless, for some giddy moments
A television
Blinked from the wolf's lookout.

Cock-Crows

I stood on a dark summit, among dark summits –
Tidal dawn was splitting heaven from earth,
The oyster
Opening to taste gold.

And I heard the cock-crows kindling in the valley
Under the mist –
They were sleepy,
Bubbling deep in the valley cauldron.

Then one or two tossed clear, like soft rockets
And sank back again dimming.

Then soaring harder, brighter, higher
Tearing the mist,
Bubble-glistenings flung up and bursting to light
Brightening the undercloud,
The fire-crests of the cocks – the sickle shouts,
Challenge against challenge, answer to answer,
Hooking higher,
Clambering up the sky as they melted,
Hanging smouldering from the night's fringes.

Till the whole valley brimmed with cock-crows,
A magical soft mixture boiling over,
Spilling and sparkling into other valleys

Lobbed-up horse-shoes of glow-swollen metal
From sheds in back-gardens, hen-cotes, farms
Sinking back mistily

Till the last spark died, and embers paled

And the sun climbed into its wet sack
For the day's work

While the dark rims hardened
Over the smoke of towns, from holes in earth.

The Long Tunnel Ceiling

Of the main-road canal bridge
Cradled black stalactite reflections.
That was the place for dark loach!

At the far end, the Moderna blanket factory
And the bushy mask of Hathershelf above it
Peered in through the cell-window.

Lorries from Bradford, baled with plump and towering
Wools and cottons met, above my head,
Lorries from Rochdale, and ground past each other
Making that cavern of air and water tremble –

Suddenly a crash!
The long gleam-ponderous watery echo shattered.

And at last it had begun!
That could only have been a brick from the ceiling!
The bridge was starting to collapse!

But the canal swallowed its scare,
The heavy mirror reglassed itself,
And the black arch gazed up at the black arch.

Till a brick
Rose through its eruption – hung massive
Then slammed back with a shock and a shattering.

An ingot!
Holy of holies! A treasure!
A trout
Nearly as long as my arm, solid
Molten pig of many a bronze loach!

There he lay – lazy – a free lord,
Ignoring me. Caressing, dismissing

The eastward easing traffic of drift,
Master of the Pennine Pass!

Found in some thin glitter among mean gritstone,
High under ferns, high up near sour heather,

Brought down on a midnight cloudburst
In a shake-up of heaven and the hills
When the streams burst with zig-zags and explosions

A seed
Of the wild god now flowering for me
Such a tigerish, dark, breathing lily
Between the tyres, under the tortured axles.

Heptonstall Old Church

A great bird landed here.

Its song drew men out of rock,
Living men out of bog and heather.

Its song put a light in the valleys
And harness on the long moors.

Its song brought a crystal from space
And set it in men's heads.

Then the bird died.

Its giant bones
Blackened and became a mystery.

The crystal in men's heads
Blackened and fell to pieces.

The valleys went out.
The moorland broke loose.

Emily Brontë

The wind on Crow Hill was her darling.
His fierce, high tale in her ear was her secret.
But his kiss was fatal.

Through her dark Paradise ran
The stream she loved too well
That bit her breast.

The shaggy sodden king of that kingdom
Followed through the wall
And lay on her love-sick bed.

The curlew trod in her womb.

The stone swelled under her heart.

Her death is a baby-cry on the moor.

Rain

Rain. Floods. Frost. And after frost, rain.
Dull roof-drumming. Wraith-rain pulsing across purple-bare woods
Like light across heaved water. Sleet in it.
And the poor fields, miserable tents of their hedges.
Mist-rain off-world. Hills wallowing
In and out of a grey or silvery dissolution. A farm gleaming,
Then all dull in the near drumming. At field-corners
Brown water backing and brimming in grass.
Toads hop across rain-hammered roads. Every mutilated leaf there
Looks like a frog or a rained-out mouse. Cattle
Wait under blackened backs. We drive post-holes.
They half fill with water before the post goes in.
Mud-water spurts as the iron bar slam-burns
The oak stake-head dry. Cows
Tamed on the waste mudded like a rugby field
Stand and watch, come very close for company
In the rain that goes on and on, and gets colder.
They sniff the wire, sniff the tractor, watch. The hedges
Are straggles of gap. A few haws. Every half-ton cow
Sinks to the fetlock at every sliding stride.
They are ruining their field and they know it.
They look out sideways from under their brows which are
Their only shelter. The sunk scrubby wood
Is a pulverized wreck, rain riddles its holes
To the drowned roots. A pheasant looking black
In his waterproofs, bends at his job in the stubble.
The mid-afternoon dusk soaks into
The soaked thickets. Nothing protects them.
The fox corpses lie beaten to their bare bones,
Skin beaten off, brains and bowels beaten out.
Nothing but their blueprint bones last in the rain,

Sodden soft. Round their hay racks, calves
Stand in a shine of mud. The gateways
Are deep obstacles of mud. The calves look up, through plastered forelocks,
Without moving. Nowhere they can go
Is less uncomfortable. The brimming world
And the pouring sky are the only places
For them to be. Fieldfares squeal over, sodden
Toward the sodden wood. A raven,
Cursing monotonously, goes over fast
And vanishes in rain-mist. Magpies
Shake themselves hopelessly, hop in the spatter. Misery.
Surviving green of ferns and brambles is tumbled
Like an abandoned scrapyard. The calves
Wait deep beneath their spines. Cows roar
Then hang their noses to the mud.
Snipe go over, invisible in the dusk,
With their squelching cries.

4 December 1973

Tractor

The tractor stands frozen – an agony
To think of. All night
Snow packed its open entrails. Now a head-pincering gale,
A spill of molten ice, smoking snow,
Pours into its steel.
At white heat of numbness it stands
In the aimed hosing of ground-level fieriness.

It defies flesh and won't start.
Hands are like wounds already
Inside armour gloves, and feet are unbelievable
As if the toe-nails were all just torn off.
I stare at it in hatred. Beyond it
The copse hisses – capitulates miserably
In the fleeing, failing light. Starlings,
A dirtier sleetier snow, blow smokily, unendingly, over
Towards plantations eastward.
All the time the tractor is sinking
Through the degrees, deepening
Into its hell of ice.

The starter lever
Cracks its action, like a snapping knuckle.
The battery is alive – but like a lamb
Trying to nudge its solid-frozen mother –
While the seat claims my buttock-bones, bites
With the space-cold of earth, which it has joined
In one solid lump.

I squirt commercial sure-fire
Down the black throat – it just coughs.
It ridicules me – a trap of iron stupidity
I've stepped into. I drive the battery
As if I were hammering and hammering

The frozen arrangement to pieces with a hammer
And it jabbers laughing pain-crying mockingly
Into happy life.

And stands
Shuddering itself full of heat, seeming to enlarge slowly
Like a demon demonstrating
A more-than-usually-complete materialization –
Suddenly it jerks from its solidarity
With the concrete, and lurches towards a stanchion
Bursting with superhuman well-being and abandon
Shouting Where Where?

Worse iron is waiting. Power-lift kneels,
Levers awake imprisoned deadweight,
Shackle-pins bedded in cast-iron cow-shit.
The blind and vibrating condemned obedience
Of iron to the cruelty of iron,
Wheels screeched out of their night-locks –

Fingers
Among the tormented
Tonnage and burning of iron

Eyes
Weeping in the wind of chloroform

And the tractor, streaming with sweat,
Raging and trembling and rejoicing.

31 January 1976

Sketching a Thatcher

Bird-bones is on the roof. Seventy-eight
And still a ladder squirrel,
Three or four nitches at a time, up forty rungs,
Then crabbing out across the traverse,
Cock-crows of insulting banter, liberated
Into his old age, like a royal fool
But still tortured with energy. Thatching
Must be the sinless job. Weathered
Like a weathercock, face bright as a ploughshare,
Skinny forearms of steely cable, batting
The reeds flush, crawling, cliff-hanging,
Lizard-silk of his lizard-skinny hands,
Hands never still, twist of body never still –
Bounds in for a cup of tea, 'Caught you all asleep!'
Markets all the gossip – cynical old goblin
Cackling with wicked joy. Bounds out –
Trips and goes full length, bounces back upright,
'Haven't got the weight to get hurt with!' Cheers
Every departure – 'Off for a drink?' and 'Off
To see his fancy woman again!' – leans from the sky,
Sun-burned-out pale eyes, eyes bleached
As old thatch, in the worn tool of his face,
In his haggard pants and his tired-out shirt –
They can't keep up with him. He just can't
Stop working. 'I don't want the money!' He'd
Prefer a few years. 'Have to sell the house to pay me!'
Alertness built into the bird-stare,
The hook of his nose, bill-hook of his face.
Suns have worn him, like an old sun-tool
Of the day-making, an old shoe-tongue
Of the travelling weathers, the hand-palm, ageless,
Of all winds on all roofs. He lams the roof
And the house quakes. Was everybody

Once like him? He's squirmed through
Some tight cranny of natural selection.
The nut-stick yealm-twist's got into his soul,
He didn't break. He's proof
As his crusty roofs. He ladder-dances
His blood light as spirit. His muscles
Must be clean as horn.
And the whole house
Is more pleased with itself, him on it,
Cresting it, and grooming it, and slapping it
Than if an eagle rested there. Sitting
Drinking his tea, he looks like a tatty old eagle,
And his yelping laugh of derision
Is just like a tatty old eagle's.

Ravens

As we came through the gate to look at the few new lambs
On the skyline of lawn smoothness,
A raven bundled itself into air from midfield
And slid away under hard glistenings, low and guilty.
Sheep nibbling, kneeling to nibble the reluctant nibbled
grass.
Sheep staring, their jaws pausing to think, then chewing
again,
Then pausing. Over there a new lamb
Just getting up, bumping its mother's nose
As she nibbles the sugar coating off it
While the tattered banners of her triumph swing and drip
from her rear-end.
She sneezes and a glim of water flashes from her rear-end.
She sneezes again and again, till she's emptied.
Shc carries on investigating her new present and seeing how
it works.
Over here is something else. But you are still interested
In that new one, and its new spark of voice,
And its tininess.
Now over here, where the raven was,
Is what interests you next. Born dead,
Twisted like a scarf, a lamb of an hour or two,
Its insides, the various jellies and crimsons and
transparencies
And threads and tissues pulled out
In straight lines, like tent ropes
From its upward belly opened like a lamb-wool slipper,
The fine anatomy of silvery ribs on display and the cavity,
The head also emptied through the eye-sockets,
The woolly limbs swathed in birth-yolk and impossible
To tell now which in all this field of quietly nibbling sheep
Was its mother. I explain

That it died being born. We should have been here, to help it.
So it died being born. 'And did it cry?' you cry.
I pick up the dangling greasy weight by the hooves soft as
    dogs' pads
That had trodden only womb-water
And its raven-drawn strings dangle and trail,
Its loose head joggles, and 'Did it cry?' you cry again.
Its two-fingered feet splay in their skin between the pressures
Of my fingers and thumb. And there is another,
Just born, all black, splaying its tripod, inching its new points
Towards its mother, and testing the note
It finds in its mouth. But you have eyes now
Only for the tattered bundle of throwaway lamb.
'Did it cry?' you keep asking, in a three-year-old field-wide
Piercing persistence. 'Oh yes' I say 'it cried.'

Though this one was lucky insofar
As it made the attempt into a warm wind
And its first day of death was blue and warm
The magpies gone quiet with domestic happiness
And skylarks not worrying about anything
And the blackthorn budding confidently
And the skyline of hills, after millions of hard years,
Sitting soft.

15 April 1974

February 17th

A lamb could not get born. Ice wind
Out of a downpour dishclout sunrise. The mother
Lay on the mudded slope. Harried, she got up
And the blackish lump bobbed at her back-end
Under her tail. After some hard galloping,
Some manoeuvring, much flapping of the backward
Lump head of the lamb looking out,
I caught her with a rope. Laid her, head uphill
And examined the lamb. A blood-ball swollen
Tight in its black felt, its mouth gap
Squashed crooked, tongue stuck out, black-purple,
Strangled by its mother. I felt inside,
Past the noose of mother-flesh, into the slippery
Muscled tunnel, fingering for a hoof,
Right back to the port-hole of the pelvis.
But there was no hoof. He had stuck his head out too early
And his feet could not follow. He should have
Felt his way, tip-toe, his toes
Tucked up under his nose
For a safe landing. So I kneeled wrestling
With her groans. No hand could squeeze past
The lamb's neck into her interior
To hook a knee. I roped that baby head
And hauled till she cried out and tried
To get up and I saw it was useless. I went
Two miles for the injection and a razor.
Sliced the lamb's throat-strings, levered with a knife
Between the vertebrae and brought the head off
To stare at its mother, its pipes sitting in the mud
With all earth for a body. Then pushed
The neck-stump right back in, and as I pushed
She pushed. She pushed crying and I pushed gasping.
And the strength

Of the birth push and the push of my thumb
Against that wobbly vertebra were deadlock,
A to-fro futility. Till I forced
A hand past and got a knee. Then like
Pulling myself to the ceiling with one finger
Hooked in a loop, timing my effort
To her birth push groans, I pulled against
The corpse that would not come. Till it came.
And after it the long, sudden, yolk-yellow
Parcel of life
In a smoking slither of oils and soups and syrups –
And the body lay born, beside the hacked-off head.

17 February 1974

The Day He Died

Was the silkiest day of the young year,
The first reconnaissance of the real spring,
The first confidence of the sun.

That was yesterday. Last night, frost.
And as hard as any of all winter.
Mars and Saturn and the Moon dangling in a bunch
On the hard, littered sky.
Today is Valentine's day.

Earth toast-crisp. The snowdrops battered.
Thrushes spluttering. Pigeons gingerly
Rubbing their voices together, in stinging cold.
Crows creaking, and clumsily
Cracking loose.

The bright fields look dazed.
Their expression is changed.
They have been somewhere awful
And come back without him.

The trustful cattle, with frost on their backs,
Waiting for hay, waiting for warmth,
Stand in a new emptiness.

From now on the land
Will have to manage without him.
But it hesitates, in this slow realization of light,
Childlike, too naked, in a frail sun,
With roots cut
And a great blank in its memory.

A Motorbike

We had a motorbike all through the war
In an outhouse – thunder, flight, disruption
Cramped in rust, under washing, abashed, outclassed
By the Brens, the Bombs, the Bazookas elsewhere.

The war ended, the explosions stopped.
The men surrendered their weapons
And hung around limply.
Peace took them all prisoner.
They were herded into their home towns.
A horrible privation began
Of working a life up out of the avenues
And the holiday resorts and the dance-halls.

Then the morning bus was as bad as any labour truck,
The foreman, the boss, as bad as the S.S.
And the ends of the street and the bends of the road
And the shallowness of the shops and the shallowness of the beer
And the sameness of the next town
Were as bad as electrified barbed wire
The shrunk-back war ached in their testicles
And England dwindled to the size of a dog-track.

So there came this quiet young man
And he bought our motorbike for twelve pounds.
And he got it going, with difficulty.
He kicked it into life – it erupted
Out of the six-year sleep, and he was delighted.

A week later, astride it, before dawn,
A misty frosty morning,
He escaped

Into a telegraph pole
On the long straight west of Swinton.

Do not Pick up the Telephone

That plastic Buddha jars out a Karate screech

Before the soft words with their spores
The cosmetic breath of the gravestone

Death invented the phone it looks like the altar of death
Do not worship the telephone
It drags its worshippers into actual graves
With a variety of devices, through a variety of disguised voices

Sit godless when you hear the religious wail of the telephone

Do not think your house is a hide-out it is a telephone
Do not think you walk your own road, you walk down a telephone
Do not think you sleep in the hand of God you sleep in the mouthpiece of a telephone
Do not think your future is yours it waits upon a telephone
Do not think your thoughts are your own thoughts they are the toys of the telephone
Do not think these days are days they are the sacrificial priests of the telephone
The secret police of the telephone

O phone get out of my house
You are a bad god
Go and whisper on some other pillow
Do not lift your snake head in my house
Do not bite any more beautiful people

You plastic crab
Why is your oracle always the same in the end?
What rake-off for you from the cemeteries?

Your silences are as bad
When you are needed, dumb with the malice of the
  clairvoyant insane
The stars whisper together in your breathing
World's emptiness oceans in your mouthpiece
Stupidly your string dangles into the abysses
Plastic you are then stone a broken box of letters
And you cannot utter
Lies or truth, only the evil one
Makes you tremble with sudden appetite to see somebody
  undone

Blackening electrical connections
To where death bleaches its crystals
You swell and you writhe
You open your Buddha gape
You screech at the root of the house

Do not pick up the detonator of the telephone
A flame from the last day will come lashing out of the
  telephone
A dead body will fall out of the telephone

Do not pick up the telephone

In the Likeness of a Grasshopper

A trap
Waits on the field path.

A wicker contraption, with working parts,
Its spring tensed and set.

So flimsily made, out of grass
(Out of the stems, the joints, the raspy-dry flags).

Baited with a fur-soft caterpillar,
A belly of amorous life, pulsing signals.

Along comes a love-sick, perfume-footed
Music of the wild earth.

The trap, touched by a breath,
Jars into action, its parts blur –

And music cries out.

A sinewy violin
Has caught its violinist.

Cloud-fingered summer, the beautiful trapper,
Picks up the singing cage

And takes out the Song, adds it to the Songs
With which she robes herself, which are her wealth,

Sets her trap again, a yard further on.

New Foal

Yesterday he was nowhere to be found
In the skies or under the skies.

Suddenly he's here – a warm heap
Of ashes and embers, fondled by small draughts.

A star dived from outer space – flared
And burned out in the straw.
Now something is stirring in the smoulder.
We call it a foal.

Still stunned
He has no idea where he is.
His eyes, dew-dusky, explore gloom walls and a glare
doorspace.
Is this the world?
It puzzles him. It is a great numbness.

He pulls himself together, getting used to the weight of
things
And to that tall horse nudging him, and to this straw.

He rests
From the first blank shock of light, the empty daze
Of the questions –
What has happened? What am I?

His ears keep on asking, gingerly.

But his legs are impatient,
Recovering from so long being nothing
They are restless with ideas, they start to try a few out,
Angling this way and that,
Feeling for leverage, learning fast –

And suddenly he's up

And stretching – a giant hand
Strokes him from nose to heel
Perfecting his outline, as he tightens
The knot of himself.
                                        Now he comes teetering
Over the weird earth. His nose
Downy and magnetic, draws him, incredulous,
Towards his mother. And the world is warm
And careful and gentle. Touch by touch
Everything fits him together.

Soon he'll be almost a horse.
He wants only to be Horse,
Pretending each day more and more Horse
Till he's perfect Horse. Then unearthly Horse
Will surge through him, weightless, a spinning of flame
Under sudden gusts,

It will coil his eyeball and his heel
In a single terror – like the awe
Between lightning and thunderclap.

And curve his neck, like a sea-monster emerging
Among foam,

And fling the new moons through his stormy banner,
And the full moons and the dark moons.

Low Water

This evening
The river is a beautiful idle woman.

The day's August burn-out has distilled
A heady sundowner.
She lies back, bored and tipsy.

She lolls on her deep couch. And a long thigh
Lifts from the flash of her silks.

Adoring trees, kneeling, ogreish eunuchs
Comb out her spread hair, massage her fingers.

She stretches – and an ecstasy tightens
Over her skin, and deep in her gold body

Thrills spasm and dissolve. She drowses.

Her half-dreams lift out of her, light-minded
Love-pact suicides. Copulation and death.

She stirs her love-potion – ooze of balsam
Thickened with fish-mucus and algae.

You stand under leaves, your feet in shallows.
She eyes you steadily from the beginning of the world.

Go Fishing

Join water, wade in underbeing
Let brain mist into moist earth
Ghost loosen away downstream
Gulp river and gravity

Lose words
Cease
Be assumed into glistenings of lymph
As if creation were a wound
As if this flow were all plasm healing

Be supplanted by mud and leaves and pebbles
By sudden rainbow monster-structures
That materialize in suspension gulping
And dematerialize under pressure of the eye

Be cleft by the sliding prow
Displaced by the hull of light and shadow

Dissolved in earth-wave, the soft sun-shock,
Dismembered in sun-melt

Become translucent – one untangling drift
Of water-mesh, and a weight of earth-taste light
Mangled by wing-shadows
Everything circling and flowing and hover-still

Crawl out over roots, new and nameless
Search for face, harden into limbs

Let the world come back, like a white hospital
Busy with urgency words

Try to speak and nearly succeed
Heal into time and other people

An Eel

I

The strange part is his head. Her head. The strangely ripened
Domes over the brain, swollen nacelles
For some large containment. Lobed glands
Of some large awareness. Eerie the eel's head.
This full, plum-sleeked fruit of evolution.
Beneath it, her snout's a squashed slipper-face,
The mouth grin-long and perfunctory,
Undershot predatory. And the iris, dirty gold
Distilled only enough to be different
From the olive lode of her body,
The grained and woven blacks. And ringed larger
With a vaguer vision, an earlier eye
Behind her eye, paler, blinder,
Inward. Her buffalo hump
Begins the amazement of her progress.
Her mid-shoulder pectoral fin – concession
To fish-life – secretes itself
Flush with her concealing suit: under it
The skin's a pale exposure of deepest eel
As her belly is, a dulled pearl.
Strangest, the thumb-print skin, the rubberized weave
Of her insulation. Her whole body
Damascened with identity. This is she
Suspends the Sargasso
In her inmost hope. Her life is a cell
Sealed from event, her patience
Global and furthered with love
By the bending stars as if she
Were earth's sole initiate. Alone
In her millions, the moon's pilgrim,
The nun of water.

II

Where does the river come from?
And the eel, the night-mind of water –
The river within the river and opposite –
The night-nerve of water?

Not from the earth's remembering mire
Not from the air's whim
Not from the brimming sun. Where from?

From the bottom of the nothing pool
Sargasso of God
Out of the empty spiral of stars

A glimmering person

Night Arrival of Sea-Trout

Honeysuckle hanging her fangs.
Foxglove rearing her open belly.
Dogrose touching the membrane.

Through the dew's mist, the oak's mass
Comes plunging, tossing dark antlers.

Then a shattering
Of the river's hole, where something leaps out –

An upside-down, buried heaven
Snarls, moon-mouthed, and shivers.

Summer dripping stars, biting at the nape.
Lobworms coupling in saliva.
Earth singing under her breath.

And out in the hard corn a horned god
Running and leaping
With a bat in his drum.

October Salmon

He's lying in poor water, a yard or so depth of poor safety,
Maybe only two feet under the no-protection of an
  outleaning small oak,
Half under a tangle of brambles.

After his two thousand miles, he rests,
Breathing in that lap of easy current
In his graveyard pool.

About six pounds weight,
Four years old at most, and hardly a winter at sea –
But already a veteran,
Already a death-patched hero. So quickly it's over!

So briefly he roamed the gallery of marvels!
Such sweet months, so richly embroidered into earth's
  beauty-dress,
Her life-robe –
Now worn out with her tirelessness, her insatiable quest,
Hangs in the flow, a frayed scarf –

An autumnal pod of his flower,
The mere hull of his prime, shrunk at shoulder and flank,

With the sea-going Aurora Borealis
Of his April power –
The primrose and violet of that first upfling in the estuary –
Ripened to muddy dregs,
The river reclaiming his sea-metals.

In the October light
He hangs there, patched with leper-cloths.

Death has already dressed him
In her clownish regimentals, her badges and decorations,
Mapping the completion of his service,

His face a ghoul-mask, a dinosaur of senility, and his whole body
A fungoid anemone of canker –

Can the caress of water ease him?
The flow will not let up for a minute.

What a change! from that covenant of polar light
To this shroud in a gutter!
What a death-in-life – to be his own spectre!
His living body become death's puppet,
Dolled by death in her crude paints and drapes
He haunts his own staring vigil
And suffers the subjection, and the dumbness,
And the humiliation of the role!

And that is how it is,
That is what is going on there, under the scrubby oak tree, hour after hour,
That is what the splendour of the sea has come down to,
And the eye of ravenous joy – king of infinite liberty
In the flashing expanse, the bloom of sea-life,

On the surge-ride of energy, weightless,
Body simply the armature of energy
In that earliest sea-freedom, the savage amazement of life,
The salt mouthful of actual existence
With strength like light –

Yet this was always with him. This was inscribed in his egg.
This chamber of horrors is also home.
He was probably hatched in this very pool.

And this was the only mother he ever had, this uneasy channel of minnows
Under the mill-wall, with bicycle wheels, car tyres, bottles
And sunk sheets of corrugated iron.
People walking their dogs trail their evening shadows across him.

If boys see him they will try to kill him.

All this, too, is stitched into the torn richness,
The epic poise
That holds him so steady in his wounds, so loyal to his doom,
  so patient
In the machinery of heaven.

That Morning

We came where the salmon were so many
So steady, so spaced, so far-aimed
On their inner map, England could add

Only the sooty twilight of South Yorkshire
Hung with the drumming drift of Lancasters
Till the world had seemed capsizing slowly.

Solemn to stand there in the pollen light
Waist-deep in wild salmon swaying massed
As from the hand of God. There the body

Separated, golden and imperishable,
From its doubting thought – a spirit-beacon
Lit by the power of the salmon

That came on, came on, and kept on coming
As if we flew slowly, their formations
Lifting us toward some dazzle of blessing

One wrong thought might darken. As if the fallen
World and salmon were over. As if these
Were the imperishable fish

That had let the world pass away –

There, in a mauve light of drifted lupins,
They hung in the cupped hands of mountains

Made of tingling atoms. It had happened.
Then for a sign that we were where we were
Two gold bears came down and swam like men

Beside us. And dived like children.
And stood in deep water as on a throne
Eating pierced salmon off their talons.

So we found the end of our journey.

So we stood, alive in the river of light
Among the creatures of light, creatures of light.

Little Whale Song

for Charles Causley

What do they think of themselves
With their global brains –
The tide-power voltage illumination
Of those brains? Their X-ray all-dimension

Grasp of this world's structures, their brains budded
Clone replicas of the electron world
Lit and re-imagining the world,
Perfectly tuned receivers and perceivers,

Each one a whole tremulous world
Feeling through the world? What
Do they make of each other?

'We are beautiful. We stir

Our self-colour in the pot of colours
Which is the world. At each
Tail-stroke we deepen
Our being into the world's lit substance,

And our joy into the world's
Spinning bliss, and our peace
Into the world's floating, plumed peace.'

Their body-tons, echo-chambered,

Amplify the whisper
Of currents and airs, of sea-peoples

And planetary manoeuvres,
Of seasons, of shores, and of their own

Moon-lifted incantation, as they dance
Through the original Earth-drama
In which they perform, as from the beginning,

The Royal House.

The loftiest, spermiest

Passions, the most exquisite pleasures,
The noblest characters, the most god-like
Oceanic presence and poise –

The most terrible fall.

Rain-Charm for the Duchy

for H.R.H. Prince Harry

After the five-month drought
My windscreen was frosted with dust.
Sight itself had grown a harsh membrane
Against glare and particles.

Now the first blobby tears broke painfully.

Big, sudden thunderdrops. I felt them sploshing like vapoury
  petrol
Among the ants
In Cranmere's cracked heath-tinder. And into the ulcer craters
Of what had been river pools.

Then, like taking a great breath, we were under it.
Thunder gripped and picked up the city.
Rain didn't so much fall as collapse.
The pavements danced, like cinders in a riddle.

Flash in the pan, I thought, as people scampered.
Soon it was falling vertical, precious, pearled.
Thunder was a brass-band accompaniment
To some festive, civic event. Squeals and hurry. With tourist
  bunting.

The precinct saplings lifted their arms and faces. And the
  heaped-up sky
Moved in mayoral pomp, behind buildings,
With flash and thump. It had almost gone by
And I almost expected the brightening. Instead, something
  like a shutter

Jerked and rattled – and the whole county darkened.
Then rain really came down. You scrambled into the car
Scattering oxygen like a drenched bush.
What a weight of warm Atlantic water!

The car-top hammered. The Cathedral jumped in and out
Of a heaven that had obviously caught fire
And couldn't be contained.
A girl in high heels, her handbag above her head,

Risked it across the square's lit metals.
We saw surf cuffed over her and the car jounced.
Grates, gutters, clawed in the backwash.
She kept going. Flak and shrapnel

Of thundercracks
Hit the walls and roofs. Still a swimmer
She bobbed off, into sea-smoke,
Where headlights groped. Already

Thunder was breaking up the moors.
It dragged tors over the city –
Uprooted chunks of map. Smeltings of ore, pink and violet,
Spattered and wriggled down

Into the boiling sea
Where Exeter huddled –
A small trawler, nets out.
'Think of the barley!' you said.

You remembered earlier harvests.
But I was thinking
Of joyful sobbings –
The throb

In the rock-face mosses of the Chains,
And of the exultant larvae in the Barle's shrunk trench, their filaments ablur like propellers, under the churned ceiling of light,

And of the Lyn's twin gorges, clearing their throats, deepening their voices, beginning to hear each other
Rehearse forgotten riffles,

And the Mole, a ditch's choked whisper
Rousing the stagnant camps of the Little Silver, the Crooked
Oak and the Yeo
To a commotion of shouts, muddied oxen
A rumbling of wagons,

And the red seepage, the smoke of life
Lowering its ringlets into the Taw,

And the Torridge, rising to the kiss,
Plunging under sprays, new-born,
A washed cherub, clasping the breasts of light,

And the Okement, nudging her detergent bottles, tugging at
her nylon stockings, starting to trundle her Pepsi-Cola
cans,

And the Tamar, roused and blinking under the fifty-mile
drumming,
Declaiming her legend – her rusty knights tumbling out of
their clay vaults, her cantrevs assembling from shillets,
With a cheering of aged stones along the Lyd and the Lew,
the Wolf and the Thrushel,

And the Tavy, jarred from her quartzy rock-heap, feeling the
moor shift
Rinsing her stale mouth, tasting tin, copper, ozone,

And the baby Erme, under the cyclone's top-heavy, toppling
sea-fight, setting afloat odd bits of dead stick,

And the Dart, her shaggy horde coming down
Astride bareback ponies, with a cry,
Loosening sheepskin banners, bumping the granite,
Flattening rowans and frightening oaks,

And the Teign, startled in her den
By the rain-dance of bracken
Hearing Heaven reverberate under Gidleigh,

And the highest pool of the Exe, her coil recoiling under the sky-shock
Where a drinking stag flings its head up
From a spilled skyful of lightning –

My windscreen wipers swam as we moved.
                                        I imagined the two moors
The two stone-age hands
Cupped and brimming, lifted, an offering –
And I thought of those other, different lightnings, the patient, thirsting ones

Under Crow Island, inside Bideford Bar,
And between the Hamoaze anchor chains,
And beneath the thousand, shivering, fibreglass hulls
Inside One Gun Point, and aligned

Under the Ness, and inside Great Bull Hill:

The salmon, deep in the thunder, lit
And again lit, with glimpses of quenchings,
Twisting their glints in the suspense,
Biting at the stir, beginning to move.

The Last of the 1st/5th Lancashire Fusiliers

A Souvenir of the Gallipoli Landings

The father capers across the yard cobbles
Look, like a bird, a water-bird, an ibis going over pebbles
We laughed, like warships fluttering bunting.

Heavy-duty design, deep-seated in ocean-water
The warships flutter bunting.
A fiesta day for the warships
Where war is only an idea, as drowning is only an idea
In the folding of a wave, in the mourning
Funeral procession, the broadening wake
That follows a ship under power.

War is an idea in the muzzled calibre of the big guns.
In the grey, wolvish outline.
War is a kind of careless health, like the heart-beat
In the easy bodies of sailors, feeling the big engines
Idling between emergencies.

It is what has left the father
Who has become a bird.
Once he held war in his strong pint mugful of tea
And drank at it, heavily sugared.
It was all for him
Under the parapet, under the periscope, the look-out
Under Achi Baba and the fifty billion flies.

Now he has become a long-billed, spider-kneed bird
Bow-backed, finding his footing, over the frosty cobbles
A wader, picking curiosities from the shallows.

His sons don't know why they laughed, watching him
    through the window
Remembering it, remembering their laughter
They only want to weep

As after the huge wars
Senseless huge wars
Huge senseless weeping.

Football

I was sick of football
Before I understood
What the game was. Dad and his boyhood!
Something his feet seemed to ail.

That damned tin can he had to kick
The whole way daily to school
Then the whole way back! His iron-shod rule.
Like a blind man with a white stick.

The school handbell, rung for playtime to end,
Flew off its handle. The purest chance.
His boot couldn't resist it – mid-bounce
He put it straight through a classroom window.

A puppy-dog, in the fish and chip shop,
Jumped from somebody's arms. It was bolting
Out for the street as his foot saved it. Incredible!
It soared over the counter into the chip-fat.

Impossible! But he did it – his boot did it
While he stared appalled. Then endless
Endless running on the hills
Escaping the torment of unfitness.

Centre half, the local team,
Picked by the talent scout for the big time
Just as the trenches buried him. More muscular
He emerged a Catch-as-catch-can wrestler.

Demobbed, he'd lost patience as a footman
Of the field's niceties.
More an assault-force with a grudge for justice,
The hit-man for the opposition's hit-men.

During his last game, my brother
Crept at half-time from the crowd
That was roaring for his father's blood.
His quiet father. His gentle, thunderstorm father.

Using up his family's every last kick.
His game, the Great War – one and synonymous.
His field – our burnt-out-no-man's-land. His trophies –
Our crosses. His triumphs – our after-shock.

Comics

My brother was born blue with his head jammed
Hard against the stony dead-end
Of the industrial tunnel. The birth-cord
Tight around his neck. His escape tool
Was Comics, Westerns. Freedom
Opened away North of the Great Divide
Inside the head. His talisman, his compass,
The rifle
Fallen into his hands from the Paleolithic,
Invisibly engraved
With Bison and Cave Bear. But the Comic Mags
Collected anyhow
Were the drug that took him
Up through the smoke-hole, out through the attic skylight.

Mother feared their visions.
The Wesleyan prudery of her girlhood –
Or what? – again and again she crammed them
Into the ash-bin. Again and again he retrieved them –
Stock to trade for others. She feared
The stars in the eyes, the bear path
Leading out of the valley
Into the den of a strange woman. The snare
Of a temple harlot.
The wrong gods. 'If you do this, that or that –
You'll kill me. Those Magazines
Are my dreams being torn into tiny pieces
By godless men who dream of bad women –
This valley and all its works, all we've slaved for,
Dumped in the ash-bin. Chapels and godliness,
Next to cleanliness, torn up and dumped in an ash-bin.'

That is what she meant, dumping his comics –
As if they were true maps

Locating Gold Fields sown with spent bullets
And upturned toes. Or Paradise East of the Sun.
Or the folly-stone of the Alchemists
In a nest of hocus-pocus.
She didn't know what she was doing
That was so clairvoyant –
As when she clawed in the blazing coals
For a screwed up ten shilling note she'd idly tossed there –
Only knowing that she was desperate
And that it was all too late.

Midas

Peasants crowded to gawp at Silenus –
The end-product of a life
They could not imagine.
They chained him with flowers and dragged him,
In a harness of flowers, to their king, Midas,
As if he were some
Harmless, helpless, half-tapir or other
Charming monster.
When Midas recognised him,
And honoured him, fat and old and drunk as he was,
As the companion of Bacchus,
And restored him to the god,

Bacchus was so grateful
He offered to grant Midas any wish –
Whatever the King wanted, it would be granted.
Midas was overjoyed
To hear this first approach, so promising,
Of his peculiar horrible doom.
He did not have to rack his brains.
A certain fantasy
Hovered in his head perpetually,
Wistfully fondled all his thoughts by day,
Manipulated all his dreams by night.
Now it saw its chance and seized his tongue.
It shoved aside
The billion – infinite – opportunities
For Midas
To secure a happiness, guaranteed,
Within the human range
Of what is possible to a god.
It grasped, with a king's inane greed,
The fate I shall describe.

Midas said: 'Here is my wish.
Let whatever I touch become gold.
Yes, gold, the finest, the purest, the brightest.'
Bacchus gazed at the King and sighed gently.
He felt pity –
Yet his curiosity was intrigued
To see how such stupidity would be punished.
So he granted the wish, then stood back to watch.

The Phrygian King returned through the garden
Eager to test the power – yet apprehensive
That he had merely dreamed and now was awake,
Where alchemy never works. He broke a twig
From a low branch of oak. The leaves
Turned to heavy gold as he stared at them
And his mouth went dry.
He felt his brain move strangely, like a muscle.
He picked up a stone and weighed it in his hand
As it doubled its weight, then doubled it again,
And became bright yellow.
He brushed his hand over a clump of grass,
The blades stayed bent – soft ribbons
Of gold foil. A ripe ear of corn
Was crisp and dry and light as he plucked it
But a heavy slug of gold, intricately braided
As he rolled it between his palms.
It was then that a cold thought seemed to whisper.
He had wanted to chew the milky grains –
But none broke chaffily free from their pockets.
The ear was gold – its grain inedible,
Inaccessibly solid with the core.
He frowned. With the frown on his face
He reached for a hanging apple.
With a slight twist he took the sudden weight
No longer so happily. This was a fruit
He made no attempt to bite, as he pondered its colour.

Almost inadvertently he stroked
The door pillars, as he entered the palace,
Pausing to watch the brilliant yellow
Suffuse the dark stone.
He washed his hands under flowing water, at a fountain.
Already a hope
Told him that the gift might wash away,
As waking up will wash out a nightmare.
But the water that touched him
Coiled into the pool below as plumes
Of golden smoke, settling heavily
In a silt of gold atoms.

Suddenly his vision
Of transmuting his whole kingdom to gold
Made him sweat –
It chilled him as he sat
At the table
And reached for a roasted bird. The carcase
Toppled from his horrified fingers
Into his dish with a clunk,
As if he had picked up a table ornament.
He reached for bread
But could not break
The plaque of gold that resembled a solid puddle
Smelted from ore.
Almost in terror now
He reached for the goblet of wine –
Taking his time, he poured in water,
Swirled the mix in what had been translucent
Rhinoceros horn
But was already common and commoner metal.
He set his lips to the cold rim
And others, dumbfounded
By what they had already seen, were aghast
When they saw the wet gold shine on his lips,

And as he lowered the cup
Saw him mouthing gold, spitting gold mush –
That had solidified, like gold cinders.
He got up, reeling
From his golden chair, as if poisoned.

He fell on his bed, face down, eyes closed
From the golden heavy fold of his pillow.
He prayed
To the god who had given him the gift
To take it back. 'I have been a fool.
Forgive me, Bacchus. Forgive the greed
That made me so stupid.
Forgive me for a dream
That had not touched the world
Where gold is truly gold and nothing but.
Save me from my own shallowness,
Where I shall drown in gold
And be buried in gold.
Nothing can live, I see, in a world of gold.'

Bacchus, too, had had enough.
His kindliness came uppermost easily.
'I return you,' said the god,
'To your happier human limitations.
But now you must wash away
The last stain of the curse
You begged for and preferred to every blessing.
A river goes by Sardis. Follow it upstream.
Find the source
Which gushes from a cliff and plunges
Into a rocky pool. Plunge with it.
Go completely under. Let that river
Carry your folly away and leave you clean.'

Midas obeyed and the river's innocent water
Took whatever was left of the granted wish.

Even today the soil of its flood plain
Can be combed into a sparse glitter.
And big popcorns of gold, in its gravels,
Fever the fossicker.

Midas never got over the shock.
The sight of gold was like the thought of a bee
To one just badly stung –
It made his hair prickle, his nerves tingle.
He retired to the mountain woods
And a life of deliberate poverty. There
He worshipped Pan, who lives in the mountain caves.
King Midas was chastened
But not really changed. He was no wiser.
His stupidity
Was merely lying low. Waiting, as usual,
For another chance to ruin his life.

*

The cliff-face of Tmolus watches
Half the Mediterranean. It falls away
To Sardis on one side, and on the other
To the village of Hypaepa.
Pan lives in a high cave on that cliff.
He was amusing himself,
Showing off to the nymphs
Thrilling them out of their airy bodies
With the wild airs
He breathed through the reeds of his flute.
Their ecstasies flattered him,
Their words, their exclamations, flattered him.
But the flattered
Become fools. And when he assured them
That Apollo, no less,
Stole his tunes and rearranged his rhythms

It was a shock
For Pan
To find himself staring at the great god
Hanging there in the air off the cave mouth,
Half eclipsed with black rage,
Half beaming with a friendly challenge.
'Tmolus, the mountain,' suggested the god, 'can judge us.'

Tmolus shook out his hair,
Freed his ears of bushes, trees, bird, insects,
Then took his place at the seat of judgement,
Binding his wig with a whole oak tree –
The acorns clustering over his eyebrows,
And announced to Pan: 'Your music first.'

It so happened
Midas was within hearing
Collecting nuts and berries. Suddenly he heard
Music that froze him immobile
As long as it lasted. He did not know
What happened to him as Pan's piping
Carried him off –
Filled him with precipices,
Lifted him on weathered summits,
Poured blue icy rivers through him,
Hung him from the stars,
Replaced him
With the fluorescent earth
Spinning and dancing on the jet of a fountain.

It stopped, and Tmolus smiled,
As if coming awake –
Back, he thought, hugely refreshed
From a journey through himself.
But now he turned
To Apollo, the great, bright god.

As he turned, all his forests
Dragged like a robe.

Apollo was serious.
His illustrious hair burst
From under a wreath of laurel picked
Only moments ago on Parnassus.
The fringe of his cloak of Tyrian purple
Was all that touched the earth.
In his left hand the lyre
Was a model, in magical code,
Of the earth and the heavens –
Ivory of narwhal and elephant,
Diamonds from the interiors of stars.
In his right hand he held
The plectrum that could touch
Every wavelength in the Universe
Singly or simultaneously.
Even his posture
Was like a tone – like a tuning fork,
Vibrant, alerting the whole earth,
Bringing heaven down to listen.

Then the plectrum moved and Tmolus,
After the first chords,
Seemed to be about to decompose
Among the harmonics.
He pulled himself together – but it was no use,
He was helpless
As the music dissolved him and poured him
Through the snakes and ladders
Of the creation and the decreation
Of the elements,
And finally, bringing the sea-horizon
To an edge clean as a knife,
Restored him to his shaggy, crumpled self.

Pan was humbled. Yes, he agreed –
Apollo was the master. Tmolus was correct.
The nymphs gazed at Apollo. They agreed.
But then a petulant voice,
A hard-angled, indignant, differing voice
Came from behind a rock.

Midas stood up. 'The judgement,' he cried,
'Is ignorant, stupid, and merely favours power.
Apollo's efforts
Are nothing but interior decoration
By artificial light, for the chic, the effete.
Pan is the real thing – the true voice
Of the subatomic.'

Apollo's face seemed to writhe
Momentarily
As he converted this clown's darkness to light,
Then pointed his plectrum at the ears
That had misheard so grievously.

Abruptly those ears lolled long and animal,
On either side of Midas' impertinent face.
Revolving at the root, grey-whiskered, bristly,
The familiar ears of a big ass.
The King,
Feeling the change, grabbed to hang on to his ears.
Then he had some seconds of pure terror
Waiting for the rest of his body to follow.
But the ears used up the power of the plectrum.
This was the god's decision. The King
Lived on, human, wagging the ears of a donkey.

Midas crept away.
Every few paces he felt at his ears and groaned.
He slunk back to his palace. He needed
Comfort. He was bitterly disillusioned
With the spirit of the wilderness.

He hid those ears – in a turban superb
As compensation could be.

But a king needs a barber.
Sworn to secrecy or impalement
The barber, wetting his lips,
Clipped around the gristly roots
Of the great angling ears as if the hair there
Might be live nerve-ends.
What he was staring at,
And having to believe, was worse
For him than for their owner,
Almost. He had to hide this news
As if it were red-hot
Under his tongue, and keep it there.
The ultimate shame secret
Of the ruler of the land.
It struggled to blurt
Itself out, whenever
He opened his mouth.
It made him sweat and often
Gasp aloud, or strangle
A groan to a sigh. Or wake up
In the middle of the silent night
Certain he had just
Yelled it out, at the top of his voice,
To the whole city.
He knew, this poor barber,
He had to spit it out somehow.

In the lawn of a park he lifted a turf
After midnight. He kneeled there
And whispered into the raw hole
'Ass's ears! Midas has ass's ears!'
Then fitted the turf back, trod flat the grave
Of that insuppressible gossip,

And went off, singing
Under his breath.

But in no time,
As if the barber had grafted it there
From some far-off reed-bed,
A clump of reeds bunched out, from that very sod.
It looked strange, on the park lawn,
But sounded stranger.
Every gust brought an articulate whisper
Out of the bending stalks. At every puff
They betrayed the barber's confidence,
Broadcasting the buried secret.
Hissing to all who happened to be passing:
'Ass's ears! Midas has ass's ears!'

The Tender Place

Your temples, where the hair crowded in,
Were the tender place. Once to check
I dropped a file across the electrodes
Of a twelve-volt battery – it exploded
Like a grenade. Somebody wired you up.
Somebody pushed the lever. They crashed
The thunderbolt into your skull.
In their bleached coats, with blenched faces,
They hovered again
To see how you were, in your straps.
Whether your teeth were still whole.
The hand on the calibrated lever
Again feeling nothing
Except feeling nothing pushed to feel
Some squirm of sensation. Terror
Was the cloud of you
Waiting for these lightnings. I saw
An oak limb sheared at a bang.
You your Daddy's leg. How many seizures
Did you suffer this god to grab you
By the roots of the hair? The reports
Escaped back into clouds. What went up
Vaporized? Where lightning rods wept copper
And the nerve threw off its skin
Like a burning child
Scampering out of the bomb-flash. They dropped you
A rigid bent bit of wire
Across the Boston City grid. The lights
In the Senate House dipped
As your voice dived inwards

Right through the bolt-hole basement.
Came up, years later,

Over-exposed, like an X-ray –
Brain-map still dark-patched
With the scorched-earth scars
Of your retreat. And your words,
Faces reversed from the light,
Holding in their entrails.

Fate Playing

Because the message somehow met a goblin,
Because precedents tripped your expectations,
Because your London was still a kaleidoscope
Of names and places any jolt could scramble,
You waited mistaken. The bus from the North
Came in and emptied and I was not on it.
No matter how much you insisted
And begged the driver, probably with tears,
To produce me or to remember seeing me
Just miss getting on. I was not on it.
Eight in the evening and I was lost and at large
Somewhere in England. You restrained
Your confident inspiration
And did not dash out into the traffic
Milling around Victoria, utterly certain
Of bumping into me where I would have to be walking.
I was not walking anywhere. I was sitting
Unperturbed, in my seat on the train
Rocking towards King's Cross. Somebody,
Calmer than you, had a suggestion. So,
When I got off the train, expecting to find you
Somewhere down at the root of the platform,
I saw that surge and agitation, a figure
Breasting the flow of released passengers,
Then your molten face, your molten eyes
And your exclamations, your flinging arms
Your scattering tears
As if I had come back from the dead
Against every possibility, against
Every negative but your own prayer
To your own gods. There I knew what it was
To be a miracle. And behind you
Your jolly taxi-driver, laughing, like a small god,

To see an American girl being so American,
And to see your frenzied chariot-ride –
Sobbing and goading him, and pleading with him
To make happen what you needed to happen –
Succeed so completely, thanks to him.
Well, it was a wonder
That my train was not earlier, even much earlier,
That it pulled in, late, the very moment
You irrupted onto the platform. It was
Natural and miraculous and an omen
Confirming everything
You wanted confirmed. So your huge despair,
Your cross-London panic dash
And now your triumph, splashed over me,
Like love forty-nine times magnified,
Like the first thunder cloudburst engulfing
The drought in August
When the whole cracked earth seems to quake
And every leaf trembles
And everything holds up its arms weeping.

You Hated Spain

Spain frightened you. Spain
Where I felt at home. The blood-raw light,
The oiled anchovy faces, the African
Black edges to everything, frightened you.
Your schooling had somehow neglected Spain.
The wrought-iron grille, death and the Arab drum.
You did not know the language, your soul was empty
Of the signs, and the welding light
Made your blood shrivel. Bosch
Held out a spidery hand and you took it
Timidly, a bobby-sox American.
You saw right down to the Goya funeral grin
And recognized it, and recoiled
As your poems winced into chill, as your panic
Clutched back towards college America.
So we sat as tourists at the bullfight
Watching bewildered bulls awkwardly butchered,
Seeing the grey-faced matador, at the barrier
Just below us, straightening his bent sword
And vomiting with fear. And the horn
That hid itself inside the blowfly belly
Of the toppled picador punctured
What was waiting for you. Spain
Was the land of your dreams: the dust-red cadaver
You dared not wake with, the puckering amputations
No literature course had glamorized.
The juju land behind your African lips.
Spain was what you tried to wake up from
And could not. I see you, in moonlight,
Walking the empty wharf at Alicante
Like a soul waiting for the ferry,
A new soul, still not understanding,
Thinking it is still your honeymoon

In the happy world, with your whole life waiting,
Happy, and all your poems still to be found.

The Earthenware Head

Who modelled your head of terracotta?
Some American student friend.
Life-size, the lips half-pursed, raw-edged
With crusty tooling – a naturalistic attempt
At a likeness that just failed. You did not like it.
I did not like it. Unease magnetized it
For a perverse rite. What possessed us
To take it with us, in your red bucket bag?
November fendamp haze, the river unfurling
Dark whorls, ferrying slender willow yellows.
The pollard willows wore comfortless antlers,
Switch-horns, leafless. Just past where the field
Broadens and the path strays up to the right
To lose the river and puzzle for Grantchester,
A chosen willow leaned towards the water.
Above head height, the socket of a healed bole-wound,
A twiggy crotch, nearly an owl's porch,
Made a mythic shrine for your double.
I fitted it upright, firm. And a willow tree
Was a Herm, with your head, watching East
Through those tool-stabbed pupils. We left it
To live the world's life and weather forever.

You ransacked Thesaurus in your poem about it,
Veiling its mirror, rhyming yourself into safety
From its orphaned fate.
But it would not leave you. Weeks later
We could not seem to hit on the tree. We did not
Look too hard – just in passing. Already
You did not want to fear, if it had gone,
What witchcraft might ponder it. You never
Said much more about it.
What happened?

Maybe nothing happened. Perhaps
It is still there, representing you
To the sunrise, and happy
In its cold pastoral, lips pursed slightly
As if my touch had only just left it.
Or did boys find it – and shatter it? Or
Did the tree too kneel finally?
Surely the river got it. Surely
The river is its chapel. And keeps it. Surely
Your deathless head, fired in a furnace,
Face to face at last, kisses the Father
Mudded at the bottom of the Cam,
Beyond recognition or rescue,
All our fears washed from it, and perfect,
Under the stained mournful flow, saluted
Only in summer briefly by the slender
Punt-loads of shadows flitting towards their honey
And the stopped clock.
Evil.
That was what you called the head. Evil.

Flounders

Was that a happy day? From Chatham
Down at the South end of the Cape, our map
Somebody's optimistic assurance,
We set out to row. We got ourselves
Into mid-channel. The tide was flowing. We hung
Anchored. Northward-pulling, our baited leads
Bounced and bounced the bottom. For three hours –
Two or three sea-robins. Cruisers
Folded us under their bow-waves, we bobbed up,
Happy enough. But the wind
Smartened against us, and the tide turned, roughening,
Dragged seaward. We rowed. We rowed. We
Saw we weren't going to make it. We turned,
Cutting downwind for the sand-bar, beached
And wondered what next. It was there
I found a horse-shoe crab's carapace, perfect,
No bigger than a bee, in honey-pale cellophane.
No way back. But big, good America found us.
A power-boat and a pilot of no problems.
He roped our boat to his stern and with all his family
Slammed back across the channel into the wind,
The spray scything upwards, our boat behind
Twisting across the wake-boil – a hectic
Four or five minutes and he cast us off
In the lee of the land, but a mile or more
From our dock. We toiled along inshore. We came
To a back-channel, under beach-house gardens – marsh grass,
Wild, original greenery of America,
Mud-slicks and fiddler-crab warrens, as we groped
Towards the harbour. Gloom-rich water. Something
Suggested easy plenty. We lowered baits,
And out of about six feet of water

Six or seven feet from land, we pulled up flounders
Big as big plates, till all our bait had gone.
After our wind-burned, head-glitter day of emptiness,
And the slogging row for our lives, and the rescue,
Suddenly out of water easy as oil
The sea piled our boat with its surplus. And the day
Curled out of brilliant, arduous morning,
Through wind-hammered perilous afternoon,
Salt-scoured, to a storm-gold evening, a luxury
Of rowing among the dream-yachts of the rich
Lolling at anchor off the play-world pier.

How tiny an adventure
To stay so monumental in our marriage,
A slight ordeal of all that might be,
And a small thrill-breath of what many live by,
And a small prize, a toy miniature
Of the life that might have bonded us
Into a single animal, a single soul –

It was a visit from the goddess, the beauty
Who was poetry's sister – she had come
To tell poetry she was spoiling us.
Poetry listened, maybe, but we heard nothing
And poetry did not tell us. And we
Only did what poetry told us to do.

The Blue Flannel Suit

I had let it all grow. I had supposed
It was all OK. Your life
Was a liner I voyaged in.
Costly education had fitted you out.
Financiers and committees and consultants
Effaced themselves in the gleam of your finish.
You trembled with the new life of those engines.

That first morning,
Before your first class at College, you sat there
Sipping coffee. Now I know, as I did not,
What eyes waited at the back of the class
To check your first professional performance
Against their expectations. What assessors
Waited to see you justify the cost
And redeem their gamble. What a furnace
Of eyes waited to prove your metal. I watched
The strange dummy stiffness, the misery,
Of your blue flannel suit, its straitjacket, ugly
Half-approximation to your idea
Of the proprieties you hoped to ease into,
And your horror in it. And the tanned
Almost green undertinge of your face
Shrunk to its wick, your scar lumpish, your plaited
Head pathetically tiny.
                    You waited,
Knowing yourself helpless in the tweezers
Of the life that judged you, and I saw
The flayed nerve, the unhealable face-wound
Which was all you had for courage.
I saw that what gripped you, as you sipped,
Were terrors that had killed you once already.
Now, I see, I saw, sitting, the lonely

Girl who was going to die.
That blue suit.
A mad, execution uniform,
Survived your sentence. But then I sat, stilled,
Unable to fathom what stilled you
As I looked at you, as I am stilled
Permanently now, permanently
Bending so briefly at your open coffin.

Daffodils

Remember how we picked the daffodils?
Nobody else remembers, but I remember.
Your daughter came with her armfuls, eager and happy,
Helping the harvest. She has forgotten.
She cannot even remember you. And we sold them.
It sounds like sacrilege, but we sold them.
Were we so poor? Old Stoneman, the grocer,
Boss-eyed, his blood-pressure purpling to beetroot
(It was his last chance,
He would die in the same great freeze as you),
He persuaded us. Every Spring
He always bought them, sevenpence a dozen,
'A custom of the house'.

Besides, we still weren't sure we wanted to own
Anything. Mainly we were hungry
To convert everything to profit.
Still nomads – still strangers
To our whole possession. The daffodils
Were incidental gilding of the deeds,
Treasure trove. They simply came,
And they kept on coming.
As if not from the sod but falling from heaven.
Our lives were still a raid on our own good luck.
We knew we'd live for ever. We had not learned
What a fleeting glance of the everlasting
Daffodils are. Never identified
The nuptial flight of the rarest ephemera –
Our own days!
                                        We thought they were a windfall.
Never guessed they were a last blessing.
So we sold them. We worked at selling them
As if employed on somebody else's

Flower-farm. You bent at it
In the rain of that April – your last April.
We bent there together, among the soft shrieks
Of their jostled stems, the wet shocks shaken
Of their girlish dance-frocks –
Fresh-opened dragonflies, wet and flimsy,
Opened too early.

We piled their frailty lights on a carpenter's bench,
Distributed leaves among the dozens –
Buckling blade-leaves, limber, groping for air, zinc-
  silvered –
Propped their raw butts in bucket water,
Their oval, meaty butts,
And sold them, sevenpence a bunch –

Wind-wounds, spasms from the dark earth,
With their odourless metals,
A flamy purification of the deep grave's stony cold
As if ice had a breath –

We sold them, to wither.
The crop thickened faster than we could thin it.
Finally, we were overwhelmed
And we lost our wedding-present scissors.

Every March since they have lifted again
Out of the same bulbs, the same
Baby-cries from the thaw,
Ballerinas too early for music, shiverers
In the draughty wings of the year.
On that same groundswell of memory, fluttering
They return to forget you stooping there
Behind the rainy curtains of a dark April,
Snipping their stems.

But somewhere your scissors remember. Wherever they
  are.

Here somewhere, blades wide open,
April by April
Sinking deeper
Through the sod – an anchor, a cross of rust.

The Bee God

When you wanted bees I never dreamed
It meant your Daddy had come up out of the well.

I scoured the old hive, you painted it,
White, with crimson hearts and flowers, and bluebirds.

So you became the Abbess
In the nunnery of the bees.

But when you put on your white regalia,
Your veil, your gloves, I never guessed a wedding.

That Maytime, in the orchard, that summer,
The hot, shivering chestnuts leaned towards us.

Their great gloved hands again making their offer
I never know how to accept.

But you bowed over your bees
As you bowed over your Daddy.

Your page a dark swarm
Clinging under the lit blossom.

You and your Daddy there in the heart of it,
Weighing your slender neck.

I saw I had given you something
That had carried you off in a cloud of gutturals –

The thunderhead of your new selves
Tending your golden mane.

You did not want me to go but your bees
Had their own ideas.

You wanted the honey, you wanted those big blossoms
Clotted like first milk, and the fruit like babies.

But the bees' orders were geometric –
Your Daddy's plans were Prussian.

When the first bee touched my hair
You were peering into the cave of thunder.

That outrider tangled, struggled, stung –
Marking the target.

And I was flung like a headshot jackrabbit
Through sunlit whizzing tracers

As bees planted their volts, their thudding electrodes,
In on their target.

Your face wanted to save me
From what had been decided.

You rushed to me, your dream-time veil off,
Your ghost-proof gloves off,

But as I stood there, where I thought I was safe,
Clawing out of my hair

Sticky, disembowelled bees,
A lone bee, like a blind arrow,

Soared over the housetop and down
And locked onto my brow, calling for helpers

Who came –
Fanatics for their God, the God of the Bees,

Deaf to your pleas as the fixed stars
At the bottom of the well.

Being Christlike

You did not want to be Christlike. Though your father
Was your God and there was no other, you did not
Want to be Christlike. Though you walked
In the love of your father. Though you stared
At the stranger your mother.
What had she to do with you
But tempt you from your father?
When her great hooded eyes lowered
Their moon so close
Promising the earth you saw
Your fate and you cried
Get thee behind me. You did not
Want to be Christlike. You wanted
To be with your father
In wherever he was. And your body
Barred your passage. And your family
Who were your flesh and blood
Burdened it. And a god
That was not your father
Was a false god. But you did not
Want to be Christlike.

Red

Red was your colour.
If not red, then white. But red
Was what you wrapped around you.
Blood-red. Was it blood?
Was it red-ochre, for warming the dead?
Haematite to make immortal
The precious heirloom bones, the family bones.

When you had your way finally
Our room was red. A judgement chamber.
Shut casket for gems. The carpet of blood
Patterned with darkenings, congealments.
The curtains – ruby corduroy blood,
Sheer blood-falls from ceiling to floor.
The cushions the same. The same
Raw carmine along the window-seat.
A throbbing cell. Aztec altar – temple.

Only the bookshelves escaped into whiteness.

And outside the window
Poppies thin and wrinkle-frail
As the skin on blood,
Salvias, that your father named you after,
Like blood lobbing from a gash,
And roses, the heart's last gouts,
Catastrophic, arterial, doomed.

Your velvet long full skirt, a swathe of blood,
A lavish burgundy,
Your lips a dipped, deep crimson.

You revelled in red.
I felt it raw – like the crisp gauze edges
Of a stiffening wound. I could touch
The open vein in it, the crusted gleam.

Everything you painted you painted white
Then splashed it with roses, defeated it,
Leaned over it, dripping roses,
Weeping roses, and more roses,
Then sometimes, among them, a little bluebird.

Blue was better for you. Blue was wings.
Kingfisher blue silks from San Francisco
Folded your pregnancy
In crucible caresses.
Blue was your kindly spirit – not a ghoul
But electrified, a guardian, thoughtful.

In the pit of red
You hid from the bone-clinic whiteness.

But the jewel you lost was blue.

Snow

Snow falling. Snowflakes clung and melted
In the sparkly black fox fur of your hat.
Soft chandeliers, ghostly wreckage
Of the Moscow Opera. Flakes perching and
Losing their hold on the heather tips. An unending
Walk down the cobbled hill into the oven
Of empty fire. Among the falling
Heavens. A short walk
That could never end was
Never ending. Down, on down
Under the thick, loose flocculence
Of a life
Burning out in the air. Between char-black buildings
Converted to closed cafés and Brontë gift-shops.
Beyond them, the constellations falling
Through the Judaean thorns, into the fleeces
Of the Pennine sheep. Deepening
Over the faces of your school-friends,
Beside their snowed-under tanks, locked into the Steppe
Where the mud had frozen again
While they drank their coffee. You escaped
Deeper into the falling flakes. They were clinging
To the charcoal crimped black ponyskin
Coat you wore. Words seemed warm. They
Melted in our mouths
Whatever was trying to cling.
                                        Leaning snow
Folded you under its cloak and ushered you away
Down the hill. Back to where you came from.

I watched you. Feeling the snow's touch.

Already, it was burying your footprints,
Drawing its white sheet over everything,
Closing the air behind you.

A Dove

Snaps its twig-tether – mounts –
Dream-yanked up into vacuum
Wings snickering.

Another, in a shatter, hurls dodging away up.

They career through tree-mazes –
Nearly uncontrollable love-weights.

Or now
Temple-dancers, possessed, and steered
By solemn powers
Through insane, stately convulsions.

Porpoises
Of dove-lust and blood splendour
With arcs
And plungings, and spray-slow explosions.

Now violently gone
Riding the snake of the long love-whip
Among flarings of mares and stallions

Now staying
Coiled on a bough
Bubbling molten, wobbling top-heavy
Into one and many.

W. B. YEATS Poems selected by SEAMUS HEANEY

W. B. YEATS

Poems selected by SEAMUS HEANEY

faber and faber

First published in 2000
by Faber and Faber Limited
3 Queen Square London WC1N 3AU

Photoset by Parker Typesetting Service, Leicester
Printed in Italy

All rights reserved

Introduction and this selection © Seamus Heaney, 2000
The poems of W. B. Yeats © Michael B. Yeats

Seamus Heaney is hereby identified as editor
of this work in accordance with Section 77
of the Copyright, Designs and Patents Act 1988

This book is sold subject to the condition that it shall not, by way of trade or otherwise, be lent, resold, hired out or otherwise circulated without the publisher's prior consent in any form of binding or cover other than that in which it is published and without a similar condition including this condition being imposed on the subsequent purchaser

A CIP record for this book
is available from the British Library

ISBN 0–571–20378–7

10 9 8 7 6 5 4 3 2 1

Contents

Note of Acknowledgement

The Introduction of this book is a revised version of the Introduction to a slightly less comprehensive selection of W. B. Yeats's poems published in Volume II of *The Field Day Anthology of Irish Writing* (1991). I am grateful to Seamus Deane, General Editor of the anthology, for permission to reprint the material in this series. As before, the texts used are those in the second edition of *The Collected Poems of W. B. Yeats* (London: Macmillan, 1950). The order in which the poems from *New Poems* (1938) and *Last Poems* (1939) appear is that established by Richard J. Finneran in *W. B. Yeats: The Poems, A New Edition* (New York and London, Macmillan, 1983).

Introduction

When W. B. Yeats was born in Dublin on 13 June 1865, the Irish poet best known at home and abroad was Thomas Moore (1779–1852), author of *Irish Melodies*, songs that maintained a sentiment of Irish nationality after the Act of Union had dissolved the Dublin parliament in 1800. The *Melodies* evoked the martial splendours of the ancient Gaelic race, but their effect was more palliative than inflammatory and as the nineteenth century proceeded Moore's conciliatory style began to lose favour. Increasingly, the decisive developments in Irish affairs depended upon what happened in committee rooms at home rather than in drawing rooms in England. Moore's songs remained popular, but in the changing literary and political conditions of the 1890s, William Hazlitt's taunt that he had turned the wild harp of Erin into a musical snuff-box was falling on ever more sympathetic ears. Early in the new century, for example, in his novel *A Portrait of the Artist as a Young Man*, James Joyce has a scene where the hero walks beneath the statue of Moore on College Green and observes its 'servile head'; and he then goes on to conceive of this representation of Ireland's 'national poet' in terms of its 'indignity'.

By the time of Yeats's death in 1939, however, 'indomitableness' had replaced 'indignity' as the distinguishing mark of the 'national' poet and the role he played. From the moment he formulated his artistic and cultural ambitions –

Know, that I would accounted be
True brother of a company
That sang, to sweeten Ireland's wrong,
Ballad and story, rann and song
('To Ireland in the Coming Times')

– to the moment when he took leave of the world and had an epitaph cut in stone 'by his command' –

Cast a cold eye
On life, on death.
Horseman, pass by!

– 'command' had indeed characterized the Yeatsian style. However insecure the inner man may have been, the outer mask appeared purposeful and uningratiating. Yeats managed to create a heroic rôle for the poet in the modern world, so much so that T. S. Eliot's evocation of 'the shade of some dead master' in 'Little Gidding' (1943) is commonly taken to be a tribute to the recently dead Irishman. And the canonization continues. Nowadays, whether he is thought of as a national bard or a world poet, Yeats figures in the mind as a translated force, an energy released and a destiny fulfilled.

Still, as a poet with a strong histrionic streak and a readiness to identify himself with variously anti-establishment and anti-populist causes in the course of a long lifetime, Yeats was never without his detractors. Yet from the beginning, those most intent upon debunking the man or demythologizing the poet could never deny that his commitments were as selfless as they were ardent. Neither George Moore (Yeats's senior) nor James Joyce (his junior) ever doubted that the phenomenon known as the Irish Literary Revival represented the execution of high artistic purpose, although both of them found fault with Yeats's ways of discharging that purpose. Moore, as a fellow member of the middle-class, mocked him for affecting a Renaissance *hauteur* and for getting carried away by his aristocratic fantasies. Joyce, more indigent and less socially advantaged, was oddly enough enraged by what he perceived as the poet's *downward* mobility and castigated him in his pamplet *The Day of the Rabblement* (1901) for his association with 'a platform from which even self-respect should have urged him to refrain'.

Joyce was here referring to Yeats's association, from the late 1890s onwards, with the cultural ambitions of the Irish Literary Theatre, soon to become the Abbey Theatre. Yeats was thereby lending his gift to the nationalist political lobby and, in Joyce's view, abdicating from the artist's proper stance as vigilant solitary, neither susceptible nor attentive to 'the emotion of the multitude'. What Joyce could not know, of course, was that a new, convulsive energy was building in the poet as the effort to bind himself to a national purpose – 'Theatre business, management of men' – collided with his antithetical and more powerful drive to assert the claims of individual personality over every solidarity. A decade later, in *Responsibilities* (1914) and *The Wild Swans at Coole* (1919), a poetry of singular clarity and detachment would spring from the tension generated in him between his ideal of service to a new, imagined Ireland and his recognition of the demeaned standards actually preferred by the Ireland in which he was living. It all contributed to the emergence of a new poetic voice, intellectually pugnacious, emotionally renovated and rhetorically high-spirited.

Yeats's active involvement with cultural and political movements in turn-of-the-century Ireland was important to his work as a lyric poet. *The Wind Among the Reeds* (1899) was continuous with the propagandist essays and reviews of the previous decade, part of an overall effort on behalf of 'the Celtic movement': the cadences of 'He Wishes for the Cloths of Heaven' were another register of a voice that was just as capable when engaged in controversy on the letters pages of British and Irish newspapers. But equally (if more unknowably) Yeats's poetry, from the mid-nineties onwards, was affected by his entry into sexual maturity and the full creative confidence that came with it. The cry of the sedge and the curlew may be present in the twilit atmosphere of the 1899 volume, but behind the Celtic landscape of the poems there was the very different townscape of Bloomsbury and the Tottenham Court Road where the poet bought the double bed he and Mrs Olivia Shakespear occupied with such clandestine joy during the happy year of 1896.

And all the while, of course, there was Maud Gonne, 'high and solitary and most stern' according to one of the poems about her, 'foremost among those I would hear praised' according to another, and 'the troubling of my life' according to a famous sentence in his *Autobiographies*. The passion she inspired – and as readers we experience it more as creative power than erotic need – made her a figure of primary poetic radiance, a Dublin Beatrice, an archetype as much as a daily presence. Nevertheless, Yeats's poetry, his politics and his involvement with the occult received an extra charge of intensity from her day to day reality in his life, and when she appeared in the title role of his subversive play *Cathleen Ni Houlihan* (1902), another kind of maturity was achieved. Yeats was able for the first time to 'engross the present and dominate memory' with an artistic work that was on the one hand a resolution of inner tensions and compulsions and, on the other, a public gesture by the representative poet, one who had set out deliberately to carry on the work of his nineteenth-century forerunners, that 'company/ That sang, to sweeten Ireland's wrong'.

Thomas Davis, Samuel Ferguson, James Clarence Mangan: the young Yeats honoured their patriotic fervour and wanted his own work to be coloured by the same sentiments – chthonic, national, Celtic – that had coloured theirs. But he was intent on avoiding their propagandist rhetoric and set himself the task of combining a commitment to Irish themes with an exploration of his own psyche and an account of his own spiritual quest. It was typical of him to maintain that a dream had been the inspiration for *Cathleen Ni Houlihan* – the drama that prompted him to wonder in old age whether 'that play of mind sent out/ Certain men the English shot'. The play might serve a cause but it was also one of those 'things discovered in the deep'. True poetry, Yeats would declare, had to be the speech of the whole man. It was not sufficient that it be the artful expression of daylight opinion and conviction; it had to emerge from a more profound consciousness and be, in the words of his friend Arthur Symons, the voice of 'the mystery which lies about us, out of which we have come and into which we shall return'.

The cadence and melancholy of these words recall the 'red-rose-bordered hem' of mystical thought in Yeats's early poetry, a kind of thought that he was determined to unite with more expected thoughts of Irish cultural and political regeneration. Yet national regeneration was of original and vital importance to him. Even though subsequent efforts to enshrine the dream in a constituted state might outrage him – his famous Senate speech of 1925 when he deplored the imposition of a ban on divorce upon the Irish protestant minority is one instance of this – and even though the War of Independence and the Civil War would darken his understanding of historical process (always dependent upon 'bitter and violent men'), Yeats's radical devotion to the potential and otherness of a specifically Irish reality should never be underestimated. Moreover, the transformation of Irish life which he envisaged would involve neither prescription nor coercion. In his early conjunction of Neo-Platonic tradition with the deposits of Irish folklore, and in the mature symbolism of his dwelling in a Norman tower conjoined with a thatched cabin, Yeats intended to open and complicate the meaning of Irishness. In fact, his imagined Ireland represented not only a regenerative breakaway from the imperium of Britain but also from the magisterium of orthodox Christianity:

Nor may I less be counted one
With Davis, Mangan, Ferguson,
Because, to him who ponders well,
My rhymes more than their rhyming tell
Of things discovered in the deep,
Where only body's laid asleep.

For the elemental creatures go
About my table to and fro,
That hurry from unmeasured mind
To rant and rage in flood and wind;
Yet he who treads in measured ways
May surely barter gaze for gaze.
('To Ireland in the Coming Times')

This poetry admittedly strikes a more cajoling note than Stephen Dedalus's celebrated line about forging in the smithy of his soul the uncreated conscience of his race; but still, by affirming his poetic entitlement – he treads in 'measured ways' – and by claiming the prerogative to 'barter gaze for gaze' with a pristine source of authority, Yeats here inaugurates his own campaign for 'the spiritual liberation of [his] country'. Hence the search for a style that would have universal command, and the ambition to establish a poetic note that would sound every bit as given, self-born and unquestionable as the myths and symbols of traditional systems of belief.

Reading Yeats, we are under the sway of a voice that offers both expansiveness and containment, and this is as true of the early work as it is of a magnificent late set-piece such as 'A Dialogue of Self and Soul'. The expansiveness arises from a confidence that the mind is its own place and within it great distances can be imagined and traversed at will. The containment is present as a sensation of strong emotional and intellectual pressure coming up against formal limits and straining within them. Even a poem as apparently candid and technically uncalculating as 'To Ireland in the Coming Times' harks back to the measure of Milton's 'Il Penseroso', and displays an incipient ability – as Yeatsian as it was Miltonic – to string the sentence out with reinforced syntactical effect over a sequence of rhymes and line-endings. The poem is a written melody as much as it is the formulation of aims and hopes; its formality operates as transparently between itself and its subjects as the eye-piece made of hare-bone operates between the enchanted poet and the quotidian world in 'The Collar-Bone of a Hare':

I would find by the edge of that water
The collar-bone of a hare
Worn thin by the lapping of water,
And pierce it through with a gimlet, and stare
At the old bitter world where they marry in churches,
And laugh over the untroubled water
At all who marry in churches,
Through the white thin bone of a hare.

Yeats's singularity as a writer depended upon this uniquely elaborated command of the strategies of English verse; but it derived also from the off-centre viewpoint he deliberately maintained as a member of occult societies, a student of mystical thought and a practitioner of magic. Even an intelligence as strong and antagonistic as James Joyce's functioned within a set of cultural and intellectual forms that were generally shared and assented to. Homer and classical learning, Roman Catholic liturgy and dogma, the medieval corpus of knowledge as represented by Dante and Aquinas – when Joyce began to write, such a keyboard of reference looked as solidly in place as the contours of nature. The weapons in his lifelong campaign of detachment and affirmation were at least agreed weapons; calling his protagonist Dedalus, for example, meant that he harnessed a whole system to his own ends. But when Yeats called a character Red Hanrahan or Michael Robartes, the names had no such resonance in the cultural memory. He did, of course, attempt to endow the characters with an archetypal aura, but he was always starting from scratch. So while Joyce might disdain 'the monkish philosophy' that was his birthright and apparatus, it was, *qua* apparatus, far more immediately efficient than the 'fardel of stories, and of personages, and of emotions' that Yeats had gathered from sources variously poetic, folkloric and esoteric.

We must therefore take special cognizance of the fact that the Dublin of the young Yeats included the Hermetic Society, where he met the Brahmin Mohini Chatterjee, as well as the Contemporary Club, where he met the founder of the Gaelic League, Douglas Hyde; and that his London included the Order of the Golden Dawn and the magician MacGregor Mathers, as well as soirées with Oscar Wilde and others at the home of W. E. Henley. As a consequence, his everyday routine included practices and meditations based upon 'secret disciplines', just as the everyday routine of his pious Victorian contemporaries might include the rites and prayers of Christianity. One has to conceive of an intelligence naturally solitary, readily combative and happily beset, mounting in confidence and strategy as the wayward, 'unchristened' pursuit of nourishment through symbol and arcane dogma yielded more and more riches. In fact, one has to remember to grant to the occult at least as much formative influence in Yeats's project as one might unthinkingly grant to Catholicism in Joyce's. Once this recognition is made, the courage of Yeats's creative undertaking and the far-fetched elaboration of his *oeuvre* stand forth in all their self-born splendour. His endeavour was not only to create an Irish literature independent of the imperial, empirical sway of Britain; it was also an attempt to launch upon the world a vision of reality that possessed no surer basis than the ground of his own imagining.

Admittedly, that imagining was conducted in terms that had been 'passed on from generation to generation by poets and painters with some help from philosophers and theologians'. The reality of a world of spirit, the immortality of the soul and its fated reincarnations, the cyclical relations pertaining between the land of the living and the land of the dead, the perviousness of these realms to each other's influence, the possibility of gaining knowledge of reality and destiny through the study of arcane books and symbols – Yeats's mind was hospitable to these ideas. Ultimately his belief in them may have been provisional, but that did not weaken their heuristic virtue within his writing. All of Yeats's poems have a ring of conviction produced by the fit he always contrived between metre, rhyme and syntax, but the ones which arise from 'the half-read wisdom of daemonic images' have an extra strangeness about them. Poems like 'The Magi' and 'The Second Coming' seem to dwell within their own imaginative ozone layer, translucent yet non-illusory, revelations that are here to stay.

Still, while it is important to insist upon the centrality of unorthodox spiritual disciplines in Yeats's life, it is a mistake to think of him as a gullible consumer of superstitions. He possessed a robust, sceptical intelligence and his grasp of what was happening in his own times was at least equal to that of the most secular and topically focussed minds of his generation. His career as a poet spanned fifty years, from *The Wandering of Oisin* in 1889 to *Last Poems*, posthumously published in 1939, the year of his death. Born in 1865, he lived a life that coincided with an era of great social and political change. Britain and other European powers moved out of the confidence of the high imperial epoch into the devastation of World War I and its aftermath: the final decades of the poet's life coincided with the Russian Revolution, the rise of fascism in Italy, the Nazi takeover in Germany, the Spanish Civil War and, finally, the months of haunted apprehension before the outbreak of World War II. In Ireland too, drastic events occurred. The Easter Rising in 1916 and the ensuing violence issued first in the Anglo-Irish Treaty of 1921 and the creation of the Irish Free State, and then in the outbreak of the Irish Civil War. And to all of these crises Yeats responded in his own idiom, at his own pace. He did record *direct* responses to some events in Ireland, most notably in his poem 'Easter 1916', but generally the poems did not arise from the immediate stimulus of happenings or from any desire to set down the story. They arose, rather, from the resonance that the happenings produced within his consciousness and from the meditations and disconsolateness they engendered there.

Obviously, then, although the historical shocks that ran through the world did affect Yeats, his imagination did not function like an obedient seismograph. Indeed the whole force of his thought worked against those philosophies which regarded the mind's activity as something determined by circumstance. He loved Bishop Berkeley's idealist confidence that all things were 'a dream' and was bold to aver

That this pragmatical, preposterous pig of a world,
its farrow that so solid seem,
Must vanish on the instant if the mind but change
its theme.

Yeats's capacity to rekindle the flame of his inspiration at different periods of his life appears therefore as a triumphant fulfilment of his own prophetic belief in the mind's indomitable resource. Constantly he affirmed the necessity of self-renewal, compulsively he pushed the limits of his own artistic and existential possibilities. Style, he declared, was the equivalent of self-conquest in a writer; early on he professed his belief that we must labour to be beautiful, and described the source and secret of his art as 'the fascination of what's difficult'.

Conquest, difficulty, labour: these terms indicate the nature of Yeats's creative disposition. From the start, he was enamoured of Blake's conviction that energy is eternal delight, yet the development of his own thought brought him more and more to the conclusion that conflict was the inescapable condition of being human. So, as his art matured and the articulation of his beliefs became more clarified and forceful, Yeats's poems typically conveyed a sensation of certitude achieved by great effort and of contradictions quelled. Poems in which the defiant self is pitted against hostile or disabling conditions – 'An Irish Airman Foresees his Death', 'September 1913', 'Meditations in Time of Civil War' – are complemented by poems that read like discharges of pure, self-possessed energy, poems from which the accidental circumstances have been excluded so that all that remains is the melody and stamina of resurgent spirit – 'The Cold Heaven', 'Byzantium', 'Long-legged Fly'.

The greatest consolidation of his powers happened during his fifties and sixties, when several occasions conspired to inaugurate a period of abundant creativity. Like Thomas Hardy's 'darkling thrush', which surprised itself and its creator with a song of 'joy illimited', Yeats too made the unpredictable choice 'to fling his soul/ Upon the growing gloom'. In poems that were both a reprise and a resonantly amplified promulgation of all that he had already thought and imagined, he performed new feats of vision and rhetoric. This onset of authority derived from a natural enlargement that came with age and eminence, but it was given further impetus by two related developments in his life: his marriage in 1917 to George Hyde-Lees, and his purchase of a Norman tower at Ballylee in Co. Galway, which he had restored as a home for himself and his new bride. Yet it was less as a family man setting up house than as an acclaimed poet entering ritually into his imagined kingdom that Yeats took possession of Thoor Ballylee. The three volumes deriving from occupation of that site are the indispensable harvest of his mature years. The speculations of *A Vision* (1925) and the poems of *The Tower* (1928) and *The Winding Stair and Other Poems* (1933) have a planetary range and splendour, and incorporate haphazard yet powerfully registered incidents of personal and public life within the orbit of a single, ardent intelligence.

This unifying drive had always been central to Yeats's mind, but its operations reached a climax with the composition of *A Vision*. Although this bold formulation of his system of thought was born out of the automatic writings that George began to produce a few days after their marriage, its dominant motifs had been present in Yeats's writings throughout his career. It was as much an arrangement of images into a paradigm of reality as it was a sustained philosophic discourse, and old preoccupations – such as the idea of apocalyptic reversals in history, the doctrine of reincarnation, and the discipline of the mask – began to be reimagined in terms of new conceptions, such as the phases of the moon and the diagram of the gyres. Many of Yeats's endeavours were now converging and reinforcing each other. His life as a husband and householder was at one with his life as a mage and a poet within the symbolic tower, and his work of original ratiocination and enquiry was issuing in a sacred book that both augmented and belonged within an already ancient tradition. Yeats now lived not as a 'bundle of accident and incoherence' but as 'something intended, complete'. He merged his biographical self into the traditional figure of the poet/seer; what spoke in the poems was not so much the voice of a private self as the voice of the bard. Thus, sequences like 'Meditations in Time of Civil War' and 'Nineteen Hundred and Nineteen' have about them the high pitch of sacred rite, and poems like 'Among School Children' and 'A Dialogue of Self and Soul' go beyond the lyric's usual function of giving perfected form to a privileged state of mind and rise to a note that is oracular, passionate and empowered. More and more, Yeats evacuated all traces of the domestic creature and became instead the mouthpiece of daring and extravagant imagination:

Labour is blossoming or dancing where
The body is not bruised to pleasure soul,
Nor beauty born out of its own despair,
Nor blear-eyed wisdom out of midnight oil.
O chestnut-tree, great-rooted blossomer,
Are you the leaf, the blossom or the bole?
O body swayed to music, O brightening glance,
How can we know the dancer from the dance?

The ambition to write such exorbitant poetry had its penalties, and the need for an utterance that would overwhelm produced a certain overweening and theatricality. Although it is true that Yeats managed to break the lyric barrier in poems like 'The Statues', where his leaps of association brought him to a realm of extreme intuition and rhetorical daring, it is also true that a certain coarsening of tone occurred in some of his poetry during the 1930s. What he may have intended as nonchalance can now strike a reader as callousness. His own self-absolution – 'Why should not old men be mad?' – does not necessarily extenuate the rant and licence, and the unease generated by his political leanings at this period is complemented by an aesthetic resistance to a strain of violence that disfigures some of the verse.

Nevertheless, the last poems do set a crown upon the lifetime's effort. 'Long-legged Fly' triumphantly celebrates the stamina and quarantine of the heroic artist, yet the very absolutism and exclusiveness of that heroic stance are questioned in 'The Man and the Echo' and 'Cuchulain Comforted'. In the end, the Man's fortitude is at worst cancelled, at best condoned by the Echo's empty rebound, and the rattle of Cuchulain's arms is subsumed into the life-in-death music of the bird-shades. These poems correct the histrionic streak Yeats was indulging when he planned to conclude his *Last Poems* – and therefore *Collected Poems* as well – with 'Politics'. 'Politics' is as full of fight as a calf on a rope and has about it the haleness of folk song; it is both a taunt and a protest, but emotionally it harks back to an earlier time. The conclusion of 'The Man and the Echo', on the other hand, is fully alive to the tragic present, the moment of complete consciousness which is also the moment of complete powerlessness in the face of pain:

But hush, for I have lost the theme,
Its joy or night seem but a dream;
Up there some hawk or owl has struck,
Dropping out of sky or rock,
A stricken rabbit is crying out,
And its cry distracts my thought.

'Politics', for all its commendable jauntiness, does not possess the force of lines like these. Here the paradoxical privileges of art are exemplified in a poem that is responsive to the cry of suffering but unable to prevent or to assist; a poem that gives pleasure by enlightening, even as it reveals its helplessness to alleviate.

It is because of this unconsoled modernity that Yeats abides many of our questions, and while it is right that the questions continue to be pressed, it is imperative to recognize the immense contribution his work makes to our general intellectual and imaginative resource. Nobody doubts his fundamental importance as the creator of a cultural idea in and for Ireland, but that is only the beginning of his greatness. His extreme exploration of the possibilities of reconciling the human impulse to transcendence with the antithetical project of consolidation is universally and inexhaustibly relevant. Naturally, some political aspects of his work have been particularly assailed – and justly defended, as when Elizabeth Cullingford concluded her study of Yeats as a political poet with the proposition that his fascist sympathies are best regarded as part of his 'fantasies' rather than as part of his 'convictions'; but perhaps the general implications of his tough-minded insight that all reality comes to us as the reward of labour have been insufficiently pondered. There is surely political meaning, at once realistic and visionary, in his sense of life as an abounding conflict of energies; in his recognition of the necessity as well as the impossibility of the attempt 'to hold in a single thought reality and justice'; and in his conviction – overriding his sense of hierarchy and election – that even among the Paudeens of this earth, 'There cannot be . . . A single soul that lacks a sweet crystalline cry.'

When all the objections have been lodged, Yeats's work survives as a purely motivated, greatly active power for good. What Andrew Marvell presented as a challenging fantasy – 'roll all our strength, and all/ Our sweetness, up into one ball'

– Yeats actually achieved. To encounter an *oeuvre* that embodies 'thoughts long knitted into a single thought' is to experience the force of what he called 'the spiritual intellect's great work'. This force transmits itself, of course, by poetic means: Yeats's essential gift is his ability to raise a temple in the ear, to make a vaulted space in language through the firmness, in-placeness and undislodgeableness of stanzaic form. But the force is also present in his persistent drive to 'teach the free man how to praise'.

Yeats's incitements to generous self-transcendence, his fostering of all that is unconstrained and enjoys full scope, contribute greatly to the value of his work. Its range is ample, from the autumnal serenities of 'The Wild Swans at Coole' through the jubilation of 'Coole Park and Ballylee, 1931' to the limb-sweetening fullness of the last stanza of 'Among School Children'. We certainly do not encounter in such work any image of life's surfaces as we know them in our world of consumer capitalism; but its sufficiency and recalcitrance encourage us to be more resolutely and abundantly alive, whatever the conditions. It raises the standards. As I wrote elsewhere:

What's the use of a held note or held line
That cannot be assailed for reassurance?

Seamus Heaney

W. B. YEATS

The Indian upon God

I passed along the water's edge below the humid trees,
My spirit rocked in evening light, the rushes round my knees,
My spirit rocked in sleep and sighs; and saw the moorfowl pace
All dripping on a grassy slope, and saw them cease to chase
Each other round in circles, and heard the eldest speak:
Who holds the world between His bill and made us strong or weak
Is an undying moorfowl, and He lives beyond the sky.
The rains are from His dripping wing, the moonbeams from His eye.
I passed a little further on and heard a lotus talk:
Who made the world and ruleth it, He hangeth on a stalk,
For I am in His image made, and all this tinkling tide
Is but a sliding drop of rain between His petals wide.
A little way within the gloom a roebuck raised his eyes
Brimful of starlight, and he said: *The Stamper of the Skies,*
He is a gentle roebuck; for how else, I pray, could He
Conceive a thing so sad and soft, a gentle thing like me?
I passed a little further on and heard a peacock say:
Who made the grass and made the worms and made my feathers gay,
He is a monstrous peacock, and He waveth all the night
His languid tail above us, lit with myriad spots of light.

The Stolen Child

Where dips the rocky highland
Of Sleuth Wood in the lake
There lies a leafy island
Where flapping herons wake
The drowsy water-rats;
There we've hid our faery vats,
Full of berries
And of reddest stolen cherries.
And of reddest stolen cherries.
Come away, O human child!
To the waters and the wild
With a faery, hand in hand,
For the world's more full of weeping than you can understand.

Where the wave of moonlight glosses
The dim grey sands with light,
Far off by furthest Rosses
We foot it all the night,
Weaving olden dances,
Mingling hands and mingling glances
Till the moon has taken flight;
To and fro we leap
And chase the frothy bubbles,
While the world is full of troubles
And is anxious in its sleep.
Come away, O human child!
To the waters and the wild
With a faery, hand in hand,
For the world's more full of weeping than you can understand.

Where the wandering water gushes
From the hills above Glen-Car,
In pools among the rushes
That scarce could bathe a star,

We seek for slumbering trout
And whispering in their ears
Give them unquiet dreams;
Leaning softly out
From ferns that drop their tears
Over the young streams.
Come away, O human child!
To the waters and the wild
With a faery, hand in hand,
For the world's more full of weeping than you can understand.

Away with us he's going,
The solemn-eyed:
He'll hear no more the lowing
Of the calves on the warm hillside
Or the kettle on the hob
Sing peace into his breast,
Or see the brown mice bob
Round and round the oatmeal-chest.
For he comes, the human child,
To the waters and the wild
With a faery, hand in hand,
For the world's more full of weeping than he can understand.

Down by the Salley Gardens

Down by the salley gardens my love and I did meet;
She passed the salley gardens with little snow-white feet.
She bid me take love easy, as the leaves grow on the tree;
But I, being young and foolish, with her would not agree.

In a field by the river my love and I did stand,
And on my leaning shoulder she laid her snow-white hand.
She bid me take life easy, as the grass grows on the weirs;
But I was young and foolish, and now am full of tears.

The Meditation of the Old Fisherman

You waves, though you dance by my feet like children at
play,
Though you glow and you glance, though you purr and you
dart;
In the Junes that were warmer than these are, the waves were
more gay,
When I was a boy with never a crack in my heart.

The herring are not in the tides as they were of old;
My sorrow! for many a creak gave the creel in the cart
That carried the take to Sligo town to be sold,
When I was a boy with never a crack in my heart.

And ah, you proud maiden, you are not so fair when his oar
Is heard on the water, as they were, the proud and apart,
Who paced in the eve by the nets on the pebbly shore,
When I was a boy with never a crack in my heart.

Cuchulain's Fight with the Sea

A man came slowly from the setting sun,
To Emer, raddling raiment in her dun,
And said, 'I am that swineherd whom you bid
Go watch the road between the wood and tide,
But now I have no need to watch it more.'

Then Emer cast the web upon the floor,
And raising arms all raddled with the dye,
Parted her lips with a loud sudden cry.

That swineherd stared upon her face and said,
'No man alive, no man among the dead,
Has won the gold his cars of battle bring.'

'But if your master comes home triumphing
Why must you blench and shake from foot to crown?'
Thereon he shook the more and cast him down
Upon the web-heaped floor, and cried his word:
'With him is one sweet-throated like a bird.'

'You dare me to my face,' and thereupon
She smote with raddled fist, and where her son
Herded the cattle came with stumbling feet,
And cried with angry voice, 'It is not meet
To idle life away, a common herd.'

'I have long waited, mother, for that word:
But wherefore now?'
'There is a man to die;
You have the heaviest arm under the sky.'

'Whether under its daylight or its stars
My father stands amid his battle-cars.'

'But you have grown to be the taller man.'

'Yet somewhere under starlight or the sun
My father stands.'
                    'Aged, worn out with wars
On foot, on horseback or in battle-cars.'

'I only ask what way my journey lies,
For He who made you bitter made you wise.'

'The Red Branch camp in a great company
Between wood's rim and the horses of the sea.
Go there, and light a camp-fire at wood's rim;
But tell your name and lineage to him
Whose blade compels, and wait till they have found
Some feasting man that the same oath has bound.'

Among those feasting men Cuchulain dwelt,
And his young sweetheart close beside him knelt,
Stared on the mournful wonder of his eyes,
Even as Spring upon the ancient skies,
And pondered on the glory of his days;
And all around the harp-string told his praise,
And Conchubar, the Red Branch king of kings,
With his own fingers touched the brazen strings.

At last Cuchulain spake, 'Some man has made
His evening fire amid the leafy shade.
I have often heard him singing to and fro,
I have often heard the sweet sound of his bow.
Seek out what man he is.'

                              One went and came.
'He bade me let all know he gives his name
At the sword-point, and waits till we have found
Some feasting man that the same oath has bound.'

Cuchulain cried, 'I am the only man
Of all this host so bound from childhood on.'

After short fighting in the leafy shade,
He spake to the young man, 'Is there no maid

Who loves you, no white arms to wrap you round,
Or do you long for the dim sleepy ground,
That you have come and dared me to my face?'

'The dooms of men are in God's hidden place.'

'Your head awhile seemed like a woman's head
That I loved once.'
                                        Again the fighting sped,
But now the war-rage in Cuchulain woke,
And through that new blade's guard the old blade broke,
And pierced him.
                                        'Speak before your breath is done.'

'Cuchulain I, mighty Cuchulain's son.'

'I put you from your pain. I can no more.'

While day its burden on to evening bore,
With head bowed on his knees Cuchulain stayed;
Then Conchubar sent that sweet-throated maid,
And she, to win him, his grey hair caressed;
In vain her arms, in vain her soft white breast.
Then Conchubar, the subtlest of all men,
Ranking his Druids round him ten by ten,
Spake thus: 'Cuchulain will dwell there and brood
For three days more in dreadful quietude,
And then arise, and raving slay us all.
Chaunt in his ear delusions magical,
That he may fight the horses of the sea.'
The Druids took them to their mystery,
And chaunted for three days.
                                                        Cuchulain stirred,
Stared on the horses of the sea, and heard
The cars of battle and his own name cried;
And fought with the invulnerable tide.

The Rose of the World

Who dreamed that beauty passes like a dream?
For these red lips, with all their mournful pride,
Mournful that no new wonder may betide,
Troy passed away in one high funeral gleam,
And Usna's children died.

We and the labouring world are passing by:
Amid men's souls, that waver and give place
Like the pale waters in their wintry race,
Under the passing stars, foam of the sky,
Lives on this lonely face.

Bow down, archangels, in your dim abode:
Before you were, or any hearts to beat,
Weary and kind one lingered by His seat;
He made the world to be a grassy road
Before her wandering feet.

The Lake Isle of Innisfree

I will arise and go now, and go to Innisfree,
And a small cabin build there, of clay and wattles made:
Nine bean-rows will I have there, a hive for the honey-bee,
And live alone in the bee-loud glade.

And I shall have some peace there, for peace comes dropping slow,
Dropping from the veils of the morning to where the cricket sings;
There midnight's all a glimmer, and noon a purple glow,
And evening full of the linnet's wings.

I will arise and go now, for always night and day
I hear lake water lapping with low sounds by the shore;
While I stand on the roadway, or on the pavements grey,
I hear it in the deep heart's core.

When You Are Old

When you are old and grey and full of sleep,
And nodding by the fire, take down this book,
And slowly read, and dream of the soft look
Your eyes had once, and of their shadows deep;

How many loved your moments of glad grace,
And loved your beauty with love false or true,
But one man loved the pilgrim soul in you,
And loved the sorrows of your changing face;

And bending down beside the glowing bars,
Murmur, a little sadly, how Love fled
And paced upon the mountains overhead
And hid his face amid a crowd of stars.

Who Goes with Fergus?

Who will go drive with Fergus now,
And pierce the deep wood's woven shade,
And dance upon the level shore?
Young man, lift up your russet brow,
And lift your tender eyelids, maid,
And brood on hopes and fear no more.

And no more turn aside and brood
Upon love's bitter mystery;
For Fergus rules the brazen cars,
And rules the shadows of the wood,
And the white breast of the dim sea
And all dishevelled wandering stars.

The Lamentation of the Old Pensioner

Although I shelter from the rain
Under a broken tree,
My chair was nearest to the fire
In every company
That talked of love or politics,
Ere Time transfigured me.

Though lads are making pikes again
For some conspiracy,
And crazy rascals rage their fill
At human tyranny,
My contemplations are of Time
That has transfigured me.

There's not a woman turns her face
Upon a broken tree,
And yet the beauties that I loved
Are in my memory;
I spit into the face of Time
That has transfigured me.

To Ireland in the Coming Times

Know, that I would accounted be
True brother of a company
That sang, to sweeten Ireland's wrong,
Ballad and story, rann and song;
Nor be I any less of them,
Because the red-rose-bordered hem
Of her, whose history began
Before God made the angelic clan,
Trails all about the written page.
When Time began to rant and rage
The measure of her flying feet
Made Ireland's heart begin to beat;
And Time bade all his candles flare
To light a measure here and there;
And may the thoughts of Ireland brood
Upon a measured quietude.

Nor may I less be counted one
With Davis, Mangan, Ferguson,
Because, to him who ponders well,
My rhymes more than their rhyming tell
Of things discovered in the deep,
Where only body's laid asleep.
For the elemental creatures go
About my table to and fro,
That hurry from unmeasured mind
To rant and rage in flood and wind;
Yet he who treads in measured ways
May surely barter gaze for gaze.
Man ever journeys on with them
After the red-rose-bordered hem.
Ah, faeries, dancing under the moon,
A Druid land, a Druid tune!

While still I may, I write for you
The love I lived, the dream I knew.
From our birthday, until we die,
Is but the winking of an eye;
And we, our singing and our love,
What measurer Time has lit above,
And all benighted things that go
About my table to and fro,
Are passing on to where may be,
In truth's consuming ecstasy,
No place for love and dream at all;
For God goes by with white footfall.
I cast my heart into my rhymes,
That you, in the dim coming times,
May know how my heart went with them
After the red-rose-bordered hem.

The Host of the Air

O'Driscoll drove with a song
The wild duck and the drake
From the tall and the tufted reeds
Of the drear Hart Lake.

And he saw how the reeds grew dark
At the coming of night-tide,
And dreamed of the long dim hair
Of Bridget his bride.

He heard while he sang and dreamed
A piper piping away,
And never was piping so sad,
And never was piping so gay.

And he saw young men and young girls
Who danced on a level place,
And Bridget his bride among them,
With a sad and a gay face.

The dancers crowded about him
And many a sweet thing said,
And a young man brought him red wine
And a young girl white bread.

But Bridget drew him by the sleeve
Away from the merry bands,
To old men playing at cards
With a twinkling of ancient hands.

The bread and the wine had a doom,
For these were the host of the air;
He sat and played in a dream
Of her long dim hair.

He played with the merry old men
And thought not of evil chance,
Until one bore Bridget his bride
Away from the merry dance.

He bore her away in his arms,
The handsomest young man there,
And his neck and his breast and his arms
Were drowned in her long dim hair.

O'Driscoll scattered the cards
And out of his dream awoke:
Old men and young men and young girls
Were gone like a drifting smoke;

But he heard high up in the air
A piper piping away,
And never was piping so sad,
And never was piping so gay.

The Song of Wandering Aengus

I went out to the hazel wood,
Because a fire was in my head,
And cut and peeled a hazel wand,
And hooked a berry to a thread;
And when white moths were on the wing,
And moth-like stars were flickering out,
I dropped the berry in a stream
And caught a little silver trout.

When I had laid it on the floor
I went to blow the fire aflame,
But something rustled on the floor,
And some one called me by my name:
It had become a glimmering girl
With apple blossom in her hair
Who called me by my name and ran
And faded through the brightening air.

Though I am old with wandering
Through hollow lands and hilly lands,
I will find out where she has gone,
And kiss her lips and take her hands;
And walk among long dappled grass,
And pluck till time and times are done
The silver apples of the moon,
The golden apples of the sun.

The Heart of the Woman

O what to me the little room
That was brimmed up with prayer and rest;
He bade me out into the gloom,
And my breast lies upon his breast.

O what to me my mother's care,
The house where I was safe and warm;
The shadowy blossom of my hair
Will hide us from the bitter storm.

O hiding hair and dewy eyes,
I am no more with life and death,
My heart upon his warm heart lies,
My breath is mixed into his breath.

He hears the Cry of the Sedge

I wander by the edge
Of this desolate lake
Where wind cries in the sedge:
Until the axle break
That keeps the stars in their round,
And hands hurl in the deep
The banners of East and West,
And the girdle of light is unbound,
Your breast will not lie by the breast
Of your beloved in sleep.

He wishes for the Cloths of Heaven

Had I the heavens' embroidered cloths,
Enwrought with golden and silver light,
The blue and the dim and the dark cloths
Of night and light and the half-light,
I would spread the cloths under your feet:
But I, being poor, have only my dreams;
I have spread my dreams under your feet;
Tread softly because you tread on my dreams.

He thinks of his Past Greatness when a Part of the Constellations of Heaven

I have drunk ale from the Country of the Young
And weep because I know all things now:
I have been a hazel-tree, and they hung
The Pilot Star and the Crooked Plough
Among my leaves in times out of mind:
I became a rush that horses tread:
I became a man, a hater of the wind,
Knowing one, out of all things, alone, that his head
May not lie on the breast nor his lips on the hair
Of the woman that he loves, until he dies.
O beast of the wilderness, bird of the air,
Must I endure your amorous cries?

The Fiddler of Dooney

When I play on my fiddle in Dooney,
Folk dance like a wave of the sea;
My cousin is priest in Kilvarnet,
My brother in Mocharabuiee.

I passed my brother and cousin:
They read in their books of prayer;
I read in my book of songs
I bought at the Sligo fair.

When we come at the end of time
To Peter sitting in state,
He will smile on the three old spirits,
But call me first through the gate;

For the good are always the merry,
Save by an evil chance,
And the merry love the fiddle,
And the merry love to dance:

And when the folk there spy me,
They will all come up to me,
With 'Here is the fiddler of Dooney!'
And dance like a wave of the sea.

The Folly of Being Comforted

One that is ever kind said yesterday:
'Your well-belovèd's hair has threads of grey,
And little shadows come about her eyes;
Time can but make it easier to be wise
Though now it seems impossible, and so
All that you need is patience.'
                                        Heart cries, 'No,
I have not a crumb of comfort, not a grain.
Time can but make her beauty over again:
Because of that great nobleness of hers
The fire that stirs about her, when she stirs,
Burns but more clearly. O she had not these ways
When all the wild summer was in her gaze.'

O heart! O heart! if she'd but turn her head,
You'd know the folly of being comforted.

Adam's Curse

We sat together at one summer's end,
That beautiful mild woman, your close friend,
And you and I, and talked of poetry.
I said, 'A line will take us hours maybe;
Yet if it does not seem a moment's thought,
Our stitching and unstitching has been naught.

Better go down upon your marrow-bones
And scrub a kitchen pavement, or break stones
Like an old pauper, in all kinds of weather;
For to articulate sweet sounds together
Is to work harder than all these, and yet
Be thought an idler by the noisy set
Of bankers, schoolmasters, and clergymen
The martyrs call the world.'

And thereupon
That beautiful mild woman for whose sake
There's many a one shall find out all heartache
On finding that her voice is sweet and low
Replied, 'To be born woman is to know –
Although they do not talk of it at school –
That we must labour to be beautiful.'

I said, 'It's certain there is no fine thing
Since Adam's fall but needs much labouring.
There have been lovers who thought love should be
So much compounded of high courtesy
That they would sigh and quote with learned looks
Precedents out of beautiful old books;
Yet now it seems an idle trade enough.'

We sat grown quiet at the name of love;
We saw the last embers of daylight die,
And in the trembling blue-green of the sky

A moon, worn as if it had been a shell
Washed by time's waters as they rose and fell
About the stars and broke in days and years.

I had a thought for no one's but your ears:
That you were beautiful, and that I strove
To love you in the old high way of love;
That it had all seemed happy, and yet we'd grown
As weary-hearted as that hollow moon.

Red Hanrahan's Song about Ireland

The old brown thorn-trees break in two high over Cummen
Strand,
Under a bitter black wind that blows from the left hand;
Our courage breaks like an old tree in a black wind and dies,
But we have hidden in our hearts the flame out of the eyes
Of Cathleen, the daughter of Houlihan.

The wind has bundled up the clouds high over Knocknarea,
And thrown the thunder on the stones for all that Maeve can
say.
Angers that are like noisy clouds have set our hearts abeat;
But we have all bent low and low and kissed the quiet feet
Of Cathleen, the daughter of Houlihan.

The yellow pool has overflowed high up on Clooth-na-Bare,
For the wet winds are blowing out of the clinging air;
Like heavy flooded waters our bodies and our blood;
But purer than a tall candle before the Holy Rood
Is Cathleen, the daughter of Houlihan.

No Second Troy

Why should I blame her that she filled my days
With misery, or that she would of late
Have taught to ignorant men most violent ways,
Or hurled the little streets upon the great,
Had they but courage equal to desire?
What could have made her peaceful with a mind
That nobleness made simple as a fire,
With beauty like a tightened bow, a kind
That is not natural in an age like this,
Being high and solitary and most stern?
Why, what could she have done, being what she is?
Was there another Troy for her to burn?

The Fascination of What's Difficult

The fascination of what's difficult
Has dried the sap out of my veins, and rent
Spontaneous joy and natural content
Out of my heart. There's something ails our colt
That must, as if it had not holy blood
Nor on Olympus leaped from cloud to cloud,
Shiver under the lash, strain, sweat and jolt
As though it dragged road-metal. My curse on plays
That have to be set up in fifty ways,
On the day's war with every knave and dolt,
Theatre business, management of men.
I swear before the dawn comes round again
I'll find the stable and pull out the bolt.

The Coming of Wisdom with Time

Though leaves are many, the root is one;
Through all the lying days of my youth
I swayed my leaves and flowers in the sun;
Now I may wither into the truth.

Upon a House Shaken by the Land Agitation

How should the world be luckier if this house,
Where passion and precision have been one
Time out of mind, became too ruinous
To breed the lidless eye that loves the sun?
And the sweet laughing eagle thoughts that grow
Where wings have memory of wings, and all
That comes of the best knit to the best? Although
Mean roof-trees were the sturdier for its fall,
How should their luck run high enough to reach
The gifts that govern men, and after these
To gradual Time's last gift, a written speech
Wrought of high laughter, loveliness and ease?

At Galway Races

There where the course is,
Delight makes all of the one mind,
The riders upon the galloping horses,
The crowd that closes in behind:
We, too, had good attendance once,
Hearers and hearteners of the work;
Aye, horsemen for companions,
Before the merchant and the clerk
Breathed on the world with timid breath.
Sing on: somewhere at some new moon,
We'll learn that sleeping is not death,
Hearing the whole earth change its tune,
Its flesh being wild, and it again
Crying aloud as the racecourse is,
And we find hearteners among men
That ride upon horses.

September 1913

What need you, being come to sense,
But fumble in a greasy till
And add the halfpence to the pence
And prayer to shivering prayer, until
You have dried the marrow from the bone?
For men were born to pray and save:
Romantic Ireland's dead and gone,
It's with O'Leary in the grave.

Yet they were of a different kind,
The names that stilled your childish play,
They have gone about the world like wind,
But little time had they to pray
For whom the hangman's rope was spun,
And what, God help us, could they save?
Romantic Ireland's dead and gone,
It's with O'Leary in the grave.

Was it for this the wild geese spread
The grey wing upon every tide;
For this that all that blood was shed,
For this Edward Fitzgerald died,
And Robert Emmet and Wolfe Tone,
All that delirium of the brave?
Romantic Ireland's dead and gone,
It's with O'Leary in the grave.

Yet could we turn the years again,
And call those exiles as they were
In all their loneliness and pain,
You'd cry, 'Some woman's yellow hair
Has maddened every mother's son':
They weighed so lightly what they gave.
But let them be, they're dead and gone,
They're with O'Leary in the grave.

To a Friend whose Work has come to Nothing

Now all the truth is out,
Be secret and take defeat
From any brazen throat,
For how can you compete,
Being honour bred, with one
Who, were it proved he lies,
Were neither shamed in his own
Nor in his neighbours' eyes?
Bred to a harder thing
Than Triumph, turn away
And like a laughing string
Whereon mad fingers play
Amid a place of stone,
Be secret and exult,
Because of all things known
That is most difficult.

Paudeen

Indignant at the fumbling wits, the obscure spite
Of our old Paudeen in his shop, I stumbled blind
Among the stones and thorn-trees, under morning light;
Until a curlew cried and in the luminous wind
A curlew answered; and suddenly thereupon I thought
That on the lonely height where all are in God's eye,
There cannot be, confusion of our sound forgot,
A single soul that lacks a sweet crystalline cry.

To a Shade

If you have revisited the town, thin Shade,
Whether to look upon your monument
(I wonder if the builder has been paid)
Or happier-thoughted when the day is spent
To drink of that salt breath out of the sea
When grey gulls flit about instead of men,
And the gaunt houses put on majesty:
Let these content you and be gone again;
For they are at their old tricks yet.
                                        A man
Of your own passionate serving kind who had brought
In his full hands what, had they only known,
Had given their children's children loftier thought,
Sweeter emotion, working in their veins
Like gentle blood, has been driven from the place,
And insult heaped upon him for his pains,
And for his open-handedness, disgrace;
Your enemy, an old foul mouth, had set
The pack upon him.
                              Go, unquiet wanderer,
And gather the Glasnevin coverlet
About your head till the dust stops your ear,
The time for you to taste of that salt breath
And listen at the corners has not come:
You had enough of sorrow before death –
Away, away! You are safer in the tomb.

September 29, 1913

Running to Paradise

As I came over Windy Gap
They threw a halfpenny into my cap,
For I am running to Paradise;
And all that I need do is to wish
And somebody puts his hand in the dish
To throw me a bit of salted fish:
And there the king is *but as the beggar.*

My brother Mourteen is worn out
With skelping his big brawling lout,
And I am running to Paradise;
A poor life, do what he can,
And though he keep a dog and a gun,
A serving-maid and a serving-man:
And there the king is *but as the beggar.*

Poor men have grown to be rich men,
And rich men grown to be poor again,
And I am running to Paradise;
And many a darling wit's grown dull
That tossed a bare heel when at school,
Now it has filled an old sock full:
And there the king is *but as the beggar.*

The wind is old and still at play
While I must hurry upon my way
For I am running to Paradise;
Yet never have I lit on a friend
To take my fancy like the wind
That nobody can buy or bind:
And there the king is *but as the beggar.*

Fallen Majesty

Although crowds gathered once if she but showed her face,
And even old men's eyes grew dim, this hand alone,
Like some last courtier at a gypsy camping-place
Babbling of fallen majesty, records what's gone.

The lineaments, a heart that laughter has made sweet,
These, these remain, but I record what's gone. A crowd
Will gather, and not know it walks the very street
Whereon a thing once walked that seemed a burning cloud.

The Cold Heaven

Suddenly I saw the cold and rook-delighting heaven
That seemed as though ice burned and was but the more ice,
And thereupon imagination and heart were driven
So wild that every casual thought of that and this
Vanished, and left but memories, that should be out of
  season
With the hot blood of youth, of love crossed long ago;
And I took all the blame out of all sense and reason,
Until I cried and trembled and rocked to and fro,
Riddled with light. Ah! when the ghost begins to quicken,
Confusion of the death-bed over, is it sent
Out naked on the roads, as the books say, and stricken
By the injustice of the skies for punishment?

The Magi

Now as at all times I can see in the mind's eye,
In their stiff, painted clothes, the pale unsatisfied ones
Appear and disappear in the blue depth of the sky
With all their ancient faces like rain-beaten stones,
And all their helms of silver hovering side by side,
And all their eyes still fixed, hoping to find once more,
Being by Calvary's turbulence unsatisfied,
The uncontrollable mystery on the bestial floor.

The Wild Swans at Coole

The trees are in their autumn beauty,
The woodland paths are dry,
Under the October twilight the water
Mirrors a still sky;
Upon the brimming water among the stones
Are nine-and-fifty swans.

The nineteenth autumn has come upon me
Since I first made my count;
I saw, before I had well finished,
All suddenly mount
And scatter wheeling in great broken rings
Upon their clamorous wings.

I have looked upon those brilliant creatures,
And now my heart is sore.
All's changed since I, hearing at twilight,
The first time on this shore,
The bell-beat of their wings above my head,
Trod with a lighter tread.

Unwearied still, lover by lover,
They paddle in the cold
Companionable streams or climb the air;
Their hearts have not grown old;
Passion or conquest, wander where they will,
Attend upon them still.

But now they drift on the still water,
Mysterious, beautiful;
Among what rushes will they build,
By what lake's edge or pool
Delight men's eyes when I awake some day
To find they have flown away?

In Memory of Major Robert Gregory

I

Now that we're almost settled in our house
I'll name the friends that cannot sup with us
Beside a fire of turf in th' ancient tower,
And having talked to some late hour
Climb up the narrow winding stair to bed:
Discoverers of forgotten truth
Or mere companions of my youth,
All, all are in my thoughts to-night being dead.

II

Always we'd have the new friend meet the old
And we are hurt if either friend seem cold,
And there is salt to lengthen out the smart
In the affections of our heart,
And quarrels are blown up upon that head;
But not a friend that I would bring
This night can set us quarrelling,
For all that come into my mind are dead.

III

Lionel Johnson comes the first to mind,
That loved his learning better than mankind,
Though courteous to the worst; much falling he
Brooded upon sanctity
Till all his Greek and Latin learning seemed
A long blast upon the horn that brought
A little nearer to his thought
A measureless consummation that he dreamed.

IV

And that enquiring man John Synge comes next,
That dying chose the living world for text
And never could have rested in the tomb
But that, long travelling, he had come
Towards nightfall upon certain set apart
In a most desolate stony place,
Towards nightfall upon a race
Passionate and simple like his heart.

V

And then I think of old George Pollexfen,
In muscular youth well known to Mayo men
For horsemanship at meets or at racecourses,
That could have shown how pure-bred horses
And solid men, for all their passion, live
But as the outrageous stars incline
By opposition, square and trine;
Having grown sluggish and contemplative.

VI

They were my close companions many a year,
A portion of my mind and life, as it were,
And now their breathless faces seem to look
Out of some old picture-book;
I am accustomed to their lack of breath,
But not that my dear friend's dear son,
Our Sidney and our perfect man,
Could share in that discourtesy of death.

VII

For all things the delighted eye now sees
Were loved by him: the old storm-broken trees
That cast their shadows upon road and bridge;

The tower set on the stream's edge;
The ford where drinking cattle make a stir
Nightly, and startled by that sound
The water-hen must change her ground;
He might have been your heartiest welcomer.

VIII

When with the Galway foxhounds he would ride
From Castle Taylor to the Roxborough side
Or Esserkelly plain, few kept his pace;
At Mooneen he had leaped a place
So perilous that half the astonished meet
Had shut their eyes; and where was it
He rode a race without a bit?
And yet his mind outran the horses' feet.

IX

We dreamed that a great painter had been born
To cold Clare rock and Galway rock and thorn,
To that stern colour and that delicate line
That are our secret discipline
Wherein the gazing heart doubles her might.
Soldier, scholar, horseman, he,
And yet he had the intensity
To have published all to be a world's delight.

X

What other could so well have counselled us
In all lovely intricacies of a house
As he that practised or that understood
All work in metal or in wood,
In moulded plaster or in carven stone?
Soldier, scholar, horseman, he,
And all he did done perfectly
As though he had but that one trade alone.

XI

Some burn damp faggots, others may consume
The entire combustible world in one small room
As though dried straw, and if we turn about
The bare chimney is gone black out
Because the work had finished in that flare.
Soldier, scholar, horseman, he,
As 'twere all life's epitome.
What made us dream that he could comb grey hair?

XII

I had thought, seeing how bitter is that wind
That shakes the shutter, to have brought to mind
All those that manhood tried, or childhood loved
Or boyish intellect approved,
With some appropriate commentary on each;
Until imagination brought
A fitter welcome; but a thought
Of that late death took all my heart for speech.

An Irish Airman Foresees his Death

I know that I shall meet my fate
Somewhere among the clouds above;
Those that I fight I do not hate
Those that I guard I do not love;
My country is Kiltartan Cross,
My countrymen Kiltartan's poor,
No likely end could bring them loss
Or leave them happier than before.
Nor law, nor duty bade me fight,
Nor public men, nor cheering crowds,
A lonely impulse of delight
Drove to this tumult in the clouds;
I balanced all, brought all to mind,
The years to come seemed waste of breath,
A waste of breath the years behind
In balance with this life, this death.

The Collar-Bone of a Hare

Would I could cast a sail on the water
Where many a king has gone
And many a king's daughter,
And alight at the comely trees and the lawn,
The playing upon pipes and the dancing,
And learn that the best thing is
To change my loves while dancing
And pay but a kiss for a kiss.

I would find by the edge of that water
The collar-bone of a hare
Worn thin by the lapping of water,
And pierce it through with a gimlet, and stare
At the old bitter world where they marry in churches,
And laugh over the untroubled water
At all who marry in churches,
Through the white thin bone of a hare.

The Fisherman

Although I can see him still,
The freckled man who goes
To a grey place on a hill
In grey Connemara clothes
At dawn to cast his flies,
It's long since I began
To call up to the eyes
This wise and simple man.
All day I'd looked in the face
What I had hoped 'twould be
To write for my own race
And the reality;
The living men that I hate,
The dead man that I loved,
The craven man in his seat,
The insolent unreproved,
And no knave brought to book
Who has won a drunken cheer,
The witty man and his joke
Aimed at the commonest ear,
The clever man who cries
The catch-cries of the clown,
The beating down of the wise
And great Art beaten down.

Maybe a twelvemonth since
Suddenly I began,
In scorn of this audience,
Imagining a man,
And his sun-freckled face,
And grey Connemara cloth,
Climbing up to a place
Where stone is dark under froth,

And the down-turn of his wrist
When the flies drop in the stream;
A man who does not exist,
A man who is but a dream;
And cried, 'Before I am old
I shall have written him one
Poem maybe as cold
And passionate as the dawn.'

Memory

One had a lovely face,
And two or three had charm,
But charm and face were in vain
Because the mountain grass
Cannot but keep the form
Where the mountain hare has lain.

Her Praise

She is foremost of those that I would hear praised.
I have gone about the house, gone up and down
As a man does who has published a new book,
Or a young girl dressed out in her new gown,
And though I have turned the talk by hook or crook
Until her praise should be the uppermost theme,
A woman spoke of some new tale she had read,
A man confusedly in a half dream
As though some other name ran in his head.
She is foremost of those that I would hear praised.
I will talk no more of books or the long war
But walk by the dry thorn until I have found
Some beggar sheltering from the wind, and there
Manage the talk until her name come round.
If there be rags enough he will know her name
And be well pleased remembering it, for in the old days,
Though she had young men's praise and old men's blame,
Among the poor both old and young gave her praise.

Broken Dreams

There is grey in your hair.
Young men no longer suddenly catch their breath
When you are passing;
But maybe some old gaffer mutters a blessing
Because it was your prayer
Recovered him upon the bed of death.
For your sole sake – that all heart's ache have known,
And given to others all heart's ache,
From meagre girlhood's putting on
Burdensome beauty – for your sole sake
Heaven has put away the stroke of her doom,
So great her portion in that peace you make
By merely walking in a room.

Your beauty can but leave among us
Vague memories, nothing but memories.
A young man when the old men are done talking
Will say to an old man, 'Tell me of that lady
The poet stubborn with his passion sang us
When age might well have chilled his blood.'

Vague memories, nothing but memories,
But in the grave all, all, shall be renewed.
The certainty that I shall see that lady
Leaning or standing or walking
In the first loveliness of womanhood,
And with the fervour of my youthful eyes,
Has set me muttering like a fool.

You are more beautiful than any one,
And yet your body had a flaw:
Your small hands were not beautiful,
And I am afraid that you will run
And paddle to the wrist

In that mysterious, always brimming lake
Where those that have obeyed the holy law
Paddle and are perfect. Leave unchanged
The hands that I have kissed,
For old sake's sake.

The last stroke of midnight dies.
All day in the one chair
From dream to dream and rhyme to rhyme I have ranged
In rambling talk with an image of air:
Vague memories, nothing but memories.

To a Squirrel at Kyle-na-no

Come play with me;
Why should you run
Through the shaking tree
As though I'd a gun
To strike you dead?
When all I would do
Is to scratch your head
And let you go.

Ego Dominus Tuus

Hic. On the grey sand beside the shallow stream
Under your old wind-beaten tower, where still
A lamp burns on beside the open book
That Michael Robartes left, you walk in the moon,
And, though you have passed the best of life, still trace,
Enthralled by the unconquerable delusion,
Magical shapes.

Ille. By the help of an image
I call to my own opposite, summon all
That I have handled least, least looked upon.

Hic. And I would find myself and not an image.

Ille. That is our modern hope, and by its light
We have lit upon the gentle, sensitive mind
And lost the old nonchalance of the hand;
Whether we have chosen chisel, pen or brush,
We are but critics, or but half create,
Timid, entangled, empty and abashed,
Lacking the countenance of our friends.

Hic. And yet
The chief imagination of Christendom,
Dante Alighieri, so utterly found himself
That he has made that hollow face of his
More plain to the mind's eye than any face
But that of Christ.

Ille. And did he find himself
Or was the hunger that had made it hollow
A hunger for the apple on the bough
Most out of reach? and is that spectral image
The man that Lapo and that Guido knew?
I think he fashioned from his opposite

An image that might have been a stony face
Staring upon a Bedouin's horse-hair roof
From doored and windowed cliff, or half upturned
Among the coarse grass and the camel-dung.
He set his chisel to the hardest stone.
Being mocked by Guido for his lecherous life,
Derided and deriding, driven out
To climb that stair and eat that bitter bread,
He found the unpersuadable justice, he found
The most exalted lady loved by a man.

Hic. Yet surely there are men who have made their art
Out of no tragic war, lovers of life,
Impulsive men that look for happiness
And sing when they have found it.

Ille. No, not sing,
For those that love the world serve it in action,
Grow rich, popular and full of influence,
And should they paint or write, still it is action:
The struggle of the fly in marmalade.
The rhetorician would deceive his neighbours,
The sentimentalist himself; while art
Is but a vision of reality.
What portion in the world can the artist have
Who has awakened from the common dream
But dissipation and despair?

Hic. And yet
No one denies to Keats love of the world;
Remember his deliberate happiness.

Ille. His art is happy, but who knows his mind?
I see a schoolboy when I think of him,
With face and nose pressed to a sweet-shop window,
For certainly he sank into his grave
His senses and his heart unsatisfied,
And made – being poor, ailing and ignorant,

Shut out from all the luxury of the world,
The coarse-bred son of a livery-stable keeper –
Luxuriant song.

Hic. Why should you leave the lamp
Burning alone beside an open book,
And trace these characters upon the sands?
A style is found by sedentary toil
And by the imitation of great masters.

Ille. Because I seek an image, not a book.
Those men that in their writings are most wise
Own nothing but their blind, stupefied hearts.
I call to the mysterious one who yet
Shall walk the wet sands by the edge of the stream
And look most like me, being indeed my double,
And prove of all imaginable things
The most unlike, being my anti-self,
And, standing by these characters, disclose
All that I seek; and whisper it as though
He were afraid the birds, who cry aloud
Their momentary cries before it is dawn,
Would carry it away to blasphemous men.

Easter 1916

I have met them at close of day
Coming with vivid faces
From counter or desk among grey
Eighteenth-century houses.
I have passed with a nod of the head
Or polite meaningless words,
Or have lingered awhile and said
Polite meaningless words,
And thought before I had done
Of a mocking tale or a gibe
To please a companion
Around the fire at the club,
Being certain that they and I
But lived where motley is worn:
All changed, changed utterly:
A terrible beauty is born.

That woman's days were spent
In ignorant good-will,
Her nights in argument
Until her voice grew shrill.
What voice more sweet than hers
When, young and beautiful,
She rode to harriers?
This man had kept a school
And rode our wingèd horse;
This other his helper and friend
Was coming into his force;
He might have won fame in the end,
So sensitive his nature seemed,
So daring and sweet his thought.
This other man I had dreamed
A drunken, vainglorious lout.

He had done most bitter wrong
To some who are near my heart,
Yet I number him in the song;
He, too, has resigned his part
In the casual comedy;
He, too, has been changed in his turn,
Transformed utterly:
A terrible beauty is born.

Hearts with one purpose alone
Through summer and winter seem
Enchanted to a stone
To trouble the living stream.
The horse that comes from the road,
The rider, the birds that range
From cloud to tumbling cloud,
Minute by minute they change;
A shadow of cloud on the stream
Changes minute by minute;
A horse-hoof slides on the brim,
And a horse plashes within it;
The long-legged moor-hens dive,
And hens to moor-cocks call;
Minute by minute they live:
The stone's in the midst of all.

Too long a sacrifice
Can make a stone of the heart.
O when may it suffice?
That is Heaven's part, our part
To murmur name upon name,
As a mother names her child
When sleep at last has come
On limbs that had run wild.
What is it but nightfall?
No, no, not night but death;
Was it needless death after all?

For England may keep faith
For all that is done and said.
We know their dream; enough
To know they dreamed and are dead;
And what if excess of love
Bewildered them till they died?
I write it out in a verse –
MacDonagh and MacBride
And Connolly and Pearse
Now and in time to be,
Wherever green is worn,
Are changed, changed utterly:
A terrible beauty is born.

Sixteen Dead Men

O but we talked at large before
The sixteen men were shot,
But who can talk of give and take,
What should be and what not
While those dead men are loitering there
To stir the boiling pot?

You say that we should still the land
Till Germany's overcome;
But who is there to argue that
Now Pearse is deaf and dumb?
And is their logic to outweigh
MacDonagh's bony thumb?

How could you dream they'd listen
That have an ear alone
For those new comrades they have found,
Lord Edward and Wolfe Tone,
Or meddle with our give and take
That converse bone to bone?

The Second Coming

Turning and turning in the widening gyre
The falcon cannot hear the falconer;
Things fall apart; the centre cannot hold;
Mere anarchy is loosed upon the world,
The blood-dimmed tide is loosed, and everywhere
The ceremony of innocence is drowned;
The best lack all conviction, while the worst
Are full of passionate intensity.

Surely some revelation is at hand;
Surely the Second Coming is at hand.
The Second Coming! Hardly are those words out
When a vast image out of *Spiritus Mundi*
Troubles my sight: somewhere in sands of the desert
A shape with lion body and the head of a man,
A gaze blank and pitiless as the sun,
Is moving its slow thighs, while all about it
Reel shadows of the indignant desert birds.
The darkness drops again; but now I know
That twenty centuries of stony sleep
Were vexed to nightmare by a rocking cradle,
And what rough beast, its hour come round at last,
Slouches towards Bethlehem to be born?

To Be Carved on a Stone at Thoor Ballylee

I, the poet William Yeats,
With old mill boards and sea-green slates,
And smithy work from the Gort forge,
Restored this tower for my wife George;
And may these characters remain
When all is ruin once again.

Sailing to Byzantium

I

That is no country for old men. The young
In one another's arms, birds in the trees
– Those dying generations – at their song,
The salmon-falls, the mackerel-crowded seas,
Fish, flesh, or fowl, commend all summer long
Whatever is begotten, born, and dies.
Caught in that sensual music all neglect
Monuments of unageing intellect.

II

An aged man is but a paltry thing,
A tattered coat upon a stick, unless
Soul clap its hands and sing, and louder sing
For every tatter in its mortal dress,
Nor is there singing school but studying
Monuments of its own magnificence;
And therefore I have sailed the seas and come
To the holy city of Byzantium.

III

O sages standing in God's holy fire
As in the gold mosaic of a wall,
Come from the holy fire, perne in a gyre,
And be the singing-masters of my soul.
Consume my heart away; sick with desire
And fastened to a dying animal
It knows not what it is; and gather me
Into the artifice of eternity.

IV

Once out of nature I shall never take
My bodily form from any natural thing,
But such a form as Grecian goldsmiths make
Of hammered gold and gold enamelling
To keep a drowsy Emperor awake;
Or set upon a golden bough to sing
To lords and ladies of Byzantium
Of what is past, or passing, or to come.

1927

Meditations in Time of Civil War

I *Ancestral Houses*

Surely among a rich man's flowering lawns,
Amid the rustle of his planted hills,
Life overflows without ambitious pains;
And rains down life until the basin spills,
And mounts more dizzy high the more it rains
As though to choose whatever shape it wills
And never stoop to a mechanical
Or servile shape, at others' beck and call.

Mere dreams, mere dreams! Yet Homer had not sung
Had he not found it certain beyond dreams
That out of life's own self-delight had sprung
The abounding glittering jet, though now it seems
As if some marvellous empty sea-shell flung
Out of the obscure dark of the rich streams,
And not a fountain, were the symbol which
Shadows the inherited glory of the rich.

Some violent bitter man, some powerful man
Called architect and artist in, that they,
Bitter and violent men, might rear in stone
The sweetness that all longed for night and day,
The gentleness none there had ever known;
But when the master's buried mice can play,
And maybe the great-grandson of that house,
For all its bronze and marble, 's but a mouse.

O what if gardens where the peacock strays
With delicate feet upon old terraces,
Or else all Juno from an urn displays
Before the indifferent garden deities;
O what if levelled lawns and gravelled ways
Where slippered Contemplation finds his ease

And Childhood a delight for every sense,
But take our greatness with our violence?

What if the glory of escutcheoned doors,
And buildings that a haughtier age designed,
The pacing to and fro on polished floors
Amid great chambers and long galleries, lined
With famous portraits of our ancestors;
What if those things the greatest of mankind
Consider most to magnify, or to bless,
But take our greatness with our bitterness?

II *My House*

An ancient bridge, and a more ancient tower,
A farmhouse that is sheltered by its wall,
An acre of stony ground,
Where the symbolic rose can break in flower,
Old ragged elms, old thorns innumerable,
The sound of the rain or sound
Of every wind that blows;
The stilted water-hen
Crossing stream again
Scared by the splashing of a dozen cows;

A winding stair, a chamber arched with stone,
A grey stone fireplace with an open hearth,
A candle and written page.
Il Penseroso's Platonist toiled on
In some like chamber, shadowing forth
How the daemonic rage
Imagined everything.
Benighted travellers
From markets and from fairs
Have seen his midnight candle glimmering.

Two men have founded here. A man-at-arms
Gathered a score of horse and spent his days

In this tumultuous spot,
Where through long wars and sudden night alarms
His dwindling score and he seemed castaways
Forgetting and forgot;
And I, that after me
My bodily heirs may find,
To exalt a lonely mind,
Befitting emblems of adversity.

III *My Table*

Two heavy trestles, and a board
Where Sato's gift, a changeless sword,
By pen and paper lies,
That it may moralise
My days out of their aimlessness.
A bit of an embroidered dress
Covers its wooden sheath.
Chaucer had not drawn breath
When it was forged. In Sato's house,
Curved like new moon, moon-luminous,
It lay five hundred years.
Yet if no change appears
No moon; only an aching heart
Conceives a changeless work of art.
Our learned men have urged
That when and where 'twas forged
A marvellous accomplishment,
In painting or in pottery, went
From father unto son
And through the centuries ran
And seemed unchanging like the sword.
Soul's beauty being most adored,
Men and their business took
The soul's unchanging look;
For the most rich inheritor,

Knowing that none could pass Heaven's door
That loved inferior art,
Had such an aching heart
That he, although a country's talk
For silken clothes and stately walk,
Had waking wits; it seemed
Juno's peacock screamed.

IV *My Descendants*

Having inherited a vigorous mind
From my old fathers, I must nourish dreams
And leave a woman and a man behind
As vigorous of mind, and yet it seems
Life scarce can cast a fragrance on the wind,
Scarce spread a glory to the morning beams,
But the torn petals strew the garden plot;
And there's but common greenness after that.

And what if my descendants lose the flower
Through natural declension of the soul,
Through too much business with the passing hour,
Through too much play, or marriage with a fool?
May this laborious stair and this stark tower
Become a roofless ruin that the owl
May build in the cracked masonry and cry
Her desolation to the desolate sky.

The Primum Mobile that fashioned us
Has made the very owls in circles move;
And I, that count myself most prosperous,
Seeing that love and friendship are enough,
For an old neighbour's friendship chose the house
And decked and altered it for a girl's love,
And know whatever flourish and decline
These stones remain their monument and mine.

V *The Road at My Door*

An affable Irregular,
A heavily-built Falstaffian man,
Comes cracking jokes of civil war
As though to die by gunshot were
The finest play under the sun.

A brown Lieutenant and his men,
Half dressed in national uniform,
Stand at my door, and I complain
Of the foul weather, hail and rain,
A pear-tree broken by the storm.

I count those feathered balls of soot
The moor-hen guides upon the stream,
To silence the envy in my thought;
And turn towards my chamber, caught
In the cold snows of a dream.

VI *The Stare's Nest by My Window*

The bees build in the crevices
Of loosening masonry, and there
The mother birds bring grubs and flies.
My wall is loosening; honey-bees,
Come build in the empty house of the stare.

We are closed in, and the key is turned
On our uncertainty; somewhere
A man is killed, or a house burned,
Yet no clear fact to be discerned:
Come build in the empty house of the stare.

A barricade of stone or of wood;
Some fourteen days of civil war;
Last night they trundled down the road
That dead young soldier in his blood:
Come build in the empty house of the stare.

We had fed the heart on fantasies,
The heart's grown brutal from the fare;
More substance in our enmities
Than in our love; O honey-bees,
Come build in the empty house of the stare.

VII *I see Phantoms of Hatred and of the Heart's Fullness and of the Coming Emptiness*

I climb to the tower-top and lean upon broken stone,
A mist that is like blown snow is sweeping over all,
Valley, river, and elms, under the light of a moon
That seems unlike itself, that seems unchangeable,
A glittering sword out of the east. A puff of wind
And those white glimmering fragments of the mist sweep by.
Frenzies bewilder, reveries perturb the mind;
Monstrous familiar images swim to the mind's eye.

'Vengeance upon the murderers,' the cry goes up,
'Vengeance for Jacques Molay.' In cloud-pale rags, or in lace,
The rage-driven, rage-tormented, and rage-hungry troop,
Trooper belabouring trooper, biting at arm or at face,
Plunges towards nothing, arms and fingers spreading wide
For the embrace of nothing; and I, my wits astray
Because of all that senseless tumult, all but cried
For vengeance on the murderers of Jacques Molay.

Their legs long, delicate and slender, aquamarine their eyes,
Magical unicorns bear ladies on their backs.
The ladies close their musing eyes. No prophecies,
Remembered out of Babylonian almanacs,
Have closed the ladies' eyes, their minds are but a pool
Where even longing drowns under its own excess;
Nothing but stillness can remain when hearts are full
Of their own sweetness, bodies of their loveliness.

The cloud-pale unicorns, the eyes of aquamarine,
The quivering half-closed eyelids, the rags of cloud or of lace,

Or eyes that rage has brightened, arms it has made lean,
Give place to an indifferent multitude, give place
To brazen hawks. Nor self-delighting reverie,
Nor hate of what's to come, nor pity for what's gone,
Nothing but grip of claw, and the eye's complacency,
The innumerable clanging wings that have put out the
moon.

I turn away and shut the door, and on the stair
Wonder how many times I could have proved my worth
In something that all others understand or share;
But O! ambitious heart, had such a proof drawn forth
A company of friends, a conscience set at ease,
It had but made us pine the more. The abstract joy,
The half-read wisdom of daemonic images,
Suffice the ageing man as once the growing boy.

1923

Nineteen Hundred and Nineteen

I

Many ingenious lovely things are gone
That seemed sheer miracle to the multitude,
Protected from the circle of the moon
That pitches common things about. There stood
Amid the ornamental bronze and stone
An ancient image made of olive wood –
And gone are Phidias' famous ivories
And all the golden grasshoppers and bees.

We too had many pretty toys when young:
A law indifferent to blame or praise,
To bribe or threat; habits that made old wrong
Melt down, as it were wax in the sun's rays;
Public opinion ripening for so long
We thought it would outlive all future days.
O what fine thought we had because we thought
That the worst rogues and rascals had died out.

All teeth were drawn, all ancient tricks unlearned,
And a great army but a showy thing;
What matter that no cannon had been turned
Into a ploughshare? Parliament and king
Thought that unless a little powder burned
The trumpeters might burst with trumpeting
And yet it lack all glory; and perchance
The guardsmen's drowsy chargers would not prance.

Now days are dragon-ridden, the nightmare
Rides upon sleep: a drunken soldiery
Can leave the mother, murdered at her door,
To crawl in her own blood, and go scot-free;
The night can sweat with terror as before
We pieced our thoughts into philosophy,

And planned to bring the world under a rule,
Who are but weasels fighting in a hole.

He who can read the signs nor sink unmanned
Into the half-deceit of some intoxicant
From shallow wits; who knows no work can stand,
Whether health, wealth or peace of mind were spent
On master-work of intellect or hand,
No honour leave its mighty monument,
Has but one comfort left: all triumph would
But break upon his ghostly solitude.

But is there any comfort to be found?
Man is in love and loves what vanishes,
What more is there to say? That country round
None dared admit, if such a thought were his,
Incendiary or bigot could be found
To burn that stump on the Acropolis
Or break in bits the famous ivories
Or traffic in the grasshoppers or bees.

II

When Loie Fuller's Chinese dancers enwound
A shining web, a floating ribbon of cloth,
It seemed that a dragon of air
Had fallen among dancers, had whirled them round
Or hurried them off on its own furious path;
So the Platonic Year
Whirls out new right and wrong,
Whirls in the old instead;
All men are dancers and their tread
Goes to the barbarous clangour of a gong.

III

Some moralist or mythological poet
Compares the solitary soul to a swan;

I am satisfied with that,
Satisfied if a troubled mirror show it,
Before that brief gleam of its life be gone,
An image of its state;
The wings half spread for flight,
The breast thrust out in pride
Whether to play, or to ride
Those winds that clamour of approaching night.

A man in his own secret meditation
Is lost amid the labyrinth that he has made
In art or politics;
Some Platonist affirms that in the station
Where we should cast off body and trade
The ancient habit sticks,
And that if our works could
But vanish with our breath
That were a lucky death,
For triumph can but mar our solitude.

The swan has leaped into the desolate heaven:
That image can bring wildness, bring a rage
To end all things, to end
What my laborious life imagined, even
The half-imagined, the half-written page;
O but we dreamed to mend
Whatever mischief seemed
To afflict mankind, but now
That winds of winter blow
Learn that we were crack-pated when we dreamed.

IV

We, who seven years ago
Talked of honour and of truth,
Shriek with pleasure if we show
The weasel's twist, the weasel's tooth.

V

Come let us mock at the great
That had such burdens on the mind
And toiled so hard and late
To leave some monument behind,
Nor thought of the levelling wind.

Come let us mock at the wise;
With all those calendars whereon
They fixed old aching eyes,
They never saw how seasons run,
And now but gape at the sun.

Come let us mock at the good
That fancied goodness might be gay,
And sick of solitude
Might proclaim a holiday:
Wind shrieked – and where are they?

Mock mockers after that
That would not lift a hand maybe
To help good, wise or great
To bar that foul storm out, for we
Traffic in mockery.

VI

Violence upon the roads: violence of horses;
Some few have handsome riders, are garlanded
On delicate sensitive ear or tossing mane,
But wearied running round and round in their courses
All break and vanish, and evil gathers head:
Herodias' daughters have returned again,
A sudden blast of dusty wind and after
Thunder of feet, tumult of images,
Their purpose in the labyrinth of the wind;
And should some crazy hand dare touch a daughter

All turn with amorous cries, or angry cries,
According to the wind, for all are blind.
But now wind drops, dust settles; thereupon
There lurches past, his great eyes without thought
Under the shadow of stupid straw-pale locks,
That insolent fiend Robert Artisson
To whom the love-lorn Lady Kyteler brought
Bronzed peacock feathers, red combs of her cocks.

1919

Leda and the Swan

A sudden blow: the great wings beating still
Above the staggering girl, her thighs caressed
By the dark webs, her nape caught in his bill,
He holds her helpless breast upon his breast.

How can those terrified vague fingers push
The feathered glory from her loosening thighs?
And how can body, laid in that white rush,
But feel the strange heart beating where it lies?

A shudder in the loins engenders there
The broken wall, the burning roof and tower
And Agamemnon dead.
                                        Being so caught up,
So mastered by the brute blood of the air,
Did she put on his knowledge with his power
Before the indifferent beak could let her drop?

1923

Among School Children

I

I walk through the long schoolroom questioning;
A kind old nun in a white hood replies;
The children learn to cipher and to sing,
To study reading-books and histories,
To cut and sew, be neat in everything
In the best modern way – the children's eyes
In momentary wonder stare upon
A sixty-year-old smiling public man.

II

I dream of a Ledaean body, bent
Above a sinking fire, a tale that she
Told of a harsh reproof, or trivial event
That changed some childish day to tragedy –
Told, and it seemed that our two natures blent
Into a sphere from youthful sympathy,
Or else, to alter Plato's parable,
Into the yolk and white of the one shell.

III

And thinking of that fit of grief or rage
I look upon one child or t'other there
And wonder if she stood so at that age –
For even daughters of the swan can share
Something of every paddler's heritage –
And had that colour upon cheek or hair,
And thereupon my heart is driven wild:
She stands before me as a living child.

IV

Her present image floats into the mind –
Did Quattrocento finger fashion it
Hollow of cheek as though it drank the wind
And took a mess of shadows for its meat?
And I though never of Ledaean kind
Had pretty plumage once – enough of that,
Better to smile on all that smile, and show
There is a comfortable kind of old scarecrow.

V

What youthful mother, a shape upon her lap
Honey of generation had betrayed,
And that must sleep, shriek, struggle to escape
As recollection or the drug decide,
Would think her son, did she but see that shape
With sixty or more winters on its head,
A compensation for the pang of his birth,
Or the uncertainty of his setting forth?

VI

Plato thought nature but a spume that plays
Upon a ghostly paradigm of things;
Solider Aristotle played the taws
Upon the bottom of a king of kings;
World-famous golden-thighed Pythagoras
Fingered upon a fiddle-stick or strings
What a star sang and careless Muses heard:
Old clothes upon old sticks to scare a bird.

VII

Both nuns and mothers worship images,
But those the candles light are not as those
That animate a mother's reveries,

But keep a marble or a bronze repose.
And yet they too break hearts – O Presences
That passion, piety or affection knows,
And that all heavenly glory symbolise –
O self-born mockers of man's enterprise;

VIII

Labour is blossoming or dancing where
The body is not bruised to pleasure soul,
Nor beauty born out of its own despair,
Nor blear-eyed wisdom out of midnight oil.
O chestnut-tree, great-rooted blossomer,
Are you the leaf, the blossom or the bole?
O body swayed to music, O brightening glance,
How can we know the dancer from the dance?

In Memory of Eva Gore-Booth and Con Markiewicz

The light of evening, Lissadell,
Great windows open to the south,
Two girls in silk kimonos, both
Beautiful, one a gazelle.
But a raving autumn shears
Blossom from the summer's wreath;
The older is condemned to death,
Pardoned, drags out lonely years
Conspiring among the ignorant.
I know not what the younger dreams –
Some vague Utopia – and she seems,
When withered old and skeleton-gaunt,
An image of such politics.
Many a time I think to seek
One or the other out and speak
Of that old Georgian mansion, mix
Pictures of the mind, recall
That table and the talk of youth,
Two girls in silk kimonos, both
Beautiful, one a gazelle.

Dear shadows, now you know it all,
All the folly of a fight
With a common wrong or right.
The innocent and the beautiful
Have no enemy but time;
Arise and bid me strike a match
And strike another till time catch;
Should the conflagration climb,
Run till all the sages know.
We the great gazebo built,
They convicted us of guilt;
Bid me strike a match and blow.

October 1927

A Dialogue of Self and Soul

I

My Soul. I summon to the winding ancient stair;
Set all your mind upon the steep ascent,
Upon the broken, crumbling battlement,
Upon the breathless starlit air,
Upon the star that marks the hidden pole;
Fix every wandering thought upon
That quarter where all thought is done:
Who can distinguish darkness from the soul?

My Self. The consecrated blade upon my knees
Is Sato's ancient blade, still as it was,
Still razor-keen, still like a looking-glass
Unspotted by the centuries;
That flowering, silken, old embroidery, torn
From some court-lady's dress and round
The wooden scabbard bound and wound,
Can, tattered, still protect, faded adorn.

My Soul. Why should the imagination of a man
Long past his prime remember things that are
Emblematical of love and war?
Think of ancestral night that can,
If but imagination scorn the earth
And intellect its wandering
To this and that and t'other thing,
Deliver from the crime of death and birth.

My Self. Montashigi, third of his family, fashioned it
Five hundred years ago, about it lie
Flowers from I know not what embroidery –
Heart's purple – and all these I set
For emblems of the day against the tower
Emblematical of the night,

And claim as by a soldier's right
A charter to commit the crime once more.

My Soul. Such fullness in that quarter overflows
And falls into the basin of the mind
That man is stricken deaf and dumb and blind,
For intellect no longer knows
Is from the *Ought*, or *Knower* from the *Known* –
That is to say, ascends to Heaven;
Only the dead can be forgiven;
But when I think of that my tongue's a stone.

II

My Self. A living man is blind and drinks his drop.
What matter if the ditches are impure?
What matter if I live it all once more?
Endure that toil of growing up;
The ignominy of boyhood; the distress
Of boyhood changing into man;
The unfinished man and his pain
Brought face to face with his own clumsiness;

The finished man among his enemies? –
How in the name of Heaven can he escape
That defiling and disfigured shape
The mirror of malicious eyes
Casts upon his eyes until at last
He thinks that shape must be his shape?
And what's the good of an escape
If honour find him in the wintry blast?

I am content to live it all again
And yet again, if it be life to pitch
Into the frog-spawn of a blind man's ditch,
A blind man battering blind men;
Or into that most fecund ditch of all,
The folly that man does

Or must suffer, if he woos
A proud woman not kindred of his soul.

I am content to follow to its source
Every event in action or in thought;
Measure the lot; forgive myself the lot!
When such as I cast out remorse
So great a sweetness flows into the breast
We must laugh and we must sing,
We are blest by everything,
Everything we look upon is blest.

Coole Park and Ballylee, 1931

Under my window-ledge the waters race,
Otters below and moor-hens on the top,
Run for a mile undimmed in Heaven's face
Then darkening through 'dark' Raftery's 'cellar' drop,
Run underground, rise in a rocky place
In Coole demesne, and there to finish up
Spread to a lake and drop into a hole.
What's water but the generated soul?

Upon the border of that lake's a wood
Now all dry sticks under a wintry sun,
And in a copse of beeches there I stood,
For Nature's pulled her tragic buskin on
And all the rant's a mirror of my mood:
At sudden thunder of the mounting swan
I turned about and looked where branches break
The glittering reaches of the flooded lake.

Another emblem there! That stormy white
But seems a concentration of the sky;
And, like the soul, it sails into the sight
And in the morning's gone, no man knows why;
And is so lovely that it sets to right
What knowledge or its lack had set awry,
So arrogantly pure, a child might think
It can be murdered with a spot of ink.

Sound of a stick upon the floor, a sound
From somebody that toils from chair to chair;
Beloved books that famous hands have bound,
Old marble heads, old pictures everywhere;
Great rooms where travelled men and children found
Content or joy; a last inheritor
Where none has reigned that lacked a name and fame
Or out of folly into folly came.

A spot whereon the founders lived and died
Seemed once more dear than life; ancestral trees,
Or gardens rich in memory glorified
Marriages, alliances and families,
And every bride's ambition satisfied.
Where fashion or mere fantasy decrees
We shift about – all that great glory spent –
Like some poor Arab tribesman and his tent.

We were the last romantics – chose for theme
Traditional sanctity and loveliness;
Whatever's written in what poets name
The book of the people; whatever most can bless
The mind of man or elevate a rhyme;
But all is changed, that high horse riderless,
Though mounted in that saddle Homer rode
Where the swan drifts upon a darkening flood.

For Anne Gregory

'Never shall a young man,
Thrown into despair
By those great honey-coloured
Ramparts at your ear,
Love you for yourself alone
And not your yellow hair.'

'But I can get a hair-dye
And set such colour there,
Brown, or black, or carrot,
That young men in despair
May love me for myself alone
And not my yellow hair.'

'I heard an old religious man
But yesternight declare
That he had found a text to prove
That only God, my dear,
Could love you for yourself alone
And not your yellow hair.'

Swift's Epitaph

Swift has sailed into his rest;
Savage indignation there
Cannot lacerate his breast.
Imitate him if you dare,
World-besotted traveller; he
Served human liberty.

The Choice

The intellect of man is forced to choose
Perfection of the life, or of the work,
And if it take the second must refuse
A heavenly mansion, raging in the dark.

When all that story's finished, what's the news?
In luck or out the toil has left its mark:
That old perplexity an empty purse,
Or the day's vanity, the night's remorse.

Mohini Chatterjee

I asked if I should pray,
But the Brahmin said,
'Pray for nothing, say
Every night in bed,
"I have been a king,
I have been a slave,
Nor is there anything,
Fool, rascal, knave,
That I have not been,
And yet upon my breast
A myriad heads have lain." '

That he might set at rest
A boy's turbulent days
Mohini Chatterjee
Spoke these, or words like these.
I add in commentary,
'Old lovers yet may have
All that time denied –
Grave is heaped on grave
That they be satisfied –
Over the blackened earth
The old troops parade,
Birth is heaped on birth
That such cannonade
May thunder time away,
Birth-hour and death-hour meet,
Or, as great sages say,
Men dance on deathless feet.'

1928

Byzantium

The unpurged images of day recede;
The Emperor's drunken soldiery are abed;
Night resonance recedes, night-walkers' song
After great cathedral gong;
A starlit or a moonlit dome disdains
All that man is,
All mere complexities,
The fury and the mire of human veins.

Before me floats an image, man or shade,
Shade more than man, more image than a shade;
For Hades' bobbin bound in mummy-cloth
May unwind the winding path;
A mouth that has no moisture and no breath
Breathless mouths may summon;
I hail the superhuman;
I call it death-in-life and life-in-death.

Miracle, bird or golden handiwork,
More miracle than bird or handiwork,
Planted on the star-lit golden bough,
Can like the cocks of Hades crow,
Or, by the moon embittered, scorn aloud
In glory of changeless metal
Common bird or petal
And all complexities of mire or blood.

At midnight on the Emperor's pavement flit
Flames that no faggot feeds, nor steel has lit,
Nor storm disturbs, flames begotten of flame,
Where blood-begotten spirits come
And all complexities of fury leave,
Dying into a dance,
An agony of trance,
An agony of flame that cannot singe a sleeve.

Astraddle on the dolphin's mire and blood,
Spirit after spirit! The smithies break the flood,
The golden smithies of the Emperor!
Marbles of the dancing floor
Break bitter furies of complexity,
Those images that yet
Fresh images beget,
That dolphin-torn, that gong-tormented sea.

1930

Crazy Jane Talks with the Bishop

I met the Bishop on the road
And much said he and I.
'Those breasts are flat and fallen now,
Those veins must soon be dry;
Live in a heavenly mansion,
Not in some foul sty.'

'Fair and foul are near of kin,
And fair needs foul,' I cried.
'My friends are gone, but that's a truth
Nor grave nor bed denied,
Learned in bodily lowliness
And in the heart's pride.

'A woman can be proud and stiff
When on love intent;
But Love has pitched his mansion in
The place of excrement;
For nothing can be sole or whole
That has not been rent.'

After Long Silence

Speech after long silence; it is right,
All other lovers being estranged or dead,
Unfriendly lamplight hid under its shade,
The curtains drawn upon unfriendly night,
That we descant and yet again descant
Upon the supreme theme of Art and Song:
Bodily decrepitude is wisdom; young
We loved each other and were ignorant.

Mad as the Mist and Snow

Bolt and bar the shutter,
For the foul winds blow:
Our minds are at their best this night,
And I seem to know
That everything outside us is
Mad as the mist and snow.

Horace there by Homer stands,
Plato stands below,
And here is Tully's open page.
How many year ago
Were you and I unlettered lads
Mad as the mist and snow?

You ask what makes me sigh, old friend,
What makes me shudder so?
I shudder and I sigh to think
That even Cicero
And many-minded Homer were
Mad as the mist and snow.

The Delphic Oracle upon Plotinus

Behold that great Plotinus swim,
Buffeted by such seas;
Bland Rhadamanthus beckons him,
But the Golden Race looks dim,
Salt blood blocks his eyes.

Scattered on the level grass
Or winding through the grove
Plato there and Minos pass,
There stately Pythagoras
And all the choir of Love.

August 19, 1931

A Last Confession

What lively lad most pleasured me
Of all that with me lay?
I answer that I gave my soul
And loved in misery,
But had great pleasure with a lad
That I loved bodily.

Flinging from his arms I laughed
To think his passion such
He fancied that I gave a soul
Did but our bodies touch,
And laughed upon his breast to think
Beast gave beast as much.

I gave what other women gave
That stepped out of their clothes,
But when this soul, its body off,
Naked to naked goes,
He it has found shall find therein
What none other knows,

And give his own and take his own
And rule in his own right;
And though it loved in misery
Close and cling so tight,
There's not a bird of day that dare
Extinguish that delight.

Ribh at the Tomb of Baile and Aillinn

Because you have found me in the pitch-dark night
With open book you ask me what I do.
Mark and digest my tale, carry it afar
To those that never saw this tonsured head
Nor heard this voice that ninety years have cracked.
Of Baile and Aillinn you need not speak,
All know their tale, all know what leaf and twig,
What juncture of the apple and the yew,
Surmount their bones; but speak what none have heard.

The miracle that gave them such a death
Transfigured to pure substance what had once
Been bone and sinew; when such bodies join
There is no touching here, nor touching there,
Nor straining joy, but whole is joined to whole;
For the intercourse of angels is a light
Where for its moment both seem lost, consumed.

Here in the pitch-dark atmosphere above
The trembling of the apple and the yew,
Here on the anniversary of their death,
The anniversary of their first embrace,
Those lovers, purified by tragedy,
Hurry into each other's arms; these eyes,
By water, herb and solitary prayer
Made aquiline, are open to that light.
Though somewhat broken by the leaves, that light
Lies in a circle on the grass; therein
I turn the pages of my holy book.

Whence had they Come?

Eternity is passion, girl or boy
Cry at the onset of their sexual joy
'For ever and for ever'; then awake
Ignorant what Dramatis Personae spake;
A passion-driven exultant man sings out
Sentences that he has never thought;
The Flagellant lashes those submissive loins
Ignorant what that dramatist enjoins,
What master made the lash. Whence had they come,
The hand and lash that beat down frigid Rome?
What sacred drama through her body heaved
When world-transforming Charlemagne was conceived?

The Four Ages of Man

He with body waged a fight,
But body won; it walks upright.

Then he struggled with the heart;
Innocence and peace depart.

Then he struggled with the mind;
His proud heart he left behind.

Now his wars on God begin;
At stroke of midnight God shall win.

Meru

Civilisation is hooped together, brought
Under a rule, under the semblance of peace
By manifold illusion; but man's life is thought,
And he, despite his terror, cannot cease
Ravening through century after century,
Ravening, raging, and uprooting that he may come
Into the desolation of reality:
Egypt and Greece, good-bye, and good-bye, Rome!
Hermits upon Mount Meru or Everest,
Caverned in night under the drifted snow,
Or where that snow and winter's dreadful blast
Beat down upon their naked bodies, know
That day brings round the night, that before dawn
His glory and his monuments are gone.

Lapis Lazuli

For Harry Clifton

I have heard that hysterical women say
They are sick of the palette and fiddle-bow,
Of poets that are always gay,
For everybody knows or else should know
That if nothing drastic is done
Aeroplane and Zeppelin will come out,
Pitch like King Billy bomb-balls in
Until the town lie beaten flat.

All perform their tragic play,
There struts Hamlet, there is Lear,
That's Ophelia, that Cordelia;
Yet they, should the last scene be there,
The great stage curtain about to drop,
If worthy their prominent part in the play,
Do not break up their lines to weep.
They know that Hamlet and Lear are gay;
Gaiety transfiguring all that dread.
All men have aimed at, found and lost;
Black out; Heaven blazing into the head:
Tragedy wrought to its uttermost.
Though Hamlet rambles and Lear rages,
And all the drop-scenes drop at once
Upon a hundred thousand stages,
It cannot grow by an inch or an ounce.

On their own feet they came, or on shipboard,
Camel-back, horse-back, ass-back, mule-back,
Old civilisations put to the sword.
Then they and their wisdom went to rack:
No handiwork of Callimachus,
Who handled marble as if it were bronze,
Made draperies that seemed to rise

When sea-wind swept the corner, stands;
His long lamp-chimney shaped like the stem
Of a slender palm, stood but a day;
All things fall and are built again,
And those that build them again are gay.

Two Chinamen, behind them a third,
Are carved in lapis lazuli,
Over them flies a long-legged bird,
A symbol of longevity;
The third, doubtless a serving-man,
Carries a musical instrument.

Every discoloration of the stone,
Every accidental crack or dent,
Seems a water-course or an avalanche,
Or lofty slope where it still snows
Though doubtless plum or cherry-branch
Sweetens the little half-way house
Those Chinamen climb towards, and I
Delight to imagine them seated there;
There, on the mountain and the sky,
On all the tragic scene they stare.
One asks for mournful melodies;
Accomplished fingers begin to play.
Their eyes mid many wrinkles, their eyes,
Their ancient, glittering eyes, are gay.

An Acre of Grass

Picture and book remain,
An acre of green grass
For air and exercise,
Now strength of body goes;
Midnight, an old house
Where nothing stirs but a mouse.

My temptation is quiet.
Here at life's end
Neither loose imagination,
Nor the mill of the mind
Consuming its rag and bone,
Can make the truth known.

Grant me an old man's frenzy,
Myself must I remake
Till I am Timon and Lear
Or that William Blake
Who beat upon the wall
Till Truth obeyed his call;

A mind Michael Angelo knew
That can pierce the clouds,
Or inspired by frenzy
Shake the dead in their shrouds;
Forgotten else by mankind,
An old man's eagle mind.

What Then?

His chosen comrades thought at school
He must grow a famous man;
He thought the same and lived by rule,
All his twenties crammed with toil;
'*What then?' sang Plato's ghost. 'What then?*'

Everything he wrote was read,
After certain years he won
Sufficient money for his need,
Friends that have been friends indeed;
'What then?' sang Plato's ghost. 'What then?'

All his happier dreams came true –
A small old house, wife, daughter, son,
Grounds where plum and cabbage grew,
Poets and Wits about him drew;
'What then?' sang Plato's ghost. 'What then?'

'The work is done,' grown old he thought,
'According to my boyish plan;
Let the fools rage, I swerved in naught,
Something to perfection brought';
But louder sang that ghost, 'What then?'

Beautiful Lofty Things

Beautiful lofty things: O'Leary's noble head;
My father upon the Abbey stage, before him a raging crowd:
'This Land of Saints,' and then as the applause died out,
'Of plaster Saints'; his beautiful mischievous head thrown back.
Standish O'Grady supporting himself between the tables
Speaking to a drunken audience high nonsensical words;
Augusta Gregory seated at her great ormolu table,
Her eightieth winter approaching: 'Yesterday he threatened my life.
I told him that nightly from six to seven I sat at this table,
The blinds drawn up'; Maud Gonne at Howth station waiting a train,
Pallas Athene in that straight back and arrogant head:
All the Olympians; a thing never known again.

The Curse of Cromwell

You ask what I have found, and far and wide I go:
Nothing but Cromwell's house and Cromwell's murderous
  crew,
The lovers and the dancers are beaten into the clay,
And the tall men and the swordsmen and the horsemen,
  where are they?
And there is an old beggar wandering in his pride –
His fathers served their fathers before Christ was crucified.
      O what of that, O what of that.,
      What is there left to say?

All neighbourly content and easy talk are gone,
But there's no good complaining, for money's rant is on.
He that's mounting up must on his neighbour mount,
And we and all the Muses are things of no account.
They have schooling of their own, but I pass their schooling
  by,
What can they know that we know that know the time to die?
      O what of that, O what of that,
      What is there left to say?

But there's another knowledge that my heart destroys,
As the fox in the old fable destroyed the Spartan boy's,
Because it proves that things both can and cannot be:
That the swordsmen and the ladies can still keep company,
Can pay the poet for a verse and hear the fiddle sound,
That I am still their servant though all are under-ground.
      O what of that, O what of that,
      What is there left to say?

I came on a great house in the middle of the night,
Its open lighted doorway and its windows all alight,
And all my friends were there and made me welcome too;
But I woke in an old ruin that the winds howled through;

And when I pay attention I must out and walk
Among the dogs and horses that understand my talk.
O what of that, O what of that,
What is there left to say?

The O'Rahilly

Sing of the O'Rahilly,
Do not deny his right;
Sing a 'the' before his name;
Allow that he, despite
All those learned historians,
Established it for good;
He wrote out that word himself,
He christened himself with blood.
How goes the weather?

Sing of the O'Rahilly
That had such little sense
He told Pearse and Connolly
He'd gone to great expense
Keeping all the Kerry men
Out of that crazy fight;
That he might be there himself
Had travelled half the night.
How goes the weather?

'Am I such a craven that
I should not get the word
But for what some travelling man
Had heard I had not heard?'
Then on Pearse and Connolly
He fixed a bitter look:
'Because I helped to wind the clock
I come to hear it strike.'
How goes the weather?

What remains to sing about
But of the death he met
Stretched under a doorway
Somewhere off Henry Street;

They that found him found upon
The door above his head
'Here died the O'Rahilly.
R.I.P.' writ in blood.
How goes the weather?

Come Gather round me, Parnellites

Come gather round me, Parnellites,
And praise our chosen man;
Stand upright on your legs awhile,
Stand upright while you can,
For soon we lie where he is laid,
And he is underground;
Come fill up all those glasses
And pass the bottle round.

And here's a cogent reason,
And I have many more,
He fought the might of England
And saved the Irish poor,
Whatever good a farmer's got
He brought it all to pass;
And here's another reason,
That Parnell loved a lass.

And here's a final reason,
He was of such a kind
Every man that sings a song
Keeps Parnell in his mind.
For Parnell was a proud man,
No prouder trod the ground,
And a proud man's a lovely man,
So pass the bottle round.

The Bishops and the Party
That tragic story made,
A husband that had sold his wife
And after that betrayed;
But stories that live longest
Are sung above the glass,
And Parnell loved his country,
And Parnell loved his lass.

The Great Day

Hurrah for revolution and more cannon-shot!
A beggar upon horseback lashes a beggar on foot.
Hurrah for revolution and cannon come again!
The beggars have changed places, but the lash goes on.

The Pilgrim

I fasted for some forty days on bread and buttermilk,
For passing round the bottle with girls in rags or silk,
In country shawl or Paris cloak, had put my wits astray,
And what's the good of women, for all that they can say
Is fol de rol de rolly O.

Round Lough Derg's holy island I went upon the stones,
I prayed at all the Stations upon my marrow-bones,
And there I found an old man, and though I prayed all day
And that old man beside me, nothing would he say
But fol de rol de rolly O.

All know that all the dead in the world about that place are stuck,
And that should mother seek her son she'd have but little luck
Because the fires of Purgatory have ate their shapes away;
I swear to God I questioned them, and all they had to say.
Was fol de rol de rolly O.

A great black ragged bird appeared when I was in the boat;
Some twenty feet from tip to tip had it stretched rightly out,
With flopping and with flapping it made a great display,
But I never stopped to question, what could the boatman say
But fol de rol de rolly O.

Now I am in the public-house and lean upon the wall,
So come in rags or come in silk, in cloak or country shawl,
And come with learned lovers or with what men you may,
For I can put the whole lot down, and all I have to say
Is fol de rol de rolly O.

The Municipal Gallery Revisited

I

Around me the images of thirty years:
An ambush; pilgrims at the water-side;
Casement upon trial, half hidden by the bars,
Guarded; Griffith staring in hysterical pride;
Kevin O'Higgins' countenance that wears
A gentle questioning look that cannot hide
A soul incapable of remorse or rest;
A revolutionary soldier kneeling to be blessed;

II

An Abbot or Archbishop with an upraised hand
Blessing the Tricolour. 'This is not,' I say,
'The dead Ireland of my youth, but an Ireland
The poets have imagined, terrible and gay.'
Before a woman's portrait suddenly I stand,
Beautiful and gentle in her Venetian way.
I met her all but fifty years ago
For twenty minutes in some studio.

III

Heart-smitten with emotion I sink down,
My heart recovering with covered eyes;
Wherever I had looked I had looked upon
My permanent or impermanent images:
Augusta Gregory's son; her sister's son,
Hugh Lane, 'onlie begetter' of all these;
Hazel Lavery living and dying, that tale
As though some ballad-singer had sung it all;

IV

Mancini's portrait of Augusta Gregory,
'Greatest since Rembrandt,' according to John Synge;
A great ebullient portrait certainly;
But where is the brush that could show anything
Of all that pride and that humility?
And I am in despair that time may bring
Approved patterns of women or of men
But not that selfsame excellence again.

V

My mediaeval knees lack health until they bend,
But in that woman, in that household where
Honour had lived so long, all lacking found.
Childless I thought, 'My children may find here
Deep-rooted things,' but never foresaw its end,
And now that end has come I have not wept;
No fox can foul the lair the badger swept –

VI

(An image out of Spenser and the common tongue).
John Synge, I and Augusta Gregory, thought
All that we did, all that we said or sang
Must come from contact with the soil, from that
Contact everything Antaeus-like grew strong.
We three alone in modern times had brought
Everything down to that sole test again,
Dream of the noble and the beggar-man.

VII

And here's John Synge himself, that rooted man,
'Forgetting human words,' a grave deep face.
You that would judge me, do not judge alone
This book or that, come to this hallowed place

Where my friends' portraits hang and look thereon;
Ireland's history in their lineaments trace;
Think where man's glory most begins and ends,
And say my glory was I had such friends.

from Under Ben Bulben

V

Irish poets, learn your trade,
Sing whatever is well made,
Scorn the sort now growing up
All out of shape from toe to top,
Their unremembering hearts and heads
Base-born products of base beds.
Sing the peasantry, and then
Hard-riding country gentlemen,
The holiness of monks, and after
Porter-drinkers' randy laughter;
Sing the lords and ladies gay
That were beaten into the clay
Through seven heroic centuries;
Cast your mind on other days
That we in coming days may be
Still the indomitable Irishry.

VI

Under bare Ben Bulben's head
In Drumcliff churchyard Yeats is laid.
An ancestor was rector there
Long years ago, a church stands near,
By the road an ancient cross.
No marble, no conventional phrase;
On limestone quarried near the spot
By his command these words are cut:
Cast a cold eye
On life, on death.
Horseman, pass by!

September 4, 1938

Cuchulain Comforted

A man that had six mortal wounds, a man
Violent and famous, strode among the dead;
Eyes stared out of the branches and were gone.

Then certain Shrouds that muttered head to head
Came and were gone. He leant upon a tree
As though to meditate on wounds and blood.

A Shroud that seemed to have authority
Among those bird-like things came, and let fall
A bundle of linen. Shrouds by two and three

Came creeping up because the man was still.
And thereupon that linen-carrier said:
'Your life can grow much sweeter if you will

'Obey our ancient rule and make a shroud;
Mainly because of what we only know
The rattle of those arms makes us afraid.

'We thread the needles' eyes, and all we do
All must together do.' That done, the man
Took up the nearest and began to sew.

'Now must we sing and sing the best we can,
But first you must be told our character:
Convicted cowards all, by kindred slain

'Or driven from home and left to die in fear.'
They sang, but had nor human tunes nor words,
Though all was done in common as before;

They had changed their throats and had the throats of birds.

January 13, 1939

The Statues

Pythagoras planned it. Why did the people stare?
His numbers, though they moved or seemed to move
In marble or in bronze, lacked character.
But boys and girls, pale from the imagined love
Of solitary beds, knew what they were,
That passion could bring character enough,
And pressed at midnight in some public place
Live lips upon a plummet-measured face.

No! Greater than Pythagoras, for the men
That with a mallet or a chisel modelled these
Calculations that look but casual flesh, put down
All Asiatic vague immensities,
And not the banks of oars that swam upon
The many-headed foam at Salamis.
Europe put off that foam when Phidias
Gave women dreams and dreams their looking-glass.

One image crossed the many-headed, sat
Under the tropic shade, grew round and slow,
No Hamlet thin from eating flies, a fat
Dreamer of the Middle Ages. Empty eyeballs knew
That knowledge increases unreality, that
Mirror on mirror mirrored is all the show.
When gong and conch declare the hour to bless
Grimalkin crawls to Buddha's emptiness.

When Pearse summoned Cuchulain to his side,
What stalked through the Post Office? What intellect,
What calculation, number, measurement, replied?
We Irish, born into that ancient sect
But thrown upon this filthy modern tide
And by its formless spawning fury wrecked,

Climb to our proper dark, that we may trace
The lineaments of a plummet-measured face.

April 9, 1938

News for the Delphic Oracle

I

There all the golden codgers lay,
There the silver dew,
And the great water sighed for love,
And the wind sighed too.
Man-picker Niamh leant and sighed
By Oisin on the grass;
There sighed amid his choir of love
Tall Pythagoras.
Plotinus came and looked about,
The salt-flakes on his breast,
And having stretched and yawned awhile
Lay sighing like the rest.

II

Straddling each a dolphin's back
And steadied by a fin,
Those Innocents re-live their death,
Their wounds open again.
The ecstatic waters laugh because
Their cries are sweet and strange,
Through their ancestral patterns dance,
And the brute dolphins plunge
Until, in some cliff-sheltered bay
Where wades the choir of love
Proffering its sacred laurel crowns,
They pitch their burdens off.

III

Slim adolescence that a nymph has stripped,
Peleus on Thetis stares.

Her limbs are delicate as an eyelid,
Love has blinded him with tears;
But Thetis' belly listens.
Down the mountain walls
From where Pan's cavern is
Intolerable music falls.
Foul goat-head, brutal arm appear,
Belly, shoulder, bum,
Flash fishlike; nymphs and satyrs
Copulate in the foam.

Long-legged Fly

That civilisation may not sink,
Its great battle lost,
Quiet the dog, tether the pony
To a distant post;
Our master Caesar is in the tent
Where the maps are spread,
His eyes fixed upon nothing,
A hand under his head.
Like a long-legged fly upon the stream
His mind moves upon silence.

That the topless towers be burnt
And men recall that face,
Move most gently if move you must
In this lonely place.
She thinks, part woman, three parts a child,
That nobody looks; her feet
Practise a tinker shuffle
Picked up on a street.
Like a long-legged fly upon the stream
Her mind moves upon silence.

That girls at puberty may find
The first Adam in their thought,
Shut the door of the Pope's chapel,
Keep those children out.
There on that scaffolding reclines
Michael Angelo.
With no more sound than the mice make
His hand moves to and fro.
Like a long-legged fly upon the stream
His mind moves upon silence.

High Talk

Processions that lack high stilts have nothing that catches the eye.
What if my great-granddad had a pair that were twenty foot high,
And mine were but fifteen foot, no modern stalks upon higher,
Some rogue of the world stole them to patch up a fence or a fire.
Because piebald ponies, led bears, caged lions, make but poor shows,
Because children demand Daddy-long-legs upon his timber toes,
Because women in the upper storeys demand a face at the pane,
That patching old heels they may shriek, I take to chisel and plane.

Malachi Stilt-Jack am I, whatever I learned has run wild,
From collar to collar, from stilt to stilt, from father to child.
All metaphor, Malachi, stilts and all. A barnacle goose
Far up in the stretches of night; night splits and the dawn breaks loose;
I, through the terrible novelty of light, stalk on, stalk on;
Those great sea-horses bare their teeth and laugh at the dawn.

The Circus Animals' Desertion

I

I sought a theme and sought for it in vain,
I sought it daily for six weeks or so.
Maybe at last, being but a broken man,
I must be satisfied with my heart, although
Winter and summer till old age began
My circus animals were all on show,
Those stilted boys, that burnished chariot,
Lion and woman and the Lord knows what.

II

What can I but enumerate old themes?
First that sea-rider Oisin led by the nose
Through three enchanted islands, allegorical dreams,
Vain gaiety, vain battle, vain repose,
Themes of the embittered heart, or so it seems,
That might adorn old songs or courtly shows;
But what cared I that set him on to ride,
I, starved for the bosom of his faery bride?

And then a counter-truth filled out its play,
The Countess Cathleen was the name I gave it;
She, pity-crazed, had given her soul away,
But masterful Heaven had intervened to save it.
I thought my dear must her own soul destroy,
So did fanaticism and hate enslave it,
And this brought forth a dream and soon enough
This dream itself had all my thought and love.

And when the Fool and Blind Man stole the bread
Cuchulain fought the ungovernable sea;
Heart-mysteries there, and yet when all is said
It was the dream itself enchanted me:

Character isolated by a deed
To engross the present and dominate memory.
Players and painted stage took all my love,
And not those things that they were emblems of.

III

Those masterful images because complete
Grew in pure mind, but out of what began?
A mound of refuse or the sweepings of a street,
Old kettles, old bottles, and a broken can,
Old iron, old bones, old rags, that raving slut
Who keeps the till. Now that my ladder's gone,
I must lie down where all the ladders start,
In the foul rag-and-bone shop of the heart.

The Man and the Echo

Man

In a cleft that's christened Alt
Under broken stone I halt
At the bottom of a pit
That broad noon has never lit,
And shout a secret to the stone.
All that I have said and done,
Now that I am old and ill,
Turns into a question till
I lie awake night after night
And never get the answers right.
Did that play of mine send out
Certain men the English shot?
Did words of mine put too great strain
On that woman's reeling brain?
Could my spoken words have checked
That whereby a house lay wrecked?
And all seems evil until I
Sleepless would lie down and die.

Echo

Lie down and die.

Man

That were to shirk
The spiritual intellect's great work,
And shirk it in vain. There is no release
In a bodkin or disease,
Nor can there be work so great
As that which cleans man's dirty slate.
While man can still his body keep

Wine or love drug him to sleep,
Waking he thanks the Lord that he
Has body and its stupidity,
But body gone he sleeps no more,
And till his intellect grows sure
That all's arranged in one clear view,
Pursues the thoughts that I pursue,
Then stands in judgment on his soul,
And, all work done, dismisses all
Out of intellect and sight
And sinks at last into the night.

Echo

Into the night.

Man

O Rocky Voice,
Shall we in that great night rejoice?
What do we know but that we face
One another in this place?
But hush, for I have lost the theme,
Its joy or night seem but a dream;
Up there some hawk or owl has struck,
Dropping out of sky or rock,
A stricken rabbit is crying out,
And its cry distracts my thought.

Politics

'In our time the destiny of man presents its meaning in political terms.' – Thomas Mann

How can I, that girl standing there,
My attention fix
On Roman or on Russian
Or on Spanish politics?
Yet here's a travelled man that knows
What he talks about,
And there's a politician
That has read and thought,
And maybe what they say is true
Of war and war's alarms,
But O that I were young again
And held her in my arms!

20th-CENTURY SCOTTISH POEMS

20th-CENTURY SCOTTISH POEMS

Selected by DOUGLAS DUNN

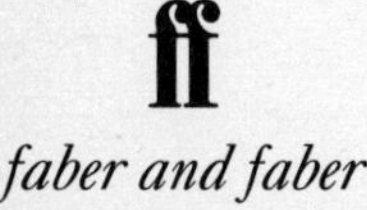

First published in 2000
by Faber and Faber Limited
3 Queen Square London WC1N 3AU

Photoset by Parker Typesetting Service, Leicester
Printed in Italy

All rights reserved
This anthology © Douglas Dunn, 1992, 2000

Douglas Dunn is hereby identified as editor of
this work in accordance with Section 77
of the Copyright, Designs and Patents Act 1988

This book is sold subject to the condition that it shall not, by way of trade or otherwise, be lent, resold, hired out or otherwise circulated without the publisher's prior consent in any form of binding or cover other than that in which it is published and without a similar condition including this condition being imposed on the subsequent purchaser

A CIP record for this book
is available from the British Library
ISBN 0–571–20388–4

10 9 8 7 6 5 4 3 2 1

IN MEMORIAM

Norman MacCaig
Sorley MacLean
George Mackay Brown
Iain Crichton Smith

Contents

Preface

Editing *The Faber Book of Twentieth-Century Scottish Poetry* (1992; revised paperback edition, 1993) was an arduous but rewarding task. This book is based on it, but it is not an epitome. Much of the most impressive poetry by Scots has been at length, and a book of this kind precluded spacious representation. It can be read as a sampler. Readers who find what they like here can go to the fuller anthology or to the poets' individual collections. However, I hope the book stands by itself as an anthology of poems worth reprinting and of poets worth recommending for further reading.

Younger poets have been productive since my original selections, and I have changed their inclusions accordingly. Interesting new poets have also appeared since 1993, and I have included a poem by as many as space permitted.

When the original anthology appeared, some reviewers were kind enough to mention that I hadn't included any of my own poems. It was nice to be noticed where I was absent. But an anthologist ought not to include poems which he or she cannot discuss critically. Besides, previous anthologies of Scottish poetry included much by their editors and closest friends, and I hope to be incapable of creating that kind of suspicion. My editorial principles are those of commitment to the subject and disinterestedness. Include me out; or, exclude me in – or whatever Sam Goldwyn's wise howler was.

The term 'twentieth-century' is, of course, an anachronism, or historical. Let it be read as a prelude to 'twenty-first century', and in a spirit that hopes for the perpetuation of good things and an end (as far as possible) to bad.

If there is one point I would like to make it is that the struggles and contests of elder or dead (alas) poets would seem to have been of assistance to the enhanced confidence and relaxation of younger generations of writers.

Douglas Dunn
Dairsie, 20 IX 99

20th-CENTURY SCOTTISH POEMS

VIOLET JACOB (1863–1946)

The Baltic

'Whaur are ye gaen sae fast, my bairn,
  It's no tae the schule ye'll win?'
'*Doon tae the shore at the fit o' the toon*
  Tae bide till the brigs come in.'

'Awa' noo wi' ye and turn ye hame,
  Ye'll no hae the time tae bide;
It's twa lang months or the brigs come back
  On the lift o' a risin' tide.'

'*I'll sit me doon at the water's mou'*
  Till there's niver a blink o' licht,
For my feyther bad' me tae tryst wi' him
  In the dairkness o' yesternicht.

' "*Rise ye an' rin tae the shore*", *says he,*
  "*At the cheep o' the waukin' bird,*
And I'll bring ye a tale o' a foreign land
  The like that ye niver heard." '

'Oh, haud yer havers, ye feckless wean,
  It was but a dream ye saw,
For he's far, far north wi' the Baltic men
  I' the hurl o' the Baltic snaw;

And what did he ca' yon foreign land?'
  '*He tell'tna its name tae me,*
But I doot it's no by the Baltic shore,
  For he said there was nae mair sea.'

blink o' licht, *beam of light*; haud yer havers, *stop your nonsense*; hurl, *violent fall*

MARION ANGUS (1866–1946)

Alas! Poor Queen

She was skilled in music and the dance
And the old arts of love
At the court of the poisoned rose
And the perfumed glove,
And gave her beautiful hand
To the pale Dauphin
A triple crown to win –
And she loved little dogs
        And parrots
    And red-legged partridges
And the golden fishes of the Duc de Guise
And a pigeon with a blue ruff
She had from Monsieur d'Elbœuf.

Master John Knox was no friend to her;
She spoke him soft and kind,
Her honeyed words were Satan's lure
The unwary soul to bind
'Good sir, doth a lissome shape
And a comely face
Offend your God His Grace
Whose Wisdom maketh these
Golden fishes of the Duc de Guise?'

She rode through Liddesdale with a song;
'Ye streams sae wondrous strang,
Oh, mak' me a wrack as I come back
But spare me as I gang,'
While a hill-bird cried and cried
Like a spirit lost
By the grey storm-wind tost.

Consider the way she had to go.
Think of the hungry snare,
The net she herself had woven,
Aware or unaware,
Of the dancing feet grown still,
The blinded eyes –
Queens should be cold and wise,
And she loved little things,
        Parrots
    And red-legged partridges
And the golden fishes of the Duc de Guise
And the pigeon with the blue ruff
She had from Monsieur d'Elbœuf.

LEWIS SPENCE (1874–1955)

The Prows O' Reekie

O wad this braw hie-heapit toun
Sail aff like an enchanted ship,
Drift owre the warld's seas up and doun,
And kiss wi' Venice lip to lip,
Or anchor into Naples' Bay
A misty island far astray
Or set her rock to Athens' wa',
Pillar to pillar, stane to stane,
The cruikit spell o' her backbane,
Yon shadow-mile o' spire and vane,
Wad ding them a', wad ding them a'!
Cadiz wad tine the admiralty
O' yonder emerod fair sea,
Gibraltar frown for frown exchange
Wi' Nigel's crags at elbuck-range,
The rose-red banks o' Lisbon make
Mair room in Tagus for her sake.

A hoose is but a puppet-box
To keep life's images frae knocks,
But mannikins scrieve oot their sauls
Upon its craw-steps and its walls;
Whaur hae they writ them mair sublime
Than on yon gable-ends o' time?

braw, *fine*; ding them a', *surpass them all*; tine, *lose*; emerod, *emerald*; elbuck, *elbow*; scrieve, *scrape*; craw-steps, *stepped gables*

RACHEL ANNAND TAYLOR (1876–1960)

The Princess of Scotland

'Who are you that so strangely woke,
   And raised a fine hand?'
Poverty wears a scarlet cloke
               In my land.

'Duchies of dreamland, emerald, rose
   Lie at your command?'
Poverty like a princess goes
               In my land.

'Wherefore the mask of silken lace
   Tied with a golden band?'
Poverty walks with wanton grace
               In my land.

'Why do you softly, richly speak
   Rhythm so sweetly-scanned?'
Poverty hath the Gaelic and Greek
               In my land.

'There's a far-off scent about you seems
   Born in Samarkand.'
Poverty hath luxurious dreams
               In my land.

'You have wounds that like passion-flowers you hide:
   I cannot understand.'
Poverty hath one name with Pride
               In my land.

'Oh! Will you draw your last sad breath
   'Mid bitter bent and sand?'
Poverty begs from none but Death
               In my land.

ANDREW YOUNG (1885–1971)

On the Pilgrims' Road

That I had hit the Road
  I partly knew
From a great Roman snail
  And sombre yew;
But that my steps went from
  And not towards
The shrine of good St Thomas,
  I thought of afterwards.

So I adored today
  No, not his ghost,
But the saints in Westwell window,
  And her the most
Who knelt there with no head
  But was so very
Adorable a saint
  In dress of crushed strawberry.

The Shepherd's Hut

The smear of blue peat smoke
That staggered on the wind and broke,
The only sign of life,
Where was the shepherd's wife,
Who left those flapping clothes to dry,
Taking no thought for her family?
For, as they bellied out
And limbs took shape and waved about,
I thought, She little knows
That ghosts are trying on her children's clothes.

EDWIN MUIR (1887–1959)

The Horses

Barely a twelvemonth after
The seven days war that put the world to sleep,
Late in the evening the strange horses came.
By then we had made our covenant with silence,
But in the first few days it was so still
We listened to our breathing and were afraid.
On the second day
The radios failed; we turned the knobs; no answer.
On the third day a warship passed us, heading north,
Dead bodies piled on the deck. On the sixth day
A plane plunged over us into the sea. Thereafter
Nothing. The radios dumb;
And still they stand in corners of our kitchens,
And stand, perhaps, turned on, in a million rooms
All over the world. But now if they should speak,
If on a sudden they should speak again,
If on the stroke of noon a voice should speak,
We would not listen, we would not let it bring
That old bad world that swallowed its children quick
At one great gulp. We would not have it again.
Sometimes we think of the nations lying asleep,
Curled blindly in impenetrable sorrow,
And then the thought confounds us with its strangeness.

The tractors lie about our fields; at evening
They look like dank sea-monsters couched and waiting.
We leave them where they are and let them rust:
'They'll moulder away and be like other loam'.
We make our oxen drag our rusty ploughs,
Long laid aside. We have gone back
Far past our fathers' land.
                                        And then, that evening

Late in the summer the strange horses came.
We heard a distant tapping on the road,
A deepening drumming; it stopped, went on again
And at the corner changed to hollow thunder.
We saw the heads
Like a wild wave charging and were afraid.
We had sold our horses in our fathers' time
To buy new tractors. Now they were strange to us
As fabulous steeds set on an ancient shield
Or illustrations in a book of knights.
We did not dare go near them. Yet they waited,
Stubborn and shy, as if they had been sent
By an old command to find our whereabouts
And that long-lost archaic companionship.
In the first moment we had never a thought
That they were creatures to be owned and used.
Among them were some half-a-dozen colts
Dropped in some wilderness of the broken world,
Yet new as if they had come from their own Eden.
Since then they have pulled our ploughs and borne our loads
But that free servitude still can pierce our hearts.
Our life is changed; their coming our beginning.

HUGH MACDIARMID (Christopher Murray Grieve) (1892–1978)

The Bonnie Broukit Bairn

For Peggy

Mars is braw in crammasy,
Venus in a green silk goun,
The auld mune shak's her gowden feathers,
Their starry talk's a wheen o' blethers,
Nane for thee a thochtie sparin',
Earth, thou bonnie broukit bairn!
– But greet, an' in your tears ye'll droun
The haill clanjamfrie!

braw in crammasy, *fine in crimson*; wheen o' blethers, *bit of nonsense*; broukit bairn, *neglected child;* greet, *weep*; the haill clanjamfrie, *the whole of worthless humanity*

The Watergaw

Ae weet forenicht i' the yow-trummle
I saw yon antrin thing,
A watergaw wi' its chitterin' licht
Ayont the on-ding;
An' I thocht o' the last wild look ye gied
Afore ye deed!

There was nae reek i' the laverock's hoose
That nicht – an' nane i' mine;
But I hae thocht o' that foolish licht
Ever sin' syne;

An' I think that mebbe at last I ken
What your look meant then.

watergaw, *broken rainbow*; weet forenicht, *wet dusk*; yow-trummle, *ewe-tremble (a cold spell in summer after sheep-shearing)*; antrin, *rare*; ayont the on-ding, *beyond the downpour*; reek, *quarrel*; laverock, *lark*; sin' syne, *since then*

The Eemis Stane

I' the how-dumb-deid o' the cauld hairst nicht
The warl' like an eemis stane
Wags i' the lift;
An' my eerie memories fa'
Like a yowdendrift.

Like a yowdendrift so's I couldna read
The words cut oot i' the stane
Had the fug o' fame
An' history's hazelraw
No' yirdit thaim.

eemis, *unsteady*; how-dumb-deid, *at the very heart*; hairst, *harvest*; i' the lift, *in the sky*; yowdendrift, *snow blown in the air*; fug, *moss*; hazelraw, *lichen*; yirdit, *buried*

O Wha's the Bride?

(*from* A Drunk Man Looks at the Thistle)

O wha's the bride that cairries the bunch
O' thistles blinterin' white?
Her cuckold bridegroom little dreids
What he sall ken this nicht.

For closer than gudeman can come
And closer to'r than hersel',

Wha didna need her maidenheid
Has wrocht his purpose fell.

O wha's been here afore me, lass,
And hoo did he get in?
  – A man that deed or I was born
  This evil thing has din.

And left, as it were on a corpse
Your maidenheid to me?
  – Nae lass, gudeman, sin' Time began
  'S hed ony mair to gi'e.

But I can gi'e ye kindness, lad,
And a pair o' willin' hands,
And you sall ha'e my briests like stars,
My limbs like willow wands,

And on my lips ye'll heed nae mair,
And in my hair forget,
The seed o' a' the men that in
My virgin womb ha'e met . . .

blinterin, *glimmering*; dreids, *suspects*; gudeman, *husband*

WILLIAM SOUTAR (1898–1943)

The Tryst

O luely, luely cam she in
And luely she lay doun:
I kent her by her caller lips
And her breists sae sma' and roun'.

A' thru the nicht we spak nae word
Nor sinder'd bane frae bane:
A' thru the nicht I heard her hert
Gang soundin' wi' my ain.

It was about the waukrife hour
Whan cocks begin to craw
That she smool'd saftly thru the mirk
Afore the day wud daw.

Sae luely, luely, cam she in
Sae luely was she gaen
And wi' her a' my simmer days
Like they had never been.

luely, *softly*; caller, *cool*; sinder'd bane frae bane, *parted bone from bone*; waukrife, *wakeful*; smool'd saftly, *slipped away*

NORMAN CAMERON (1905–53)

Green, Green is El Aghir

Sprawled on the crates and sacks in the rear of the truck,
I was gummy-mouthed from the sun and the dust of the
track.
And the two Arab soldiers I'd taken on as hitch-hikers
At a torrid petrol-dump, had been there on their hunkers
Since early morning. I said, in a kind of French
'On m'a dit, qu'il y a une belle source d'eau fraîche.
Plus loin, à El Aghir' . . .

It was eighty more kilometres
Until round a corner we heard a splashing of waters,
And there, in a green, dark street, was a fountain with two
faces
Discharging both ways, from full-throated faucets
Into basins, thence into troughs and thence into brooks.
Our negro corporal driver slammed his brakes,
And we yelped and leapt from the truck and went at the
double
To fill our bidons and bottles and drink and dabble.
Then, swollen with water, we went to an inn for wine.
The Arabs came, too, though their faith might have stood
between.
'After all,' they said, 'it's a boisson,' without contrition.

Green, green is El Aghir. It has a railway-station,
And the wealth of its soil has borne many another fruit,
A mairie, a school and an elegant Salle de Fêtes.
Such blessings, as I remarked, in effect, to the waiter,
Are added unto them that have plenty of water.

ROBERT GARIOCH (Robert Garioch Sutherland) (1909–81)

Glisk of the Great

I saw him comin out the N.B. Grill,
creashy and winey, wi his famous voice
crackin some comic bawr to please three choice
notorious bailies, lauchan fit to kill.

Syne thae fowre crousie cronies clam intill
a muckle big municipal Rolls-Royce,
and disappeared, aye lauchan, wi a noise
that droont the traffic, towards the Calton Hill.

As they rade by, it seemed the sun was shinin
brichter nor usual roun thae cantie three
that wi thon weill-kent Heid-yin had been dinin.

Nou that's the kinna thing I like to see;
tho ye and I look on and canna jyne in,
it gies our toun some tone, ye'll aa agree.

glisk, *glimpse*; creashy, *greasy*; bawr, *joke*; bailies, *magistrates*; lauchan, *laughing*; crousie, *merry*; clam, *climbed*; muckle big, *great big*; cantie, *cheerful*; weill-kent Heid-yin, *well-known magnifico*

Heard in the Cougate

'Whu's aa thae fflagpoles ffur in Princes Street?
Chwoich! Ptt! Hechyuch! Ab-boannie cairry-on.
Seez-owre the wa'er. Whu' the deevil's thon
inaidie, heh?' 'The Queen's t'meet

The King o Norway wi his royal suite.'
'His royal wh'?' 'The hale jing-bang. It's aw in
the papur. Whaur's ma speck-sh? Aye they're gaun
t'day-cor-ate the toun. It's a fair treat,

something ye dinnae see jist ivry day,
foun'uns in the Gairdens, muckle spates
dancing t'music, an thir's t'be nae

chairge t'gi'in, it aw gaes on the Rates.'
'Ah ddae-ken whu' the pplace is comin tae
wi aw thae, hechyuch! fforeign po'entates.'

NORMAN MACCAIG (1910–96)

Summer Farm

Straws like tame lightnings lie about the grass
And hang zigzag on hedges. Green as glass
The water in the horse-trough shines.
Nine ducks go wobbling by in two straight lines.

A hen stares at nothing with one eye,
Then picks it up. Out of an empty sky
A swallow falls and, flickering through
The barn, dives up again into the dizzy blue.

I lie, not thinking, in the cool, soft grass,
Afraid of where a thought might take me – as
This grasshopper with plated face
Unfolds his legs and finds himself in space.

Self under self, a pile of selves I stand
Threaded on time, and with metaphysic hand
Lift the farm like a lid and see
Farm within farm, and in the centre, me.

Byre

The thatched roof rings like heaven where mice
Squeak small hosannahs all night long,
Scratching its golden pavements, skirting
The gutter's crystal river-song.

Wild kittens in the world below
Glare with one flaming eye through cracks,
Spurt in the straw, are tawny brooches
Splayed on the chests of drunken sacks.

The dimness becomes darkness as
Vast presences come mincing in,
Swagbellied Aphrodites, swinging
A silver slaver from each chin.

And all is milky, secret, female.
Angels are hushed and plain straws shine.
And kittens miaow in circles, stalking
With tail and hindleg one straight line.

Old Edinburgh

Down the Canongate
down the Cowgate
go vermilion dreams
snake's tongues of bannerets
trumpets with words from their mouths
saying *Praise me, praise me.*

Up the Cowgate
up the Canongate
lice on the march
tar on the amputated stump
Hell speaking with the tongue of Heaven
a woman tied to the tail of a cart.

And history leans by a dark entry
with words from his mouth
that say *Pity me, pity me*
but never forgive.

SORLEY MACLEAN (Somhairle Macgill-Eain) (1911–96)

Glac a' Bhàis

Thubhairt Nàsach air choireigin gun tug am Furair air ais do fhir na Gearmailte 'a' chòir agus an sonas bàs fhaotainn anns an àraich'

'Na shuidhe marbh an 'Glaic a' Bhàis'
fo Dhruim Ruidhìseit,
gill' òg 's a logan sìos m' a ghruaidh
's a thuar grìsionn.

Smaoinich mi air a' chòir's an àgh
a fhuair e bho Fhurair,
bhith tuiteam ann an raon an àir
gun éirigh tuilleadh;

air a' ghreadhnachas's air a' chliù
nach d' fhuair e 'na aonar,
ged b' esan bu bhrònaiche snuadh
ann an glaic air laomadh

le cuileagan mu chuirp ghlas'
air gainmhich lachduinn
's i salach-bhuidhe 's làn de raip
's de sprùidhlich catha.

An robh an gille air an dream
a mhàb na h-Iùdhaich
's na Comunnaich, no air an dream
bu mhotha, dhiùbh-san

a threòraicheadh bho thoiseach àl
gun deòin gu buaireadh
agus bruaillean cuthaich gach blàir
air sgàth uachdaran?

Ge b'e a dheòin-san no a chàs,
a neoichiontas no mhìorun,
cha do nochd e toileachadh 'na bhàs
fo Dhruim Ruidhìseit.

Death Valley

Some Nazi or other has said that the Fuehrer had restored to German manhood the 'right and joy of dying in battle'

*Sitting dead in 'Death Valley'
below the Ruweisat Ridge
a boy with his forelock down about his cheek
and his face slate-grey;*

*I thought of the right and the joy
that he got from his Fuehrer,
of falling in the field of slaughter
to rise no more;*

*of the pomp and the fame
that he had, not alone,
though he was the most piteous to see
in a valley gone to seed*

*with flies about grey corpses
on a dun sand
dirty yellow and full of the rubbish
and fragments of battle.*

*Was the boy of the band
who abused the Jews
and Communists, or of the greater
band of those*

*led, from the beginning of generations,
unwillingly to the trial
and mad delirium of every war
for the sake of rulers?*

Whatever his desire or mishap,
his innocence or malignity,
he showed no pleasure in his death
below the Ruweisat Ridge.

Hallaig

'Tha tìm, am fiadh, an coille Hallaig'

Tha bùird is tàirnean air an uinneig
troimh 'm faca mi an Aird an Iar
's tha mo ghaol aig Allt Hallaig
'na craoibh bheithe, 's bha i riamh

eadar an t-Inbhir 's Poll a' Bhainne,
thall 's a bhos mu Bhaile-Chùirn:
tha i 'na beithe, 'na calltuinn,
'na caorunn dhìreach sheang ùir.

Ann an Screapadal mo chinnidh,
far robh Tarmad 's Eachunn Mór,
tha 'n nigheanan 's am mic 'nan coille
ag gabhail suas ri taobh an lóin.

Uaibhreach a nochd na coilich ghiuthais
ag gairm air mullach Cnoc an Rà,
dìreach an druim ris a' ghealaich –
chan iadsan coille mo ghràidh.

Fuirichidh mi ris a' bheithe
gus an tig i mach an Càrn,
gus am bi am bearradh uile
o Bheinn na Lice f' a sgàil.

Mura tig 's ann theàrnas mi a Hallaig
a dh'ionnsaigh sàbaid nam marbh,
far a bheil an sluagh a' tathaich,
gach aon ghinealach a dh' fhalbh.

Tha iad fhathast ann a Hallaig,
Clann Ghill-Eain's Clann MhicLeòid,
na bh' ann ri linn Mhic Ghille-Chaluim:
Chunnacas na mairbh beò.

Na fir 'nan laighe air an lianaig
aig ceann gach taighe a bh' ann,
na h-igheanan 'nan coille bheithe,
direach an druim, crom an ceann.

Eadar an Leac is na Feàrnaibh
tha 'n rathad mór fo chóinnich chiùin,
's na h-igheanan 'nam badan sàmhach
s' dol a Chlachan mar o thùs.

Agus a' tilleadh as a' Chlachan,
á Suidhisnis 's á tir nam beò;
a chuile té òg uallach
gun bhristeadh cridhe an sgeòil.

O Allt na Feàrnaibh gus an fhaoilinn
tha soilleir an dìomhaireachd nam beann
chan eil ach coimhthional nan nighean
ag cumail na coiseachd gun cheann.

A' tilleadh a Hallaig anns an fheasgar,
anns a' chamhanaich bhalbh bheò,
a' lìonadh nan leathadan casa,
an gàireachdaich 'nam chluais 'na ceò,

's am bòidhche 'na sgleò air mo chridhe
mun tig an ciaradh air na caoil,
's nuair theàrnas grian air cùl Dhùn Cana
thig peileir dian á gunna Ghaoil;

's buailear am fiadh a tha 'na thuaineal
a' snòtach nan làraichean feòir;
thig reothadh air a shùil 'sa' choille:
chan fhaighear lorg air fhuil ri m' bheò.

Hallaig

'Time, the deer, is in the wood of Hallaig'

The window is nailed and boarded
through which I saw the West
and my love is at the Burn of Hallaig,
a birch tree, and she has always been

between Inver and Milk Hollow,
here and there about Baile-chuirn:
she is a birch, a hazel,
a straight, slender young rowan.

In Screapadal of my people
where Norman and Big Hector were,
their daughters and their sons are a wood
going up beside the stream.

Proud tonight the pine cocks
crowing on the top of Cnoc an Ra,
straight their backs in the moonlight –
they are not the wood I love.

I will wait for the birch wood
until it comes up by the cairn,
until the whole ridge from Beinn na Lice
will be under its shade.

If it does not, I will go down to Hallaig,
to the Sabbath of the dead,
where the people are frequenting,
every single generation gone.

They are still in Hallaig,
MacLeans and MacLeods,
all who were there in the time of Mac Gille Chaluim
the dead have been seen alive.

The men lying on the green
at the end of every house that was,
the girls a wood of birches,
straight their backs, bent their heads.

Between the Leac and Fearns
the road is under mild moss
and the girls in silent bands
go to Clachan as in the beginning,

and return from Clachan,
from Suisnish and the land of the living;
each one young and light-stepping,
without the heartbreak of the tale.

From the Burn of Fearns to the raised beach
that is clear in the mystery of the hills,
there is only the congregation of the girls
keeping up the endless walk,

coming back to Hallaig in the evening,
in the dumb living twilight,
filling the steep slopes,
their laughter a mist in my ears,

and their beauty a film on my heart
before the dimness comes on the kyles,
and when the sun goes down behind Dun Cana
a vehement bullet will come from the gun of Love;

and will strike the deer that goes dizzily,
sniffing at the grass-grown ruined homes;
his eye will freeze in the wood,
his blood will not be traced while I live.

SYDNEY TREMAYNE (1912–86)

A Burial

Of one who was much to me,
Nothing to anyone else,
I shall have least to say,
For silence is not false.
Once when I walked in iron
Through dead formalities,
I wished that I need not summon
The barbarous preaching voice.
So simple an act as death
Needs no pomp to excuse,
Nor any expense of breath
To magnify what is.
The sun shot the red apples,
Flies swung on summer air,
The world swam in green ripples
As a slow sea might stir.
There is no more to do
But to turn and go away,
Turn and finally go
From one who was much to me,
Nothing to anyone else.
Often it must be so
And always words be false.
Child, do you blame what is?
Child, do you blame what was?

DOUGLAS YOUNG (1913–73)

For a Wife in Jizzen

Lassie, can ye say
  whaur ye ha been,
whaur ye ha come frae,
  whatna ferlies seen?

Eftir the bluid and swyte,
  the warsslin o yestreen,
ye ligg forfochten, whyte,
  prouder nor onie Queen.

Albeid ye hardly see me
  I read it i your een,
sae saft blue and dreamy,
  mindan whaur ye've been.

Anerly wives ken
  the ruits of joy and tene,
    the march o daith and birth,
      the tryst o love and strife
i the howedumbdeidsuinsheen,
  fire, air, water, yirth
    mellan to mak new life,
lauchan and greetan, feiman and serene.

Dern frae aa men
  the ferlies ye ha seen.

jizzen, *childbed*; ferlies, *marvels*; warsslin, *struggling*; forfochten, *exhausted*; nor, *than*; albeid, *although*; mindan, *remembering*; anerly, *only*; tene, *grief*; howedumbdeidsuinsheen, *midnight sunshine*; mellan, *mixing*; lauchan, *laughing*; greetan, *weeping*; feiman, *passionate*; dern, *hide*

RUTHVEN TODD (1914–1978)

Trout Flies

for J.K.M.

Ten years of age and intent upon a tea-brown burn
Across a moor in Lanarkshire, brass reel and greenheart
Rod, my first, I tried them out and came to learn
These magic names, from which I now can never part.

The insignificant ones were best, so ran the story
Of the old man who slowly taught me how to cast:
Dark Snipe, perhaps, Cow Dung, or favourite Greenwell's
  Glory,
Would attract the sleek trout that moved so fast

To attack and suck the right and only fly.
Gaudy Partridge & Orange could be used, he said,
By those who fished on lochs, *his* fish would shy
From bright Butcher, Cardinal, or Teal & Red.

Now, on a clear day, a Wickham's Fancy might
Deceive a hungry trout, or even a Red Spinner,
But Coch-y-Bondu, or March Brown, in failing light,
Were more certain to bring home the dinner.

Watching the dull fly settle gently on the water
I would await the tug and make my strike,
While these names became a permanent mortar
Between my memories, names that I like

And tongue familiarly, Black Midge and August Dun,
Blue Upright, Cinnamon Sedge, Coachman and Pheasant
  Tail,
Red Ant, Red Hackle, Furnace Palmer, and Yellow Sally, in
  the sun,
Ghost, Green Midge, Half Stone and, sometimes, Never Fail.

G. S. FRASER (1914–80)

Home Town Elegy

For Aberdeen in Spring

Glitter of mica at the windy corners,
Tar in the nostrils, under blue lamps budding
Like bubbles of glass the blue buds of a tree,
Night-shining shopfronts, or the sleek sun flooding
The broad abundant dying sprawl of the Dee:
For these and for their like my thoughts are mourners
That yet shall stand, though I come home no more,
Gas-works, white ballroom, and the red brick baths
And salmon nets along a mile of shore,
Or beyond the municipal golf-course, the moorland paths
And the country lying quiet and full of farms.
This is the shape of a land that outlasts a strategy
And is not to be taken with rhetoric or arms.
Or my own room, with a dozen books on the bed
(Too late, still musing what I mused, I lie
And read too lovingly what I have read),
Brantôme, Spinoza, Yeats, the bawdy and wise,
Continuing their interminable debate,
With no conclusion, they conclude too late,
When their wisdom has fallen like a grey pall on my eyes.
Syne we maun part, their sall be nane remeid –
Unless my country is my pride, indeed,
Or I can make my town that homely fame
That Byron has, from boys in Carden Place,
Struggling home with books to midday dinner,
For whom he is not the romantic sinner,
The careless writer, the tormented face,

The hectoring bully or the noble fool,
But, just like Gordon or like Keith, a name:
A tall, proud statue at the Grammar School.

SYDNEY GOODSIR SMITH (1915–75)

Slugabed (*from* Under the Eildon Tree)

Here I ligg, Sydney Slugabed Godless Smith,
The Smith, the Faber, ποιητής and Makar,
And Oblomov has nocht to learn me,
Auld Oblomov has nocht on me
Liggan my lane in bed at nune
Gantan at gray December haar,
A cauld, scummie, hauf-drunk cup o' tea
        At my bed-side,
        Luntan Virginian fags
– The New World thus I haud in fief
And levie kyndlie tribute. Black men slave
Aneath a distant sun to mak for me
Cheroots at hauf-a-croun the box.
    Wi ase on the sheets, ase on the cod,
And crumbs of toast under my bum,
Scrievan the last great coronach
O' the westren flickeran bourgeois world.
    Eheu fugaces!
                                        Lacrimæ rerum!
Nil nisi et cætera ex cathedra
                                        Requiescat up your jumper.

O, michtie Stalin in the Aist!
Could ye but see me nou,
The type, endpynt and final blume
O' decadent capitalistical thirldom
    – It took five hunder year to produce me –
Och, could ye but see me nou
What a sermon could ye gie
    Further frae the Hailie Kremlin
Bummlan and thunderan owre the Steppes,

Athort the mountains o' Europe humman
Till Swack! at my front door, the great *Schloss Schmidt*
That's *Numéro Cinquante* (ПЯТЬДЕСЯТ* ye ken)
In the umquhile pairk o' Craigmillar House
Whar Marie Stewart o the snawie blee
Aince plantit ane o' a thousand treen.
  Losh, what a sermon yon wad be!
For Knox has nocht on Uncle Joe
And Oblomov has nocht on Smith
  And sae we come by a route maist devious
  Til the far-famed Aist-West Synthesis!
  Beluved by Hugh that's beluved by me
And the baith o' us loe the barley-bree –
But wha can afford to drink the stuff?
  Certies no auld Oblomov!
  – And yet he does! Whiles!
But no as muckle as Uncle Joe – I've smaa dout!
НА ЗГОРОВЬЕ* then, auld Muscovite!

Thus are the michtie faaen,
Thus the end o' a michtie line,
Dunbar til Smith the Slugabed
Whas luve burns brichter nor them aa
And whas dounfaain is nae less,
  Deid for a ducat deid
By the crueltie o' his ain maistress.

ligg, *lie*; my lane, *alone*; gantan, *gaping*; haar, *mist*; ase, *ash*; cod, *pillow*; coronach, *elegy*; thirldom, *servitude*; bummlan, *bustling*; humman, *humming*; umquhile, *former*; blee, *complexion*; loe, *love*; barley-bree, *whisky*; no as muckle, *not as much*; dounfaain, *downfall*

* piat' desiat, *fifty*; Na zdrorovye, *good health*

GEORGE CAMPBELL HAY (Deorsa Caimbeul Hay) (1915–84)

Bisearta

Chi mi rè geàrd na h-oidhche
dreòs air chrith 'na fhroidhneas thall air fàire,
a' clapail le a sgiathaibh,
a' sgapadh 's a' ciaradh rionnagan na h-àird' ud.

Shaoileadh tu gun cluinnte,
ge cian, o 'bhuillsgein ochanaich no caoineadh,
ràn corruich no gàir fuatha,
comhart chon cuthaich uaidh no ulfhairt fhaolchon,
gun ruigeadh drannd an fhòirneirt
o'n fhùirneis òmair iomall fhéin an t-saoghail;
ach sud a' dol an leud e
ri oir an speur an tosdachd olc is aognaidh.

C' ainm nochd a th' orra,
na sràidean bochda anns an sgeith gach uinneag
a lasraichean 's a deatach,
a sradagan is sgreadail a luchd thuinidh,
is taigh air thaigh 'ga reubadh
am broinn a chéile am brùchdadh toit a' tuiteam?
Is có an nochd tha 'g atach
am Bàs a theachd gu grad 'nan cainntibh uile,
no a' spàirn measg chlach is shailthean
air bhàinidh a' gairm air cobhair, is nach cluinnear?
Cò an nochd a phàidheas
sean chìs àbhaisteach na fala cumant?

Uair dearg mar lod na h-àraich,
uair bàn mar ghile thràighte an eagail éitigh,
a' dìreadh 's uair a' teàrnadh,
a' sìneadh le sitheadh àrd 's a' call a mheudachd,

a' fannachadh car aitil
's ag at mar anail dhiabhail air dhéinead,
an t-Olc 'na chridhe 's 'na chuisle,
chì mi 'na bhuillean a' sìoladh 's a' leum e.
Tha 'n dreòs 'na oillt air fàire,
'na fhàinne ròis is òir am bun nan speuran,
a' breugnachadh 's ag àicheadh
le shoillse sèimhe àrsaidh àrd nan reultan.

Bizerta

I see during the night guard
a blaze flickering, fringing the skyline over yonder,
beating with its wings
and scattering and dimming the stars of that airt.

You would think that there would be heard
from its midst, though far away, wailing and lamentation,
the roar of rage and the yell of hate,
the barking of the dogs from it or the howling of wolves,
that the snarl of violence would reach
from yon amber furnace the very edge of the world;
but yonder it spreads
along the rim of the sky in evil ghastly silence.

What is their name tonight,
the poor streets where every window spews
its flame and smoke,
its sparks and the screaming of its inmates,
while house upon house is rent
and collapses in a gust of smoke?
And who tonight are beseeching
Death to come quickly in all their tongues,
or are struggling among stones and beams,
crying in frenzy for help, and are not heard?

Who tonight is paying
the old accustomed tax of common blood?

Now red like a battlefield puddle,
now pale like the drained whiteness of foul fear,
climbing and sinking,
reaching and darting up and shrinking in size,
growing faint for a moment
and swelling like the breath of a devil in intensity,
I see Evil as a pulse
and a heart declining and leaping in throbs.
The blaze, a horror on the skyline,
a ring of rose and gold at the foot of the sky,
belies and denies
with its light the ancient high tranquillity of the stars.

W. S. GRAHAM (1918–86)

The Lying Dear

At entrance cried out but not
For me (Should I have needed it?)
Her bitching eyes under
My pressing down shoulder
Looked up to meet the face
In cracks on the flaking ceiling
Descending. The map of damp
Behind me, up, formed
Itself to catch the look
Under the closed (now)
Lids of my lying dear.

Under my pinning arm
I suddenly saw between
The acting flutters, a look
Catch on some image not me.

With a hand across her eyes
I changed my weight of all
Knowledge of her before.
And like a belly sledge
I steered us on the run
Mounting the curves to almost
The high verge. Her breath
Flew out like smoke. Her beauty
Twisted into another
Beauty and we went down
Into the little village
Of a new language.

The Stepping Stones

I have my yellow boots on to walk
Across the shires where I hide
Away from my true people and all
I can't put easily into my life.

So you will see I am stepping on
The stones between the runnels getting
Nowhere nowhere. It is almost
Embarrassing to be alive alone.

Take my hand and pull me over from
The last stone on to the moss and
The three celandines. Now my dear
Let us go home across the shires.

TOM SCOTT (1918–95)

The Mankind Toun

For Shirley Bridges

Hou lang we've socht
I dinna ken
For a toun that micht
Be fit for men.
Ten thousant year
Or mair or less
But yond or here
Wi smaa success.

We've fled mirk Thebes
Wi Ikhnaton,
Fleggit the grebes
By Babylon
And sat in quorum,
Man til man
In Karakorum
Wi Jenghis Khan.

Seen Nineveh,
Byzantium,
Sidon, Troy,
Cartaga, Rome;
Corinth, wi its
Wreathit touers,
Damascan streets
Wi Asterte's whures;
Been amang the tents
Round Samarkan
And alang the bents
By Trebizon.

Frae Nippur, Tyre,
Jerusalem,
Athens, Palmyra,
Pergamum
Til Florence, Venice,
The toun on Thames,
Imperial Vienna's
Waltzan dames,
Braw touns we've seen,
And will again,
But nane that hes been
Fit for men.

Shall we never find
The toun whaur love
Rules mankind?
Whaur the hawk, the dove,
And houlet form
A trinitie
That keeps frae hairm
Ilk chimney tree?
Whaur first is laist
And ilk and ane
Gie free their best
Til brither-men?

Whiles it seems
It canna be,
Binna in dreams;
Or till we see
The minarets,
The spires that rise
Abuin the yetts
O paradise.

But na, we'll find
Midnicht or noon,
Our vaigin's end,
The mankind toun:
Yet bidan true
Til the Sender's aims
Seek further new
Jerusalems.

fleggit, *startled*; bents, *bent-grass*; houlet, *owl*; ilk, *each*; binna, *unless*; abuin the yetts, *above the gates*; vaigin, *journey*

MURIEL SPARK (b. 1918)

Elegy in a Kensington Churchyard

Lady who lies beneath this stone,
Pupil of Time pragmatical,
Though in a lifetime's cultivation
You did not blossom, summer shall.

The fierce activity of grass
Assaults a century's constraint.
Vigour survives the vigorous,
Meek as you were, or proud as paint.

And bares its fist for insurrection
Clenched in the bud; lady who lies
Those leaves will spend in disaffection
Your fond estate and purposes.

Death's a contagion: spring's a bright
Green fit; the blight will overcome
The plague that overcame the blight
That laid this lady low and dumb,

And laid a parish on its back
So soon amazed, so long enticed
Into an earthy almanack,
And musters now the spring attack;
Which render passive, latent Christ.

HAMISH HENDERSON (b. 1919)

Seven Good Germans (Seventh Elegy)

The track running between Mekili and Tmimi was at one time a kind of no-man's-land. British patrolling was energetic, and there were numerous brushes with German and Italian elements. El Eleba lies about half-way along this track.

Of the swaddies
who came to the desert with Rommel
there were few who had heard (or would hear) of El Eleba.

They recce'd,
or acted as medical orderlies
or patched up their tanks in the camouflaged workshops
and never gave a thought to a place like El Eleba.

To get there, you drive into the blue, take a bearing
and head for damn-all. Then you're there. And where are
you?

– Still, of some few who did cross our path at El Eleba
there are seven who bide under their standing crosses.

The first a Lieutenant.
When the medicos passed him
for service overseas, he had jotted in a note-book
to the day and the hour keep me steadfast there
is only the decision and the will
the rest has no importance

The second a Corporal.
He had been in the Legion
and had got one more chance to redeem his lost honour.

What he said was
Listen here, I'm fed up with your griping –
If you want extra rations, go get 'em from Tommy!
You're green, that's your trouble. Dodge the column, pass the buck
and scrounge all you can – that's our law in the Legion.
You know Tommy's got 'em. . . . He's got mineral waters,
and beer, and fresh fruit in that white crinkly paper
and God knows what all! Well, what's holding you back?
Are you windy or what?
Christ, you 'old Afrikaners'!
If you're wanting the eats, go and get 'em from Tommy!

The third had been a farm-hand in the March of Silesia
and had come to the desert as fresh fodder for machine guns.
His dates are inscribed on the files, and on the cross-piece.

The fourth was a lance-jack.
He had trusted in Adolf
while working as a chemist in the suburb of Spandau.
His loves were his 'cello, and the woman who had borne him
two daughters and a son. He had faith in the Endsieg.
THAT THE NEW REICH MAY LIVE prayed the flyleaf of his Bible.

The fifth a mechanic.
All the honour and glory,
the siege of Tobruk and the conquest of Cairo
meant as much to that Boche as the Synod of Whitby.
Being wise to all this, he had one single headache,
which was, how to get back to his sweetheart (called Ilse).
– He had said
Can't the Tommy wake up and get weaving?
If he tried, he could put our whole Corps in the bag.
May God damn this Libya and both of its palm-trees!

The sixth was a Pole
– or to you, a Volksdeutscher –
who had put off his nation to serve in the Wehrmacht.
He siegheiled, and talked of 'the dirty Polacken,'
and said what he'd do if let loose among Russkis.
His mates thought that, though 'just a polnischer
Schweinhund',
he was not a bad bloke.
On the morning concerned
he was driving a truck with mail, petrol and rations.
The MP on duty shouted five words of warning.
He nodded
laughed
revved
and drove straight for El Eleba
not having quite got the chap's Styrian lingo.

The seventh a young swaddy.
Riding cramped in a lorry
to death along the road which winds eastward to Halfaya
he had written three verses in appeal against his sentence
which soften for an hour the anger of Lenin.

Seven poor bastards
dead in African deadland
(tawny tousled hair under the issue blanket)
wie einst Lili
dead in African deadland
einst Lili Marlene

ALEXANDER SCOTT (1920–89)

Coronach

For the dead of the 5/7th Battalion, The Gordon Highlanders

Waement the deid
I never did,
Owre gled I was ane o the lave
That somewey baid alive
To trauchle my thowless hert
Wi ithers' hurt.

But nou that I'm far
Frae the fechtin's fear,
Nou I hae won awa frae aa thon pain
Back til my beuks and my pen,
They croud aroun me out o the grave
Whaur love and langourie sae lanesome grieve.

Cryan the cauld words:
'We hae dree'd our weirds,
But you that byde ahin,
Ayont our awesome hyne,
You are the flesh we aince had been,
We that are bruckle brokken bane.'

Cryan a drumlie speak:
'You hae the words we spak,
You hae the sang
We canna sing,
Sen death maun skail
The makar's skill.

'Makar, frae nou ye maun
Be singan for us deid men,
Sing til the warld we loo'd
(For aa that its brichtness lee'd)
And tell hou the sudden nicht
Cam doun and made us nocht.'

Waement the deid
I never did,
But nou I am safe awa
I hear their wae
Greetan greetan dark and daw,
Their death the-streen my darg the-day.

coronach, *lament*; waement, *lament*; ane o the lave, *one of the remainder*; baid, *stayed*; trauchle, *trouble*; thowless, *spiritless*; fechtin, *fighting*; beuks, *books*; langourie, *longing*; dree'd our weirds, *endured our fates*; byde ahin, *remain behind*; ayont, *beyond*; hyne, *haven*; bruckle, *brittle*; brokken, *broken*; drumlie speak, *dull speech*; maun skail, *must disperse*; makar, *poet*; loo'd, *loved*; lee'd, *lied*; nocht, *nothing*; greetan, *weeping*; daw, *dawn*; the-streen, *yesterday*; darg, *work*

EDWIN MORGAN (b. 1920)

Cinquevalli

Cinquevalli is falling, falling.
The shining trapeze kicks and flirts free,
solo performer at last.
The sawdust puffs up with a thump,
settles on a tangle of broken limbs.
St Petersburg screams and leans.
His pulse flickers with the gas-jets. He lives.

Cinquevalli has a therapy.
In his hospital bed, in his hospital chair
he holds a ball, lightly, lets it roll round his hand,
or grips it tight, gauging its weight and resistance,
begins to balance it, to feel its life attached to his
by will and knowledge, invisible strings
that only he can see. He throws it
from hand to hand, always different,
always the same, always
different, always the
same.
His muscles learn to think, his arms grow very strong.

Cinquevalli in sepia
looks at me from an old postcard: bundle of enigmas.
Half faun, half military man; almond eyes, curly hair,
conventional moustache; tights, and a tunic loaded
with embroideries, tassels, chains, fringes; hand on hip
with a large signet-ring winking at the camera
but a bull neck and shoulders and a cannon-ball
at his elbow as he stands by the posing pedestal;
half reluctant, half truculent,
half handsome, half absurd,
but let me see you forget him: not to be done.

Cinquevalli is a juggler.
In a thousand theatres, in every continent,
he is the best, the greatest. After eight years perfecting
he can balance one billiard ball on another billiard ball
on top of a cue on top of a third billiard ball
in a wine-glass held in his mouth. To those
who say the balls are waxed, or flattened,
he patiently explains the trick will only work
because the spheres are absolutely true.
There is no deception in him. He is true.

Cinquevalli is juggling with a bowler,
a walking-stick, a cigar, and a coin.
Who foresees? How to please.
The last time round, the bowler
flies to his head, the stick sticks in his hand,
the cigar jumps into his mouth, the coin
lands on his foot – ah, but
is kicked into his eye
and held there as the miraculous monocle
without which the portrait would be incomplete.

Cinquevalli is practising.
He sits in his dressing-room talking to some friends,
at the same time writing a letter with one hand
and with the other juggling four balls.
His friends think of demons, but
'You could do all this,' he says,
sealing the letter with a billiard ball.

Cinquevalli is on the high wire in Odessa.
The roof cracks, he is falling, falling
into the audience, a woman breaks his fall,
he cracks her like a flea, but lives.

Cinquevalli broods in his armchair in Brixton Road.
He reads in the paper about the shells whining
at Passchendaele, imagines the mud and the dead.
He goes to the window and wonders through that dark
evening
what is happening in Poland where he was born.
His neighbours call him a German spy.
'Kestner, Paul Kestner, that's his name!'
'Keep Kestner out of the British music-hall!'
He frowns; it is cold; his fingers seem stiff and old.

Cinquevalli tosses up a plate of soup
and twirls it on his forefinger; not a drop spills.
He laughs, and well may he laugh
who can do that. The astonished table
breathe again, laugh too, think the world
a spinning thing that spills, for a moment, no drop.

Cinquevalli's coffin sways through Brixton
only a few months before the Armistice.
Like some trick they cannot get off the ground
it seems to burden the shuffling bearers, all their arms
cross-juggle that displaced person, that man
of balance, of strength, of delights and marvels,
in his unsteady box at last into the earth.

The Coin

We brushed the dirt off, held it to the light.
The obverse showed us *Scotland*, and the head
of a red deer; the antler-glint had fled
but the fine cut could still be felt. All right:
we turned it over, read easily *One Pound*,
but then the shock of Latin, like a gloss,
Respublica Scotorum, sent across
such ages as we guessed but never found

at the worn edge where once the date had been
and where as many fingers had gripped hard
as hopes their silent race had lost or gained.
The marshy scurf crept up to our machine,
sucked at our boots. Yet nothing seemed ill-starred.
And least of all the realm the coin contained.

The First Men on Mercury

– We come in peace from the third planet.
Would you take us to your leader?

– Bawr stretter! Bawr. Bawr. Stretterhawl?

– This is a little plastic model
of the solar system, with working parts.
You are here and we are there and we
are now here with you, is this clear?

– Gawl horrop. Bawr. Abawrhannahanna!

– Where we come from is blue and white
with brown, you see we call the brown
here 'land', the blue is 'sea', and the white
is 'clouds' over land and sea, we live
on the surface of the brown land
all round is sea and clouds. We are 'men'.
Men come –

– Glawp men! Gawrbenner menko. Menhawl?

– Men come in peace from the third planet
which we call 'earth'. We are earthmen.
Take us earthmen to your leader.

– Thmen? Thmen? Bawr. Bawrhossop.
Yuleeda tan hanna. Harrabost yuleeda.

– I am the yuleeda. You see my hands,
we carry no benner, we come in peace.
The spaceways are all stretterhawn.

– Glawn peacemen all horrabhanna tantko!
Tan come at'mstrossop. Glawp yuleeda!

– Atoms are peacegawl in our harraban.
Menbat worrabost from tan hannahanna.

– You men we know bawrhossoptant. Bawr.
We know yuleeda. Go strawg backspetter quick.

– We cantantabawr, tantingko backspetter now!

– Banghapper now! Yes, third planet back.
Yuleeda will go back blue, white, brown
nowhanna! There is no more talk.

– Gawl han fasthapper?

– No. You must go back to your planet.
Go back in peace, take what you have gained
but quickly.

– Stretterworra gawl, gawl . . .

– Of course, but nothing is ever the same,
now is it? You'll remember Mercury.

DERICK THOMSON (Ruaraidh MacThomais) (b. 1921)

An Tobar

Tha tobar beag am meadhon a' bhaile
's am feur ga fhalach,
am feur gorm sùghor ga dhlùth thughadh,
fhuair mi brath air bho sheann chaillich,
ach thuirt i, 'Tha 'm frith-rathad fo raineach
far am minig a choisich mi le'm chogan,
's tha'n cogan fhèin air dèabhadh.'
Nuair sheall mi 'na h-aodann preasach
chunnaic mi 'n raineach a' fàs mu thobar a sùilean
's ga fhalach bho shireadh 's bho rùintean,
's ga dhùnadh 's ga dhùnadh.

'Cha teid duine an diugh don tobar tha sin'
thuirt a' chailleach, 'mar a chaidh sinne
nuair a bha sinn òg,
ged tha 'm bùrn ann cho brèagh 's cho geal.'
'S nuair sheall mi troimhn raineach 'na sùilean
chunnaic mi lainnir a' bhùirn ud
a ni slàn gach ciùrradh
gu ruig ciùrradh cridhe.

'Is feuch an tadhail thu dhòmhsa,'
thuirt a' chailleach, 'ga b'ann le meòirean,
's thoir thugam boinne den uisge chruaidh sin
a bheir rudhadh gu m' ghruaidhean.'
Lorg mi an tobar air èiginn
's ged nach b'ise bu mhotha feum air
'sann thuice a thug mi 'n eudail.

Dh' fhaodadh nach eil anns an tobar
ach nì a chunnaic mi 'm bruadar,
oir nuair chaidh mi an diugh ga shireadh
cha d'fhuair mi ach raineach is luachair,
's tha sùilean na caillich dùinte
's tha lì air tighinn air an luathghair.

The Well

Right in the village there's a little well
and the grass hides it,
green grass in sap closely thatching it.
I heard of it from an old woman
but she said: 'The path is overgrown with bracken
where I often walked with my cogie,
and the cogie itself is warped.'
When I looked in her lined face
I saw the bracken growing round the well of her eyes,
and hiding it from seeking and from desires,
and closing it, closing it.

'Nobody goes to that well now,'
said the old woman, 'as we once went,
when we were young,
though its water is lovely and white.'
And when I looked in her eyes through the bracken
I saw the sparkle of that water
that makes whole every hurt
till the hurt of the heart.

'And will you go there for me,'
said the old woman, 'even with a thimble,
and bring me a drop of that hard water

that will bring colour to my cheeks.'
I found the well at last,
and though her need was not the greatest
it was to her I brought the treasure.

It may be that the well
is something I saw in a dream,
for today when I went to seek it
I found only bracken and rushes,
and the old woman's eyes are closed
and a film has come over their merriment.

Srath Nabhair

Anns an adhar dhubh-ghorm ud,
àirde na sìorraidheachd os ar cionn,
bha rionnag a' priobadh ruinn
'S i freagairt mireadh an teine
ann an cabair taigh m' athar
a' bhlianna thugh sinn an taigh le bleideagan sneachda.

Agus siud a' bhlianna cuideachd
a shlaod iad a' chailleach don t-sitig,
a shealltainn cho eòlach 's a bha iad air an Fhìrinn,
oir bha nid aig eunlaith an adhair
(agus cròthan aig na caoraich)
ged nach robh àit aice-se anns an cuireadh i a ceann fòidhpe.

A Shrath Nabhair 's a Shrath Chill Donnain,
is beag an t-iongnadh ged a chinneadh am fraoch àlainn
oirbh,
a' falach nan lotan a dh' fhàg Pàdraig Sellar 's a sheòrsa,
mar a chunnaic mi uair is uair boireannach cràbhaidh
a dh' fhiosraich dòrainn an t-saoghail-sa
is sìth Dhè 'na sùilean.

Strathnaver

In that blue-black sky,
as high above us as eternity,
a star was winking at us,
answering the leaping flames of fire
in the rafters of my father's house,
that year we thatched the house with snowflakes.

And that too was the year
they hauled the old woman out on to the dung-heap,
to demonstrate how knowledgeable they were in Scripture,
for the birds of the air had nests
(and the sheep had folds)
though she had no place in which to lay down her head.

O Strathnaver and Strath of Kildonan,
it is little wonder that the heather should bloom on your slopes,
hiding the wounds that Patrick Sellar, and such as he, made,
just as time and time again I have seen a pious woman
who has suffered the sorrow of this world,
with the peace of God shining from her eyes.

Old Fisherman with Guitar

A formal exercise for withered fingers.
The head is bent,
The eyes half closed, the tune
Lingers
And beats, a gentle wing the west had thrown
Against his breakwater wall with salt savage lament.

So fierce and sweet the song on the plucked string,
Know now for truth
Those hands have cut from the net
The strong
Crag-eaten corpse of Jock washed from a boat
One old winter, and gathered the mouth of Thora to his mouth.

Trout Fisher

Semphill, his hat stuck full of hooks
Sits drinking ale
Among the English fishing visitors,
Probes in detail
Their faults in casting, reeling, selection of flies.
'Never,' he urges, 'do what it says in the books'.
Then they, obscurely wise,
Abandon by the loch their dripping oars
And hang their throttled tarnish on the scale.

'Forgive me, every speckled trout',
Says Semphill then,
'And every swan and eider on these waters.
Certain strange men
Taking advantage of my poverty
Have wheedled all my subtle loch-craft out
So that their butchery
Seem fine technique in the ear of wives and daughters.
And I betray the loch for a white coin.'

Kirkyard

A silent conquering army,
The island dead,
Column on column, each with a stone banner
Raised over his head.

A green wave full of fish
Drifted far
In wavering westering ebb-drawn shoals beyond
Sinker or star.

A labyrinth of celled
And waxen pain.
Yet I come to the honeycomb often, to sip the finished
Fragrance of men.

WILLIAM NEILL (b. 1922)

Map Makers

When Irongray grew out of *Earran Reidh*
the culture could not stand on level ground.
Grey dominies of unmalleable will
invented newer legends of their own
to satisfy the blacksmith and his children.

After *Cill Osbran* closed up to Closeburn
more books were shut than Osbran's psalter.
Seeking to baptize the new born name
the pedants hurried to the nearest water
which wasn't even warm.

When *Seann Bhaile* swelled to Shambelly
the old steading became a glutton's belch.
Every tourist pointed a magic finger
padding lean Fingal to a flabby Falstaff.

The cold men in the city
who circumscribe all latitude
wiped their bullseye glasses
laid down the stabbing pens
that had dealt the mortal wounds
slaying the history of a thousand years
in the hour between lunch and catching the evening train.

dominies, *schoolmasters*

IVOR CUTLER (b. 1923)

The Railway Sleepers

The railway sleepers
heavy and dry
from old workingwomen's bones.

Trains press over like stout husbands.

Jacket vest and trousers
smelling of cloth and husband
lay black on a chair
not responding to light.

My nose on the pillow.
Breath flows along the cotton hollows.

A bare bulb
yellow in the signal box.

The heavy sleepers lie dark.
Creak under the frost.

A starving bush
perched on the verge
shrieks at dense air out the tunnel
tearing its twigs.
Ends of roots
suck cinders for organic compounds.

The signalman
is noticing his painted tea-flask
on the sill.
He picks his nose without knowing.
Snot drops about his feet.

Dawn
gleams like mercury
afraid to come up.

ALASTAIR REID (b. 1926)

Scotland

It was a day peculiar to this piece of the planet,
when larks rose on long thin strings of singing
and the air shifted with the shimmer of actual angels.
Greenness entered the body. The grasses
shivered with presences, and sunlight
stayed like a halo on hair and heather and hills.
Walking into town, I saw, in a radiant raincoat,
the woman from the fish-shop. 'What a day it is!'
cried I, like a sunstruck madman.
And what did she have to say for it?
Her brow grew bleak, her ancestors raged in their graves
as she spoke with their ancient misery:
'We'll pay for it, we'll pay for it, we'll pay for it!'

IAIN CRICHTON SMITH (1928–98)

The Law and the Grace

It's law they ask of me and not grace.
'Conform,' they say, 'your works are not enough.
Be what we say you should be,' even if
graceful hypocrisy obscures my face.

'We know no angels. If you say you do
that's blasphemy and devilry.' Yet I have
known some bright angels, of spontaneous love.
Should I deny them, be to falsehood true,

the squeeze of law which has invented torture
to bring the grace to a malignant head?
Do you want me, angels, to be wholly dead?
Do you need, black devils, steadfastly to cure

life of itself? And you to stand beside
the stone you set on me? No, I have angels. Mine
are free and perfect. They have no design
on anyone else, but only on my pride,

my insufficiency, imperfect works.
They often leave me but they sometimes come
to judge me to the core, till I am dumb.
Is this not law enough, you patriarchs?

Chinese Poem

1

To Seumas Macdonald,
now resident in Edinburgh –
I am alone here, sacked from the Department
for alcoholic practices and disrespect.
A cold wind blows from Ben Cruachan.
There is nothing here but sheep and large boulders.
Do you remember the nights with *Reliquae Celticae*
and those odd translations by Calder?
Buzzards rest on the wires. There are many seagulls.
My trousers grow used to the dung.
What news from the frontier? Is Donald still Colonel?
Are there more pupils than teachers in Scotland?
I send you this by a small boy with a pointed head.
Don't trust him. He is a Campbell.

2

The dog brought your letter today
from the red postbox on the stone gate
two miles away and a bit.
I read it carefully with tears in my eyes.
At night the moon is high over Cladach
and the big mansions of prosperous Englishmen.
I drank a half bottle thinking of Meg
and the involved affairs of Scotland.
When shall we two meet again
in thunder, lightning or in rain?
The carrots and turnips are healthy,
the *Farmers' Weekly* garrulous.
Please send me a *Radio Times* and a book
on cracking codes. I have much sorrow.
Mrs Macleod has a blue lion on her pants.
They make a queenly swish in a high wind.

3

There is a man here who has been building a house
for twenty years and a day.
He has a barrow in which he carries large stones.
He wears a canvas jacket.
I think I am going out of my mind.
When shall I see the city again,
its high towers and insurance offices,
its glare of unprincipled glass?
The hens peck at the grain.
The wind brings me pictures of exiles,
ghosts in tackety boots, lies,
adulteries in cornfields and draughty cottages.
I hear Donald is a brigadier now
and that there is fighting on the frontier.
The newspapers arrive late with strange signs on them.
I go out and watch the road.

4

Today I read five books.
I watched Macleod weaving a fence
to keep the eagles from his potatoes.
A dull horse is cobwebbed in rain.
When shall our land consider itself safe
from the assurance of the third rate mind?
We lack I think nervous intelligence.
Tell them I shall serve in any capacity,
a field officer, even a private,
so long as I can see the future
through uncracked field glasses.

5

A woman arrived today
in a brown coat and a brown muff.
She says we are losing the war,
that the Emperor's troops are everywhere
in their blue armour and bluc gloves.
She says there are men in a stupor
in the ditches among the marigolds
crying 'Alas, alas.'
I refuse to believe her.
She is, I think, an agent provocateur.
She pretends to breed thistles.

Listen

Listen, I have flown through darkness towards joy,
I have put the mossy stones away from me,
and the thorns, the thistles, the brambles.
I have swum upward like a fish

through the black wet earth, the ancient roots
which insanely fight with each other
in a grave which creates a treasure house
of light upward-springing leaves.

Such joy, such joy! Such airy drama
the clouds compose in the heavens,
such interchange of comedies,
disguises, rhymes, denouements.

I had not believed that the stony heads
would change to actors and actresses,
and that the grooved armour of statues
would rise and walk away

into a resurrection of villages,
townspeople, citizens, dead exiles,
who sing with the salt in their mouths,
winged nightingales of brine.

BURNS SINGER (1928–64)

Peterhead in May

Small lights pirouette
Among these brisk little boats.
A beam, cool as a butler,
Steps from the lighthouse.

Wheelroom windows are dark.
Reflections of light quickly
Skip over them tipsily like
A girl in silk.

One knows there is new paint
And somehow an intense
Suggestion of ornament
Comes into mind.

Imagine elephants here.
They'd settle, clumsily sure
of themselves and of us and of four
Square meals and of water.

Then you will have it. This
Though a grey and quiet place
Finds nothing much amiss.
It keeps its stillness.

There is no wind. A thin
Mist fumbles above it and,
Doing its best to be gone,
Obscures the position.

This place is quiet or,
Better, impersonal. There
Now you have it. No verdict
Is asked for, no answer.

Yet nets will lie all morning,
Limp like stage scenery,
Unused but significant
Of something to come.

GEORGE MACBETH (1932–92)

Draft for an Ancestor

When I was young, and wrote about him first,
My Uncle Hugh was easier to hold.
        Now, in my age, at worst
    I take him by some outer fold
Of what was his. His Humber, by the door.
    That, at the least, if nothing more

Creates an image of his prosperous time
And thumbs in waistcoats to suggest their power.
        I hear tall glasses chime
    And clocks from walnut sound the hour
As they drive to Derby, where their horse will lose.
    At last, it seems, men have to choose

What traits in relatives they will to raise
To the height of models, awkward, fey, or strong,
        And there arrange as praise
    For the unhooked soul, keen to belong
To its family, some tree of love and grace
    In which there blossoms no mean face.

I feel this drive. As years go by, it grows
And I want an ancestry of heroic mould
        Fit for a world that knows
    How to accept the subtly bold
Who grasp at shields and leaves with a sprig of wit
    And honours their effrontery with it.

So Uncle Hugh, that self-made, stubborn man
I see in photographs, and hear in my head,
            Provides a flash of élan
      To the ranks of my more sombre dead
And, startling, floods their quarters with his brash
      And flighty Scottish kind of dash.

CHRISTOPHER SALVESEN (b. 1935)

History of Strathclyde

How earth was made, I might have had it sung,
How life began – hushed rocking of the tide
Lapping the sleepy margins of the world.

But – searching back into almost unsearchable
Time (and yet, the waters have always stirred) –
Footprints tell a different order of fact:
Three-toed, Batrachian, printed in the rocks,
In the flaggy sandstone of Euchan Water
In the upper reaches of Nithsdale – early
Exploratory steps as the moment passed;
Petrified, along with suncracks and ripples,
Like those of any casual hen or dog
On a wet concrete path – the same sun shone.

Ah but the earth, this grassy land, has changed.
These pitted marks I long to think are raindrops
More properly interpreted as sea-spray:
No fossil bones or plants remain to help us
But – carcasses and all organic debris
Devoured by scavengers and scouring tides –
It was a coast, the glaring salty shore
Where bushy banks run now and the rowans sway.

A kingdom in the history of man,
A Dark Age kingdom and in that well named –
So little known of family and fighting,
Thus easily guessed at but so hard to grasp –
It was a border, and a middle ground,
As the power of Rome withdrew: other tides,
Less tied to the moon's control, carried on
The moves of life, washed over them as well.

Today in the bright afternoon I saw,
As I walked a drove-road towards the north,
The black-faced ewes cropping the heathery hills,
One, by the track, seeming asleep: except –
A neat dark-red pit in the bony face –
The crows had pecked its eyes out: for a moment,
As the sun went on with its mindless work,
In that wool hulk, a history of Strathclyde.

KENNETH WHITE (b. 1936)

from Late August on the Coast

A SHORT INTRODUCTION TO WHITE POETICS

Consider first the Canada Goose
brown body, whitish breast
black head, long black neck
with a white patch from throat to cheek
bill and legs black
flies in regular chevron or line formation
flight note: *aa-honk*
(that's the one old Walt heard on Long Island)

Then there's the Barnacle Goose
black and white plumage
white face and forehead
(in German, it's *Weisswangengans*)
flight in close ragged packs
flight note
a rapidly repeated *gnuk:*
gnuk gnuk gnuk gnuk gnuk gnuk gnuk
(like an ecstatic Eskimo)

Look now at the Brent Goose
small and dark
black head, neck and breast
brilliant white arse
more sea-going than other geese
feeds along the coast
by day or by night
rapid flight
seldom in formation

irregularly changing flocks
her cry:
a soft, throaty gut-bucket *rronk*

The Red-Breasted Goose
has a combination of
black, white and chestnut plumage
legs and bill blackish
quick and agile, this beauty
seldom flies in regular formation
cry:
a shrill *kee-kwa kee-kwa*
(who, what? who, what?)

The Greylag
pale grey forewings
thick orange bill
lives near the coastline
flies to grazing grounds at dawn
usually in regular formation
cry: *aahng ung-ung*
(like a Chinese poet
exiled in Mongolia)

As to the Bean Goose
she has a dark forewing
and a long black bill
talks a lot less than other geese
just a low, rich, laconic *ung-unk*

The Snow Goose
has a pure white plumage
with blacktipped wings
dark pink bill and legs
(in North America turns blue
a dusky blue-grey)
in Europe you might take her for a swan
or maybe a gannet

till she lets you know abruptly
with one harsh *kaank*
she's all goose

so
there they go
through the wind, the rain, the snow

wild spirits
knowing what they know

STEWART CONN (b. 1936)

Todd

My father's white uncle became
   Arthritic and testamental in
   Lyrical stages. He held cardinal sin
Was misuse of horses, then any game

Won on the sabbath. A Clydesdale
   To him was not bells and sugar or declension
   From paddock, but primal extension
Of rock and soil. Thundered nail

Turned to sacred bolt. And each night
   In the stable he would slaver and slave
   At cracked hooves, or else save
Bowls of porridge for just the right

Beast. I remember I lied
   To him once, about oats: then I felt
   The brand of his loving tongue, the belt
Of his own horsey breath. But he died,

When the mechanised tractor came to pass.
   Now I think of him neighing to some saint
   In a simple heaven or, beyond complaint,
Leaning across a fence and munching grass.

On Craigie Hill

The farmhouse seems centuries ago,
The steadings slouched under a sifting of snow
For weeks on end, lamps hissing, logs stacked
Like drums in the shed, the ice having to be cracked
To let the shaggy cats drink. Or
Back from the mart through steaming pastures
Men would come riding – their best
Boots gleaming, rough tweeds pressed
To a knife-edge, pockets stuffed with notes.

Before that even, I could visualise (from coloured
Prints) traps rattling, wheels spinning; furred
Figures posing like sepia dolls
In a waxen world of weddings and funerals.
When Todd died, last of the old-stagers,
Friends of seventy years followed the hearse.
Soon the farm went out of the family; the Cochranes
Going to earth or, like their cousins,
Deciding it was time to hit town.

The last link broken, the farm-buildings stand
In a clutter below the quarry. The land
Retains its richness – but in other hands.
Kilmarnock has encroached. It is hard to look
Back with any sense of belonging.
Too much has changed, is still changing.
This blustery afternoon on Craigie Hill
I regard remotely the muddy track
My father used to trudge along, to school.

ROBIN FULTON (b. 1937)

Resolutions

All day the air got harder and harder.
I woke in the small hours, rooftops

frozen seas of tranquillity, while far
below the first flakes fell on the street.

The air of another planet come down to earth,
we breathe harshly between familiar stones.

No place for flesh. Spirit and bone
at odds, the nerves caught between, singing:

'Must it be?' It must be must be must be
bouncing like a ball in a small room without windows.

D. M. BLACK (b. 1941)

Kew Gardens

In memory of Ian A. Black, died January 1971

Distinguished scientist, to whom I greatly defer
(old man, moreover, whom I dearly love),
I walk today in Kew Gardens, in sunlight the colour of honey
which flows from the cold autumnal blue of the heavens to
light these tans and golds,
these ripe corn and leather and sunset colours of the East
Asian liriodendrons,
of the beeches and maples and plum-trees and the stubborn
green banks of the holly hedges –
and you walk always beside me, you with your knowledge of
names
and your clairvoyant gaze, in what for me is sheer panorama
seeing the net or web of connectedness. But today it is I who
speak
(and you are long dead, but it is to you I say it):

'The leaves are green in summer because of chlorophyll
and the flowers are bright to lure the pollinators,
and without remainder (so you have often told me)
these marvellous things that shock the heart the head can
account for;
but I want to sing an excess which is not so simply
explainable,
to say that the beauty of the autumn is a redundant beauty,
that the sky had no need to be this particular shade of blue,
nor the maple to die in flames of this particular yellow,
nor the heart to respond with an ecstasy that does not beget
children.
I want to say that I do not believe your science

although I believe every word of it, and intend to understand
it
that although I rate that unwavering gaze higher than almost
everything
there is another sense, a hearing, to which I more deeply
attend.
Thus I withstand and contradict you, I, your child,
who have inherited from you the passion which causes me to
oppose you.'

AONGHAS MACNEACAIL (b. 1942)

from an cathadh mor

3

mìorbhail an t-sneachda
gach criostal àraid
gach criostal gun chàraid
meanbh-chlachaireachd
gach lóineag a' tàthadh
saoghal fo chidhis

sneachda fiorghlan
  (ìocshlaint nan galair
  fras chalman air iteal
  mealltach mesmearach)
sneachda gun lochd
  (cléireach ag ùrnaigh
  an cille stàilinn
  ghlas a chreideimh
  cléireach a' guidhe
  fhradharc 'na bhoisean
  ag àicheadh a bhruadar)

sneachda lainnireach
  (leanabh a' ruidhleadh aig uinneig
  sùilean a' dealradh)
sneachda grioglannach
  (speuran brùite dùinte)
sneachda brìodalach
  snàigeach sniagach
sneachda lìonmhorachadh
  sàmhach sàmhach

sneachda càrnach
sneachda fillteach
sneachda casgrach

6

sìneadh a h-éididh air
cathair   caisteal   clachan

sgaoileadh a còt' air
gach buaile   gach bealach
gach sgurr is gach rubha
h-uile sràid anns gach baile
geal   geal   geal

plangaid air saoghal
brat-sìth do threubhan domhain

an gilead gealltanach   gluasadach

8

chan fhaic an t-iasgair ach cobhar
sgorran is sgeirean fo chobhar
sgaothan a' gluasad
                                        thar a' chala
                                        thar an raoin
                                        thar an t-sléibh
cha dhearc a shùil air cuan air cala
chan fhaic e ach cobhar nan sgaoth
a' traoghadh air raointean

an eathar 'na taibhse air teadhair
a lìn nan greasain gheal bhreòiteach
oillsginn gun anam a' crochadh is
        bòtainnean laighe mar chuirp

sluaghan a' chuain do-ruigsinn

from *the great snowbattle*

3

marvel of snow
every crystal unique
every crystal without peer
micro-masonry
every flake cementing
a world beneath its mask

virginal snow
(balm for plagues
flurry of flying doves
deceptive, deadening)
faultless snow
(a cleric prays
in the steel cell
of his credo
cleric beseeches,
his sight in his palms
denying his dreams)

brilliant snow
(child dancing at window
eyes reflect glitter)
constellated snow
(the skies are bruised   enclosed)
cajoling snow
snaking sneaking
multiplying snow
silent silent
mounding snow
pleating snow
slaughtering snow

6

stretching her raiment on
city   castle   clachan

spreading her coat on
each meadow   each pass
each peak and each reef
all the streets in each town
white   white   white

a blanket on the world
a flag of truce for
all the tribes in a universe

the whiteness promising   shifting

8

the fisher sees nothing but foam
summits and skerries are under the spray
shoals are moving
                    over harbours
                    across fields
                    across the moors
his eye cannot see ocean, anchorage
he sees only foaming shoals
subsiding on meadows

the boat is a tethered ghost
his nets white friable webs
his oilskins hang soulless while
      boots are outstretched corpses

ocean's multitudes are out of reach

ALAN BOLD (1943–98)

A Special Theory of Relativity

According to Einstein
There's no still centre of the universe:
Everything is moving
Relative to something else.
My love, I move myself towards you,
Measure my motion
In relation to yours.

According to Einstein
The mass of a moving body
Exceeds its mass
When standing still.
My love, in moving
Through you
I feel my mass increase.

According to Einstein
The length of a moving body
Diminishes
As speed increases.
My love, after accelerating
Inside you
I spectacularly shrink.

According to Einstein
Time slows down
As we approach
The speed of light.
My love, as we approach
The speed of light
Time is standing still.

ALISON FELL (b. 1944)

Pushing Forty

Just before winter
we see the trees show
their true colours:
the mad yellow of chestnuts
two maples like blood sisters
the orange beech
braver than lipstick

Pushing forty, we vow
that when the time comes
rather than wither
ladylike and white
we will henna our hair
like Colette, we too
will be gold and red
and go out
in a last wild blaze

IAN ABBOT (1944–89)

A Body of Work

Do you not see, finally,
how the earth is moving to inhabit me?

My teeth
are the white stones of the river-bed;
throughout the day
an otter dozes in the dank holt of my mouth.
The sinews of my legs
go down into the earth like roots, and knots of shifting clay
compose the muscles of my face.
My hair, my sex becoming
clumps of hoary winter grass.

Seasons are manifest in me:
I know their white, their green, their turning yellow.
Laughing, my voice is the fever of stags; the pure
transparency of leaves is in my speech. Constellations
sift their burning atoms through my veins.

But in singing, weeping,
waking in the night and crying out,
my language is a deer dismembered under pines,
bloody and netted with shadows.
An intricate labyrinth of entrails,
lit from within
and patiently transfigured to the lightning grin of bones.

TOM LEONARD (b. 1944)

from Unrelated Incidents

1

its thi lang-
wij a thi
guhtr thaht hi
said its thi
langwij a
thi guhtr

awright fur
funny stuff
ur
Stanley Bax-
ter ur but
luv n science
n thaht naw

thi langwij
a thi
intillect hi
said thi lang-
wij a thi intill-
ects Inglish

then whin thi
doors slid
oapn hi raised
his hat geen
mi a fare-
well nod flung
oot his right

fit boldly n
fell eight
storeys
doon thi
empty
lift-shaft

from Ghostie Men

right inuff
ma language is disgraceful

ma maw tellt mi
ma teacher tellt mi
thi doactir tellt mi
thi priest tellt mi

ma boss tellt mi
ma landlady in carrington street tellt mi
thi lassie ah tried tay get aff way in 1969 tellt mi
sum wee smout thit thoat ah hudny read chomsky tellt mi
a calvinistic communist thit thoat ah wuz revisionist tellt mi

po-faced literati grimly kerryin thi burden a thi past tellt mi
po-faced literati grimly kerryin thi burden a thi future tellt
mi
ma wife tellt mi jist-tay-get-inty-this-poem tellt mi
ma wainz came hame fray school an tellt mi
jist aboot ivry book ah oapnd tellt mi
even thi introduction tay thi Scottish National Dictionary
tellt mi

ach well
all livin language is sacred
fuck thi lohta thim

LIZ LOCHHEAD (b. 1947)

The Grim Sisters

And for special things
(weddings, school-
concerts) the grown up girls next door
would do my hair.

Luxembourg announced *Amami Night.*

I sat at peace passing bobbipins
from a marshmallow pink cosmetic purse
embossed with jazzmen,
girls with pony tails and a November
topaz lucky birthstone.
They doused my cow's-lick, rollered
and skewered tightly.
I expected that to be lovely
would be worth the hurt.

They read my Stars,
tied chiffon scarves to doorhandles, tried
to teach me tight dancesteps
you'd no guarantee
any partner you might find would ever be able to
keep up with as far as I could see.

There were always things to burn
before the men came in.

For each disaster
you were meant to know the handy hint.
Soap at a pinch
but better nailvarnish (clear) for ladders.
For kisscurls, spit.

Those days womanhood was quite a sticky thing
and that was what these grim sisters came to mean.

'You'll know all about it soon enough.'
But when the clock struck they
stood still, stopped dead.
And they were left there
out in the cold with the wrong skirtlength
and bouffant hair,
dressed to kill,

who'd been
all the rage in fifty-eight,
a swish of Persianelle
a slosh of perfume.
In those big black mantrap handbags
they snapped shut at any hint of *that*
were hedgehog hairbrushes
cottonwool mice and barbed combs to tease.
Their heels spiked bubblegum, dead leaves.

Wasp waist and cone breast, I see them yet.
I hope, I hope
there's been a change of more than silhouette.

My Mother's Suitors

have come to court me
have come to call oh
yes with their wonderful world
war two moustaches their long
stem roses their cultivated
accents (they're English aren't they
at very least they're
educated-Scots).
They are absolutely
au fait with menu-French

they know the language of flowers
& oh they'd die
rather than send a dozen yellow
they always get them right & red.
Their handwriting on the florist's card
slants neither too much to the left or right.

They are good sorts.
They have the profile for it – note
the not too much nose
the plenty chin. The
stockings they bring have no strings
& their square
capable hands are forever
lifting your hair and gently
pushing your head away from them
to fumble endearingly at your nape
with the clasp of the pretty heirloom
little necklace they know their
grandmother would have wanted
you to have.
(Never opals – they know
that pearls mean tears).

They have come to call & we'll all
go walking under the black sky's
droning big bombers
among the ratatat of ack-ack.
We'll go dancing & tonight
shall I wear the lilac, or the
scarlet, or the white?

VALERIE GILLIES (b. 1948)

The Ericstane Brooch

The gold cross-bow brooch,
The Emperors' gift to an officer,
Was lost on the upland moor.
The pierced work and the inscription
Lay far from human habitation.

It worked on time and space
And they were at work on it.
What could withstand them?
But it was waiting for the human,
To address itself to a man or woman.

In the wilderness it meant nothing.
The great spaces dissolved its image,
Time obliterated its meaning.
Without being brought in,
It was less than the simplest safety-pin.

Now the brooch is transporting the past
To the present, the far to the near.
Between the two, its maker and wearer
And watcher live mysteriously.
Who is this who values it so seriously?

It exists, it has been seen by him.
If it speaks, it can only say
'He lost me.' And we reply, 'Who?
For he can also be our loss,
This moment floating face-down in the moss.'

Dumb replica: the original is in Los Angeles.
How is it, the man once destroyed,
His brooch continues boundlessly?
Our very existence is what it defies:
We no longer see what once we scrutinized.

RON BUTLIN (b. 1949)

This Evening

You placed yellow roses by the window, then,
leaning forwards, began combing your red hair;
perhaps you were crying.
To make the distance less I turned away
and faced you across the earth's circumference.

The window-pane turns black:
across its flawed glass suddenly your image
runs on mine.
I stare at the vase until yellow
is no longer a colour, nor the roses flowers.

TOM POW (b. 1950)

from The Gift of Sight

SAINT MEDAN

That Medan was beautiful,
        there was no doubt.
Wherever she went,
        hearts were routed.

But, to her, these looks
        were but a costume
she couldn't cast off.
        She saw her fortune

not in the fancy
        of romantic play –
it was in inner things
        her interests lay.

Medan took a vow
        of chastity; her life
she bound to Christ.
        It was a sharp knife

in the hearts of men.
        But one noble knight
did not believe her.
        To quit his sight

she left Ireland
        for green Galloway.
To the Rhinns she came,
        to live in poverty.

The knight followed.
He would die or wed
his heart's crusade.
Pure Medan now fled

to a rock in the sea.
With prayer, the rock
became a boat;
the boat she took

thirty miles away.
Still, he followed;
blindly obeying
what the hollow

in his heart called for.
He'd have been lost,
but a crowing cock –
to both their costs –

told him the house
where Medan lay.
Shaken, she climbed
and she prayed

as she climbed
into a thorn tree.
From there, she asked,
'What do you see

in me to excite
your passion?' 'Your face
and eyes,' he replied.
She sighed, 'In which case . . .'

then impaled her eyes
on two sharp thorns
and flung them at him.
Desire was torn

forever from that knight.
    He looked at his feet,
where the eyes had rolled –
    lustrous jade, now meat

for ants. Horror-struck,
    he left – a penitent.
Medan washed her face,
    for a spring – heaven-sent –

gurgled from the dry earth.
    The rest of her days
were lived in poverty
    and sanctity. (*Praise*

the Lord, sang Ninian.)
    The proud cock half-lived,
but crowed no more.
    And sight became the gift

Saint Medan gave,
    so that all could suffer
in equal measure,
    beauty and terror.

BRIAN MCCABE (b. 1951)

Slug

Don't you fancy me in my black
figure-hugging bodystocking
skin?

Watch me arch my agile back,
show my underside's pale line –
like an inky, questing tongue.

Do I disgust you?
I am not the only libido
to ooze from this dark earth.

Haven't we met somewhere
before? What are you doing here
on this rainy afternoon, alone?

My tapering finger is beckoning
you to your likeness.
Come on.

GERALD MANGAN (b. 1951)

Heraclitus at Glasgow Cross

Where Gallowgate meets London Road
   and the world walks out with his wife,
umbrellas sail in long flotillas
   through streets you can't cross twice.

The old home town looks just the same
   when you step down off the Sixty-Three.
The jukebox music takes you back
   to the green, green grass of Polmadie.

Everything swarms and eddies in smirr.
   Wine flows out from the Saracen's Head.
Mascara runs, like soot from a guttering.
   Day-glo signs glow green on red.

Something for Everyone. Nothing for Nothing.
   Social Security Estimates Free.
It's Scotland's Friendliest Market-Place.
   Watch Your Handbags, Ladies, Please.

Watch the Do-nuts fry in grease,
   the tailgate-auctioneers compete
with the broken-winded squeezebox player,
   wheezing through his leaking pleats.

Or under Clyde Street's railway arches,
   see the stubbled dossers soak
like debris snagged in shallows, blowing
   old Virginia up in smoke.

Down where the fishwives trade in rags,
   they curl like snails in paper shells:
lips of sponge, skins of mould,
   eyes like cinders doused in hell.

They're watching concrete fill the docks,
the bollards rust on the graving-quays.
The green green grass grows overhead,
on gantries still as gallows-trees.

Where Gorbals faces Broomielaw,
the river's black and still as ice.
When the ferryman takes the fare, he says
You can cross this river twice.

smirr, *drizzle*

ANDREW GREIG (b. 1951)

In the Tool-shed

'Hummingbirds' he said, and spat. Winged tongues
hovered in the half-light of their names;
cat, cobra, cockatoo rose hissing from the juice.
Piece-time in Africa, amid the terrapins
and jerrycans! Steam swirled above the Congo
of his cup, mangrove-rooted fingers plugged the air –
'Baboons? Make sure you look them in the eyes.' Birds
of paradise! Parrots, paraffin, parakeets
flashed blue and raucous through
thickets of swoe, scythe, riddle, adze.
He sat bow-backed and slack in the dark
heart of his kingdom – creator, guide
in that jungle of sounds, boxes, cloches, canes,
twine, twill, galoshes, jumbled all
across, over, through and into one another
from floor to roof, prowled by fabled carnivores,
the jaguar! the secateurs! Words poke
wet muzzles through reeds of sound
grown enormous overnight. Twin depths
of pitch and pitcher! Elephants lean
patiently upon their ponderous names.
They come in clutches: azaleas, zebras, zambesi.
Orchids, oranges, oran-utangs hang
from their common mouth. Lemming, gorilla, lynx
slink nose to tail through mango groves,
drenched in this sibilant monsoon: moonstone, machetes,
peacocks, paw-paws, lepers, leopards – the walls
are creaking but hold them all, swaying, sweating,
in that dark continent between the ears.
Easy, easy genesis! Old witchdoctor, gardener,
deity of the shed, I grew that garden

from his words, caught the fever
pitch of his Niagara; I follow still
the Orinoco of his blue forearm veins
that beat among the talking drums
of all my childhood afternoons.

FRANK KUPPNER (b. 1951)

from Passing Through Doorways (Part I)

i

I can no longer remain in this building,
Not after this latest turn of events;
After I have shut the door, my watch says 9.26;
I walk down those few stairs again, determined, above all, to
pass time.

ii

Having spent all my life not merely in one city,
But in a tightly circumscribed part of one city,
I find that most of the significant doors in my life
Opened and shut within a few minutes of each other.

iii

A leisurely evening walk could unite the four of them;
Have I really never gone on such a walk before?
It is autumn, and again the sky is completely dark;
It is the wrong time of the evening to have crowds on the
streets.

ANGUS MARTIN (b. 1952)

Forest

For Sid Gallagher

Since I lately came to live
in an old house with a fire in it,
wood has got into my vision.

I put my saw to wood
and glance a nick, and then I cut
wood into bits that please me.

Weight and form may please me,
and I am pleased to own
what at last I have to burn.

I am a Scottish wood-collector;
I belong to a great tradition
of bleeding hands and thick coats.

Wood accumulates about me;
I build it into piles,
I bag it and I lug it.

I love the look of wood:
its surfaces are maps and pictures,
and staring eyes and voiceless mouths.

Wood to the end is unresisting:
it lets me lift and drag it
far from that place that it lay down.

Wood will never fight
the blade's truncating stroke
or scream when fire consumes it.

But I had dreams of wood.
I was alone in a high forest,
sun and seasons banished.

The trees bent down their silent heads
and closed their branches round about
and I was gathered into air.

I burn in my dreams of wood,
a melting torch suspended
in the dark heart of a silent forest.

JOHN GLENDAY (b. 1952)

The Apple Ghost

A musty smell of dampness filled the room
Where wrinkled green and yellow apples lay
On folded pages from an August newspaper.

She said:
'*My husband brought them in, you understand,*
Only a week or two before he died.
He never had much truck with waste, and
I can't bring myself to throw them out.
He passed away so soon . . .'

I understood then how the wonky kitchen door,
And the old Austin, settling upon its
Softened tyres in the wooden shed,
Were paying homage to the absence of his quiet hands.

In the late afternoon, I opened
Shallow cupboards where the sunlight leaned on
Shelf over shelf of apples, weightless with decay.
Beneath them, sheets of faded wallpaper
Showed ponies prancing through a summer field.
This must have been the only daughter's room
Before she left for good.

I did not sleep well.

The old woman told me over breakfast
How the boards were sprung in that upper hall;
But I knew I had heard his footsteps in the night,
As he dragged his wasted body to the attic room
Where the angles of the roof slide through the walls,
And the fruit lay blighted by his helpless gaze.

I knew besides that, had I crossed to the window
On the rug of moonlight,
I would have seen him down in the frosted garden,
Trying to hang the fruit back on the tree.

DILYS ROSE (b. 1954)

Fetish

Whisper if you must
But the walls absorb all confession
    – I've run through this ritual so often
    If he insists, I make a confession
    Kid on his demand has me truly enthralled
    If that's not sufficient try *deeply appalled*.

Your wish, for the moment, is my command
I'm mistress of every disguise
Is it rubber fur leather or silk I've to use
To pull the wool over your eyes?
Watch me concoct your burning obsession
Spell out your lust, own up to your passion.

So that's all it was that you wanted
A secret so paltry – I'd never have guessed
It could send a man scouring the town.
A scrap of mock silk – I'm no longer impressed.
You looked like the type who'd know I don't tout
My quality goods. See yourself out.

ROBIN ROBERTSON (b. 1955)

Fugue for Phantoms

This is the heart's thorn: the red rinse of memory;
this is the call of the coronach – keening, keening
over the water, haunted water,
the pitched grey, gull-swept sea.

This is the net and trident, thrown and retrieved,
thrown again; this is the death we live through –
our own thoughts are the mesh that's cast,
that let in the past with a stabbing spear.

These are the strange stigmata, the memories that bleed;
these are the luminous ghosts: lures
on the barb that pulls the heart from darkness
and silence, to the surface of the sea.

Where they have risen, the sea-dead, bobbing in effigy:
skin gone to curd, and worn now like a fragile dress,
water behind the eyes like the insides of oyster shells;
their huge heads puckered, their faces pursed like lips.

I would commit it all to the deep;
I want never to remember anything of this.

JOHN BURNSIDE (b. 1955)

The Blind

On Tuesdays they walked from the school
to the public baths,

passing our window, leaving us unseen
in every weather: flecked with snow or rain,

they marched in pairs, a good eight hundred yards
of guesswork.

All afternoon I pictured them
swimming in silence,

attuned to one another through the play
of water and skin,

imagining some kinship with the drowned
they might possess, unknowing: how they would guess

at motion and other lives
through the palm-smooth tiles;

and later, through trig,
I heard them walking back

and waited for the first blithe face to show
beyond the fence, the tap of whited canes

tracing a current home, through bricks and tar:
magnetic; guided; rooting in the darkness.

Out of Exile

When we are driving through the border towns
we talk of houses, empty after years
of tea and conversation;
of afternoons marooned against a clock
and silences elected out of fear,
of lives endured for what we disbelieved.

We recognise the shop fronts and the names,
the rushing trees and streets into the dark;
we recognise a pattern in the sky:
blackness flapping like a broken tent,
shadow foxes running in the stars,
But what we recognise is what we bring.

Driving, early, through the border towns,
the dark stone houses clanging at our wheels,
and we invent things as they might have been:
a light switched on, some night, against the cold,
and children at the door, with bags and coats,
telling stories, laughing, coming home.

CAROL ANN DUFFY (b. 1955)

Plainsong

Stop. Along this path, in phrases of light,
trees sing their leaves. No Midas touch
has turned the wood to gold, late in the year
when you pass by, suddenly sad, straining
to remember something you're sure you knew.

Listening. The words you have for things die
in your heart, but grasses are plainsong,
patiently chanting the circles you cannot repeat
or understand. This is your homeland,
Lost One, Stranger who speaks with tears.

It is almost impossible to be here and yet
you kneel, no one's child, absolved by late sun
through the branches of a wood, distantly
the evening bell reminding you, *Home, Home,*
Home, and the stone in your palm telling the time.

Pilate's Wife

Firstly, his hands – a woman's. Softer than mine,
with pearly nails, like shells from Galilee.
Indolent hands. Camp hands that clapped for grapes.
Their pale, mothy touch made me flinch. Pontius.

I longed for Rome, home, someone else. When the Nazarene
entered Jerusalem, my maid and I crept out,
bored stiff, disguised, and joined the frenzied crowd.
I tripped, clutched the bridle of an ass, looked up

and there he was. His face? Ugly. Talented.
He looked at me. I mean he looked at *me*. My God.
His eyes were eyes to die for. Then he was gone,
his rough men shouldering a pathway to the gates.

The night before his trial, I dreamt of him.
His brown hands touched me. Then it hurt.
Then blood. I saw that each tough palm was skewered
by a nail. I woke up, sweating, sexual, terrified.

Leave him alone. I sent a warning note, then quickly dressed.
When I arrived, the Nazarene was crowned with thorns.
The crowd was baying for Barabbas. Pilate saw me,
looked away, then carefully turned up his sleeves

and slowly washed his useless, perfumed hands.
They seized the prophet then and dragged him out,
up to the Place of Skulls. My maid knows all the rest.
Was he God? Of course not. Pilate believed he was.

MICK IMLAH (b. 1956)

Goldilocks

This is a story about the possession of beds.
It begins at the foot of a staircase in Oxford, one midnight,
When (since my flat in the suburbs of London entailed
A fiancée whose claims I did not have the nerve to evict)

I found myself grateful for climbing alone on a spiral
To sleep I could call with assurance exclusively mine,
For there was the name on the oak that the Lodge had
   assigned
Till the morning to me (how everything tends to its place!)

And flushed with the pleasing (if not unexpected) success
Of the paper on 'Systems of Adult-to-Infant Regression'
With which the Young Fireball had earlier baffled his betters
At the Annual Excuse for Genetics to let down its ringlets,

I'd just sniggered slightly (pushing the unlocked door
Of the room where I thought there was nothing of mine to
   protect)
To observe that my theory, so impudent in its address
To the Masters of Foetal Design and their perfect disciples,

Was rubbish – and leant to unfasten the window a notch,
When I suddenly grasped with aversion before I could see it
The fact that the bed in the corner directly behind me
Had somebody in it. A little ginger chap,

Of the sort anthropologists group in the genus of *tramp*,
Was swaddled, as though with an eye to the state of the
   sheets,
With half of his horrible self in the pouch of the bedspread
And half (both his raggled and poisonous trouser-legs) out;

Whose snore, like the rattle of bronchial stones in a bucket,
Resounded the length and the depth and the breadth of the
problem
Of how to establish in safety a climate conducive
To kicking him out – till at last I could suffer no longer

The sight of his bundle of curls on my pillow, the proof
That even the worst of us look in our sleep like the angels
Except for a few. I closed to within a yard
And woke him, with a curt hurrahing sound.

And he reared in horror, like somebody late for work
Or a debutante subtly apprised of a welcome outstayed,
To demand (not of me, but more of the dreary familiar
Who exercised in its different styles the world's

Habit of persecution, and prodded him now)
Phit time is it? – so you'd think that it made any difference –
So you'd think after all that the berth had a rota attached
And Ginger was wise to some cynical act of encroachment;

But when, with a plausible echo of fatherly firmness,
I answered, 'It's bedtime' – he popped out and stood in a
shiver,
And the released smell of his timid existence swirled
Like bracing coffee between our dissimilar stances.

Was there a dim recollection of tenement stairways
And jam and the Rangers possessed him, and sounded a
moment
In creaks of remorse? 'Ah'm sorry, son – Ah couldnae tell
They'd hae a wee boy sleepin here – ye know?'

(And I saw what a file of degradations queued
In his brown past, to explain how Jocky there
Could make me out to be innocent and wee:
As if to be wee was not to be dying of drink;

As if to be innocent meant that you still belonged
Where beds were made for one in particular.)
Still, the lifespan of sociable feelings is shortest of all
In the breast of the migrant Clydesider; and soon he relapsed

Into patterns of favourite self-pitying sentiments. 'Son –
Ah'm warse than – Ah cannae, ye know? Ah'm off tae ma
  dandy!
Ah've done a wee josie – aye, wheesh! – it's warse what Ah'm
  gettin –
Aye – warse!' And again the appeal to heredity – 'Son.'

(In the course of his speech, the impostor had gradually
  settled
Back on the bed, and extended as visual aids
His knocked-about knuckles; tattoed with indelible foresight
On one set of these was the purple imperative SAVE.)

Now I'm keen for us all to be just as much worse as we want,
In our own time and space – but not, after midnight, in my
  bed;
And to keep his inertia at bay, I went for the parasite,
Scuttling him off with a shout and the push of a boot

That reminded his ribs I suppose of a Maryhill barman's,
Until I had driven him out of the door and his cough
Could be heard to deteriorate under a clock in the landing.
(Och, if he'd known *I* was Scottish! Then I'd have got it.)

*

But of course he came back in the night, when I
                                        dreamed I was coughing
And he stood by the door in the composite guise of a
  woman –
A mother, a doting landlady, a shadowy wife –
Sleepless as always, relieved nonetheless to have found me,

Or half-relieved – given what I had become;
Saying – 'It's just from the coughing and so on I wondered
If maybe a tramp had got into your bedroom' – and then,
Disappointedly: 'Couldn't you spare a wee thought for your
dad?'

(I thought I was dreaming again on the train in the morning
To hear at my shoulder, before I had properly settled,
'Excuse me – is this seat taken?' spastically spoken;
But it wasn't our friend that I humoured through Didcot,
and Reading,

No, but an anoracked spotter of diesels from Sheffield
Whose mind was apparently out in the sidings at Crewe:
Only one more in a world of unwanted connexions,
Who waved like a child when I fled for the toilet at Ealing.)

*

This is my gloss on the story of Goldilocks. Note:
It uncovers a naked and difficult thought about beds,
Namely, that seldom again will there ever be one
With only you in it; take that however you will.

ELIZABETH BURNS (b. 1957)

The Oddity

She is a crooked planet: does not fit
in the thin universe of this house
that peoples itself with gentlefolk
who blink as though they do not see her
when she asks to use the library.

There is a clanking housekeeper
whose spiked mouth, licked, would give off poison,
and a cluster of maidservants
who, in the mothballed linen cupboard,
will gossip on the newcomer.

It's whispered that she's delicate
is delivered of bowls of sopped bread
bland milk puddings
but Cook sees her, the little witch,
sneaking herbs from the kitchen garden.

This household's under the thumb
of the chimes of the grandfather clock
Nothing here is tainted by imagination's kiss
and nothing queer-eyed or peculiarly skinned
gets out to roam the corridors

so that she, with her silences and pencils
her barefoot tiptoeing over the flagstones
in her old grey muslin dress
that billows out in draughty stairwells
feels freak: hears laughter

frothing in the steamy kitchen
whispers bubbling under doors,
is trailed by soft footsteps, rustling silks,
but reaches the room: a fastness:
turns the brass key in the lock behind her.

Soon there will be apron-smothered giggles
outside her door: she will rise
stuff the keyhole with a handkerchief
to block the peering eyes
then draw the shades against the lilac sky

and in thin dusk-light, take ink,
begin, in copperplate,
though hot tears plop, and blot the page,
and voices batter at her head
like scatty moths, to write.

ROBERT CRAWFORD (b. 1959)

Scotland in the 1890s

'I came across these facts which, mixed with others ...'
Thinking of Helensburgh, J. G. Frazer
Revises flayings and human sacrifice;
Abo of the Celtic Twilight, St Andrew Lang
Posts him a ten-page note on totemism
And a coloured fairy book – an Oxford man
From Selkirk, he translates Homer in his sleep.

'When you've lived here, even for a short time,
Samoa's a bit like Scotland – there's the sea ...
Back in Auld Reekie with a pen that sputtered
I wrote my ballad, "Ticonderoga" or
"A Legend of the West Highlands", then returned
To King Kalakaua's beach and torches –
You know my grandfather lit Lismore's south end?'

Mr Carnegie has bought Skibo Castle.
His Union Jack's sewn to the stars and stripes.
James Murray combs the dialect from his beard
And files slips for his massive *Dictionary*.
Closing a fine biography of mother,
Remembering Dumfries, and liking boys,
James Barrie, caught in pregnant London silence,
Begins to conceive the Never Never Land.

Knowledge

Ferrier invents the word *epistemology*
Sitting in a doorway wiped across with light

From an early flashgun. Round him, young buck students
Scatter in the aftershock, vanish.

*

Euclidean rain stots on cobbles
In wintry St Andrews. Ferrier hunches with cold,

Drawing his black gown over his head
Like a photographer, abolishing himself.

*

A sore has developed, a gland gone syphilitic.
He reads up the chemistry of mercuric oxide,

Hears his Aunt Susan, the famour author
Of *Marriage*, has died in her sleep.

*

Frail, he blocks a lecture-room entrance.
A New Woman confronts him: 'I wish to know

By what right you keep me from these Chemistry lectures.'
He can't move, at one with the stone.

IAIN BAMFORTH (b. 1959)

Men on Fire

Being a land of dissent and magnificent defeats
it evolved a subtle theology of failure, stealing its own
  thunder
wherever two or three were gathered together
and the occult plumbing groaned querulously beneath the
  boards.

These days, it grows owlish with hindsight –
recounting itself as a salvo of rain far north on mappamundi,
who's who of a supernumerary Creation myth
that swallowed the serpent's tail, ate the offspring whole.

When Rousseau exhumed the weather over Waverley
its civil imaginary became a fast diminishing return.
Few Encyclopaedists recall the genealogy backpacked out of
  Troy
or the vernacular of a silver-tongued Golden Age.

Later it saw itself arsy-versy, a nation after the letter;
but common cause outreaching the Dutch
it sold its birthright for a cut of the glory . . .
a mere idea, it seemed invincible.

Yet it thrived on its own lost cause, and the mark of Cain
was a lefthandedness it practised righteously –
its sentinel cities on the plain a gritty paradigm
for an industry of calloused hands.

Guilt was one thing it exported to the new world;
ballast to the quantum energy ascending through midnight
  suns
as a monument of candour, men on fire:
here, in the old, sorrow recurs as a brief downpour,

dream-fug, supplements to a Journal of the Plague Year
when the gospel of virtues, that manic uprightness,
laid blame at nobody's door but its own . . .
beyond reach of heaven was a legislature pining for hell.

Out of it, sons and daughters have no clear sighting
of how an apple-tree opens the debate
but know it does, since they find themselves
on a mission without a motor, reciting the plot backwards

while pavements become rain-sleeked and lustral
and an oddly buoyant cargo gospel
swims through anti-matter to the hard edge of the landscape.
Like a native technology, it starts from what's left

and salvages its own future, a startled Doric narrative
stalking the wet track, tongue and tinder
to its radical children, shy to touch the incontrovertible ores
of a faith that has lately outgrown its disappointment.

DAVID KINLOCH (b. 1959)

The Voyage
for Donny O'Rourke

Baudelaire's mother sent him to sea
To cure him of the vice of verse.

But at Saint-Denis de Bourbon
He tried to disembark

Through rough waves to a sea-saw
Jetty with selected Balzac

Tucked beneath his arm.

Through twelve feet of ocean
The poet climbed the small boat's

Ladder but in the elevator
Of Mauritian water

Found himself alone at last
With the Human Comedy,

Swept up in its mane of emerald eyes,
Heard poems swimming striped

And suddenly yellow in his brain,
Then stepped like Aphrodite

Up to dry land, books fast
But opening in his hands.

DONNY O'ROURKE (b. 1959)

Clockwork

Broken clocks and watches were my father's hobby,
Killing time, he'd say, no irony intended, –
So grandfathers loitered dumbstruck in our lobby,
Hands salaaming as if begging to be mended.

Testimonial tokens of lifetimes on the job
Added to his pile their grateful mollusc gape.
Stammering snuff-stain waistcoat fob –
Tick corrected by puff and scrape.

Eyeglass squinched, he'd read the auguries,
Pronounce and whistle, arrange his tiny tools,
Wind the watch until we'd hear it wheeze,
Teaching me to prod among the cogs and spools

Though my cack-handedness loomed larger through his
glass
He didn't mind the knack not passing on
It's a stoic's pastime, letting time pass,
He knew with quartz and plastic his day had gone

Now Dad's hands are slow and he's lost his spring
His face is scuffed by the emery-paper years
But he can value a clock by its pendulum swing
Or a watch, by the tact, of the tick, that he hears

And on Sundays sometimes we still repair
To smile at every bang on mantel chime
So many hunched gloamings unwinding there
My father and I keeping perfect time.

GERRY CAMBRIDGE (b. 1959)

Praise of a Crofter

You'd shove, unknocking, into the croft on the hill where I sat in easy despairing
Over the page's bounded snow, and mutter about the rain-soaked hay,
The tatties you brought in your bucket, and how the beasts were faring –
Storm-unignorable, sweeping my bland blue heaven of choices away

With the one word, *Now*. Old drunkard, stubbly abstraction-hater, washer 'Wunce a week',
When you'd strip to a vest that hung there in rags as if you were freshly tiger-mauled,
Mocker, your laughter bright as the skies, of the folly of what I sought, or seek;
Jim Harcus, Jim Harcus, if forever's a lifetime, the name you are forever called,

When I went to the North expecting to praise elementals and skies,
There you awaited, wheezing like a steam-train, blunt as a hail shower –
And more remarkable soon your gale-blazed cheeks and ship-containing blue of your eyes
Than argosies dreamt on the seas in a golden hour;

Exemplar of the actual, of the sense I'd have in my every line,
You, clang-solid, brine-bitter, standing over the West's
Atlantic, clouds arranged about your head,
Or hunching, tractor-borne, through showers, to mend a
fence to keep in your beasts with twine,
No sipper at bottles, drinker at the fresh original spring of the
unread,

Dreader of the kirkyard's harbour, you hoarded in boxes and
letters a life, served up dire home-brew;
Island Apemantus, godless religious man, digger of friends'
deep graves,
Funeral attender out in unboundaried air on your tractor,
beside the expansive blue
Drowning the sight of the eye, the final resolving brine that
dooms and saves,

Thank you, for the many a dark-encircled night we sat up
late;
No case of liking you or not: simply there, in your wire-twist-
buttoned coat;
Reliable as tatties in your bucket, and strong as an iron gate;
Perching the bird of the real in my mind – and anchor, for
the spirit's boat.

W. N. HERBERT (b. 1961)

The Black Wet*

It's raining stair-rods and chairlegs,
it's raining candelabra and microwaves,
it's raining eyesockets.
When the sun shines through the shower
it's raining the hair of Sif,
each strand of which is real gold
(carat unknown).

It's raining jellyfish,
it's raining nuts, bolts and pineal glands,
it's raining a legion of fly noyades,
it's raining marsupials and echnidae,
it's raining anoraks in profusion.
It's siling, it's spittering, it's stotting, it's teeming,
it's pouring, it's snoring, it's plaining, it's Spaining.

People look up, open their mouths momentarily,
and drown.
People look out of windows and say,
'Send it down, David.'
Australians remark, 'Huey's missing the bowl.'
Americans reply, 'Huey, Dewie and Louie
are missing the bowl.'

It's not merely raining,
it's Windering and Thirling, it's Buttering down.
It's raining lakes, it's raining grass-snakes,
it's raining Bala, Baikal, and balalaikas,
it's raining soggy sidewinders and sadder adders.
It's raining flu bugs, Toby jugs and hearth-rugs,
it's raining vanity.

The sky is one vast water-clock
and it's raining seconds, it's raining years:
already you have spent more of your life looking at the rain
than you have sleeping, cooking, shopping and making love.
It's raining fusilli and capeletti,
it's raining mariners and albatrosses,
it's raining iambic pentameters.

Let's take a rain-check:
it's raining houndstooth and pinstripe,
it's raining tweed. This is the tartan of McRain.
This is the best test of the wettest west:
it is not raining locusts – just.
Why rain pests
when you can rain driving tests?

It is raining through the holes in God's string vest.

* *The black wet* (Scots): rain as opposed to snow.

JACKIE KAY (b. 1961)

Dance of the Cherry Blossom

Both of us are getting worse
Neither knows who had it first

He thinks I gave it to him
I think he gave it to me

Nights chasing clues where
One memory runs into another like dye.

Both of us are getting worse
I know I'm wasting precious time

But who did he meet between
May 87 and March 89.

I feel his breath on my back
A slow climb into himself then out.

In the morning it all seems different
Neither knows who had it first

We eat breakfast together – newspapers
And silence except for the slow slurp of tea

This companionship is better than anything
He thinks I gave it to him.

By lunchtime we're fighting over some petty thing
He tells me I've lost my sense of humour

I tell him I'm not Glaswegian
You all think death is a joke

It's not funny. I'm dying for fuck's sake
I think he gave it to me.

Just think he says it's every couple's dream
I won't have to wait for you up there

I'll have you night after night – your glorious legs
Your strong hard belly, your kissable cheeks

I cry when he says things like that
My shoulders cave in, my breathing trapped

Do you think you have a corner on dying
You self-pitying wretch, pathetic queen.

He pushes me; we roll on the floor like whirlwind;
When we are done in, our lips find each other

We touch soft as breeze, caress the small parts
Rocking back and forth, his arms become mine

There's nothing outside but the noise of the wind
The cherry blossom's dance through the night.

KATHLEEN JAMIE (b. 1962)

The Way We Live

Pass the tambourine, let me bash out praises
to the Lord God of movement, to Absolute
non-friction, flight, and the scary side:
death by avalanche, birth by failed contraception.
Of chicken tandoori and reggae, loud, from tenements,
commitment, driving fast and unswerving
friendship. Of tee-shirts on pulleys, giros and Bombay,
barmen, dreaming waitresses with many fake-gold
bangles. Of airports, impulse, and waking to uncertainty,
to strip-lights, motorways, or that pantheon –
the mountains. To overdrafts and grafting

and the fit slow pulse of wipers as you're
creeping over Rannoch, while the God of moorland
walks abroad with his entourage of freezing fog,
his bodyguard of snow.
Of endless gloaming in the North, of Asiatic swelter,
to launderettes, anecdotes, passions and exhaustion,
Final Demands and dead men, the skeletal grip
of government. To misery and elation; mixed,
the sod and caprice of landlords.
To the way it fits, the way it is, the way it seems
to be: let me bash out praises – pass the tambourine.

Arraheids

See thon raws o flint arraheids
in oor gret museums o antiquities
awful grand in Embro –
Dae'ye near'n daur wunner at wur histrie?
Weel then, Bewaur!

The museums of Scotland are wrang.
They urnae arraheids
but a show o grannies' tongues,
the hard tongues o grannies
aa deid an gaun
back to thur peat and burns,
but for thur sherp
chert tongues, that lee
fur generations in the land
like wicked cherms, that lee
aa douce in the glessy cases in the gloom
o oor museums, an
they arnae lettin oan. But if you daur
sorn aboot an fancy
the vanished hunter, the wise deer runnin on;
wheesht . . . an you'll hear them,
fur they cannae keep fae muttering
ye arnae here tae wonder,
whae dae ye think ye ur?

DON PATERSON (b. 1963)

Nil Nil

Just as any truly accurate representation of a particular geography can only exist on a scale of 1:1 (imagine the vast, rustling map of Burgundy, say, settling over it like a freshly starched sheet!) so it is with all our abandoned histories, those ignoble lines of succession that end in neither triumph nor disaster, but merely plunge on into deeper and deeper obscurity; only in the infinite ghost-libraries of the imagination – their only possible analogue – can their ends be pursued, the dull and terrible facts finally authenticated.

François Aussemain, *Pensées*

From the top, then, the zenith, the silent footage:
McGrandle, majestic in ankle-length shorts,
his golden hair shorn to an open book, sprinting
the length of the park for the long hoick forward,
his balletic toe-poke nearly bursting the roof
of the net; a shaky pan to the Erskine St End
where a plague of grey bonnets falls out of the clouds.
But ours is a game of two halves, and this game
the semi they went on to lose; from here
it's all down, from the First to the foot of the Second,
McGrandle, Visocchi and Spankie detaching
like bubbles to speed the descent into pitch-sharing,
pay-cuts, pawned silver, the Highland Division,
the absolute sitters ballooned over open goals,
the dismal nutmegs, the scores so obscene
no respectable journal will print them; though one day
Farquhar's spectacular bicycle-kick
will earn him a name-check in Monday's obituaries.
Besides the one setback – the spell of giant-killing
in the Cup (Lochee Violet, then Aberdeen Bon Accord,
the deadlock with Lochee Harp finally broken
by Farquhar's own-goal in the replay)

nothing inhibits the fifty-year slide
into Sunday League, big tartan flasks,
open hatchbacks parked squint behind goal-nets,
the half-time satsuma, the dog on the pitch,
then the Boy's Club, sponsored by Skelly Assurance,
then Skelly Dry Cleaners, then nobody;
stud-harrowed pitches with one-in-five inclines,
grim fathers and perverts with Old English Sheepdogs
lining the touch, moaning softly.
Now the unrefereed thirty-a-sides,
terrified fat boys with calipers minding
four jackets on infinite, notional fields;
ten years of dwindling, half-hearted kickabouts
leaves two little boys – Alastair Watt,
who answers to 'Forty', and wee Horace Madden,
so smelly the air seems to quiver above him –
playing desperate two-touch with a bald tennis ball
in the hour before lighting-up time.
Alastair cheats, and goes off with the ball
leaving wee Horace to hack up a stone
and dribble it home in the rain;
past the stopped swings, the dead shanty-town
of allotments, the black shell of Skelly Dry Cleaners
and into his cul-de-sac, where, accidentally,
he neatly back-heels it straight into the gutter
then tries to swank off like he meant it.

Unknown to him, it is all that remains
of a lone fighter-pilot, who, returning at dawn
to find Leuchars was not where he'd left it,
took time out to watch the Sidlaws unsheathed
from their great black tarpaulin, the haar burn off Tayport
and Venus melt into Carnoustie, igniting
the shoreline; no wind, not a cloud in the sky
and no one around to admire the discretion
of his unscheduled exit: the engine plopped out

and would not re-engage, sending him silently
twirling away like an ash-key,
his attempt to bail out only partly successful,
yesterday having been April the 1st –
the ripcord unleashing a flurry of socks
like a sackful of doves rendered up to the heavens
in private irenicon. He caught up with the plane
on the ground, just at the instant the tank blew
and made nothing of him, save for his fillings,
his tackets, his lucky half-crown and his gallstone,
now anchored between the steel bars of a stank
that looks to be biting the bullet on this one.

In short, this is where you get off, reader;
I'll continue alone, on foot, in the failing light,
following the trail as it steadily fades
into road-repairs, birdsong, the weather, nirvana,
the plot thinning down to a point so refined
not even the angels could dance on it. Goodbye.

00:00: Law Tunnel

(leased to the Scottish Mushroom Company after its closure in 1927)

(i)

In the airy lull
between the wars
they cut the rails
and closed the doors

on the stalled freight:
crate on crate
of blood and earth –
the shallow berth

of the innocents,
their long room
stale and tense
with the same dream

(ii)

Strewn among
the ragged queue –
the snoring king
and his retinue,

Fenrir, Pol Pot,
Captain Oates
and the leprechauns –
are the teeth, the bones

and begging-cup
of the drunken piper.
The rats boiled up
below the sleepers

(iii)

The crippled boy
of Hamelin
pounds away
at the locked mountain

waist-deep in thorn
and all forlorn,
he tries to force
the buried doors

I will go to my mother
and sing of my shame
I will grow up to father
the race of the lame

ANGELA MCSEVENEY (b. 1964)

The Lump

Rolling over in a hot June night
I cradled my breasts in my arms
and felt a hard knot of tissue.

I was fifteen.
My life rose up in my throat
and threatened to stifle me.

It took three attempts to tell my mother.
She promised that my appointment would be
with a woman doctor.

A nurse called my name.
I didn't have cancer.

The stitches in my skin reminded me
of a chicken trussed for the oven.

I felt ashamed
that the first man to see me
had only been doing his job.

GILLIAN FERGUSON (b. 1965)

The Winter Rose

for Dr James Hawkins

Blue-handed, with difficult string,
I staked the broken winter rose,

unbending fibres of green spine,
lifting a crumpled white face –

rain-teared, blinded with earth;
finished by axing winds.

So many thorns hid in the leaves,
and light so thin,

my task lasted even as snow
rehearsed Christmas in the garden.

And when I would have drowned
in snow, an angel came –
I had no words or gold.

But I saw the crushed bush
ghosted with buds;

her face now upturned – furred,
snug in snow – to stars;

after sleeping summer
ironing new petals with air.

And when I would have drowned
in snow, an angel came –
I had no words or gold.

KATE CLANCHY (b. 1965)

Poem for a Man with No Sense of Smell

This is simply to inform you:

that the thickest line in the kink of my hand
smells like the feel of an old school desk,
the deep carved names worn sleek with sweat;

that beneath the spray of my expensive scent
my armpits sound a bass note strong
as the boom of a palm on a kettle drum;

that the wet flush of my fear is sharp
as the taste of an iron pipe, midwinter,
on a child's hot tongue; and that sometimes,

in a breeze, the delicate hairs on the nape
of my neck, just where you might bend
your head, might hesitate and brush your lips,

hold a scent frail and precise as a fleet
of tiny origami ships, just setting out to sea.

RODDY LUMSDEN (b. 1966)

Yeah Yeah Yeah

No matter what you did to her, she said,
There's times, she said, she misses you, your face
Will pucker in her dream, and times the bed's
Too big. Stray hairs will surface in a place
You used to leave your shoes. A certain phrase,
Some old song on the radio, a joke
You had to be there for, she said, some days
It really gets to her; the way you smoked
Or held a cup, or her, and how you woke
Up crying in the night sometimes, the way
She'd stroke and hush you back, and how you broke
Her still. All this she told me yesterday,
Then she rolled over, laughed, began to do
To me what she so rarely did with you.

TRACEY HERD (b. 1968)

Coronach

The skylark's melody is sealed in ice:
a coronach as blue as the winter
sky. The moon wobbles over the rock face,
throwing into high relief the climber
in a gully below the glittering maze.

He is a brilliant figure in this frieze.
His genius walked him into space
and left him to find a foothold there.
The moon is sheer ice or a cracked watch-face
that swings on its fragile chain of stars.

Night is falling at its own modest pace.

ACKNOWLEDGEMENTS

For permission to reprint copyright material the publishers gratefully acknowledge the following:

IAN ABBOT: 'A Body of Work' from *Avoiding the Gods* (Chapman, 1988) by permission of Chapman. MARION ANGUS: 'Alas! Poor Queen' from *Selected Poems* (Serif Books, 1950) by permission of Faber and Faber Limited. IAIN BAMFORTH: 'Men on Fire' from *Sons and Pioneers* (Carcanet, 1992) by permission of Carcanet Press Ltd. D.M. BLACK: 'Kew Gardens' from *Collected Poems 1964–87* (Polygon, 1991) by permission of Polygon. ALAN BOLD: 'A Special Theory of Relativity' by permission of the late Alan Bold. GEORGE MACKAY BROWN: 'Old Fisherman with Guitar', 'Trout Fisher' and 'Kirkyard' from *Selected Poems 1954–1983* (John Murray, 1991) by permission of John Murray (Publishers) Ltd. ELIZABETH BURNS: 'The Oddity' from *Ophelia and Other Poems* (Polygon, 1991) by permission of Polygon. JOHN BURNSIDE: 'Out of Exile' from *The Hoop* (Carcanet Press, 1988) by permission of Carcanet Press Limited; 'The Blind', from *A Normal Skin* (Jonathan Cape, 1997) by permission of Random House UK. RON BUTLIN: 'This Evening' from *Ragtime in Unfamiliar Bars* (Secker & Warburg, 1985) © Ron Butlin, 1985, by permission of Martin Secker and Warburg Limited. GERRY CAMBRIDGE: 'Praise of a Crofter' from *The Shell House* (Scottish Cultural Press, 1995). NORMAN CAMERON: 'Green Green, is El Aghir' from *Collected Poems*, edited by W. Hope and J. Barker (Anvil Press, 1989) by permission of Anvil Press Poetry Ltd. KATE CLANCHY: 'Poem for a man with no sense of smell' from *Slattern* (Chatto & Windus, 1995). STEWART CONN: 'Todd' and 'On Craigie Hill' from *In the Kibble Palace: New and Selected Poems* (Bloodaxe Books, 1987) by permission of Bloodaxe Books Ltd. ROBERT CRAWFORD: 'Scotland in the 1890s' from *A Scottish Assembly* (Chatto & Windus, 1990) and 'Knowledge' from *Spirit Machines* (Jonathan Cape, 1999) by permission of Random Century Group. IVOR CUTLER: 'The Railway Sleepers' from *A Flat Man* (Trigram Press, 1977) by permission of the author. CAROL ANN DUFFY: 'Plainsong' from *Selling Manhattan* (Anvil Press, 1987), by permission of Anvil Press Poetry Ltd; and 'Pilate's Wife' from *The*

World's Wife (Picador, 1999) by permission. ALISON FELL: 'Pushing Forty' from *Kisses for Mayakovsky* (Virago Press, 1984) by permission of Peake Associates. GILLIAN FERGUSON: 'The Winter Rose' from *Air for Sleeping Fish* (Bloodaxe, 1997) by permission of Bloodaxe Books Ltd. ROBIN FULTON: 'Resolutions' from *Fields of Focus* (Anvil Press, 1982) by permission of Anvil Press Poetry Ltd. ROBERT GARIOCH: 'Glisk of the Great' and 'Heard in the Cougate' from *Complete Poetical Works* (Macdonald Publishers, 1983) by permission of The Saltire Society. VALERIE GILLIES: 'The Ericstane Brooch' from *The Chanter's Tune* (Canongate, 1990) by permission of Canongate Press Plc. JOHN GLENDAY: 'The Apple Ghost' from *The Apple Ghost* (Peterloo Poets, 1989) by permission of Peterloo Poets. W.S. GRAHAM: 'The Lying Dear' from *Collected Poems 1942–1977* (Faber, 1979) by permission of the Estate of W. S. Graham. ANDREW GREIG: 'In the Tool-shed' from *Surviving Passages* (Canongate, 1982) by permission of the author. GEORGE CAMPBELL HAY: 'Bisearta'/'Bizerta' from *Modern Scottish Gaelic Poems*, edited by D. Macaulay (Southside, 1976) by permission of Canongate Press Plc. HAMISH HENDERSON: 'Seven Good Germans' from *Elegies for the Dead in Cyrenaica* (Polygon, 1990) by permission of Polygon. W. N. HERBERT: 'The Black Wet' from *The Laurelude.* TRACEY HERD: 'Coronach' from *No Hiding Place* (Bloodaxe, 1998), by permission of Bloodaxe Books. MICK IMLAH: 'Goldilocks' from *Birthmarks* (Chatto & Windus, 1988) by permission of Random Century Group. KATHLEEN JAMIE: 'The Way We Live' from *The Way We Live* (Bloodaxe Books, 1987) and 'Arraheids' from *The Queen of Sheba* (Bloodaxe, 1994) by permission of Bloodaxe Books Ltd. JACKIE KAY; 'Dance of the Cherry Blossom' from *The Adoption Papers* (Bloodaxe Books, 1991) by permission of Bloodaxe Books Ltd. DAVID KINLOCH: 'The Voyage' from *Paris–Forfar* (Polygon, 1994). FRANK KUPPNER: 'Passing Through Doorways' from *The Intelligent Observation of Naked Women* (Carcanet Press, 1987) by permission of Carcanet Press Limited. TOM LEONARD: *from* 'Unrelated Incidents' and *from* 'Ghostie Men' from *Intimate Voices: Selected Work 1965–1983* (Galloping Dog Press, 1984) by permission of the author. LIZ LOCHHEAD: 'The Grim Sisters' and 'My Mother's Suitors' from *Dreaming Frankenstein and Collected Poems* (Polygon, 1984) by permission of Polygon. RODDY LUMSDEN: 'Yeah Yeah Yeah' from *Yeah, Yeuh, Yeah* (Bloodaxc, 1997). GEORGE MACBETH:

'Draft for an Ancestor' from *Collected Poems 1958–1982* (Hutchinson, 1989), copyright © George MacBeth, 1989, by permission of Sheil Land Associates Ltd. BRIAN MCCABE: 'Slug' from *Body Parts* (Cannongate, 1999). NORMAN MCCAIG: 'Summer Farm', 'Byre' and 'Old Edinburgh' from *Collected Poems* (Chatto & Windus, 1990) by permission of Random Century Group. HUGH MACDIARMID (Christopher Murray Grieve): 'The Bonnie Broukit Bairn', 'The Watergaw' and 'The Eemis Stane' from *Selected Poems of Hugh MacDiarmid* (Carcanet Press, 1992) by permission of Carcanet Press Limited. SORLEY MACLEAN: 'Glac a' Bhàis'/'Death Valley' and 'Hallaig'/'Hallaig' from *From Wood to Ridge: Collected Poems in Gaelic and English* (Carcanet Press, 1989) by permission of Carcanet Press Limited. AONGHAS MACNEACAIL: *from* 'an cathadh mor'/ *from* 'the great snowbattle' from *an seachnadh agus dain eile. The avoiding and other poems* (Macdonald Publishers, 1986) by permission of The Saltire Society. ANGELA MCSEVENEY: 'The Lump' from *Coming Out with It* (Polygon, 1992) by permission of Polygon. GERALD MANGAN: 'Heraclitus at Glasgow Cross' from *Waiting for the Storm* (Bloodaxe Books, 1990) by permission of Bloodaxe Books Ltd. ANGUS MARTIN: 'Forest' from *The Larch Plantation* (Macdonald Publishers, 1990) by permission of The Saltire Society. EDWIN MORGAN: 'The First Men on Mercury' and 'Cinquevalli', *from* 'Sonnets from Scotland': 'The Coin' from *Collected Poems* (Carcanet Press, 1990) by permission of Carcanet Press Limited. EDWIN MUIR: 'The Horses' from *Collected Poems* (Faber, 1960) by permission of Faber and Faber Limited. WILLIAM NEILL: 'Map Makers' from *Wild Places* (Luath Press, 1985) by permission of the author. DONNY O'ROURKE: 'Clockwork' from *The Waistband* (Polygon, 1997). DON PATERSON: 'Nil Nil' from *Nil Nil* (Faber, 1993) and '00:00: Law Tunnel; from *God's Gift to Women* (Faber, 1997) by permission of Faber and Faber Limited. TOM POW: 'Saint Medan' from *The Moth Trap* (Canongate, 1990) by permission of Canongate Press Plc. ALASTAIR REID: 'Scotland' from *Weathering* (Canongate, 1978) by permission of Canongate Press Plc. ROBIN ROBERTSON: 'Fugue for Phantoms' from *A Painted Field* (Picador, 1997) by permission. DILYS ROSE: 'Fetish' from *Madame Doubtfire's Dilemma* (Chapman, 1989) by permission of Chapman. CHRISTOPHER SALVESEN: 'History of Strathclyde' from *Among the Goths* (Mariscat, 1986) by permission of Mariscat Publishers. TOM

SCOTT: 'The Mankind Toun' from *The Ship, and Ither Poems* (OUP, 1963) by permission of the late Tom Scott. BURNS SINGER: 'Peterhead in May' from *Selected Poems*, edited by A. Cluysenaar (Carcanet Press, 1977) by permission of Carcanet Press Limited. IAIN CRICHTON SMITH: 'The Law and the Grace', *from* 'The White Air of March' and 'Chinese Poem' from *Selected Poems* (Carcanet Press, 1985), 'Listen' from *The Village* (Carcanet Press, 1989) by permission of Carcanet Press Limited. SYDNEY GOODSIR SMITH: *from* 'Under the Eildon Tree – V: Slugabed' from *Collected Poems* (John Calder, 1975) Copyright © John Calder (Publishers) Ltd 1975, by permission of Calder Publications Ltd. WILLIAM SOUTAR: 'The Tryst' from *The Poems of William Soutar* edited by W. R. Aitken (Scottish Academic Press, 1988) by permission of The Trustees of The National Library of Scotland. MURIEL SPARK: 'Elegy in a Kensington Churchyard' from *Going Up to Sotheby's, and Other Poems* (Granada Publishing, 1982) by permission of David Higham Associates Limited. DERICK THOMSON: 'An Tobar'/'The Well', 'Srath Nabhair'/'Strathnaver' from *Creachadh na clarsaich . . . : Plundering the Harp. Collected Poems 1940–1980* (Macdonald Publishers, 1982) by permission of The Saltire Society. RUTHVEN TODD: 'Trout Flies' from *Garland for the Winter Solstice* (Dent, 1961) by permission of David Higham Associates Limited. SYDNEY TREMAYNE: 'A Burial' from *Selected and New Poems* (Chatto & Windus, 1973) Copyright © Sydney Tremayne, 1973, by permission of Sheil Land Associates Ltd. KENNETH WHITE: *from* 'Late August on the Coast' from *The Bird Path: Collected Longer Poems* (Mainstream Publishing, 1989) by permission of Mainstream Publishing Co. (Edinburgh) Ltd. ANDREW YOUNG: 'On the Pilgrim's Road' and 'The Shepherd's Hut' from *The Poetical Works* (Secker & Warburg, 1985) by permission of The Estate of Andrew Young. DOUGLAS YOUNG: 'For a Wife in Jizzen' from *A Clear Voice: Douglas Young, Poet and Polymath*, edited by C. Young and D. Murison (Macdonald Publishers, 1976) by permission of The Saltire Society.

Faber and Faber Limited apologize for any errors or omissions in the above list and would be grateful to be notified of any corrections that should be incorporated in the next edition or reprint of this volume.

INDEX OF POETS

JOHN KEATS Poems selected by ANDREW MOTION

JOHN KEATS

Poems selected by

ANDREW MOTION

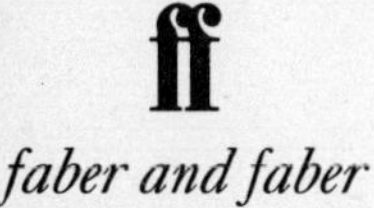

faber and faber

First published in 2000
by Faber and Faber Limited
3 Queen Square London WC1N 3AU

Photoset by Parker Typesetting Service, Leicester
Printed in Italy

All rights reserved

Introduction and this selection © Andrew Motion, 2000

Andrew Motion is hereby identified as editor
of this work in accordance with Section 77
of the Copyright, Designs and Patents Act 1988

This book is sold subject to the condition that it shall not, by way of trade or otherwise, be lent, resold, hired out or otherwise circulated without the publisher's prior consent in any form of binding or cover other than that in which it is published and without a similar condition including this condition being imposed on the subsequent purchaser

A CIP record for this book
is available from the British Library
ISBN 0–571–20373–6

10 9 8 7 6 5 4 3 2 1

Contents

Introduction

When Keats died in 1821, at the age of twenty-five, he was virtually unknown as a poet, except as an object of suspicion and ridicule. The best-received of his three volumes had sold a measly 250 copies; *Blackwood's Magazine* and the *Quarterly Review* had been scathing about his long poem *Endymion* (1818); he himself had been accused of luxuriousness and effeminacy.

Not surprisingly, his small band of admirers leapt to his defence – but several of them only made matters worse. Shelley, in his elegy *Adonais* (1821), Leigh Hunt in his memoir *Lord Byron and Some Contemporaries* (1828) and Richard Monckton Milnes in the first full-length biography (1848), all helped to enshrine Keats as the archetype of the stricken Romantic. According to them, he was a supersensitive soul who had lived apart from the world, and who had immediately shrivelled up when exposed to its cruelties.

The Victorians accepted this version of events, and sentimentalised it even more thoroughly. Their Keats was a pre-Pre-Raphaelite, sugared and swooning. 'O for a life of sensation rather than thoughts', they found him saying in one of his letters – and took the remark at face value. It suited them, as part of their drive towards national cohesion, to suppose that significant poets in the past had never paid much attention to troublesome ideas of any kind – let alone actually dissenting ones. It especially suited Tennyson – a champion of Keats's – since it provided a kind of cover for his own more thoughtful moments.

This polite version of 'little Keats' lasted an astonishingly long time – until almost the end of the twentieth century, in fact. Then, at long last, the picture began to change. People began to realise that those early bad reviews were not just examples of critical stupidity, but proof of a very particular kind of disapproval. *Blackwood's* and the *Quarterly* were hard-core Tory journals, and as far as they were concerned, Keats was a dangerously subversive figure – lower class (his father had been an ostler), badly educated (he had not been to university), and the friend of radicals (Leigh Hunt, Shelley and their circle). Furthermore, his poems proved this in all respects – not just in their explicit remarks about liberty and oppression, but in their very fabric: their suburban references, their luscious music and their pulsing eroticism.

Actually, 'explicit remarks' about liberal politics are pretty few and far between in Keats's poems. There are some early pieces, such as the lines 'Written on the Day that Mr Leigh Hunt Left Prison', and a few later swipes (such as the attack on money-grubbing in 'Isabella') – but generally Keats, like his idol Shakespeare, does not come to the front of the page and wag his finger at his readers. 'We hate poems that have a palpable design on us', he says in one of his letters, and elsewhere 'Axioms in philosophy are not axioms until they are proved upon our pulses'. In other words, Keats's radicalism is invariably not something we see spelt out in his poems, but something we experience at a fundamental and sensuous level. It exists in a brilliantly realised world of stories, myths and legends, where we are continually required (as we also are in Shakespeare) to make morally responsible interpretations. It occurs in lyrics and odes which are shaped by distinct historical forces, but which have transmuted these forces. (We can see this in 'To Autumn', for instance, which was written shortly after the Peterloo Massacre.)

To read Keats in this way – as a man of the world (a qualified doctor, a sociable spirit) who was in love with the world of the imagination – is to do him justice as an individual, and to prove his kinship with his great Romantic contemporaries. It also shows why he matters to us now. As he resisted the pressures of his history, and absorbed and recast them in his work, he made a connection between his own time and all time – between a particular truth and all beauty. In the process, he made himself exemplary.

Andrew Motion

JOHN KEATS

On First Looking into Chapman's Homer

Much have I travelled in the realms of gold,
   And many goodly states and kingdoms seen;
   Round many western islands have I been
Which bards in fealty to Apollo hold.
Oft of one wide expanse had I been told
   That deep-browed Homer ruled as his demesne;
   Yet did I never breathe its pure serene
Till I heard Chapman speak out loud and bold:
Then felt I like some watcher of the skies
   When a new planet swims into his ken;
Or like stout Cortez when with eagle eyes
   He stared at the Pacific – and all his men
Looked at each other with a wild surmise –
   Silent, upon a peak in Darien.

from Sleep and Poetry

LINES 96-154

O for ten years, that I may overwhelm
Myself in poesy; so I may do the deed
That my own soul has to itself decreed.
Then will I pass the countries that I see
In long perspective, and continually
Taste their pure fountains. First the realm I'll pass
Of Flora, and old Pan: sleep in the grass,
Feed upon apples red, and strawberries,
And choose each pleasure that my fancy sees;
Catch the white-handed nymphs in shady places,
To woo sweet kisses from averted faces –
Play with their fingers, touch their shoulders white
Into a pretty shrinking with a bite
As hard as lips can make it, till, agreed,
A lovely tale of human life we'll read.
And one will teach a tame dove how it best
May fan the cool air gently o'er my rest;
Another, bending o'er her nimble tread,
Will set a green robe floating round her head,
And still will dance with ever varied ease,
Smiling upon the flowers and the trees:
Another will entice me on, and on
Through almond blossoms and rich cinnamon;
Till in the bosom of a leafy world
We rest in silence, like two gems upcurled
In the recesses of a pearly shell.

And can I ever bid these joys farewell?
Yes, I must pass them for a nobler life,
Where I may find the agonies, the strife
Of human hearts – for lo! I see afar,
O'er-sailing the blue cragginess, a car

And steeds with streamy manes – the charioteer
Looks out upon the winds with glorious fear:
And now the numerous tramplings quiver lightly
Along a huge cloud's ridge; and now with sprightly
Wheel downward come they into fresher skies,
Tipped round with silver from the sun's bright eyes.
Still downward with capacious whirl they glide;
And now I see them on a green-hill's side
In breezy rest among the nodding stalks.
The charioteer with wondrous gesture talks
To the trees and mountains; and there soon appear
Shapes of delight, of mystery, and fear,
Passing along before a dusky space
Made by some mighty oaks: as they would chase
Some ever-fleeting music on they sweep.
Lo! how they murmur, laugh, and smile, and weep –
Some with upholden hand and mouth severe;
Some with their faces muffled to the ear
Between their arms; some, clear in youthful bloom,
Go glad and smilingly athwart the gloom;
Some looking back, and some with upward gaze;
Yes, thousands in a thousand different ways
Flit onward – now a lovely wreath of girls
Dancing their sleek hair into tangled curls;
And now broad wings. Most awfully intent
The driver of those steeds is forward bent,
And seems to listen: O that I might know
All that he writes with such a hurrying glow.

from Endymion

BOOK I, lines 1–33

A thing of beauty is a joy for ever:
Its loveliness increases; it will never
Pass into nothingness; but still will keep
A bower quiet for us, and a sleep
Full of sweet dreams, and health, and quiet breathing.
Therefore, on every morrow, are we wreathing
A flowery band to bind us to the earth,
Spite of despondence, of the inhuman dearth
Of noble natures, of the gloomy days,
Of all the unhealthy and o'er-darkened ways
Made for our searching: yes, in spite of all,
Some shape of beauty moves away the pall
From our dark spirits. Such the sun, the moon,
Trees old, and young, sprouting a shady boon
For simple sheep; and such are daffodils
With the green world they live in; and clear rills
That for themselves a cooling covert make
'Gainst the hot season; the mid forest brake,
Rich with a sprinkling of fair musk-rose blooms:
And such too is the grandeur of the dooms
We have imagined for the mighty dead;
All lovely tales that we have heard or read –
An endless fountain of immortal drink,
Pouring unto us from the heaven's brink.

Nor do we merely feel these essences
For one short hour; no, even as the trees
That whisper round a temple become soon
Dear as the temple's self, so does the moon,
The passion poesy, glories infinite,
Haunt us till they become a cheering light
Unto our souls, and bound to us so fast,

That, whether there be shine, or gloom o'ercast,
They always must be with us, or we die.

BOOK I, lines 769–842

'Peona! ever have I longed to slake
My thirst for the world's praises: nothing base,
No merely slumbrous phantasm, could unlace
The stubborn canvas for my voyage prepared –
Though now 'tis tattered, leaving my bark bared
And sullenly drifting: yet my higher hope
Is of too wide, too rainbow-large a scope,
To fret at myriads of earthly wrecks.
Wherein lies happiness? In that which becks
Our ready minds to fellowship divine,
A fellowship with essence; till we shine,
Full alchemized, and free of space. Behold
The clear religion of heaven! Fold
A rose leaf round thy finger's taperness,
And soothe thy lips; hist, when the airy stress
Of music's kiss impregnates the free winds,
And with a sympathetic touch unbinds
Aeolian magic from their lucid wombs;
Then old songs waken from enclouded tombs;
Old ditties sigh above their father's grave;
Ghosts of melodious prophesyings rave
Round every spot where trod Apollo's foot;
Bronze clarions awake, and faintly bruit,
Where long ago a giant battle was;
And, from the turf, a lullaby doth pass
In every place where infant Orpheus slept.
Feel we these things? – that moment have we stepped
Into a sort of oneness, and our state
Is like a floating spirit's. But there are
Richer entanglements, enthralments far
More self-destroying, leading, by degrees,

To the chief intensity: the crown of these
Is made of love and friendship, and sits high
Upon the forehead of humanity.
All its more ponderous and bulky worth
Is friendship, whence there ever issues forth
A steady splendour; but at the tip-top,
There hangs by unseen film, an orbèd drop
Of light, and that is love: its influence,
Thrown in our eyes, genders a novel sense,
At which we start and fret; till in the end,
Melting into its radiance, we blend,
Mingle, and so become a part of it –
Nor with aught else can our souls interknit
So wingedly. When we combine therewith,
Life's self is nourished by its proper pith,
And we are nurtured like a pelican brood.
Ay, so delicious is the unsating food,
That men, who might have towered in the van
Of all the congregated world, to fan
And winnow from the coming step of time
All chaff of custom, wipe away all slime
Left by men-slugs and human serpentry,
Have been content to let occasion die,
Whilst they did sleep in love's elysium.
And, truly, I would rather be struck dumb,
Than speak against this ardent listlessness:
For I have ever thought that it might bless
The world with benefits unknowingly,
As does the nightingale, up-perchèd high,
And cloistered among cool and bunchèd leaves –
She sings but to her love, nor e'er conceives
How tip-toe Night holds back her dark-grey hood.
Just so may love, although 'tis understood
The mere commingling of passionate breath,
Produce more than our searching witnesseth –
What I know not: but who, of men, can tell

That flowers would bloom, or that green fruit would swell
To melting pulp, that fish would have bright mail,
The earth its dower of river, wood, and vale,
The meadows runnels, runnels pebble-stones,
The seed its harvest, or the lute its tones,
Tones ravishment, or ravishment its sweet,
If human souls did never kiss and greet?

BOOK II, lines 387–427

After a thousand mazes overgone,
At last, with sudden step, he came upon
A chamber, myrtle walled, embowered high,
Full of light, incense, tender minstrelsy,
And more of beautiful and strange beside:
For on a silken couch of rosy pride,
In midst of all, there lay a sleeping youth
Of fondest beauty; fonder, in fair sooth,
Than sighs could fathom, or contentment reach:
And coverlids gold-tinted like the peach,
Or ripe October faded marigolds,
Fell sleek about him in a thousand folds –
Not hiding up an Apollonian curve
Of neck and shoulder, nor the tenting swerve
Of knee from knee, nor ankles pointing light;
But rather, giving them to the fillèd sight
Officiously. Sideway his face reposed
On one white arm, and tenderly unclosed,
By tenderest pressure, a faint damask mouth
To slumbery pout; just as the morning south
Disparts a dew-lipped rose. Above his head,
Four lily stalks did their white honours wed
To make a coronal; and round him grew
All tendrils green, of every bloom and hue,
Together intertwined and trammelled fresh:
The vine of glossy sprout; the ivy mesh,

Shading its Ethiope berries; and woodbine,
Of velvet leaves and bugle-blooms divine;
Convolvulus in streakèd vases flush;
The creeper, mellowing for an autumn blush;
And virgin's bower, trailing airily;
With others of the sisterhood. Hard by,
Stood serene Cupids watching silently.
One, kneeling to a lyre, touched the strings,
Muffling to death the pathos with his wings;
And, ever and anon, uprose to look
At the youth's slumber; while another took
A willow-bough, distilling odorous dew,
And shook it on his hair; another flew
In through the woven roof, and fluttering-wise
Rained violets upon his sleeping eyes.

BOOK III, lines 1–40

There are who lord it o'er their fellow-men
With most prevailing tinsel: who unpen
Their baaing vanities, to browse away
The comfortable green and juicy hay
From human pastures; or – O torturing fact! –
Who, through an idiot blink, will see unpacked
Fire-branded foxes to sear up and singe
Our gold and ripe-eared hopes. With not one tinge
Of sanctuary splendour, not a sight
Able to face an owl's, they still are dight
By the blear-eyed nations in empurpled vests,
And crowns, and turbans. With unladen breasts,
Save of blown self-applause, they proudly mount
To their spirit's perch, their being's high account,
Their tip-top nothings, their dull skies, their thrones –
Amid the fierce intoxicating tones
Of trumpets, shoutings, and belaboured drums,
And sudden cannon. Ah! how all this hums,

In wakeful ears, like uproar passed and gone –
Like thunder clouds that spake to Babylon,
And set those old Chaldeans to their tasks. –
Are then regalities all gilded masks?
No, there are thronèd seats unscalable
But by a patient wing, a constant spell,
Or by ethereal things that, unconfined,
Can make a ladder of the eternal wind,
And poise about in cloudy thunder-tents
To watch the abysm-birth of elements.
Ay, 'bove the withering of old-lipped Fate
A thousand Powers keep religious state,
In water, fiery realm, and airy bourne,
And, silent as a consecrated urn,
Hold sphery sessions for a season due.
Yet few of these far majesties – ah, few! –
Have bared their operations to this globe –
Few, who with gorgeous pageantry enrobe
Our piece of heaven – whose benevolence
Shakes hand with our own Ceres, every sense
Filling with spiritual sweets to plenitude,
As bees gorge full their cells.

BOOK IV, lines 513–62

There lies a den,
Beyond the seeming confines of the space
Made for the soul to wander in and trace
Its own existence, of remotest glooms.
Dark regions are around it, where the tombs
Of buried griefs the spirit sees, but scarce
One hour doth linger weeping, for the pierce
Of new-born woe it feels more inly smart:
And in these regions many a venomed dart
At random flies; they are the proper home
Of every ill: the man is yet to come

Who hath not journeyed in this native hell.
But few have ever felt how calm and well
Sleep may be had in that deep den of all.
There anguish does not sting; nor pleasure pall:
Woe-hurricanes beat ever at the gate,
Yet all is still within and desolate.
Beset with plainful gusts, within ye hear
No sound so loud as when on curtained bier
The death-watch tick is stifled. Enter none
Who strive therefore: on the sudden it is won.
Just when the sufferer begins to burn,
Then it is free to him; and from an urn,
Still fed by melting ice, he takes a draught –
Young Semele such richness never quaffed
In her maternal longing! Happy gloom!
Dark Paradise! where pale becomes the bloom
Of health by due; where silence dreariest
Is most articulate; where hopes infest;
Where those eyes are the brightest far that keep
Their lids shut longest in a dreamless sleep.
O happy spirit-home! O wondrous soul! –
Pregnant with such a den to save the whole
In thine own depth. Hail, gentle Carian!
For, never since thy griefs and woes began,
Hast thou felt so content: a grievous feud
Hath led thee to this Cave of Quietude.
Ay, his lulled soul was there, although upborne
With dangerous speed, and so he did not mourn
Because he knew not whither he was going.
So happy was he, not the aerial blowing
Of trumpets at clear parley from the east
Could rouse from that fine relish, that high feast.
They stung the feathered horse: with fierce alarm
He flapped towards the sound. Alas, no charm
Could lift Endymion's head, or he had viewed
A skyey masque, a pinioned multitude –

And silvery was its passing. Voices sweet
Warbling the while as if to lull and greet
The wanderer in his path. Thus warbled they,
While past the vision went in bright array.

'In drear-nighted December'

I

In drear-nighted December,
Too happy, happy tree,
Thy branches ne'er remember
Their green felicity:
The north cannot undo them,
With a sleety whistle through them,
Nor frozen thawings glue them
From budding at the prime.

II

In drear-nighted December,
Too happy, happy brook,
Thy bubblings ne'er remember
Apollo's summer look;
But with a sweet forgetting,
They stay their crystal fretting,
Never, never petting
About the frozen time.

III

Ah! would 'twere so with many
A gentle girl and boy!
But were there ever any
Writhed not of passèd joy?
The feel of not to feel it,
When there is none to heal it,
Nor numbèd sense to steel it,
Was never said in rhyme.

‘When I have fears that I may cease to be’

When I have fears that I may cease to be
   Before my pen has gleaned my teeming brain,
Before high-pilèd books, in charactery,
   Hold like rich garners the full-ripened grain;
When I behold, upon the night’s starred face,
   Huge cloudy symbols of a high romance,
And think that I may never live to trace
   Their shadows, with the magic hand of chance;
And when I feel, fair creature of an hour!
   That I shall never look upon thee more,
Never have relish in the faery power
   Of unreflecting love! – then on the shore
Of the wide world I stand alone, and think
Till love and fame to nothingness do sink.

To J. H. Reynolds, Esq.

Dear Reynolds, as last night I lay in bed,
There came before my eyes that wonted thread
Of shapes, and shadows, and remembrances,
That every other minute vex and please:
Things all disjointed come from North and South –
Two witch's eyes above a cherub's mouth,
Voltaire with casque and shield and habergeon,
And Alexander with his nightcap on,
Old Socrates a-tying his cravat,
And Hazlitt playing with Miss Edgeworth's cat,
And Junius Brutus, pretty well so so,
Making the best of's way towards Soho.

Few are there who escape these visitings –
Perhaps one or two whose lives have patient wings,
And through whose curtains peeps no hellish nose,
No wild-boar tushes, and no mermaid's toes;
But flowers bursting out with lusty pride,
And young Aeolian harps personified,
Some, Titian colours touched into real life –
The sacrifice goes on; the pontiff knife
Gloams in the sun, the milk-white heifer lows,
The pipes go shrilly, the libation flows;
A white sail shows above the green-head cliff,
Moves round the point, and throws her anchor stiff.
The mariners join hymn with those on land.

You know the Enchanted Castle – it doth stand
Upon a rock, on the border of a lake,
Nested in trees, which all do seem to shake
From some old magic-like Urganda's sword.
O Phoebus! that I had thy sacred word
To show this castle, in fair dreaming wise,
Unto my friend, while sick and ill he lies!

You know it well enough, where it doth seem
A mossy place, a Merlin's Hall, a dream.
You know the clear lake, and the little isles,
The mountains blue, and cold near-neighbour rills,
All which elsewhere are but half animate;
Here do they look alive to love and hate,
To smiles and frowns; they seem a lifted mound
Above some giant, pulsing underground.

Part of the building was a chosen see,
Built by a banished santon of Chaldee;
The other part, two thousand years from him,
Was built by Cuthbert de Saint Aldebrim;
Then there's a little wing, far from the sun,
Built by a Lapland witch turned maudlin nun;
And many other juts of agèd stone
Founded with many a mason-devil's groan.

The doors all look as if they oped themselves,
The windows as if latched by fays and elves,
And from them comes a silver flash of light,
As from the westward of a summer's night;
Or like a beauteous woman's large blue eyes
Gone mad through olden songs and poesies –

See! what is coming from the distance dim!
A golden galley all in silken trim!
Three rows of oars are lightening, moment-whiles,
Into the verdurous bosoms of those isles.
Towards the shade, under the castle wall,
It comes in silence – now 'tis hidden all.
The clarion sounds, and from a postern-grate
An echo of sweet music doth create
A fear in the poor herdsman, who doth bring
His beasts to trouble the enchanted spring.
He tells of the sweet music, and the spot,
To all his friends – and they believe him not.

O that our dreamings all, of sleep or wake,
Would all their colours from the sunset take,
From something of material sublime,
Rather than shadow our own soul's daytime
In the dark void of night. For in the world
We jostle – but my flag is not unfurled
On the admiral staff – and to philosophize
I dare not yet! O, never will the prize,
High reason, and the lore of good and ill,
Be my award! Things cannot to the will
Be settled, but they tease us out of thought.
Or is it that imagination brought
Beyond its proper bound, yet still confined,
Lost in a sort of purgatory blind,
Cannot refer to any standard law
Of either earth or heaven? It is a flaw
In happiness, to see beyond our bourne –
It forces us in summer skies to mourn;
It spoils the singing of the nightingale.

Dear Reynolds, I have a mysterious tale,
And cannot speak it. The first page I read
Upon a lampit rock of green seaweed
Among the breakers. 'Twas a quiet eve;
The rocks were silent, the wide sea did weave
An untumultuous fringe of silver foam
Along the flat brown sand. I was at home
And should have been most happy – but I saw
Too far into the sea, where every maw
The greater on the less feeds evermore. –
But I saw too distinct into the core
Of an eternal fierce destruction,
And so from happiness I far was gone.
Still am I sick of it; and though, today,
I've gathered young spring-leaves, and flowers gay
Of periwinkle and wild strawberry,

Still do I that most fierce destruction see –
The shark at savage prey, the hawk at pounce,
The gentle robin, like a pard or ounce,
Ravening a worm. – Away, ye horrid moods!
Moods of one's mind! You know I hate them well,
You know I'd sooner be a clapping bell
To some Kamchatkan missionary church,
Than with these horrid moods be left in lurch.
Do you get health – and Tom the same – I'll dance,
And from detested moods in new romance
Take refuge. Of bad lines a centaine dose
Is sure enough – and so 'here follows prose' . . .

Isabella; or, The Pot of Basil

I

Fair Isabel, poor simple Isabel!
Lorenzo, a young palmer in Love's eye!
They could not in the self-same mansion dwell
Without some stir of heart, some malady;
They could not sit at meals but feel how well
It soothed each to be the other by;
They could not, sure, beneath the same roof sleep
But to each other dream, and nightly weep.

II

With every morn their love grew tenderer,
With every eve deeper and tenderer still;
He might not in house, field, or garden stir,
But her full shape would all his seeing fill;
And his continual voice was pleasanter
To her than noise of trees or hidden rill;
Her lute-string gave an echo of his name,
She spoilt her half-done broidery with the same.

III

He knew whose gentle hand was at the latch
Before the door had given her to his eyes;
And from her chamber-window he would catch
Her beauty farther than the falcon spies;
And constant as her vespers would he watch,
Because her face was turned to the same skies;
And with sick longing all the night outwear,
To hear her morning-step upon the stair.

IV

A whole long month of May in this sad plight
Made their cheeks paler by the break of June:
'To-morrow will I bow to my delight,
To-morrow will I ask my lady's boon.'

'O may I never see another night,
   Lorenzo, if thy lips breathe not love's tune.'
So spake they to their pillows; but, alas,
Honeyless days and days did he let pass –

V

Until sweet Isabella's untouched cheek
   Fell sick within the rose's just domain,
Fell thin as a young mother's, who doth seek
   By every lull to cool her infant's pain:
'How ill she is,' said he, 'I may not speak,
   And yet I will, and tell my love all plain:
If looks speak love-laws, I will drink her tears,
And at the least 'twill startle off her cares.'

VI

So said he one fair morning, and all day
   His heart beat awfully against his side;
And to his heart he inwardly did pray
   For power to speak; but still the ruddy tide
Stifled his voice, and pulsed resolve away –
   Fevered his high conceit of such a bride,
Yet brought him to the meekness of a child:
Alas! when passion is both meek and wild!

VII

So once more he had waked and anguishèd
   A dreary night of love and misery,
If Isabel's quick eye had not been wed
   To every symbol on his forehead high.
She saw it waxing very pale and dead,
   And straight all flushed; so, lispèd tenderly,
'Lorenzo!' – here she ceased her timid quest,
But in her tone and look he read the rest.

VIII

'O Isabella, I can half-perceive
   That I may speak my grief into thine ear.

If thou didst ever anything believe,
  Believe how I love thee, believe how near
My soul is to its doom: I would not grieve
  Thy hand by unwelcome pressing, would not fear
Thine eyes by gazing; but I cannot live
Another night, and not my passion shrive.

IX

Love! thou art leading me from wintry cold,
  Lady! thou leadest me to summer clime,
And I must taste the blossoms that unfold
  In its ripe warmth this gracious morning time.'
So said, his erewhile timid lips grew bold,
  And poesied with hers in dewy rhyme:
Great bliss was with them, and great happiness
Grew, like a lusty flower, in June's caress.

X

Parting they seemed to tread upon the air,
  Twin roses by the zephyr blown apart
Only to meet again more close, and share
  The inward fragrance of each other's heart.
She, to her chamber gone, a ditty fair
  Sang, of delicious love and honeyed dart;
He with light steps went up a western hill,
And bade the sun farewell, and joyed his fill.

XI

All close they met again, before the dusk
  Had taken from the stars its pleasant veil,
All close they met, all eves, before the dusk
  Had taken from the stars its pleasant veil,
Close in a bower of hyacinth and musk,
  Unknown of any, free from whispering tale.
Ah! better had it been for ever so,
Than idle ears should pleasure in their woe.

XII

Were they unhappy then? – It cannot be –
  Too many tears for lovers have been shed,
Too many sighs give we to them in fee,
  Too much of pity after they are dead,
Too many doleful stories do we see,
  Whose matter in bright gold were best be read;
Except in such a page where Theseus' spouse
Over the pathless waves towards him bows.

XIII

But, for the general award of love,
  The little sweet doth kill much bitterness;
Though Dido silent is in under-grove,
  And Isabella's was a great distress,
Though young Lorenzo in warm Indian clove
  Was not embalmed, this truth is not the less –
Even bees, the little almsmen of spring-bowers,
Know there is richest juice in poison-flowers.

XIV

With her two brothers this fair lady dwelt,
  Enrichèd from ancestral merchandise,
And for them many a weary hand did swelt
  In torchèd mines and noisy factories,
And many once proud-quivered loins did melt
  In blood from stinging whip – with hollow eyes
Many all day in dazzling river stood,
To take the rich-ored driftings of the flood.

XV

For them the Ceylon diver held his breath,
  And went all naked to the hungry shark;
For them his ears gushed blood; for them in death
  The seal on the cold ice with piteous bark
Lay full of darts; for them alone did seethe
  A thousand men in troubles wide and dark:

Half-ignorant, they turned an easy wheel,
That set sharp racks at work to pinch and peel.

XVI

Why were they proud? Because their marble founts
   Gushed with more pride than do a wretch's tears? –
Why were they proud? Because fair orange-mounts
   Were of more soft ascent than lazar stairs? –
Why were they proud? Because red-lined accounts
   Were richer than the songs of Grecian years? –
Why were they proud? again we ask aloud,
Why in the name of Glory were they proud?

XVII

Yet were these Florentines as self-retired
   In hungry pride and gainful cowardice,
As two close Hebrews in that land inspired,
   Paled in and vineyarded from beggar-spies –
The hawks of ship-mast forests – the untired
   And panniered mules for ducats and old lies –
Quick cat's-paws on the generous stray-away –
Great wits in Spanish, Tuscan, and Malay.

XVIII

How was it these same ledger-men could spy
   Fair Isabella in her downy nest?
How could they find out in Lorenzo's eye
   A straying from his toil? Hot Egypt's pest
Into their vision covetous and sly!
   How could these money-bags see east and west? –
Yet so they did – and every dealer fair
Must see behind, as doth the hunted hare.

XIX

O eloquent and famed Boccaccio!
   Of thee we now should ask forgiving boon,
And of thy spicy myrtles as they blow,
   And of thy roses amorous of the moon,

And of thy lilies, that do paler grow
  Now they can no more hear thy gittern's tune.
For venturing syllables that ill beseem
The quiet glooms of such a piteous theme.

XX

Grant thou a pardon here, and then the tale
  Shall move on soberly, as it is meet;
There is no other crime, no mad assail
  To make old prose in modern rhyme more sweet:
But it is done – succeed the verse or fail –
  To honour thee, and thy gone spirit greet,
To stead thee as a verse in English tongue,
An echo of thee in the north wind sung.

XXI

These brethren having found by many signs
  What love Lorenzo for their sister had,
And how she loved him too, each unconfines
  His bitter thoughts to other, well nigh mad
That he, the servant of their trade designs,
  Should in their sister's love be blithe and glad,
When 'twas their plan to coax her by degrees
To some high noble and his olive-trees.

XXII

And many a jealous conference had they,
  And many times they bit their lips alone,
Before they fixed upon a surest way
  To make the youngster for his crime atone;
And at the last, these men of cruel clay
  Cut Mercy with a sharp knife to the bone,
For they resolvèd in some forest dim
To kill Lorenzo, and there bury him.

XXIII

So on a pleasant morning, as he leant
  Into the sunrise, o'er the balustrade

Of the garden-terrace, towards him they bent
   Their footing through the dews; and to him said,
'You seem there in the quiet of content,
   Lorenzo, and we are most loth to invade
Calm speculation; but if you are wise,
Bestride your steed while cold is in the skies.

XXIV

'To-day we purpose, ay, this hour we mount
   To spur three leagues towards the Apennine;
Come down, we pray thee, ere the hot sun count
   His dewy rosary on the eglantine.'
Lorenzo, courteously as he was wont,
   Bowed a fair greeting to these serpents' whine;
And went in haste, to get in readiness,
With belt, and spur, and bracing huntsman's dress.

XXV

And as he to the court-yard passed along,
   Each third step did he pause, and listened oft
If he could hear his lady's matin-song,
   Or the light whisper of her footstep soft;
And as he thus over his passion hung,
   He heard a laugh full musical aloft,
When, looking up, he saw her features bright
Smile through an in-door lattice, all delight.

XXVI

'Love, Isabel!' said he, 'I was in pain
   Lest I should miss to bid thee a good morrow:
Ah! what if I should lose thee, when so fain
   I am to stifle all the heavy sorrow
Of a poor three hours' absence? but we'll gain
   Out of the amorous dark what day doth borrow.
Good bye! I'll soon be back.' 'Good bye!' said she –
And as he went she chanted merrily.

XXVII

So the two brothers and their murdered man
  Rode past fair Florence, to where Arno's stream
Gurgles through straitened banks, and still doth fan
  Itself with dancing bulrush, and the bream
Keeps head against the freshets. Sick and wan
  The brothers' faces in the ford did seem,
Lorenzo's flush with love. – They passed the water
Into a forest quiet for the slaughter.

XXVIII

There was Lorenzo slain and buried in,
  There in that forest did his great love cease.
Ah! when a soul doth thus its freedom win,
  It aches in loneliness – is ill at peace
As the break-covert blood-hounds of such sin.
  They dipped their swords in the water, and did tease
Their horses homeward, with convulsèd spur,
Each richer by his being a murderer.

XXIX

They told their sister how, with sudden speed,
  Lorenzo had ta'en ship for foreign lands,
Because of some great urgency and need
  In their affairs, requiring trusty hands.
Poor girl! put on thy stifling widow's weed,
  And 'scape at once from Hope's accursèd bands;
To-day thou wilt not see him, nor to-morrow,
And the next day will be a day of sorrow.

XXX

She weeps alone for pleasures not to be;
  Sorely she wept until the night came on,
And then, instead of love, O misery!
  She brooded o'er the luxury alone:
His image in the dusk she seemed to see,
  And to the silence made a gentle moan,

Spreading her perfect arms upon the air,
And on her couch low murmuring 'Where? O where?'

XXXI

But Selfishness, Love's cousin, held not long
Its fiery vigil in her single breast.
She fretted for the golden hour, and hung
Upon the time with feverish unrest –
Not long – for soon into her heart a throng
Of higher occupants, a richer zest,
Came tragic – passion not to be subdued,
And sorrow for her love in travels rude.

XXXII

In the mid days of autumn, on their eves
The breath of Winter comes from far away,
And the sick west continually bereaves
Of some gold tinge, and plays a roundelay
Of death among the bushes and the leaves,
To make all bare before he dares to stray
From his north cavern. So sweet Isabel
By gradual decay from beauty fell,

XXXIII

Because Lorenzo came not. Oftentimes
She asked her brothers, with an eye all pale,
Striving to be itself, what dungeon climes
Could keep him off so long? They spake a tale
Time after time, to quiet her. Their crimes
Came on them, like a smoke from Hinnom's vale;
And every night in dreams they groaned aloud,
To see their sister in her snowy shroud.

XXXIV

And she had died in drowsy ignorance,
But for a thing more deadly dark than all.
It came like a fierce potion, drunk by chance,
Which saves a sick man from the feathered pall

For some few gasping moments; like a lance,
   Waking an Indian from his cloudy hall
With cruel pierce, and bringing him again
Sense of the gnawing fire at heart and brain.

XXXV

It was a vision. – In the drowsy gloom,
   The dull of midnight, at her couch's foot
Lorenzo stood, and wept: the forest tomb
   Had marred his glossy hair which once could shoot
Lustre into the sun, and put cold doom
   Upon his lips, and taken the soft lute
From his lorn voice, and past his loamèd ears
Had made a miry channel for his tears.

XXXVI

Strange sound it was, when the pale shadow spake;
   For there was striving, in its piteous tongue,
To speak as when on earth it was awake,
   And Isabella on its music hung.
Languor there was in it, and tremulous shake,
   As in a palsied Druid's harp unstrung;
And through it moaned a ghostly under-song,
Like hoarse night-gusts sepulchral briars among.

XXXVII

Its eyes, though wild, were still all dewy bright
   With love, and kept all phantom fear aloof
From the poor girl by magic of their light,
   The while it did unthread the horrid woof
Of the late darkened time – the murderous spite
   Of pride and avarice, the dark pine roof
In the forest, and the sodden turfèd dell,
Where, without any word, from stabs he fell.

XXXVIII

Saying moreover, 'Isabel, my sweet!
   Red whortle-berries droop above my head,

And a large flint-stone weighs upon my feet;
  Around me beeches and high chestnuts shed
Their leaves and prickly nuts; a sheep-fold bleat
  Comes from beyond the river to my bed:
Go, shed one tear upon my heather-bloom,
And it shall comfort me within the tomb.

XXXIX

'I am a shadow now, alas! alas!
  Upon the skirts of human-nature dwelling
Alone. I chant alone the holy mass,
  While little sounds of life are round me knelling,
And glossy bees at noon do fieldward pass,
  And many a chapel bell the hour is telling,
Paining me through: those sounds grow strange to me,
And thou art distant in humanity.

XL

'I know what was, I feel full well what is,
  And I should rage, if spirits could go mad;
Though I forget the taste of earthly bliss,
  That paleness warms my grave, as though I had
A seraph chosen from the bright abyss
  To be my spouse: thy paleness makes me glad;
Thy beauty grows upon me, and I feel
A greater love through all my essence steal.'

XLI

The Spirit mourn'd 'Adieu!' – dissolved and left
  The atom darkness in a slow turmoil;
As when of healthful midnight sleep bereft,
  Thinking on rugged hours and fruitless toil,
We put our eyes into a pillowy cleft,
  And see the spangly gloom froth up and boil:
It made sad Isabella's eyelids ache,
And in the dawn she started up awake –

XLII

'Ha! ha!' said she, 'I knew not this hard life,
  I thought the worst was simple misery;
I thought some Fate with pleasure or with strife
  Portioned us – happy days, or else to die;
But there is crime – a brother's bloody knife!
  Sweet Spirit, thou hast schooled my infancy:
I'll visit thee for this, and kiss thine eyes,
And greet thee morn and even in the skies.'

XLIII

When the full morning came, she had devised
  How she might secret to the forest hie;
How she might find the clay, so dearly prized,
  And sing to it one latest lullaby;
How her short absence might be unsurmised,
  While she the inmost of the dream would try.
Resolved, she took with her an agèd nurse,
And went into that dismal forest-hearse.

XLIV

See, as they creep along the river side,
  How she doth whisper to that agèd dame,
And, after looking round the champaign wide,
  Shows her a knife. – 'What feverous hectic flame
Burns in thee, child? – What good can thee betide,
  That thou shouldst smile again?' The evening came,
And they had found Lorenzo's earthy bed –
The flint was there, the berries at his head.

XLV

Who hath not loitered in a green church-yard,
  And let his spirit, like a demon-mole,
Work through the clayey soil and gravel hard,
  To see skull, coffined bones, and funeral stole;
Pitying each form that hungry Death hath marred
  And filling it once more with human soul?

Ah! this is holiday to what was felt
When Isabella by Lorenzo knelt.

XLVI

She gazed into the fresh-thrown mould, as though
  One glance did fully all its secrets tell;
Clearly she saw, as other eyes would know
  Pale limbs at bottom of a crystal well;
Upon the murderous spot she seemed to grow,
  Like to a native lily of the dell –
Then with her knife, all sudden, she began
To dig more fervently than misers can.

XLVII

Soon she turned up a soilèd glove, whereon
  Her silk had played in purple phantasies,
She kissed it with a lip more chill than stone,
  And put it in her bosom, where it dries
And freezes utterly unto the bone
  Those dainties made to still an infant's cries:
Then 'gan she work again, nor stayed her care,
But to throw back at times her veiling hair.

XLVIII

That old nurse stood beside her wondering,
  Until her heart felt pity to the core
At sight of such a dismal labouring,
  And so she kneelèd, with her locks all hoar,
And put her lean hands to the horrid thing.
  Three hours they laboured at this travail sore –
At last they felt the kernel of the grave,
And Isabella did not stamp and rave.

XLIX

Ah! wherefore all this wormy circumstance?
  Why linger at the yawning tomb so long?
O for the gentleness of old Romance,
  The simple plaining of a minstrel's song!

Fair reader, at the old tale take a glance,
  For here, in truth, it doth not well belong
To speak – O turn thee to the very tale,
And taste the music of that vision pale.

L

With duller steel than the Persèan sword
  They cut away no formless monster's head,
But one, whose gentleness did well accord
  With death, as life. The ancient harps have said,
Love never dies, but lives, immortal Lord:
  If Love impersonate was ever dead,
Pale Isabella kissed it, and low moaned.
'Twas Love – cold, dead indeed, but not dethroned.

LI

In anxious secrecy they took it home,
  And then the prize was all for Isabel.
She calmed its wild hair with a golden comb,
  And all around each eye's sepulchral cell
Pointed each fringèd lash; the smeared loam
  With tears, as chilly as a dripping well,
She drenched away – and still she combed, and kept
Sighing all day – and still she kissed, and wept.

LII

Then in a silken scarf – sweet with the dews
  Of precious flowers plucked in Araby,
And divine liquids come with odorous ooze
  Through the cold serpent-pipe refreshfully –
She wrapped it up; and for its tomb did choose
  A garden-pot, wherein she laid it by,
And covered it with mould, and o'er it set
Sweet basil, which her tears kept ever wet.

LIII

And she forgot the stars, the moon, and sun,
  And she forgot the blue above the trees,

And she forgot the dells where waters run,
   And she forgot the chilly autumn breeze;
She had no knowledge when the day was done,
   And the new morn she saw not, but in peace
Hung over her sweet basil evermore,
And moistened it with tears unto the core.

LIV

And so she ever fed it with thin tears,
   Whence thick, and green, and beautiful it grew,
So that it smelt more balmy than its peers
   Of basil-tufts in Florence; for it drew
Nurture besides, and life, from human fears,
   From the fast mouldering head there shut from view:
So that the jewel, safely casketed,
Came forth, and in perfumèd leafits spread.

LV

O Melancholy, linger here awhile!
   O Music, Music, breathe despondingly!
O Echo, Echo, from some sombre isle,
   Unknown, Lethean, sigh to us – O sigh!
Spirits in grief, lift up your heads, and smile.
   Lift up your heads, sweet Spirits, heavily,
And make a pale light in your cypress glooms,
Tinting with silver wan your marble tombs.

LVI

Moan hither, all ye syllables of woe,
   From the deep throat of sad Melpomene!
Through bronzèd lyre in tragic order go,
   And touch the strings into a mystery;
Sound mournfully upon the winds and low;
   For simple Isabel is soon to be
Among the dead. She withers, like a palm
Cut by an Indian for its juicy balm.

LVII

O leave the palm to wither by itself;
  Let not quick Winter chill its dying hour! –
It may not be – those Baälites of pelf,
  Her brethren, noted the continual shower
From her dead eyes; and many a curious elf,
  Among her kindred, wondered that such dower
Of youth and beauty should be thrown aside
By one marked out to be a Noble's bride.

LVIII

And, furthermore, her brethren wondered much
  Why she sat drooping by the basil green,
And why it flourished, as by magic touch.
  Greatly they wondered what the thing might mean:
They could not surely give belief, that such
  A very nothing would have power to wean
Her from her own fair youth, and pleasures gay,
And even remembrance of her love's delay.

LIX

Therefore they watched a time when they might sift
  This hidden whim; and long they watched in vain:
For seldom did she go to chapel-shrift,
  And seldom felt she any hunger-pain;
And when she left, she hurried back, as swift
  As bird on wing to breast its eggs again;
And, patient as a hen-bird, sat her there
Beside her basil, weeping through her hair.

LX

Yet they contrived to steal the basil-pot,
  And to examine it in secret place.
The thing was vile with green and livid spot,
  And yet they knew it was Lorenzo's face:
The guerdon of their murder they had got,
  And so left Florence in a moment's space,

Never to turn again. Away they went,
With blood upon their heads, to banishment.

LXI

O Melancholy, turn thine eyes away!
   O Music, Music, breathe despondingly!
O Echo, Echo, on some other day,
   From isles Lethean, sigh to us – O sigh!
Spirits of grief, sing not your 'Well-a-way!'
   For Isabel, sweet Isabel, will die –
Will die a death too lone and incomplete,
Now they have ta'en away her basil sweet.

LXII

Piteous she looked on dead and senseless things,
   Asking for her lost basil amorously;
And with melodious chuckle in the strings
   Of her lorn voice, she oftentimes would cry
After the pilgrim in his wanderings,
   To ask him where her basil was, and why
'Twas hid from her: 'For cruel 'tis,' said she,
To steal my basil-pot away from me.'

LXIII

And so she pined, and so she died forlorn,
   Imploring for her basil to the last.
No heart was there in Florence but did mourn
   In pity of her love, so overcast.
And a sad ditty on this story born
   From mouth to mouth through all the country passed:
Still is the burthen sung – 'O cruelty,
To steal my basil-pot away from me!'

A Song about Myself

I

There was a naughty boy,
A naughty boy was he,
He would not stop at home,
He could not quiet be –
He took
In his knapsack
A book
Full of vowels
And a shirt
With some towels –
A slight cap
For night-cap –
A hair brush,
Comb ditto,
New stockings,
For old ones
Would split O!
This knapsack
Tight at's back
He rivetted close
And followed his nose
To the North,
To the North,
And followed his nose
To the North.

II

There was a naughty boy
And a naughty boy was he,
For nothing would he do
But scribble poetry –
He took

An inkstand
In his hand
And a pen
Big as ten
In the other
And away
In a pother
He ran
To the mountains
And fountains
And ghostès
And postès
And witches
And ditches,
And wrote
In his coat
When the weather
Was cool –
Fear of gout –
And without
When the weather
Was warm,
Och, the charm
When we choose
To follow one's nose
To the North,
To the North,
To follow one's nose
To the North!

III

There was a naughty boy
And a naughty boy was he,
He kept little fishes
In washing tubs three
In spite

Of the might
Of the maid,
Nor afraid
Of his granny-good,
He often would
Hurly burly
Get up early
And go,
By hook or crook,
To the brook
And bring home
Miller's thumb,
Tittlebat
Not over fat,
Minnows small
As the stall
Of a glove,
Not above
The size
Of a nice
Little baby's
Little finger –
O he made
('Twas his trade)
Of fish a pretty kettle,
A kettle –
A kettle,
Of fish a pretty kettle,
A kettle!

IV

There was a naughty boy,
And a naughty boy was he,
He ran away to Scotland
The people for to see –
There he found

That the ground
Was as hard,
That a yard
Was as long,
That a song
Was as merry,
That a cherry
Was as red,
That lead
Was as weighty,
That fourscore
Was as eighty,
That a door
Was as wooden
As in England –
So he stood in his shoes
And he wondered,
He wondered,
He stood in his
Shoes and he wondered.

from Hyperion. A Fragment

BOOK I, lines 1–71

Deep in the shady sadness of a vale
Far sunken from the healthy breath of morn,
Far from the fiery noon, and eve's one star,
Sat grey-haired Saturn, quiet as a stone,
Still as the silence round about his lair;
Forest on forest hung above his head
Like cloud on cloud. No stir of air was there,
Not so much life as on a summer's day
Robs not one light seed from the feathered grass,
But where the dead leaf fell, there did it rest.
A stream went voiceless by, still deadened more
By reason of his fallen divinity
Spreading a shade: the Naiad 'mid her reeds
Pressed her cold finger closer to her lips.

Along the margin-sand large foot-marks went,
No further than to where his feet had strayed,
And slept there since. Upon the sodden ground
His old right hand lay nerveless, listless, dead,
Unsceptred; and his realmless eyes were closed;
While his bowed head seemed listening to the Earth,
His ancient mother, for some comfort yet.

It seemed no force could wake him from his place;
But there came one, who with a kindred hand
Touched his wide shoulders, after bending low
With reverence, though to one who knew it not.
She was a Goddess of the infant world;
By her in stature the tall Amazon
Had stood a pigmy's height: she would have ta'en
Achilles by the hair and bent his neck;
Or with a finger stayed Ixion's wheel.

Her face was large as that of Memphian sphinx,
Pedestalled haply in a palace court,
When sages looked to Egypt for their lore.
But O! how unlike marble was that face,
How beautiful, if sorrow had not made
Sorrow more beautiful than Beauty's self.
There was a listening fear in her regard,
As if calamity had but begun;
As if the vanward clouds of evil days
Had spent their malice, and the sullen rear
Was with its storèd thunder labouring up.
One hand she pressed upon that aching spot
Where beats the human heart, as if just there,
Though an immortal, she felt cruel pain;
The other upon Saturn's bended neck
She laid, and to the level of his ear
Leaning with parted lips, some words she spake
In solemn tenor and deep organ tone –
Some mourning words, which in our feeble tongue
Would come in these like accents (O how frail
To that large utterance of the early Gods!)
'Saturn, look up! – though wherefore, poor old King?
I have no comfort for thee, no, not one:
I cannot say, "O wherefore sleepest thou?"
For heaven is parted from thee, and the earth
Knows thee not, thus afflicted, for a God;
And ocean too, with all its solemn noise,
Has from thy sceptre passed; and all the air
Is emptied of thine hoary majesty.
Thy thunder, conscious of the new command,
Rumbles reluctant o'er our fallen house;
And thy sharp lightning in unpractised hands
Scorches and burns our once serene domain.
O aching time! O moments big as years!
All as ye pass swell out the monstrous truth,
And press it so upon our weary griefs

That unbelief has not a space to breathe.
Saturn, sleep on – O thoughtless, why did I
Thus violate thy slumbrous solitude?
Why should I ope thy melancholy eyes?
Saturn, sleep on, while at thy feet I weep!'

BOOK I, lines 158–200

Meanwhile in other realms big tears were shed,
More sorrow like to this, and such like woe,
Too huge for mortal tongue or pen of scribe.
The Titans fierce, self-hid, or prison-bound,
Groaned for the old allegiance once more,
And listened in sharp pain for Saturn's voice.
But one of the whole mammoth-brood still kept
His sovereignty, and rule, and majesty –
Blazing Hyperion on his orbèd fire
Still sat, still snuffed the incense, teeming up
From man to the sun's God – yet unsecure:
For as among us mortals omens drear
Fright and perplex, so also shuddered he –
Not at dog's howl, or gloom-bird's hated screech,
Or the familiar visiting of one
Upon the first toll of his passing-bell,
Or prophesyings of the midnight lamp;
But horrors, portioned to a giant nerve,
Oft made Hyperion ache. His palace bright
Bastioned with pyramids of glowing gold,
And touched with shade of bronzèd obelisks,
Glared a blood-red through all its thousand courts,
Arches, and domes, and fiery galleries;
And all its curtains of Aurorian clouds
Flushed angerly, while sometimes eagle's wings,
Unseen before by Gods or wondering men,
Darkened the place, and neighing steeds were heard,
Not heard before by Gods or wondering men.

Also, when he would taste the spicy wreaths
Of incense, breathed aloft from sacred hills,
Instead of sweets, his ample palate took
Savour of poisonous brass and metal sick:
And so, when harboured in the sleepy west,
After the full completion of fair day,
For rest divine upon exalted couch
And slumber in the arms of melody,
He paced away the pleasant hours of ease
With stride colossal, on from hall to hall;
While far within each aisle and deep recess,
His wingèd minions in close clusters stood,
Amazed and full of fear; like anxious men
Who on wide plains gather in panting troops,
When earthquakes jar their battlements and towers.

BOOK I, lines 214–50

He entered, but he entered full of wrath;
His flaming robes streamed out beyond his heels,
And gave a roar, as if of earthly fire,
That scared away the meek ethereal Hours
And made their dove-wings tremble. On he flared,
From stately nave to nave, from vault to vault,
Through bowers of fragrant and enwreathèd light,
And diamond-pavèd lustrous long arcades,
Until he reached the great main cupola.
There standing fierce beneath, he stamped his foot,
And from the basement deep to the high towers
Jarred his own golden region; and before
The quavering thunder thereupon had ceased,
His voice leapt out, despite of god-like curb,
To this result: 'O dreams of day and night!
O monstrous forms! O effigies of pain!
O spectres busy in a cold, cold gloom!
O lank-eared Phantoms of black-weeded pools!

Why do I know ye? Why have I seen ye? Why
Is my eternal essence thus distraught
To see and to behold these horrors new?
Saturn is fallen, am I too to fall?
Am I to leave this haven of my rest,
This cradle of my glory, this soft clime,
This calm luxuriance of blissful light,
These crystalline pavilions, and pure fanes,
Of all my lucent empire? It is left
Deserted, void, nor any haunt of mine.
The blaze, the splendour, and the symmetry,
I cannot see – but darkness, death and darkness.
Even here, into my centre of repose,
The shady visions come to domineer,
Insult, and blind, and stifle up my pomp. –
Fall! – No, by Tellus and her briny robes!
Over the fiery frontier of my realms
I will advance a terrible right arm
Shall scare that infant thunderer, rebel Jove,
And bid old Saturn take his throne again.'

BOOK II, lines 167–242

So ended Saturn; and the God of the Sea,
Sophist and sage from no Athenian grove,
But cogitation in his watery shades,
Arose, with locks not oozy, and began,
In murmurs which his first-endeavouring tongue
Caught infant-like from the far-foamèd sands.
'O ye, whom wrath consumes! who, passion-stung,
Writhe at defeat, and nurse your agonies!
Shut up your senses, stifle up your ears,
My voice is not a bellows unto ire.
Yet listen, ye who will, whilst I bring proof
How ye, perforce, must be content to stoop;
And in the proof much comfort will I give,

If ye will take that comfort in its truth.
We fall by course of Nature's law, not force
Of thunder, or of Jove. Great Saturn, thou
Hast sifted well the atom-universe;
But for this reason, that thou art the King,
And only blind from sheer supremacy,
One avenue was shaded from thine eyes,
Through which I wandered to eternal truth.
And first, as thou wast not the first of powers,
So art thou not the last; it cannot be:
Thou art not the beginning nor the end.
From Chaos and parental Darkness came
Light, the first fruits of that intestine broil,
That sullen ferment, which for wondrous ends
Was ripening in itself. The ripe hour came,
And with it Light, and Light, engendering
Upon its own producer, forthwith touched
The whole enormous matter into life.
Upon that very hour, our parentage,
The Heavens, and the Earth, were manifest:
Then thou first born, and we the giant race,
Found ourselves ruling new and beauteous realms.
Now comes the pain of truth, to whom 'tis pain –
O folly! for to bear all naked truths,
And to envisage circumstance, all calm,
That is the top of sovereignty. Mark well!
As Heaven and Earth are fairer, fairer far
Than Chaos and blank Darkness, though once chiefs;
And as we show beyond that Heaven and Earth
In form and shape compact and beautiful,
In will, in action free, companionship,
And thousand other signs of purer life;
So on our heels a fresh perfection treads,
A power more strong in beauty, born of us
And fated to excel us, as we pass
In glory that old Darkness: nor are we

Thereby more conquered, than by us the rule
Of shapeless Chaos. Say, doth the dull soil
Quarrel with the proud forests it hath fed,
And feedeth still, more comely than itself?
Can it deny the chiefdom of green groves?
Or shall the tree be envious of the dove
Because it cooeth, and hath snowy wings
To wander wherewithal and find its joys?
We are such forest-trees, and our fair boughs
Have bred forth, not pale solitary doves,
But eagles golden-feathered, who do tower
Above us in their beauty, and must reign
In right thereof. For 'tis the eternal law
That first in beauty should be first in might.
Yea, by that law, another race may drive
Our conquerors to mourn as we do now.
Have ye beheld the young God of the Seas,
My dispossessor? Have ye seen his face?
Have ye beheld his chariot, foamed along
By noble wingèd creatures he hath made?
I saw him on the calmèd waters scud,
With such a glow of beauty in his eyes,
That it enforced me to bid sad farewell
To all my empire: farewell sad I took,
And hither came, to see how dolorous fate
Had wrought upon ye; and how I might best
Give consolation in this woe extreme.
Receive the truth, and let it be your balm.'

The Eve of St Agnes

I

St Agnes' Eve – Ah, bitter chill it was!
The owl, for all his feathers, was a-cold;
The hare limped trembling through the frozen grass,
And silent was the flock in woolly fold:
Numb were the Beadsman's fingers, while he told
His rosary, and while his frosted breath,
Like pious incense from a censer old,
Seemed taking flight for heaven, without a death,
Past the sweet Virgin's picture, while his prayer he saith.

II

His prayer he saith, this patient, holy man;
Then takes his lamp, and riseth from his knees,
And back returneth, meagre, barefoot, wan,
Along the chapel aisle by slow degrees:
The sculptured dead, on each side, seem to freeze,
Emprisoned in black, purgatorial rails;
Knights, ladies, praying in dumb orat'ries,
He passeth by; and his weak spirit fails
To think how they may ache in icy hoods and mails.

III

Northward he turneth through a little door,
And scarce three steps, ere Music's golden tongue
Flattered to tears this agèd man and poor;
But no – already had his deathbell rung:
The joys of all his life were said and sung:
His was harsh penance on St Agnes' Eve.
Another way he went, and soon among
Rough ashes sat he for his soul's reprieve,
And all night kept awake, for sinners' sake to grieve.

IV

That ancient Beadsman heard the prelude soft;
And so it chanced, for many a door was wide,
From hurry to and fro. Soon, up aloft,
The silver, snarling trumpets 'gan to chide:
The level chambers, ready with their pride,
Were glowing to receive a thousand guests:
The carvèd angels, ever eager-eyed,
Stared, where upon their heads the cornice rests,
With hair blown back, and wings put cross-wise on their breasts.

V

At length burst in the argent revelry,
With plume, tiara, and all rich array,
Numerous as shadows haunting faerily
The brain, new-stuffed, in youth, with triumphs gay
Of old romance. These let us wish away,
And turn, sole-thoughted, to one Lady there,
Whose heart had brooded, all that wintry day,
On love, and winged St Agnes' saintly care,
As she had heard old dames full many times declare.

VI

They told her how, upon St Agnes' Eve,
Young virgins might have visions of delight,
And soft adorings from their loves receive
Upon the honeyed middle of the night,
If ceremonies due they did aright;
As, supperless to bed they must retire,
And couch supine their beauties, lily white;
Nor look behind, nor sideways, but require
Of Heaven with upward eyes for all that they desire.

VII

Full of this whim was thoughtful Madeline:
The music, yearning like a God in pain,

She scarcely heard: her maiden eyes divine,
Fixed on the floor, saw many a sweeping train
Pass by – she heeded not at all: in vain
Came many a tip-toe, amorous cavalier,
And back retired – not cooled by high disdain,
But she saw not: her heart was otherwhere.
She sighed for Agnes' dreams, the sweetest of the year.

VIII

She danced along with vague, regardless eyes,
Anxious her lips, her breathing quick and short:
The hallowed hour was near at hand: she sighs
Amid the timbrels, and the thronged resort
Of whisperers in anger, or in sport;
'Mid looks of love, defiance, hate, and scorn,
Hoodwinked with faery fancy – all amort,
Save to St Agnes and her lambs unshorn,
And all the bliss to be before to-morrow morn.

IX

So, purposing each moment to retire,
She lingered still. Meantime, across the moors,
Had come young Porphyro, with heart on fire
For Madeline. Beside the portal doors,
Buttressed from moonlight, stands he, and implores
All saints to give him sight of Madeline
But for one moment in the tedious hours,
That he might gaze and worship all unseen;
Perchance speak, kneel, touch, kiss – in sooth such things
have been.

X

He ventures in – let no buzzed whisper tell,
All eyes be muffled, or a hundred swords
Will storm his heart, Love's fev'rous citadel:
For him, those chambers held barbarian hordes,
Hyena foemen, and hot-blooded lords,

Whose very dogs would execrations howl
Against his lineage: not one breast affords
Him any mercy, in that mansion foul,
Save one old beldame, weak in body and in soul.

XI
Ah, happy chance! the agèd creature came,
Shuffling along with ivory-headed wand,
To where he stood, hid from the torch's flame,
Behind a broad hall-pillar, far beyond
The sound of merriment and chorus bland:
He startled her; but soon she knew his face,
And grasped his fingers in her palsied hand,
Saying, 'Mercy, Porphyro! hie thee from this place:
They are all here to-night, the whole blood-thirsty race!

XII
'Get hence! get hence! there's dwarfish Hildebrand –
He had a fever late, and in the fit
He cursèd thee and thine, both house and land:
Then there's that old Lord Maurice, not a whit
More tame for his grey hairs – Alas me! flit!
Flit like a ghost away.' 'Ah, gossip dear,
We're safe enough; here in this arm-chair sit,
And tell me how –' 'Good Saints! not here, not here;
Follow me, child, or else these stones will be thy bier.'

XIII
He followed through a lowly archèd way,
Brushing the cobwebs with his lofty plume,
And as she muttered, 'Well-a – well-a-day!'
He found him in a little moonlight room,
Pale, latticed, chill, and silent as a tomb.
'Now tell me where is Madeline,' said he,
'O tell me, Angela, by the holy loom
Which none but secret sisterhood may see,
When they St Agnes' wool are weaving piously.'

XIV

'St Agnes? Ah! it is St Agnes' Eve –
Yet men will murder upon holy days:
Thou must hold water in a witch's sieve,
And be liege-lord of all the Elves and Fays,
To venture so: it fills me with amaze
To see thee, Porphyro! – St Agnes' Eve!
God's help! my lady fair the conjuror plays
This very night. Good angels her deceive!
But let me laugh awhile, I've mickle time to grieve.'

XV

Feebly she laugheth in the languid moon,
While Porphyro upon her face doth look,
Like puzzled urchin on an agèd crone
Who keepeth closed a wondrous riddle-book,
As spectacled she sits on chimney nook.
But soon his eyes grew brilliant, when she told
His lady's purpose; and he scarce could brook
Tears, at the thought of those enchantments cold,
And Madeline asleep in lap of legends old.

XVI

Sudden a thought came like a full-blown rose,
Flushing his brow, and in his painèd heart
Made purple riot; then doth he propose
A stratagem, that makes the beldame start:
'A cruel man and impious thou art:
Sweet lady, let her pray, and sleep, and dream
Alone with her good angels, far apart
From wicked men like thee. Go, go! – I deem
Thou canst not surely be the same that thou didst seem.'

XVII

'I will not harm her, by all saints I swear,'
Quoth Porphyro: 'O may I ne'er find grace
When my weak voice shall whisper its last prayer,

If one of her soft ringlets I displace,
Or look with ruffian passion in her face:
Good Angela, believe me by these tears,
Or I will, even in a moment's space,
Awake, with horrid shout, my foeman's ears,
And beard them, though they be more fanged than wolves
and bears.'

XVIII

'Ah! why wilt thou affright a feeble soul?
A poor, weak, palsy-stricken, churchyard thing,
Whose passing-bell may ere the midnight toll;
Whose prayers for thee, each morn and evening,
Were never missed.' – Thus plaining, doth she bring
A gentler speech from burning Porphyro,
So woeful, and of such deep sorrowing,
That Angela gives promise she will do
Whatever he shall wish, betide her weal or woe.

XIX

Which was, to lead him, in close secrecy,
Even to Madeline's chamber, and there hide
Him in a closet, of such privacy
That he might see her beauty unespied,
And win perhaps that night a peerless bride,
While legioned faeries paced the coverlet,
And pale enchantment held her sleepy-eyed.
Never on such a night have lovers met,
Since Merlin paid his Demon all the monstrous debt.

XX

'It shall be as thou wishest,' said the Dame:
'All cates and dainties shall be storèd there
Quickly on this feast-night; by the tambour frame
Her own lute thou wilt see. No time to spare,
For I am slow and feeble, and scarce dare
On such a catering trust my dizzy head.

Wait here, my child, with patience; kneel in prayer
The while. Ah! thou must needs the lady wed,
Or may I never leave my grave among the dead.'

XXI
So saying, she hobbled off with busy fear.
The lover's endless minutes slowly passed;
The dame returned, and whispered in his ear
To follow her; with agèd eyes aghast
From fright of dim espial. Safe at last,
Through many a dusky gallery, they gain
The maiden's chamber, silken, hushed, and chaste;
Where Porphyro took covert, pleased amain.
His poor guide hurried back with agues in her brain.

XXII
Her faltering hand upon the balustrade,
Old Angela was feeling for the stair,
When Madeline, St Agnes' charmèd maid,
Rose, like a missioned spirit, unaware:
With silver taper's light, and pious care,
She turned, and down the agèd gossip led
To a safe level matting. Now prepare,
Young Porphyro, for gazing on that bed –
She comes, she comes again, like ring-dove frayed and fled.

XXIII
Out went the taper as she hurried in;
Its little smoke, in pallid moonshine, died:
She closed the door, she panted, all akin
To spirits of the air, and visions wide –
No uttered syllable, or, woe betide!
But to her heart, her heart was voluble,
Paining with eloquence her balmy side;
As though a tongueless nightingale should swell
Her throat in vain, and die, heart-stiflèd, in her dell.

XXIV

A casement high and triple-arched there was,
All garlanded with carven imag'ries
Of fruits, and flowers, and bunches of knot-grass,
And diamonded with panes of quaint device,
Innumerable of stains and splendid dyes,
As are the tiger-moth's deep-damasked wings;
And in the midst, 'mong thousand heraldries,
And twilight saints, and dim emblazonings,
A shielded scutcheon blushed with blood of queens and
kings.

XXV

Full on this casement shone the wintry moon,
And threw warm gules on Madeline's fair breast,
As down she knelt for heaven's grace and boon;
Rose-bloom fell on her hands, together pressed,
And on her silver cross soft amethyst,
And on her hair a glory, like a saint:
She seemed a splendid angel, newly dressed,
Save wings, for Heaven – Porphyro grew faint;
She knelt, so pure a thing, so free from mortal taint.

XXVI

Anon his heart revives; her vespers done,
Of all its wreathèd pearls her hair she frees;
Unclasps her warmèd jewels one by one;
Loosens her fragrant bodice; by degrees
Her rich attire creeps rustling to her knees:
Half-hidden, like a mermaid in sea-weed,
Pensive awhile she dreams awake, and sees,
In fancy, fair St Agnes in her bed,
But dares not look behind, or all the charm is fled.

XXVII

Soon, trembling in her soft and chilly nest,
In sort of wakeful swoon, perplexed she lay

Until the poppied warmth of sleep oppressed
Her soothèd limbs, and soul fatigued away –
Flown, like a thought, until the morrow-day;
Blissfully havened both from joy and pain;
Clasped like a missal where swart Paynims pray;
Blinded alike from sunshine and from rain,
As though a rose should shut, and be a bud again.

XXVIII

Stolen to this paradise, and so entranced,
Porphyro gazed upon her empty dress,
And listened to her breathing, if it chanced
To wake into a slumbrous tenderness;
Which when he heard, that minute did he bless,
And breathed himself: then from the closet crept,
Noiseless as fear in a wide wilderness,
And over the hushed carpet, silent, stepped,
And 'tween the curtains peeped, where, lo! – how fast she slept.

XXIX

Then by the bed-side, where the faded moon
Made a dim, silver twilight, soft he set
A table, and, half anguished, threw thereon
A cloth of woven crimson, gold, and jet –
O for some drowsy Morphean amulet!
The boisterous, midnight, festive clarion,
The kettle-drum, and far-heard clarinet,
Affray his ears, though but in dying tone;
The hall door shuts again, and all the noise is gone.

XXX

And still she slept an azure-lidded sleep,
In blanchèd linen, smooth, and lavendered,
While he from forth the closet brought a heap
Of candied apple, quince, and plum, and gourd,
With jellies soother than the creamy curd,

And lucent syrups, tinct with cinnamon;
Manna and dates, in argosy transferred
From Fez; and spicèd dainties, every one,
From silken Samarkand to cedared Lebanon.

XXXI

These delicates he heaped with glowing hand
On golden dishes and in baskets bright
Of wreathèd silver; sumptuous they stand
In the retirèd quiet of the night,
Filling the chilly room with perfume light.
'And now, my love, my seraph fair, awake!
Thou art my heaven, and I thine eremite:
Open thine eyes, for meek St Agnes' sake,
Or I shall drowse beside thee, so my soul doth ache.'

XXXII

Thus whispering, his warm, unnervèd arm
Sank in her pillow. Shaded was her dream
By the dusk curtains – 'twas a midnight charm
Impossible to melt as icèd stream.
The lustrous salvers in the moonlight gleam;
Broad golden fringe upon the carpet lies.
It seemed he never, never could redeem
From such a steadfast spell his lady's eyes;
So mused awhile, entoiled in woofèd fantasies.

XXXIII

Awakening up, he took her hollow lute,
Tumultuous, and, in chords that tenderest be,
He played an ancient ditty, long since mute,
In Provence called, 'La belle dame sans mercy',
Close to her ear touching the melody –
Wherewith disturbed, she uttered a soft moan:
He ceased – she panted quick – and suddenly
Her blue affrayèd eyes wide open shone.
Upon his knees he sank, pale as smooth-sculptured stone.

XXXIV

Her eyes were open, but she still beheld,
Now wide awake, the vision of her sleep –
There was a painful change, that nigh expelled
The blisses of her dream so pure and deep.
At which fair Madeline began to weep,
And moan forth witless words with many a sigh,
While still her gaze on Porphyro would keep;
Who knelt, with joinèd hands and piteous eye,
Fearing to move or speak, she looked so dreamingly.

XXXV

'Ah, Porphyro!' said she, 'but even now
Thy voice was at sweet tremble in mine ear,
Made tuneable with every sweetest vow,
And those sad eyes were spiritual and clear:
How changed thou art! How pallid, chill, and drear!
Give me that voice again, my Porphyro,
Those looks immortal, those complainings dear!
O leave me not in this eternal woe,
For if thou diest, my Love, I know not where to go.'

XXXVI

Beyond a mortal man impassioned far
At these voluptuous accents, he arose,
Ethereal, flushed, and like a throbbing star
Seen mid the sapphire heaven's deep repose;
Into her dream he melted, as the rose
Blendeth its odour with the violet –
Solution sweet. Meantime the frost-wind blows
Like Love's alarum pattering the sharp sleet
Against the window-panes; St Agnes' moon hath set.

XXXVII

'Tis dark: quick pattereth the flaw-blown sleet.
'This is no dream, my bride, my Madeline!'
'Tis dark: the icèd gusts still rave and beat.

'No dream, alas! alas! and woe is mine!
Porphyro will leave me here to fade and pine. –
Cruel! what traitor could thee hither bring?
I curse not, for my heart is lost in thine,
Though thou forsakest a deceivèd thing –
A dove forlorn and lost with sick unprunèd wing.'

XXXVIII

'My Madeline! sweet dreamer! lovely bride!
Say, may I be for aye thy vassal blessed?
Thy beauty's shield, heart-shaped and vermeil dyed?
Ah, silver shrine, here will I take my rest
After so many hours of toil and quest,
A famished pilgrim – saved by miracle.
Though I have found, I will not rob thy nest
Saving of thy sweet self; if thou think'st well
To trust, fair Madeline, to no rude infidel.

XXXIX

Hark! 'tis an elfin-storm from faery land,
Of haggard seeming, but a boon indeed:
Arise – arise! the morning is at hand,
The bloated wassaillers will never heed –
Let us away, my love, with happy speed –
There are no ears to hear, or eyes to see,
Drowned all in Rhenish and the sleepy mead;
Awake! arise! my love, and fearless be,
For o'er the southern moors I have a home for thee.'

XL

She hurried at his words, beset with fears,
For there were sleeping dragons all around,
At glaring watch, perhaps, with ready spears –
Down the wide stairs a darkling way they found.
In all the house was heard no human sound.
A chain-drooped lamp was flickering by each door;
The arras, rich with horseman, hawk, and hound,

Fluttered in the besieging wind's uproar;
And the long carpets rose along the gusty floor.

XLI

They glide, like phantoms, into the wide hall;
Like phantoms, to the iron porch, they glide;
Where lay the Porter, in uneasy sprawl,
With a huge empty flaggon by his side:
The wakeful bloodhound rose, and shook his hide,
But his sagacious eye an inmate owns.
By one, and one, the bolts full easy slide –
The chains lie silent on the footworn stones –
The key turns, and the door upon its hinges groans.

XLII

And they are gone – ay, ages long ago
These lovers fled away into the storm.
That night the Baron dreamt of many a woe,
And all his warrior-guests, with shade and form
Of witch, and demon, and large coffin-worm,
Were long be-nightmared. Angela the old
Died palsy-twitched, with meagre face deform;
The Beadsman, after thousand aves told,
For aye unsought for slept among his ashes cold.

La Belle Dame sans Merci. A Ballad

I

O what can ail thee, knight-at-arms,
Alone and palely loitering?
The sedge has withered from the lake,
And no birds sing.

II

O what can ail thee, knight-at-arms,
So haggard and so woe-begone?
The squirrel's granary is full,
And the harvest's done.

III

I see a lily on thy brow,
With anguish moist and fever-dew,
And on thy cheeks a fading rose
Fast withereth too.

IV

I met a lady in the meads,
Full beautiful – a faery's child,
Her hair was long, her foot was light,
And her eyes were wild.

V

I made a garland for her head,
And bracelets too, and fragrant zone;
She looked at me as she did love,
And made sweet moan.

VI

I set her on my pacing steed,
And nothing else saw all day long,
For sidelong would she bend, and sing
A faery's song.

VII

She found me roots of relish sweet,
And honey wild, and manna-dew,
And sure in language strange she said –
'I love thee true'.

VIII

She took me to her elfin grot,
And there she wept and sighed full sore,
And there I shut her wild wild eyes
With kisses four.

IX

And there she lullèd me asleep
And there I dreamed – Ah! woe betide! –
The latest dream I ever dreamt
On the cold hill side.

X

I saw pale kings and princes too,
Pale warriors, death-pale were they all;
They cried – 'La Belle Dame sans Merci
Thee hath in thrall!'

XI

I saw their starved lips in the gloam,
With horrid warning gapèd wide,
And I awoke and found me here,
On the cold hill's side.

XII

And this is why I sojourn here
Alone and palely loitering,
Though the sedge is withered from the lake,
And no birds sing.

Ode to Psyche

O Goddess! hear these tuneless numbers, wrung
  By sweet enforcement and remembrance dear,
And pardon that thy secrets should be sung
  Even into thine own soft-conchèd ear:
Surely I dreamt to-day, or did I see
  The wingèd Psyche with awakened eyes?
I wandered in a forest thoughtlessly,
  And, on the sudden, fainting with surprise,
Saw two fair creatures, couchèd side by side
  In deepest grass, beneath the whispering roof
  Of leaves and tremblèd blossoms, where there ran
    A brooklet, scarce espied:
'Mid hushed, cool-rooted flowers, fragrant-eyed,
  Blue, silver-white, and budded Tyrian,
They lay calm-breathing on the bedded grass;
  Their arms embraced, and their pinions too;
  Their lips touched not, but had not bade adieu,
As if disjoinèd by soft-handed slumber,
And ready still past kisses to outnumber
  At tender eye-dawn of aurorean love:
    The wingèd boy I knew;
  But who wast thou, O happy, happy dove?
    His Psyche true!

O latest born and loveliest vision far
  Of all Olympus' faded hierarchy!
Fairer than Phoebe's sapphire-regioned star
  Or Vesper, amorous glow-worm of the sky;
Fairer than these, though temple thou hast none,
    Nor altar heaped with flowers;
Nor virgin-choir to make delicious moan
    Upon the midnight hours;
No voice, no lute, no pipe, no incense sweet

From chain-swung censer teeming;
No shrine, no grove, no oracle, no heat
Of pale-mouthed prophet dreaming.

O brightest! though too late for antique vows,
Too, too late for the fond believing lyre,
When holy were the haunted forest boughs,
Holy the air, the water, and the fire;
Yet even in these days so far retired
From happy pieties, thy lucent fans,
Fluttering among the faint Olympians,
I see, and sing, by my own eyes inspired.
So let me be thy choir, and make a moan
Upon the midnight hours;
Thy voice, thy lute, thy pipe, thy incense sweet
From swingèd censer teeming –
Thy shrine, thy grove, thy oracle, thy heat
Of pale-mouthed prophet dreaming.

Yes, I will be thy priest, and build a fane
In some untrodden region of my mind,
Where branchèd thoughts, new grown with pleasant pain,
Instead of pines shall murmur in the wind:
Far, far around shall those dark-clustered trees
Fledge the wild-ridgèd mountains steep by steep;
And there by zephyrs, streams, and birds, and bees,
The moss-lain Dryads shall be lulled to sleep;
And in the midst of this wide quietness
A rosy sanctuary will I dress
With the wreathed trellis of a working brain,
With buds, and bells, and stars without a name,
With all the gardener Fancy e'er could feign,
Who breeding flowers, will never breed the same:
And there shall be for thee all soft delight
That shadowy thought can win,
A bright torch, and a casement ope at night,
To let the warm Love in!

Ode on a Grecian Urn

I

Thou still unravished bride of quietness,
  Thou foster-child of silence and slow time,
Sylvan historian, who canst thus express
  A flowery tale more sweetly than our rhyme:
What leaf-fringed legend haunts about thy shape
  Of deities or mortals, or of both,
    In Tempe or the dales of Arcady?
  What men or gods are these? What maidens loth?
What mad pursuit? What struggle to escape?
    What pipes and timbrels? What wild ecstasy?

II

Heard melodies are sweet, but those unheard
  Are sweeter; therefore, ye soft pipes, play on;
Not to the sensual ear, but, more endeared,
  Pipe to the spirit ditties of no tone:
Fair youth, beneath the trees, thou canst not leave
  Thy song, nor ever can those trees be bare;
    Bold Lover, never, never canst thou kiss,
Though winning near the goal – yet, do not grieve:
  She cannot fade, though thou hast not thy bliss,
    For ever wilt thou love, and she be fair!

III

Ah, happy, happy boughs! that cannot shed
  Your leaves, nor ever bid the Spring adieu;
And, happy melodist, unwearièd,
  For ever piping songs for ever new;
More happy love! more happy, happy love!
  For ever warm and still to be enjoyed,

For ever panting, and for ever young –
All breathing human passion far above,
That leaves a heart high-sorrowful and cloyed,
A burning forehead, and a parching tongue.

IV

Who are these coming to the sacrifice?
To what green altar, O mysterious priest,
Lead'st thou that heifer lowing at the skies,
And all her silken flanks with garlands dressed?
What little town by river or sea shore,
Or mountain-built with peaceful citadel,
Is emptied of this folk, this pious morn?
And, little town, thy streets for evermore
Will silent be; and not a soul to tell
Why thou art desolate, can e'er return.

V

O Attic shape! Fair attitude! with brede
Of marble men and maidens overwrought,
With forest branches and the trodden weed;
Thou, silent form, dost tease us out of thought
As doth eternity: Cold Pastoral!
When old age shall this generation waste,
Thou shalt remain, in midst of other woe
Than ours, a friend to man, to whom thou say'st,
'Beauty is truth, truth beauty, – that is all
Ye know on earth, and all ye need to know.'

Ode to a Nightingale

I

My heart aches, and a drowsy numbness pains
  My sense, as though of hemlock I had drunk,
Or emptied some dull opiate to the drains
  One minute past, and Lethe-wards had sunk:
'Tis not through envy of thy happy lot,
  But being too happy in thine happiness –
    That thou, light-wingèd Dryad of the trees,
      In some melodious plot
  Of beechen green, and shadows numberless,
    Singest of summer in full-throated ease.

II

O, for a draught of vintage! that hath been
  Cooled a long age in the deep-delvèd earth,
Tasting of Flora and the country green,
  Dance, and Provençal song, and sunburnt mirth!
O for a beaker full of the warm South,
  Full of the true, the blushful Hippocrene,
    With beaded bubbles winking at the brim,
      And purple-stainèd mouth,
  That I might drink, and leave the world unseen,
    And with thee fade away into the forest dim –

III

Fade far away, dissolve, and quite forget
  What thou among the leaves hast never known,
The weariness, the fever, and the fret
  Here, where men sit and hear each other groan;
Where palsy shakes a few, sad, last grey hairs,
  Where youth grows pale, and spectre-thin, and dies;

Where but to think is to be full of sorrow
And leaden-eyed despairs;
Where Beauty cannot keep her lustrous eyes,
Or new Love pine at them beyond to-morrow.

IV

Away! away! for I will fly to thee,
Not charioted by Bacchus and his pards,
But on the viewless wings of Poesy,
Though the dull brain perplexes and retards.
Already with thee! tender is the night,
And haply the Queen-Moon is on her throne,
Clustered around by all her starry Fays;
But here there is no light,
Save what from heaven is with the breezes blown
Through verdurous glooms and winding mossy ways.

V

I cannot see what flowers are at my feet,
Nor what soft incense hangs upon the boughs,
But, in embalmèd darkness, guess each sweet
Wherewith the seasonable month endows
The grass, the thicket, and the fruit-tree wild –
White hawthorn, and the pastoral eglantine;
Fast fading violets covered up in leaves;
And mid-May's eldest child,
The coming musk-rose, full of dewy wine,
The murmurous haunt of flies on summer eves.

VI

Darkling I listen; and, for many a time
I have been half in love with easeful Death,
Called him soft names in many a musèd rhyme,
To take into the air my quiet breath;

Now more than ever seems it rich to die,
To cease upon the midnight with no pain,
While thou art pouring forth thy soul abroad
In such an ecstasy!
Still wouldst thou sing, and I have ears in vain –
To thy high requiem become a sod.

VII

Thou wast not born for death, immortal Bird!
No hungry generations tread thee down;
The voice I hear this passing night was heard
In ancient days by emperor and clown:
Perhaps the self-same song that found a path
Through the sad heart of Ruth, when, sick for home,
She stood in tears amid the alien corn;
The same that oft-times hath
Charmed magic casements, opening on the foam
Of perilous seas, in faery lands forlorn.

VIII

Forlorn! the very word is like a bell
To toll me back from thee to my sole self!
Adieu! the fancy cannot cheat so well
As she is famed to do, deceiving elf.
Adieu! adieu! thy plaintive anthem fades
Past the near meadows, over the still stream,
Up the hill-side; and now 'tis buried deep
In the next valley-glades:
Was it a vision, or a waking dream?
Fled is that music – Do I wake or sleep?

Ode on Melancholy

I

No, no, go not to Lethe, neither twist
  Wolf's-bane, tight-rooted, for its poisonous wine:
Nor suffer thy pale forehead to be killed
  By nightshade, ruby grape of Proserpine;
Make not your rosary of yew-berries,
  Nor let the beetle, not the death-moth be
    Your mournful Psyche, nor the downy owl
A partner in your sorrow's mysteries;
  For shade to shade will come too drowsily,
    And drown the wakeful anguish of the soul.

II

But when the melancholy fit shall fall
  Sudden from heaven like a weeping cloud,
That fosters the droop-headed flowers all,
  And hides the green hill in an April shroud;
Then glut thy sorrow on a morning rose,
  Or on the rainbow of the salt sand-wave,
    Or on the wealth of globèd peonies;
Or if thy mistress some rich anger shows,
  Emprison her soft hand, and let her rave,
    And feed deep, deep upon her peerless eyes.

III

She dwells with Beauty – Beauty that must die;
  And Joy, whose hand is ever at his lips
Bidding adieu; and aching Pleasure nigh,
  Turning to poison while the bee-mouth sips:
Ay, in the very temple of Delight
  Veiled Melancholy has her sovran shrine,

Though seen of none save him whose strenuous tongue
Can burst Joy's grape against his palate fine;
His soul shall taste the sadness of her might,
And be among her cloudy trophies hung.

Ode on Indolence

They toil not, neither do they spin

I

One morn before me were three figures seen,
  With bowèd necks, and joinèd hands, side-faced;
And one behind the other stepped serene,
  In placid sandals, and in white robes graced;
They passed, like figures on a marble urn,
  When shifted round to see the other side;
    They came again; as when the urn once more
Is shifted round, the first seen shades return;
  And they were strange to me, as may betide
    With vases, to one deep in Phidian lore.

II

How is it, Shadows! that I knew ye not?
  How came ye muffled in so hush a masque?
Was it a silent deep-disguisèd plot
  To steal away, and leave without a task
My idle days? Ripe was the drowsy hour;
  The blissful cloud of summer-indolence
    Benumbed my eyes; my pulse grew less and less;
Pain had no sting, and pleasure's wreath no flower:
  O, why did ye not melt, and leave my sense
    Unhaunted quite of all but – nothingness?

III

A third time passed they by, and, passing, turned
  Each one the face a moment whiles to me;
Then faded, and to follow them I burned
  And ached for wings because I knew the three;
The first was a fair Maid, and Love her name;

The second was Ambition, pale of cheek,
    And ever watchful with fatiguèd eye;
The last, whom I love more, the more of blame
  Is heaped upon her, maiden most unmeek –
    I knew to be my demon Poesy.

IV

They faded, and, forsooth! I wanted wings.
  O folly! What is love! and where is it?
And, for that poor Ambition – it springs
  From a man's little heart's short fever-fit.
For Poesy! – no, she has not a joy –
  At least for me – so sweet as drowsy noons,
    And evenings steeped in honeyed indolence.
O, for an age so sheltered from annoy,
  That I may never know how change the moons,
    Or hear the voice of busy common-sense!

V

A third time came they by – alas! wherefore?
  My sleep had been embroidered with dim dreams;
My soul had been a lawn besprinkled o'er
  With flowers, and stirring shades, and baffled beams:
The morn was clouded, but no shower fell,
  Though in her lids hung the sweet tears of May;
    The open casement pressed a new-leaved vine,
  Let in the budding warmth and throstle's lay;
O Shadows! 'twas a time to bid farewell!
    Upon your skirts had fallen no tears of mine.

VI

So, ye three Ghosts, adieu! Ye cannot raise
  My head cool-bedded in the flowery grass;
For I would not be dieted with praise,

A pet-lamb in a sentimental farce!
Fade softly from my eyes, and be once more
In masque-like figures on the dreamy urn.
Farewell! I yet have visions for the night,
And for the day faint visions there is store.
Vanish, ye Phantoms! from my idle sprite,
Into the clouds, and never more return!

Lamia

PART I

Upon a time, before the faery broods
Drove Nymph and Satyr from the prosperous woods,
Before King Oberon's bright diadem,
Sceptre, and mantle, clasped with dewy gem,
Frighted away the Dryads and the Fauns
From rushes green, and brakes, and cowslipped lawns,
The ever-smitten Hermes empty left
His golden throne, bent warm on amorous theft:
From high Olympus had he stolen light,
On this side of Jove's clouds, to escape the sight
Of his great summoner, and made retreat
Into a forest on the shores of Crete.
For somewhere in that sacred island dwelt
A nymph, to whom all hoofèd Satyrs knelt,
At whose white feet the languid Tritons poured
Pearls, while on land they withered and adored.
Fast by the springs where she to bathe was wont,
And in those meads where sometime she might haunt,
Were strewn rich gifts, unknown to any Muse,
Though Fancy's casket were unlocked to choose.
Ah, what a world of love was at her feet!
So Hermes thought, and a celestial heat
Burnt from his wingèd heels to either ear,
That from a whiteness, as the lily clear,
Blushed into roses 'mid his golden hair,
Fallen in jealous curls about his shoulders bare.

From vale to vale, from wood to wood, he flew,
Breathing upon the flowers his passion new,
And wound with many a river to its head
To find where this sweet nymph prepared her secret bed.
In vain; the sweet nymph might nowhere be found,

And so he rested, on the lonely ground,
Pensive, and full of painful jealousies
Of the Wood-Gods, and even the very trees.
There as he stood, he heard a mournful voice,
Such as, once heard, in gentle heart destroys
All pain but pity; thus the lone voice spake:
'When from this wreathèd tomb shall I awake!
When move in a sweet body fit for life,
And love, and pleasure, and the ruddy strife
Of hearts and lips! Ah, miserable me!'
The God, dove-footed, glided silently
Round bush and tree, soft-brushing, in his speed,
The taller grasses and full-flowering weed,
Until he found a palpitating snake,
Bright, and cirque-couchant in a dusky brake.

She was a gordian shape of dazzling hue,
Vermilion-spotted, golden, green, and blue;
Striped like a zebra, freckled like a pard,
Eyed like a peacock, and all crimson barred;
And full of silver moons, that, as she breathed,
Dissolved, or brighter shone, or interwreathed
Their lustres with the gloomier tapestries –
So rainbow-sided, touched with miseries,
She seemed, at once, some penanced lady elf,
Some demon's mistress, or the demon's self.
Upon her crest she wore a wannish fire
Sprinkled with stars, like Ariadne's tiar;
Her head was serpent, but ah, bitter-sweet!
She had a woman's mouth with all its pearls complete;
And for her eyes – what could such eyes do there
But weep, and weep, that they were born so fair,
As Proserpine still weeps for her Sicilian air.
Her throat was serpent, but the words she spake
Came, as through bubbling honey, for Love's sake,
And thus – while Hermes on his pinions lay,

Like a stooped falcon ere he takes his prey –

'Fair Hermes, crowned with feathers, fluttering light,
I had a splendid dream of thee last night:
I saw thee sitting, on a throne of gold,
Among the Gods, upon Olympus old,
The only sad one; for thou didst not hear
The soft, lute-fingered Muses chanting clear,
Nor even Apollo when he sang alone,
Deaf to his throbbing throat's long, long melodious moan.
I dreamt I saw thee, robed in purple flakes,
Break amorous through the clouds, as morning breaks,
And, swiftly as a bright Phoebean dart,
Strike for the Cretan isle; and here thou art!
Too gentle Hermes, hast thou found the maid?'
Whereat the star of Lethe not delayed
His rosy eloquence, and thus inquired:
'Thou smooth-lipped serpent, surely high inspired!
Thou beauteous wreath, with melancholy eyes,
Possess whatever bliss thou canst devise,
Telling me only where my nymph is fled –
Where she doth breathe!' 'Bright planet, thou hast said,'
Returned the snake, 'but seal with oaths, fair God!'
'I swear,' said Hermes, 'by my serpent rod,
And by thine eyes, and by thy starry crown!'
Light flew his earnest words, among the blossoms blown.
Then thus again the brilliant feminine:
'Too frail of heart! for this lost nymph of thine,
Free as the air, invisibly, she strays
About these thornless wilds; her pleasant days
She tastes unseen; unseen her nimble feet
Leave traces in the grass and flowers sweet;
From weary tendrils, and bowed branches green,
She plucks the fruit unseen, she bathes unseen;
And by my power is her beauty veiled
To keep it unaffronted, unassailed
By the love-glances of unlovely eyes

Of Satyrs, Fauns, and bleared Silenus' sighs.
Pale grew her immortality, for woe
Of all these lovers, and she grievèd so
I took compassion on her, bade her steep
Her hair in weïrd syrops, that would keep
Her loveliness invisible, yet free
To wander as she loves, in liberty.
Thou shalt behold her, Hermes, thou alone,
If thou wilt, as thou swearest, grant my boon!'
Then, once again, the charmèd God began
An oath, and through the serpent's ears it ran
Warm, tremulous, devout, psalterian.
Ravished, she lifted her Circean head,
Blushed a live damask, and swift-lisping said,
'I was a woman, let me have once more
A woman's shape, and charming as before.
I love a youth of Corinth – O the bliss!
Give me my woman's form, and place me where he is.
Stoop, Hermes, let me breathe upon thy brow,
And thou shalt see they sweet nymph even now.'
The God on half-shut feathers sank serene,
She breathed upon his eyes, and swift was seen
Of both the guarded nymph near-smiling on the green.
It was no dream; or say a dream it was,
Real are the dreams of Gods, and smoothly pass
Their pleasures in a long immortal dream.
One warm, flushed moment, hovering, it might seem
Dashed by the wood-nymph's beauty, so he burned;
Then, lighting on the printless verdure, turned
To the swooned serpent, and with languid arm,
Delicate, put to proof the lithe Caducean charm.
So done, upon the nymph his eyes he bent
Full of adoring tears and blandishment,
And towards her stepped: she, like a moon in wane,
Faded before him, cowered, nor could restrain
Her fearful sobs, self-folding like a flower

That faints into itself at evening hour:
But the God fostering her chillèd hand,
She felt the warmth, her eyelids opened bland,
And, like new flowers at morning song of bees,
Bloomed, and gave up her honey to the lees.
Into the green-recessèd woods they flew;
Nor grew they pale, as mortal lovers do.

Left to herself, the serpent now began
To change; her elfin blood in madness ran,
Her mouth foamed, and the grass, therewith besprent,
Withered at dew so sweet and virulent;
Her eyes in torture fixed, and anguish drear,
Hot, glazed, and wide, with lid-lashes all sear,
Flashed phosphor and sharp sparks, without one cooling tear.
The colours all inflamed throughout her train,
She writhed about, convulsed with scarlet pain:
A deep volcanian yellow took the place
Of all her milder-moonèd body's grace;
And, as the lava ravishes the mead,
Spoilt all her silver mail, and golden brede;
Made gloom of all her frecklings, streaks and bars,
Eclipsed her crescents, and licked up her stars.
So that, in moments few, she was undressed
Of all her sapphires, greens, and amethyst,
And rubious-argent; of all these bereft,
Nothing but pain and ugliness were left.
Still shone her crown; that vanished, also she
Melted and disappeared as suddenly;
And in the air, her new voice luting soft,
Cried, 'Lycius! gentle Lycius!' – Borne aloft
With the bright mists about the mountains hoar
These words dissolved: Crete's forests heard no more.

Whither fled Lamia, now a lady bright,
A full-born beauty new and exquisite?
She fled into that valley they pass o'er

Who go to Corinth from Cenchreas' shore;
And rested at the foot of those wild hills,
The rugged founts of the Peræan rills,
And of that other ridge whose barren back
Stretches, with all its mist and cloudy rack,
South-westward to Cleone. There she stood
About a young bird's flutter from a wood,
Fair, on a sloping green of mossy tread,
By a clear pool, wherein she passionèd
To see herself escaped from so sore ills,
While her robes flaunted with the daffodils.

Ah, happy Lycius! – for she was a maid
More beautiful than ever twisted braid,
Or sighed, or blushed, or on spring-flowered lea
Spread a green kirtle to the minstrelsy:
A virgin purest lipped, yet in the lore
Of love deep learnèd to the red heart's core;
Not one hour old, yet of sciential brain
To unperplex bliss from its neighbour pain,
Define their pettish limits, and estrange
Their points of contact, and swift counterchange;
Intrigue with the specious chaos, and dispart
Its most ambiguous atoms with sure art;
As though in Cupid's college she had spent
Sweet days a lovely graduate, still unshent,
And kept his rosy terms in idle languishment.

Why this fair creature chose so faerily
By the wayside to linger, we shall see;
But first 'tis fit to tell how she could muse
And dream, when in the serpent prison-house,
Of all she list, strange or magnificent:
How, ever, where she willed, her spirit went;
Whether to faint Elysium, or where
Down through tress-lifting waves the Nereids fair
Wind into Thetis' bower by many a pearly stair;

Or where God Bacchus drains his cups divine,
Stretched out, at ease, beneath a glutinous pine;
Or where in Pluto's gardens palatine
Mulciber's columns gleam in far piazzian line.
And sometimes into cities she would send
Her dream, with feast and rioting to blend;
And once, while among mortals dreaming thus,
She saw the young Corinthian Lycius
Charioting foremost in the envious race,
Like a young Jove with calm uneager face,
And fell into a swooning love of him.
Now on the moth-time of that evening dim
He would return that way, as well she knew,
To Corinth from the shore; for freshly blew
The eastern soft wind, and his galley now
Grated the quaystones with her brazen prow
In port Cenchreas, from Egina isle
Fresh anchored; whither he had been awhile
To sacrifice to Jove, whose temple there
Waits with high marble doors for blood and incense rare.
Jove heard his vows, and bettered his desire;
For by some freakful chance he made retire
From his companions, and set forth to walk,
Perhaps grown wearied of their Corinth talk:
Over the solitary hills he fared,
Thoughtless at first, but ere eve's star appeared
His fantasy was lost, where reason fades,
In the calmed twilight of Platonic shades.
Lamia beheld him coming, near, more near –
Close to her passing, in indifference drear,
His silent sandals swept the mossy green;
So neighboured to him, and yet so unseen
She stood: he passed, shut up in mysteries,
His mind wrapped like his mantle, while her eyes
Followed his steps, and her neck regal white
Turned – syllabling thus, 'Ah, Lycius bright,

And will you leave me on the hills alone?
Lycius, look back! and be some pity shown.'
He did – not with cold wonder fearingly,
But Orpheus-like at an Eurydice –
For so delicious were the words she sung,
It seemed he had loved them a whole summer long.
And soon his eyes had drunk her beauty up,
Leaving no drop in the bewildering cup,
And still the cup was full – while he, afraid
Lest she should vanish ere his lip had paid
Due adoration, thus began to adore
(Her soft look growing coy, she saw his chain so sure):
'Leave thee alone! Look back! Ah, Goddess, see
Whether my eyes can ever turn from thee!
For pity do not this sad heart belie –
Even as thou vanished so I shall die.
Stay! though a Naiad of the rivers, stay!
To thy far wishes will thy streams obey.
Stay! though the greenest woods be thy domain,
Alone they can drink up the morning rain:
Though a descended Pleiad, will not one
Of thine harmonious sisters keep in tune
Thy spheres, and as thy silver proxy shine?
So sweetly to these ravished ears of mine
Came thy sweet greeting, that if thou shouldst fade
Thy memory will waste me to a shade –
For pity do not melt!' – 'If I should stay,'
Said Lamia, 'here, upon this floor of clay,
And pain my steps upon these flowers too rough,
What canst thou say or do of charm enough
To dull the nice remembrance of my home?
Thou canst not ask me with thee here to roam
Over these hills and vales, where no joy is –
Empty of immortality and bliss!
Thou art a scholar, Lycius, and must know
That finer spirits cannot breathe below

In human climes, and live. Alas! poor youth,
What taste of purer air hast thou to soothe
My essence? What serener palaces,
Where I may all my many senses please,
And by mysterious sleights a hundred thirsts appease?
It cannot be – Adieu!' So said, she rose
Tip-toe with white arms spread. He, sick to lose
The amorous promise of her lone complain,
Swooned, murmuring of love, and pale with pain.
The cruel lady, without any show
Of sorrow for her tender favourite's woe,
But rather, if her eyes could brighter be,
With brighter eyes and slow amenity,
Put her new lips to his, and gave afresh
The life she had so tangled in her mesh;
And as he from one trance was wakening
Into another, she began to sing,
Happy in beauty, life, and love, and every thing,
A song of love, too sweet for earthly lyres,
While, like held breath, the stars drew in their panting fires.
And then she whispered in such trembling tone,
As those who, safe together met alone
For the first time through many anguished days,
Use other speech than looks; bidding him raise
His drooping head, and clear his soul of doubt,
For that she was a woman, and without
Any more subtle fluid in her veins
Than throbbing blood, and that the self-same pains
Inhabited her frail-strung heart as his.
And next she wondered how his eyes could miss
Her face so long in Corinth, where, she said,
She dwelt but half retired, and there had led
Days happy as the gold coin could invent
Without the aid of love; yet in content
Till she saw him, as once she passed him by,
Where 'gainst a column he leant thoughtfully

At Venus' temple porch, 'mid baskets heaped
Of amorous herbs and flowers, newly reaped
Late on that eve, as 'twas the night before
The Adonian feast; whereof she saw no more,
But wept alone those days, for why should she adore?
Lycius from death awoke into amaze,
To see her still, and singing so sweet lays;
Then from amaze into delight he fell
To hear her whisper woman's lore so well;
And every word she spake enticed him on
To unperplexed delight and pleasure known.
Let the mad poets say whate'er they please
Of the sweets of Faeries, Peris, Goddesses,
There is not such a treat among them all,
Haunters of cavern, lake, and waterfall,
As a real woman, lineal indeed
From Pyrrha's pebbles or old Adam's seed.
Thus gentle Lamia judged, and judged aright,
That Lycius could not love in half a fright,
So threw the goddess off, and won his heart
More pleasantly by playing woman's part,
With no more awe than what her beauty gave,
That, while it smote, still guaranteed to save.
Lycius to all made eloquent reply,
Marrying to every word a twinborn sigh;
And last, pointing to Corinth, asked her sweet,
If 'twas too far that night for her soft feet.
The way was short, for Lamia's eagerness
Made, by a spell, the triple league decrease
To a few paces; not at all surmised
By blinded Lycius, so in her comprised.
They passed the city gates, he knew not how,
So noiseless, and he never thought to know.

As men talk in a dream, so Corinth all,
Throughout her palaces imperial,

And all her populous streets and temples lewd,
Muttered, like tempest in the distance brewed,
To the wide-spreaded night above her towers.
Men, women, rich and poor, in the cool hours,
Shuffled their sandals o'er the pavement white,
Companioned or alone; while many a light
Flared, here and there, from wealthy festivals,
And threw their moving shadows on the walls,
Or found them clustered in the corniced shade
Of some arched temple door, or dusky colonnade.

Muffling his face, of greeting friends in fear,
Her fingers he pressed hard, as one came near
With curled grey beard, sharp eyes, and smooth bald crown,
Slow-stepped, and robed in philosophic gown:
Lycius shrank closer, as they met and passed,
Into his mantle, adding wings to haste,
While hurried Lamia trembled: 'Ah,' said he,
'Why do you shudder, love, so ruefully?
Why does your tender palm dissolve in dew?' –
'I'm wearied,' said fair Lamia, 'tell me who
Is that old man? I cannot bring to mind
His features – Lycius! wherefore did you blind
Yourself from his quick eyes?' Lycius replied,
' 'Tis Apollonius sage, my trusty guide
And good instructor; but tonight he seems
The ghost of folly haunting my sweet dreams.'

While yet he spake they had arrived before
A pillared porch, with lofty portal door,
Where hung a silver lamp, whose phosphor glow
Reflected in the slabbèd steps below,
Mild as a star in water; for so new,
And so unsullied was the marble hue,
So through the crystal polish, liquid fine,
Ran the dark veins, that none but feet divine
Could e'er have touched there. Sounds Aeolian

Breathed from the hinges, as the ample span
Of the wide doors disclosed a place unknown
Some time to any, but those two alone,
And a few Persian mutes, who that same year
Were seen about the markets: none knew where
They could inhabit; the most curious
Were foiled, who watched to trace them to their house.
And but the flitter-wingèd verse must tell,
For truth's sake, what woe afterwards befell,
'Twould humour many a heart to leave them thus,
Shut from the busy world, of more incredulous.

PART II

Love in a hut, with water and a crust,
Is – Love, forgive us! – cinder, ashes, dust;
Love in a palace is perhaps at last
More grievous torment than a hermit's fast.
That is a doubtful tale from faery land,
Hard for the non-elect to understand.
Had Lycius lived to hand his story down,
He might have given the moral a fresh frown,
Or clenched it quite: but too short was their bliss
To breed distrust and hate, that make the soft voice hiss.
Besides, there, nightly, with terrific glare,
Love, jealous grown of so complete a pair,
Hovered and buzzed his wings, with fearful roar,
Above the lintel of their chamber door,
And down the passage cast a glow upon the floor.

For all this came a ruin: side by side
They were enthronèd, in the eventide,
Upon a couch, near to a curtaining
Whose airy texture, from a golden string,
Floated into the room, and let appear
Unveiled the summer heaven, blue and clear,
Betwixt two marble shafts. There they reposed,

Where use had made it sweet, with eyelids closed,
Saving a tithe which love still open kept,
That they might see each other while they almost slept;
When from the slope side of a suburb hill,
Deafening the swallow's twitter, came a thrill
Of trumpets – Lycius started – the sounds fled,
But left a thought, a buzzing in his head.
For the first time, since first he harboured in
That purple-linèd palace of sweet sin,
His spirit passed beyond its golden bourne
Into the noisy world almost forsworn.
The lady, ever watchful, penetrant,
Saw this with pain, so arguing a want
Of something more, more than her empery
Of joys; and she began to moan and sigh
Because he mused beyond her, knowing well
That but a moment's thought is passion's passing-bell.
'Why do you sigh, fair creature?' whispered he:
'Why do you think?' returned she tenderly,
'You have deserted me – where am I now?
Not in your heart while care weighs on your brow:
No, no, you have dismissed me; and I go
From your breast houseless – ay, it must be so.'
He answered, bending to her open eyes,
Where he was mirrored small in paradise,
'My silver planet, both of eve and morn!
Why will you plead yourself so sad forlorn,
While I am striving how to fill my heart
With deeper crimson, and a double smart?
How to entangle, trammel up and snare
Your soul in mine, and labyrinth you there
Like the hid scent in an unbudded rose?
Ay, a sweet kiss – you see your mighty woes.
My thoughts! shall I unveil them? Listen then!
What mortal hath a prize, that other men
May be confounded and abashed withal,

But lets it sometimes pace abroad majestical,
And triumph, as in thee I should rejoice
Amid the hoarse alarm of Corinth's voice.
Let my foes choke, and my friends shout afar,
While through the throngèd streets your bridal car
Wheels round its dazzling spokes.' – The lady's cheek
Trembled; she nothing said, but, pale and meek,
Arose and knelt before him, wept a rain
Of sorrows at his words; at last with pain
Beseeching him, the while his hand she wrung,
To change his purpose. He thereat was stung,
Perverse, with stronger fancy to reclaim
Her wild and timid nature to his aim:
Besides, for all his love, in self-despite,
Against his better self, he took delight
Luxurious in her sorrows, soft and new.
His passion, cruel grown, took on a hue
Fierce and sanguineous as 'twas possible
In one whose brow had no dark veins to swell.
Fine was the mitigated fury, like
Apollo's presence when in act to strike
The serpent – Ha, the serpent! Certes, she
Was none. She burnt, she loved the tyranny,
And, all subdued, consented to the hour
When to the bridal he should lead his paramour.
Whispering in midnight silence, said the youth,
'Sure some sweet name thou hast, though, by my truth,
I have not asked it, ever thinking thee
Not mortal, but of heavenly progeny,
As still I do. Hast any mortal name,
Fit appellation for this dazzling frame?
Or friends or kinsfolk on the citied earth,
To share our marriage feast and nuptial mirth?'
'I have no friends,' said Lamia, 'no, not one;
My presence in wide Corinth hardly known:
My parents' bones are in their dusty urns

Sepulchred, where no kindled incense burns,
Seeing all their luckless race are dead, save me,
And I neglect the holy rite for thee.
Even as you list invite your many guests;
But if, as now it seems, your vision rests
With any pleasure on me, do not bid
Old Apollonius – from him keep me hid.'
Lycius, perplexed at words so blind and blank,
Made close inquiry; from whose touch she shrank,
Feigning a sleep; and he to the dull shade
Of deep sleep in a moment was betrayed.

It was the custom then to bring away
The bride from home at blushing shut of day,
Veiled, in a chariot, heralded along
By strewn flowers, torches, and a marriage song,
With other pageants: but this fair unknown
Had not a friend. So being left alone,
(Lycius was gone to summon all his kin)
And knowing surely she could never win
His foolish heart from its mad pompousness,
She set herself, high-thoughted, how to dress
The misery in fit magnificence.
She did so, but 'tis doubtful how and whence
Came, and who were her subtle servitors.
About the halls, and to and from the doors,
There was a noise of wings, till in short space
The glowing banquet-room shone with wide-archèd grace.
A haunting music, sole perhaps and lone
Supportress of the faery-roof, made moan
Throughout, as fearful the whole charm might fade.
Fresh carvèd cedar, mimicking a glade
Of palm and plantain, met from either side,
High in the midst, in honour of the bride;
Two palms and then two plantains, and so on,
From either side their stems branched one to one

All down the aislèd place; and beneath all
There ran a stream of lamps straight on from wall to wall.
So canopied, lay an untasted feast
Teeming with odours. Lamia, regal dressed,
Silently paced about, and as she went,
In pale contented sort of discontent,
Missioned her viewless servants to enrich
The fretted splendour of each nook and niche.
Between the tree-stems, marbled plain at first,
Came jasper panels; then anon, there burst
Forth creeping imagery of slighter trees,
And with the larger wove in small intricacies.
Approving all, she faded at self-will,
And shut the chamber up, close, hushed and still,
Complete and ready for the revels rude,
When dreadful guests would come to spoil her solitude.

The day appeared, and all the gossip rout.
O senseless Lycius! Madman! wherefore flout
The silent-blessing fate, warm cloistered hours,
And show to common eyes these secret bowers?
The herd approached; each guest, with busy brain,
Arriving at the portal, gazed amain,
And entered marvelling – for they knew the street,
Remembered it from childhood all complete
Without a gap, yet ne'er before had seen
That royal porch, that high-built fair demesne.
So in they hurried all, mazed, curious and keen –
Save one, who looked thereon with eye severe,
And with calm-planted steps walked in austere.
'Twas Apollonius: something too he laughed,
As though some knotty problem, that had daffed
His patient thought, had now begun to thaw,
And solve and melt – 'twas just as he foresaw.

He met within the murmurous vestible
His young disciple. ' 'Tis no common rule,

Lycius,' said he, 'for uninvited guest
To force himself upon you, and infest
With an unbidden presence the bright throng
Of younger friends; yet must I do this wrong,
And you forgive me.' Lycius blushed, and led
The old man through the inner doors broad-spread;
With reconciling words and courteous mien
Turning into sweet milk the sophist's spleen.

Of wealthy lustre was the banquet-room,
Filled with pervading brilliance and perfume:
Before each lucid panel fuming stood
A censer fed with myrrh and spicèd wood,
Each by a sacred tripod held aloft,
Whose slender feet wide-swerved upon the soft
Wool-woofèd carpets; fifty wreaths of smoke
From fifty censers their light voyage took
To the high roof, still mimicked as they rose
Along the mirrored walls by twin-clouds odorous.
Twelve spherèd tables, by silk seats ensphered,
High as the level of a man's breast reared
On libbard's paws, upheld the heavy gold
Of cups and goblets, and the store thrice told
Of Ceres' horn, and, in huge vessels, wine
Come from the gloomy tun with merry shine.
Thus loaded with a feast the tables stood,
Each shrining in the midst the image of a God.

When in an antechamber every guest
Had felt the cold full sponge to pleasure pressed,
By ministering slaves, upon his hands and feet,
And fragrant oils with ceremony meet
Poured on his hair, they all moved to the feast
In white robes, and themselves in order placed
Around the silken couches, wondering
Whence all this mighty cost and blaze of wealth could spring.

Soft went the music the soft air along,
While fluent Greek a vowelled undersong
Kept up among the guests, discoursing low
At first, for scarcely was the wine at flow;
But when the happy vintage touched their brains,
Louder they talk, and louder come the strains
Of powerful instruments. The gorgeous dyes,
The space, the splendour of the draperies,
The roof of awful richness, nectarous cheer,
Beautiful slaves, and Lamia's self, appear,
Now, when the wine has done its rosy deed,
And every soul from human trammels freed,
No more so strange; for merry wine, sweet wine,
Will make Elysian shades not too fair, too divine.

Soon was God Bacchus at meridian height;
Flushed were their cheeks, and bright eyes double bright:
Garlands of every green, and every scent
From vales deflowered, or forest-trees branch-rent,
In baskets of bright osiered gold were brought
High as the handles heaped, to suit the thought
Of every guest – that each, as he did please,
Might fancy-fit his brows, silk-pillowed at his ease.

What wreath for Lamia? What for Lycius?
What for the sage, old Apollonius?
Upon her aching forehead be there hung
The leaves of willow and of adder's tongue;
And for the youth, quick, let us strip for him
The thyrsus, that his watching eyes may swim
Into forgetfulness; and, for the sage,
Let spear-grass and the spiteful thistle wage
War on his temples. Do not all charms fly
At the mere touch of cold philosophy?
There was an awful rainbow once in heaven:
We know her woof, her texture; she is given
In the dull catalogue of common things.

Philosophy will clip an Angel's wings,
Conquer all mysteries by rule and line,
Empty the haunted air, and gnomèd mine –
Unweave a rainbow, as it erewhile made
The tender-personed Lamia melt into a shade.

By her glad Lycius sitting, in chief place,
Scarce saw in all the room another face,
Till, checking his love trance, a cup he took
Full brimmed, and opposite sent forth a look
'Cross the broad table, to beseech a glance
From his old teacher's wrinkled countenance,
And pledge him. The bald-head philosopher
Had fixed his eye, without a twinkle or stir
Full on the alarmèd beauty of the bride,
Brow-beating her fair form, and troubling her sweet pride.
Lycius then pressed her hand, with devout touch,
As pale it lay upon the rosy couch:
'Twas icy, and the cold ran through his veins;
Then sudden it grew hot, and all the pains
Of an unnatural heat shot to his heart.
'Lamia, what means this? Wherefore dost thou start?
Know'st thou that man?' Poor Lamia answered not.
He gazed into her eyes, and not a jot
Owned they the lovelorn piteous appeal;
More, more he gazed; his human senses reel;
Some hungry spell that loveliness absorbs;
There was no recognition in those orbs.
'Lamia!' he cried – and no soft-toned reply.
The many heard, and the loud revelry
Grew hush; the stately music no more breathes;
The myrtle sickened in a thousand wreaths.
By faint degrees, voice, lute, and pleasure ceased;
A deadly silence step by step increased,
Until it seemed a horrid presence there,
And not a man but felt the terror in his hair.

'Lamia!' he shrieked; and nothing but the shriek
With its sad echo did the silence break.
'Begone, foul dream!' he cried, gazing again
In the bride's face, where now no azure vein
Wandered on fair-spaced temples; no soft bloom
Misted the cheek; no passion to illume
The deep-recessèd vision. All was blight;
Lamia, no longer fair, there sat a deadly white.
'Shut, shut those juggling eyes, thou ruthless man!
Turn them aside, wretch! or the righteous ban
Of all the Gods, whose dreadful images
Here represent their shadowy presences,
May pierce them on the sudden with the thorn
Of painful blindness; leaving thee forlorn,
In trembling dotage to the feeblest fright
Of conscience, for their long offended might,
For all thine impious proud-heart sophistries,
Unlawful magic, and enticing lies.
Corinthians! look upon that grey-beard wretch!
Mark how, possessed, his lashless eyelids stretch
Around his demon eyes! Corinthians, see!
My sweet bride withers at their potency.'
'Fool!' said the sophist, in an undertone
Gruff with contempt; which a death-nighing moan
From Lycius answered, as heart-struck and lost,
He sank supine beside the aching ghost.
'Fool! Fool!' repeated he, while his eyes still
Relented not, nor moved: 'From every ill
Of life have I preserved thee to this day,
And shall I see thee made a serpent's prey?'
Then Lamia breathed death-breath; the sophist's eye,
Like a sharp spear, went through her utterly,
Keen, cruel, perceant, stinging: she, as well
As her weak hand could any meaning tell,
Motioned him to be silent; vainly so,
He looked and looked again a level – *No!*

'A Serpent!' echoed he; no sooner said,
Than with a frightful scream she vanishèd:
And Lycius' arms were empty of delight,
As were his limbs of life, from that same night.
On the high couch he lay! – his friends came round –
Supported him – no pulse, or breath they found,
And, in its marriage robe, the heavy body wound.

To Autumn

I

Season of mists and mellow fruitfulness,
  Close bosom-friend of the maturing sun,
Conspiring with him how to load and bless
  With fruit the vines that round the thatch-eves run;
To bend with apples the mossed cottage-trees,
  And fill all fruit with ripeness to the core;
    To swell the gourd, and plump the hazel shells
  With a sweet kernel; to set budding more,
And still more, later flowers for the bees,
Until they think warm days will never cease,
    For Summer has o'er-brimmed their clammy cells.

II

Who hath not seen thee oft amid thy store?
  Sometimes whoever seeks abroad may find
Thee sitting careless on a granary floor,
  Thy hair soft-lifted by the winnowing wind;
Or on a half-reaped furrow sound asleep,
  Drowsed with the fume of poppies, while thy hook
    Spares the next swath and all its twinèd flowers;
And sometimes like a gleaner thou dost keep
  Steady thy laden head across a brook;
  Or by a cider-press, with patient look,
    Thou watchest the last oozings hours by hours.

III

Where are the songs of Spring? Ay, where are they?
  Think not of them, thou hast thy music too –
While barrèd clouds bloom the soft-dying day,
  And touch the stubble-plains with rosy hue:

Then in a wailful choir the small gnats mourn
  Among the river sallows, borne aloft
    Or sinking as the light wind lives or dies;
And full-grown lambs loud bleat from hilly bourn;
  Hedge-crickets sing; and now with treble soft
  The red-breast whistles from a garden-croft;
    And gathering swallows twitter in the skies.

from The Fall of Hyperion. A Dream

CANTO I, lines 1–57

Fanatics have their dreams, wherewith they weave
A paradise for a sect; the savage too
From forth the loftiest fashion of his sleep
Guesses at Heaven: pity these have not
Traced upon vellum or wild Indian leaf
The shadows of melodious utterance.
But bare of laurel they live, dream, and die;
For Poesy alone can tell her dreams,
With the fine spell of words alone can save
Imagination from the sable charm
And dumb enchantment. Who alive can say,
'Thou art no Poet – mayst not tell thy dreams'?
Since every man whose soul is not a clod
Hath visions, and would speak, if he had loved,
And been well nurtured in his mother tongue.
Whether the dream now purposed to rehearse
Be Poet's or Fanatic's will be known
When this warm scribe my hand is in the grave.

Methought I stood where trees of every clime,
Palm, myrtle, oak, and sycamore, and beech,
With plantain, and spice-blossoms, made a screen –
In neighbourhood of fountains, by the noise
Soft-showering in mine ears, and, by the touch
Of scent, not far from roses. Turning round,
I saw an arbour with a drooping roof
Of trellis vines, and bells, and larger blooms,
Like floral censers, swinging light in air;
Before its wreathèd doorway, on a mound
Of moss, was spread a feast of summer fruits,
Which, nearer seen, seemed refuse of a meal
By angel tasted, or our Mother Eve;

For empty shells were scattered on the grass,
And grape-stalks but half bare, and remnants more,
Sweet-smelling, whose pure kinds I could not know.
Still was more plenty than the fabled horn
Thrice emptied could pour forth at banqueting
For Proserpine returned to her own fields,
Where the white heifers low. And appetite
More yearning than on earth I ever felt
Growing within, I ate deliciously;
And, after not long, thirsted, for thereby
Stood a cool vessel of transparent juice,
Sipped by the wandered bee, the which I took,
And, pledging all the mortals of the world,
And all the dead whose names are in our lips,
Drank. That full draught is parent of my theme.
No Asian poppy, nor elixir fine
Of the soon-fading jealous Caliphat;
No poison gendered in close monkish cell,
To thin the scarlet conclave of old men,
Could so have rapt unwilling life away.
Among the fragrant husks and berries crushed,
Upon the grass I struggled hard against
The domineering potion; but in vain –
The cloudy swoon came on, and down I sunk,
Like a Silenus on an antique vase.
How long I slumbered 'tis a chance to guess.

CANTO I, lines 93-220

Towards the altar sober-paced I went,
Repressing haste, as too unholy there;
And, coming nearer, saw beside the shrine
One ministering; and there arose a flame.
When in mid-May the sickening East wind
Shifts sudden to the south, the small warm rain
Melts out the frozen incense from all flowers,

And fills the air with so much pleasant health
That even the dying man forgets his shroud –
Even so that lofty sacrificial fire,
Sending forth Maian incense, spread around
Forgetfulness of everything but bliss,
And clouded all the altar with soft smoke,
From whose white fragrant curtains thus I heard
Language pronounced: 'If thou canst not ascend
These steps, die on that marble where thou art.
Thy flesh, near cousin to the common dust,
Will parch for lack of nutriment – thy bones
Will wither in few years, and vanish so
That not the quickest eye could find a grain
Of what thou now art on that pavement cold.
The sands of thy short life are spent this hour,
And no hand in the universe can turn
Thy hourglass, if these gummèd leaves be burnt
Ere thou canst mount up these immortal steps.'
I heard, I looked: two senses both at once,
So fine, so subtle, felt the tyranny
Of that fierce threat, and the hard task proposed.
Prodigious seemed the toil; the leaves were yet
Burning – when suddenly a palsied chill
Struck from the pavèd level up my limbs,
And was ascending quick to put cold grasp
Upon those streams that pulse beside the throat.
I shrieked; and the sharp anguish of my shriek
Stung my own ears – I strove hard to escape
The numbness, strove to gain the lowest step.
Slow, heavy, deadly was my pace: the cold
Grew stifling, suffocating, at the heart;
And when I clasped my hands I felt them not.
One minute before death, my iced foot touched
The lowest stair; and as it touched, life seemed
To pour in at the toes: I mounted up,
As once fair Angels on a ladder flew

From the green turf to Heaven. 'Holy Power,'
Cried I, approaching near the hornèd shrine,
'What am I that should so be saved from death?
What am I that another death come not
To choke my utterance sacrilegious, here?'
Then said the veilèd shadow: 'Thou hast felt
What 'tis to die and live again before
Thy fated hour. That thou hadst power to do so
Is thy own safety; thou hast dated on
Thy doom.' 'High Prophetess,' said I, 'purge off,
Benign, if so it please thee, my mind's film.'
'None can unsurp this height,' returned that shade,
'But those to whom the miseries of the world
Are misery, and will not let them rest.
All else who find a haven in the world,
Where they may thoughtless sleep away their days,
If by a chance into this fane they come,
Rot on the pavement where thou rotted'st half.'
'Are there not thousands in the world,' said I,
Encouraged by the sooth voice of the shade,
'Who love their fellows even to the death;
Who feel the giant agony of the world;
And more, like slaves to poor humanity,
Labour for mortal good? I sure should see
Other men here: but I am here alone.'
'They whom thou spak'st of are no visionaries,'
Rejoined that voice – 'They are no dreamers weak,
They seek no wonder but the human face;
No music but a happy-noted voice –
They come not here, they have no thought to come –
And thou art here, for thou art less than they –
What benefit canst thou do, or all thy tribe,
To the great world? Thou art a dreaming thing,
A fever of thyself. Think of the Earth;
What bliss even in hope is there for thee?
What haven? Every creature hath its home;

Every sole man hath days of joy and pain,
Whether his labours be sublime or low –
The pain alone; the joy alone; distinct:
Only the dreamer venoms all his days,
Bearing more woe than all his sins deserve.
Therefore, that happiness be somewhat shared,
Such things as thou art are admitted oft
Into like gardens thou didst pass erewhile,
And suffered in these temples; for that cause
Thou standest safe beneath this statue's knees.'
'That I am favoured for unworthiness,
By such propitious parley medicined
In sickness not ignoble, I rejoice –
Ay, and could weep for love of such award.'
So answered I, continuing, 'If it please,
Majestic shadow, tell me: sure not all
Those melodies sung into the world's ear
Are useless: sure a poet is a sage,
A humanist, physician to all men.
That I am none I feel, as vultures feel
They are no birds when eagles are abroad.
What am I then? Thou spakest of my tribe:
What tribe?' – The tall shade veiled in drooping white
Then spake, so much more earnest, that the breath
Moved the thin linen folds that drooping hung
About a golden censer from the hand
Pendant. – 'Art thou not of the dreamer tribe?
The poet and the dreamer are distinct,
Diverse, sheer opposite, antipodes.
The one pours out a balm upon the world,
The other vexes it.' Then shouted I,
Spite of myself, and with a Pythia's spleen,
'Apollo! faded, far-flown Apollo!
Where is thy misty pestilence to creep
Into the dwellings, through the door crannies,
Of all mock lyrists, large self-worshippers

And careless hectorers in proud bad verse.
Though I breathe death with them it will be life
To see them sprawl before me into graves.
Majestic shadow, tell me where I am,
Whose altar this; for whom this incense curls;
What image this, whose face I cannot see,
For the broad marble knees; and who thou art,
Of accent feminine so courteous?'

CANTO I, lines 232–71

There was a silence, while the altar's blaze
Was fainting for sweet food: I looked thereon,
And on the pavèd floor, where nigh were piled
Faggots of cinnamon, and many heaps
Of other crispèd spice-wood – then again
I looked upon the altar, and its horns
Whitened with ashes, and its languorous flame,
And then upon the offerings again;
And so by turns – till sad Moneta cried:
'The sacrifice is done, but not the less
Will I be kind to thee for thy goodwill.
My power, which to me is still a curse,
Shall be to thee a wonder; for the scenes
Still swooning vivid through my globèd brain,
With an electral changing misery,
Thou shalt with those dull mortal eyes behold,
Free from all pain, if wonder pain thee not.'
As near as an immortal's spherèd words
Could to a mother's soften, were these last:
But yet I had a terror of her robes,
And chiefly of the veils, that from her brow
Hung pale, and curtained her in mysteries
That made my heart too small to hold its blood.
This saw that Goddess, and with sacred hand
Parted the veils. Then saw I a wan face,

Not pined by human sorrows, but bright-blanched
By an immortal sickness which kills not;
It works a constant change, which happy death
Can put no end to; deathwards progressing
To no death was that visage; it had passed
The lily and the snow; and beyond these
I must not think now, though I saw that face –
But for her eyes I should have fled away.
They held me back, with a benignant light,
Soft-mitigated by divinest lids
Half-closed, and visionless entire they seemed
Of all external things – they saw me not,
But in blank splendour beamed like the mild moon,
Who comforts those she sees not, who knows not
What eyes are upward cast.

'Bright star! would I were steadfast as thou art'

Bright star! would I were steadfast as thou art –
  Not in lone splendour hung aloft the night
And watching, with eternal lids apart,
  Like nature's patient, sleepless Eremite,
The moving waters at their priestlike task
  Of pure ablution round earth's human shores,
Or gazing on the new soft-fallen mask
  Of snow upon the mountains and the moors –
No – yet still steadfast, still unchangeable,
  Pillowed upon my fair love's ripening breast,
To feel for ever its soft swell and fall,
  Awake for ever in a sweet unrest,
Still, still to hear her tender-taken breath,
And so live ever – or else swoon to death.

'This living hand, now warm and capable'

This living hand, now warm and capable
Of earnest grasping, would, if it were cold
And in the icy silence of the tomb,
So haunt thy days and chill thy dreaming nights
That thou would wish thine own heart dry of blood
So in my veins red life might stream again,
And thou be conscience-calmed – see here it is –
I hold it towards you.

To Fanny

I

Physician Nature! let my spirit blood!
  O ease my heart of verse and let me rest;
Throw me upon thy tripod till the flood
  Of stifling numbers ebbs from my full breast.
A theme! a theme! Great Nature! give a theme;
    Let me begin my dream.
I come – I see thee, as thou standest there,
Beckon me out into the wintry air.

II

Ah! dearest love, sweet home of all my fears,
  And hopes, and joys, and panting miseries,
Tonight, if I may guess, thy beauty wears
    A smile of such delight,
    As brilliant and as bright,
  As when with ravished, aching, vassal eyes,
    Lost in a soft amaze,
    I gaze, I gaze!

III

Who now, with greedy looks, eats up my feast?
  What stare outfaces now my silver moon!
Ah! keep that hand unravished at the least;
    Let, let, the amorous burn –
    But, prithee, do not turn
  The current of your heart from me so soon.
    O save, in charity,
    The quickest pulse for me!

IV

Save it for me, sweet love! though music breathe
  Voluptuous visions into the warm air,
Though swimming through the dance's dangerous wreath,
    Be like an April day,
    Smiling and cold and gay,
  A temperate lily, temperate as fair;
    Then, Heaven! there will be
    A warmer June for me.

V

Why, this – you'll say, my Fanny! – is not true:
  Put your soft hand upon your snowy side,
Where the heart beats; confess – 'tis nothing new –
    Must not a woman be
    A feather on the sea,
  Swayed to and fro by every wind and tide?
    Of as uncertain speed
    As blow-ball from the mead?

VI

I know it – and to know it is despair
  To one who loves you as I love, sweet Fanny!
Whose heart goes fluttering for you everywhere,
    Nor, when away you roam,
    Dare keep its wretched home.
  Love, Love alone, has pains severe and many:
    Then, loveliest! keep me free
    From torturing jealousy.

VII

Ah! if you prize my subdued soul above
  The poor, the fading, brief, pride of an hour,
Let none profane my Holy See of Love,

Or with a rude hand break
The sacramental cake;
Let none else touch the just new-budded flower;
If not – may my eyes close,
Love! on their last repose.

WAR MUSIC

WAR MUSIC

An Account of Books 16 to 19 of Homer's *Iliad*

CHRISTOPHER LOGUE

faber and faber

First published in Great Britain in 1981
by Jonathan Cape Ltd
Published by Penguin Books Ltd 1984
Published in the USA in 1987
by Farrar, Straus & Giroux, Inc., New York
Published in paperback in 1988
by Faber and Faber Limited
3 Queen Square London WC1N 3AU
This paperback edition first published in 2000

Photoset by Parker Typesetting Service, Leicester
Printed in Italy

All rights reserved
© Christopher Logue, 1981, 1988

Christopher Logue is hereby identified as author
of this work in accordance with Section 77
of the Copyright, Designs and Patents Act 1988

All performing rights in this work are fully protected
and permission to perform in whole or in part must be
obtained in advance from David Godwin Associates,
55 Monmouth Street, London WC2H 9DG, or from
Faber and Faber Limited

This book is sold subject to the condition that it shall not, by way of trade or otherwise, be lent, resold, hired out or otherwise circulated without the publisher's prior consent in any form of binding or cover other than that in which it is published and without a similar condition including this condition being imposed on the subsequent purchaser

A CIP record for this book
is available from the British Library

ISBN 0–571–20383–3

10 9 8 7 6 5 4 3 2 1

Contents

Introduction

Either the translations of the *Iliad* on which *War Music* is based did not exist or they had had only a passing interest for me until 1959, when Donald Carne-Ross suggested I contribute to a new version of the poem he was about to commission for the BBC.

Knowing no Greek I began work on the passage he chose for me by studying the same passage in the translations published by Chapman (1611), Pope (1720), Lord Derby (1865), A. T. Murray (1924), and Rieu (1950).

While Pope was the most and Murray the least accomplished of these authors, Murray, according to learned gossip, possessed the most and Pope the least information about Homer's Greek – though Chapman had tried to abort the charge that his translation was based on a French crib by calling his judges 'envious Windfuckers'; Lord Derby was high-Victorian- and Rieu mid-Windsor-steady.

Whatever these guides knew about the language in which the *Iliad* was composed they gave me a dissimilar impression of the work that had inspired their own, and this variety, plus regular 'On Homer' tutorials from Carne-Ross, supported my plan to retain Homer's story line, to cut or amplify or add to its incidents, vary its similes, and (mostly) omit Homer's descriptive epithets: 'ten-second-miler-Achilles', 'never-defeated Ajax', and so forth.

As the work progressed I paid less attention to my guides. Carne-Ross provided translations retaining the Greek word order; I concocted a new story line; and then, knowing the gist of what this or that character said, tried to make their voices come alive and to keep the action on the move.

Rather than a translation in the accepted sense of the word, I was writing what I hoped would turn out to be a poem in English dependent upon whatever, through reading and through conversation, I could guess about a small part of the *Iliad*, a poem whose composition is reckoned to have preceded the beginnings of our own written language by fifteen centuries.

My reading on the subject of translation had produced at least one important opinion: 'We must try its effect as an English poem,' Boswell reports Johnson as saying; 'that is the way to judge of the merit of a translation.'

Even though it owes its life to ridicule or to the power of bad taste, any poem that survives outside literary circles for more than one generation is noteworthy.

For a poem of over 15,000 lines representing an age as remote from its own as it is from ours to survive the collapse of, not just one society (a critical test no poem in English has, as yet, had to pass), but two, could mean that those who have kept it alive are mad.

And if it follows that those who read the *Iliad* in translation or in recomposition are merely a bit touched, some of our problems become clearer: Pope earned the equivalent of £100,000 from his Homer work; my edition of Lord Derby's *Iliad* is its fifth; two million copies of Rieu's version have been sold. In fact, any deficiencies of length or of vigour you may find in what follows may be ascribed to my concern for public health.

War Music comprises Books (as scholars call them) 16 to 19 of the *Iliad*.

My choosing these passages derives from the advice of Carne-Ross. 'Book 16, or *Patrocleia*,' he said, 'might be described as a miniature version of the *Iliad*. It has a quarrel, a making-up, a concession, several battles, the death of a famous leader (Sarpedon), disagreement in Heaven, a human cheeking the Gods, and, as a result of that human's death, an irreversible change.

'In addition to these things *Patrocleia* contains the *Iliad*'s crucial twist: through the death of Patroclus, Achilles returns to the fight, thereby assuring the destruction of Troy.'

Pax, or Book 19, is its opposite: disaffected allies settling their differences in order to avoid defeat at the hands of a mutual enemy. *Pax* lacks fighting; it exemplifies the public confession of common sins righted by material compensation and absolved by formal sacrifice.

With *Pax* completed I realised that conflating Books 17 and 18 as *GBH* (Grievous Bodily Harm, an English legal term for serious forms of criminal assault) would allow me to try my hand at something new – 600-odd lines devoted almost entirely to violent, mass action, which, once done, would unite *Patrocleia* and *Pax* into a narrative capable of being read independently of its guessed-at parent.

After *Patrocleia* was published I started to get critical support not only from those connected with the composition and publication of verse but from those whom we may choose to count among the hopelessly insane: the hard core of Unprofessional Ancient Greek Readers, Homer's lay fans.

Welcome as the support of my like had been, as encouraging, and critically speaking more useful, were my contacts with such fans. 'Quite good that bit of Homer you did,' one might say. 'If you do more of it, have a look at' – citing a favourite passage – 'and in case you need any help with the words – take my card.'

I took up three such offers. What I learned from those Homerniks clarified the guesses I made about the transmitted text, and my debt to them is considerable.

In addition to Carne-Ross I would like to thank Colin Leach, Peter Levi, Bernard Pomerance, Kathleen Raine, George Rapp, Stephen Spender and George Steiner for their critical support; and the Bollingen Foundation and the Arts Council of Great Britain for their financial support.

C.L., 1988

WAR MUSIC

Prologue

In the ninth summer of the Trojan War Achilles withdrew his forces from the Greek Confederacy because Agamemnon appropriated one of his female slaves.

Thereafter the Trojans gained the upper hand. Hector raided the Greek beach-head, crossed the ditch protecting their fleet, and burned one of its ships. It looked as if the Greeks would be destroyed.

At this moment Patroclus came to Achilles and begged for his help.

PATROCLEIA

Now hear this:
While they fought around the ship from Thessaly,
Patroclus came crying to the Greek.

'Why tears, Patroclus?' Achilles said.
'Why hang about my ankles like a child
Pestering its mother, wanting to be picked up,
Expecting her to stop what she is at, and,
In the end, getting its way through snivels?
You have bad news from home?
Someone is dead, Patroclus? Your father? Mine?
But news like that is never confidential.
If such was true, you, me, and all the Myrmidons
Would cry together.
It's the Greeks, Patroclus, isn't it?
You weep because a dozen Greeks lie dead beside their ships.
But did you weep when those same Greeks condoned my wrongs?
If I remember rightly, you said – nothing.'

And Patroclus:
'Save your hate, Achilles. It will keep.
Our cause is sick enough without your grudging it my tears.
You know Odysseus is wounded?
Orontes, too – his thigh: King Agamemnon, even. Yet
Still you ask: *Why tears?*
Is there to be no finish to your grudge?
No, no; don't shrug me off. Mind who it is that asks:
Not the smart Ithacan; not Agamemnon. Me.
And God forbid I share the niceness of a man
Who, when his friends go down, sits tight
And finds his vindication in their pain.
They are dying, Achilles. Dying like flies.

Think, if you cannot think of them, of those
Who will come after them; what they will say:
  Achilles the Resentful – can you hear it? –
Achilles, strong? . . . *The Strongest of the Strong* –
And just as well, because his sense of wrong was heavy.
  Shameful that I can talk to you this way.'
  All still.
  'And yet, among the many who do not,
As I believe that God and she who bore
You to a mortal husband back your claim,
So I believe they will not censor mine:
  Let me go out and help the Greeks, Achilles.
Let me command your troops. Part of them, then?
And let me wear your armour.'
  Still.
  'Man – it will be enough!
Me, dressed as you, pointing the Myrmidons . . .
The sight alone will make Troy pause, and say:
"It's him," a second look will check them, turn them,
Give the Greeks a rest (although war has no rest) and turned,
Nothing will stop us till they squat behind their Wall.'

  And so he begged for death.

  'Better to ask yourself,' Achilles said,
'If you would stay my friend or not
Than speculate which god, or whether God Himself,
Packaged the specious quibbles with my mouth
Your insolence delivers to my face.
  Why not add Agamemnon to your whine?
King vain, king fretful, truthless Agamemnon,
Eager to eat tomorrow's fame today.
  Go on . . . *He was a sick man at the time, Achilles.*
He did it to avoid unpleasantness, Achilles.
Achilles, he was not too well advised.'
  Staring each other down until he said:

'O love,
I am so glutted with resentment that I ache.
Tell me, have I got it wrong?
Did he not take the girl I won? –
And all my fine fair-weather friends agree
That she was mine by right of rape and conquest? Yet,
When it comes to it, they side with him; the royal slug
Who robs the man on whom his crown depends.
Yet done is done; I cannot grudge forever.
Take what you want: men, armour, cars, the lot.'
Easy to see his loss was on the run;
Him standing, saying:
'Muster the troops and thrust them, hard,
Just here' – marking the sand – 'between the enemy
And the Fleet.
Aie! . . . they are impudent, these Trojans . . .
They stroke our ships,
Fondle their slim black necks, and split them, yes --
Agamemnon's itchy digits make me absent,
My absence makes them brave, and so, Patroclus,
Dear Agamemnon's grab-all/lose-all flows.
All right: if not Achilles, then his vicar.
Forget the spear. Take this '– one half its length – 'instead.
You say Odysseus is out? Bad. Bad. And Ajax, too?
No wonder all I hear is
Hector, Hector, Hector, everywhere Hector,
As if he were a god split into sixty!
Hurry, Patroclus, or they will burn us out . . .
But listen first. Hard listening? Good.
Hear what I want:
My rights, and my apologies. No less.
And that is all.
I want the Greeks saved, yes;
Thereafter – Agamemnon at my tent,
With her, Briseis, willing, at my feet;
And many gifts. Be clear about the gifts.

And one thing more before you go:
Don't overreach yourself, Patroclus.
Without me you are something, but not much.
Let Hector be. He's mine – God willing.
In any case he'd make a meal of you,
And I don't want you killed.
But neither do I want to see you shine
At my expense.
So mark my word:
No matter how, how much, how often, or how easily you win,
Once you have forced the Trojans back, you stop.
There is a certain brightness in the air,
Meaning the Lord Apollo is too close
For you to disobey me and be safe.
You know Apollo loves the Trojans; and you know
That even God our Father hesitates
To contradict Apollo . . .
O friend,
I would be glad if all the Greeks lay dead
While you and I demolished Troy alone.'

*

Cut to the Fleet.

The air near Ajax was so thick with arrows, that,
As they came, their shanks tickered against each other;
And under them the Trojans swarmed so thick
Ajax outspread his arms, turned his spear flat,
And simply *pushed*. Yet they came clamouring back until
So many Trojans had a go at him
The iron chaps of Ajax' helmet slapped his cheeks
To soft red pulp, and his head reached back and forth
Like a clapper inside a bell made out of sword blades.
Maybe, even with no breath left,

Big Ajax might have stood it yet; yet
Big and all as he was, Prince Hector meant to burn that ship:
And God was pleased to let him.

Pulling the Trojans out a yard or two,
He baited Ajax with his throat; and Ajax took.
As the spear lifted, Hector skipped in range;
As Ajax readied, Hector bared his throat again;
And, as Ajax lunged, Prince Hector jived on his right heel
And snicked the haft clean through its neck,
Pruning the bronze nose of – Aie! – it was good to watch
Big Ajax and his spear, both empty topped,
Blundering about for – Oh, a minute went
Before he noticed it had gone.
But when he noticed it he knew
God stood by Hector's elbow, not by his;
That God was pleased with Hector, not with Ajax;
And, sensibly enough, he fled.

The ship was burned.

*

October.
The hungry province grows restive.
The Imperial army must visit the frontier.
Dawn.
The Captains arrive behind standards;
A tiger's face carved on each lance-butt;
And equipment for a long campaign
Is issued to every soldier.
First light.
Men stand behind the level feathers of their breath.
A messenger runs from the pearl-fringed tent.
The Captains form a ring. They read.
The eldest one points north. The others nod.

Likewise his Captains stood around Achilles: listening.
And the Myrmidons began to arm and tramp about the
beach,
First sunlight off the sea like thousands of white birds.
Salt haze.

Imagine wolves: an hour ago the pack
Hustled a stag, then tore it into shreds.
And now that they have gorged upon its haunch
They need a drink to wash their curry down.
So, sniffing out a pool, they loll their long,
Thin, sharp-pointed tongues therein; and as they lap
Rose-coloured billows idle off their chops,
Drifting throughout the water like pink smoke.

Likewise his soldiers ready for his eye,
Their five commanders on his right,
Patroclus on his left,
And the onshore wind behind Achilles' voice:

'Excellent killers of men!
Today Patroclus leads; and by tonight,
You, behind him, will clear the Trojans from our ditch.
And who at twilight fails to bring
At least one Trojan head to deck
The palings of our camp, can sleep outside
With Agamemnon's trash.'

The columns tightened.
The rim of each man's shield
Overlapped the face of his neighbour's shield
Like clinkered hulls – as shipwrights call them when they lay
Strake over strake, caulked against seas.
As they moved off, the columns tightened more;
Until, to one above, it seemed, five wide black straps,
Studded with bolts, were being drawn across the sand.

*

Before Achilles sailed to Troy
His women packed and put aboard his ship
A painted oak box filled with winter clothes;
Rugs for his feet, a fleece-lined windcheater –
You know the sort of thing. And in this box
He kept an eye bowl made from ivory and horn
Which he, and only he, used for Communion.
And having spoken to his troops he took it out,
Rubbed sulphur crystals on its inner face,
And washed and dried his hands before,
Spring water rinsed, brimming with altar-wine,
He held it at arm's length, and prayed:

'Our Father, Who rules the Heaven,
Because Your will is done where will may be,
Grant me this prayer
As You have granted other prayers of mine:
Give my Patroclus Your victory;
Let him show Hector he can win
Without me at his side;
And grant, above all else, O Lord,
That when the Trojans are defeated, he
Returns to me unharmed.'

God heard his prayer and granted half of it.
Patroclus would rout the Trojans; yes;
But not a word was said about his safe return.
No, my Achilles, God promised nothing of the kind,
As carefully you dried your cup,
As carefully replaced it in its box,
And stood outside your tent and watched
Your men and your Patroclus go by.

*

Hornets occasionally nest near roads.
In the late spring they breed, feeding their grubs
And feeding off the tacky sweat those grubs exude.
Ignorant children sometimes poke
Sticks into such a nest, and stir. The hornets swarm.
Often a swollen child dies that night.
Sometimes they menace passers-by instead.

No such mistake today.

Swarming up and off the beach
Patroclus swung Achilles' Myrmidons
Left at the ditch.
Keeping it on their right they streamed
Along the camp's main track; one side, the rampart;
On the other, ships.
Things were so close you could not see your front;
And from the footplate of his wheels, Patroclus cried:
'For Achilles!'
As the enemies closed.

The Trojans lay across the ship,
Most of them busy seeing that it burned.
Others slid underneath and were so occupied
Knocking away the chocks that kept it upright,
They did not see Patroclus stoop.
But those above did.
In less time than it takes to dip and light a match
Achilles' helmet loomed above their cheeks
With Myrmidons splayed out on either side
Like iron wings.
Dropping the pitch
They reached for javelins, keelspikes, boat-hooks, Oh,
Anything to keep Achilles off –
Have he and Agamemnon patched things up?

Patroclus aimed his spear where they were thickest.
That is to say, around
The chariot commander, Akafact.
But as Patroclus threw
The ship's mast flamed from stem to peak, and fell
Lengthwise across the incident.
Its fat waist clubbed the hull's top deck
And the ship flopped sideways.
Those underneath got crunched.
And howling Greeks ran up
To pike the others as they slithered off.
This fate was not for Akafact:
Because the mast's peak hit the sand no more than six
Feet from Patroclus' car, the horses shied,
Spoiling his cast. Nothing was lost.
As he fell back, back arched,
God blew the javelin straight; and thus
Mid-air, the cold bronze apex sank
Between his teeth and tongue, parted his brain,
Pressed on, and stapled him against the upturned hull.
His dead jaw gaped. His soul
Crawled off his tongue and vanished into sunlight.

Often at daybreak a salty moon
Hangs over Ida; and the wind that comes
More than a thousand miles across Asia
Knocks a tile off Priam's roof.
About this time each day for nine long years
His men marched down the Skean road,
Their spears like nettles stirred by wind;
And round about this time each day
The Greek commanders shade their eyes
And squinny through the morning sun;
And since no battle has returned
All of its soldiers, the Trojans wave,
Look back towards the wall, and think

Of those who may require new men next day.

The battle swayed.
Half-naked men hacked slowly at each other
As the Greeks eased back the Trojans.
They stood close;
Closer; thigh in thigh; mask twisted over iron mask
Like kissing.
One moment fifty chariots break out; head for the ditch;
Three cross; the rest wheel back; vanish in ochre dust.
For an instant the Greeks falter. One is killed. And then
The Trojans are eased back a little more;
The ship is cleared, the fire smothered, and who cares
That Hector's chariot opens a new way,
Now moving, pausing now, now moving on again,
And his spear's tip flickers in the smoky light
Like the head of a crested adder over fern? –
Always the Trojans shift towards the ditch.

Of several incidents, consider two:
Panotis' chariot yawed and tipped him
Back off the plate by Little Ajax' feet.
Neither had room to strike; and so the Greek
Knocked his head back with a forearm smash,
And in the space his swaying made, close lopped.
Blood dulled both sides of the leafy blade.
Fate caught Panotis' body; death his head.
Nearer the ditch Arcadeum met Lycon:
Catching each other's eye both cast, both missed,
Both ran together, and both struck; but
Only Lycon missed both times.
His neck was cut clean through
Except for a skein of flesh off which
His head hung down like a melon.

You will have heard about the restless mice

Called lemmings; how, at no set time, and why,
No one is sure, they form a grey cascade that pours
Out of the mountains, down, across the flat,
Until they rush into the sea and drown.

Likewise the Trojans as they crossed the ditch.

From the far bank Hector tried to help them
Impossible . . .
He did not guess
So many cars, so many infantry, had crossed;
Engaged, there never seemed enough; but now
They crammed the edge,
The big-eyed horses rearing at the drop,
Their mouths wrenched sideways,
Neck yokes dragged back like saddles.
And though the drivers looped their reins,
Pegged themselves in, and hauled,
The teetering jam eased forward.
Only the soft edge held them;
And as the wheels notched into it, the dirt came up
Over the bolts that pinned the axles to the centre-poles,
Horses on one side of the rim,
Cars and men the other.
Stuck.
While other men, infantry,
Meant to be rearguard, climbed into, pulled friends into,
Shouted, struck at who tried to check them, jammed
Spear-poles through spokes –
Aie . . .
And Patroclus let them, let them,
Let them balance, let them, then cried:
'For Achilles!'
And drove in.

As you, Hector, drove off.

So the Trojans nearest to Patroclus squirmed
Away from him towards the ditch; and those
Near falling into it clawed back
Towards Patroclus; and those cram-packed between
Just clawed and squirmed and –
   Why did you leave them, Hector? You
Who had generals like clouds, soldiers like drops of rain,
As you were partway back to Priam's capital
The soft edge gave, and all your glittering soldiery
Toppled into the ditch like swill.

   On certain winter days the land seems grey,
   And the no-headroom left between it and the grey
   Masses of downthrust cloud, fills with wet haze:
   Lines of cold rain weld mile on sightless mile
   Of waste to air: floods occupy the state; and still
   The rains continue, grey on grey;
   God's punishment, say some, on those who bear
   False witness; and some say, on those
   Judges divorced from justice by contempt
   Of those they judge; plus the accomplices of both,
   Perched on their fencing through the vacant day,
   Until the water takes them all in all
   In one enormous wave into the sea.

   The Trojan horses made like this.
As they went up the far side of the ditch
They dragged behind them dead or half-dead charioteers
Who had looped themselves inside their reins.
Better like this, perhaps, than left to Greeks.

   Patroclus split the rump.
Some (only a few) followed their horses up
Onto the plain and ran for Troy. The rest
Scurried along the ditch and hid themselves
Among Scamander's fens.

Nothing was left of Hector's raid except
Loose smoke-swaths like blue hair above the dunes,
And Agamemnon's ditch stained crimson where
Some outraged god five miles tall had stamped on glass.

A movement in the air. Gulls lift;
Then sideslip; land again. No more.
Mindless of everything Achilles said
Patroclus went for Troy.

*

See if you can imagine how it looked:

An opened fan, held flat; its pin
(That marks the ditch) towards yourself; its curve
(That spans the plain) remote:
The left guard points at Troy; the right
Covers the dunes that front the Aegean coast:
Like crabs disturbed by flame the Trojans run
This way and that across its radiants.
Patroclus thrusts his soldiers at the mid
Point of the pleated leaf; a painted sun.

And it was here that Thestor, Enop's boy,
Met that circumstance in nature
Gods call fate, and on this day, men called Patroclus.
Thestor was not a Trojan.
But when King Priam's satraps came from Troy
And asked Sarpedon, Lycia's Prince, for aid,
And he said, 'Yes' – Thestor, the apple of old Enop's eye,
Applied to leave his management and fight
With all his clan. And as he reined away, he called:
'Do not forsake me, O my seven meadows,
Until I conquer Greece!'
Though all he conquered was six foot of sand.

Fate's sister, Fortune, favours those
Who keep their nerve.
Thestor was not like this.
He lost his head, first; then his life.
His chariot bucked too slow over the rutted corpses,
And as Patroclus drew abreast of him,
The terrified boy let the horses baulk,
Leaving the reins to flow beside the car,
And cowered in its varnished basket,
Weeping.
They passed so close that hub skinned hub.
Ahead, Patroclus braked a shade, and then,
And gracefully as men in oilskins cast
Fake insects over trout, he speared the boy,
And with his hip his pivot, prised Thestor up and out
As easily as later men detach
A sardine from an opened tin.

Nine more Lycians died on the long run for Troy –
And they were no great trouble.
If a spear missed, Patroclus watched
Their white heels flutter up the plain through dust,
Picked a fresh haft, waited, and pinned his next.
The day seemed done; dust could be left to dust;
Flies had laid eggs in many of the dead;
Until Sarpedon wedged his car across the rout,
Pushed up his mask, and said:
'Well run, my soldiers, but from what?' –
Selecting two light javelins – 'Who will wait
To see their known Prince spit
Once and for all this big, anonymous Greek' –
And vaulted off his chariot plate –
'That makes you sweat?' – and flexed himself,
Running his thumb across his points, and scuffed
Dirt toward Patroclus, who climbed down
More slowly; pleased beneath his iron.

It was noon.

God and His wife (who is His sister, too)
Watched them prepare. He, with regret; She,
With satisfaction heard Him out:
'Surely Fate has marked enough good men without
Sarpedon?
Shall I return him to his waving plains
Or let . . .'
And She:
'Others beside Yourself have children due today.
If one God saves his bud – why not the rest?
My dear, I know You love Sarpedon; and I know
His death goes hard. Why not do this:
Let him fight bravely fora while; then, when
Patroclus severs him from care and misery,
Sleep and Death shall carry him to Lycia by Taurus,
Remembered by wise men throughout the world
And buried royally.'
Noon. Striped mosquitoes. Nothing stirs.

Under the white sun, back and forth
Across a disk of yellow earth, midway
Between the sea and closed stone capital,
The heroes fought like Pharaoh's bare-necked hens
Wrangling over carrion in the air.
They sight each other, stand on their tails,
Lock claws, lie back inside their wings, and hang
High in between the white-faced pyramids,
Each savaging the other's craw.

Likewise the human champions until
Patroclus' spear nosed past Sarpedon's busy heart
And the ground sense in his body leached away.
Kneeling at first, then laid full length,
Teeth clenched and saying: 'Glaucos, be quick

Or they will strip me while I live.
    And if they do it, Glaucos, if
My captured weapons prove their jubilee,
Shame on you, Glaucos, till your dying day.
    So get our best.
Anaxapart, Aeneas, Hector, too – do not miss him-
And cover me with moving blades till sunset.
Then . . .' he was going,
'For my sake, Glaucos . . .' going,
'Kill!'
    And he was gone.
Sunlight reflecting in his dry brown eyes.
    Patroclus in his chariot again,
Wiping his neck, his smiling beard,
About to signal the advance.

    'Listen, Master!'
Glaucos prayed to Lord Apollo,
    'Wherever You may be,
    And You are everywhere,
    And everywhere You hear
    Men in their trouble;
    Trouble has come to me.
    Our best is dead and I
    Am wounded, Lord! O Lord
    Apollo hear my prayer!
    You know me, and You know
    That I shall fight until I die,
    But I can barely lift my arm!
    Lord, put my pain to sleep,
    And grant me strength enough to keep
    My sword above Sarpedon's corpse
    Until the sun obeys Your call to set.'

    And Apollo, Mousegod, Lord of the Morning, He
Whose face is brighter than a thousand suns,

Mollified his wound with sacred thought,
And let delight in fighting warm his loins.
And He did more: as Glaucos fetched their best,
Apollo called:
  'Sun, stand thou still over Ilium,
And guard Sarpedon's body till their blades
Move over it as grasses over stone.'

  Air into azure steel;
The daylight stiffens to translucent horn;
  And through it,
Falling,
  One sun's cord
Opening out into a radiant cone around Sarpedon's corpse;
And him inside that light, as if
A god asleep upon his outstretched hand.

*

  Dust like red mist.
Pain like chalk on slate. Heat like Arctic.
The light withdrawn from Sarpedon's body.
The enemies swirling over it.
Bronze flak.
  Man against man; banner behind raised banner;
The torn gold overwhelming the faded blue;
Blue overcoming gold; both up again; both frayed
By arrows that drift like bees, thicker than autumn rain.
  The left horse falls. The right, prances through blades,
Tearing its belly like a silk balloon.
And the shields inch forward under bowshots.
And under the shields the half-lost soldiers think:
'We fight when the sun rises; when it sets we count the dead.
What has the beauty of Helen to do with us?' Half-lost,
With the ochre mist swirling around their knees,
They shuffle forward, lost, until the shields clash:

– AOI!
   Lines of black ovals eight feet high, clash:
– AOI!
And in the half-light who will be first to hesitate,
Or, wavering, draw back, and Yes! . . . the slow
Wavering begins, and, Yes! . . . they bend away from us,
As spear points flicker in between black hide
Bronze glows vaguely, and bones show
Like pink drumsticks.
   And over it all,
As flies shift up and down a haemorrhage alive with ants,
The captains in their iron masks drift past each other,
Calling, calling, gathering light on their breastplates;
So stained they think that they are friends
And do not turn, do not salute, or else salute their enemies.
   But we who are under the shields know
Our enemy marches at the head of the column;
And yet we march!
The voice we obey is the voice of the enemy,
Yet we obey!
And he who is forever talking about enemies
Is himself the enemy!

   Light circling the dunes. The flying white.
Larks soar above the soldiers, breathing haze.
And them above, their faces pressed against eternal glass,
The Gods . . .

   'The one I fancy,' Hera says, 'is him.'
'The Redhead?'
   'Yes . . . ' and whispered over space into his ear:
'King human. Menelaos. If you stick
Him, him, and *him*, I promise you will get your Helen back.'

   See how that Royal fights:
Flaking his blade on Python's hip,

He rakes its splintered edge down Cazca's back,
Tosses aside the stump,
And with his ever-vengeful, empty hands,
Grabs Midon, old King Raphno's eldest son
– Known as Count Suckle to his enemies –
Expert at dicing, good in bed, who once
(Just for a joke, of course) ate thirty vulture's eggs
At one of Helen's parties on the wall.
And later men recalled how he was slain;
One swearing 'gutted,' one 'that he was ripped
Up the front until his belly grinned,'
And some were quite convinced he ran away
And lived ten thousand days beside a cool
And amethystine lake in Phrygia;
But if you want the truth, well . . .
King Menelaos got him by the ears
Bowed back his chubby neck and bit
A lump out of his jugular –
'Sweet God, his dirty blood is in my eyes!
Some Trojan runt will stick me . . .' but
She who admired him wiped the mess away.

    If Hector waved,
His wounded and his sick got up to fight;
And if Patroclus called, the Myrmidons
Struck, and called back; with them, as with Patroclus,
To die in battle was like going home.

    Try to recall the pause, thock, pause,
    Made by axe blades as they pace
    Each other through a valuable wood.
    Though the work takes place on the far
    Side of a valley, and the axe strokes are
    Muted by depths of warm, still standing air,
    They throb, throb, closely in your ear;
    And now and then you catch a phrase

Exchanged between the men who work
More than a mile away, with perfect clarity.

Likewise the sound of spear on spear,
Shield against shield, shield against spear
Around Sarpedon's body.

And all this time God watched His favourite enemies:
Minute Patroclus, like a fleck
Of radium on His right hand,
Should he die now – or push the Trojans back still more?
And on His left, Prince Hector, like a silver mote,
Should he turn coward for an hour
And let Patroclus steal Sarpedon's gear?
The left goes down.
In the half-light Hector's blood turns milky
And he runs for Troy.

It is true that men are clever;
But the least of gods is cleverer than their best.
And it was here, before God's hands
(Moons poised on either side of their earth's agate)
You overreached yourself, Patroclus.
Yes, my darling,
Not only God was out that day but Lord Apollo.
'*You know Apollo loves the Trojans: so,*
Once you have forced them back, you stop.'
Remember it, Patroclus? Or was it years ago
Achilles cautioned you outside his tent?
Remembering or not you stripped Sarpedon's gear,
And went for Troy alone.

And God turned to Apollo, saying:
'Mousegod, take my Sarpedon out of range
And clarify his wounds with mountain water.
Moisten his body with tinctures of white myrrh

And violet iodine; and when these chrysms dry,
Fold him in miniver that never wears
And lints that never fade,
And call my two blind footmen, Sleep and Death,
To carry him to Lycia by Taurus,
Where, playing stone chimes and tambourines,
His tribe will consecrate his death,
Before whose memory the stones shall fade.'
   And Apollo took Sarpedon out of range
And clarified his wounds with mountain water;
Moistened his body with tinctures of white myrrh
And violet iodine; and when these chrysms dried
He folded him in miniver and lints
That never wear, that never fade,
And called God's two blind footmen, Sleep and Death,
Who carried him
Before whose memory the stones shall fade
To Lycia by Taurus.

*

   Three times Patroclus climbed Troy's wall.
Three times his fingers scraped the parapet.
Three times, and every time he tried it on
The smiling Mousegod flicked him back.
But when he came a fourth, last time,
The smile was gone.
   Instead, from parapet to plain to beach-head, on,
Across the rucked, sunstruck Aegean, the Mousegod's voice,
Loud as ten thousand crying together,
Cried:

'Greek,
Get back where you belong!'

So loud
Even the Yellow Judges giving law
Half-way across the world's circumference paused.

'Get back where you belong!
Troy will fall in God's good time,
But not to you!'

It was Patroclus' turn to run, wide-armed,
Staring into the fight, and desperate to hide
(To blind that voice) to hide
Among the stainless blades.
And as he ran
Apollo dressed as Priam's brother stood
Above the Skean Gate, and strolled
With Hector for a while, and took his arm,
And mentioning the ways of duty, courage, love,
And other perishable joys infecting men,
Dissolved his cowardice with promises.
Observe the scene:
They stand like relatives: the man, the God,
Chatting together on the parapet
That spans the Gate.
The elder points. The other nods. And the plumes nod
Over them both. Patroclus cannot see
The uncle's finger leading Hector's eye
Towards his flesh.
Nor can he hear Apollo whispering:
'Achilles' heart will break . . .' And neither man
Thinks that a god discusses mortals with a mortal.

Patroclus fought like dreaming:
His head thrown back, his mouth – wide as a shrieking
mask –
Sucked at the air to nourish his infuriated mind
And seemed to draw the Trojans onto him,
To lock them round his waist, red water, washed against his
chest,
To lay their tired necks against his sword like birds.
– Is it a god? Divine? Needing no tenderness? –
Yet instantly they touch, he butts them,
Cuts them back:
– Kill them!
My sweet Patroclus,
– Kill them!
As many as you can,
For
Coming behind you through the dust you felt
– What was it? – felt creation part, and then

APO

LLO!

Who had been patient with you

Struck.

His hand came from the east,
And in his wrist lay all eternity;
And every atom of his mythic weight
Was poised between his fist and bent left leg.
Your eyes lurched out. Achilles' helmet rang
Far and away beneath the cannon-bones of Trojan horses,
And you were footless . . . staggering . . . amazed . . .
Between the clumps of dying, dying yourself,
Dazed by the brilliance in your eyes,
The noise – like weirs heard far away –
Dabbling your astounded fingers
In the vomit on your chest.
And all the Trojans lay and stared at you;
Propped themselves up and stared at you;
Feeling themselves as blest as you felt cursed.
All of them lay and stared;
And one, a boy called Thackta, cast.
His javelin went through your calves,
Stitching your knees together, and you fell,
Not noticing the pain, and tried to crawl
Towards the Fleet, and – even now – feeling
For Thackta's ankle – ah! – and got it? No . . .
Not a boy's ankle that you got,
But Hector's.

Standing above you,
His bronze mask smiling down into your face,
Putting his spear through . . . ach, and saying:
'Why tears, Patroclus?
Did you hope to melt Troy down
And make our women fetch the ingots home?
I can imagine it!
You and your marvellous Achilles;
Him with an upright finger, saying:

Don't show your face again, Patroclus,
Unless it's red with Hector's blood.'
And Patroclus,
Shaking the voice out of his body, says:
'Big mouth.
Remember it took three of you to kill me.
A god, a boy, and, last and least, a hero.
I can hear Death pronounce my name, and yet
Somehow it sounds like *Hector.*
And as I close my eyes I see Achilles' face
With Death's voice coming out of it.'

Saying these things Patroclus died.
And as his soul went through the sand
Hector withdrew his spear and said:
'Perhaps.'

GBH

And Helen walks beneath a burning tree.
Over her nearest arm her olive stole;
Beneath her see-through shift, her nudity;
A gelded cupidon depletes her woe.

*

Faultless horizon. Flattish sea.
Wet shore. Wide plain. Look west:
King Menelaos sees Patroclus fall
And thinks: 'His death will get us home.'
Under a mile away Prince Hector says:
'Thackta, keep watch,'
Who wants Achilles' chariot and pair.
Then climbs into his own. Full lock. And goes.

*

Before it disappears beneath the sea
The plain due west of Troy accumulates
Into a range of whalebacked, hairy dunes,
Two days' ride long, parallel to the coast,
And, at their greatest, half a bowshot thick:
White, empty beaches, supervised by Greece,
Stretch from the tidemark to their crested cliffs;
But on the landward side, and long before
Their yellows fade through buff into the black
Alluvial plain supporting distant Troy,
Sickle-shaped bays of deep, loose sand, embraced
By corniced horns, appear; and over there
– Much like the foothill of a parent range –
A knoll of osier and grassbound scree,
Known to the enemies as Leto's Chair,

Trespasses on the buff and masks the mouth
Of one such windless bay, in which
Patroclus lies and crouching Thackta dreams:

'I got his love. If I could get his head . . .'

*

Picture a yacht
Canting at speed
Over ripple-ribbed sand.
Change its mast to a man,
Change its boom to a bow,
Change its sail to a shield:
See Menelaos
Breasting the whalebacks to picket the corpse of Patroclus.
His face is sad behind his mask; but not sad-soft,
Sad-up-the-hill and contemplate the moon
Until times change.

Thackta, get lost: he has not seen you – yet;
A child beheading parsley grass
Is all you'll be to him, who knows –
If he can get it out – Patroclus' corpse
Will breach Achilles' strike, the Skean Gate,
And Helen's porch; an ample beast, who vaults
The tufted hussock between you and him
And lets his long, grey, bronze-pronged spear,
Sweep, sweep, Patroclus' vacant face, and guards him gone
Raptly as speechless breathers guard their young:
So run!
But he does not. Prince Hector is his god.
Instead:
'Get off my meat, Greek king.
I got him first' (a lie) 'his flesh is mine.'
Smooth as a dish that listens to the void

The Redhead's face swings up.
  'Dear God,' he thinks,
'Who is this lily-wristed titch?'
Picking a blob of dried froth from his lips,
Locking his mud-green eyes on Thackta's blue,
And saying: 'Boy,
I can hear your heart.
Who hopes to hold your children on her knee?'

  Hector has found Achilles' sacred pair.
He idles in: 'Hi'e . . . hi'e . . .,' his chariot in,
Dapple and grey they are, their reins in sand,
'Hi'e. Hi'e,' who move away from him,
No hint of Troy or Thackta in his head.
  Air into lips; speech into Hector's ear.
Apollo's presence, Priam's voice: 'My son,'
Who does not hear . . .
  Louder the god. The horses vanish. 'Son,
King Menelaos wants Patroclus' corpse.
Thackta has just one spear.'

  Whenever Thackta fought he wore
Slung from an oiled tendon round his neck
A cleverly articulated fish;
Each jacinth scale a moving part; each eye, a pearl.
His luck; his glittering christopher; a gift.
  'My name is Thackta, Greek,' he said,
And fingered it.
  'Thackta, the son of Raphno, Lord of Tus?'
  'Indeed.'
  'And brother of Lord Midon?'
  'Yes.'
  'Here is the news. I killed him earlier today.
Not that his death was worth an ounce of fluff.'
  Answer him, Thackta; keep him at his chat;
Tell him you like the colour of his horns –

That Helen left a man too old to fuck.
We can see Hector. Hector reads your fix
And will return before this king-sized wart
Upon the body of your world can cast;
So do not cast . . . And yet he does,
And notes – arm up, toe down – the spear approach
King Menelaos' needling mouth, who wills it near,
Observes it streaking through the sunburnt air,
Waits till his face is half its haft's length off,
Then bows – as if to Helen on their wedding day.
　And as that often polished leaf slid past,
Offhandedly the bitter Greek reached up
And hooked the tendon around Thackta's neck
And smashed his downwards moving cry against his knee,
And poached his eyes, and smashed and smashed
That baby face, loose as a bag of nuts; and then –
When Thackta's whimpering gained that fine, high shriek,
Dear to a mind inspired by vengefulness – the Greek
Posted his blade between the runny lips,
Increased the number of the dead by one,
Eased his malignant vigour with a sigh,
And scratched; then snapped the thong
And wiggled Thackta's jacinth fish
Between the Heavenly and his royal eye.

　No sound. No movement in the bay.
Stripping his victim with professional speed;
Plate-straps between his teeth; Patroclus up –
And – hup! – knees bowed; one last look round;
Now up the whalebacks to the coast.
　Not your day, Menelaos, not your day:
Dust in the air? or smoke? a shout –
Source out of sight, but near, but out of sight
Behind the crest, trough, crest, trough, crest;
Now soon, now soon to see
– Put down that armour isolated king –

Hector, with Glaucos and Anaxapart,
Outdistancing the wind that comes from Greece
– 'If I leave you, Patroclus, what' –
And Hector's blood-cry, Hector's plume
– 'If I do not, what will become of me?' –
Among the other, nodding, orange plumes.
And all their banners rising one by one;
One after one; and then another one
– 'Prince Hector's one of them' –
Come between Leto's Chair, the corniced horn,
Fast as a rested python over tile,
Into the yellow bay.
   Bronze tyres. Reflecting breast-straps. You must set
Patroclus' body back upon the sand,
And as the arrows start to splash, back off,
Running towards the backslope, up, a cat
Airborne a moment, one glance back: 'Dear God,
Their chariots will slice,' splash, 'corpse,' splash, splash,
'In half,' and reach the crest,
And:
   'Ajax!'
And:
   'Odysseus!'
You shout, and run, and run . . .
   And who would not?
   Then Hector's hand goes up.
Up go the horses. Zigzagged sand. Wheels lock.
   And you are off,
As he climbs down.
   Eyelight like sun on tin.
   'My Prince?'
Turning Patroclus over with his foot,
   'Yes, Glaucos.' Looking up.
No sign of Troy therein.
   'The Greek has gone for help.'
   'I know,'

His nostrils fluttering,
'Give me your axe,'
His mouth like twine.
'My axe?'
'You, Manto:
Shell this lookalike and load the armour up.'
Tall plumes go bob.
'And you –'
(Sarpedon's armourer)
'Anaxapart'
(Who once had fifty stitches in his face)
'Up with its shoulders. Yes, like that.'
(And you could strike a match upon the scar.)
'Now stretch its neck across that rock,'
His arm held out behind; still looking down:
'Glaucos, I asked you for your axe.'
Zephyrs disturb their bearskins. Mask meets mask.
Then Glaucos said:
'Before you use Patroclus' fat to grease
Your chariot hubs, Overlord Hector, ask yourself how
Troy can be held without Sarpedon's men.
Dog in the forehead but at heart a deer,
Recall the luckless morning when you kicked
Your silk-and-silver counterpane aside
And found your coast alive with shrieking Greeks.
After the shock of it, was not Sarpedon's name
The first to cross your lips? whose help you begged?
Though all you brought was "*We would be obliged*"
And "*Thankyou, thankyou*" when he promised it –
Keeping his promise with half Lycia.
And on the day we came,
Before Aeneas and yourself had stopped
Mow multiplying thanks by previous thanks
Sarpedon and Anaxapart had armed,
Gotten our troops together and engaged.
That day, and every long successive fighting day,

He was first out, last home; with laughter,
Golden wounds, good words; always the first,
First across Agamemnon's ditch today.
    But now that he is dead and has no fellow,
How do you keep your obligation, Hector?
    Begging my axe to violate the one
Greek corpse sufficiently revered to change for his;
Wanting Achilles' gear to pod your beef;
And giving Helen's reject time to fetch
More of our enemies up.
    I know . . . I know . . .'
Ingathering his reins:
    'Day one, a friend; day two, a guest; day three, a chore.
Sarpedon's death makes me the Lycian chief.
Why should we risk ourselves for Hector's Wall
Who leaves his ally naked in a ditch?'

    Thin
Wavering heat. Big flakes of sand. Live things
Blown right and left.
    The tail-end of a banner wraps
A soldier's face: 'Why fight?
The wind brings leaves enough to light a fire.'

    'You will not die saluting, Glaucos – will you?'
Prince Hector said. And to the rest:
    'Get the bones home. When Greece comes back
I shall be good enough to watch.'

    Patroclus naked now.
The armour stacked beneath a chariot rug.
Manto beside the horses, eyes cast down,
Awaiting Hector's word.

    'Lead on.'

Silent as men grown old while following sheep
They watch him wheel away.

*

Sea-bird's eye view:
Soldiers around Patroclus: centaur ants
Hoisting a morsel,
And,
On the whalebacks' tidal side,
Ajax and Little Ajax, Helen's man,
Odysseus and his driver, Bombax, head
A wedge of plate-faced Greeks.
Close-up on Bombax; 45; fighting since 2;
Who wears his plate beneath his skin; one who has killed
More talking bipeds than Troy's wall has bricks;
Whose hair is long, is oiled, is white, is sprung,
Plaited with silver wire, twice plaited – strong? –
Why, he could swing a city to and fro with it
And get no crick; whose eye can fix
A spider's web yoking a tent peg to its guy
Five miles downbeach – and count its spokes:
'By night?'
See them come padding down the coastal lane,
Flow up the low-browed, crested cliffs, across the backs;
Two hundred plus; then, at Odysseus' sign, drop flat,
And steer their helmets through the sabre grass,
Lining the shoulders of the bay to look
Down upon Glaucos and the corpse.
'Ready?' Odysseus says.
Their massed plumes nod.

*

Moving at speed, but absolutely still,
The arrow in the air. Death in a man

As something first perceived by accident.
    Massed hands; massed glare;
The piston-kneed, blade-flailing Greeks pour down,
Like a gigantic fan with razored vanes,
Leaping the hummock-studded slope, up-down,
As if the ground between each clump was taut,
Was trampoline, up-down, so slow they fly,
So quick upon the sand.
    Glaucos an instant blinded by the sky
White backflash off their polished front; but in the next,
Scanning them through its after-image, cool
As the atrium of a mossy shrine, and shouts:
    'Close! Close!'
Too late, alas. Before his voice is out
Their masks are on him like a waterfall!
    Who was it said
That one long day's more work will see it done?
Up to the waist in dead:
    '*Dear Lord,*' he prays,
    '*Dear Lord,*' his soldiers dead,
    '*By day,*'
Their souls like babies rising from their lips,
    '*A river in the sky,*'
'Keep close!'
    '*By night, an Amazon.*
    Save us from this and I will build a stone.'
'Close! Closer still!'
    '*Temple that bears*'
'Now slope your shields!'
    '*Shadows of deer at sunset and Thy name.*'
    Clenching his men about Patroclus' corpse;
Faced by a fly; all eyes; an egg with eyes;
'We have it still!' – attacked by eyes – 'Edge out . . .'
Arrows that thock, that enter eyes, that pass
Close as a layer of paint, that blind,
That splash about them like spring rain.

Bombax takes heads
Like chopping twelve-inch logs for exercise;
Feathers of blood surround him like a bronze
On decorative water; 'Hector, where? –
Dog in the forehead but at heart a doe,'
As sunlight jumps from cheek to shiny cheek,
Eager to glorify their transience.
'Not to climb Leto's Chair. That way lies death,
Anaxapart,' who does not hear, his eyes
On Pyrop, *The Macedonian Ham*
(As Little Ajax christened him)
The richest and the fattest Greek
(A chariot factory plus numerous farms)
To sail from Liminaria to Troy;
Who looks behind him, half crouched down,
As timid and as fearful as a dog
About to shit.
'Run, Greek – run, run,'
Anaxapart insists. And (fool!) instead
Of burrowing among the shields, he does,
And running cries:
'My mother is alone, and old, and sick,'
But what fear urged obesity held back.
Six arrows in the Lycian's fist:
'My' – one,
'Is' – two,
'And' – three,
Then – four, – five, – six
In the air at once . . . Wi'eeee!
Even Odysseus paused to catch that trick.
– And the arrows go so fast their shanks ignite!
– And the hits make Pyrop flounce!
– And he cannot hold his mud!
Six hammer blows upon his neck; and long before his voice,
So high, so piteous and profound, died out,
Anaxapart's keen zanies sheared his tin.

Pleasure maybe
But not a sign of victory in this.
Glaucos shows red:
Bent as if seen through water, split tip hooked,
Both edges blunted on Greek flesh, his sword.
'*This is our end, my Lord,*'
His feet go backwards, treading on the dead
That sigh and ooze like moss.
'*Heaven is silent;*
Earth does not confide;
I turn around,
The way to Troy is barred.'
Patroclus in their midst. Around him, shields.
Around the shields, the masks.
'Close! Close!'

*

Achilles' armour was not made on earth.
A lame god yoked its spacious particles.
Deliberate inattention has
Only enhanced its light-collecting planes;
Into whose depth, safe, safe, amid the dunes
Prince Hector looks, amazed, and strips his own;
Stands naked in the light, amazed, and lifts
Its bodice up, and kisses it; then holds it out,
And, like a man long kept from water, lets
Its radiance pour down; and sees within
The clouds that pass, the gulls that stall,
His own hope-governed face, and near its rim,
Distorted as the brilliant surface bends
Its rivetless, near-minus weight away,
His patient horses, and his men.

Then,
Through the azure vacancy in which

Our cooling onion floats: clouds long as lips,
God's lips above the mountain, saying:
  'Worm:
Your death is nearer than your nose.
"*Perhaps,*" you told Patroclus as he went.
Perhaps was wrong. But I will let you fight
Dressed as the gods are dressed,
And give your heart a priceless boost, until
Oblivion's resistless whisper bids
Its pulse, a drum between two torches in the night,
To follow your creation on their way.'

  The clouds have altered now:
Upgathered like a continental shelf
Crowned by mauve air, and down their pillowed range
Emerald-stained chrome through leaf to orange-grey,
Clear to the listening eye their caves read dusk:
Though that dim porch is Ganges' length away.

  Hector is in the armour. Boran lifts
A coiling oxhorn to his lips. And though
Its summons bumps the tower where Priam sits
Beside a lip that slides
Out of a stone lion's mouth into a pool,
The king is old and deaf, and does not move.

*

  One thousand Trojan soldiers form a ring.
They link their arms; they breathe in unison;
Lay back their faces till each throat stands wide,
And wait; and wait; then, on the masterbeat,
Shatter the empyrean with a cry!
Then stamp! Then cry! Then stamp again! Then cry!
Cry overfollowing cry, concordant stamp
On stamp, until the far, translucent hue

Augments their promising to die, and rides
Forward to sunset on their 'God for Troy!'
  Hector is in the middle of that ring;
Crouched on his toes; his knees braced wide; palms up;
White dactyls tigered; arms outspread.
And now his certain, triple-armoured mind
(By God, the holy metal, and his men)
Grows light, grows lucent, clarified for death.
And as their voices mix above their prince,
He rocks from toe to toe; and as they stamp,
First one and then the other of his feet
Lifts from the sand; and as they lean and lead
Into a skip-step sunwise traipse around,
Though Hector keeps his body jack-knifed down,
Adding his voice to theirs he starts to turn
Counter their turn, to lift himself, to spin,
Becoming in their eyes a source, a sun,
A star, whose force is theirs, who leaps –
Unfolds his body in the air,
Prances upon the air, and in the air
Unsheaths Achilles' sword and makes it sing . . .
  See how they flow towards him, arms upraised,
Table their shields to keep his dance aloft,
And cry again, and cry, and start to pour
Over the dunes, him spinning on that top,
Across the buff and onward to the bay,
Achilles' blade about his waist, so fast,
A cymbal struck by voices, shimmer struck,
Out of whose metal centre Hector's own,
Seething between his teeth, wails up the sky
On one insatiable note.
  And as his wail spread outward on the air,
And as the stolen armour ate the light,
Those fighting round Patroclus' body thought
Earth had upthrust a floe of luminous malt
That swamped their world and pitched the famous Greeks

Back to the crest and filled the bay with waves.
  And surfacing upon that molten sludge
With Glaucos in his arms, Prince Hector said,
As he wiped the crawling stains away:
  'Remember me?'
Aeneas going by so close
His slipstream pats their cheeks,
  'Remember me?'
And rings Patroclus with a horse-high,
Set-too-close-for-the-point-of-a-spear's-tip
Wall of a hundred oxhide shields.

*

  Impacted battle; dust above a herd.
Trachea, source of tears, sliced clean.
Deckle-edged wounds: 'Poor Jataphact, to know,' knocked
    clean
Out of his armour like a half-set jelly,
'Your eyes to be still open yet not see,' or see
By an abandoned chariot a dog
With something like your forearm in its mouth;
A face split off,
Sent skimming lidlike through the crunch,
Still smiling, but its pupils dots on dice:
  Bodies so intermixed
The tremor of their impact keeps the dead
Upright within the mass. Half-dragged, half-borne,
Killed five times over, Caphno – rose with his oar,
Sang as his rapt ship ran its sunside strake
Through the lace of an oncoming wave –now splashed
With blood plus slaver from his chest to chin,
Borne back into the mass, itself borne back
And forth across the bay like cherry froth.
  Someone breaks out; another follows him;
Throws, hits, rides on; the first – transfixed –

Hauls on the carefully selected pole
Trembling within his groin, and drags
His bladder out with it;
Then doubles popeyed back into the jam.
  Notice the Cretans, Little A. & Big – some team!
Prince Little loves to tease them with his arse:
  'I'll screw your widow, Badedas,'
Shouting head down, his face between his knees;
And when the angered Trojan throws, *he* throws,
Twisting and catching what the other threw,
And has the time to watch his leaf divide
His fellow soldier from the light and goes
'No third green generation from his tree,'
Whistling away.
  The Greeks swear by their dead. The Trojans by their
    home.
'Not one step back –' 'If I should die –' and does.
Water through water: who can tell whose red, whose roar
It is? Their banners overclouding one by one;
One after one; and then another one.
  Anaxapart has tied Patroclus' body to a shield:
Spreadeagled on its front,
With Zeeteez and Opknocktophon as crucifers.
And much as their posterity will spurn
Vampires with garlic, ignorance with thought,
Those Trojans elevate his corpse and claim:
  'Gangway for Troy!'
While in the chariot length their idol gains,
With fingerbells and feathered necklaces,
Molo the Dancer from Cymatriax tugs
At its penis as he squeaks:
  'Achilles' love!'
  Trumpets behind the corpse; more Trojan masks;
Then tambourines and drums: 'Not one step back . . .'
But must! 'Troy!' 'Troy!' 'If I –' and does.

Seeking a quiet eddy in the flood;
Blood flowing from his nostrils; he who fights
Without the aid of anger says: 'Antilochos.
Run to the Fleet. Give Wondersulk our news.
His love is dead. His armour gone.
Prince Hector has the corpse.
And as an afterthought, that we are lost.'
'Why me, Odysseus?'
'That is the why. Now go,
And not so gloomy, if you wish to please.'
Fast as the strongest wing can fly
Between the twilight and the setting sun,
He goes.

Big Ajax is not one for thought.
Monkeys and rats avoid his company.
Now he is lost. He looks about. He stands
As one who listens for a far-off call,
And now and then, refocussed, knocks
An optimistic blade aside,
Or reaches out and grabs what passes by.
And all the while his huge, packed heart,
Trying to squeeze an answer from its brain:
'Lord, we will crack. I know it. We will crack.'
Until young Manto, Hector's ward,
Came to the stymied giant's aid.

'*Stay here. We do not cut green wheat,*'
Prince Hector ordered as he led the dance.
Five minutes later Hector's word became
'I am at least a mile away' from where
Arrows like raindrops slash through boiling dust;
Then walked; then dropped; then: 'Only ten lengths more'
– Though on your hands and knees it still seems far –
And saw – head up – dead Caphno's chariot and pair
Come wandering down the outskirt of that day:

'My prize! My prize!' – on, up, flick, off – 'My prince,
You will be proud of me!' – away . . .
    But once upon the plate the battle's roar
– Wind larruped flame through stands of dry garrigue –
Inspired his disobedience, swamped his car;
And how the fights blur by, and how the wind
Snaffles the yellow tatter of his hair:
'Did Hector lie? There is no danger here.
And who is that Greek beast, breathless and faint,
Leaning upon his spear, so out of time
That I can run him down?' O downy sprat,
That crocodile is Ajax.
And though his mind is worlds away his eye
Has registered your blip long since,
Signalled his back to bend, his fingers to select
A stone, young Manto, bigger than your head,
Rowed back his elbow, thrown it true, and, true,
It did not, was not aimed at you, that hit
The left horse – splat! – between its gentle eyes,
Dead on the hoof and dragged its tracemate down,
And forwarding your body through the air,
Your please-Prince-Hector-help-me open mouth
Swallowed the nose of Ajax' canted spear.

    Harder than painting snowfields in full sunlight
The light in Ajax' eye, his answer come:
    Out with your sword; up, aim, and in-
To the living horse with it. The traces cut.
Then feel the shaft rise freely to your hand.
    And like a man who thrusts a glowing rake
Into an opened furnace, Ajax picked
Dandiprat Manto off his spear,
Then rammed dead Caphno's chariot through the Greek-
Cum-Trojan flux.
    And now the Greeks are speaking with one voice:
'Patroclus ours!' across the dark they call,

And echoing this counted chicken, Troy:
'Who gets the body shares the gold with me!'
And all: 'Are these my arms,
So tired they go on, and on, alone?'

*

  Elsewhere late afternoon goes lazily enough.
No sign of cloud. Small noises cross the air intact.
  And yawning as he leaves his tent
To sigh and settle back against a rope –
As some men settle into life
Quiet in quiet rooms, supplied
With all they need by mute, obedient hands –
Achilles: who does his best to blimp
The queasy premonitions that explode beneath his heart:
  '*No matter how, how much, how often, or how easily you*
    win –
O my Patroclus, are you bitten off?'

  Antilochos appearing through these words.
Hateful the voice that springs between his clear-edged lips,
Weakening Odysseus' message to: 'Is gone.'

  Down on your knees, Achilles. Farther down.
Now forward on your hands and put your face into the dirt,
And scrub it to and fro.
  Grief has you by the hair with one
And with the forceps of its other hand
Uses your mouth to trowel the dogshit up;
Watches you lift your arms to Heaven; and then
Pounces and screws your nose into the filth.
  Gods have plucked drawstrings from your head,
And from the template of your upper lip
Modelled their bows.
  Not now. Not since

Your grieving reaches out and pistol-whips
That envied face, until
Frightened to bear your black, backbreaking agony alone,
You sank, throat back, thrown back, your voice
Thrown out across the sea to reach your Source.

*

Salt-water woman,
Eternal,
She heard him;
Long-bodied Thetis who lives in the wave,
In the coral,
Fluorescent;
Green over grey over olive forever;
The light falling sideways from Heaven,
She heard him,
Achilles,
Her marvellous son.

Surge in her body;
Head ferns grow wider,
Grow paler;
Her message, his message,
Goes through the water:
'Sisters,'
Nayruesay,
'Sisters,'
Eternal,
Salt-water women,
Came when she called to them,
Came through the waves to her, swam as she swam
Towards Greece; beyond Greece; now she passes the Islands,
Arm over arm swimming backways, peaked nipples,
Full fifty green-grey palely shimmering kith of King Nayruce,
Those who leave eddies, who startle, her sisters:

Derna, Leucate, lithe Famagusta,
Isso, Nifaria, black chevroned Cos,
Panope, beaded, entwining Galethiel,
Thasos, Talita, Hymno and Phyle,
Sleek Manapharium, Jithis, Bardia,
Serpentine Xanthe, Nemix and Simi,
Came from the iodine, surfaced through azure
Onto the beach-head and lay round Achilles.

'What cause have you to weep?' his mother said.
'It was your hands God saw, your voice He heard
Uplifted, saying: "*Lord, until they feel my lack,*
Let the Greeks burn; let them taste pain." '
And heard him say:
'Poor Source –
Wet-cheeked, much-wronged, long-suffering Thetis,
Famous in time as the Eternal Moan,
That dowry of Heaven-sent weapons you brought
My brutal father when your father forced
You to divide your legs for oafish him,
Pods Hector now; and I, the paradigm
Of all creation's violent hierarchy,
Sit naked by the sea and number waves.
Excellent that my Greekish aides taste pain;
And better that they die. But not enough.
Not agony enough. Increase that pain;
Without appeal and without delay
Let death come down – and not, please God
(For I will be His master either way),
Exclusively to Agamemnon's led;
But onto Troy; and onto Troy Beyond; and until all of us
Brain-damaged, stinking herd of God-foxed sheep,
Chiefs of our loathsome, thought-polluted dot –
Bar two: Hector's dark head is mine.'
'You cannot have it without armour, child,'
His mother said.

And vanished through the waves with all her school.

Sunfade. Sea breathing. Sea-lice trot
Over warm stones.
Achilles and Antilochos:
How small they look beneath the disappearing sky!
Sap rises in them both. An opening breeze
Ruffles their hair; but only A. hears:

'Greek . . .'
'Yes?'
'Greek . . .'
'Who?'
'Iris.'
'Speak.'
'Go to the ditch.
Let Troy know you are back.
Until your strength is operational
Your voice must serve.
You know what fighting is:
When things are at their worst an extra shout
Can save the day.'

He goes.

*

Consider planes at touchdown – how they poise;
Or palms beneath a numbered hurricane;
Or birds wheeled sideways over windswept heights;
Or burly salmon challenging a weir;
Right-angled, dreamy fliers, as they ride
The instep of a dying wave, or trace
Diagonals on snowslopes:

Quick cuts like these may give

Some definition to the mind's wild eye
That follow-spots Achilles' sacred pair –
No death, no dung, no loyalty to man
In them – come Troyside down the dunes towards the bay,
Achilles' charioteer, Alastor, lost
On their basket's plate, locked to their reins,
Pulling with all his might to make them stay,
That also Iris heard, that know their Care,
Their semi-human Clay, their half-loved, half-obeyed,
Half-childlike lord, Achilles, will demand
Their services: each worth at least
An income of ten thousand men a day.

*

At night at Priam's table Hector sits
Beside Aeneas. So it is now.
Square into Greece their two-edged axe heads go,
Sledgehammers on detested statuary,
The bar from which all Trojan wires are drawn.

Head-lock, body-slam,
Hector attacking;
His anger, his armour, his:
'Now, now, or never, O Infinite, Endless Apollo,'
But silent,
*'I, in my weakness, beseech you to cast
All thought of peace on earth for me away
Without possession of that corpse.'*
Hard to say who is who: the soldiers, the captains,
Their guts look alike.

Ajax alone between it and their thirst:
Pivoting on his toes, his arms looped up,
Safe in his hands his spear's moist butt, that whirrs
– Who falls into that airscrew, kiss goodbye . . .

And for a moment Hector driven back,
And when, and if, and here it comes:
'On! On! On! On!' he cries. 'Die on that spear!'
The Trojans try to snake beneath its point,
And Ajax down on one, and with the other foot
Thrusts himself round until the spear's bronze torque
Hisses a finger's width above Patroclus' face,
As Bombax shouts: 'Here, Ajax, here,'
As Menelaos: 'Here . . .'

And while his brother keeps his back, Aeneas taunts:
'Crapulous mammoth! Thicker than the wall!
Ajax the wordless chattel of his strength!' –
And spits, and runs, and, yes, the Greek is hooked!
Who follows him, and throws . . . A hit?
Odysseus holds his breath: 'Alas – Apollo hates that shot':
Forth went the hand of clarity across the twilit air
And tipped the straight-grained, bronze-fanged pole aside.

'God scum,' said Bombax – only to himself.

Aeneas through the blades, brushing their strokes aside,
Up the far slope, with Ajax far behind,
And sees Alastor entering the bay
Between the horn and Leto's Chair,
And sprints towards its brink,
And . . . two, one, off! –
Free fall –
Free fall –
Swooping upon Alastor in his car,
As angels in commemorative stone
Still swoop on unknown soldiers as they die
For some at best but half-remembered cause.
And as Alastor swerved, Aeneas' axe
Enhanced the natural crackage of his skull,
And he quit being, while his pair

Skid-slithered through the tumult, flailed that mass,
And overran Patroclus' tattered corpse.
    Hector triumphant:
Dropping his spear, clenching his fists,
Raising his fists in the air, shaking his fists with delight:
    'Who brings it out will share the fame with me!'
Anaxapart has got it by the chin.
Knees bent, spine bowed, feet braced into the clavicles,
Wrenching the nut right left right right, thinks:
'Screw the bastard off . . .'
Leaning across Anaxapart Prince Hector shouts, 'On! On!'
Trying to slash at Bombax and the Greeks,
Who have Patroclus by the feet, and tug:
    'Ah . . .'
They tug.
    'Ah . . .'
The body stretched between them like a hide.

*

Five miles due north.
Achilles on the rampart by the ditch:
    He lifts his face to ninety; draws his breath;
And from the bottom of his heart emits
So long and loud and terrible a scream,
The icy scabs at either end of earth
Winced in their sleep; and in the heads that fought
It seemed as if, and through his voice alone,
The whole world's woe could be abandoned to the sky.

    And in that instant all the fighting glassed.

    Odysseus excepted.

    Quick as a priest who waits for passing birds
To form a letter in the air, he has

Patroclus' body up and out.
    And as Prince Hector shouts:
'The Greeks have got their carrion intact!'
    The sun,
Head of a still-surviving kingdom, drew
The earth between them and himself,
    And so the plain grew dark.

*

    Starred sky. Calm sky.
Only the water's luminosity
Marks the land's end.

    A light is moving down the beach.
It wavers. Comes towards the fleet.
The hulls like upturned glasses made of jet.

    Is it a God?
No details

    Yet.

    Now we can hear a drum.

    And now we see it:
Six warriors with flaming wands,
Eight veteran bearers, and one prince,
Patroclus, dead, crossed axes on his chest,
Upon a bier.

    Gold on the wrists that bear the prince aloft.
Tears on the cheeks of those who lead with wands.
Multiple injuries adorn the corpse.
And we, the army, genuflect in line.

*

Five years ago Achilles robbed a Phrygian citadel
And kept the temple cauldron for himself.
The poet who accompanied him to Troy
Deciphered the inscriptions on its waist.
One said:
I AM THE EARTH
The other:
VOID.

And when from zigzagged ewers his female slaves
Had filled and built a fire beneath its knees,
Achilles laved the flesh and pinned the wounds
And dressed the yellow hair and spread
Ointments from Thetis' cave on every mark
Of what Patroclus was, and kissed its mouth,
And wet its face with tears, and kissed and kissed again,
And said: 'My love, I swear you will not burn
Till Hector's severed head is in my lap.'

PAX

Rat.
Pearl.
Onion.
Honey:
These colours came before the Sun
Lifted above the ocean,
Bringing light
Alike to mortals and Immortals.

And through this falling brightness,
Through the by now:
Mosque,
Eucalyptus,
Utter blue,
Came Thetis,
Gliding across the azimuth,
With armour the colour of moonlight laid on her forearms;
Her palms upturned;
Her hovering above the fleet;
Her skyish face towards her son,

Achilles,
Gripping the body of Patroclus
Naked and dead against his own,
While Thetis spoke:
'Son . . .'
His soldiers looking on;
Looking away from it; remembering their own;
'Grieving will not amend what Heaven has done.
Suppose you throw your hate after Patroclus' soul.
Who besides Troy will gain?
See what I've brought . . .'

And as she laid the moonlit armour on the sand
It chimed;
And the sound that came from it
Followed the light that came from it,
Like sighing,
Saying,
Made in Heaven.

And those who had the neck to watch Achilles weep
Could not look now.
Nobody looked. They were afraid.

Except Achilles: looked,
Lifted a piece of it between his hands;
Turned it; tested the weight of it; and then
Spun the holy tungsten, like a star between his knees,
Slitting his eyes against the flare, some said,
But others thought the hatred shuttered by his lids
Made him protect the metal.

His eyes like furnace doors ajar.

When he had got its weight
And let its industry console his grief a bit:
'I'll fight,'
He said. Simple as that. 'I'll fight.'

And so Troy fell.

'But while I fight, what will become of this' –
Patroclus – 'Mother?
Inside an hour a thousand slimy things will burrow.
And if the fight drags on his flesh will swarm
Like water boiling.'
And she:
'Son, while you fight,

Nothing shall taint him;
Sun will not touch him,
Nor the slimy things.'

  Promising this she slid
Rare ichors in the seven born openings of Patroclus' head,
Making the carrion radiant.
  And her Achilles went to make amends,
Walking alone beside the broken lace that hung
Over the sea's green fist.

  The sea that is always counting.

  Ever since men began in time, time and
  Time again they met in parliaments,
  Where, in due turn, letting the next man speak,
  With mouthfuls of soft air they tried to stop
  Themselves from ravening their talking throats;
  Hoping enunciated airs would fall
  With verisimilitude in different minds,
  And bring some concord to those minds; soft air
  Between the hatred dying animals
  Monotonously bear towards themselves;
  Only soft air to underwrite the in-
  Built violence of being, to meld it to
  Something more civil, rarer than true forgiveness.
  No work was lovelier in history;
  And nothing failed so often: knowing this
  The army came to hear Achilles say:
  'Pax, Agamemnon.' And Agamemnon's: 'Pax.'
  Now I must ask you to forget reality,
To be a momentary bird above those men
And watch their filings gather round
The rumour of a conference until
Magnetic grapevines bind them close.
  From a low angle the army looks oval, whitish centered,

Split at one end, prised slightly open, and,
Opposite to the opening, Achilles
(Who they have come to hear) with hard-faced veterans
On either side, lance-butts struck down,
And here and there a flag. Even the chariot mechanics,
Tentmakers, priests, and whores came up
To hear their Lords say pax.

And as men will, they came, the limping kings;
Odysseus first, chatting to Little Ajax, through the ring,
Sitting them down; and after them, a trifle slow
But coming all the same, doomed Agamemnon,
King of Kings, his elbow gummed with blood.

The ring is shut. Enormous calm.
King Agamemnon and Achilles face to face,
Distinct as polygon and square.

Achilles first:
'King,
I have been a fool.
The arid bliss self-righteousness provokes
Addled my mind.'
Odysseus nods.
'Remembering how I took Briseis' town,
And how its women offered me their flesh –
Like simple creatures looking for a passage to the sea –
It would have been far better for us both
If, when the winnings were aligned,
I had ignored her urgent vulnerability.
But, having made it so, I like my own.
And if another man – my King, what's more –
Takes what is mine and lets the army know it,
What are they both to do?
Kings can admit so little.
Kings know: what damages their principality

Endangers all.
    If he is inconsiderate,
He is the king; if greedy, greedy king,
And if at noon the king says: '*It is night.*' –
Behold, the stars!
    What if he damages the man
On whom his principality depends?
He's still the king. His war goes on. The man must give.
    But if the man in question cannot give
Because the god in him that makes the king his chief
        dependant
Is part and parcel of the god that cries *Revenge*! when he is
        wronged,
What happens then?
    Stamp on my foot, my heart is stunned;
I cannot help it; it is stunned; it rankles –
Here,' touching his chest.
    'I am not angry anymore.
My heart is broken. Done is done, it says.
And yet its pain can only mask my rancour.
So let pride serve.
When all is said and done – I am Achilles.'

    And the army love their darling, and they cry:
'Achil! Achil! Achil!'
Louder than any counting sea;
And sentries on the eastern wall of Troy
Sweat by their spears.

    King Agamemnon waits.

    And waits.

    Then rising, says:

    'Heroes . . .

I do not think your zeal will be injured
If those who are the farthest off stand still,
And those in front stop muttering to themselves.'
    Bad start.
'Everyone can't hear everything, of course.'
    Gulls cry.
'However, even clear-voiced heralds,
Accustomed as they are to public speaking,
Can lose their audience if inattention makes them feel
Indifference to their message.'
    Gulls.

    'In fact, the things I have to say, are, in a sense,
Meant for Achilles' ears alone.
But if the army and his peers witness our settlement
My purpose will be better served.
    Like him, I am a man.
But I am also king. His king. Your king.
And as your king I have received
What most of you have not unwillingly agreed was mine:
The best part of the blame.'
    He has them now.
    'BUT I AM NOT TO BLAME!'
    And now.
    'Undoubtedly I took, unfairly, pulling rank,
The girl Achilles won.
I tell you it was not my wish.
Between my judgement and my action Ahtay fell;
God's eldest girl, contentious Ahtay . . . Oh,
Soft are her footsteps but her performance keeps no day;
Nor does she walk upon the ground, but drifts
Into our human wishes like the sticky flecks of down
Tickling our lips in endless summertime;
And with her episode comes misery.
    Let me remind you how God walked
Into the courtyard of the Sun and told his cabinet:
    'Rejoice with me!

For unto men this day a child is born
Whose blood is royal with my eminence;
And who, all in good time, will be
A king called *Hercules.*'
And looking at her fingers, Hera said:
'We have been fooled before.
However; if you swear
That any child of yours born on this day . . .'
God swore; and Ahtay sat between His eyes.
Soon as the oath had crossed His mythic lips
Hera went quick as that from Heaven to Greece,
And with her right hand masked the womb
Swaddling Hercules, and with her left
Parted the body of another girl whose child was His
But only eight months gone,
And held it up and jeered:
'See what your oath has done!'
God made the early boy a king, and Hercules a serf
And wept as men must weep.
If you will lead the Greeks, Achilles,
I will give Briseis back;
And may we be forgiven.'

The sun is smaller now.

Achilles says: 'Let us fight now – *at once* –'
'Wait' – slipping the word in like a bolt –
'Marvellous boy,' Odysseus says.
'You can do what you like with us except make men fight hungry.
Well . . . you could do that too, but . . .'
Turning away from him towards the ranks –
'Wait!
The king will keep his promise now.
Young lords will fetch his penal gifts
For everyone to see and be amazed.

Everyone knows that men who get
Angry without good reason will
Conciliate without free gifts.
Therefore Achilles gladly takes
Everything Agamemnon gives.
And he who gives steps free of blame,
As he adopts the wrong.
God bless them both.'

Then, squatting by Achilles, says:
'Boy – you are the best of us. Your strength is fabulous.
But in my way I know some things you don't.
In any case, I'm old. Let me play wise.
What we have got to do is not embroidery.
For you, the battle may be gold.
The men will enter it like needles,
Breaking or broken, but either way,
Emerging naked as they went.
Think of the moment when they see
The usual loot is missing from this fight
Although the usual risks are not.
They do not own the swords with which they fight;
Nor the ships that brought them here;
Orders are handed down to them in words
They barely understand; frankly,
They do not give a whit who fucks soft Helen.
Ithaca's mine; Pythia yours; but what are they defending?
They love you? Yes. They do. They also loved Patroclus;
And he is dead, they say; bury the dead, they say;
A hundred of us singing angels died for every knock
Patroclus took – so why the fuss? – that's war, they say,
Who came to eat in Troy and not to prove how much
Dear friends are missed.
Certainly, they are fools.
But they are right. Fools often are.
Bury the dead, Achil,

And I will help you pitch Troy in the sea.'

*

Cobalt in Heaven,
And below it
Polar blue.
The body of the air is lapis, and
Where it falls
Behind the soft horizon,
The light turns back to Heaven.

A soldier pisses by his chariot;
Another
Sweetens his axe blade on a soapy stone;
And up between the dunes,
With ribbons, tambourines, and little drums,
Come twelve white horses led by seven women,
Briseis in their midst,
Her breasts so lovely that they envy one another.
And they pass by . . .
And after them young lords, escorting
Twenty ewers of bright silver, each in a polished trivet,
Their shining cheeks engraved by silversmiths
With files of long-nosed soldiers on the march.
And they pass by . . .
And after them, a sledge
Piled with twelve lots of Asian gold,
Carefully weighed, worth a small city.
And they pass by . . .
And last of all, guarding a sacrificial hog,
Talthibios, Chief Herald of the Greeks,
Passed by into the centre of the ring.

Yellow mists over Mount Ida.
The hog lowers its gilded tusks.
Is still.

By Agamemnon's feet, Talthibios sprinkles barley;
Snips a tuft from the hog's nape;
Waits for a breeze to nudge it off his palm
Into the flames that burn between the army and its king.

Haze covers Mount Ida.
Sand falls down sand.
Even the Gods are listless.

And Agamemnon spreads his arms,
Raises his face towards the sun, and cries:

'GOD
Be my witness;
EARTH
My witness;
SUN, SKY, WATER, WIND,
My witness.
I have not tampered with the girl
I took unjustly from Achilles.'

And drags his knife across the hog's silk throat.

Mists over Ida.

Slaves gut and throw the dead hog in the sea.

The army like ten thousand yellow stones.

Achilles says:
'So be it.
Eat, and prepare to fight.'

And took Briseis to his ship.

*

Under the curve the keel makes
Where it sweeps upright to the painted beak,
Achilles' tetrarchs placed their gilded oars,
Set twelve carved thwarts across them, then
Surfaced this stage with wolf- and beaver-fleece;
Amid whose stirring nap Patroclus lay:
The damaged statue of a prince awaiting transportation.
Near it Achilles sat, Odysseus beside,
And women brought them food.
'Patroclus liked to eat,' Achilles said,
'And you cooked well, Patroclus, didn't you?
Particularly well that summer when
The royal cuckold, crown in hand, came visiting from Argos
Whining 'wife' and 'theft' and 'war' and 'please' and –
What is this *eat*, Odysseus?
If you were telling me: He's dead, your father; well . . .
I might eat a bit; troubled, it's true; but eat
Like any fool who came God knows how many mist-
And danger-mixed sea-miles to salvage Helen.
Oh, I know you, Odysseus. You think:
Achilles will fight better if he feeds.
Don't be so sure.
I do not care about his gifts. I do not care, Odysseus,
Do not care!
Patroclus was my life's sole love.
The only living thing that called
Love out of me.
At night I used to dream of how, when he came home to Greece,
He'd tell them of my death – for I must die – and show my son
This house, for instance; or that stone beside the stream;
My long green meadows stretching through the light
So clear it seems to magnify . . .'

And here Achilles falls asleep beside his dead;

Odysseus goes off, as close to tears
As he will ever be;
    And,
At a window of the closed stone capital,
Helen wipes the sweat from under her big breasts.
    Aoi! . . . she is beautiful.

    But there is something foul about her, too.

    Now I shall ask you to imagine how
    Men under discipline of death prepare for war.
    There is much more to it than armament,
    And kicks from those who could not catch an hour's sleep,
    Waking the ones who dozed like rows of spoons;
    Or those with everything to lose, the kings,
    Asleep like pistols in red velvet.
    Moments like these absolve the needs dividing men.
    Whatever caught and brought and kept them here,
    Under Troy's ochre wall for ten burnt years,
    Is lost: and for a while they join a terrible equality;
    Are virtuous, self-sacrificing, free;
    And so insidious is this liberty
    That those surviving it will bear
    An even greater servitude to its root:
    Believing they were whole, while they were brave,
    That they were rich, because their loot was great;
    That war was meaningful, because they lost their friends.
    They rise! – the Greeks with smiling iron mouths.
    They are like Nature; like a mass of flame;
    Great lengths of water struck by changing winds;
    A forest of innumerable trees;
    Boundless sand; snowfall across broad steppes at dusk.
    As a huge beast stands and turns around itself,
    The well-fed, glittering army, stands and turns.

    Nothing can happen till Achilles wakes.

He wakes.

Those who have slept with sorrow in their hearts
Know all too well how short but sweet
The instant of their coming-to can be:
The heart is strong, as if it never sorrowed;
The mind's dear clarity intact; and then,
The vast, unhappy stone from yesterday
Rolls down these vital units to the bottom of oneself.

Achilles saw his armour in that instant,
And its ominous radiance flooded his heart.
Bright pads with toggles crossed behind the knees,
Bodice of fitted tungsten, pliable straps;
His shield as round and rich as moons in spring;
His sword's haft parked between sheaves of grey obsidian,
From which a lucid blade stood out, leaf-shaped, adorned
With running spirals.
And for his head a welded cortex; yes,
Though it is noon, the helmet screams against the light;
Scratches the eye; so violent it can be seen
Across three thousand years.

Achilles stands; he stretches; turns on his heel;
Punches the sunlight, bends, then – jumps! . . .
And lets the world turn fractionally beneath his feet.

Noon. In the foothills
Melons emerge from their green hidings.
Heat.

He walks towards the chariot.
Greece waits.

Over the wells in Troy mosquitoes hover.

Beside the chariot.
Soothing the sacred horses; watching his driver cinch,
Shake out the reins, and lay them on the rail;
Dapple and white the horses are; perfect they are;
Sneezing to clear their cool black muzzles.

He mounts.

The chariot's basket dips. The whip
Fires in between the horses' ears;
And as in dreams, or at Cape Kennedy, they rise,
Slowly it seems, their chests like royals, yet
Behind them in a double plume the sand curls up,
Is barely dented by their flying hooves,
And wheels that barely touch the world,
And the wind slams shut behind them.

'Fast as you are,' Achilles says,
'When twilight makes the armistice,
Take care you don't leave me behind
As you left my Patroclus.'

And as it ran the white horse turned its tall face back
And said:
'Prince,
This time we will, this time we can, but this time cannot last.
And when we leave you, not for dead – but dead –
God will not call us negligent as you have done.'

And Achilles, shaken, says:
'I know I will not make old bones.'

And laid his scourge against their racing flanks.

Someone has left a spear stuck in the sand.

Guide to Pronunciation

PLACES

Cymatriax	Cy·**mat**·tri·ax
Ida	Ey·der
Ithaca	**Ith**·tha·ka
Liminaria	Lim·in·**ah**·ree·ah
Lycia	Ly·see·ah
Phrygia	**Phri**·gee·ah
Pythia	**Pi**·thee·ah
Scamander	Ska·**man**·der
Skean	**Skee**·an
Taurus	**Taor**·us
Thessaly	**Thess**·a·ly

MORTALS AND IMMORTALS

Aeneas	Ae·**nee**·as
Ahtay	**Ah**·tay
Akafact	**Ak**·a·fact
Alastor	Al·**ass**·tor
Anaxapart	An·**ax**·a·part
Antilochos	An·**til**·o·kos
Arcadeum	Ar·**kay**·de·um
Badedas	Bad·**day**·das
Bardia	Bar·**dee**·ah
Bombax	**Bom**·bax
Boran	**Bore**·an
Briseis	Bri·**see**·is
Caphno	**Caph**·no
Cazca	**Caz**·ca
Cos	Coss
Derna	**Der**·na
Enop	**Ee**·nop
Famagusta	Fa·ma·**gust**·ta

Galethiel	Gal·ee·thiel
Glaucos	**Glau**·cos
Hera	**Hear**·a
Hymno	**Him**·no
Isso	**Iss**·o
Jataphact	**Ja**·ta·phact
Jithis	**Gee**·this
Leto	**Lee**·toh
Leucate	Leu·**ka**·tay
Lycon	**Ly**·con
Manapharium	Ma·na·**pha**·ree·um
Manto	**Man**·toh
Menelaos	Men·na·**lay**·us
Midon	**My**·don
Molo	Mow·lo
Myrmidons	**Myr**·mi·dons
Nayruce	**Nay**·ruce
Nayruesay	**Nay**·rue·say
Nemix	**Ne**·mix
Nifaria	Ni·**far**·ia
Opknocktophon	Op·**knock**·toh·phon
Orontes	O·**ron**·tes
Panope	**Pan**·oh·pe
Panotis	Pan·**oh**·tis
Patroclus	Pa·**trock**·lus
Phyle	**Phy**·lee
Priam	**Pry**·am
Pyrop	**Py**·rop
Raphno	**Raph**·no
Sarpedon	Sar·**pee**·don
Simi	**See**·me
Talita	Tal·**lee**·ta
Talthibios	Tal·**thy**·bios
Thackta	**Thack**·ta
Thasos	**Thas**·sos
Thestor	**Thess**·tor

Thetis	**Theet**·is
Xanthe	**Xan**·thee
Zeeteez	Zee·teez

SHOUTS

Aie	Eye·**eeee**
Aoi	**A**·oy

T. S. ELIOT Four Quartets

T. S. ELIOT Four Quartets

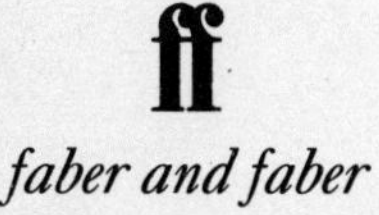

This edition first published in 2000
by Faber and Faber Limited
3 Queen Square, London, WC1N 3AU

'Burnt Norton' (1936), 'East Coker' (1940),
'The Dry Salvages' (1941) and 'Little Gidding' (1942)
first published in one volume as *Four Quartets* in 1944
by Faber and Faber Limited
First published in paperback in 1959

Photoset by Parker Typesetting Service, Leicester
Printed in Italy

All rights reserved
© T. S. Eliot, 1944
© Valerie Eliot, 1979

T. S. Eliot is hereby identified as author
of this work in accordance with Section 77
of the Copyright, Designs and Patents Act 1988

This book is sold subject to the condition that it shall not, by way of trade or otherwise, be lent, resold, hired out or otherwise circulated without the publisher's prior consent in any form of binding or cover other than that in which it is published and without a similar condition including this condition being imposed on the subsequent purchaser

A CIP catalogue record for this book
is available from the British Library

ISBN 0–571–20343–4

10 9 8 7 6 5 4 3 2 1

Contents

τοῦ λόγου δ᾽ἐόντος ξυνοῦ ζώουσιν οἱ πολλοί
ὡς ἰδίαν ἔχοντες φρόνησιν.

I. p. 77. Fr. 2.

ὁδὸς ἄνω κάτω μία καὶ ὡυτή.

I. p. 89. Fr. 60.

Diels: *Die Fragmente der Vorsokratiker* (Herakleitos).

I wish to acknowledge my obligation to friends for their criticism, and particularly to Mr John Hayward for improvements of phrase and construction.

BURNT NORTON

I

Time present and time past
Are both perhaps present in time future,
And time future contained in time past.
If all time is eternally present
All time is unredeemable.
What might have been is an abstraction
Remaining a perpetual possibility
Only in a world of speculation.
What might have been and what has been
Point to one end, which is always present.
Footfalls echo in the memory
Down the passage which we did not take
Towards the door we never opened
Into the rose-garden. My words echo
Thus, in your mind.
                                        But to what purpose
Disturbing the dust on a bowl of rose-leaves
I do not know.
                              Other echoes
Inhabit the garden. Shall we follow?
Quick, said the bird, find them, find them,
Round the corner. Through the first gate,
Into our first world, shall we follow
The deception of the thrush? Into our first world.
There they were, dignified, invisible,
Moving without pressure, over the dead leaves,
In the autumn heat, through the vibrant air,
And the bird called, in response to
The unheard music hidden in the shrubbery,
And the unseen eyebeam crossed, for the roses
Had the look of flowers that are looked at.
There they were as our guests, accepted and accepting.
So we moved, and they, in a formal pattern,

Along the empty alley, into the box circle,
To look down into the drained pool.
Dry the pool, dry concrete, brown edged,
And the pool was filled with water out of sunlight,
And the lotos rose, quietly, quietly,
The surface glittered out of heart of light,
And they were behind us, reflected in the pool.
Then a cloud passed, and the pool was empty.
Go, said the bird, for the leaves were full of children,
Hidden excitedly, containing laughter.
Go, go, go, said the bird: human kind
Cannot bear very much reality.
Time past and time future
What might have been and what has been
Point to one end, which is always present.

II

Garlic and sapphires in the mud
Clot the bedded axle-tree.
The trilling wire in the blood
Sings below inveterate scars
Appeasing long forgotten wars.
The dance along the artery
The circulation of the lymph
Are figured in the drift of stars
Ascend to summer in the tree
We move above the moving tree
In light upon the figured leaf
And hear upon the sodden floor
Below, the boarhound and the boar
Pursue their pattern as before
But reconciled among the stars.

At the still point of the turning world. Neither flesh nor fleshless;
Neither from nor towards; at the still point, there the dance is,

But neither arrest nor movement. And do not call it fixity,
Where past and future are gathered. Neither movement from
nor towards,
Neither ascent nor decline. Except for the point, the still
point,
There would be no dance, and there is only the dance.
I can only say, *there* we have been: but I cannot say
where.
And I cannot say, how long, for that is to place it in time.
The inner freedom from the practical desire,
The release from action and suffering, release from the inner
And the outer compulsion, yet surrounded
By a grace of sense, a white light still and moving,
Erhebung without motion, concentration
Without elimination, both a new world
And the old made explicit, understood
In the completion of its partial ecstasy,
The resolution of its partial horror.
Yet the enchainment of past and future
Woven in the weakness of the changing body,
Protects mankind from heaven and damnation
Which flesh cannot endure.
Time past and time future
Allow but a little consciousness.
To be conscious is not to be in time
But only in time can the moment in the rose-garden,
The moment in the arbour where the rain beat,
The moment in the draughty church at smokefall
Be remembered; involved with past and future.
Only through time time is conquered.

III

Here is a place of disaffection
Time before and time after
In a dim light: neither daylight

Investing form with lucid stillness
Turning shadow into transient beauty
With slow rotation suggesting permanence
Nor darkness to purify the soul
Emptying the sensual with deprivation
Cleansing affection from the temporal.
Neither plenitude nor vacancy. Only a flicker
Over the strained time-ridden faces
Distracted from distraction by distraction
Filled with fancies and empty of meaning
Tumid apathy with no concentration
Men and bits of paper, whirled by the cold wind
That blows before and after time,
Wind in and out of unwholesome lungs
Time before and time after.
Eructation of unhealthy souls
Into the faded air, the torpid
Driven on the wind that sweeps the gloomy hills of London,
Hampstead and Clerkenwell, Campden and Putney,
Highgate, Primrose and Ludgate. Not here
Not here the darkness, in this twittering world.

Descend lower, descend only
Into the world of perpetual solitude,
World not world, but that which is not world,
Internal darkness, deprivation
And destitution of all property,
Desiccation of the world of sense,
Evacuation of the world of fancy,
Inoperancy of the world of spirit;
This is the one way, and the other
Is the same, not in movement
But abstention from movement; while the world moves
In appetency, on its metalled ways
Of time past and time future.

IV

Time and the bell have buried the day,
The black cloud carries the sun away.
Will the sunflower turn to us, will the clematis
Stray down, bend to us; tendril and spray
Clutch and cling?
Chill
Fingers of yew be curled
Down on us? After the kingfisher's wing
Has answered light to light, and is silent, the light is still
At the still point of the turning world.

V

Words move, music moves
Only in time; but that which is only living
Can only die. Words, after speech, reach
Into the silence. Only by the form, the pattern,
Can words or music reach
The stillness, as a Chinese jar still
Moves perpetually in its stillness.
Not the stillness of the violin, while the note lasts,
Not that only, but the co-existence,
Or say that the end precedes the beginning,
And the end and the beginning were always there
Before the beginning and after the end.
And all is always now. Words strain,
Crack and sometimes break, under the burden,
Under the tension, slip, slide, perish,
Decay with imprecision, will not stay in place,
Will not stay still. Shrieking voices
Scolding, mocking, or merely chattering,
Always assail them. The Word in the desert
Is most attacked by voices of temptation,
The crying shadow in the funeral dance,
The loud lament of the disconsolate chimera.

The detail of the pattern is movement,
As in the figure of the ten stairs.
Desire itself is movement
Not in itself desirable;
Love is itself unmoving,
Only the cause and end of movement,
Timeless, and undesiring
Except in the aspect of time
Caught in the form of limitation
Between un-being and being.
Sudden in a shaft of sunlight
Even while the dust moves
There rises the hidden laughter
Of children in the foliage
Quick now, here, now, always –
Ridiculous the waste sad time
Stretching before and after.

EAST COKER

I

In my beginning is my end. In succession
Houses rise and fall, crumble, are extended,
Are removed, destroyed, restored, or in their place
Is an open field, or a factory, or a by-pass.
Old stone to new building, old timber to new fires,
Old fires to ashes, and ashes to the earth
Which is already flesh, fur and faeces,
Bone of man and beast, cornstalk and leaf.
Houses live and die: there is a time for building
And a time for living and for generation
And a time for the wind to break the loosened pane
And to shake the wainscot where the field-mouse trots
And to shake the tattered arras woven with a silent motto.

In my beginning is my end. Now the light falls
Across the open field, leaving the deep lane
Shuttered with branches, dark in the afternoon,
Where you lean against a bank while a van passes,
And the deep lane insists on the direction
Into the village, in the electric heat
Hypnotised. In a warm haze the sultry light
Is absorbed, not refracted, by grey stone.
The dahlias sleep in the empty silence.
Wait for the early owl.
In that open field
If you do not come too close, if you do not come too close,
On a summer midnight, you can hear the music
Of the weak pipe and the little drum
And see them dancing around the bonfire
The association of man and woman
In daunsinge, signifying matrimonie –
A dignified and commodious sacrament.
Two and two, necessarye coniunction,

Holding eche other by the hand or the arm
Whiche betokeneth concorde. Round and round the fire
Leaping through the flames, or joined in circles,
Rustically solemn or in rustic laughter
Lifting heavy feet in clumsy shoes,
Earth feet, loam feet, lifted in country mirth
Mirth of those long since under earth
Nourishing the corn. Keeping time,
Keeping the rhythm in their dancing
As in their living in the living seasons
The time of the seasons and the constellations
The time of milking and the time of harvest
The time of the coupling of man and woman
And that of beasts. Feet rising and falling.
Eating and drinking. Dung and death.

Dawn points, and another day
Prepares for heat and silence. Out at sea the dawn wind
Wrinkles and slides. I am here
Or there, or elsewhere. In my beginning.

II

What is the late November doing
With the disturbance of the spring
And creatures of the summer heat,
And snowdrops writhing under feet
And hollyhocks that aim too high
Red into grey and tumble down
Late roses filled with early snow?
Thunder rolled by the rolling stars
Simulates triumphal cars
Deployed in constellated wars
Scorpion fights against the Sun
Until the Sun and Moon go down
Comets weep and Leonids fly
Hunt the heavens and the plains

Whirled in a vortex that shall bring
The world to that destructive fire
Which burns before the ice-cap reigns.

That was a way of putting it – not very satisfactory:
A periphrastic study in a worn-out poetical fashion,
Leaving one still with the intolerable wrestle
With words and meanings. The poetry does not matter
It was not (to start again) what one had expected.
What was to be the value of the long looked forward to,
Long hoped for calm, the autumnal serenity
And the wisdom of age? Had they deceived us
Or deceived themselves, the quiet-voiced elders,
Bequeathing us merely a receipt for deceit?
The serenity only a deliberate hebetude,
The wisdom only the knowledge of dead secrets
Useless in the darkness into which they peered
Or from which they turned their eyes. There is, it seems to us,
At best, only a limited value
In the knowledge derived from experience.
The knowledge imposes a pattern, and falsifies,
For the pattern is new in every moment
And every moment is a new and shocking
Valuation of all we have been. We are only undeceived
Of that which, deceiving, could no longer harm.
In the middle, not only in the middle of the way
But all the way, in a dark wood, in a bramble,
On the edge of a grimpen, where is no secure foothold,
And menaced by monsters, fancy lights,
Risking enchantment. Do not let me hear
Of the wisdom of old men, but rather of their folly,
Their fear of fear and frenzy, their fear of possession,
Of belonging to another, or to others, or to God.
The only wisdom we can hope to acquire
Is the wisdom of humility: humility is endless.

The houses are all gone under the sea.

The dancers are all gone under the hill.

III

O dark dark dark. They all go into the dark,
The vacant interstellar spaces, the vacant into the vacant,
The captains, merchant bankers, eminent men of letters,
The generous patrons of art, the statesmen and the rulers,
Distinguished civil servants, chairmen of many committees,
Industrial lords and petty contractors, all go into the dark,
And dark the Sun and Moon, and the Almanach de Gotha
And the Stock Exchange Gazette, the Directory of Directors,
And cold the sense and lost the motive of action.
And we all go with them, into the silent funeral,
Nobody's funeral, for there is no one to bury.
I said to my soul, be still, and let the dark come upon you
Which shall be the darkness of God. As, in a theatre,
The lights are extinguished, for the scene to be changed
With a hollow rumble of wings, with a movement of
darkness on darkness,
And we know that the hills and the trees, the distant
panorama
And the bold imposing façade are all being rolled away –
Or as, when an underground train, in the tube, stops too
long between stations
And the conversation rises and slowly fades into silence
And you see behind every face the mental emptiness deepen
Leaving only the growing terror of nothing to think about;
Or when, under ether, the mind is conscious but conscious
of nothing –
I said to my soul, be still, and wait without hope
For hope would be hope for the wrong thing; wait without
love
For love would be love of the wrong thing; there is yet faith
But the faith and the love and the hope are all in the waiting.

Wait without thought, for you are not ready for thought:
So the darkness shall be the light, and the stillness the
  dancing.
Whisper of running streams, and winter lightning.
The wild thyme unseen and the wild strawberry,
The laughter in the garden, echoed ecstasy
Not lost, but requiring, pointing to the agony
Of death and birth.

                You say I am repeating
Something I have said before. I shall say it again.
Shall I say it again? In order to arrive there,
To arrive where you are, to get from where you are not,
  You must go by a way wherein there is no ecstasy.
In order to arrive at what you do not know
  You must go by a way which is the way of ignorance.
In order to possess what you do not possess
  You must go by the way of dispossession.
In order to arrive at what you are not
  You must go through the way in which you are not.
And what you do not know is the only thing you know
And what you own is what you do not own
And where you are is where you are not.

IV

The wounded surgeon plies the steel
That questions the distempered part;
Beneath the bleeding hands we feel
The sharp compassion of the healer's art
Resolving the enigma of the fever chart.

Our only health is the disease
If we obey the dying nurse
Whose constant care is not to please
But to remind of our, and Adam's curse,
And that, to be restored, our sickness must grow worse.

The whole earth is our hospital
Endowed by the ruined millionaire,
Wherein, if we do well, we shall
Die of the absolute paternal care
That will not leave us, but prevents us everywhere.

The chill ascends from feet to knees,
The fever sings in mental wires.
If to be warmed, then I must freeze
And quake in frigid purgatorial fires
Of which the flame is roses, and the smoke is briars.

The dripping blood our only drink,
The bloody flesh our only food:
In spite of which we like to think
That we are sound, substantial flesh and blood –
Again, in spite of that, we call this Friday good.

V

So here I am, in the middle way, having had twenty years –
Twenty years largely wasted, the years of *l'entre deux guerres* –
Trying to learn to use words, and every attempt
Is a wholly new start, and a different kind of failure
Because one has only learnt to get the better of words
For the thing one no longer has to say, or the way in which
One is no longer disposed to say it. And so each venture
Is a new beginning, a raid on the inarticulate
With shabby equipment always deteriorating
In the general mess of imprecision of feeling,
Undisciplined squads of emotion. And what there is to conquer
By strength and submission, has already been discovered
Once or twice, or several times, by men whom one cannot hope
To emulate – but there is no competition –

There is only the fight to recover what has been lost
And found and lost again and again: and now, under
  conditions
That seem unpropitious. But perhaps neither gain nor loss.
For us, there is only the trying. The rest is not our business.

Home is where one starts from. As we grow older
The world becomes stranger, the pattern more complicated
Of dead and living. Not the intense moment
Isolated, with no before and after,
But a lifetime burning in every moment
And not the lifetime of one man only
But of old stones that cannot be deciphered.
There is a time for the evening under starlight,
A time for the evening under lamplight
(The evening with the photograph album).
Love is most nearly itself
When here and now cease to matter.
Old men ought to be explorers
Here or there does not matter
We must be still and still moving
Into another intensity
For a further union, a deeper communion
Through the dark cold and the empty desolation,
The wave cry, the wind cry, the vast waters
Of the petrel and the porpoise. In my end is my beginning.

THE DRY SALVAGES

The Dry Salvages – presumably *les trois sauvages* – is a small group of rocks, with a beacon, off the N.E. coast of Cape Ann, Massachusetts.
Salvages is pronounced to rhyme with *assuages.*
Groaner: a whistling buoy.

I

I do not know much about gods; but I think that the river
Is a strong brown god – sullen, untamed and intractable,
Patient to some degree, at first recognised as a frontier;
Useful, untrustworthy, as a conveyor of commerce;
Then only a problem confronting the builder of bridges.
The problem once solved, the brown god is almost forgotten
By the dwellers in cities – ever, however, implacable,
Keeping his seasons and rages, destroyer, reminder
Of what men choose to forget. Unhonoured, unpropitiated
By worshippers of the machine, but waiting, watching and
waiting.
His rhythm was present in the nursery bedroom,
In the rank ailanthus of the April dooryard,
In the smell of grapes on the autumn table,
And the evening circle in the winter gaslight.

The river is within us, the sea is all about us;
The sea is the land's edge also, the granite
Into which it reaches, the beaches where it tosses
Its hints of earlier and other creation:
The starfish, the horseshoe crab, the whale's backbone;
The pools where it offers to our curiosity
The more delicate algae and the sea anemone.
It tosses up our losses, the torn seine,
The shattered lobsterpot, the broken oar
And the gear of foreign dead men. The sea has many voices,
Many gods and many voices.
The salt is on the briar rose,
The fog is in the fir trees.
The sea howl
And the sea yelp, are different voices
Often together heard: the whine in the rigging,
The menace and caress of wave that breaks on water,

The distant rote in the granite teeth,
And the wailing warning from the approaching headland
Are all sea voices, and the heaving groaner
Rounded homewards, and the seagull:
And under the oppression of the silent fog
The tolling bell
Measures time not our time, rung by the unhurried
Ground swell, a time
Older than the time of chronometers, older
Than time counted by anxious worried women
Lying awake, calculating the future,
Trying to unweave, unwind, unravel
And piece together the past and the future,
Between midnight and dawn, when the past is all deception,
The future futureless, before the morning watch
When time stops and time is never ending;
And the ground swell, that is and was from the beginning,
Clangs
The bell.

II

Where is there an end of it, the soundless wailing,
The silent withering of autumn flowers
Dropping their petals and remaining motionless;
Where is there an end to the drifting wreckage,
The prayer of the bone on the beach, the unprayable
Prayer at the calamitous annunciation?

There is no end, but addition: the trailing
Consequence of further days and hours,
While emotion takes to itself the emotionless
Years of living among the breakage
Of what was believed in as the most reliable –
And therefore the fittest for renunciation.

There is the final addition, the failing
Pride or resentment at failing powers,

The unattached devotion which might pass for devotionless,
In a drifting boat with a slow leakage,
The silent listening to the undeniable
Clamour of the bell of the last annunciation.

Where is the end of them, the fishermen sailing
Into the wind's tail, where the fog cowers?
We cannot think of a time that is oceanless
Or of an ocean not littered with wastage
Or of a future that is not liable
Like the past, to have no destination.

We have to think of them as forever bailing,
Setting and hauling, while the North East lowers
Over shallow banks unchanging and erosionless
Or drawing their money, drying sails at dockage;
Not as making a trip that will be unpayable
For a haul that will not bear examination.

There is no end of it, the voiceless wailing,
No end to the withering of withered flowers,
To the movement of pain that is painless and motionless,
To the drift of the sea and the drifting wreckage,
The bone's prayer to Death its God. Only the hardly, barely
  prayable
Prayer of the one Annunciation.

It seems, as one becomes older,
That the past has another pattern, and ceases to be a mere
  sequence –
Or even development: the latter a partial fallacy
Encouraged by superficial notions of evolution,
Which becomes, in the popular mind, a means of disowning
  the past.
The moments of happiness – not the sense of well-being,
Fruition, fulfilment, security or affection,
Or even a very good dinner, but the sudden illumination –
We had the experience but missed the meaning,

And approach to the meaning restores the experience
In a different form, beyond any meaning
We can assign to happiness. I have said before
That the past experience revived in the meaning
Is not the experience of one life only
But of many generations – not forgetting
Something that is probably quite ineffable:
The backward look behind the assurance
Of recorded history, the backward half-look
Over the shoulder, towards the primitive terror.
Now, we come to discover that the moments of agony
(Whether, or not, due to misunderstanding,
Having hoped for the wrong things or dreaded the wrong
things,
Is not in question) are likewise permanent
With such permanence as time has. We appreciate this better
In the agony of others, nearly experienced,
Involving ourselves, than in our own.
For our own past is covered by the currents of action,
But the torment of others remains an experience
Unqualified, unworn by subsequent attrition.
People change, and smile: but the agony abides.
Time the destroyer is time the preserver,
Like the river with its cargo of dead negroes, cows and
chicken coops,
The bitter apple and the bite in the apple.
And the ragged rock in the restless waters,
Waves wash over it, fogs conceal it;
On a halcyon day it is merely a monument,
In navigable weather it is always a seamark
To lay a course by: but in the sombre season
Or the sudden fury, is what it always was.

III

I sometimes wonder if that is what Krishna meant –
Among other things – or one way of putting the same thing:

That the future is a faded song, a Royal Rose or a lavender spray
Of wistful regret for those who are not yet here to regret,
Pressed between yellow leaves of a book that has never been opened.
And the way up is the way down, the way forward is the way back.
You cannot face it steadily, but this thing is sure,
That time is no healer: the patient is no longer here.
When the train starts, and the passengers are settled
To fruit, periodicals and business letters
(And those who saw them off have left the platform)
Their faces relax from grief into relief
To the sleepy rhythm of a hundred hours.
Fare forward, travellers! not escaping from the past
Into different lives, or into any future;
You are not the same people who left that station
Or who will arrive at any terminus,
While the narrowing rails slide together behind you;
And on the deck of the drumming liner
Watching the furrow that widens behind you,
You shall not think 'the past is finished'
Or 'the future is before us'.
At nightfall, in the rigging and the aerial,
Is a voice descanting (though not to the ear,
The murmuring shell of time, and not in any language)
'Fare forward, you who think that you are voyaging;
You are not those who saw the harbour
Receding, or those who will disembark.
Here between the hither and the farther shore
While time is withdrawn, consider the future
And the past with an equal mind.
At the moment which is not of action or inaction
You can receive this: "on whatever sphere of being
The mind of a man may be intent
At the time of death" – that is the one action

(And the time of death is every moment)
Which shall fructify in the lives of others:
And do not think of the fruit of action.
Fare forward.
                    O voyagers, O seamen,
You who come to port, and you whose bodies
Will suffer the trial and judgement of the sea,
Or whatever event, this is your real destination.'
So Krishna, as when he admonished Arjuna
On the field of battle.
                              Not fare well,
But fare forward, voyagers.

IV

Lady, whose shrine stands on the promontory,
Pray for all those who are in ships, those
Whose business has to do with fish, and
Those concerned with every lawful traffic
And those who conduct them.

Repeat a prayer also on behalf of
Women who have seen their sons or husbands
Setting forth, and not returning:
Figlia del tuo figlio,
Queen of Heaven.

Also pray for those who were in ships, and
Ended their voyage on the sand, in the sea's lips
Or in the dark throat which will not reject them
Or wherever cannot reach them the sound of the sea bell's
Perpetual angelus.

V

To communicate with Mars, converse with spirits,
To report the behaviour of the sea monster,
Describe the horoscope, haruspicate or scry,

Observe disease in signatures, evoke
Biography from the wrinkles of the palm
And tragedy from fingers; release omens
By sortilege, or tea leaves, riddle the inevitable
With playing cards, fiddle with pentagrams
Or barbituric acids, or dissect
The recurrent image into pre-conscious terrors –
To explore the womb, or tomb, or dreams; all these are usual
Pastimes and drugs, and features of the press:
And always will be, some of them especially
When there is distress of nations and perplexity
Whether on the shores of Asia, or in the Edgware Road.
Men's curiosity searches past and future
And clings to that dimension. But to apprehend
The point of intersection of the timeless
With time, is an occupation for the saint –
No occupation either, but something given
And taken, in a lifetime's death in love,
Ardour and selflessness and self-surrender.
For most of us, there is only the unattended
Moment, the moment in and out of time,
The distraction fit, lost in a shaft of sunlight,
The wild thyme unseen, or the winter lightning
Or the waterfall, or music heard so deeply
That it is not heard at all, but you are the music
While the music lasts. These are only hints and guesses,
Hints followed by guesses; and the rest
Is prayer, observance, discipline, thought and action.
The hint half guessed, the gift half understood, is
    Incarnation.
Here the impossible union
Of spheres of existence is actual,
Here the past and future
Are conquered, and reconciled,
Where action were otherwise movement
Of that which is only moved

And has in it no source of movement –
Driven by dæmonic, chthonic
Powers. And right action is freedom
From past and future also.
For most of us, this is the aim
Never here to be realised;
Who are only undefeated
Because we have gone on trying;
We, content at the last
If our temporal reversion nourish
(Not too far from the yew-tree)
The life of significant soil.

LITTLE GIDDING

I

Midwinter spring is its own season
Sempiternal though sodden towards sundown,
Suspended in time, between pole and tropic.
When the short day is brightest, with frost and fire,
The brief sun flames the ice, on pond and ditches,
In windless cold that is the heart's heat,
Reflecting in a watery mirror
A glare that is blindness in the early afternoon.
And glow more intense than blaze of branch, or brazier,
Stirs the dumb spirit: no wind, but pentecostal fire
In the dark time of the year. Between melting and freezing
The soul's sap quivers. There is no earth smell
Or smell of living thing. This is the spring time
But not in time's covenant. Now the hedgerow
Is blanched for an hour with transitory blossom
Of snow, a bloom more sudden
Than that of summer, neither budding nor fading,
Not in the scheme of generation.
Where is the summer, the unimaginable
Zero summer?

If you came this way,
Taking the route you would be likely to take
From the place you would be likely to come from,
If you came this way in may time, you would find the hedges
White again, in May, with voluptuary sweetness.
It would be the same at the end of the journey,
If you came at night like a broken king,
If you came by day not knowing what you came for,
It would be the same, when you leave the rough road
And turn behind the pig-sty to the dull façade
And the tombstone. And what you thought you came for
Is only a shell, a husk of meaning

From which the purpose breaks only when it is fulfilled
If at all. Either you had no purpose
Or the purpose is beyond the end you figured
And is altered in fulfilment. There are other places
Which also are the world's end, some at the sea jaws,
Or over a dark lake, in a desert or a city –
But this is the nearest, in place and time,
Now and in England.

If you came this way,
Taking any route, starting from anywhere,
At any time or at any season,
It would always be the same: you would have to put off
Sense and notion. You are not here to verify,
Instruct yourself, or inform curiosity
Or carry report. You are here to kneel
Where prayer has been valid. And prayer is more
Than an order of words, the conscious occupation
Of the praying mind, or the sound of the voice praying.
And what the dead had no speech for, when living,
They can tell you, being dead: the communication
Of the dead is tongued with fire beyond the language of the living.
Here, the intersection of the timeless moment
Is England and nowhere. Never and always.

II

Ash on an old man's sleeve
Is all the ash the burnt roses leave.
Dust in the air suspended
Marks the place where a story ended.
Dust inbreathed was a house –
The wall, the wainscot and the mouse.
The death of hope and despair,
This is the death of air.

There are flood and drouth
Over the eyes and in the mouth,
Dead water and dead sand
Contending for the upper hand.
The parched eviscerate soil
Gapes at the vanity of toil,
Laughs without mirth.
    This is the death of earth.

Water and fire succeed
The town, the pasture and the weed.
Water and fire deride
The sacrifice that we denied.
Water and fire shall rot
The marred foundations we forgot,
Of sanctuary and choir.
    This is the death of water and fire.

In the uncertain hour before the morning
    Near the ending of interminable night
    At the recurrent end of the unending
After the dark dove with the flickering tongue
    Had passed below the horizon of his homing
    While the dead leaves still rattled on like tin
Over the asphalt where no other sound was
    Between three districts whence the smoke arose
    I met one walking, loitering and hurried
As if blown towards me like the metal leaves
    Before the urban dawn wind unresisting.
    And as I fixed upon the down-turned face
That pointed scrutiny with which we challenge
    The first-met stranger in the waning dusk
    I caught the sudden look of some dead master
Whom I had known, forgotten, half recalled
    Both one and many; in the brown baked features
    The eyes of a familiar compound ghost
Both intimate and unidentifiable.

So I assumed a double part, and cried
And heard another's voice cry: 'What! are *you* here?'
Although we were not. I was still the same,
Knowing myself yet being someone other –
And he a face still forming; yet the words sufficed
To compel the recognition they preceded.
And so, compliant to the common wind,
Too strange to each other for misunderstanding,
In concord at this intersection time
Of meeting nowhere, no before and after,
We trod the pavement in a dead patrol.
I said: 'The wonder that I feel is easy,
Yet ease is cause of wonder. Therefore speak:
I may not comprehend, may not remember.'
And he: 'I am not eager to rehearse
My thought and theory which you have forgotten.
These things have served their purpose: let them be.
So with your own, and pray they be forgiven
By others, as I pray you to forgive
Both bad and good. Last season's fruit is eaten
And the fullfed beast shall kick the empty pail.
For last year's words belong to last year's language
And next year's words await another voice.
But, as the passage now presents no hindrance
To the spirit unappeased and peregrine
Between two worlds become much like each other,
So I find words I never thought to speak
In streets I never thought I should revisit
When I left my body on a distant shore.
Since our concern was speech, and speech impelled us
To purify the dialect of the tribe
And urge the mind to aftersight and foresight,
Let me disclose the gifts reserved for age
To set a crown upon your lifetime's effort.
First, the cold friction of expiring sense
Without enchantment, offering no promise

But bitter tastelessness of shadow fruit
As body and soul begin to fall asunder.
Second, the conscious impotence of rage
At human folly, and the laceration
Of laughter at what ceases to amuse.
And last, the rending pain of re-enactment
Of all that you have done, and been; the shame
Of motives late revealed, and the awareness
Of things ill done and done to others' harm
Which once you took for exercise of virtue.
Then fools' approval stings, and honour stains.
From wrong to wrong the exasperated spirit
Proceeds, unless restored by that refining fire
Where you must move in measure, like a dancer.'
The day was breaking. In the disfigured street
He left me, with a kind of valediction,
And faded on the blowing of the horn.

III

There are three conditions which often look alike
Yet differ completely, flourish in the same hedgerow:
Attachment to self and to things and to persons, detachment
From self and from things and from persons; and, growing between them, indifference
Which resembles the others as death resembles life,
Being between two lives – unflowering, between
The live and the dead nettle. This is the use of memory:
For liberation – not less of love but expanding
Of love beyond desire, and so liberation
From the future as well as the past. Thus, love of a country
Begins as attachment to our own field of action
And comes to find that action of little importance
Though never indifferent. History may be servitude,
History may be freedom. See, now they vanish,
The faces and places, with the self which, as it could, loved them,

To become renewed, transfigured, in another pattern.
Sin is Behovely, but
All shall be well, and
All manner of thing shall be well.
If I think, again, of this place,
And of people, not wholly commendable,
Of no immediate kin or kindness,
But some of peculiar genius,
All touched by a common genius,
United in the strife which divided them;
If I think of a king at nightfall,
Of three men, and more, on the scaffold
And a few who died forgotten
In other places, here and abroad,
And of one who died blind and quiet,
Why should we celebrate
These dead men more than the dying?
It is not to ring the bell backward
Nor is it an incantation
To summon the spectre of a Rose.
We cannot revive old factions
We cannot restore old policies
Or follow an antique drum
These men, and those who opposed them
And those whom they opposed
Accept the constitution of silence
And are folded in a single party.
Whatever we inherit from the fortunate
We have taken from the defeated
What they had to leave us – a symbol:
A symbol perfected in death.
And all shall be well and
All manner of thing shall be well
By the purification of the motive
In the ground of our beseeching.

IV

The dove descending breaks the air
With flame of incandescent terror
Of which the tongues declare
The one discharge from sin and error.
The only hope, or else despair
    Lies in the choice of pyre or pyre –
    To be redeemed from fire by fire.

Who then devised the torment? Love.
Love is the unfamiliar Name
Behind the hands that wove
The intolerable shirt of flame
Which human power cannot remove.
    We only live, only suspire
    Consumed by either fire or fire.

V

What we call the beginning is often the end
And to make an end is to make a beginning.
The end is where we start from. And every phrase
And sentence that is right (where every word is at home,
Taking its place to support the others,
The word neither diffident nor ostentatious,
An easy commerce of the old and the new,
The common word exact without vulgarity,
The formal word precise but not pedantic,
The complete consort dancing together)
Every phrase and every sentence is an end and a beginning,
Every poem an epitaph. And any action
Is a step to the block, to the fire, down the sea's throat
Or to an illegible stone: and that is where we start.
We die with the dying:
See, they depart, and we go with them.
We are born with the dead:

See, they return, and bring us with them.
The moment of the rose and the moment of the yew-tree
Are of equal duration. A people without history
Is not redeemed from time, for history is a pattern
Of timeless moments. So, while the light fails
On a winter's afternoon, in a secluded chapel
History is now and England.

With the drawing of this Love and the voice of this Calling

We shall not cease from exploration
And the end of all our exploring
Will be to arrive where we started
And know the place for the first time.
Through the unknown, remembered gate
When the last of earth left to discover
Is that which was the beginning;
At the source of the longest river
The voice of the hidden waterfall
And the children in the apple-tree
Not known, because not looked for
But heard, half-heard, in the stillness
Between two waves of the sea.
Quick now, here, now, always –
A condition of complete simplicity
(Costing not less than everything)
And all shall be well and
All manner of thing shall be well
When the tongues of flame are in-folded
Into the crowned knot of fire
And the fire and the rose are one.